VICTORIA

in the 1880s

The Rush to be Rich

The Rush to be Rich

A HISTORY OF THE
COLONY OF VICTORIA, 1883–1889

GEOFFREY SERLE

Reader in History
Monash University

Myer Senior Research Fellow
University of Melbourne, 1970

MELBOURNE UNIVERSITY PRESS

First published 1971

Printed in Australia by
Halstead Press Pty Ltd, Kingsgrove, N.S.W. 2208, for
Melbourne University Press, Carlton, Victoria 3053
Great Britain and Europe: ISBS Inc., London
USA and Canada: ISBS Inc., Portland, Oregon 97208

Registered in Australia for transmission by post as a book

Designed by Norman Quaintance

ISBN 0 522 84009 4
Dewey Decimal Classification Number 994.03

Preface

I regard this book primarily as a blocking-in of an important undeveloped area of Australian history. I have written it in the conviction that an examination of one colony over a short term of years is the most useful way of opening up a period and topics of which little is known, and that the degree of difference of the colonies from each other in the late nineteenth century needs demonstration. Something like the equivalent of two years' full-time work has been invested. However, the diversity and complexity of Victorian society in the 1880s, compared to the 1850s, and the range and quantity of sources have meant that this is not as thorough a study as *The Golden Age*. I hope that it will stimulate work in the period by others, and that I shall have the opportunity of revising and refining my work in future editions. For much of what appears here is a first attempt to explore complicated subjects—and inevitably is superficial to some degree, as all general history in any case must be.

This book has been planned as the first of two volumes covering the period 1883 to 1900. It sets out to be an overall history of the eighties, with only a few topics receiving much less than due attention. The most notable of these are education, culture and feminism—all of which will be featured in the next volume.

The book is neither as authoritative nor as biographically interesting as it might have been, because of the almost entire absence of collections of private papers. Prominent Victorians and their descendants, compared to New South Welshmen—let alone Englishmen and Americans—have been reprehensibly careless and ignorant in destroying or failing to take care to preserve diaries, correspondence and other papers. We are all the losers. It may be that Victorian history can never be written satisfactorily and that, in the absence of their papers, many distinguished men will never receive full biographical recognition.

Nearly every person mentioned in the book is or will be included in volumes 3 to 6 of the *Australian Dictionary of Biography*. Hence I have not included biographical notes on men of lesser importance. I hope the lay reader will forgive the fairly thorough annotation, which is justifiable as a guide to further research.

The advice of many friends and colleagues has improved my work. They include Marian Aveling, Colin Badger, John Bennett, Geoff Blainey,

Gordon Buxton, Michael Cannon, Manning Clark, Graeme Davison, Gwen Dow, James Grant, Denis Grundy, Alan Hall, Sid Ingham, John La Nauze, John McCarty, Sam McCulloch, Noel McLachlan, Allan Martin, Ann Mitchell, George Parsons, John Rickard, Peter Ryan, Barry Smith and Frank Strahan. I owe a special debt to Mrs Kathleen Thomson and Carole Woods for their careful assistance and to Mrs Jean Thompson and others who typed the manuscript. My wife, Jessie, remains my best critic.

I am grateful for permission to use and quote from documents, and for their hospitality, to the governing bodies of the State Library of Victoria, the National Library of Australia, the Mitchell Library, the Dixson Library, the University of Melbourne Archives, and the British Museum; and to the Royal Commonwealth Society, London, the directors of the Australia and New Zealand Bank Limited, and the Marquess of Salisbury. I am especially indebted to the skilful officers of the La Trobe Library (State Library of Victoria) where I carried out most of my work; most of the illustrations are from its files. I thank the Australian Research Grants Committee for providing research assistance, my colleagues at Monash University for a generous allowance of research time, and the University of Melbourne for its hospitality in 1970 (by use of the Myer Fund) which enabled me to complete this book a year earlier than would otherwise have been the case.

G.S.

Monash University

Contents

Preface v

Prologue: The Years Between, 1861–1882 1

POLITICS

1 Political Framework, 1883–1886 17
The 1883 election and the formation of the coalition—ideological assumptions and influences; the nature of politics—the Service–Berry ministry—Gillies and Deakin take over; the 1886 election

ECONOMICS

2 Economic Sketch 45
General aspects—pastoralism—agriculture and land settlement—the gold-mining industry—banking and commerce—manufacturing; the effects of protection—the growth of Melbourne—the public sector; transport—application of inventions; women at work—rising prosperity

3 Class Relations and the Rise of Labour 86
Class and class-consciousness—standard of living—the trade union movement—the eight-hours movement—the factory reform and early closing movements; the tailoresses' strike—industrial conflicts: bootmakers and wharf labourers—miners', shearers' and transport unions—harmony of interests; the Board of Conciliation—the unions and politics—summing-up

RELIGION

4 The Churches under Stress 127
The challenge to faith—Moorhouse and Strong; theological conflicts; the denominations—the Secularists—the Salvation Army—reassessment

5 Evangelicals in Action 153
Secular education—Sabbatarianism—temperance—morals—the extent of wowser influence

NATIONALITY

6 Crisis in the Pacific and the Campaign for Federation, 1883–1887 179
New Guinea, the New Hebrides and the federal Convention—Victoria and New South Wales—1884: the New Guinea crisis—General Gordon, defence and imminent war, 1885—the Federal Council established—the New Hebrides crisis, 1886–7, and the Colonial Conference—naval defence—Victorian diplomacy and the imperial response

7 Migrants, Native-born and Irish-Australians 216
Imperial loyalty and migrant patriotism—the future of the imperial relationship; Imperial Federation—native-born Australians; the A.N.A. to 1887—Irish-Australians; the Home Rule movement

THE HIGH BOOM YEARS

8 Fools' Paradise, 1887–1888 247
The land boom develops—peak of the boom—government, politicians and the boom; boom morality

9 'Marvellous Melbourne', 1887–1888 272
Boom Melbourne described; style of life—the seamy side: the stench; larrikins—the Queen's Jubilee, the centennial Exhibition, culture, sport, and incidents of the day—drift to the city

10 National Issues, 1888 295
The Chinese 'menace'—the formal imperial relationship—towards a decision on nationality; the A.N.A.—the federal campaign bogged down

11 Close of an Era, 1888–1889 318
Political developments; dissident farmers—the boom, 1889—imperial relations and defence—towards federation—economic doubts, late 1889; Labour and the London dock strike—conclusion

Abbreviations 341

Notes 343

Bibliography 373

Index 381

Illustrations

H. J. Wrixon, 1886		19
J. B. Patterson, 1888		21
David Syme, 1888		28
F. W. Haddon, 1888		29
James Service, *c.* 1885	*facing*	36
Graham Berry, *c.* 1885	„	36
George Higinbotham, *c.* 1890	„	36
C. H. Pearson, *c.* 1890	„	36
Duncan Gillies, *c.* 1885	„	37
Alfred Deakin, 1886	„	37
The Ministerial Bench	„	37
Goldsbrough & Co., warehouse	„	52
Mining revival at Bendigo: the Beehive	„	52
Wheat-threshing in the Goulburn Valley	„	53
A Victorian selector's homestead, 1880	„	53
Newly felled tree, Mirboo South	„	100
First store at Warragul, 1876	„	100
MacRobertson's works	„	101
J. Buncle and Son, works	„	101
The demands of Labour		109
William Trenwith, *c.* 1885	*facing*	116
Benjamin Douglass, *c.* 1885	„	116
Interior of Council Room, Trades Hall	„	116
Collins Street East on a Sunday morning	„	117
The 'Christian' of today		131
The case of the Rev. Charles Strong		137
Bishop Moorhouse	*facing*	148
Rev. Charles Strong	„	148
Chloë	„	149
The Victorian Navy	„	164
Headquarters Staff, Victorian Military Forces, 1884	„	164
Governor Sir Henry Loch, family and staff, *c.* 1885	„	165
A patriotic meeting, 1885		197
Land sale, 1888	*facing*	212
Matthew Davies, 1887	„	213

James Mirams, *c.* 1887	*facing*	213
James Munro	,,	213
Tommy Bent	,,	213
The old story		225
Federal Hotel, Collins Street, 1888	*facing*	228
E.S. & A. Bank, 1887	,,	228
Kamesburgh, Brighton	,,	229
Goodrest, South Yarra	,,	229
Henry Gyles Turner, 1886		250
B. J. Fink, 1888		263
Catalogue of the Impression Exhibition		289
Elizabeth Street and Collins Street, 1889	*facing*	292
Opening of the Centennial Exhibition	,,	293
Collins Street, looking east, 1886	,,	308
Sturt Street, Ballarat	,,	309

PROLOGUE

The Years Between, 1861–1882

'Romance is at an end; capital has reasserted its sway, and pride of purse is triumphant. It needs must be so,' a visitor remarked of Victoria of the mid-eighteen-sixties.[1] The gold rushes were over, a famous colony had been established, and many mature ex-diggers had cause to be grateful for the improved living standards and prospects they had gained from migration. Soberly they settled back to the conventional routine of organized society, married and brought up families, and nostalgically and fretfully day-dreamed of their restless years of hope and freedom on the diggings. Their children were to inherit a legend of bold, enterprising men for whom anything had been possible and who had totally transformed the primitive society they found.

The post-gold-rush decades were, however, a period of prolonged and painful adjustment. Once gold production began to decline after 1858, the harsh truth began to emerge that the colony could not possibly cater for a large proportion of its work-force. Early in the sixties tens of thousands of men were attracted away to rushes in New Zealand and New South Wales. Many of those who remained sometimes felt that the fierceness of competition for wives was the colony's chief drawback; in 1861 there were three times as many bachelors of marrying age as spinsters. State-assisted immigration of females, the growth to adulthood of the children of the fifties, and the departure of disconsolate bachelors eventually balanced the sexes. Over a period of twenty years, more adult males left Victoria (especially to New Zealand) than arrived from overseas, although a steady flow continued from the British Isles of men who paid their own way or were brought out by relatives or friends. The male work-force grew only by about 13 per cent, and only by means of natural increase. The impressive 60 per cent addition to population between 1861 and 1881, from 537,000 (46 per cent of the Australian colonies) to 860,000 (38 per cent), was nearly all of women and children. Over the same period the number of bread-winners in New South Wales increased at twice the rate. The sixties were years of slow economic growth; the years 1871 to 1874 saw more lively expansion, but they were followed by a levelling-off and then a marked down-turn in 1878–9 when unemployment was again high. Only from 1880 did Victoria once again share conspicuously in the economic growth of the Australian colonies, which since the fifties had been so remarkable by world standards.

The massive immigration of young diggers in their twenties in the eighteen-fifties and the subsequent decline of immigration left a lasting kink in the population. The marriage- and birth-rates in the late fifties and sixties were extraordinarily high; by the seventies there were relatively few people in their twenties but large numbers in their forties and many teenagers and young children. Victoria's history in the later nineteenth century must be written largely in terms of the migrant generation of the fifties who continued to dominate through the eighties, when most of their children were coming of age. Between 1870 and 1893 all eleven Victorian premiers were migrants, nine of them having arrived in the fifties, whereas only one of the twenty premiers of New South Wales and South Australia was a migrant of the fifties and five were native-born.

The basic economic change of the sixties and seventies is shown simply by the figures: in 1861 goldminers numbered 80,000 or more (one-third of the male work-force) and in 1881 some 35,000 (one-eighth); in 1861 there were about 35,000 farmers and farm-workers (one-seventh of the male work-force) and in 1881 about 70,000 (one-quarter). Meanwhile the pastoral industry was expanding to its confined limits and manufacturing was growing steadily. Melbourne, with huge capital for investment from gold-winnings, had established its dominance as the financial centre of Australia.

Year by year gold production fell, except for slight rallies in 1868, 1871–3 and 1880–2; in 1880 it was half that of 1862 and about one-quarter the figure for marvellous 1852. By the mid-seventies wool had again become the more valuable product (and wool and gold together long continued to provide more than three-quarters of overseas export income). In the early sixties the dwindling few thousand surface alluvial diggers worked out the last new fields at the head of the Goulburn River and in the Gippsland ranges; Wood's Point and Walhalla were the last gold towns of any size. The deep buried alluvial rivers of Ballarat and the deeper quartz reefs of Bendigo and Stawell were the major deposits still to be exploited. By 1872 mechanized quartz mines were producing as much gold as alluvial workings; dynamite, the percussion rock-drill, the diamond drill and the safety-cage had revolutionized mining by 1880. During the sixties the great majority of miners became wage-employees, though co-operative companies (often with complicated arrangements for proxy workers) and the co-operative tributing system remained common. Most miners invested in the hundreds of companies financed in the gold towns. Bendigo saw wild speculation in 1871, the year of its greatest revival; later that year the passing of the radical No Liability Act made it temporarily possible to attract the more cautious city investors who had largely boycotted the industry because of its deplorable reputation.

Ballarat and Bendigo were the showplaces, the miracle cities which vied with each other in fierce local patriotism. Ballarat, which about 1870 was briefly the fourth city of Australia with some 50,000 inhabitants, had declined to 40,000 by 1881; Bendigo, with more than 35,000 residents, was still growing. Ballarat had already dubbed itself 'the Garden City of Victoria'. Some visitors described it as like a handsome inland capital, 'a perfect Arcadia'; the public gardens and tree-lined streets reminded others of German watering-places. The working mines were well hidden, gums had grown again to partly conceal the scars, and the rich surrounding farming areas gave an impression of long-established contented plenty. At Bendigo, on the other hand, the poppet-heads and mullock-heaps of glistening white quartz defied attempts at municipal improvement, and the neighbourhood was comparatively barren. Smaller gold towns remained hideous, until local enterprise and nature began to restore landscapes which suggested 'a combination of new railway-works, brickfield, stone-quarry, and rubbish-heap'.[2] All the gold towns reflected in their cultural and intellectual life the outstanding quality of the migrants of the fifties; judging by the number of distinguished Australians born and educated in the gold towns, a disproportionate number of the more intelligent migrants settled there compared to Melbourne. The high standard of the newspapers, the level of political participation and church membership, the number of outstanding schools like Grenville College and Loreto Convent at Ballarat were not paralleled elsewhere in Australia outside the capitals. Charles and Ellen Kean, the actors, found their Ballarat audiences more intelligent than those in Melbourne or Sydney and equal to London's.[3] No other gold town now compared in size with Ballarat and Bendigo. By 1881 Castlemaine and Chewton had declined to a population of about 7,500, Stawell at 7,300 and Clunes at 5,800 were holding fairly well, while Daylesford, Creswick, Maryborough, Maldon, Ararat, St Arnaud, Beechworth and Talbot ranged in order between 3,900 and 2,300. Of all these struggling towns, only Maryborough, Ararat and St Arnaud had prospects of growth because of their surrounding farmlands or importance as railway junctions.

Despite the onslaught on the squatters, wool production continued to expand slowly until the mid-seventies when the industry levelled out. In 1860 Victoria and New South Wales both had about six million sheep; the Victorian figure grew to around ten million by the early eighties, but New South Wales then had nearly forty million. Meanwhile, as the land Acts took effect, the number of runs was halved and the area of pastoral occupation was cut back by two-thirds. The squatters consolidated in the Western District but elsewhere were largely forced out. With little back country except the inhospitable Mallee to which to retreat, Victorian pastoral investors moved into the Riverina, which 'speedily became the property of Melbourne residents, either absolutely or by way of mortgage'.[4] Most of the runs by now were owned or largely owned by the pastoral finance houses and banks. For many of the squatters had outreached themselves by converting to freehold, or by buying off selectors and paying dummies, or by investing heavily in fencing and building lavish mansions; others were brought down by the fluctuations of the seasons and the dips in wool prices about 1870 and in 1879. Leviathans like 'Big' Clarke and Sir Samuel Wilson might remain unscathed, but Hugh Glass and many others were ruined.

Agricultural progress was slow in the sixties; it is likely that the increase from about 400,000 to 700,000 acres under crop occurred much more on lands bought by auction in the fifties than on the new selections. The intense land hunger of so many migrants, the urgent need to find employment for the colony's bloated population, and envious determination to 'Upset squatterdom's domination, Give every poor man a home' (as Thatcher, the songster, put it) forced governments to make earnest attempts to convert the bulk of the colony's land from pastoral to agricultural use. They had to acknowledge in part the poor migrant's right to land against the rights of capital and first occupation. The migrant's desire for property was so strong that the selection Acts made minimal provision for long leasehold; those few who argued for it could not gain a hearing. In contemporary terms £1 an acre was astonishingly dear when compared to the almost free land of the United States and Canada, especially as Victorian land was on the whole of poorer quality. The Wakefieldian technique of using land revenue to pay for migrants was abandoned and the revenue from land sales conveniently helped governments to avoid direct taxation for many years.

The earlier selection Acts were calamitous in their effects. The Nicholson Act of 1860 was so emasculated by the Legislative Council that it was almost useless. Gavan Duffy's Act of 1862 was drafted so badly that the Council, knowing that it would prove to be futile, allowed it to pass; the selection provisions had to be suspended after nine weeks. Meanwhile squatters' dummies and sham selectors waiting to be bought off had proved as numerous as genuine settlers; in the end the squatters lost very little land under the Act, although there was some successful settlement here and there. A brief period began when perjury became a commonplace, evading the law was socially acceptable and corruption among politicians and public servants flourished as never before or since. The main provisions of J. M. Grant's equally well-meant Act of 1865 worked little better, for much dummying and speculative selection continued. But Grant's ruthless interpretation of clause 42, providing for occupation before survey of twenty-acre lots near the goldfields, was very effective. Grant allowed four or more adjacent blocks to the one settler, up to thirty miles from a goldfield; in five years some 17,000 men joined 'the 42nd, or home-making brigade', many of them working miners who spent part of their time on their selections.

The 1869 amending Act, drafted by Grant, proved at last to be almost knave-proof; nearly all the colony not yet alienated was thrown open for selection before survey, and by 1880 practically all that could optimistically be described as agricultural land had been sold. Eleven million acres were alienated in nine years. Victoria north of the ranges, apart from the Mallee, was occupied for the third time, following on the squatters and the miners

—and occupied permanently. Wheatgrowing was almost entirely transferred inland; the inhabitants of the Wimmera and northern Victoria increased by 70,000 in the seventies, while the older-settled rural areas actually lost population. Fifty or more new townships began to grow fast, Horsham and Shepparton conspicuous among them. The Wimmera was largely settled—and very successfully—by South Australians from exhausted wheatlands, while much of the lower Goulburn valley and the north was populated from the Ballarat-Creswick-Clunes area. In Gippsland, the Sale and Bairnsdale region made good progress, while the first brave forays began in west and south Gippsland. The working male farming population increased in the seventies from under 50,000 to about 70,000 on half that number of farms. The doubling of cultivated area is much more striking, especially the growth of the Wimmera and the north to about two-thirds of the whole cultivated area while less ground was ploughed in the old areas. The breakthrough came in the late seventies; in 1877 Victoria became self-supporting in wheat at last, with the aid of protective duties from 1868, and began to accumulate export surpluses.* Victoria's area under crop was now well over twice that of New South Wales, but South Australia had developed even faster in the seventies and remained well ahead.

The breakthrough may be explained in various ways. Cheap railway transport was crucial. It is no coincidence that great expansion of production coincided with the arrival of the railway tracks at Horsham, St Arnaud and Shepparton in 1878–9; when at last the Gippsland railway went through to Sale in 1877–8 large areas were opened which had not previously been viable because transport costs to Melbourne had been prohibitive. Some of the new farms were financed by urban investors or successful farmers who could afford to equip themselves adequately and expand to the most economic size. The growth of experience of Australian conditions and modification of European assumptions about farming were perhaps most important of all. Very many of the successful selectors of the seventies were men with ten to twenty years' experience in Victoria or South Australia. Yet, despite the extent of success, perhaps half the selectors failed utterly and abandoned their blocks. The assumptions of self-sufficiency, which had buoyed the hopes of so many land-hungry migrants, died hard. The farmer without capital who did not realize that farming was a business requiring specialized production for market was condemned to grinding poverty, eked out by work on the roads or employment as contract-labour on fencing or dam-sinking.

The second answer to the problem of providing employment in the post-gold-rush period was to foster local industries by protection. Although between 1862 and 1871 by far the greater part of the increase in the Australian manufacturing population was in Victoria, this was essentially a natural response to the needs for food, clothing and shelter. For the political

* In 1860–1 area under crop was about 387,000 acres (wheat 161,000), in 1869–76 between 681,000 and 737,000 (wheat 284,000–350,000); then there was a quick climb to about 1,549,000 (wheat 977,000) in 1880–1.

battle for protection was not easily won: the tariffs of 1866 and 1867 were the first victories, but the rates were not increased to markedly protective levels until 1871 and no major increases followed until 1879. The numbers employed in manufacturing rose from roughly 10,000 in 1861 to about 45,000 in 1883. The number of workmen in quarries, brickyards and saw-mills increased steadily till the mid-seventies, while light engineering, machinery and carriage-manufacturing boomed in the early seventies. The clothing and footwear industries especially depended on protection, while flour mills, bakeries, breweries and tanneries accounted for most of the others employed in 'factories'. Glass and paper were first manufactured, and the first woollen mill was established, in the later sixties. An industrial base was painfully being laid.

Most of this manufacturing expansion was naturally in Melbourne, whose population grew from the unnaturally low 23 per cent of the colony in 1861 to 33 per cent in 1881 when its residents numbered 283,000. In the sixties Melbourne grew no faster than the urban population of the colony as a whole. But in the seventies the notorious long-term trend of metropolitan expansion became clear, when many country towns declined and Melbourne grew at twice the rate of the rest of the colony, despite the success of northern and Wimmera farming settlement. Melbourne's dominant expansion east and south of the Yarra was yet to come; in 1881 more than two-thirds lived north and west of the river and about the same proportion in the city and inner suburbs of Fitzroy, Collingwood, Richmond, North and South Melbourne, Carlton and Prahran. Over the same period, Geelong's slow growth during the gold-rush period was checked; in the seventies its population declined slightly to about 19,000.

'Victorian society is like English,' remarked John Martineau, 'with a thick slice cut off the top and a thin slice off the bottom.'[5] The formulation is useful in assessing the extent to which these migrants reproduced Britain, though 'thick' and 'thin' might be better omitted. Certainly the aristocracy was unrepresented, but there was a sprinkling of pastoralists, farmers, former army officers and clergy of landed gentry (often Anglo-Irish) background. The next levels were perhaps over-represented: lawyers, doctors and schoolmasters with the highest training, gentlemen in the senior civil service, bankers and merchants with good education, genteel clerks and governesses (and well-bred remittance-men) were all abundant. Artisan craftsmen had also arrived in great numbers during the gold rushes; most of the new manufacturers were artisans with more ambition and financial backing than their fellows. Outside these occupations all was flux. Older farmers and newer selectors were of the most diverse origins, though preponderantly with rural labouring backgrounds. Some of the professional miners of Ballarat and Bendigo had been tin- or coal-miners in England and many had been common labourers, but again there was a large minority with varied class and occupational backgrounds. The huge labouring class of navvies, cab-drivers, barmen, swaggies and others were largely representative of the unskilled labourers of Britain and Ireland, but also included many who had sunk in the social scale. The lowest slice of Old England, the depressed and chronically poverty-stricken, were almost entirely unrepresented. However, some of the many ex-convicts, mostly from neighbouring colonies, who had remained formed a criminal class which was possibly as large, relatively, as England's.

Political power hardly reflected the balance of classes. Charles Pearson briefly summed up Victoria's post-gold-rush political achievement as

> the carrying out by Englishmen, Scotchmen, and Irishmen, on virgin soil, of the reforms they had dreamed of at home. Grote's vote by ballot; the manhood suffrage, which was an article in the charter of 1848; [Fox's] ideal separation of Church and State; O'Connell's Home Rule; the Birmingham League's free and secular education; John Mill's yeoman proprietorship, have all become realities here, while they are for the most part still nothing more than aspirations in England.[6]

True, and yet largely misleading: for Pearson has mentioned all the major legislative achievements of a quarter-century, except the establishment of protection. A grotesque constitution nullified the democratic potential, reduced the parliamentary process almost to futility, and added immensely to class bitterness. For the representatives of the well-to-do in the Legislative Council, which had one-tenth of the Assembly's electorate in the sixties and one-sixth in the seventies, had a veto over all legislation. The squatters in the Council wrecked several land Bills and delayed extensive land settlement, held up abolition of state aid to the churches for eighteen years, and revoked numerous lesser popular decisions. Most of the Council's obstructionism amounted to no more than naked defence of recently acquired privileges by those whom George Higinbotham labelled the 'wealthy lower orders'. Yet there was also a strong core of coherent conservative opinion among the landed, mercantile and professional classes, to whom democracy was abhorrent. The chief characteristic of this upper-class party was its pessimism and lack of faith in the future of a colony in which democratic assumptions inevitably set the tone. Many of them still saw themselves as migrants in temporary exile waiting to amass enough to retire home; meanwhile they were disgusted by the trends of colonial life.

Few such Tories were to be found in the popular Assembly. But with the passing of time, new classes of 'conservatives' arose to resist the demands of radical political interests. Self-made men of substance, often radicals and democrats in earlier days, now defended the neo-democratic system which had given them opportunity, and resented suggestion of further radical change. Moreover, as protection became central in radical democratic policies, the classical liberal, especially if a merchant, was driven to the right; free trade was so fundamental a truth to educated men that few could compromise. The *Argus* was driven to identify itself with the conservatives of the Council as much from intellectual outrage as because its rival, the *Age*, was convincing workingmen that protection guaranteed both job and good wage. Similarly, the workingman's hostility to assisted migration, which was virtually eliminated from 1873, was a radical policy which liberal freetraders found intolerable.

The mass of popular representatives in the lower house were liberals and democrats at least to the extent that they believed, first and foremost, in equality of opportunity—that all should 'start fair'—and in the desirability of wide diffusion of wealth and property. In the sixties and seventies the tone of Victorian politics was more radical than elsewhere in the colonies and, despite its Council, Victoria pioneered most radical legislation. Most members of the Assembly represented three broad economic interests—farming-selecting, mining and manufacturing-artisan. When these interests came together in support of protection, land legislation and reform of the Council, and were opposed by the pastoral and financial interests, politics took on a violent class aspect. In periods when the radical alliance broke apart, governments tended to be formed by groupings of factions. And at any time politics largely consisted of the business of developing the colony by providing finance for public works and the bargaining of local members for public money, rather than ideological issues or conflicts of sectional interests.

There were two periods of prolonged crisis between Assembly and Council with accompanying popular fervour. In 1865 the McCulloch ministry, inspired by George Higinbotham, set out again to carry a workable selection Act and to coerce the Council over the issue of protection. The defiant Council eventually gave way on the practical issues, but maintained its constitutional principles by withstanding the Assembly's techniques of coercion. In the meantime the Governor, Sir Charles Darling, trying to do his duty by carrying out the advice of his responsible ministers, had acquiesced in illegal methods and made partisan statements and was recalled by the Colonial Office. He left the colony to the cheers of the 'Melbourne mob' while the government again carried the battle to the Council by insisting on a compensatory grant to Lady Darling. Another deadlock followed, which was ultimately resolved by the Colonial Office agreeing to reinstate Darling in the service. The Council, having come through its ordeal unscathed, made the gesture of slightly broadening its constituency. The late seventies saw an even more serious conflict when an alliance of selectors, miners, manufacturers and trade unionists organized the National Reform and Protection League and rallied behind Graham Berry's Liberals to win a sweeping electoral victory in 1877. The League had 150 branches, pledged its candidates to a platform, and was virtually a political party. The Berry ministry's key policies were high protection and a land tax aimed at soaking the squatters, both of which were eventually carried, and fundamental reform of the Council. The upper house chose to fight on the issue of payment of members of the Assembly, a crucial democratic demand. The government retaliated by on 'Black Wednesday', 8 January 1878, dismissing the lesser judiciary, all magistrates, several departmental heads and more than one hundred other civil servants, in order both to cow the Council and to ensure better attention to duty by officers who had been notoriously partisan. The atmosphere was hysterical, sensible men spoke seriously of the possibility of civil war, the Premier's life was said to be threatened. Outraged conservatives identified the ministry and its supporters with communism; members of the ministry, who were anything but revolutionary by inclination, seriously considered extreme methods of smashing capitalist power. Sir George Bowen, the Governor, and his lady were ostracized by Society because of what he regarded as proper constitutional support for the ministry. Capital took fright and fled the colony, accentuating the down-turn in the economy which reflected the world-wide depression. Yet the Council again survived a determined attempt to break its powers. The Secretary of State for the Colonies refused a request by Berry, on embassy to England, to reform the constitution; drought conditions and governmental misunderstanding of their problems alienated the farmers; and the Catholics were demanding redress of their grievances. Berry's Liberal coalition began to break up. Its determined assault ended in ignominious failure, for the Council's powers were left untouched and a widening of its electorate to about half the Assembly's strengthened its position. Eventually in 1881 the Constitutionalist or 'Conservative' anti-Berryites combined with the Catholics under Sir Bryan O'Loghlen to dismiss the reformers. The war fought for political democracy was lost.

Victorian England was one of the most devout societies the world has known. Victoria's church- and chapel-going migrants possibly were relatively as numerous as South Australia's. Although in 1871 35 per cent of the population described themselves as Church of England, 23 per cent Roman Catholic, 15 per cent Presbyterian and 12 per cent Methodist, the largest denomination by far in terms of active church membership was the Methodist. An astonishing revival campaign in the early sixties had increased its strength, especially in the gold towns, where its adherents numbered about one in five. The Church of England was handicapped by poverty and inability to attract first-rate clergy, and was struggling; but when Bishop Moorhouse arrived in 1877 it gained new life. The Scottish and Northern Irish Presbyterians held their ground well after reunification in 1859. Bishop Goold and his clergy—Irish almost to a man—were slowly but steadily extending provision for their flock. New sees were created at Ballarat and Bendigo in 1874, before the Anglicans created a second bishopric at Ballarat. The strength of the Presbyterians, nonconformists, and evangelicals in the Church of England had already lent a note of pious respectability to most Victorian institutions and to the treatment of social issues.

Despite their numerical strength, the churches were on the defensive. Liberal assumptions eroded doctrinaire theological positions and ecclesiastical claims to privilege or state sustenance. State aid continued against the will both of governments and most Christians until 1875; its earlier withdrawal would have been of serious concern to both Anglican and Catholic bishops. The challenge of science, however, though ignored by Catholics and most evangelicals, forced thinking Christians into grave reappraisal of fundamentals. The debate was necessarily just as passionate and disturbing as in England, and was certainly the crucial intellectual issue of the age. Rationalist propaganda was circulating in the late sixties; in 1869 Bishop Perry and Dr Bromby were speaking and pamphleteering against each other within the Anglican faith; in the early seventies spiritualism began to gain strength. By 1879 Moorhouse, though relatively modern and liberal, was under attack from the agnostic Marcus Clarke in a famous debate. A slight relative decline in church membership in the seventies reflected the increase of doubt, anti-clericalism, and criticism of dogmatic theology. The evangelicals were under assault, but by the test of numbers still dominated the field.

The Education Act of 1872 embodied the far-reaching decision that the state would supply almost-free education for every child. The Common Schools Act of 1862, which provided for the administration of state and denominational schools by a board of honorary, spare-time commissioners, had succeeded in placing only about half the colony's children at school. In a community in which liberal and democratic ideas were so strong, it is not surprising that there were vehement assertions of the duty to establish a comprehensive educational system at as little cost to parents as possible. Practical arguments in support were plentiful: crime was the product of ignorance, industrial civilization demanded full utilization of potential abilities, political democracy required educated voters. It was obvious that the churches were not up to the task; hence the state must provide. When the government department was created, 300 private and church schools closed; but the school population almost immediately rose by half, although the compulsory clause was not to be fully carried out for many years. The seventies saw a massive programme of neo-Gothic school-building and teacher-recruitment.

The Act had been delayed for many years by religious differences, and in the end made no concessions to the Catholics. Protestant voluntarists and most evangelicals had been willing to see state aid to church schools abolished. However, a stand by the Church of England was chiefly responsible for the withdrawal of the Bill produced in 1867 by the Higinbotham royal commission which provided for religious instruction in the state system. Yet the Anglicans clearly lacked the strength to build up their own school system. Their unwillingness to forgo state aid and the inability of the Protestant churches to agree together on a formula for religious teaching in the state system drove Higinbotham and many other politicians, urged on by the *Age* and *Argus* both, to an extreme secular position. The Victorian Act as passed was far more secularist than that of any other colony; religious teaching was excluded, unless local boards of advice made after-hours arrangements for visiting instructors (a provision inserted by the Legislative Council). The Catholic hierarchy, deeming that all education must have a religious framework, were determined to develop their own system, bitterly fought the withdrawal of state aid, and railed against the 'scheme of Godless compulsory education'. In the context they stood no chance, and suffered the liberal and Protestant backlash against papal attacks on liberalism and the declaration of papal infallibility. Some liberals hoped idealistically that coercing the Catholics into the state system would ultimately help to eliminate inherited old-world sectarian strife, but in the final stages of the controversy most set out gleefully to 'dish the Catholics'. The Catholics were not to be coerced. Although in the late seventies they could still handle barely half their children, mighty efforts continued to close the gap.

In October 1878 the Kelly gang murdered three policemen. Twenty months later, after they had been declared outlaws, had stuck up banks at Euroa and Jerilderie, had made a laughing-stock of the police, and cost the state an immense amount of money, Ned Kelly was captured at Glenrowan and hanged, after his mates had perished. They were 'mere boys', wild colonial boys, second-generation delinquents, ill-educated dead-enders in a rural slum, who having declared war on society were inevitably destroyed. They were the last expression of the lawless frontier in what was becoming a highly organized and educated society, the last protest of the mighty bush now tethered with iron rails to Melbourne and the world. For they were made by direct convict tradition, by traditional Irish attitudes to an alien ruling class, and by the protest of the landless against the landowner. The essential background to their tragedy was the determination of magistrates and police to stamp out by savage sentences the local trade of horse-, sheep- and cattle-stealing. Ned at least, however madly and inchoately, was a class rebel who had sufficient vision to dream of an armed rebellion by the discontented of the north-east. Bourgeois society saw the episode as shameful and disgraceful, especially because there had been alarmingly widespread support in the district. But the myth which survived so strongly was based not merely on Ned's remarkable personal qualities but deeply in social grievances and universal attitudes to authority. As so often in Australia, artists and writers have recognized significance which historians have missed.

Constitutional obscurity and the imperial habit of allowing vital issues to resolve themselves confused the process of developing self-government. There were in fact no important disputes with the Colonial Office over the Victorian government's right to legislate in any particular area. Following the Canadian precedent, the first moves towards protection were tolerated, and the colonies' claim to the right to make trade agreements with each other was grudgingly conceded in 1873. The first major conflict with the mother country since the demand for self-government was the campaign in 1863 and 1864 to have convict transportation to Western Australia abolished. A remarkable public agitation, which culminated in the government threatening to withdraw the mail subsidy, ended when the imperial government agreed to stop sending convicts. The internal political crises of the sixties then had serious repercussions on the imperial relationship.

The justified recall of the popular Governor Darling in 1866, followed by the Duke of Buckingham's foolish intervention on the side of the Legislative Council in January 1868, set Victorian politicians and the Colonial Office at loggerheads. Higinbotham's resolutions of 1869, which denied the right of the imperial government to intervene in any way in domestic affairs, were passed by the Assembly in an atmosphere of resentful suspicion; at this time and only at this time, separation appeared as likely as not. Throughout the seventies the Colonial Office handled Victorian governments gingerly; Sir Robert Herbert of the Colonial Office told Governor Bowen in 1877 that 'it is now held here that the power of self-misgovernment conceded to the Australian colonies has hardly any conceivable limitation, so far as intra-colonial questions are concerned'.[7] In the crisis of the late seventies the Colonial Office was again popularly linked with the conservatives and the Council who looked to it for protection against the democratic hordes. Despite these tensions, there were fewer conflicts over self-government than in most of the other colonies. In a period when it appeared that predominant opinion in England saw little future in Empire, the Victorians wistfully craved for recognition and hoped desperately that they could remain part of Greater Britain—always provided there was no interference in their domestic affairs. Their real feelings were shown in the fervent welcomes to the Duke of Edinburgh in 1867–8 and to the princes, Albert and George, in 1881.

The sense of isolation from home which tortured so many colonists was dramatically reduced by the telegraph link in 1872; now at least the outline of great events was known daily from the tantalizingly brief cables. Moreover, the details followed ever more speedily as steam replaced sail and the Suez Canal was opened. The passage from England to Melbourne was more than halved over fifteen years; by 1880 thirty-eight days was normal—often less than from London to New York thirty years before. It was almost possible now to pretend that Victoria was part of Britain—a provincial part certainly, but hardly more so than Scotland or Ulster. Economically and culturally Victoria was indeed no more and no less than an offshoot of Britain. The first important foreign influences, apart from some small American trading contacts, followed on Melbourne's grandiose International Exhibition of 1880. While primarily protectionist propaganda and a braggart display of colonial achievement, it also created economic links with several European nations which exposed Melbourne to new cosmopolitan influences.

Through the long night of colonial particularism, governments went to extraordinary lengths not to co-operate with each other. Provincial rivalry and jealousy found extreme expression in the battle with New South Wales for control of the Riverina. The occasional attempts by Gavan Duffy, Parkes and governors to raise the question of federation were futile. Despite large movements of population, the colonies remained largely isolated from each other; Victoria had as close links with New Zealand as with New South Wales in the sixties and seventies. The skiting which Anthony

Trollope found so distasteful everywhere in Australia was much more in terms of individual 'colonial' than Australian superiority—and no doubt 'the blast of the trumpet as heard in Victoria'[8] was the loudest of all. There was some basis to the sense of difference between the colonies which, about 1880, had grown further apart from each other and varied more widely in character than perhaps at any other time. In no real sense yet was there an Australian economy, but rather loosely linked economies fluctuating independently. In comparison with New South Wales, Victoria had many more farmers, goldminers and factory-workers, few pastoral workers and almost no coalminers; hence the occupational class structures of the two colonies and the sectional class groupings in politics were very different. Victoria had many more Presbyterians, more nonconformists, and more church members and church attenders. Victoria, alone of the colonies, was overwhelmingly peopled by unassisted migrants—and by migrants of one generation—whereas New South Wales had many more adult native-born and a relatively even spread of migrants of different periods. The contrast of Victoria with Queensland is even more marked, but less so with South Australia. Hence variations in beliefs and attitudes between the colonies, despite all their basic similarities, were striking.[9]

1883 was an eventful year of new departures and old conflicts coming to a head. The formation of a coalition government ended a period of bitter and fruitless conflict and began a season of productive political achievement. The election was dominated by sectarian bitterness, which sharpened with the arrival of the Redmond brothers preaching Home Rule for Ireland. The movement for annexation of New Guinea and the New Hebrides for the first time brought Victoria prominently on to the international stage. The Victorian government committed itself to the cause of federation and forced an agreement to create a Federal Council. Higinbotham's lecture on science and religion precipitated a disruption of Presbyterianism over the case of Charles Strong. The Salvation Army was invading the colony; the Secularists were joining battle on another front. 'Wowsers' and liberals clashed over the opening of the National Gallery on Sundays. The tailoresses' strike introduced a new era in industrial relations. The civil service was basically reformed. 'Peace, Progress and Prosperity' had recently been the political slogan of the day as the boom got under way. Yet the colony was torn with conflicts breaking out through the surface unity.

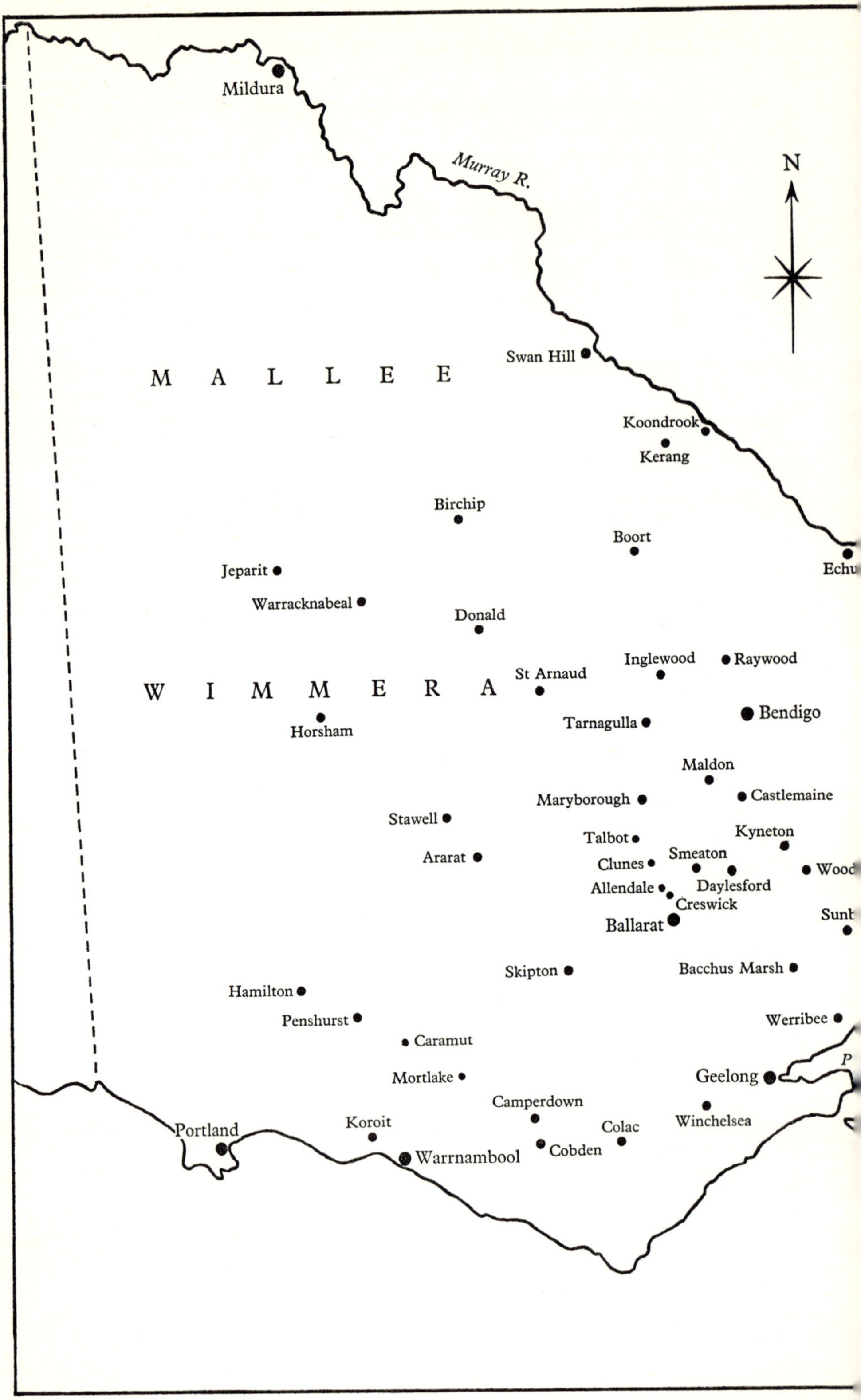
Mildura
Murray R.
N
MALLEE
Swan Hill
Koondrook
Kerang
Birchip
Boort
Echu
Jeparit
Warracknabeal
Donald
Inglewood
Raywood
St Arnaud
WIMMERA
Bendigo
Horsham
Tarnagulla
Maldon
Maryborough
Castlemaine
Stawell
Talbot
Kyneton
Ararat
Smeaton
Clunes
Wood
Daylesford
Allendale
Creswick
Ballarat
Sunb
Skipton
Bacchus Marsh
Hamilton
Penshurst
Werribee
Caramut
P
Mortlake
Geelong
Camperdown
Winchelsea
Portland
Koroit
Colac
Warrnambool
Cobden

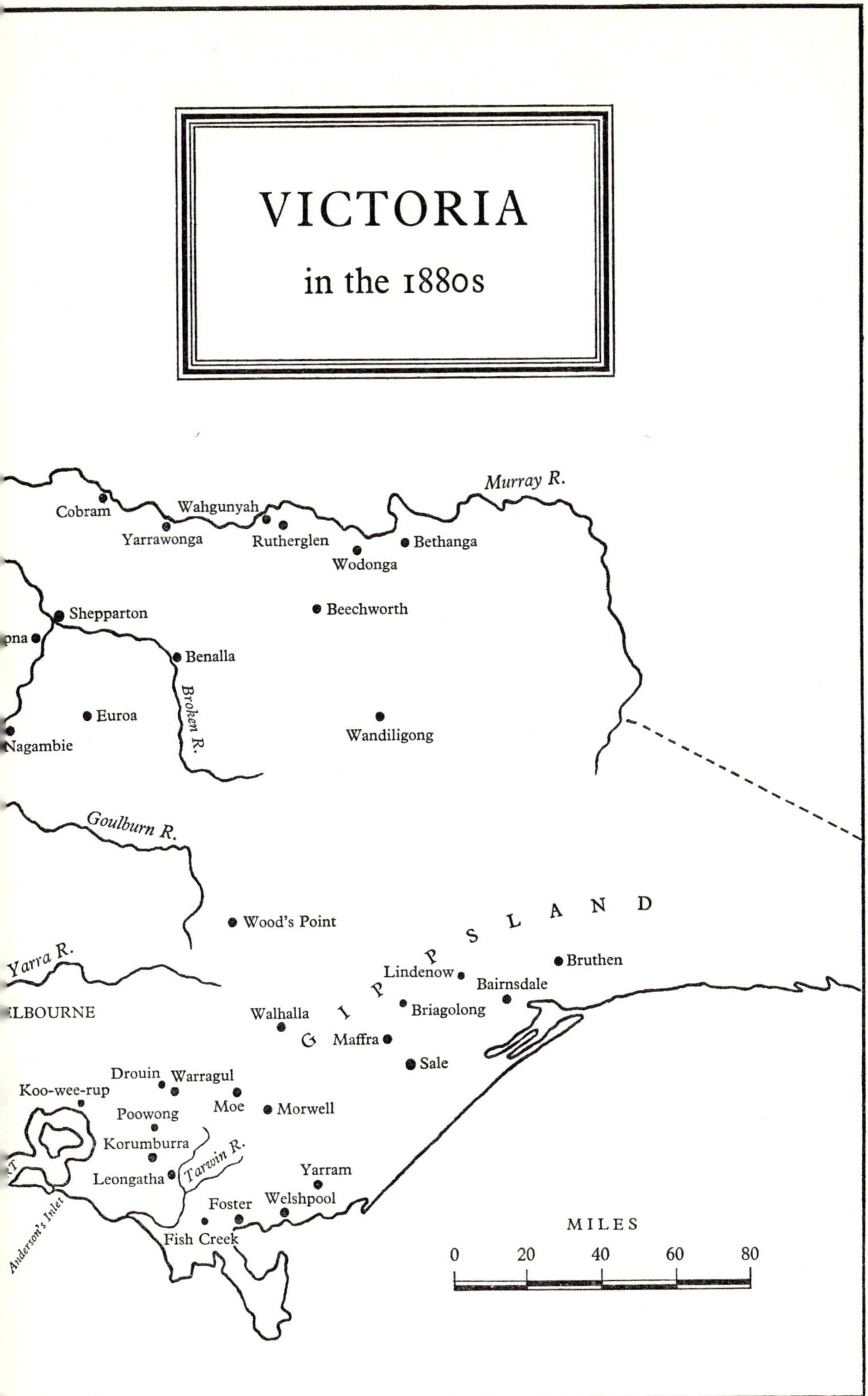
VICTORIA
in the 1880s
Murray R.
Cobram
Wahgunyah
Yarrawonga
Rutherglen
Bethanga
Wodonga
Beechworth
Shepparton
Benalla
Broken R.
Euroa
Wandiligong
Nagambie
Goulburn R.
Wood's Point
GIPPSLAND
Yarra R.
Bruthen
Lindenow
Bairnsdale
Briagolong
Walhalla
Maffra
Sale
Drouin
Warragul
Koo-wee-rup
Moe
Morwell
Poowong
Korumburra
Tarwin R.
Leongatha
Yarram
Foster
Welshpool
Fish Creek
Anderson's Inlet
MILES
0
20
40
60
80

Politics

1

Political Framework, 1883–1886

The 1883 election and formation of the coalition

On 30 January 1883 Sir Bryan O'Loghlen, Irish-Catholic baronet and stop-gap Premier, announced a snap election. His minority ministry of Catholics, party rebels and opportunists, dominated by 'Tommy' Bent, had been kept in office by the Constitutionalists since July 1881. The long session of 1882 had been barren and futile. O'Loghlen had bungled a major overseas loan and the banks, whose advice he had refused, were hostile to him. He told the Governor, Lord Normanby, that the Assembly was 'divided into numerous sections of parties'. But the strict party division of the Berry period had by no means died out; about three-fifths of the members still met regularly in Constitutionalist and Liberal caucuses. The major complication was the single-minded determination of the Catholics to gain grants for their schools. From 1879, when the Catholic Education Defence Association was formed, the bishops and Sir John O'Shanassy had manipulated the Catholic vote. At the first election in 1880 they had helped to eject Berry; at the second they had helped to bring him back. Bishop O'Connor warned that the vote would continue to change sides until justice was done. In 1881 O'Shanassy conspired successfully to bring Berry down again; the clergy then persuaded a rather unwilling O'Loghlen to appoint a royal commission on education. Irritation with the Catholics was sharpened in 1881 and 1882 by local support for the Irish National League and news of the terrorist murders in Phoenix Park, Dublin.* In the Liberal party-room J. B. Patterson and other Orangemen demanded an overt anti-papist policy and several Catholics were expelled from caucus.[1]

Party allegiances held firmly enough to shape the broad course of the brief election campaign. Yet Protestant-liberal defence of the Education Act was the only major issue to emerge; both parties, while genuinely concerned to restore a viable political system by eliminating the Catholic wreckers, were spurred on to sectarian extremism by the Orangemen in their ranks. The Liberal *Age* viciously distorted the Irish issue, as part of its attack on Catholics for 'always bringing the altar to the polling booth',[2] and accused the Constitutionalists of allying themselves with the

* See p. 238.

Catholics. Not to be so smeared, some of the conservative organs like *Punch* replied in kind:

> Thumbs down on the Thursday to come;
> From priest and the pig let's be free;
> No more of priest's craft or Home Rule;
> Cast off the old man of the see.[3]

The government was so unpopular that O'Loghlen had difficulty in finding candidates and was himself defeated. The result of the election was inconclusive. Berry claimed a victory but according to the *Argus* about thirty-eight Constitutionalists were returned, thirty-two Liberals and fifteen supporters of the ministry and independents. Hardly any Catholics survived except those who supported the Education Act.[4]

Neither party could form a secure ministry so, despite long-standing enmities, it was agreed to coalesce—but exactly when the agreement was made is uncertain. There are persistent stories that the coalition was a brain-child of David Syme and his men. But the possibility had been canvassed long before. Berry and Henry Wrixon had almost brought it off in August 1880, and Wrixon continued to work for it; the probability of a coalition was common gossip a fortnight before the election. Simon Fraser, a leading Orangeman, claimed that he and Patterson were mainly responsible.[5] It seems likely that the men from the *Age* made the broad proposal to James Service, a freetrader, that he should join on equal terms with Berry, on the understanding that protection would be a settled policy and that the *Age* would support the ministry. Service demanded the premiership and worked out the details with Berry; each vetoed two or three of the other's choice of colleagues, but there was little difficulty in agreeing on a programme. On 6 March, when the Assembly met, Service's no-confidence motion was quickly carried without a division. Charles Pearson rejoiced that 'the decent men of the two parties fused into one strong following' and that many of the less reputable from both went into opposition. The bankers congratulated themselves that the finances were in Service's safe hands.[6]

James Service, who had just returned from two years in Britain, appeared very much as a saviour. A 'sturdy, stiff-necked, indomitable and canny' Scot now touching sixty, he had been intended for the kirk until his father, Robert, was converted to Baptism. Father and son had been staunch moral-force Chartists. James was a schoolmaster for several years, then joined a Glasgow tea and coffee firm of which he became a partner, migrated in 1853, and prospered as a merchant specializing in the distribution of Robur tea. Robert followed his son to the colony and became prominent as a preacher and temperance worker; his ideas broadened and by 1870, when he founded the Sunday Free Discussion Society, he was something of a sceptic. James became first mayor of Emerald Hill, was a member of the Assembly from 1857 to 1862, carried the Torrens reform of land transfers, introduced as Lands Minister the first radical selection

H. J. Wrixon, 1886

Bill, and resigned in disgust while it was being cut down to the innocuous Nicholson Act. He was indeed a classical advanced liberal—though not a democrat, for he continued to support a dual property vote and the rights of an upper house based on property. But he fervently believed in equality of opportunity, was sympathetic to trade unions, and worked enthusiastically to elevate the underprivileged. He was vehemently anti-clerical and anti-papist; his remark that the Catholic grievance was not a question of conscience but only of cash was long held against him. Though a religious sceptic, he was still concerned with matters of faith and used to investigate spiritualist phenomena with his friend and banking associate, Gyles Turner. His belief in free trade led to electoral defeats for several years. Throughout the seventies he was chairman of directors of the Commercial Bank and an active president of the Alfred Hospital. On returning to the Assembly he became Treasurer in the Kerferd coalition ministry; then after condemning McCulloch's opportunism he supported the Berry ministry of 1877 but broke with them after 'Black Wednesday'. He succeeded McCulloch as Opposition Leader and came briefly to power in 1880. Service was a lean, sprightly, tallish man, grey-eyed, balding with full grey beard. Courteous, sociable and popular, he was a natural conciliator, bore few grudges and did not resort to personalities; he had no trace of snobbishness. His honesty was patent, he could not dissemble, and while adept at compromise was no trimmer. He was not an orator but, as Deakin wrote, his

> strength lay in the lucidity of his thought and the simplicity of his language, his skill in marshalling masses of facts or figures, in grouping and grasping, in interpreting, clarifying, and contrasting them; sum-

> ming up the argument or situation by homely metaphors or terse epigrammatic phrases . . . the note of his speeches was almost purely intellectual, for though capable of being strongly moved, keenly sensitive, and greatly swayed by his deeper feelings, the heat which glowed within him was generally disguised under an apparent *sang froid*.

His precise mind was shown in his financial ability, and his emotional fervour in the zeal for imperialism and federation he was yet to reveal. He was highly cultivated and well-read; J. A. Froude was impressed by his reflective conversation which reminded him of a philosopher or English bishop. Most extraordinary of all in Victorian Melbourne—having separated from his wife in the eighteen-fifties, he took another 'wife' by whom he had several daughters, lived down the gossip, and won wide approval and affection as a public man.[7]

Graham Berry and Service respected and liked each other, despite the bitter conflicts of the previous decade. Berry had been a small Chelsea draper with little interest in politics before he migrated in 1852 at the age of thirty and opened a grocery in South Yarra. He closely resembled his near-contemporary, Henry Parkes, in his humble origins, determination to improve himself by study of history and literature, and entry into journalism to finance a political career. Both were forceful orators (who scattered aspirates erratically), had a genius for debate and instinctive political insight, and grew from demagogues almost to statesmen. Even before his first election to the Assembly in 1861, Berry had become a leading protectionist spokesman; by 1878 he was idolized by the masses and hated more by the upper classes than any radical in Victorian history, before or since. Yet his radicalism was moderate; except in that one crisis, he did not use the language of class antagonism or recommend any fundamental modification of society. 'All I see in politics worth troubling about is the good of the working classes,' he once said, and claimed that what was being achieved in Victoria made him feel that he had 'something worth living for'—the relief of hardship, and the material, educational and moral elevation of the workingman. He had a vain streak, was jaunty in demeanour with a rather prancing walk, and had such magnetic attractiveness that people often stopped and stared after him in the street. By now much of the old fire had died, though he was by no means an extinct volcano; he had mellowed, was more polished and polite and content to rest on his political laurels, but any rude opponent still found him a tough customer.*[8]

Of the eighty-six members of the Assembly, approximately thirty-six were born in England, nineteen in Scotland and sixteen in Ireland, while

* Service nominated as colleagues Duncan Gillies (see p. 40), G. B. Kerferd, a Beechworth brewer, lawyer and former Premier, and J. F. Levien. Berry gathered Alfred Deakin (see pp. 40-41), A. L. Tucker, a Fitzroy accountant, and G. D. Langridge, the popular Collingwood estate agent. R. S. Anderson was at first the only member from the Council, but after his death in October 1883, F. T. Sargood was brought in as Minister of Defence, and James Campbell and N. Thornley were added to the ministry in 1884.

J. B. Patterson, 1888

only twelve were native-born.* About fifty-four—almost two-thirds—were migrants from the United Kingdom in the fifties; thirteen had arrived before gold and six after 1860. About thirty were Anglicans, twenty Presbyterians (mostly on the 'Conservative' side), fifteen Wesleyans (nearly all Liberals), nine Catholics, three Congregationalists and three Jews. There were only three pastoralists, and nine were farmers; five were city merchants and four financiers, while seven were lawyers and five practised other professions. Fully half the members were small businessmen of the most diverse kind: retailers, auctioneers, stock and station agents, manufacturers, mining agents and local newspaper proprietors.[9] When some trade unionists began a movement for direct representation of Labour in Parliament, a politician commented that almost exactly half his colleagues had been 'tradesmen' of the following occupations: miners, publicans, carpenters, draymen, grocers, drapers, engineers, printers, chemists, nailer, gardener, calico printer, tailor, bookseller, butcher, mason, builder, sawyer, saddler, boilermaker, nurseryman, cabinetmaker, blacksmith, jeweller, patternmaker, currier, teamster, wheelwright, hosier, brewer, shoemaker and capmaker.[10] Most of these men now owned their own businesses, though not always in their earlier trade, while others were professional politicians with minor business interests on the side. One adverse critic summed them up as 'supple Bourgeois' and 'respectable cunning middlemen'.[11]

The formation of the coalition was widely popular. Prolonged wrangles about reform of the Legislative Council had exhausted the contestants; the

* Information is lacking in a few cases and definition is sometimes impossible, but all these figures are very close to the mark.

even division between two parties and an unstable centre had produced a stalemate; and the protection-free trade issue was largely settled. Ideological differences were now allowed to remain latent and common assumptions to prevail; the neglected business of developing the colony could proceed.

Ideological assumptions and influences; the nature of politics

Despite their blatant sectional and personal objectives, nearly all politicians agreed that it was their opportune task to build a society based on British institutions and traditions of freedom, but materially far superior to Britain, and hence happier and morally superior. Equality of opportunity was the most commonly accepted objective: all should start fair in life; inherited inequality and privilege were anathema. 'Equality such a people as ours will have at all hazards, and at any cost,' Wrixon had written. 'We may well hope that our descendants will preserve freedom, but we may be perfectly certain that they will insist on equality.'[12] To increase opportunities and raise living standards by development of the colony was the chief business of politics. As Patterson once said: 'Our only object in representing the community should be . . . to improve the conditions of the community—to find employment and plenty of it, and to see that the people have a fair field and plenty of chances of doing well.'[13]

Nevertheless, ideological divisions still had some force in the coalition period from 1883 to 1890, despite the party truce, criss-crossing religious and regional loyalties, and the activities of parochial and place-hunting politicians. Party caucus meetings continued; the class and interest basis of the parties remained obvious, though it was becoming less clear-cut. There was a grain of truth in R. E. N. Twopeny's description of the Liberals and Constitutionalists as 'the present and the past lower orders'. Wrixon, for one, had been deploring the degree to which liberalism had become 'a cry of the worse-off against the better-off'.[14] The pastoralist, the merchant and the banker looked still to the Constitutionalists; the Trades Hall and most of the mining towns remained loyal to the Liberals. Yet the precarious Liberal alliance of miner, selector, and manufacturer and artisan had largely broken up. Time had almost healed the mutual hatred of squatter and selector; most of the farming seats north of the Range had swung against Berry in the election. Few merchants and manufacturers were fighting still over the tariff and many were finding a common interest in extending Victoria's intercolonial trade. The National Reform and Protection League machine had almost run down and the weakness of other political organizations demonstrated the decline of ideological fervour. None the less, the two groups in the coalition remained distinct, and Cabinet had frequently to be conducted on the basis of compromise.

An illustration of the power of the *Age* is the historical confusion it caused by dubbing the Constitutionalists 'Conservatives', a title which they rightly never accepted. However, it became popular usage, was adopted by Deakin and his friend Sir Charles Dilke in their writings, and has been followed by subsequent historians. 'There is not another member . . . who is half so much a liberal as I am, and as I was in the very early days', complained John McIntyre; 'because I happen to believe in freedom of trade I have been dubbed Conservative'. Tell a lie often enough and it will be believed, Bruce Smith protested.[15] However often the Constitutionalists proclaimed themselves as liberals at election-time, the dreadful charge stuck. No shorthand tag will suffice; but to name the 'Conservatives' Liberals and the 'Liberals' Democrats would be nearer the mark.

There were plenty of conservatives in the colony in a stronger political position than has commonly been allowed. Philosophical conservatives, whose pessimistic view of human nature allowed no support for legislative amelioration, may have been few. But there were numerous products of the jungle, well represented in the Legislative Council, whose politics consisted merely of naked defence of recently acquired property. Wrixon had described them:

> The distinguishing mark of our upper class is its wealth, but in no quarter of the globe could there be a less trustworthy test of merit or intelligence. Some of the least deserving have grown rich by sharp business habits,—some of the most ignorant by chance or cunning. . . . Wealth is the only badge of our aristocracy, but it confers a nobility neither exclusive nor enduring.[16]

Moreover, important social groups—most pastoralists and bankers, many merchants, most of the judiciary and lawyers, higher civil servants and Anglican and Presbyterian clergy—had brought with them or adopted unalloyed Toryism. These groups had not accepted democracy or the egalitarian assumptions of the majority; their support enabled the Council to hold out through all crises with its powers unimpaired. Despite the radical tone of Victorian politics, conservatism had not been defeated but was merely kept constantly on the defensive. In practice, the chief spokesmen for the conservatives and the Council were the exponents of classical *laissez-faire* liberalism who believed that the unhindered operation of free enterprise, free trade and 'enlightened self-interest' would produce the greatest material progress. These dogmatic, inflexible theorists, like the unofficial leader of the Council, Dr W. E. Hearn, Robert Murray Smith, Edward Langton, or the *Argus* editorial writers, were totally at odds with the massive state intervention being extended by governments of all complexions. In 1887 Bruce Smith published his anachronistic 683-page *Liberty and Liberalism. A Protest against the Growing Tendency toward undue Interference by the State, with individual Liberty, private Enterprise, and the Rights of Property*. He believed liberalism's task now was only '*to guard over* the equal liberties of citizens generally, with a view to their *preservation*'.[17] Some of these men and others like Gyles Turner preached social Darwinism as backing for their *laissez-faire* theory; the biological analogy of the survival of the fittest must rule out molly-coddling by the state.[18] Yet even the doctrinaire Murray Smith, who became an embarrassment to his party, would defend Victoria's limited democracy. Writing to a friend in 1882, he remarked that democracy, 'with all its drawbacks',

> is the best thing going and the most generous. Democracies are sometimes silly, hasty, unjust, but they are never coldly and deliberately cruel. You and I have made a mark in different ways. What could we ever have done at home with a dead weight of wealth and privilege hanging over us? It seems absurd to say so, but I don't believe there are any more sincere democrats than you and I, and, however unpopular I may be, nevertheless I say, 'Let democracy flourish'.[19]

About one-sixth of the members of the Assembly between 1880 and 1900 might be described as conservatives in the foregoing terms;[20] and most Legislative Councillors would have to be added. But the large majority of the Constitutionalists were at least as liberal as most of the English Liberal party. Service fairly claimed he was 'a Liberal of the Gladstone stamp', not 'within a thousand miles of being a Conservative'.[21] He and others like Gillies, Kerferd and Wrixon, had been anti-pastoralist land reformers, who wanted to equalize opportunity; they were freetraders certainly (or by now 'low protectionists') but in other respects were willing to use the state to increase opportunity without dogmatic respect for the rights of private enterprise. They properly resented being saddled with the behaviour of the Council, though they could not escape responsibility for their own right wing in the Assembly. The 'Conservatives' broadly were backed by pseudo-aristocratic, upper-middle-class and professional groups, and by thousands of other prosperous property-owners of whom Charles Pearson remarked: 'democracy has given them what they want, and they feel grateful to it, and would resent any open attack upon it, but are not disposed to carry it out in new directions'.[22] The 'Conservatives' in short were distinguished from the Liberals in that they accepted only three or four points of the Charter and were not willing to go quite so far or quite so fast.[23]

Pearson defined a large part of the Liberal creed when he wrote:

> when I speak of Democracy I mean self-government by men educated up to a common low level, and trained by the habit of self-government under institutions which secure power to the majority. I assume that such men will be disposed to look to the duties of property at least as jealously as to its rights; will sympathise with labour against capital where the two are in apparent antagonism; will wish to see property subdivided, and will be especially careful of whatever secures the independence of the poorer classes, vote by ballot, universal suffrage, and free education.[24]

The Liberals were the democratic party in that they wished to eliminate or greatly reduce the power of the Council, to bring in 'one man, one vote', and to safeguard payment of members. Backed by the Trades Hall, they were more concerned to attack economic privilege, curb capitalism, harass large landed interests, increase protection, widen state intervention, eliminate 'sweating', and reduce hours of work. Nonconformism, rationalism and nationalism were all stimulating influences, while Orangemen and temperance reformers added stern principled elements. On the left, supporters of state banking, land nationalization, Henry George's single land-tax and other forms of severe property taxation anticipated the later course of politics.

The protection issue was still a good guide to party allegiance. However, some protectionists, usually farming representatives, were on the 'Conservative' side, while Pearson and a few other freetraders stood by the Liberals. The battle for protection had been fought and won as a bread-and-butter issue by interest groups: manufacturers and farmers against merchants. Victory had been made easier by Victoria's revenue problem which led many politicians to settle for low protection as the most convenient form of taxation. Victoria had much less than half the land revenue of New South Wales; the protectionist increases of 1871, 1878 and 1879 had all been at times of budgetary difficulty; higher duties had been adopted in preference to borrowing, raising land revenue or imposing additional direct taxation. The argument over principle was now settled, vested interests had been created which could not be destroyed, and moderate politicians on either side were content. The royal commission on the tariff chaired by James Mirams, which was appointed in September 1881 and reported in October 1883, was conducted on the basis of compromise and attempted to construct a simplified and scientific tariff on the agreed basis of moderate protection.[25] A few extremists on both sides, most of whom opposed the coalition, carried on the fight. In public the propaganda battle continued unabated, especially in the columns of the *Age* and *Argus*; the dreary theologians doggedly restated their misguided claims about the beneficial or disastrous effects of protection on Victoria. But protection had become respectable. By the late eighties more than four-fifths of the Assembly found it convenient to describe themselves in the *Victorian Parliamentary Handbook* as protectionists (and liberals), and veterans looked proudly back to 'the olden times when we fought the great battle of protection'.[26]

'State socialism' or 'colonial socialism' was already well advanced in other directions: the state was a huge landlord and money-lender, monopolized the building and operation of railways, poured money into public works, subsidized mining and agriculture, and owned and operated the telegraph system. It generously succoured its creatures, the shires and municipalities, but often with strict conditions over expenditure. The degree of state economic activity which developed in the later part of the century and the weakness of doctrinaire defence of rugged individualism are a curiosity of Victorian and Australian history. Private capital was too puny to provide for major works like railways, only the state could build on such a scale; but state action went far beyond such necessities. The prevailing assumption was that massive public works and artificial state support were essential to promote settlement, increase population and provide employment; the North American technique of land grants in return for building railways and other services was deliberately rejected. Dilke noted how strong the assumption was, compared to Britain or North America, that the state could influence the level of prosperity. In the eighties and nineties state intervention developed further, towards protecting the underprivileged.[27]

Politicians usually justified state action and their unusual limited economic planning on pragmatic grounds. David Syme's propaganda in the *Age* made their task relatively easy and provided theory for those who demanded it. No other intellectual had such a coherent and forceful programme or a comparable platform. Syme was able enough as an economist to make a shrewd theoretical attack on orthodox *laissez-faire*; his *Outlines of an Industrial Science* (1876) had won him some international standing. He dismissed the conventional notion that free trade was 'in accordance with the teachings of nature'. The gardener and farmer constantly mended nature:

> In the same manner a legislature mends nature when it passes a measure for the removal of nuisances which are injurious to health . . . every positive law is an interference with natural law. Is there anything peculiarly sacred about industry that it should be looked upon as sacrilege to lay hands on it? . . . The dogma of *laissez-faire*, if applied to social life, would be the negation of all law. . . .
>
> Is it desirable, from an individual point of view, that a certain act should be performed? Then the individual should perform it. Is it desirable, from a social point of view, that a certain act should be performed? Then the state should perform it. . . .
>
> What is good for all, and not merely for an individual or a class, should be undertaken by the state; what benefits only the few should be left to private enterprise.[28]

Syme recognized the need for theoretical study of economic growth in new countries, a topic neglected by economists everywhere; he knew that the doctrine of free trade was tailored to the needs of Britain, which only followed free trade as far as it suited its interests. He was a nationalist in that he wanted to see a colonial society which was guided by its own interests and which was more than an extension of free trade England—though, to this extent, nearly all colonists agreed. It was enough for Dr Hearn, he could write, 'that the commercially fittest should survive, without reference to whether such survivors were to be his fellow-citizens or aliens at the uttermost ends of the earth'.[29] Syme was a radical, an anti-monopolist, a champion of the have-nots and the trade unions; his criticism of competition was similar to the socialists'. Well ahead of his time, he supported a state bank and state note-issue, the non-alienation of crown lands, industrial legislation, and more even distribution of wealth by means of direct taxation.[30]

This seemingly most grim and dour of Scots—tall, spare, upright, imperious, with flinty face and searching eyes—had finally achieved security and political power after establishing the *Age* in the face of violent hostility from conservatives in the business world. The long battle, following the strictest and least loving of upbringings and harsh experience on the Californian and Victorian goldfields, produced a combative, ruthless, emotionally violent man who made few reservations about means and ends. The men on the *Age* lived under iron discipline and on frugal wages. The editorial blue pencil missed little, only a rare joke slipped by; Syme's one famous joke was the figure of Mercury (who slew Argus) surmounting the pediment on the *Age* building. Syme lived for his paper, though he later developed a variety of business interests; his intellectual horizon was bounded by economics, politics and science, he was blind and deaf to the arts. He was mellowing a little by the eighties and the legend has perhaps exaggerated his austere and harsh nature. He was also a painfully shy man who was almost incapable of speaking at a public meeting. It would be difficult to find a more interesting talker, remarked Alfred Deakin, who like a few other friends found in him modest diffidence, warmth and tenderness. He was a far more successful parent than his father and was capable of many private acts of generosity.[31]

Perhaps Syme's greatest ability was in picking men. A. L. Windsor, editor from 1872 to 1900, a brilliant man who was better read and a better writer than Syme, was content to be his instrument, but may have contributed much more than we know on day-to-day policy. A. B. Robinson, father of great entrepreneurs, was an able financial and commercial editor for thirty years and Syme's private business adviser. Syme took up Deakin at the age of twenty-two and they quickly became friends. Politically, however, Deakin retained his independence and was anything but Syme's creature; it is much to both men's credit that they remained on affectionate terms for thirty years. More extraordinary was Syme's alliance with Charles Pearson, Oxford don, professor of history at King's College, London, farmer in South Australia, first headmaster of the Melbourne Presbyterian Ladies' College, and M.L.A. from 1878. Pearson was both an original and prophetic thinker and a 'colonizer' of the latest overseas ideas. In the late seventies he was anticipating and advocating much of the modern welfare state: full employment, national insurance, social services, free education through grammar school to university. Practical as so many academics are, he was an effective politician who could stand up well to the hurly-burly. In three and a half years between 1880 and 1884 he wrote some 650 articles and editorials for the *Age* and the weekly *Leader*, adding intellectual distinction and breadth and sowing many ideas which were not reaped for a decade or more. In the canon of Victorian liberalism he ranks with Higinbotham, Syme, Berry and Deakin.[32]

The *Age* far outstripped rivals in sales from 1868 when its price was reduced to one penny; in the eighties circulation rose from about 40,000 to 100,000, remaining about five times that of the twopenny *Argus*. It defined liberalism simply as 'that energetic striving after better things' as against that 'spirit of caste and changelessness which is the inner essence of

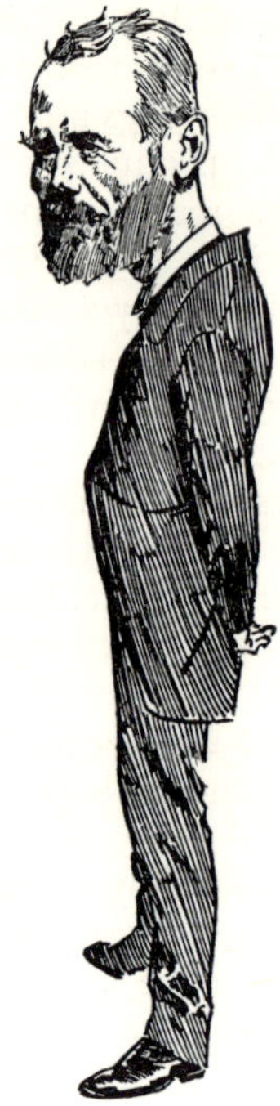

David Syme, 1888

Conservatism'.[33] Protection first and foremost, land reform, support for trade unions were the consistent planks of policy, but almost every radical idea had a hearing. It was less obsequiously colonial in outlook than any other important Australian daily newspaper of the time; but there was an uncertain tone about its handling of national and imperial questions. No person or institution was safe from the *Age*, not even its advertisers. The Governor might be attacked for neglecting his duties; the award of imperial honours was ridiculed; pretension, pomposity and flunkeyism were delightfully deflated, notably by 'Atticus' in the *Leader*. Syme had no doubts about the power of the press as an organ of progress and as an 'educating agency', or rather as a 'public instructor'.[34] But while Syme allowed very free comment, news was not sacred. One of his disillusioned reporters remarked: 'The *Age* is not a newspaper; it's a political engine.' News was frequently distorted, slanted, suppressed; there was justification for *Punch*'s nickname of 'Ananias'. Reporters sometimes as part of their duties had to discover what they could to the discredit of the *Age*'s political opponents. Sir Thomas Esmonde, a visiting Irish home-ruler, considered the *Age* and the *Argus* 'better gotten up and more capably directed than any newspaper in the United Kingdom'; at the same time the *Age* was 'the larrikin of Australian journalism' which on the Irish question lied 'hot

F. W. Haddon, 1888

and strong, and broad and deep', and insinuated and misrepresented, and suppressed and falsified, and never allowed any reply. Even Deakin judged the *Age* to be frequently 'virulent, variable and unfair' and recklessly partisan.[35] Its occasional puzzling inconsistency may be explained partly by Syme's obsession with running counter to whatever was the policy of the *Argus*.

The legend has it that Syme 'ruled the country as absolutely as a Tsar',[36] and held a 'dominant power . . . that no public man of the time dared question or rebel against'.[37] Deakin, who was in an unrivalled position to judge, pitched the claim much lower:

> The relations between [Syme] and public men were intimate to a surprising degree. He enjoyed their confidence in and out of office, shaping their programmes from time to time, governing their selection of colleagues as incoming Premiers and enjoying afterwards a knowledge of the inmost secrets of Cabinets. . . .[38]

It appears that the *Age* first achieved great influence with the Berry ministry of 1877. From then on, any politician ignored it at his peril. David Munro, a machinery manufacturer, remarked that he saw hundreds of his men reading the paper at his works every morning: 'they take their politics from the *Age*'.[39] The Trades Hall and many of the mass readership were almost captive. Editorials printed in larger type and more prominent than any news item carried great weight. When the *Age* adopted the anti-sweating or irrigation movements, they immediately became 'practical politics'. Parliamentary candidates could be squashed by writing down, or built up into prominence.[40] Yet the limitations of the *Age*'s influence in the eighties are demonstrated by the poverty of liberal achievement and the fact that so many of Syme's pet beliefs—elective ministries and the iniquity of government by party, non-alienation of land, co-operatives and profit-sharing—were almost hopeless causes. One of the advantages of coalition was that it reduced the *Age*'s influence. The peak of its power was to come in the nineties when legend and fact approximate.

In 1884 Angus Mackay, proprietor of the Bendigo *Advertiser* and founder-editor of the Sydney *Daily Telegraph*, condemned the Melbourne press for its constant political misrepresentation: 'it allows a feeling of party to enter into every walk of life, and looks upon every one outside its circle, and who holds different views and opinions, as an enemy'.[41] The charge was aimed as much at the ultra-conservative *Argus* as the *Age*. In its editorials at least, the *Argus* was just as venomous and attempted political assassination quite as frequently; it waged constant vendetta against Pearson and other 'class traitors'. Esmonde, however, thought it had a 'ghost of a conscience' compared to the *Age*. Its news columns were usually objective, though it was capable of ruthless distortion. Deakin, a prejudiced witness, believed Howard Willoughby's brilliant weekly political commentaries, 'Above the Speaker', were 'masterpieces of consistent and deliberate misrepresentation'.[42] The *Argus* nominally supported the 'Conservatives' but was usually found in full support of the Council. Free trade had been its guiding star, and total incapacity to compromise on this lost issue greatly reduced its influence. Its upper-class prejudice and blatant provocation of capital against the workingman almost justified the Sydney *Bulletin*'s contemptuous title for it of the 'Squatter's Friend and Vested Interests' Guardian'. 'Nobody minds the *Argus*,' Wrixon once comforted Mrs Pearson after one of its personal attacks.[43] While it continued to be a highly profitable enterprise, Frederick W. Haddon, editor from 1867 to 1898, was given an almost completely free hand. Haddon had been assistant-secretary of the Statistical Society of London when Edward Wilson engaged him as private secretary and then quickly raised him to the editorship. A man of cultivated literary taste, Haddon soon subordinated what independence of mind he may have had to the needs of the Victorian Establishment.* Nevertheless, he made the *Argus* into a magnificent newspaper. Twopeny and others believed it 'the best daily paper published out of England',[44] or second only to *The Times*. In size, range of news, fullness of reporting, and literary content, it left the *Age* far behind. The

* Wilson remained a radical but his partners, Lauchlan Mackinnon and Allan Spowers were able to outvote him. After Wilson's death in 1878, his trustees and the Mackinnon and Spowers families retained control.

Argus and its weekly, the *Australasian*, might, indeed, be put forward as the best evidence of Melbourne's high intellectual and cultural stature in the late nineteenth century.

There were many other journalistic influences, of which the *Daily Telegraph* and its *Weekly Times* were the most important. After fourteen undistinguished years as a morning daily, the *Telegraph* was bought in 1883 by an evangelical syndicate headed by James Balfour. 'Conservative' in politics, it was ably and energetically managed, with the Reverend W. H. Fitchett as consulting editor, and rivalled the *Argus* in circulation.[45] The *Herald*, an evening paper since 1869, had a sensational style and little political influence.* The poverty-stricken weekly *Advocate*, controlled by Joseph Winter, was spokesman for the Irish Catholics who, constantly libelled by the three morning dailies, had some influence on the *Herald* through its part-owner and editor, Samuel Vincent Winter, Joseph's brother. *Punch* was a powerful propagandist organ of the Legislative Council and was financed by conservative interests. More than two hundred newspapers and journals were published in Victoria. The country press was in its heyday and many of the provincial newspapers were of high standard. Several of the large towns carried two dailies or tri-weeklies which broadly supported the Liberal and 'Conservative' causes. The Ballarat *Courier*, which had the largest circulation of any paper outside the capital cities, was an outstanding example of a powerful democratic journal; it was edited by E. J. Bateman who was backed by able journalists like Thomas Bury and W. B. Withers.[46] The ability of Christopher Crisp, editor-proprietor of the Bacchus Marsh *Express*, won an influential circulation. Railway extensions were increasing the circulation of the metropolitan dailies, but for some time yet the metropolitan weeklies were read more widely in country areas than the dailies.

Lengthy discussion of ideology and party propaganda may give a misleading impression of political behaviour unless note is also taken of the frequency with which parliamentarians owed their election to their religious views or the influence of the licensed victuallers or prohibitionists.[47] Moreover, localism and opportunism remained very important. Many politicians firmly believed in their independence and freedom from party control; the notion of Parliament as a collection of individuals whose prime duty was to act as agents for local constituents remained strong. Governments almost always had to purchase the support of some 'independent' members and give favoured treatment to nominal supporters as well as staunch adherents; similarly, leading politicians trying to create a faction around themselves would promise future bounty. So the local member would sell himself, for a period, for establishment of a government agency or a government contract for a firm in his electorate. The railway was the great prize in rural areas, for on it the future of a town or district depended, and it greatly raised property values. Grants for roads and

* Other daily (evening) papers—the *World* (1881–5), N. Levi's *Daily News* (1885–6) and, later, the *Evening Standard* (1889–94)—were of little consequence.

bridges reduced the farmer's marketing costs, and likewise raised property values. Hence, in the developing areas especially, the member was judged more often by his lobbying prowess than by his views. This pork-barrel, pig-swill aspect of politics, with all its lamentable effects on governmental stability and coherent developmental policy, was an inevitable feature of a colony with democratic institutions.* Ambition and opportunism were to be expected, and the struggle for a well-paid Cabinet post was vigorous. The trouble was, as one old parliamentary hand remarked, 'the mother pig has not sufficient teats for the many little piggy-wiggys about her'.[48] Outright bribery and corruption of politicians, however, were now almost unknown. There is a strong case for arguing that payment of members of the Assembly (introduced in 1870) had worked for good.[49] More to the point, the watchful party press was ready to pounce. Blackguardism was confined to two or three members; one of them was said to have kept files on all his colleagues which detailed misdemeanours, scandals and family skeletons.[50] It was remarked in 1885 that only one member of the Assembly was a drunkard, that even he could speak coherently, and that the worst scenes were created by the teetotallers.[51] Rough and crude though it was in many respects, the Victorian Assembly was no discredit to the colony at this stage at least. The high boom years were to test every member's probity.

One other political factor demands separate treatment; the inspiration of George Higinbotham. No man in Australian history, perhaps, has been so taken as a model of conduct and so loved and revered. The historian, faced with a man with unique claims of character and personal influence for good, vainly struggles to grasp him; just as his obituarists and disciples movingly and ineffectively struggled to define and express their debts. This Dublin-born barrister served his political apprenticeship as radical editor of the *Argus* in the fifties, and became the driving-force of the McCulloch ministries in the sixties, when he devoted himself to smashing the power of the Legislative Council. In this period, he developed his vendetta against the Colonial Office and his peculiar views on the Victorian constitution, while remaining the most staunch of imperial loyalists. As chairman of the royal commission on education and subsequently, he made the greatest single contribution to the shape of the Education Act. He could easily have taken the leadership of the Liberal party instead of Berry; but the practice of party government was alien to him. In 1876 he retired in disillusion from parliamentary politics which he had come to regard as 'a sort of pandemonium in which a number of lost souls are endeavouring to increase one another's torture'.[52] In 1880 he was raised to the Supreme Court bench and was to become Chief Justice in 1886. In this later period of his career he stood out as the agonized proponent of Christianity without creeds and churches and also, such was his reputation as a democrat, as the idol of the trade union movement. He was, of course, obstinate,

* See (Sir) Henry Wrixon's laborious novels, closely based on experience: *Jacob Shumate* . . . (London, 1903) and *Edward Fairlie Frankfort, or Politics among the People* (London, 1912).

extreme, 'as uncompromising as chastity', utterly unrealistic in the standards he set, often impossible to deal with, and possibly profoundly mistaken in his constitutional interpretation.* But his contempt for materialist values shamed most of his political critics into muted respect. Although as orator and ideologist he stood out in his generation, his main influence was private and personal. Ben Douglass, the veteran trade unionist, was one of his closest friends; so was Service for whom there was never 'a truer man, a better man, a nobler man', whatever his extraordinary notions on how to bring about the millennium. Of the younger generation whom he nurtured, William Shiels like many others found him 'the most chivalrous, the most gentle, the most considerate' of mentors. The range of men whose lives and conduct were deeply affected by his magnetic charm, humility and example ranged from Wrixon, Gyles Turner, Deakin, H. B. Higgins and W. H. Irvine to Labour men such as Dr Maloney and Randolph Bedford.[53]

The Service-Berry ministry

The first thing the Service-Berry ministry had to do, all the press agreed and nearly every politician admitted, was to reform the public service. Its condition was lamentable. Intrigues and poor discipline characterized an overmanned and inefficient service. Men looked back in shame to the iniquitous 'Black Wednesday', when so many were summarily dismissed and several distinguished men, like the architect William Wardell, were permanently lost. The 1862 Civil Service Act had been soundly based, providing for entrance by examination and a system of classification. There were loopholes in the Act, however, and ministers habitually appointed hangers-on as supernumeraries, to whom classification did not apply, and promoted them at whim. It was now almost impossible to enter the service without help by a political patron; by 1883 there were at least twice as many supernumeraries as those who had entered in the standard manner. Clerks, policemen, railwaymen, teachers were appointed for no other reason than that they were friends, relatives or constituents of parliamentary supporters of the ministry of the day; applicants who lived in borderline constituencies were preferred. Ministers and Parliament wasted much time dealing with administrative detail relating to the service; members were badgered and embarrassed by constant requests for patronage. The demand for a secure public billet was enormous for, in the area of manual labour at least, most outside employment was temporary.[54]

The condition of the Railways department, where patronage was at its worst, alarmed the public most. A succession of inexperienced tinkering ministers had not allowed departmental officers sufficient responsibility. Already in 1876 and 1880 governments had decided to establish an independent commission which would 'take the Railways out of politics', but they lost office before they could act. In 1882 Bent's behaviour as minister and a succession of accidents roused intense public feeling which was

* See pp. 303-4.

partly whipped up by the press as anti-government propaganda. O'Loghlen hastily introduced legislation, but the election intervened; the issue was so prominent in the campaign that the new government had the clearest possible mandate to act. The Victorian Railways Commissioners Bill was passed without difficulty. A Commission of three full-time members was set up and control of the railways passed to them. Parliament of course retained full financial authority and decided what lines were to be built; the Commission's by-laws were to be subject to the approval of the Governor-in-Council. The Act was partly a compromise between those wishing to retain the Railways as a government department and those who wanted operation handed to private enterprise; the latter was a forlorn hope since private enterprise would seek highest possible profits and would be unlikely to allow low freight rates to farmers. The government appointed as chairman, Richard Speight from the English Midland Railway; his handsome salary of £3,000 (£1,200 more than the Premier's) was not high by world standards for such posts. The Commissioners made a good start, bringing in many reforms. A brief period of profit-making led other colonies to copy the technique of the independent commission for their railways. But by 1886 it was clear that the spirit of the Act was not being observed; Parliament was interfering as much as ever, and the difficult problem of the appropriate relationship between Parliament and the Commission, between policy and administration, had not been solved. But whatever the immediate consequences to the Victorian Railways, this legislation of 1883 was a landmark—for it began 'the great administrative revolution' which made the statutory corporation so important a feature of Australian government and ultimately had effects far beyond Australia.*[55]

The Public Service Act of 1883, which quickly followed, abolished ministerial patronage by setting up an independent Public Service Board (the first in Australia) to control appointment and promotion. The service could now be entered only at the foot by examination, except for professional officers; promotion was to depend on merit as well as seniority. A distinguished outsider was appointed as chairman, J. M. Templeton, an actuary who was a very efficient and difficult man. The other members were M. H. Irving, former professor of Classics and English at the University and headmaster in turn of Wesley College and the Hawthorn Grammar School, and Thomas Couchman, secretary of the Department of Mines. The Board proceeded personally to inspect the work and to classify the great majority of civil servants one by one, and to apply new scales of payment. Friendly critics lamented that the salary scales provided no attraction for the best and brightest of Victoria's youth who would do far better for themselves in the commercial world. Within two years there were one thousand appeals against the Board's decisions, as the cuckoos were found out and demoted; the newspapers were full of complaints, the Public

* If this Act was of such crucial pioneering inventive importance as administrative historians claim, work needs to be done on its conceptual origins. Gillies and Service may have been no more than midwives.

Service Association called for an enquiry into the working of the Act, and the whole service was alleged to be in a state of open revolt.[56] Templeton and the ministry were at odds about the degree of independence the Board actually had; Templeton made the elementary blunder of assuming that when the Act said the Board could request the Governor to act on its advice, it meant the Governor and not Cabinet. Eventually he was forced to resign in 1888 when, after refusing to forgo a paid directorship, an Act was passed which forbade public servants to hold outside employment. Irving also resigned, the Board fell under the control of senior public servants, and the principle of seniority reigned supreme again over merit. Meanwhile Parliament was restive about the diminution of ministers' powers over public servants; some members regarded the Board as a disastrous failure. But however disappointing the outcome of reform, the new arrangements were surely superior to the traditional patronage system.[57]

As Treasurer as well as Premier, Service was fortunate in that his financial task was straightforward. Good seasons and the prosperity of the early boom years left him with no serious budgetary problem. Even though revenue from sale of land was falling, the healthy returns from Customs (which provided more than half the revenue) allowed him to leave taxation and the tariff unaltered and thus avoid potentially the most divisive and time-consuming issues of all. Existing direct taxation, though very mild, was grossly unfair. Under the land tax imposed by Berry in 1877, the 800 or so largest landed proprietors were paying an average of £145 each; the object of 'bursting up the large estates' was not being achieved (though the tax may have hindered further growth of estates) while most of the better-off escaped direct taxation. They were ultimately catered for in small degree by the estates duty brought in in 1870 (another Victorian 'first') which was graduated so mildly that when 'Money' Miller died in 1888, leaving an estate of almost £1,500,000, his executors paid only 5 per cent in duty. The general understanding of the coalition was that existing protection would not be modified. The issue was so sensitive that the government ignored the sensible report of the Mirams commission on the tariff. It had recommended increased duties where there was genuine protective effect, the elimination of duties for which no protective case could be made, and abolition of the iniquitous tax on livestock crossing the border which was so provocative to New South Wales.[58] But the government could not escape argument on important day-to-day decisions on the application of protection to the purchase of government stores and to the terms of government contracts. Avoidance of expenditure on assisted immigration, despite the pleas of the farmers, had also been a settled policy for more than a decade.[59] Service's main financial task was to prepare for a £4 million London loan, which was triumphantly achieved in 1885. It was all plain sailing for the old banker; with the full support of the business community he carried through three straightforward budgets.

Two urgent developmental tasks—railway construction and land settlement—dominated the government's thinking. Decisions to make railway extensions, taken in 1873, 1877 and 1880, had quadrupled the length of the tracks to 1,355 miles open in 1882. The planned growth had been relatively cautious and successful. Then Bent had brought in his notorious Bill which provided for a new line or spur for almost every constituency—a gross bribe which tended to demoralize politics. He intended to saddle the country with lines 'towards infinity, towards gum trees, swamps, cemeteries and private back doors', a critic observed.[60] After five months' pushing and shoving, the Bill was still not carried when the Assembly dissolved. In 1884 Gillies brought in his 'Octopus' Bill which absorbed nearly all Bent's proposals, provided for construction of 927 miles of track—even more than Bent had recommended—and was greeted with delighted approval. The Commissioners reported favourably on forty-seven of the proposed lines, with blithely low estimates of the cost. Backed by their local railway leagues, the training-grounds of so many politicians, the country members whose lines were in jeopardy rallied for the fray. In the end, after numerous rings had bargained with each other for support,[61] Parliament added fifteen lines, often against the government's wishes, and raised the total mileage to about 1,200; nearly everyone was satisfied. Provision was also made for rounding off the suburban network.[62]

The gay abandon of the politicians (to be seen at its most extreme in the sheerly crazy proposals of 1890) cannot be understood without recognizing both the emotional fervour induced by the railway engine as the symbol of progress and civilization and the changes it made in social life. The countryman simply *had* to have the railway. Apart from the crucial economic benefits, it vastly reduced his sense of isolation and allowed him to feel he was participating in modern civilization. Friends could meet more often, the remote farmer could occasionally visit the metropolis and the provincial city, and weekend or holiday excursion trips to faraway places were possible. 'Henceforth a trip to Melbourne was an ordinary occurrence, not a staggering phenomenon,' wrote a Gippsland girl. 'The old jogtrot, simple days of almost unbroken quiet and isolation were gone.'[63] Quicker, cheaper travel also increased the diversions of suburban life. No wonder half the Cabinet and the local member, vote-gathering at every stop and banqueting in every town, were exhilarated by the rejoicing crowds meeting the first train on a new line.

Land legislation was urgently needed. In the Mallee the rabbits and dingoes had largely taken over in the late seventies and the pastoralists on annual licence were fast giving up. The chaotic state of politics had prevented any action, but in 1883 A. L. Tucker, the Lands Minister, quickly managed to pass his Mallee Pastoral Leases Act whose object was to give tenants long leases under such favourable terms that they would improve holdings and make serious efforts to wipe out the pests. No alienation was provided for, though eventual agricultural settlement was envisaged. Passing of the Act was aided by the experience of a visiting parliamentary party which managed to get itself bushed for a time in the scrub.[64]

The 1878 Land Act also had to be renewed, but as hardly any good land

James Service, *c.* 1885

Graham Berry, *c.* 1885

George Higinbotham, *c.* 1890

C. H. Pearson, *c.* 1890

Duncan Gillies, *c.* 1885

Alfred Deakin, 1886

The Ministerial Bench, 1883

remained unselected and the Mallee had been otherwise provided for, Tucker's 1884 Act was relatively uncontroversial. The old system of pastoral tenure was abolished, as little now remained under it but remnants of runs and stony mountainsides. The Act continued the trend of encouraging small farmer-graziers, and was notable for the introduction for the first time of systematic classification and also for its provisions for leasing potentially rich swamplands at Koo-wee-rup, Moe and elsewhere as they were drained.[65]

None of this legislation was very radical or more than logical extension of previous laws. Pearson's subsequent claim that Victoria had reserved a great part of its land from sale in order to 'try the experiment of State landlordism', which he implied was an example of a world trend towards land nationalization, exaggerated the importance of the leasing provisions in the two Acts.[66] The Liberals were still obsessed by the land question. From 1870 W. H. Gresham's Land Tenure Reform League, which campaigned for abolition of alienation, was supported by Syme and Higinbotham; in 1873 Higinbotham's motion in the Assembly for abolition of land sales won eight other supporters.[67] Syme and Pearson would have made Berry's land tax much more harsh and progressive, both as a means of forcing subdivision and as redress for steep increases in land values which had been partly produced by state expenditure on railways and other public works.[68] In 1882 Berry included repurchase of freehold in his programme, and Deakin came out as a strong supporter of the leasing movement. In 1883 Mirams stumped the colony, trying to drum up support for his Land Reservation League and calling for abolition of alienation,[69] and John Quick published his classic *History of Land Tenure in the Colony of Victoria*, very much as a campaign document. Henry George was beginning to attract followers: in 1884 many of the radical young men in Ballarat were land nationalizers or single-taxers and acclaimed Quick when he lectured there on the land question.[70] Much of this was a reflection of the contemporary English land reform movement,[71] but there was also a peculiarly deep-seated local vehemence on the question, though few of the Liberals were outright land nationalizers. It was all rather an academic question, however, as the good land had been alienated and it would have been politically suicidal to challenge British colonists' notions about the sacredness of freehold. Nevertheless the ideological basis was being laid for the limited compulsory reacquisition which was ultimately to occur.

Extensive land settlement had been achieved. Overdue attention now had to be given to the problems of drought, markets and scientific farming. The Service government sensibly set about gathering information as the basis for planning, and set up two major commissions. Late in 1884 Deakin was seconded from the government for six months to head the commission on irrigation, and in September 1885 a strong commission on vegetable products began systematically reviewing the prospects of developing agricultural products other than wheat. The Department of Agriculture was expanded, and the government was happy to help F. T. Derham carry his Agricultural Colleges Bill in 1884;[72] Dookie and Longerenong were founded in 1886 and 1889 and other colleges were planned.

We shall observe in the next two chapters how the state was slowly extending its functions.[73] The financial outlay for country water supply was large, and irrigation was likely to need huge investment. Bounties for coal production and new agricultural products were being freely offered. Railway construction and operation involved immense sums; those who wanted to lease the railways to private enterprise were finally defeated in the debates of 1883–4. The Melbourne tramway system, however, under legislation of 1884, although it was to be constructed by the state, was to be temporarily operated by a private company. Telephones were nationalized in 1886 after a minimum of ideological debate. Social legislation was less prominent in the coalition years, though an important new Factories Act was passed in 1885, the operation of mining machinery was regulated from 1883, and trade unions were legalized in 1884. Neglected children were covered by legislation in 1883, but the annual vote for hospitals and other charitable institutions remained almost unchanged.

The coalition inevitably steered clear of controversial issues relating to democratic reform. Payment of members of the Assembly was renewed in 1883 on a free vote only by forty-three votes to twenty-eight, but was made permanent in 1886.[74] Plural voting was not to be challenged until 1888 and the female franchise was not yet a serious question. Similarly, no attempt was made to reform the electoral system which since O'Shanassy's anti-democratic coup of 1863 had provided for automatic enrolment of ratepayers and a 'contracting in' system for other adult males, who had to establish three months' residential qualification in a constituency, pay one shilling (later sixpence) for their electoral right, and re-enrol periodically. Five-sixths of the Assembly's electorate consequently were ratepayers; taking plural voting into account, only about two-thirds of adult males were enrolled and of them only about two-thirds normally voted. 'Manhood suffrage' thus amounted to a minority of the adult male population actually voting in an election—a telling comment on colonial democracy. The Council meanwhile became comparatively quiet, in contrast to its resolute obstructionism in the sixties and seventies. The 'reform' of 1881, which trebled its constituency to roughly half the Assembly's without reducing its almost unqualified powers, had immensely strengthened its position. Some of the bitter-enders like Sir William Mitchell had died, and Sir Charles Sladen had retired in disgust at the coalition of the Constitutionalists with the terrible Berry; representatives of wider branches of capital were being elected and slightly changing its tone.[75] Most of the members asserted their right-wing position by refusing to ally themselves with the 'Conservatives', let alone the Liberals; in 1883 Dr Hearn and James Lorimer were made joint leaders of the 'independent' party which sometimes met as a caucus of almost the whole house to discuss attitudes to legislation.[76] The Council's chief contributions between 1883 and 1885 were to wreck Deakin's Factory Act, to delay the legalization of trade unions, to reject in 1885 an electoral distribution Bill for the Assembly (which admittedly was a hurried measure to adjust outstanding anomalies before the 1886 election), but also, notably, to pass in 1884 after prolonged grave discussion—safely, now that it had lost almost all relevance—a Bill to provide for mining on private property, a measure which the Council had rejected fourteen times since 1856.

The government's major concentration of interest—certainly Service's—was on events in the Pacific and the imperial handling thereof, on its federal crusade and on defence responsibilities, all of which will be considered in chapter 6. Its major legislation for reform of the civil service and railway administration, land settlement, railway construction and regulation of industry had been sensible and unspectacular, and was backed by a mass of useful minor legislation which had been pending for years. In two years more Acts were passed than in any two previous parliaments; almost every area except education and the tariff was touched. In 1885, however, reform of the liquor laws excluded much else. Financial policy was basically sound: the extravagant plan of railway construction was to extend over several years, most of the lines were justified on any count, and the programme could be checked or pruned at any time. Business, the press—all but the most doctrinaire party men—applauded the workmanlike programme of legislation and the healing of the self-inflicted wounds during the 'Berry blight'. 'No parliament can show a more imposing record of great public utility', the *Age* conceded early in 1886.[77]

The parliamentary opposition was footling; there was not one attempt to oust the government in 1883 and 1884. In March 1883 Bent took the lead in founding a 'National Liberal League' based on the O'Loghlen ministry's supporters, notably the Irish; it was hardly heard of again.[78] Apart from the O'Loghlenites, the Opposition consisted of little more than disappointed contenders for place—'the Catholics and the captious', the *Argus* remarked.[79] The old Liberal radicals rejected by Berry or vetoed by Service from the ministry, notably Mirams, W. Collard Smith and Patterson, were dangerous, but ambitious 'Conservatives' like Robert Harper and John McIntyre also sulked and sniped. The discontented lacked press support and violently disagreed with each other; their sham attacks were easily handled. Bent emerged as Opposition leader, but he was too preoccupied with business adventures and too evidently an opportunist to be a major threat. In 1885, however, the long-drawn-out complexities of the licensing Bill and astute stonewalling by Bent, Collard Smith and Gaunson put the ministry in difficulties. Yet, remarkably, for three years Service and Berry kept tight control on all other major questions except approval of some railway lines and their attempt to negotiate a commercial treaty with Tasmania. Seeking the politics of consensus, the ministry was anxious to please everyone but the Irish Catholics, and usually obliged pressure groups and deputations—the Trades Hall equally with the Chambers of Commerce and Manufactures, though the licensed victuallers and the temperance cohorts were more difficult to reconcile.

Gillies and Deakin take over; the 1886 election

The government broke up fortuitously at the close of 1885 when its three leading members dropped out. Service was feeling the strain, and decided on firm medical advice to take a long holiday overseas. Berry had his eyes on the Agent-Generalship and a knighthood. Kerferd wanted a seat on the Supreme Court bench. These three and Gillies and Deakin laid their plans from October 1885 to reconstruct the coalition, and allowed Parliament to dissolve in December without making any announcement; their Cabinet colleagues were probably informed on 18 December.[80] Duncan Gillies was to take over—Peter Lalor's mate at Ballarat in 1854, short, sturdy, dapper, florid, unfashionably cleanshaven, a bachelor and a ladies' man. He was the most professional of politicians, almost continuously a member of the Assembly since 1859, having been already a member of six ministries, a superb parliamentarian, the ablest debater in the House—lucid, incisive, logical, convincing in his broad Scottish accent. A bonny fighter with his back to the wall, a scheming tactician, he was temperamentally conservative with no religious and few political convictions, not a man who would fight to the last gasp for a principle. He was said to be a convivial clubman; most people found him reticent, cold and contemptuous in manner, a sardonic smiler. His abilities gave him great authority and wide respect, but he had little originality or imagination and was narrow-minded and shallow with little learning, despite his considerable intelligence. This self-confident man of the world, this classical practical politician, was perhaps the most crucial Premier in Victorian history, for he was to preside over Victoria's self-destruction.[81]

Somehow the *Argus* learned what was brewing and broke the news on Boxing Day. The *Age* reacted bitterly and led the outcry, especially against the jobbery of Kerferd's elevation to the bench which most of the Bar violently opposed.[82] The chief Liberal papers—the *Age*, the Ballarat *Courier* and the Bendigo *Independent*—all recommended breaking the coalition, allowing Gillies to form a new ministry, and fighting the election on party lines. The 'Conservative' caucus, numbering about twenty-six, was content to continue the coalition. About thirty members, including most of the Catholics, were unattached. Everything depended on whether the Liberal caucus, of about twenty-eight members, decided to break free and on whom it elected as leader. Berry (and Service) looked to Alfred Deakin, the young Solicitor-General and Commissioner of Public Works, who was still only twenty-nine and unsure of his ambitions and capacity. He had strayed into politics seven years earlier when, after joining the *Age* and *Leader* during a tiro barrister's usual briefless period, he had been pushed into Parliament by Syme. An omnivorous consumer of every old and new idea, he had come through his spiritualist phase and, though preoccupied with the great works of literature he was determined to write, had been knocked into shape in one of the toughest of all schools of reality —the Victorian Parliament. His intellectual capacity was backed by great natural charm, a sternly principled outlook and the gift of oratory. He was on terms of open hostility with the political rogues, but could handle savage attacks and sneers at his 'theorizing' with amusing badinage.* Already he was the chief spokesman for the native-born. In a sense he claimed the Liberal leadership by default, for antagonism to Berry had removed most of the senior men from the party. Ironically the only possible leader other than Deakin was his friend and mentor, Charles Pearson, who was recommending breaking the coalition and fighting on a radical platform. At this decisive moment, Deakin was tortured with doubts. Already he had held off a premature attempt in 1884 by the enthusiastic young men of Ballarat to draft him as leader of a new radical party.†[83] He closed his diary for 1885 with the agonized note: 'Old year closes with my nomination as Leader of the Liberal Party—Will the New Year give it—Is it worth taking—Is this all not leading me farther & farther from my true goal—In God I trust.' On 5 January he wrote to a friend: 'I do *not* wish to be leader and have not yet decided whether even if selected I could accept.'[84] Despite grave doubts he argued the case to caucus for remaining within the coalition. Caucus was evenly divided, but eventually decided on 19 January that the chances of winning the election against both 'Conservatives' and Catholics were too uncertain, agreed not to break away, and elected Deakin as leader—who no doubt decided to make the best of his unwelcome success.[85]

An immediate challenge came from the left. James Mirams, James Munro and several others who had been prominent in the powerful National Reform and Protection League formed another National Liberal League with the support of the *Age* and the backing of W. A. Trenwith and other Trades Hall men.‡ The main policy points were 'equalisation of taxation' (to include a tax on absentee investors), abolition of land sales, higher protection and electoral reform.[86] Suburban branches were quickly formed. Deakin and the coalition Liberals appeared to be in some electoral danger, especially in the gold towns where anti-coalition feeling was strong. Deakin's answer was to select most of his Liberal ministers from the left-wingers who had opposed continuation of the coalition. Pearson and J. L. Dow were both *Age* journalists (but Syme could still not be persuaded to support the coalition); two Ballarat men were included (Henry

* E.g. McIntyre's classic anti-intellectual condemnation of his 'doing the philosopher business' and putting forward 'theories which may very well be expounded in the schoolrooms or the lecture hall, but are scarcely in place when subjected to the criticism of practical men' (*P.D.*, vol. 41, pp. 2600–1).

† What, one wonders, was 'Syme's offer' of 18 June 1884 which Deakin noted and underlined in his diary? Two days later he went to Ballarat and met the young men.

‡ Other Liberal politicians involved were D. M. Davies, Dow, Laurens, Nimmo, Rose and Woods.

Cuthbert and John James, a Wesleyan) after Quick of Bendigo had refused an offer because of local Liberal hostility to the coalition.[87] The nonconformists were further pleased by the choice of W. F. Walker and John Nimmo. Deakin had possibly approached the dangerous Patterson who, however, was aiming for the premiership or nothing and hoped to rally the discontented of both parties. Invitations to him and other anti-Berry Liberals to rejoin caucus were rebuffed by nearly all. Gillies meanwhile was sweetening business interests by his choice of the merchants, James Lorimer and (later) James Bell, F. T. Derham (a biscuit-manufacturer and Deakin's bosom friend), and M. H. Davies, the financier. With the gentle and courteous Wrixon ranking third in the ministry, the churchmen were well represented and the *Telegraph* was pleased. Only Gillies and Deakin remained of the previous ministers, six of whom had been brusquely dropped.[88]

The coalition fared well in the election early in March 1886. The National Liberal League failed disastrously; Mirams lost his seat in Collingwood and none of the three Trades Hall men succeeded. The government did badly in the mining towns where James was beaten and independent gains were made by candidates pledged to the Decentralisation League. Founded in Bendigo in October 1885 by J. H. Abbott and others, the League was a protest by provincial towns rather than farmers against the Melbourne 'octopus'; its demands amounted to little more than increased expenditure of public money outside Melbourne.[89] In the city a committee of prominent members of the Chambers of Commerce and Manufactures worked hard for coalition candidates. The Catholics made no impression. Liberals fared slightly better than 'Conservatives' overall. Gillies and Deakin could face the new Parliament, confident of the staunch support of about twenty-two members each. Moreover, several more fair-weather friends usually attended caucus meetings. Nevertheless a strong group of men—Patterson, Munro, Bent, Collard Smith, McIntyre, Shiels and Harper among them—remained outside the coalition, strong enough to provide a standing alternative ministry.[90] Fewer than twenty members, however, met early in the 1886 session to re-elect Bent as 'Leader of the Opposition'.[91]

Service had earned the confidence of all businessmen, a leading banker reported home to England in January 1886. Politics in Victoria were in far better shape than in New South Wales where chaos prevailed. The only danger was extravagant railway building. It was to be hoped that Gillies would emulate Service in financial moderation.[92] Examination of the economy will demonstrate that such relative complacency was not unjustified until 1886.

Economics

2

Economic Sketch

General aspects

Early in 1883 an intelligent young English migrant, R. E. N. Twopeny,* was impressed by the dynamism of Melbourne as a business centre:

> . . . Melbourne is justly entitled to be considered the metropolis of the Southern Hemisphere. . . . it is in the Victorian city that the trade and capital, the business and pleasure of Australia chiefly centre. Is there a company to be got up to stock the wilds of Western Australia, or to form a railway on the land-grant system in Queensland, to introduce the electric light, . . . the promoters either belong to Melbourne, or go there for their capital. The headquarters of nearly all the large commercial institutions which extend their operation beyond the limits of any one colony are to be found there. If you wish to transact business well and quickly, to organize a new enterprise—in short, to estimate and understand the trade of Australia, you must go to Melbourne and not to Sydney. . . . [It is] Melbourne brains that find outlets for fresh commerce in every direction. There is a bustle and life about Melbourne which you altogether miss in Sydney. The Melbourne man is always on the look-out for business, the Sydney man waits for business to come to him. The one is always in a hurry, the other takes life more easily.[1]

The impression is both exaggerated and misleading for Victoria had for some years been running well behind New South Wales in rate of economic growth and new capital investment, as was natural in view of the relative resources of the two colonies once gold deposits had been largely exploited. Victoria's population of 862,000 in 1881 was 38 per cent of the Australian colonies (including Tasmania) and about 36 per cent (1,100,000) at the close of the eighties; but new capital formation was only about one-quarter of the Australian total for most of the decade, rising to about one-third by 1890 in the late stages of the boom.[2] However, Victorian businessmen were also directing considerable British capital and some Victorian capital into the northern colonies. Moreover, Melbourne's financial supremacy and lead in manufacturing were to continue to make it the headquarters of institutions which were ultimately to become industrial giants.

* Is there a better book of social observation than *Town Life in Australia* written by the age of twenty-five?

The Victorian economy displayed the major features common to the four chief mainland colonies. The rate of capital accumulation and population growth had been very high by world standards. Development was, however, based on exceptional importations of British capital, which by the early eighties was looking to Australia as the major area of safe overseas investment. A mixed economy was developing to a degree highly unusual in the nineteenth century; governments borrowed capital from overseas, invested it on a scale comparable with private enterprise, and were mighty entrepreneurs and employers of labour.[3] However, Victoria had an economic pattern which differed widely from the other colonies, especially in balance of occupations, more perhaps than at any other time. Victoria was far more closely settled than any other colony, having about twice the number of people Tasmania and New Zealand had per square mile, four times New South Wales and thirty times South Australia and Queensland. It remained far more a farming, manufacturing and gold mining community than New South Wales, while pastoralism was becoming relatively unimportant and coalmining still barely existed. Ernest ('Chinese') Morrison remarked on re-reaching Victoria at Echuca on his long march back from the Gulf of Carpentaria in April 1883: 'Instead of immense tracts of country owned by one man, and given up to sheep, there was a succession of beautiful little farms, each with its haystack, its neat little cottage, its substantial fence, and its scene of vigorous activity.'[4] Melbourne held one-third of Victoria's population and was Australia's biggest city by far. And Melbourne, rather than Victoria, was to have a boom in the later eighties which defied all comparisons.

By 1881 the number of men and women under forty-five was at last roughly similar. The basic demographic feature still was the concentration of men in their fifties who had been young migrants in the eighteen-fifties; the consequential high birth-rate of the sixties now meant that large numbers of boys and girls were reaching maturity. The gulf between the two generations had been deepened by the departure of many young males in the seventies when economic opportunities were still relatively limited. In 1881, astonishingly, there were more men between the ages of forty and fifty-four than between twenty-five and thirty-nine.*[5] In business life, as in other areas of society, perhaps three out of four of the higher-level decision-makers were migrants of the fifties.

Immigration from Britain picked up sharply in the early eighties as prosperity grew; between 1882 and 1889 it is likely that an average of

* A. R. Hall (*Stock Exchange of Melbourne*, p. 50) notes the following annual rates of growth:

	1871–81	*1881–91*
Males 15–39	0.8	4.9
Males 40–64	2.1	0.2

In the later eighties, when many old migrants were dying, Victoria's death-rate became the highest of the colonies. The birth-rate, which had fallen right away in the late seventies, began to climb in the later eighties but remained the lowest in the colonies until 1890.

10,000 unassisted migrants annually settled in the colony.* Most of them were attracted to the colony by the reports of relatives and friends, but little can be learned of their backgrounds. The eighties was also a period of high mobility of population; many more arrived in Victoria from other colonies than left, especially between 1886 and 1888. Most of them were migrants whom other governments, especially Queensland's, were assisting to their colonies. Only about one in twenty of the Australian-born in Victoria were natives of other colonies. Every year more people arrived from Tasmania, South Australia and Western Australia than left for those colonies, but through the decade Victoria lost more than she gained from New South Wales and Queensland. There were, perhaps, 2,000 new German migrants in the eighties, both from Germany and South Australia, but no other significant non-British accession of population; the number of Chinese declined slightly to about 10,000. In fact 1881 to 1890 were the only years between 1871 and 1906 when Victoria had more immigrants than emigrants. Even so, the surplus of 114,000 arrivals by sea over departures was less than Queensland's and much less than the figure for New South Wales, though Victoria had more new migrants than either between 1886 and 1890. New South Wales had passed Victoria in male population by 1885, but Victoria then more than held her own in total population until she suddenly lost the lead in 1891.[6]

Pastoralism

By 1880 the pastoral industry in Victoria had reached its productive limits in terms of the existing technology. New South Wales now had three or four times as many sheep; until 1887, however, Victoria regularly shipped wool to greater value than New South Wales, because Melbourne was the natural outlet for the Riverina. Sheep-raising for wool was still concentrated in the Western District and southern Wimmera on large freehold estates where substantial mansion-homesteads, clusters of outbuildings and sturdy wire fences had long been built. Few of the Port Phillip pastoralists had survived into the eighties: many had died, many had gone home, some had retired to their town houses in Melbourne and Geelong and remotely supervised their sons or managers on the property, and many were ruined. Ten outstandingly successful families owned almost two million acres between them—the Chirnsides, Robertsons, Russells, Clarkes, Wilsons, Armytages, Moffats, Austins, Manifolds and Wares—but only a few dozen others had largely unencumbered estates of a few thousand acres which they could call their own. Perhaps the most distinguished surviving Scottish patriarch was John Lang Currie (1818–98), who had migrated in 1841, acquired Larra near Camperdown in 1844, and since 1859, when he won first prize at the first Skipton Show, had been a famous

* The figures range between 13,000 in 1882 and 19,000 in 1889, but included many in transit to other colonies. It is not possible either to enumerate or classify migrants from overseas or from other colonies. See H. H. Hayter's remarks on the imperfections of migration statistics in his *Census of Victoria, 1881. General Report*, pp. 20–4.

merino breeder. He was first chairman of the pioneer cloth manufacturing firm in Geelong, backed experiments in exporting refrigerated meat, was a director of a leading pastoral finance house, owned runs in three colonies, and was an early collector of Australiana. He eventually left an estate of almost £500,000.

The industry was changing fast. There were few leaseholds now outside the Mallee and scrubby hill-country. The larger properties were steadily being partitioned as sections were sold off to relieve the load of debt and to make further improvements possible. Successful selectors going in for mixed farming were now probably running as many sheep as the pastoralists proper.[7] Absentee ownership increased as successful city men, crowning their social aspirations, invested in pastoral property. As the local meat-market grew, some of the old pastoralists specialized more in fat lambs and cattle. An important minor development was the Indian horse trade, controlled by Archibald Currie, who annually shipped several thousand horses on his vessels.[8] Rabbits were an appalling nuisance, in the Western District especially. They *could* be eliminated, but only by digging out and re-fencing at enormous cost: the Manifolds spent about £5,000 in getting rid of them from one property.[9] A growing proportion of the wool clip was being auctioned locally before export; more wool was sold at Melbourne and Geelong than Sydney until the nineties.[10] A few bales were now being bought by local manufacturers, but most pastoralists were more concerned to develop world markets, even in China and Japan,[11] than to nourish a local textile industry. The great hope was to develop meat exports. Since 1868 S. S. Ritchie's Melbourne Meat Preserving Company had been exporting tinned meat and meat extract, but it had to close in 1886 after loss of British Army contracts to Chicago and a fall in London prices.[12] Refrigeration was a more hopeful prospect. After a successful shipment of frozen meat organized by Andrew McIlwraith in 1879–80, a pastoral syndicate formed the Australian Frozen Meat Export Company and built a freezing-works at Newport. The prospect of uniting production, shipping and distribution overseas was attractive, but although the technical problems of refrigeration had been largely solved, selling in such competitive markets proved too difficult and the company was wound up late in 1885.[13]

Since the gold rushes Melbourne had dominated Australian pastoral finance. The great wool houses financed purchases of runs and stocking and fencing by individual pastoralists, made advances on the next wool clip, handled its transport and sale, supplied stores, and ultimately often took over properties when their clients ran too deeply into debt.[14] Goldsbrough's (which was converted to a public company in 1881 and amalgamated with Mort's in 1888) sold about one-tenth of the total Australian wool clip from its massive bluestone Bourke Street warehouses. Dalgety's enterprises also reached back to the forties; in 1884 they too were incorporated to bring in more British capital. The old Melbourne firm of Hastings Cuninghame converted itself in 1879 to the Australasian Mortgage and Agency Company with a large injection of Scottish capital. The Australian Mortgage (Mercantile) Land & Finance Company, London-controlled but operated from Melbourne, in twenty years lent more than £2 million of British capital to pastoralists and paid a dividend of 20 per cent throughout the eighties. Several other Anglo-Australian houses, formed in the sixties and seventies, emerged as giants in the eighties after absorbing smaller firms and many local stock and station agencies.* The banks also committed themselves deeply to mortgage-finance of the pastoral industry. The greater part of the vast amount of British capital imported to Australia in the seventies and eighties was channelled into pastoralism. From 1882 a pastoral boom began, especially in speculative quick-gain transactions and runs in western New South Wales and Queensland.[15]

The Melbourne-based finance houses naturally found their major field of operation in western New South Wales, the chief area of expansion. The Riverina had long been taken up, mainly by Victorian squatters attracted by large vacant areas, retreating from the bitter political onslaught, and seeing better prospects under the Robertson Acts. Among parliamentarians alone, ten or a dozen had Riverina interests in the eighties.[16] Pastoral pioneering in Victoria, except in the inhospitable Mallee, was long over. The loss of business confidence during the 'Berry blight' and the discriminatory land tax contributed to the flight of capital to the north. According to one exaggerated, disgruntled calculation, £15 million capital was driven out;[17] but it is likely that high wool prices, rising property values and consequent availability of capital had more to do with it. Much of the new settlement up the Darling was by Victorians, and scores took up runs in Queensland where George Fairbairn and Donald Smith Wallace each had several. The new stations were largely stocked from Victoria and a steady stream of labour followed capital to the north. In January 1883 the Squatting Investment Company, a Goldsbrough offshoot with Simon Fraser,† M.L.A., as chairman, paid £380,000 for a Queensland property of one and a half million acres; many invested in country near the Gulf of Carpentaria the same year,[18] and Victorian capitalists had an interest in McIlwraith's plan for a land-grant railway.

* E.g. William Sloane & Co., which in 1885 became the Union Mortgage & Agency Co., absorbed Jas. Turner & Co., and later became Australian Estates Ltd.; the New Zealand Loan & Mercantile Agency; the British & Australasian Trust & Agency Co.; the Australasian Agency and Banking Corporation, which amalgamated with Goldsbrough's in 1881.

† The powerful Simon Fraser (1832–1919) is surely worth a biography. Born in Canada of Scottish parentage, he migrated in 1853, was a very successful digger at Bendigo, traded in horses and produce, and built bridges. He became a leviathan railway-builder, undertaking the Bendigo-Echuca, Port Augusta and other contracts. About 1870 he was buying many of Hugh Glass's pastoral properties and runs in Queensland, where he was eventually a pioneer in artesian boring and was involved in McIlwraith's land-grant schemes. He was a director of the Moama-Deniliquin railway. By the eighties he was powerful in Melbourne financial circles and controlled the *Evening Standard*. He was a parliamentarian from 1874, topped the poll for the Senate in 1901, and was possibly the most influential Orangeman in Victoria. He was knighted in 1918.

'Queensland is keeping half Toorak,' it had been suggested from time to time; investments in Queensland, more than almost anything else, said one politician, made Melbourne the prosperous city it was. In 1885 after drought years, it was remarked that Toorak and Melbourne were keeping half Queensland.[19]

Investment in sugar plantations by Victorians between 1880 and 1884 almost rivalled pastoral investment in Queensland. The Melbourne Mackay Sugar Company owned several estates in the fast developing Mackay region. Thomas Swallow and F. T. Derham, the biscuit-makers, invested £180,000 in the Hambledon estate near Cairns. The Victoria Sugar Company, which operated at Yarraville the only refinery in Victoria, put £200,000 into the Victoria plantation in the Herbert Valley. The world sugar slump and the dumping of European beet-sugar contributed to losses by the company approaching £500,000; its works closed temporarily in 1886, and in 1887 it amalgamated with the Colonial Sugar Refining Company with which it had previously been loosely associated. The Pyramid Company fell in 1887 and an investment of £160,000 was wiped out, while the Fanning brothers were said to have lost £400,000. In 1887 the Victorian government raised the duty on beet-sugar, but failed to persuade the Queensland government to agree to a reciprocity treaty which might have guaranteed the whole Victorian market. Meanwhile the industry was in collapse and eventually almost the whole Victorian investment was lost.*[20]

The pastoral investments in western New South Wales and Queensland were based on the easy assumption that the high returns of the seventies could be repeated in the new, comparatively arid areas. Immediate experience was disillusioning. R. G. Casey senior was one of many in Queensland who, faced with falling wool prices and dry years in 1883 and 1884 and a staggering load of debt, found the going hard.[21] Better seasons and the revival of prices in the mid-eighties renewed determination to pour good money after bad in the blithe conviction that boundless prosperity was at hand. The flood of available capital made it commonplace for pastoralists to have mortgage-engagements of £100,000 and more. Yet the unrecognized turning-point for the industry, to which overstocking, rising costs and the rabbit plague in New South Wales all contributed, had come by 1884, after which overall returns on pastoral investments declined.[22] The huge capital invested from Melbourne in New South Wales and Queensland—both new British capital through the pastoral houses and the banks, and capital derived from local pastoral enterprise—and its relatively poor returns, is a crucial aspect of the Victorian economy of the eighties.

Agriculture and land settlement

The eighties was a testing period for the farmers. After great expansion in the late seventies, the value of agricultural production barely increased

* Plantations owned or financed by Victorian syndicates or companies also included Airdmillan, Gairloch, Hamleigh, Macknade, Oakenden, Pioneer and Pleystowe.

through the decade, although the area of land cultivated grew by nearly one-half. However, the 35,000 or so farmers were now contributing almost twice as much in productive value to the economy as the pastoralists and two to three times as much as the miners. The lone farmer, aided by family and seasonal labour, was the rule. Tenant-farmers could probably have been numbered only in hundreds; some remained still on the south-west coast, a few pastoralists like the Hentys and Ritchies let out parts of their properties, and Sir W. J. Clarke, the one great landlord of the colony, leased his Sunbury estate and had fifty-three contented tenants on his Dowling Forest property near Ballarat.[23] Several thousand farms, mainly near the coast or the old goldfields, dated back to the pre-selection period. A few others had come on the market when pastoralists sold their freeholds or parts of them; the Hepburn property of 36,000 acres at Smeaton, for example, was sold in farms of 50 to 240 acres at about £9 an acre. But a good three-quarters of the farmers were selectors. By the mid-eighties there had been more than 100,000 selections under the 1869 Act and its amendments.[24] This total, compared with the number of working farms, indicates how many failures and reselections and absorptions of selections there had been, as the drastic weeding-out of those with inadequate capital, vigour, talent and good fortune proceeded. Dairying had developed to the limit—Victoria had half as many again dairy cattle as New South Wales throughout the eighties—and could not expand until refrigeration and other technical innovations made exporting possible; as it was, good butter was often sent in despair to Melbourne for disposal as grease. Fruit-growing could not develop much further without large-scale irrigation and a reliable export market. Most Victorian farmers were now wheat-growers in the north and north-west—and by the mid-eighties the wheat industry was in trouble.

The area under wheat had grown in the seventies from under three hundred thousand to almost a million acres. In the eighties it did not reach a million and a quarter acres, while average annual production barely increased and remained just less than South Australia's. The home market had been safeguarded by a tariff which rose from 9d per hundredweight in 1868 to 1s in 1872, 2s in 1881 (and eventually 2s 11d in 1890). Exports had begun in the late seventies: 27 per cent of the crop was

Year	*Area cultivated '000 acres*	*Wheat cultivated '000 acres*	*Wheat '000 bushels*	*Wheat exports £'000*	*Oats '000 bushels*	*Potatoes '000 tons*	*Sheep '000*	*Cattle '000*
1881	1,822	927	8,714	689	3,612	134	10,267	1,287
1882	2,041	969	8,751	627	4,446	130	10,174	1,287
1883	2,216	1,104	15,570	356	4,718	161	10,739	1,298
1884	2,323	1,096	10,433	1,430	4,393	161	10,637	1,288
1885	2,405	1,020	9,171	409	4,692	163	10,682	1,291
1886	2,418	1,053	12,100	167	4,256	171	10,700	1,303
1887	2,576	1,233	13,329	416	4,563	198	10,624	1,334
1888	2,565	1,217	8,648	515	2,804	131	10,819	1,371
1889	2,627	1,179	11,496	84	5,645	157	10,882	1,394

exported in the earlier eighties, only 9 per cent in the later. The downward trend of world prices from the seventies to the nineties, as the new countries expanded production, explains much but only part of the story.[25]

Initial expenses and difficulties had cleaned out perhaps half the selectors within three or four years. On the northern plains, clearing–ringbarking, grubbing and burning–was usually a relatively minor problem. Fencing* was a major, and ultimately an expensive commitment, and building a dam was another essential early task. A stripper, winnower, reaper, ploughs and harrows might cost £150; horses, a couple of cows, a few sheep another £150. According to one experienced Wedderburn farmer,

> the absolutely necessary expenditure required for fencing the boundaries of the land and around the cultivation; building the very roughest hut large enough to shelter even a small family; buying implements, and putting in, say, twenty acres of crop, which was about the average of the first year; paying rent and rates, and living in the most economical fashion whilst the crop grew–would amount, at the very lowest estimate, to £250. I know that in the majority of cases this was far exceeded.[26]

Since the royal commission of 1878, which recognized some of the basic facts of land settlement, a block could be paid off at the rate of £16 a year for twenty years for 320 acres; Australian land may have been outrageously dear by North American standards, but this cost was minor in the farmer's economy.[27] Transport was the next crucial item: those too far from the inching-out tentacles of the railway system or whose local railway league was defeated by the supporters of an alternative route were often simply priced out of the market for years to come. Wife and children made a crucial contribution to the domestic economy. A vegetable patch and a few fowls went a long way to feeding the family, and fruit trees were planted in hope; where possible a dairy was set up, but only part of the year was suitable for making butter and cheese. Some farmers, especially the Germans, made brave efforts to be self-sufficient; many Warracknabeal settlers took pride in 'keeping square' with the town tradesmen by barter of butter, cheese and eggs.[28] But the selector short of capital had to have some cash income other than his crop and would go out working for his neighbours or on public works in the district. His debts in the storekeepers' ledgers were increasing and the banks, which charged lower interest–only about 10 per cent–were unlikely to give backing until he had weathered the first most difficult years.†

* In timbered country, brush fences or chock-and-log which would ultimately be sold for firewood in a nearby township were the immediate answer. On the plains, timber often had to be dragged from some distance. Hence light posts and rails (which would decay quickly and have to be replaced within a few years) were often used, while those who could afford it went in for wire immediately. A heavy stock-proof fence, however, cost three or four times as much as light wire.

† Geoffrey Blainey's claim in his history of the National Bank (*Gold and Paper*, pp. 94–5), that it made a 'notable and unsung contribution to national development' by carrying at high risk so many selectors, needs further investigation with regard to the banks in general.

Goldsbrough & Co. warehouse

Mining revival at Bendigo: the Beehive

Wheat-threshing in the Goulburn Valley

A Victorian selector's homestead, 1880

'With the great majority, the result of the first three years' work was increasing debt and mortgaged holdings. And yet the quantity of work got through was marvellous.' And in spite of everything—in spite of the rabbits, too, and the plagues of grasshoppers—optimism kept up: 'Well, now that the fencing and improvements are all right, I can go on increasing my cultivation, and 200 acres of wheat at 12 bushels per acre and 4s 6d per bushel, will give me nearly £550 for my year's work, which will pay handsomely'.[29] But nine or ten bushels an acre and 3s a bushel were often what resulted. After the good years of the early seventies, a dry cycle followed from 1876 to 1882, and in many areas overcropping soon exhausted the soil.

Machinery, if it could be afforded, brought long-term economies; between the seventies and the nineties there was a mechanical revolution. The time-honoured form of cultivation had been single-furrow ploughing, sowing by hand and harrowing for weeds. A primitive reaper cut the crop which was bound by hand, stooked, carted to a stack, and hand-threshed. The monstrous steam-thresher operated by teams of sixteen or eighteen men and drawn by bullocks from farm to farm was fairly common by the seventies. The horse- or bullock-drawn stripper—'a huge iron box travelling round and round the crop in a cloud of dust, driven by a man perched high in an iron seat, sweltering in the blazing sun, his hands black with grease and his clothes saturated with machine oil'[30]—came in slowly, forced on by the shortage of labour and its high cost. Local blacksmiths and small implement-manufacturers, knowing local needs and learning from South Australian examples, often competed successfully with the big Melbourne firms. By 1886 more than 7,000 strippers and 8,000 winnowing machines were in use, more than twice as many as six years before, and ploughs now had as many as eight furrows.[31]

The wheat-farmer learned from trial and error and by word of mouth—for example, to plough shallow instead of deep. But there seemed to be no answer to many of his problems. Smut could be controlled by pickling seed in a solution of copper sulphate, but rust was getting worse, and there was no answer to 'take-all' except grazing the land for years. Despite shooting, trapping, poisoning, gassing and digging out burrows, the rabbits got worse. The degree of overcropping—three or four crops in succession despite obvious soil exhaustion—may be explained partly by the assumption that it was always possible to move on after ruthless exploitation. Those who believed in fertilizer stuck to bone dust; superphosphate was available in the eighties, but knowledge of Custance's experiments in South Australia was slow to filter through.[32] When the Germans of the Murtoa district introduced fallowing, the practice caught on fairly quickly, but the man on only 320 acres had little alternative but to go on cropping. Science had not yet done much to help the farmer: Farrer was not experimenting until the later eighties, the Dookie and Longerenong colleges were only being founded, and the Department of Agriculture formed in 1872 appears to have had small impact. The agricultural columns of the weekly *Australasian, Leader* and *Weekly Times* and the local paper were helpful, but the farmer relied much more on yarns with his mates in the Farmers' Unions and local agricultural societies.

It was more and more commonly assumed in the early eighties that the 'grain sick' land was giving out; in 1884 it was claimed that not one man growing wheat alone was doing well and that it was not possible to survive on 320 acres. The painful answer was gradually being found: fallowing and grazing on larger farms—the alternation of wheat and wool instead of the old English system of alternate cropping. By the mid-eighties land was rapidly changing hands as the comparatively successful absorbed the unsuccessful, and by the close of the decade the great majority of wheat farms were of more than 500 acres.[33]

Water for the north became the cry as the dry years grew worse between 1880 and 1882. Carting water for domestic use and driving stock up to forty miles was constant drudgery in those summers; well-sinking and boring were rarely successful. Early in 1882 the railway extension from St Arnaud to Donald was hurried on so that water-trains could relieve Donald township. Government had not been entirely neglectful; the departmental engineers, George Gordon and Alexander Black, had been appointed as a Water Conservancy Board and their urgent reports of 1880 were the basis of the Water Conservation Act of 1881, which encouraged construction of local waterworks to satisfy domestic needs and watering of stock. The policy of decentralization, deriving from legislation of the sixties subsidizing construction of the gold towns' water supplies, was continued: government would advance money to local water trusts, based now on shires as well as boroughs, which would plan and control their systems and levy water rates to pay interest on the loans. By 1886 twenty-three trusts had been created and the government had spent more than £500,000. With J. D. Derry as engineer, the Wimmera United Water Trust had taken over the Glenorchy weir recently begun by the shire, and built the Longerenong weir and the Wartook reservoir. Pick-and-shovel navvies were slowly extending the web of channels which would eventually criss-cross the Wimmera and Mallee.

Intensive irrigation was the splendid dream, the cure-all, which (in typical period phraseology) would make the north 'blossom as a rose'. In 1871 B. H. Dods had launched his Great North Western Canal, Irrigation, Traffic and Motor Power Company which planned, in return for a three-million acre land grant, to divert the Goulburn River and build an east-west canal to the far west which would join with a north-south canal from Portland to the Murray; one or two million acres might be irrigated on the way. Governments gave no encouragement, but Hugh McColl became secretary of the company, and, aided and abetted by the active Central Irrigation League and frequent public comments by Bishop Moorhouse, devoted himself to the cause. Gordon and Black reported pessimistically in 1881 on the prospects of large-scale irrigation, claiming that a much larger population would be necessary in the north before costs and returns could be balanced. McColl, the man with 'water on the brain', who had been elected to the Assembly in 1880 almost purely as an irrigationist and was at first something of a laughing-stock, continued with Catoesque single-mindedness to condemn Gordon as a 'departmental liability' and to decry his 'gutters' as a totally inadequate basis for expansion. He now won influential allies: the *Age* and *Argus* in 1883 sent their agricultural experts, the brothers J. L. and T. K. Dow, to California to study irrigation, David Syme was converted, and so was Alfred Deakin in the government. As a preliminary move, amending water legislation of 1883 on the basis of the Gordon-Black reports provided for formation of irrigation trusts with the consent of three-quarters of landowners owning two-thirds of the land in the district. In 1884 Gordon and Black produced plans for irrigating part of the Goulburn valley. McColl was largely satisfied when the crusading Deakin had himself appointed late in 1884 as chairman of a strong royal commission on irrigation and left for the United States to investigate irrigation practice in company with J. L. Dow and Edward Cunningham of the *Age* and *Argus* and Derry, the Wimmera water engineer. McColl died in April 1885, just before Deakin returned and produced his report on irrigation in the United States, which concluded that if Victoria was to 'utilise her abundant natural advantages, bring her productiveness to the highest point, and secure to the agricultural population of her arid districts a permanent prosperity, it must be by means of irrigation'.[34] The major findings of the commission were complete in August 1885 and a series of reports followed on specific proposals by Stuart Murray, engineer of the Echuca and Waranga Trust and secretary to the commission. Meanwhile, small private irrigation schemes had been developing, especially on the banks of the Goulburn. Fruit was being grown near Shepparton in 1884, farmers near Echuca were growing lucerne in 1885, and in 1886 a syndicate founded the Ardmona fruit-growing settlement near Mooroopna.

All was ready for the major Irrigation Act of 1886 which Deakin enthusiastically piloted through, in the belief that it would be possible to irrigate several million acres and grow oranges, vines, olives, currants, lucerne and other products in huge quantities. A common assumption was that irrigation would double the colony's productive power. The Act built on the existing basis, providing for 'national works' by the state and local works controlled by local trusts using moneys lent by the government. The state asserted total ownership and control by the community of all natural waters and, unlike California, insisted on state planning of priorities. The first 'national work' was the Goulburn weir, near Nagambie, built between 1887 and 1891. But there was little surplus water for irrigation from the works and channels constructed by the local water trust which had got off to a very bad start; the Pine Lodge weir on the Broken River had failed utterly and the channels from the Goulburn were leaking, notably on the Waranga Embankment, because of the excavations of yabbies. Nevertheless by 1888 water was being pumped along 367 miles of channels in the area. Kerang and Swan Hill had developed small schemes, and more than

20,000 acres were being irrigated in the colony, much of it still by private riverbank schemes rather than under the auspices of the trusts. Two-thirds of land irrigated was used for wheat, but it was soon found that wheat-growing by irrigation was uneconomic. By 1890 £1,750,000 had been spent by the state on irrigation works or lent to twenty-five irrigation trusts of which five had schemes working. Progress had been much slower than hoped, but the enormity of the technical and economic problems involved in irrigation was not yet realized.[35]

Meanwhile, one of the largest and most extraordinary of the boom-period enterprises had begun. In California Deakin and his colleagues had met and interested George and William Chaffey in the possibilities of irrigation settlements in Victoria. George Chaffey was a remarkable man: a Canadian engineer-shipbuilder in his thirties who had already first supplied electricity to Los Angeles, built the longest telephone line in the world, and from 1882 had created the model Ontario irrigation settlement from an arid Californian cattle-run. Deakin had not actually invited the Chaffeys, who were attracted more by the assurances of an American acquaintance, who had had Australian experience, that large land grants would be made to them. George Chaffey arrived amid great publicity in 1886, was disappointed to learn there was no possibility of free land, but was impressed by the possibilities of the Murray valley. The government, after much hesitation because of popular antipathy to 'land monopolists', reached an agreement with Chaffey in October for the sale of up to 250,000 acres over twenty years at an effective price of 17s an acre. According to Chaffey, Deakin 'drove a devilish hard bargain'. Certainly the Chaffeys were to take all the risks. George Chaffey had fixed on the Mildura run, 'a Sahara of hissing hot winds' plagued with rabbits, but he had been impressed by the homestead garden. The government ran into trouble, when it attempted to legalize the Chaffey agreement, from an Opposition anxious to seize on any popular issue. After almost entirely artificial tirades against 'Yankee land-grabbers', the government weakly agreed to lay the land open for tender, after a twenty-five-hour sitting of the Assembly.[36] J. F. Levien, recently a Cabinet minister, hurried off to London to attempt to raise capital. The irritated Chaffeys turned to the South Australian government and negotiated the Renmark agreement, but when no tenders were received for Mildura they were persuaded to take up the original contract, which was signed on 31 May 1887. George Chaffey moved speedily. By the end of the year, the town and subdivision of the first 25,000 acres had been planned; he had formed a company in which he and his brother were principal shareholders; he had designed revolutionary pumping machinery; the Red Book—*The Australian Irrigation Colonies* by James Vincent, the chief publicity medium for attracting settlers—was distributed far and wide; offices were opened in Melbourne, Adelaide and London, and several thousand applications had been received for land offered at £20 an acre—cleared, ploughed, irrigated, ready for planting. The prospect of concentrated settlement with all the advantages of town life was immensely attractive, notwithstanding prohibition of the sale of alcoholic beverages; half the early settlers were to be English migrants attracted directly. In 1889 they flooded in, in 1890 there were 3,000 people in the settlement. All was going well with the exciting project—but the catastrophic failure and ultimate success of Mildura is part of the history of the nineties and later, and must be postponed.[37]

In the mid-eighties the move into the southern Mallee began. The pastoralists had done reasonably well there in the sixties but after the rabbits invaded, sixty-two runs were abandoned between 1878 and 1883 and on eighteen other runs the wool clip fell by four-fifths. The 1878 Lands royal commission described it as an 'abominable wilderness' and in 1880 John Gavan Duffy recounted:

> We went over miles and miles of the country without seeing a solitary sheep or a sign of life, except thousands of rabbits, and so thoroughly had these devastated the district that there was not a blade of grass to be seen, and the trees were stripped of their bark as high as the rabbits could reach.

Ten years later a journalist expressed its popular image as 'a country that people know very little about, that nobody has done much good with, that has broken the backs of many men, the hearts of not a few; that contains the skeleton and the ugly ghosts of many a bright dream'.[38] Some of the northern Wimmera farmers, however, who had cleared patches of mallee scrub, knew the potential of the soil, and when the Mallee Pastoral Leases Act of 1883 came into operation demand was keen; 521 leases were issued in 1884. Amending legislation of 1885 guaranteeing compensation for improvements gave further encouragement. Settlement had been delayed by remoteness, rabbits, the state of the law, and the poor prospect of railway development, but primarily by the cost of clearing. South Australians and South Australian innovations were the necessary agents. In the early seventies, 'mullenizing'—dragging a forked log or triangle with spikes driven through it over burnt ground to grub up the stumps—had been introduced. The mallee roller, to level the smaller scrub, soon followed, and in 1876 the stump-jump plough. All were extensively used in the assault on South Australian mallee lands in the late seventies. By 1884 stump-jump ploughs were being manufactured at Tarnagulla and widely used in the Wimmera, but it was only in the same year that at Nhill a trial of a mallee roller—a red-gum log, ten feet long and two feet nine inches in diameter, drawn by ten bullocks—attracted local interest.[39] Iron boilers, or anything heavy enough to roll, could clear about seven acres a day. By these methods clearing costs were reduced from about £4 an acre to less than £1 and costs could be spread over several years while roots and suckers were gradually eliminated. Meanwhile E. H. Lascelles, who was later to make a notable contribution to Mallee settlement, was proving that rabbits and wild dogs could be controlled by fencing off water and poisoning; in six years one thousand dogs were destroyed on his run alone.

In 1885 a government fence was run along the thirty-sixth parallel to keep the main army of rabbits away from expanding settlement in the south. So leases began to be subdivided from about 1885, and settlers moved north from Warracknabeal, Jeparit and Birchip, and in from Swan Hill. By 1887 scores of wagons were trekking over the South Australian border, their drivers attracted by cheap larger farms and new soil. Many of them were Germans, as were many of those moving on from the Wimmera and Western District. By 1890 there were fully 500 farmers growing wheat in the southern and eastern Mallee, and prospects of further expansion were promising.[40]

On the frontier in the Great Forest of South Gippsland an extraordinary and heroic battle was in progress. So difficult of access by land and dependent on sea communication, Gippsland had been slow to develop. One of the few relatively successful areas of settlement under the Duffy Act had been the Sale and Bairnsdale region where selectors at Maffra, Briagolong, Bruthen, Lindenow and elsewhere were establishing themselves. The first assault on the dense scrub had been about 1870 at Brandy Creek (Warragul); by the time the central railway was through to Sale in 1878, farming settlements along the line were well established. Only in the mid-seventies was it widely realized that the thick forest country to the south, about 2,000 square miles deep in decomposed vegetable matter and with a forty- to fifty-inch rainfall, would when cleared grow English grasses and clovers. The first attempt was made in 1874 in the Poowong area, where there was a small group of Danish selectors; then in the later seventies settlers moved into the hills from the Tarwin river and towards Foster and Fish Creek from Welshpool on the coast. The latter was to be a notably successful enterprise by experienced farmers with considerable capital.[41]

> Entering the scrub for the first time, [wrote one settler], what impressed one most was the wilderness of thin saplings all around. . . . Then the size of the big timber would strike you. It looked larger in the scrub, where it compared only with saplings, than on the clearings where the trees compared with one another. Often you could only see one or two of their immense trunks at a time looming up through the scrub, as any object was hidden from view at a chain or less away. The next thing that struck you especially when you attempted to move was the terrible tangle of logs, fallen saplings, swordgrass and rubbish of all kinds that . . . covered the ground entirely from sight. With arms crossed in front of you, to save your face from the swordgrass, you bored through the ruck till you struck a log or a fallen sapling, and mounting it, you might not touch ground again for a hundred yards or so, stepping from one fallen sapling to another three or four feet off the ground.[42]

Most of the big timber was at least 150 feet high; one famous hollow tree with an inside diameter of 26 feet was used for years as a church, school and hall, for it could hold fifty people. Ferns flourished in the extreme moistness of most areas; insects—flies, mosquitoes, ants, caterpillars, tarantulas—teemed everywhere; and it was the land of the lyre-bird.

It was axework all the way. The settler had to clear a track in, blaze the bounds of his block, run up a house from bush timber, then tackle years of clearing. After some experience, an area of timber would be 'nicked'—partly chopped through; then the felling of a forest giant on the higher side would induce 'a vast, crashing, smashing, splintering, roaring and thundering avalanche of falling timber'. The fern-trees were slow work for like the tangle of swordgrass and wiregrass, they could not be chopped. The American axe predominated; men carried a whetstone or oilstone for frequent use, string or copper wire for the frequently broken handle. Axe-handles varied greatly in quality; a sturdy, well-grained one, balanced to perfection by glass-scraping or sandpapering, perhaps with several inches 'bound with string, waxed thread, copper wire, pieces or strips of tin', was treasured. Although teams of contractors appeared, the hard-up settler commonly worked alone; there were frequent terrible accidents. Nearly everyone used a compass, but many a man was hopelessly bushed within a few hundred yards of his camp.

'Scrub cutting' was the winter and spring occupation; the crucial event was the summer burn, generally in dry January. By unwritten law, neighbours had to be consulted and usually took part in lighting a circle of fire round the area of fallen scrub. Much depended on a satisfactory burn, which was followed by the grimy process of picking up, stacking and further burning. Then, about April, grass was sown on the ash, and usually very satisfactorily. For many years the gaunt spars of ringbarked trees were to dominate the landscape; fallen trunks would gradually be cleared and stumps grubbed out, burned or blown out; and the second growth, especially of swordgrass, had to be hacked out after two or three years. It cost £10 an acre or much more to have this major clearing and sowing done; theoretically £1,000 needed to be spent on a block over the first two or three years before there could be any significant return.[43] The settler whose only capital was his own labour had to be strong indeed. 'I shall never forget my first experience in the Buln-Buln clearing,' Bishop Moorhouse recalled:

> When night came on we were surrounded by great red blazing trunks of trees. It reminded one of Pandemonium more than anything else. . . . Energetic, enterprising, industrious, and enduring men; but I have been frequently told by them, when smoking my pipe in their company at night by their fires, that it almost drags the heart out of a man to get the country clear. One man said to me, 'I have been ten years at it, and have not done it yet.' . . . It is a lifework, but there is something at the end of it, and there is something also for that man's sons and his son's sons.[44]

There was no road on earth like a Gippsland road, it was believed. The pack-tracks were 'unspeakably rough', often six to eighteen inches deep in mud in winter; poles were stuck in the bad 'crab-holes' to warn the nextcomer. The first government roads were bad jokes, mapped on the chess-board pattern regardless of terrain. Shire councils had to purchase land in order to re-route them and attempt to recoup expenses from rate-payers in no position to pay. The government eventually gave a special subsidy because of the peculiar difficulties. Meanwhile in some parts settlers worked together voluntarily for weeks at a time, cutting, bridging and laying corduroy.[45]

In the eighties most of South Gippsland was simply not economically viable. It was not sheep country: footrot was common and the dingoes and eagles were continually molesting. Cultivation was usually out of the question until many more stumps could be grubbed. It was great dairying country, but the Melbourne market was distant, highly competitive and ruinously expensive to get to. Butter had to be taken by pack-horse or sledge over the hills to the railway at Drouin or Morwell or to ships at Anderson's Inlet or Western Port—and then often sold for 3d a pound. 'We that are locked up cannot get out', wrote a correspondent plaintively to the *Argus* in 1889:

> We cleared the scrub on our holdings, which all know was dense. We sowed with grass, began to dairy, but found to our cost that the summer was too much, with the roads, our butter being melted before it reached market. We tried cattle and pigs, but found our area was too small for these. We tried sheep, but the wild dogs were too destructive. . . . We were driven back to dairy produce, which does not keep our families and pay the rent. We have been driven into the hands of the banks or private money-lenders, on purpose to hold on until we could get roads or railways. . . . after bringing a family into the world and working ourselves almost into the grave, using all our best days in trying to leave something for our children that our fathers could not leave us, we find that we have spent our strength for nought better than either the hospital or benevolent asylum for ourselves and orphanages for our children.[46]

Splitters could not get timber to market, calves were being knocked on the head, berry bushes rooted out. Others complained that the northern farmers who had had no clearing problems were now to get irrigation; why should there not be a clearing subsidy for the Gippslanders?[47]

The casualty rate of selectors in South Gippsland was probably higher than anywhere and included many who were exhausted and broken in body and spirit.[48] Selections could be bought for less than the cost of improvements. Capital and blind optimism carried some through, and after the southern railway went through Korumburra and Leongatha to Yarram between 1887 and 1892, and the dairying revolution of the nineties began, land values steadily climbed. The son's sons of the pioneers of the milk and butter shires eventually inherited rich portions.

Dairy exports, government was well aware, were a rich potential field, but other agricultural exports were harder to develop. Production of hops increased tenfold between 1882 and 1885 after the European crop had failed, but hopes for a permanent market proved illusory. Wattle-bark was expected to be commercially valuable as a dye in the manufacture of footwear, but diseases hit the plantations. Winegrowing appeared to have great prospects, especially in the Rutherglen area, and production almost trebled in the eighties; about 1880 Victoria grew less than New South Wales but ten years later was producing more than New South Wales and South Australia together. But the local market was limited: British migrants overwhelmingly preferred beer or spirits and Father J. J. Bleasdale's hope that Victorians would become 'a healthy, sober, jolly, wine-drinking' people was not realized, despite the large market for 'champagne' during the boom years. A few growers were producing wines of high quality: the Bordeaux merchants valued the Yarra valley wines of the de Castellas among the very best French, and a Yering wine was awarded the German Emperor's special prize for the colonial product of highest quality at the 1880–81 Exhibition. But many winegrowers knew little of the craft and produced sweet heavy wines of high alcoholic content; light dry wines were held to be 'hard' and 'sour'. Export markets were difficult to find, especially as British import duties were high. The phylloxera disease had devastated the Geelong area in 1877 and ultimately ruined the industry, although it did not reach Bendigo or the north-east until the nineties and never touched the Yarra valley. Victoria was lamentably slow in adopting the appropriate remedy: phylloxera-resistant American vines, which other wine-producing countries had long been using, were not introduced until 1900.[49]

The Victorian selector had no Henry Lawson or 'Steele Rudd' to immortalize him; nor has his life been recreated to any extent by historians. One or two thousand selectors prospered from the start; only a minority, though a sizeable one, came through at all, at least at the first attempt. Failure was so frequent that stark poverty must have been widespread. The work was 'absolutely slavery', dawn to long after dusk often, one Wimmera farmer recalled. 'Day after day on poor food and bad water you had to walk behind the plough and harrows, and following the harrows on rough-ploughed land has to be experienced before one can give any idea as to what it is like.'[50] It was very different later when one could ride on ploughs and drills. Porridge, bread and dripping, corned meat was the staple diet (and in some areas kangaroos and possums were welcome additions); no butter, no shoes for the children, no doctor except when all-important 'Father' was ill. Housing was a low priority for expense; the log huts were often plastered with mud, and sometimes in the Wimmera were built of *pisé*. Roofs were usually of bark, occasionally thatch; small saplings, tied with bullock hide, held the bark in place. In the early years milled weatherboard and galvanized iron roof were signs of 'wealth' or 'aristocratic pretension'. Cooking pots hung over the fireplace and a camp oven was used for baking and roasting. Walls were often covered with newspapers, floors were earthen, furniture home-made; a box-bookshelf might hold the Bible, Macaulay's History, an almanack, Dickens, a 'home doctor'; on the walls might be reproductions of Holman Hunt's *Light of the World* or Longstaff's *Breaking the News*. Hessian covered with paper divided off a bedroom.[51] Children might milk the cows before going to school and bring them in on the way home, and then, a boy from Boort recalled,

> we fed the fowls, gathered the eggs, chopped the kindling wood and when older and big enough to use the large axe, chopped the wood for the fires. In summer we also carted water from the dam 100 yards away—as many as 50 four gallon tins of it. This was put onto the vegetables and fruit trees. In between times we dug around the fruit trees, cut bathurst burrs, dug drains. . . . my brother and I considered ourselves lucky that Father was a sheep and wheat farmer, and not a 'Cow Cocky', as some of the neighbours were. [Their children] were indeed to be pitied. It meant, week in, week out, generally starting before dawn, milking then separating the cream just in time to get ready for school, starting the milking not long after school was out, and it seemed to us that they went on till after dark. We thought it a life not worth living.[52]

Loneliness was not so common a problem in closely-settled Victoria and the classic tragedy of the lost child rarely occurred; nevertheless, children in remote timbered areas were sometimes 'belled' and ordered never to leave the track or dismount when riding to school. Tiny townships at crossroads or creek-junctions were communal centres comprising school, recreation hall, church, hotel, store and post office, smithy—'education, recreation, salvation, damnation' on the four corners, perhaps.[53] The growing district towns were often crude and ugly, with dusty roads, straggling shacks, and creek-bed littered with rusty cans and broken bottles, before municipal improvers won the day.[54] As release from toil, men and women gathered at church and for concerts and sing-songs, dances, sporting events, agricultural fairs and ploughing matches; and their children fished, swam in the dams and creeks, hunted possums, and enjoyed days off from school slaughtering rabbits. Youths desperately looked forward to the day when they could afford to buy a horse and saddle. It may be that most selectors never expected to 'make good', and were content with independence barely above subsistence level when they could achieve it. The general impression gained of the worse-off selectors is not of long-drawn-out grinding poverty, but rather of cutting losses and selling out to neighbours and moving on or back to the city or towns.

Those who came through successfully were inevitably hard and proud men. Despite all difficulties they had tamed the land by dint of their own toughness and perseverance, had proved themselves, had achieved independence—however precarious over the decades to come—by their own efforts. They inherited now the long tradition through the ages, from Virgil to Jefferson and the French Physiocrats, which asserted the superiority and sweet contentment of the simple agricultural life. The farmer followed the noblest calling of all; living so close to nature, he was uncorrupted by society, and more virtuous and patriotic than the decadent city-dweller. The wheat-grower especially prided himself on producing the staff of life, in following a more progressive calling than the mere grazing pastoralist. The established farmer came to see himself as part of the backbone of the country and through the Farmers' Unions began to demand redress of his grievances and an appropriate share—and ultimately much more than his share—of political power. In his respectability and pride in his property he was the antithesis of the classical Australian bushworker, who indeed played only a peripheral role in Victoria.[55]

The goldmining industry

Goldmining was in slow decline. It stood to reason, most old miners faithfully proclaimed, that there *must* be lots more gold to be won. But production, which in the fifties had averaged about 2,600,000 ounces a year, had fallen to 1,350,000 in 1871 and 760,000 in 1879, then revived to 899,000 in 1882, but again fell steadily to 615,000 in 1889; the price of gold remained stable at about £4 an ounce. The fluctuating dividends from mining companies declined from a temporary peak of £864,000 in 1882 to £529,000 in 1889–90. The official estimated number of miners fell away from 36,000–37,000 (including 6,600 Chinese) in 1881 and 1882 to under 25,000 in 1889, but only about half this number could have been earning regular wages; the rest were working part-time in other jobs or were prospectors or Chinese living in poverty.* Since 1872 more had been earned from working quartz than alluvial, but until late in the eighties alluvial miners (including nearly all the Chinese) remained the majority. However, gold was still an important industry, with perhaps two-thirds as many workers early in the eighties as there were in manufacturing. The value of gold produced was still almost as great in the early eighties as that of wool. Victoria mined more gold annually, except in 1877 and 1878, than the rest of Australasia combined until 1886, and then more than the rest of Australia until 1889 when Queensland jumped to the lead for one year. Dividends from mining companies were greater in the early eighties than from all other public companies—though this indicates how few businesses were yet incorporated. The industry was now highly mechanized. Quartz was being crushed profitably when only a few pennyweights per ton could be extracted; the miners still applied more horsepower than all Victoria's factories and provided the basis for the developing engineering industry.[56]

Apart from Ballarat and Bendigo, the chief mining centres were now Creswick, Stawell and Maryborough. Bendigo (with Eaglehawk) took pride of place; 4,000 to 5,000 quartz-miners there were producing more than a quarter of Victorian gold and about twice as much as Ballarat through the eighties. In 1882 Bendigo's ninety-five companies had paid-up capital of almost £1 million.[57] By 1890 the two richest public companies, the Garden Gully United and the Great Extended Hustler's, had paid about £850,000 and £600,000 to shareholders and workers formed in tribute companies. Sinking shafts to remarkable depths was a Bendigo characteristic; by 1885

* For example, in 1884 total production was worth £3.12 million; dividends accounted for £789,000; the remainder could have provided wages for no more than 20,000 miners.

three companies were down beyond 2,000 feet, by 1889 nine, led by George Lansell's '180' mine at 2,500 feet—by 1914 more than fifty shafts were over 2,000 feet and one was down almost a mile. Lansell, who with his fellow-townsman, J. B. Watson, were the only two Victorian gold millionaires, was a responsible optimist who carried thousands of Bendigo families with him; he stood alone as a Victorian mining entrepreneur and contributed much in return for his fortune.[58] At Ballarat the deep alluvial had been exhausted; the premier mine, the Band of Hope and Albion which produced £2,500,000, was now working only in quartz at 1,200 feet. But the Star of the East and other companies were productive enough for 2,000 to 3,000 miners to be employed still. Early in the eighties deep alluvial mining revived in the Creswick and the Kingston-Smeaton area where as many were now employed as at Ballarat; in the mid-eighties returns from the Madame Berry mine climbed to over £600,000. Allendale, Creswick's satellite boom-town, had collapsed by 1888. At Clunes the Port Phillip Company, that 'mining school in practical operation', finally closed in 1887, having won almost £2 million of gold; but the New North Clunes and New Lothair companies were still doing well.[59] Stawell's deep quartz and alluvial mines were now at low ebb although a thousand miners were still employed and the revival of the Magdala in 1884 raised flagging hopes.[60] The Maryborough mines had been in danger of collapse but were saved largely by B. J. Fink's entrepreneurial skill. St Arnaud rallied when the great Lord Nelson mine began paying dividends in 1888.[61] Walhalla in 1886 celebrated the payment of the millionth pound of dividends from Victoria's richest mine, the Long Tunnel, now past its peak.[62] The Castlemaine area continued to decline and the scattered north-east workings at Wandiligong and elsewhere were producing little. There were still occasional minor rushes and rumours of great discoveries; in May 1888 300 men rushed to Marong near Inglewood; in October the *Age* reported 'NEW GOLD FINDS IN VICTORIA' at Murphy's Creek near Tarnagulla, Gordon and the head of the Broken River. But despite Ballarat's confident hopes of a great revival, little was produced to stem the long decline.[63]

In 1883 and 1884, as production dropped, mining shares fell sharply in value. An active and helpful Mines Department, government subsidies for prospecting and purchase of machinery which rose to £80,000 in 1886, and legislation at last in 1884 to compel proprietors to allow mining on private property made little apparent difference. Mining managers were weak in metallurgy and backward in innovation by American standards, but more advanced technical knowledge could only have hastened the industry's demise.[64] Shortage of capital was the constant plea; it is indeed remarkable how little capital outside the mining towns could be found in the eighties, despite the flurry in Melbourne over Tasmanian tin in 1882, Barrier Ranges silver in 1884, then the Broken Hill mania of 1887,[65] and the vast sums poured into the pastoral industry and land speculation. The Melbourne investor had been bitten too often. Even after the telegraphic link in 1872, suspicious British investors were rarely attracted to Victorian mining. Victorian promoters made several unsuccessful trips to London in the eighties; John McIntyre won some capital in 1887 on his second attempt to gain backing for a flourishing Maldon mine. Yet in 1886–7 London gave massive support to Charters Towers flotations and replaced Melbourne as the Australian goldmining promotional centre.[66] The unscrupulous minority at the 'Corner' in Ballarat and 'under the Beehive' in Bendigo had 'cruelled the pitch'. An *Argus* journalist in 1887 referred to 'the infernal gambling and swindling' involved in mining, which 'used to be manly, heroic in some of its phases. It seems coolfish as bookmaking, foxy as sprint running now.'[67] The royal commission on goldmining of 1890–91 condemned 'the gambling in shares' which had 'driven thousands from legitimate mining ventures'.[68] Hay Kirkwood, five times mayor of Eaglehawk, in the early eighties deplored 'the fast and loose style of sharebroking' at Bendigo:

> Any Jack, Tom, or Harry . . . can be a sharebroker or jobber without let, hindrance or licence. Unfortunately for the great mining industry of Victoria, many capitalists in and out of the mining districts are shy to invest in companies that can be 'bulled' and 'beared' about in such a shuttlecock style by many persons of very little standing in honorable society. The system of sharejobbing at present carried on creates a depraved means of 'making money'. There is no trusting each other's honesty in the business. Diamond cut diamond is the order of the day.[69]

The responsible members of the Ballarat and Bendigo exchanges strove to enforce a rigorous code of ethics, but the damage had been done.

The stalwart middle-aged miners of the towns remained as paradoxical as they had always been. Swindling promoter and upright broker fought the battle of morality above ground; thieving below by employees was widespread; mining life was, as Froude described it, 'a gigantic gambling system'.[70] On the other hand the large majority of these men were sober churchgoers and an industrial élite who merited Trollope's eulogy of them as 'intelligent, manly and independent—altogether free from that subservience which the domination of capital too often produces . . . in no community are the manners of the people more courteous or their conduct more decent'.[71] The gold towns led the colony in political idealism and originality. Yet the many good Methodists among them—more than one-third of Creswick's population, for example—were either inconsistent in practising what they preached about gambling, or were incapable of policing the rogues who inevitably swarmed round casinos.

Banking and commerce

At the centre of the economy stood the Collins Street banks. The long-established English banks—the Australasia (founded 1835) and the Union (1837), both of which did about half their business in Victoria—were well placed. Smaller English banks which concentrated less on Victoria were the London Chartered, the English, Scottish and Australian with Sir George Verdon as manager, and the Oriental which failed in 1884 and when reconstructed won little business. Of the locally founded note-issuing banks, the Bank of Victoria (1853), largely under the control of the Miller family, the National (1858) and the Commercial Bank of Australia (1866) were the largest; the Bank of New South Wales was bigger than any of these, but did relatively little business in Victoria. The Colonial (1856) with Sir W. J. Clarke as Governor, the City of Melbourne (1873), the Federal (founded by James Munro in 1881), and the Mercantile (1877, until 1885 named the Australian and Economic Bank) were smaller institutions. These local banks were the most valuable group of investment companies other than mining on the Melbourne stock exchanges, highly profitable enterprises which paid dividends averaging about 12 per cent. Competition was fierce. In 1887 the banks doing most business were the Victoria (14 per cent of deposits and the highest number of notes in circulation), Commercial, Australasia, National, Union and Colonial (9 per cent) in that order. E. S. Parkes, the able and vigorous Superintendent of the Australasia, believed Victoria was 'overbanked' and feared that local loyalties and the tendency of shareholders to attract and divert business to the colonial institutions would push the English banks 'out of the premier place'.[72] The Australasia, however, improved its position in Victoria in the eighties, whereas the Union declined. Of the local banks, the National under the control of Francis Grey Smith and the Commercial with Henry Gyles Turner as general manager were expanding most quickly. In 1885 the National followed most of the others in opening business in Sydney; but the Bank of Victoria, which had opened negotiations to merge with the National in 1881, continued to operate only in Victoria. All the larger banks were looking outwards, competing especially in trying to attract British deposits, and tending to lend more and more on the basis of urban and rural real estate, despite traditional inhibitions. There were great dangers, as well as opportunities, in the intensifying competition to attract new deposits, satisfy borrowers and extend into new areas—dangers which in the long run were to sort out the true banking men from the juveniles. By English standards, banking services had extended widely in the community; Victoria had relatively four times as many bank branches as England. Twopeny noticed that

> Nearly everybody who is worth £100 has a banking account, and most people who have an account have overdrafts, which are given for the most part on purely personal security. The banks also advance freely on growing crops, wool on the sheep's back, and all kinds of intangible security. Many of the largest merchants are to all intents and purposes mere bank-agents. It is quite a common thing for ordinary working-men to keep bank accounts; and all farmers, even the smallest, are obliged to keep them; for in the country specie payments are almost unknown, and the smallest sums are paid by cheque. Even in the towns, residents usually pay any sum over a pound by cheque.

Because of his relative importance and the dependence of almost every class on his good will, 'the banker occupies the highest social position, almost irrespective of his merits'.[73]

Laissez-faire assumptions about the sanctity of private enterprise prevailed, except where government had intervened to create a large public sector of the economy—by building, operating and maintaining railways, water supply, posts, telegraphs and from 1886 telephones; constructing state and municipal works; constructing but not operating tramways; and encouraging industry and agriculture by protection and bonuses and other subsidies. Otherwise, the banks continued to control investment policy. It would be interesting to know how much and how often governments attempted to influence banking credit policy—whether, for example, there were attempts to influence bankers, who were usually doctrinaire free-traders, to reduce their interest in pastoral development and give more favourable treatment to manufacturers and mining directors. The banks could not be expected to act often in conjunction, but at least from 1877 the Associated Banks of Victoria, uniquely in the Australasian colonies, had been formed to discuss policy, especially on interest rates and relations with government. Most of the banks held the government balances, supplied short-term credit, and advised on the negotiation of loans in London.[74] In 1884 and 1885 there were tense discussions with the ministry. Service, who was irritated by the lack of support by some banks for a previous loan, considered 'Government were too much in the hands of the Banks'. Some Cabinet members wanted government funds to be placed entirely with the colonial banks, and others recommended putting the government account up for tender by groups of banks. In the end a happy agreement was reached whereby the Bank of New South Wales was dropped and the City of Melbourne and the Federal were included in the new arrangement for holding government funds. But in 1885 and 1886 the government acted with surprising independence of the banks' advice in floating new loans. After sharp disagreement in 1886 over deposit rates, the Associated Banks broke up, but reconstituted themselves late in the year.[75] There was no serious movement yet to establish a national bank in addition to the flourishing Savings Bank and post-office savings banks. Only the Master of the Mint (established in 1869 to produce sovereigns and other coins) and radical politicians like Mirams and Pearson wanted a state bank to take over the private banks' note issues. When a royal commission on banking was appointed after the Oriental's failure, the private bankers had their way and legislation merely made backing of currency the first charge on a bank's assets.[76]

Victoria's volume of overseas trade was heavy, for its high production of primary products for export and its early stage of industrial development allowed the import of large quantities of manufactured equipment and consumer and luxury goods. The consistent import surplus—12 per cent in the earlier eighties—was more than balanced by the high rate of capital import. The great bulk of overseas exports went to Britain, and a little to India, the Cape and elsewhere; wool and other pastoral products and gold exported by the pastoral houses and banks made up well over four-fifths of the value. Wheat exports were handled by a few firms like Derham & Co., Fry & Co. who were also large-scale millers, and Gibbs, Bright who were general importers and pastoral financiers as well. In return more than 70 per cent of the wide variety of imports from overseas came from Britain, 10 per cent from other parts of the Empire, and small quantities from the United States (4 per cent) and the East (7 per cent); France, Germany and other European countries developed trading contacts after the Exhibition of 1880–81. Although Melbourne had geographical advantages for supplying the Riverina, Tasmania and New Zealand, intercolonial trade amounted to little more than one-third of the value of overseas trade, even including the large quantity of New South Wales wool transhipped and the continual movement of cattle and sheep. Victoria's largest local import item was coal from New South Wales, and a variety of exports—wheat and flour, butter and cheese and, increasingly, manufactured goods—were sent to the other colonies.

An outstanding feature of Melbourne's mercantile life was the small degree of specialization and the frequent combination of wholesale and retail trade. Fanning, Nankivell & Co. had their leading interest in the tea and sugar trade with India, China and Mauritius, but also owned pastoral runs and shipped wool and wheat. James Balfour & Co. imported both English manufactures and tea and other eastern goods, were general indenters, shipped wool, and were agents for overseas life, fire and marine insurance firms. The Flinders Lane softgoods houses—Sargood's, Paterson, Laing and Bruce, Robert Reid's—were more circumscribed in their activities, as were wholesale grocers like Henry Berry & Co. and wine and spirit merchants like John Connell & Co. But James McEwan & Co. were both huge importers and retailers of ironmongery, and their rivals, McLean Bros. & Rigg, imported furniture as well. The major fashionable shops were embryo department stores. Buckley & Nunn and Ball & Welch were comparatively confined, but Craig, Williamson & Thomas and the ultra-smart Alston & Brown were wholesalers and retailers, drapers, milliners, tailors and dressmakers, home furnishers and much else besides. Felton and Grimwade, the drug importers, were launching out into a wide variety of manufacturing activities. W. H. Rocke & Co. were large importers, manufacturers and retailers of furniture. Lysaght's imported about half the galvanized iron used in the colony and also manufactured wire-netting. Many of these firms were employing one or two hundred men and were large up-country suppliers. The music houses of George L. Allan, W. H. Glen and Nicholson & Co. were competing vigorously for the huge market for pianos and sheet music which they imported and retailed. The great rival booksellers and stationers, George Robertson and Samuel Mullen, respectively developed publishing and lending-library sidelines; and E. W. Cole moved from the Eastern Market, had a grand opening in Bourke

Street on Cup Day 1883, and began acquiring premises through to Collins Street, which he reached in 1900.*[77]

A dozen of the shops, according to Twopeny, were equal and perhaps superior to any in Birmingham or Manchester; some of the window-dressing was tasteful enough to be reminiscent of Paris. The general run of shops were 'English as English can be' in style. In the better ones the service was almost as obsequious as in England; on the other hand 'in the second-rate shops there is often an unnecessary assertion of the shopman's equality with his customer, and a great indifference as to whether he buys or not'. (It is, perhaps, unwise to accept any generalization about the 30,000 shop-assistants in the colony.) Twopeny's remarks of 1883 about standards of commercial morality, though only the impressions of one intelligent young man, are interesting in the light of subsequent experience. He observed that while there were many businessmen of quite the highest standards of probity, the general standard of commercial ethics was lower than in England, although colonists were more on their guard against deception. Sharp practices and tricks of the trade were very common, verbal agreements were less trustworthy: 'You are expected to be on your guard against being "taken in"; and if you are taken in, no one has any compassion for you, the general opinion being that a man who trusts to anything less than the plainest black-and-white is a fool.' Trade was more speculative and profits usually far larger than in Europe.[78]

Manufacturing; the effects of protection

Protectionist Victoria was the manufacturing centre of the colonies. Output and employment had increased steadily in the seventies, surged ahead in 1880 and 1881, and continued to grow except for a marked check in 1886; between 1881 and 1889 employment rose from about 43,000 to 57,000.[79] However, building materials, metals, machinery and carriages, and printing accounted for nearly all the growth; the clothing and textiles industries reached a peak in 1882 and then declined, and boiling-down works and tanneries were doing less business. Indeed, if building materials are omitted, manufacturing employment grew very little until 1888 and 1889. In several fields a limit seemed to have been reached for exports to the other colonies, where competition was growing and governments were retaliating against Victorian protection. The size of factories was growing rapidly. Among the 2,000 to 3,000 works which might be defined as factories, there were only about fifteen in 1882 employing more than 200

* No attempt is made here to list major firms and institutions comprehensively. Some mention should be made, however, of the development of mutual life insurance as a form of institutional saving. Among seven major Melbourne foundations rivalling the huge Sydney-based Australian Mutual Provident Society, were the National Mutual (founded in 1869 by J. M. Templeton, who originated the non-forfeiture principle when premiums were overdue), the Colonial Mutual (1871) and the Temperance and General (1876). There were nine major fire and marine insurance offices with Melbourne headquarters. Two major trustee companies were the Trustees, Executors and Agency Co., founded by William Templeton in 1880, and the National Trustees, Executors and Agency Co.

hands; two clothing factories, Langlands' Foundry and Swallow & Ariell's biscuit works were the only ones employing more than 300. By 1888 31 factories had more than 200 hands and another 61 between 100 and 200; half the manufacturing workers (and much more than half in Melbourne) were now working in factories with more than 50 employees.[80] The formation and failure of 'factories' was constant; at least 200 were closing down and being replaced each year. Numerous craftsmen, ambitiously seeking independence, were still launching out on their own and failing after a few months for want of capital and ability to snatch a share of business.[81] About one-fifth of the factory hands were women who made up about five-sixths of the clothing workers and one-quarter of those in the footwear trade.[82]

Most of the numerous food and drink establishments—more than 700 were enumerated in 1886, employing about 6,000 people—were flour-mills, bakeries and butcheries with only one or two hands. Large Melbourne millers like James Fry and Thomas Brunton were tending to drive small men out of business, especially after production methods were revolutionized by the substitution of rollers for stones.[83] Swallow & Ariell's biscuit-factory at Port Melbourne, said to be the fifth largest in the world, was

Employment in Selected Manufacturing Industries

	1883	1889
BUILDING MATERIALS AND FURNITURE	9,329	13,810
Stone quarries, etc.	1,153	1,749
Bricks and pottery	1,582	3,243
Sawmills and joinery	4,101	6,202
Furniture	1,516	1,672
ENGINEERING AND METAL WORKING	9,822	14,214
Agricultural implements	1,352	1,006
Coach and wagon works	2,124	2,980
FOOD, DRINK AND TOBACCO	6,776	7,698
Breweries	860	1,252
Soft drinks	823	1,183
Flour milling	793	807
Wool scouring and tanning	1,754	1,576
Chemicals	1,216	1,238
Clothing	5,552	5,068
Boots and shoes	4,088	3,819
Printing	3,084	4,219

(A. R. Hall, 'Victorian Manufacturing Employment 1860-1900' (unpub. paper.))

managed by F. T. Derham, Thomas Swallow's son-in-law; their fifty-seven varieties sold well in all the colonies.[84] The Red Cross Preserving Co. in Chapel Street, South Yarra, employed 150 in making jams, pickles and sauces. Evan Rowlands, the soft-drink manufacturer, whose soda-water was famous throughout the colonies, had branched out from Ballarat to Melbourne and Sydney and employed 300 all told.[85] Macpherson Robertson, aged nineteen in 1880, started making sweets in the bath at home with a sixpenny nailcan, a threepenny pannikin and a bag of sugar. He tramped the suburbs, selling his products to shops, graduated to a tricycle, and by 1887 had thirty hands.[86]

The seventy to eighty breweries were by far the largest capital element in this group. The more important of them illustrate how frequently private companies were incorporated in the eighties, when additional capital was sought in a period of expansion and the founding migrants sought to retire. The Fitzgerald family's Castlemaine brewery set up an offshoot at South Melbourne in 1885 and was soon paying a 25 per cent dividend. The McCracken brothers, who did the largest trade of all, and the Victoria and Shamrock breweries converted to public companies in 1887 and 1888. Edward Latham's Carlton Brewery was incorporated in 1882 and amalgamated as the Carlton and West End Breweries in 1889.[87] Many small provincial breweries were still adequately protected by freight charges from the Melbourne firms. The eighties saw the beginning of a crucial change of taste. Colonial beers were English-style strong ales with a definite local tang. The warm climate caused special brewing problems and it was not until after 1890 that technological advances greatly improved the taste of ordinary beer. However, about 1882 the Cohn brothers in Bendigo began brewing lager successfully on a small scale; in 1885 an attempt in Collingwood by Germans failed commercially; but in 1888 W. M. and R. Foster from New York started business. In 1889 they complained that importers of German and American lagers had cut prices by a third in an attempt to run them out of business. They asked the government for additional protection and were granted it, despite the protest of the politician, G. D. Carter of the Carlton Brewery, that 'If this beer was to take, the people must first be got to like to drink it, and at present the people did not like it as well as the ordinary colonial beer.' Lager was not brewed in Sydney until 1896.[88]

In the mid-eighties, just before the 1886 recession struck hard, the clothing and allied industries were employing perhaps 11,000 men and women and also a substantial number of 'outworkers' in their homes. More than 7,000 tailoresses and tailors, aided by fairly high protection, were supplying nearly all the made-up clothing for the local market. Skilled labour was plentiful and machinery was abundant; a few big companies were tending to force out the smaller firms. There was some local pride and amusement when Lincoln, Stuart & Co. were called on to supply the uniforms for the New South Wales Sudan contingent as a rush order.[89] Hatters had captured about three-quarters of the local market. Some 4,000 men and women were employed in the fiercely competitive boot and shoe trade centred in Collingwood and Richmond. J. C. Bedggood, an importer as well as manufacturer, spent much of his time promoting his goods far and wide in the other colonies and worrying about growing competition from Sydney.

The metals and machinery industries, which expanded from about 8,000 workers in 1880 to more than 14,000 in 1889, deserve particular notice. The great expansion of the iron trades in the seventies, which even then were beginning to export to South-east Asia, gave hope that Melbourne would become another Birmingham. Although much of this growth might be seen as the 'easy stage' of import-replacement, there were many notable achievements. Standing out from the scores of iron, brass and copper foundries, iron and tin works and wire factories and the hundreds of local smithies were great firms like Langlands', Danks', Johns' and others. Langlands', which dated back to the forties, bought out the Fulton Foundry Co. Ltd in 1881, were superbly equipped with the latest machine tools, and in 1887 were aiming to introduce the Bessemer steel-making process. John Danks, a Wesleyan family firm exemplifying thrift, industry and ploughing back of profits, had monopolized production of water taps by the seventies. In their foundry, brassworks and electroplating works they were now producing steam and safety valves, pumping machinery and plumbing goods for the intercolonial trade; in 1886 they established an English branch factory. Peter Johns, another Wesleyan, had worked as a foreman on reassembling the Crystal Palace, the Exhibition building, in London. When he migrated in 1856 he started as a builder of iron houses, and then formed Johns and Co., whose Melbourne Iron Works specialized in girders, roofing and ornamental iron. In the late seventies he was developing general engineering work and moving into lift manufacturing and installation. When the firm became a public company in 1888, it was employing 120 men and Johns owned a mansion and sixteen acres in Hawthorn.[90] David Munro & Co. had varied interests as ironworkers, machinery manufacturers, contractors and bridge-builders. John McIlwraith's Melbourne Lead Works, manufacturing gas pipes, grew with the expansion of the gas industry and by the eighties were also supplying plumbing materials, glazing and hardware for the building industry. In the mid-eighties, Mephan Ferguson, manufacturer of iron bridges and bolts and nuts, supplied a new need when Deakin returned from California with the demand that water supply pipes be made of wrought-iron and not cast-iron. Ferguson met the challenge, monopolized government contracts and was soon employing about 300 hands. Ballarat and Bendigo foundries, like Harkness & Co. in Bendigo, supplied large orders of mining machinery for Queensland in the later eighties.[91]

Of all the engineering works, Ballarat's Phoenix Foundry was the most famous, for it was builder of locomotives for the Victorian Railways. It had been a public company since 1870 under the management of W. H. Shaw and employed 300 men early in the eighties and 400 later. Until the seventies locomotives were imported from England; since 1871 the Phoenix had tendered successfully almost every time. It was undercapitalized, had rarely declared a dividend, but was paying its skilled men up to 15s a a day. There were great celebrations in April 1883 when the Phoenix delivered its hundredth engine. A public holiday was declared and 15,000 people assembled; the locomotive was covered with flags, flowers and ribbons with 'Advance Ballarat' on the front and 'Hail Victoria' on the side. The band struck up 'See the Conquering Hero Comes' as the engine slowly moved up with Service, Deakin and other politicians, mayors, councillors, directors, and railway officials hanging on, whereupon 'the funnel of the engine emitted a great deal of scalding water which fell in two or three heavy showers on the Ministers and others'. The engine was christened 'Victoria', the Union Jack was unfurled and the band played 'Rule Britannia'. The *Argus* sourly commented that the Phoenix Foundry, like the Bendigo Rolling Stock Works, was in effect subsidized by the state. Another hundred engines were produced by 1886.[92] In 1873 the Phoenix formed as a subsidiary the Lal Lal Iron Mining Co. near Ballarat as a brave attempt to avoid the expense of importing pig-iron. The company built a blast furnace, employed up to 160 men and produced more than 2,000 tons of pig-iron (800 in 1884) before it suddenly collapsed in 1885. Costs were too high and the iron too hard for general engineering work.[93]

After long struggles, the local coachbuilders were producing quality products which were mainly adaptations of American designs, and had taken almost the entire local market. G. F. Pickles, whose Bendigo and Melbourne works employed more than 300 men, was one of several flourishing firms.[94] Agricultural implement and machinery manufacturers similarly almost monopolized the market by careful attention to the peculiar needs of local farmers. Hugh Lennon was an example of a blacksmith who in less than twenty years became one of the largest producers of farm machinery in the colonies. By 1870 his plough was widely used and although he was soon producing 600 a year, shortage of skilled labour made it difficult to meet growing demand. The Kellys' use of Lennon's mouldboard steel for their armour was an advertising windfall. Lennon claimed that Victoria led the world in manufacture of agricultural implements and that English manufacturers were stealing his designs.[95] Two other leading innovators were John Buncle, whose North Melbourne ironworks concentrated increasingly on farm machinery, and James Morrow, a partner in Joseph Nicholson & Co. Morrow produced several new reapers and strippers, and from 1880 to 1883 worked on combining the stripper and the winnower. Experimental combine harvesters had been built in South Australia since 1875, but Morrow's patent of January 1884 was the first to be acknowledged as wholly successful. Hugh Victor McKay, a youth on a farm near Raywood, was building his model at the same time. At trials late in 1885 Morrow's combine was judged slightly superior to McKay's and sold well from 1886, but McKay's 'Sunshine', which was produced in quantity from the mid-nineties, predominated in the long run.[96]

Only a summary indication can be given of the wide range of other manufacturing activity. Saddlery and harness manufacture and tanning, employing some 500 and 1,500 men respectively, were both tending to decline. But Michaelis, Hallenstein, although troubled by a shortage of wattle-bark after ruthless exploitation, was a highly efficient firm with branches in Sydney, London and New Zealand.[97] Furniture manufacture, in which possibly 2,000 were employed including a large minority of Chinese, was based on small-scale enterprise in at least 100 factories. Printing was a major industry employing three to four thousand men; Sands and McDougall, the largest firm, had 320 hands in 1888.[98] The Australian Paper Mills at South Melbourne, with William Brookes and Archibald Currie in control, were laying the basis for long-term advance. The gas industry markedly developed late in the decade when George Swinburne formed the Colonial Gas Association to provide co-ordinated services to country works.[99] Tallow production was declining, but the Apollo Stearine Candle Co. maintained large intercolonial exports of tallow and soap.[1] Cuming Smith's, also on the Maribyrnong River, were successfully developing and exporting acids and fertilizers. The drug importers and manufacturers, Alfred Felton and F. S. Grimwade, both of nonconformist background, were founding an empire which over three-quarters of a century was to grow into Drug Houses of Australia and Australian Consolidated Industries. Their Melbourne Glass Bottle Works, founded in 1872 with L. Mount as manager, was a hazardous pioneering enterprise which began to show profits in the eighties. Their partnership with Joseph Bosisto in manufacturing Parrot and Emu brands eucalyptus oil, which Bosisto had been exporting since 1868 as the most Australian product of all, was more successful. But like Henry Berry before them, their attempts (on French Island) to manufacture salt failed.[2]

The near-absence of workable coal in Victoria was a major handicap and expense to industry dependent on imports from New South Wales. Black coal in the Cape Patterson-Kilcunda area of South Gippsland had long been worked; a company there had failed in the fifties and in the early eighties the Victorian Coal Company was struggling to keep up small production. Several other companies had been floated but had collapsed, and investors were wary despite the long-standing promise of a government bonus. The broken and 'faulty' character of the deposits also discouraged enterprise. The existence of brown coal in Gippsland had been known since the sixties, but the problem of working it economically seemed insuperable. The Great Morwell Brown Coal Mining Company took out a lease in 1887 (which it began to work in 1889) and the government sponsored further prospecting and testing. The serious New South Wales coal strike in August-September 1888, which caused considerable slowing up of Victorian industry and laying off of workmen, increased the sense of urgency; several Gippsland companies were floated and a royal commission was appointed in 1889 to recommend ways and means of hastening development. As it happened, promising discoveries of black coal were about to be made in the Korumburra area, where a syndicate had been prospecting since 1883.[3]

Only rough conclusions can be reached on the effects of protection on industrial growth. The tariff was almost all-embracing, covering some 200 items; most of the *ad valorem* duties were at the rate of, and none higher than, 20 and 25 per cent. The tariff was unsystematic; the Mirams commission found many duties with no protective effect whose abolition it unsuccessfully recommended. Straightout conflicts between import merchant and manufacturer still sometimes occurred when the importer in conjunction with a foreign manufacturer 'dumped' his goods, hoping to drive the local product off the market and then by raising prices to recoup temporary losses.[4] But many merchants had started manufacturing themselves; several clothing, footwear and furniture importers were doing much greater business in this way and were content with the 'protective system'.[5] Groups of manufacturers sometimes had conflicting interests over protective tariffs. Boot- and shoemakers, who imported much raw material, favoured abolition of the leather duties protecting tanners and curriers so that they could compete in New South Wales against Sydney manufacturers; David Altson, the saddler, believed he could do without protection if he could import leather free.[6] The most important conflict was between the woollen mills manufacturing cloth, and clothing manufacturers importing cloth. The Victorian Woollen Cloth Manufacturing Co. had operated successfully in Geelong from 1866, paying regular dividends and employing about 200 with the help of a government bonus and 15 per cent protection. Two other Geelong companies were the Albion and the Excelsior Woollen Mills, and there were other firms in Melbourne, Ballarat and Castlemaine; all told about 800 were employed. The Melbourne Woollen Mill Company, founded in 1871 with James Munro prominent, had to wind up in 1884 and most of the other companies were in trouble; application of the Factories Act which reduced hours from fifty-six to forty-eight, though delayed for three months for this industry, seemed the last straw. Munro and the other Geelong members moved in 1886 for prohibitive duties of 40 or 60 per cent and much more on some items. The clothing manufacturers, backed by the merchants who catered for them, rose in anger, and claimed their industry would be ruined. The government in the end gave a small increase in duties to both sides and withstood an attempt by Munro to bring it down. The concession was not enough to save the mills, most of which went out of business in the next few years because, Munro went on claiming, they did not get the protection they deserved in 1886, but really because they had been producing a limited range of mediocre goods at relatively high prices.[7]

For the sake of political harmony, the government snubbed the Mirams commission, did not attempt the herculean and probably suicidal task of systematizing the tariff and eliminating anomalies, and left it alone as much as possible. In 1886 it weakly compromised on woollen duties, and in 1887 increased duties on timber, to rescue local sawmillers, and on beet-sugar to protect Victorian capital interests in Queensland and to revive the local sugar refinery. After long resistance it finally had to cave in to the farmers in 1889 and concede further agricultural protection as well as increases on certain manufactures. Meanwhile, it had consistently given preference in government contracts to local manufacturers—in effect a policy of subsidy which was of crucial importance in the protective system. Stores and machinery, with the eagle-eyed protectionists watching, were usually purchased within the colony; a contract clause required that only colonial-made bolts and nuts could be used for railway carriages and trucks. In 1883 Parliament required all state school texts to be printed in the colony. In 1886 the government was letting contracts within the colony of £500,000 for engines and rolling stock and £150,000 more for water pipes, a dredge, and a steamer for the Customs Department.[8] The government refused the claim of Victorian shipowners for a share in protection by means of a bounty to make up for the higher wages they had to pay. There was little sympathy either for a proposal by the Victorian Artists' Society, citing the American precedent, for a duty of £10 on each imported painting; Charles Conder, in the minority, considered the request a 'degradation to art as setting it on a trade level'.[9]

The myth about protectionist Victoria has obscured the fact that until the nineties protective duties were low, compared to the United States, Canada and many other colonies.[10] Natural protection, by means of high freight charges for bulkier goods from Europe and insurance, exchange and wharfage costs, was often as substantial as the duties imposed. But the disadvantages of small-scale production, falling import prices after 1884, and the necessity of paying high wages sent many stripling manufacturers to the wall. Protectionist duties were nothing like high enough to be prohibitive. They certainly enabled some infant industries to get on their feet; it is difficult, for example, to explain the sudden spurt of the clothing industry in the early eighties except in terms of the protectionist increases of the late seventies. But in the footwear trade the effective tariff tended to produce wasteful overcompetition. The level of protection was not producing a startling growth in manufacturing, most sections of which did *not* 'boom' in the eighties.[11]

Protection was to run wild from 1889 through the crisis in the nineties. For the moment, however, most of the politicians had sensibly settled for the moderately protective system. But the rabid fury of the *Age* and *Argus* and their supporters and the confusion of the issue with intercolonial rivalry made constant controversy inescapable. The rival colonial statisticians juggled their figures to provide new evidence of superior progress for the propagandists to use in their meaningless comparisons. The *Age* announced in 1887 that 'New South Wales having had fifty years the start of Victoria, four times the territory, payable coal fields' and numerous other advantages was 'far behind Victoria industrially and financially'. Victoria was far ahead in agriculture, manufacturing, exports other than wool, and intercolonial trade; even New South Wales's pastoral advance was based on 'Victorian capital and energy': 'New South Wales adds another to the many illustrations of the national folly of being guided by "theorists" '.[12] On the other hand, Edward Pulsford, the able Sydney free trade propagandist, could claim—for the most part accurately—that New South Wales led in growth of population, wealth, revenue, trade, shipping, number of factories, horse-power and value of plant and machinery, mail transmitted, wages, and consumption of luxuries, while Victoria had more insolvencies and higher taxation.[13]

New South Wales, because of her greater resources, was inevitably taking the lead in population and production. The fanatics reacted triumphantly or gloomily, but rarely modified their obsessive opinions. Even after 1900 Gyles Turner, the historian, put ridiculous emphasis on protection to explain why Victoria had lost pride of place.[14] The distortions of the newspapers concealed the opinions of those who sensibly realized the issue was overrated. There must have been many, like Service, who eventually saw virtues on either side and, in his case to the terrible glee of the *Age* and the chagrin of the *Argus*, remarked that while free trade produced greater wealth, protection ensured fairer distribution of wealth.[15]

That Victoria had almost one-third as many again engaged in manufacturing as New South Wales illustrates the significance and limitations of protection. For New South Wales was superior or comparable in manufacturing strength where natural protection applied or local natural resources gave an advantage. Victoria was ahead in industries such as clothing which could not develop far in a free-trading community. Protection to manufacturing was crucial to no more than 20,000 workmen, less than one-tenth of the Victorian work-force. It was of immense benefit to them in ensuring some measure of job security and of indirect benefit to many more in its general bolstering of wages. Protection was the triumph of the migrant craftsman demanding opportunity to pursue his trade and sometimes to launch an industry. Protection reduced unemployment; without it, there would have been ruthless deployment of low-paid labour. It would be difficult to argue that, without protection, exports could have been increased sufficiently to make up for the industrial production which protection induced. It probably made the early foundation of some major industries possible. However, the costs to the bulk of consumers were fairly high, though they were saved from other forms of taxation. In terms of living standards, protection was a relatively minor factor compared to the fluctuating export prices of wool and wheat. Its importance lies more in the ideological side-tracking of a generation than in its effects on the economy.[16]

The growth of Melbourne

The expansion of Melbourne's population, from 283,000 (33 per cent of the colony's population) in 1881 to 491,000 (43 per cent) in 1891, is perhaps the most remarkable feature of the decade. The population of towns outside Melbourne and of rural areas increased relatively little; the proportion living outside towns fell from 43 per cent to 35 per cent. Melbourne's share of the colony's population increase over the decade was almost three-quarters, whereas Sydney's share of the New South Wales increase was a little over two-fifths. Growth of the new farming towns was barely faster than the decline of the old mining towns. But it was not rural decline which contributed to Melbourne's growth, although the limitation of employment possibilities in the pastoral and family-unit wheat-growing industries is crucial in explaining the bloated size of Australian cities. The stagnation and decline of the mining towns, however, did produce a significant accession to the city's work-force, for thousands of young men coming of age in the eighties could see no future in their home-towns. This decade was also, in a sense, an intermediate period—'after' gold and 'before' coal and irrigation which were both to be decentralizing agencies in minor degree. The growth of industry in Melbourne, while important, was only one factor of many; unlike most of the new large cities of the world, Melbourne had grown massively before manufacturing became very significant. Urbanization was now stimulating industrial development rather than the reverse. The nature of the railway system was taking full effect; Victoria's was the one Australian railway system which grossly favoured the capital city: 'Railways are the rivers of Australia, and all the Victorian rivers have but one mouth', Francis Adams remarked.[17] Melbourne's advantages and the absence of other major ports or communications centres were now having a snowballing effect. Industry continued to concentrate close to the largest market and labour supply and the sources of power, and at the hub of the transport system. Melbourne's commercial and financial supremacy and its handling of the flood of overseas capital led to expansion of commercial employment. Migrants from overseas or other colonies, whether or not they had intended to go up-country, preferred Melbourne's job opportunities and did not leave the city. The growing numbers stimulated further demand for housing, transport and other services, and for labour.[18]

Thus the building of Melbourne in the eighties—of houses, shops, offices, churches, hospitals, public buildings, streets, waterworks—became a major sector of the economy. The city itself was extensively rebuilt, as multi-storey construction became possible and great financial institutions resolved to present grander fronts to the world. Residential investment more than doubled between 1883 and 1888; the Melbourne building boom from 1882 was stimulated partly by a sharp rise in the number of young married couples and accelerated quickly from 1885 when migrants poured in.[19] Early in 1888 just on 10,000 Victorians, more than double the number in 1881, were working in brickyards and sawmills alone; brick production had trebled. Thousands of double-fronted weatherboard detached cottages were run up in Footscray, Essendon, Brunswick, Northcote, Coburg and Preston, while on the other side of the river in Hawthorn, Malvern, Caulfield and Camberwell as many brick as wooden houses were built. About sixty building societies in Melbourne, some of which dated back to the sixties, were responsible for about two-thirds of housing finance, until late in the boom when a rash of new speculative investment companies took a large share. Most of the building societies were 'permanent' and not 'terminating'; James Munro had introduced the former principle when he founded the Victorian Permanent in 1865. The societies had a high reputation and their wage- and salary-earning members repaid their loans with admirable regularity. By the mid-eighties building society deposits were so large that they were rivalling the savings banks as savings institutions; their operations depended little on loans from banks or other outside sources. One major society, the Modern Permanent Building and Investment Society, financed about one-tenth of new Melbourne housing in the eighties and also used nearly two-fifths of its funds for advances for house purchase. Many of its clients were wage-earning skilled workers, especially building workers, aiming to own their own homes, but they also included landlord-borrowers building houses for rental, and speculative builders.[20] Housing construction remained largely the business of small-scale builders, but the number of large contractors increased markedly, and 'speculative' builders, who were responsible for almost one-third of all building, kept production well ahead of demand.[21]

The public sector; transport

The public sector of the economy, as in the other Australian colonies, was on a scale relatively greater than almost any country in the world, almost equal in magnitude to the private sector in importation and outlay of capital. However haphazardly, the central government was by far the leading investor and entrepreneur in the colony. Communication was, of course, the major area of activity—not only railways, but roads, harbour works, river improvements and telegraph extensions; water supply became the next most important area, and local government and defence works were almost equally significant. Perhaps two-thirds of the capital invested by government was spent on wage-labour for construction works; as yet, however, works were usually contracted out and little direct employment for construction was given. Indirect governmental employment on such a scale had a damaging effect on the availability of labour for private enterprise, especially as the eight-hours agreement was firmly written into government contracts. Numerous petitions in the eighties pleaded for a resumption of assisted immigration and complained that government was importing huge quantities of capital but not the labour to work it.[22] Government investment gave massive stimulus to economic growth, helped to raise real wages and to improve the standard of living, but at the same time tended to handicap the growth of manufacturing and agriculture.[23]

In perspective, Victorian railway building in the eighties is not as remarkable as is sometimes implied. In the seventies Victoria had built 925 miles, and in the eighties built 1,272 compared to New South Wales's 1,345 and Queensland's 1,509 miles. Victoria's expenditure, because of the greater costs of constructing and equipping on the wider gauge, was slightly more per mile than in New South Wales and nearly twice as much as in Queensland. Victoria now had an extensive network, with many branch lines rather than a series of trunk lines, and unlike the other colonies earned as much from carriage of passengers as freight. Expenditure on construction increased steadily from 1884 to 1889, while New South Wales cut down in the later eighties. The major works were the five parallel extensions into the north-western wheatlands and to the South Australian border, the Colac-Warrnambool-Hamilton line, the South Gippsland line and an extension from Sale to Bairnsdale, new branches to the Murray in the north and the north-east, and numerous suburban lines. The main motive and achievement of the new construction was to aid the Wimmera, northern, Gippsland and other farmers. The continuation of the battle for the Riverina by new lines to Swan Hill, Koondrook, Cobram and Yarrawonga as well as Echuca, Wahgunyah and Wodonga was a minor aspect.* Following suburban extensions to Frankston and Box Hill-Lilydale in 1882, new lines were opened to Coburg (1884), Heidelberg (1888), Preston-Whittlesea (1889) and Glen Iris (1890). The two separate systems were to be effectively linked by a viaduct along Flinders Street (not completed until 1891), and Gippsland was also to be linked to Spencer Street by the Outer Circle line from Oakleigh to Fairfield (1891)—an extraordinary decision, almost but not quite indefensible for one objective was to cater conveniently for goods traffic.[24]

The Railways became a huge industry. By the end of the decade, some 10,000 men were employed in the service, including the Newport workshops which were developed from 1882 for construction of carriages and maintenance of rolling stock. In addition thousands of navvies were out building the new lines; the Phoenix Foundry at Ballarat was manufacturing engines by the hundred, and the Bendigo Rolling Stock Works employed more than 200 hands. The rails were imported, but a growing proportion of other equipment was being supplied in the colony, and sleeper cutting was no negligible part of the timber trade. When the construction gangs arrived to extend a line, roaring canvas towns sprang up almost overnight and disappeared as quickly. Local farmers had prosperous, arduous periods sub-contracting to provide water, fencing, ballast and timber. Towns waxed fat when fortunate enough to be the terminus of the line for a few years, and waned sadly when the line moved on. It was a great day for a district when the extended line or spur was finally opened with speeches by the contractor, the surveyor, the railways inspector, a Cabinet minister, the local member, the shire president—then a bottle of champagne smashed against the engine and barrels of beer for the navvies.[25]

* N. G. Butlin several times refers to the importance of intercolonial rivalry and attempts to capture trade as the 'main determinant' of railways investment in the eighties (*Investment in Australian Economic Development*, pp. 416, 330, 363, 368–9). It was very important earlier, but in the eighties barely 10 per cent of Victorian railway building was relevant to the Riverina question. Butlin's excellent map (p. 325) illustrates the point.

Under the new Commissioners' rule, the Railways made a small surplus between 1886 and 1889, taking all interest on loans into account, whereas for the five previous years there had been a deficit of about £1 million. There were notable improvements in efficiency, but Speight and his colleagues may not have stood firmly enough against political pressures by insisting on accumulating profits in the prosperous years. Fares were moderate by world standards, despite expensive coal and high wages. Freight charges on goods from New South Wales and from the marginal farming areas were kept as low as possible. The accepted assumption was that the state Railways were not to make profits but to run as a service to the public. Moreover Speight went out of his way to meet requests made of him, however uneconomic, and prices he paid for land were sometimes startling. He has been described by Geoffrey Blainey as a 'strange mixture of philanthropist and efficiency expert'. The day of reckoning for such extravagance was to come all too soon.[26]

The huge losses made by the Railways after 1889 are a crucial feature of Victoria's history and the railway policies of the eighties are a subject of sharp controversy. It is argued, on the one hand, that a 'highly inefficient and wasteful transport system' and a huge public debt were created; that the basic balance of payments problem was accentuated by 'waste, inefficiency and misdirection of investment outlays'; that the extensions of the eighties added nothing to net revenue until the nineteen-twenties, or for a long time to export earnings; that the railways were primarily built for wheat-farmers, who had not solved the problem of permanent agriculture; that unprofitable new lines were constantly defended by rationalizations, such as higher land values, less expenditure on roads, and the probability of denser settlement filling the empty spaces.[27] Against all this is the simple valid argument that 'down the railways went thousands of train loads of goods that would not have been produced if there had been no railways, and that up the railway went thousands of people to settle areas in which they would not have made a living but for railways'. Railways lessened the costs of mining and other inland industries, supplied cheaper goods to the inland consumer, and provided vast employment directly and indirectly.[28]

The argument over the costs of developmental policies is a constant one in Australian history. In this case there are safe obvious conclusions to be drawn, however banal. Most of the railway investment can be justified in the short term or long; much of the railway losses can reasonably be set off against the many concealed benefits. But a minority of the lines should never have been built, and were built only because of governmental inability to weigh priorities strictly and to resist political pressure.

The spreading railways naturally dominated other forms of transport. Expenditure on major communicating roads dwindled away; Cobb & Co. and other coaching firms were forced back to criss-cross connections and out to the periphery. Railways were killing off the river trade too, although Echuca held on through the eighties as Victoria's second port, funnelling

Riverina wool down to Melbourne and station supplies coming back up the railway to the barges. Rail transport was actually more expensive than shipping wool down the Murray, but selling and shipping through the Melbourne pastoral houses and the saving of time were overriding advantages. Some regular river traffic up the Goulburn continued through the eighties. In 1886 Wm. McCulloch & Co., 'owners of and agents for a large fleet of steamers trading on the inland rivers . . . contractors for the supply of red gum timber (any quantity) . . . Proprietors of the Melbourne "Parcels Express" ', closed down their Echuca office, while their rivals as carriers, Permewan Wright, continued to operate on the rivers.*[29] The linking of the Victorian and New South Wales railways in 1883 hardly affected the cheap intercolonial shipping trade. Wm. Howard Smith and Sons dominated the passenger trade with the east coast and were large coal shippers and coal merchants. The Melbourne Steamship Co. and Huddart, Parker & Co. were other major shipping firms. The Peninsula and Orient S.N. Co. provided the major overseas passenger line and retained the Victorian mail contract.

Melbourne's inner transport problem was most happily solved by the introduction of cable tramways in 1885, under the guidance of the brilliant American, F. B. Clapp. From 1869 his Melbourne Omnibus Company had dominated the horse-bus system and from the late seventies, when 'Tramway' was inserted in the company's name, he made determined efforts to convert government, municipalities and public to the need for trams. Legislation was eventually passed in 1883 whereby a Trust of seven members from the Melbourne City Council and eleven from other municipalities was created, with power to borrow money to construct lines which would be leased to the company until 1916; the company was to pay interest on and contribute to a sinking fund for the loan. Clapp then travelled the world in order to decide on the most appropriate system. He was most impressed by the cable trams of San Francisco and Dunedin, and imported as installing engineer, G. S. Duncan, who had had experience in both cities. The Spencer Street to Richmond line was the first completed, in November 1885, and in the six following years a forty-seven-mile network was constructed. The company was highly efficient, manufactured its own cars, sternly controlled its employees, made enormous profits and paid huge dividends.[30] By 1890 Melbourne was superbly equipped with a suburban transport system of trains and trams.

Application of inventions; women at work

Technological innovations, as always, were altering the pattern of business and domestic life. Melbourne city and the main streets of suburbs and towns and most urban houses had long been lit by gas; in 1878 the Metro-

* The Echuca wharf was 330 yards long, with a top decking 38 feet above the river's summer level. In the seventies, Echuca handled an annual average of 196 vessels, in the eighties 145, and in the nineties 74. (Allan Morris, *Rich River* (Echuca, 1952), especially ch. 12.)

politan Gas Company had been formed by amalgamation of city and suburban companies. In the seventies, after the Bunsen burner had greatly increased the heating qualities of gas, stoves began to be imported and from 1880 the local company built its own models. In the eighties the gas stove became a standard domestic amenity and gas bath-heaters were first offered in 1887.[31] Gas consumption and the number of domestic installations in Melbourne roughly doubled during the decade. Electricity could make little impact because of its cost. There were numerous demonstrations and experiments from 1878; there were even night football matches under lights in 1879,[32] and Elizabeth Street was temporarily lit by arc-lamps in 1880. A theatre changed to electric lighting in 1882 and the Public Library in April 1883. The Bank of Australasia in 1884, to the delight of its employees, installed its own plant at head office lighting fifty lamps of twenty candle-power. Other firms followed, but the Australian Electric and two other companies were struggling to convince domestic consumers that the improvement justified the cost. In 1888 there was an experimental run of a tram by electricity. But it was not until the nineties that electricity was widely adopted for street lighting, and many years were to pass before it came into common domestic use.[33] Melbourne had been ahead of London in forming a telephone company in 1880, but service was so poor that meetings of subscribers and the Chamber of Commerce in 1886 implored the government to take it over. The change gave general satisfaction and a link was made with Geelong in 1889.[34] Hydraulic goods lifts had been introduced fairly widely in the seventies; Paterson, Laing and Bruce had three in their warehouse in 1880. The introduction of passenger lifts, one of the first of which was at Parliament House in 1883, was to have a crucial effect on the skyline of the city during the boom building of the later eighties.[35] A few typewriters were being used in offices in 1886; the lawnmower, replacing scythe and roller, was one of the most exciting innovations of the period; and ice-chests were another welcome amenity—local models were replacing American imports.[36] It is not surprising that all these inventions were of overseas origin. Australian originality was most successfully applied to agricultural machinery; men like Lennon, Buncle, Morrow and McKay were outstanding innovators. Even in this broad field, however, there were occasional accusations of backwardness; in 1884 the *Argus* was deploring the absence of a single grain elevator in the colony—the Americans had been using them for a quarter of a century.[37] Other original minds at work in the colony included Louis Brennan, the inventor of the dirigible torpedo (who made a model of a helicopter in 1883), and A. U. Alcock in the electrical field (who later established the principle of the hovercraft).[38]

In the eighties little employment was open to women still, except domestic service, making clothes and teaching. Early in the decade, rather more than 20,000, of whom nearly half were under twenty-one, were employed privately as maids and cooks, and another 3,000 as waitresses. About 18,000 were dressmakers, milliners, tailoresses and shoemakers, of whom perhaps one-quarter were working in factories. The constant shortage of domestic servants reflected the preference of native-born girls for the independence of factory employment at lower wages. Some desperate ladies formed a Domestic Servants' Immigration Society in 1885. Nearly 5,000 women were teaching—a relatively small number still—of whom about one-third were private governesses or music-teachers. A standard advertisement ran: 'Wanted. Young lady as nursery governess; must be able to give instruction in French and music; salary £30 a year.' Any cook and most housemaids would have regarded such payment as outrageous. About 2,000 were shop-assistants, 1,500 washerwomen and 1,100 nurses. The number of saleswomen increased markedly in the eighties; but clerking and copying in offices, and the professions other than teaching continued briefly to remain male preserves. In 1887, however, one of the banks engaged its first lady typist.[39]

Rising prosperity

In a sense the boom had begun late in 1880. 1881 to 1885 were years of sharply rising prosperity, though there were marked fluctuations in different sections of the economy. In 1881 and 1882 bank clearing-house returns rose dramatically, wages recovered from their depressed state and rose above standard rates, and a mild property boom developed. The rise of wool prices in 1880 and the influx from London of capital for investment in wool, a mild mining revival, better seasons for the farmers after 1882, and increasing demand for metropolitan housing all contributed. Early in 1881 the banks temporarily had too much money in hand and were preaching the need for more vigorous enterprise; twelve months later they were short of deposits and began actively seeking cash in Britain. 1882 saw further large investments in pastoral property in the Riverina and Queensland, in sugar and in Melbourne land. There was a slight building recession and general slackening of growth in 1883 and no longer so obviously a condition of over-full employment. Yet in April, when Service was starting out as Treasurer, he felt it wise to strike a note of caution and warn that a 'reaction', a 'depression' was bound to come 'after all this excitement'.[40] Coghlan refers to an 'illimitable and insatiable' demand for money at this time; prosperity could be measured by increasing imports, swelling revenue and slightly falling prices. 1884 and 1885 were years of high prosperity, although pastoralists in the north were suffering from drought, there were huge losses in sugar, and the Oriental Bank failed in May 1884. (The Bank failed for no reason connected with its Australian business and eventually repaid the Victorian government and other depositors.)[41] In 1884 wheat and flour exports reached their highest point, suburban sales for villa allotments 'leapt into popularity', the building boom continued, and the National Bank increased its deposits by almost half. In the five years to 1885 city land values steadily rose at an average annual rate of 9 per cent.[42] In 1885 with a fall in wool prices, pastoral interests were feeling the pinch. However, immigration sharply rose, the building boom accelerated and real estate speculation increased, the railways were working at a profit, and Victorian credit had never stood higher in London; the loan in November 1885 was sold at £107. Victorian public borrowing was still relatively modest by the standards of New South Wales and Queensland. 1886 was to see a mild reflection of the severe recession in other colonies (which will be discussed in chapter 8, together with the wild boom of 1887–8). But until 1887, it might be argued that the boom, based on political stability, general confidence and large imports of capital, showed few signs of getting out of hand.[43]

3

Class Relations and the Rise of Labour

Class and class-consciousness

Victoria by the eighties was settling into a relatively stable mould of occupational and social classes; transformation of individual economic fortune and social position was no longer so common. The attempt to retain or recreate the old-world hierarchy of social rank was still the main issue. Egalitarians, who asserted the desirability of classlessness and refused to recognize class distinctions, provided staunch resistance. The simple overriding class division and consciousness of class, which the Labour movement was to provoke in the nineties, were still far distant.

There were numerous claims to social élitism. Ada Cambridge, the novelist, eulogized the tiny group of the type Martin Boyd was to immortalize in his novels, 'a small, inter-related, highly exclusive circle . . . , who had had time and the means to read, travel, and generally sustain the traditions of refinement to which they were born'. Some of them are to be found in the pages of 'Rolf Boldrewood's' *Old Melbourne Memories.* Money was no passport to their society, 'brains and good breeding alone counted'; their children married only their own kind.[1] At another extreme was the type of the ex-army officer-police magistrate—the 'Captain Bunderby' whom Norman Lindsay remembered as a child at Creswick, with his 'studied pose of bored insolence to the pretensions of all humanity outside the pale of its exclusive class consciousness'.* Those squatters who put up the Governor on his country tours were among the superior set. A handful of them had established local patriarchal relationships; at one Anglican church the congregation rose to its feet on the entry of the dowager lady from the mansion-homestead. Some of them automatically took the chair at shire council meetings, and had built the local church and largely maintained its incumbent. They were gentry of a sort; Trollope had found most of them very like the eighteenth century Tory squirearchy, proud 'but not fine gentlemen' and without much taste in art and literature.[2] Yet their claim to form an aristocracy had fallen flat. They were not numerous enough, their economic position was too precarious,

* '"Can you explain why I appear to be so unpopular in this demned town?", "Bunderby" asked Dr Lindsay. "Well, if you must know, Bunderby, it's because you're such an infernal snob."' 'Captain Bunderby' ultimately had to flee Creswick when he wronged a shopkeeper's daughter. ('Uncles and Others', *Southerly*, 1955, no. 1, pp. 2–3.)

and above all they were detested by the mass of the people because of their ruthless methods of acquiring land and their claim to class superiority. They soon lost all political initiative although, entrenched in the Legislative Council, they retained a power of veto. Many of the old pioneers remained totally irreconcilable to colonial democracy and merited Pearson's description: 'he dismisses the tenant or workman who votes against him, is irritated if hats are not touched to him, and denounces all proposals for the higher culture of the masses as communism.'[3] Few of their children, however, adopted such a stance.

The pastoralist in town, whether really out of the top drawer or awkwardly acting the gentleman, was at the centre of Melbourne 'Society'. Gentlemen of the old official class, many professional men, a few long-established merchants and bankers, and their ladies, formed a working alliance with the 'landed gentry' in defence of old notions of station and duty. The banker, because of his sheer power, was necessarily a social leader.[4] But it was the age of the bourgeoisie, and they refused to agree that landed property was essential for social recognition. Pastoral finance remained crucial in the economy, but most representatives of urban capital were unsympathetic to the squatters as a class, were often self-made *nouveaux riches* determined to break through the caste barriers to social climbing, and scouted social snobbery about 'trade'.* The 'upper class' found it impossible to draw a rigid social line, for too many powerful men were demanding entry. Government House had long ago succumbed. So those who set themselves up as a social élite could not be confined to those with claims to family background, education or broad acres.

In fact, the test amounted to little more than money:

> we have neither an aristocracy of birth nor one of intellect, [A. M. Topp commented]. We have simply a plutocracy—a body of men who have made their own fortunes, and in the process have acquired all the hardness of feeling and narrowness of view that have characterized plutocracies all the world over. They judge a man by his bank account, and esteem or despise him [accordingly].†[5]

Twopeny considered the plutocracy to be 'utterly selfish in character' and neglectful of its charitable duties, and remarked that artists, writers and scientists were quite without status. His astringent eye noted how much

* Ada Cambridge ironically remarks on 'that obscure line which divides the wholesale merchant's social acceptability from the lost condition of the retail trader' (*The Three Miss Kings* (Melb., 1891), p. 124). Douglas Sladen recalled the embarrassment when a squatter's daughter came to stay with her cousins in Geelong: 'The father of the cousins kept a big shop in the town, so the cousins were not in Geelong Society. . . . When a shopkeeper wanted to rank as a gentleman he bought a Station, and dropped the shop. A bank clerk was a gentleman, so the sons of rich shopkeepers liked to become bank clerks.' (*My Long Life* (London, 1939), p. 58.)

† 'Tasma' has an excellent description of the wealthy self-made man in *Uncle Piper of Piper's Hill* (London, 1892), pp. 66-9. Exulting in his wealth as proof of hard work and wisdom, he was shrewd, generous, not to be contradicted or reasoned with, contemptuous of non-material pursuits—and often appeared pigheaded and vulgar to his educated children.

more easily a lady could be manufactured than a gentleman; but despite all his absurdity the parvenu at least had 'the merit of seeking after better things'.[6] And Ada Cambridge acknowledged that one of the virtues of Melbourne Society was its freedom from the 'elaborate snobbishness' which a 'British prig' practised.[7] No doubt this was largely a woman-made world. Twopeny considered social distinctions were 'very slight' among men, that it was 'lawful to be friendly with everybody and anybody in town'; he also noted how frequently, because of the nature of migration, men had married far beneath them.[8] Another well-bred observer noted that he had found no gentleman who employed a valet.*[9] The ladies, however, suffered their daily agonies over whether their calling cards would be returned, who should be introduced to whom, whether a certain suitor was eligible, or whether some lady without her own carriage would have to be dropped.[10]

In the country towns too, the women tended to define social groupings broadly into three. The bankers, doctors, lawyers, large landowners and superior government officials cut themselves off, while shopkeepers asserted their status over those who 'worked with their hands'. The lines were drawn more or less successfully even in the mining towns, though 'men who had worked together in earlier days did not change as a rule when some struck riches and their mates didn't'.[11] Most farmers and their wives had little time for such niceties.

The gulf between commerce and manufacturing, between white-collars and those who soiled their hands, remained wide. The manufacturer was nearly always an artisan, often a nonconformist from the North-country, who had launched out for himself and made good by hard work and thrift and who continued actively to supervise his works.[12] A few who achieved wealth and property began to make their way into the upper ranks of the social hierarchy, but many who prospered refused to alter their tastes or modest style of life. The proud artisan-craftsman—temperate, thrifty, self-improving and politically aware—retained a dignified sense of self-esteem, strove to be 'respectable', and was often ambitious to improve his status by becoming a master. The skilled miner of Bendigo and Ballarat—often a small investor, a pillar of the church, and conscious of being a labour aristocrat—was of a similar mould. The small shopkeeper—independent-minded and of widely varying origins—was usually less educated and showed less concern with the world than the artisan. But all followed the business and professional man in dress, deportment and other conventions. The superior artisan was bearded or at least mustachio'd, and had his dark suit, silk hat and everyday bowler.[13] It was difficult to distinguish the classes by their dress.

* The extent to which domestic servants are employed is an illuminating aspect of class and status in society. The number of domestic servants in Victoria was relatively almost half that in Britain. About one family in ten employed a cook-maid. The number of male servants was about 3,000, most of whom were coachmen-gardeners; butlers were very very few. It is unlikely that many more than 1,000 families employed a nursemaid. See Twopeny, *Town Life*, 'Servants'.

The further gap between artisan and unskilled labourer—navvy, dock-labourer, railway porter, domestic servant—was as wide again in terms of education, income, conduct, political participation and self-esteem. Even the common labourer, however, had his black coat and bowler for Sunday wear. Beyond them again were the defeated and the outcast—the criminals, alcoholics and other demoralized or unbalanced men often on the brink of destitution.

There were, after all, only a few thousand people strongly motivated to assert an upper class superiority. Observers were almost unanimous in noting both the prevailing atmosphere of social equality and classlessness, and the dignity of workingmen. Ada Cambridge judged that manners 'do not deteriorate as the social scale descends; we were jostled on the crowded pavements, but not rudely'. E. H. Sugden, the newly-arrived Master of Queen's College, was happy that workingmen addressed him 'without any rudeness, but with perfect familiarity and ease'. There were only two classes on the railways, and few other than workingmen in working dress travelled second class. Waitresses and cabbies would not accept tips; domestic servants addressed the master of the house as 'Mr X' and not 'Sir'.[14] Francis Adams made perhaps the most exaggerated assessment of the workingman's self-respect:

> The People in Australia breathes free: it does not feel the weight of the two great divisions of the Middle-class that is above it, the well-to-do and the gentlemen. Workmen here do not go slouching down the streets, as they do in England, crushed under the sense of their inferiority. This is a true republic, the truest, as I take it, in the world. In England, the average man feels that he is an inferior: in America he feels that he is a superior: in Australia he feels that he is an equal. This is indeed delightful . . . here the People is neither servile nor insolent, but only shows its respect of itself by its respect of others. Nowhere else but in France is there, I think, anything quite like it.[15]

Urban manufacturers and artisans, selectors, and the mining promoters and workmen of the gold towns instinctively resisted any attempt to perpetuate old-world class privilege. The 'digger of the old school', according to Joseph Furphy, was 'fully alive to the privilege of release from the pressure of mildewed conventions touching squire and parson'.[16] The ideal of independence, of being one's own boss, remained potent, although most hopes were blighted and independence was often a poor reality. Yet perhaps one man in three of the older colonists had taken up a selection at some stage, thousands of miners held shares in companies or worked on co-operative principles, many artisans launched out as manufacturers—usually with quite inadequate capital—and many others set up their own shops or agencies. Nearly all of them, and most of those who became mere wage-earners too, rejected any claims of birth, old-world social standing or education to social superiority. They also frequently repudiated the whole notion of 'class',* and generally acknowledged the claims only of material success. The assumption remained dominant that opportunities for improvement of economic status were still plentiful. The degree of prosperity achieved—the wide distribution of property, which gave so many workingmen the sense of having a stake in the community—also inhibited growth of working-class consciousness. Prosperity, social mobility and class confusion had tended to promote good understanding between the better- and the worse-off.[17] But the constant venom of *Punch* and the contemptuous sniping of the *Argus* at the workingman indicated the fragility of the prevailing social harmony. The latent class-consciousness of many workingmen would revive if they came to believe that opportunities for advancement were being shut off.

Standard of living

Victoria was 'a paradise for working men', Bishop Moorhouse announced on his return home. It was 'a new England in everything but this—that it has no paupers and no destitution'.[18] Gyles Turner claimed that Australian working-class living standards were the highest in the world; in Victoria, deposits with banks, finance companies and building societies amounted to £28 per head of population. 'We have absolutely no undeserved pauperism,' he concluded.[19] Dozens of overseas observers were astonished by the prosperity of workingmen and the amount spent on dress by factory girls:

> You can see that bread-and-butter never enters into the cares of these people; it is only the cake which is sometimes endangered, or has not sufficient plums in it. . . . Except under very rare circumstances poverty . . . may fairly be considered a reproach. Every man has it in his power to earn a comfortable living; and if . . . the working-man does not become one of the capitalists . . . he has only himself to blame.

'You never see a discontented face or a hungry one,' Froude remarked. The 'happiness, cheerfulness, and all-round comfort of life' of the working class had never been equalled in the history of the world, wrote another enthusiast.[20] Short hours were the general rule and the politician trembled at the labour vote. Parliamentarians and pressmen condemned the shirking, loafing unemployed agitators with extraordinary venom.

Those who asserted that want was here a stranger and misery unknown sometimes lied, perhaps, for their own reasons but more often were simply deceiving themselves. Victoria was so evidently a success story and prosperity so easily won, they believed, that those who cried poor had to be

* Cf. the remarks, forty years on, of George Cockerill, a Bendigo boy and *Age* journalist, on a Bendigo man: 'Sir John Quick . . . supplies, in his honorable career, an answer to the loathsome, grovelling lie of "class-consciousness". In early life Sir John was a hard manual worker. . . . He knew no thought of class consciousness when he was a battery-feeder, and he knows none now that he is an honored judge. . . . It is not a question of class—of "bourgeois" or "proletariat"—as the abject foreigner would have it. It is one of manhood—Australian manhood at that.' (Quick Papers, newspaper cutting.)

either corrupt or moral weaklings. The enthusiasts were correct on the main point, however. Wages were rising through the eighties, prices had long been stable and in the mid-eighties were dropping. A high proportion of workingmen owned their own cottages or were well on the way to doing so, and their children's education was almost free. Massive government spending and the elimination of direct competition by assisted migrants ensured a high measure of employment security. Australian workingmen had more money to spend than their fellows anywhere, except possibly in North America. The cost of food in relation to income was lower than in any country but the United States and Canada. Australian meat consumption was the highest in the world by far—two or three times relatively as much as Britain's, about four times Germany's, ten times Italy's; the best mutton was fourpence a pound and many a mechanic's family ate twenty pounds or more every week. The consumption of alcohol, strangely, was low by European standards; so was the consumption of tobacco by American standards.[21] The known comparison was with Britain: wages were far higher, while the cost of living was similar or a little lower; food was cheaper, clothing cost about the same, and rent was higher. Rising standards induced the optimistic assumption that conditions would continue to improve.

The unskilled labourer was usually paid 6s to 8s a day—a maximum of £90 to £120 a year—and artisans earned about half as much again. Most building tradesmen and metal workers received 10s to 12s a day, £150 to £180 a year. A few highly skilled blacksmiths, boilermakers and turners earned £200 a year or more. Only a minority of workmen could regard their employment as 'permanent'; most payment was by the day and the job security of the civil service was hence very attractive. One acute observer believed that over a wide area of employment, there was less security than in England and more time lost between jobs.[22] In the absence of any provision by the state of financial relief for unemployment, sickness, accident or death, friendly societies flourished and the insurance function of trade unions was crucial.[23] Relatively few semi-skilled and unskilled labourers, however, had any insurance provision in the early eighties. More genteel occupations were much better rewarded. Drapers' assistants earned between £120 and £250 a year and bank clerks about £145 at the age of twenty-one; one-quarter of the National Bank's officers were paid at least £300 in the late eighties and one-tenth £450 or more. Some banks forbade their employees to marry without an income of £200 or £250, normally reached about the age of thirty. Middle-range civil servants and bank clerks both were paid much more than schoolmasters.[24] The gap between the lowest and the highest pay was wide indeed: Cabinet ministers received £1,400 to £2,000, a top civil servant £1,000, a university professor £1,000 and a house, while many business and professional men earned between £1,000 and £3,000 a year. And there was no income tax.

The artisan, as a rule, set out to own his own house, which he usually purchased through a building society. Payments were normally higher than rents, interest was high and the house had to be paid off in seven to twelve years; consequently there were many casualties. Labourers were in no position to acquire their own homes but they, like the artisans, usually lived in a separate house and took immense pride in their tiny gardens; workingmen as a whole flatly declared against living in terraces or sharing houses. Rents for cheap houses rose in the eighties to 12s or 15s a week or £1 for a better one. Suburban railway extensions both hastened the spread of factories out of the city and made it possible, with the help of cheap workmen's fares, for the factory worker to live well away from his place of employment. Nevertheless, the greatest expansion of workmen's housing in the eighties was in Footscray where the factories and workshops were fast increasing. Unlike Sydney and Adelaide, the workman's house was nearly always weatherboard—a simple oblong box with a passage down the middle and corrugated iron roofing. By world standards, Victorian workingmen were very comfortably housed, but the eighties was 'the golden age of jerry-building'[25] and many an innocent purchaser was tricked into buying the shoddiest of houses.[26]

It is true that there was no poverty remotely comparable in scale with an English city. There was no need for a poor-law and poor-rates to feed and house the destitute, because near-full employment was maintained. Most of the poverty-stricken were either physically afflicted, elderly, widowed, or deserted wives and children—people often powerless to help themselves and dependent on public or private charity. Government cared for the insane, and provided institutions for or subsidized private institutions for the blind, deaf and dumb, and orphans. Private charities, such as the Melbourne Ladies' Benevolent Society and church groups, assisted the chronically ill and families in distress from lack of a male breadwinner. Every big country town had its Benevolent Asylum, maintained largely by private subscription, for the aged poor. There remained a small pocket, only a few hundreds in Melbourne perhaps, of vagrant, homeless poor, incapable of working, for whom Dr Singleton almost alone provided at his Collingwood Mission and elsewhere in the city.[27]

The buoyant labour market ensured reasonable wages for most of those in employment. Union organization and legislation cleaned up some of the black spots of sweated female and child labour. Every winter, however, when seasonal demand for agricultural and building labourers declined, a few hundred men in Melbourne were out of work. Unemployment was ephemeral and confined largely to unskilled labourers, but short-term distress was genuine. Skilled workers often had to seek new jobs, but usually quickly found a post. Government, press and public opinion—even the *Age* and the Trades Hall Council—were hard to convince that a problem existed. The government, while refusing to establish an employment bureau, eventually came round to planning public works to take account of the seasonal labour surplus. It annually issued free railway passes up-country to those seeking work—300 were taken up in 1886—and it sometimes provided special subsistence works, though always at pay lower than market rates. 1883 and 1884 were good years, though in May 1884 there were 300 or 400 unemployed in Melbourne. The 1885 winter was worse, and winter 1886, when bad conditions in Sydney and Adelaide drove unemployed men to Melbourne, and winter 1887, when the building trade slackened, were comparatively serious. In August 1886 a procession of 300 men carried 'Food or Work' slogans, and some who attempted to rush the Chief Secretary's office were arrested; the magistrates were harsh towards demonstrators. In 1887, for the first time, Parliament admitted a serious problem. Deakin confessed that there was terrible poverty and suffering which could only be mitigated, not remedied. For as another government spokesman said, 'Whatever the Government did, there would always be suffering in large cities.' An Opposition spokesman agreed that 'upon the mantle of civilisation there must always be a fringe of poverty'; they should try to narrow the fringe, while taking care not to encourage dependence on the state.[28]

A large section of the working class—a quarter perhaps or a third—did not share in the boom and remained marginally above the breadline. It was remarkable that the proportion was so small. But the family man on a labourer's wage, even if he had 'permanent' employment, could not save or look forward to owning his own house, and continued his accustomed precarious existence. No William Lane emerged, as in Queensland, to savage the oppressors of the poor. Most workmen remained untouched by trade unions. Prosperity was weakening the reforming zeal and blunting the criticisms of radicals and humanitarians, and inhibiting acceptance of fundamental criticisms of capitalism which were beginning to filter through from overseas.

The trade union movement

In the eighties, nevertheless, trade unions emerged as a major force. Economic discipline had been reimposed about 1860 in a period of labour surplus. Most of the proud unions formed in the fifties had collapsed or maintained precarious life as little more than benefit societies, although the building unions and some others managed to retain the eight-hour day. The early seventies saw a revival; new unions were formed and frequently attempted to win shorter hours or higher wages by direct action when negotiation failed. However, there were several cases like the Agricultural Implement Makers' Union which, having won the eight hours, entered on a two-month strike for a wage increase, was defeated and collapsed in 1873, and was not re-formed until 1885.[29] There was a spurt of activity between 1878 and 1880 when many of the union leaders were closely associated with the National Reform and Protection League behind the Berry government. Some important industrial gains were made, and more new unions were founded than in the previous decade; the old spirit of '56 was revived, according to one Labour publicist.[30]

Nearly all the unions were skilled craft societies with small membership. The building unions and the Operative Bootmakers each probably had several hundred members, but most had only a few score; at this stage, only a tiny proportion of the work-force was unionized. Most were purely Melbourne unions, though a few had provincial branches and at least two—the Amalgamated Society of Engineers and the Amalgamated Society of Carpenters and Joiners—were branches of English unions. Entrance fees were often substantial and the weekly fee 1s or more; the Bootmakers' and the Printers' fee of 6d a week was unusually low and indicated an industrial rather than a benefit emphasis. Most of the societies justified Coghlan's comment:

> The Melbourne trade unions were, on the whole, narrow and exclusive bodies, with high entrance fees, designed to restrict the numbers in the trade, in order that constant employment at high wages might be obtained by those within the union circle. It was sometimes necessary for an artisan to belong to three or four unions in order that he might not be boycotted on a particular job.[31]

Many societies resisted entry of brother unionists arriving from other colonies or insisted on entrance fees and a probationary period of membership. Several small unions in the one trade sometimes went through painful years of unsuccessful negotiation before amalgamation; there were still four carpenters' unions in the late eighties and the Felt Hatters and the Silk Hatters remained rivals.[32] All of them reflected the interest of English unions in the establishment of machinery for conciliation and arbitration on the assumption that negotiation would produce reasonable solutions; but, failing this, many were prepared to withdraw their labour. Few of them yet, however, had much feeling for the trade union interest as a whole, or for any class interest, or for labourers below them in the social scale. The Trades Hall Committee supervised tenancy of the stone building erected in 1874 and had few other functions than planning extensions to it. Attempts were made in 1874 and 1880 to form a separate Trades and Labour Council with wider functions. Eventually in 1883 a Trades Hall Council was established by widening the functions of the Trades Hall Committee and not by creation of a rival organization.[33]

In 1882, as prosperity grew, union activity surged forward. A score of new societies were formed in a couple of years, existing ones expanded, and numerous improvements in wages and hours were won after disputes lasting a few days.[34] In these years most unions achieved the eight-hours principle, which traditionally had been the first objective as wages were already relatively high. The Melbourne Typographical Society was typical of many when it won the eight hours, made major wage gains in 1883 and 1889, and trebled its membership in these years.[35] Even an Accountants and Clerks' Association attracted some staunch support. Success was not always easily won by unskilled workers: for example, Howard Smith & Sons in 1883 used non-union labour under police protection to break a strike for shorter hours by their coalyard men and drivers, who lost their jobs but formed a union.[36] The growth or formation of large 'new' unions of semi-skilled or unskilled workers basically altered the balance of the movement. The Amalgamated Miners' Association revived about 1880 and late in the eighties had seven or eight thousand Victorian members; the Seamen's Union formed in 1874 was joined in 1884 by the Stewards and Cooks; the Wharf Labourers and the Timber Yard Employees, formed in 1883 and 1885, had about 1,000 and 1,500 members at the end of the decade; and, most remarkable of all, the Shearers' Union was formed in 1886. These unions tended to be less concerned with benefits than the craft societies, to charge low fees, to ignore differences of skill among members, and to seek to join with their intercolonial equivalents. The task of organizing unskilled labourers not firmly attached to an industry was far more difficult. There had been many attempts from the fifties to form local or sectional labourers' societies. There were many more attempts in the eighties, when several carters and drivers' unions and labourers' unions were co-existing; a Navvies' Union formed in 1886 did well until its secretary ran off with the funds.[37] In 1888 a Public Works Employees' Union was the largest group in the eight-hours procession.[38] In sum, by the close of the eighties, at least seventy-five unions were active with a total membership of at least 30,000 in 1888 and 40,000 in 1890.

With new rules and changed name, the Melbourne Trades Hall Council set out in 1884 to win the affiliation of as many unions as possible, and succeeded dramatically; sixty-six unions had joined by 1886. But it remained almost exclusively a Melbourne body; Ballarat, Bendigo and Geelong formed their own Trades Hall Councils and the Miners and Shearers refused to affiliate, mainly because representation was based on tenancy of the building, and outside unions, however large, were granted only one representative. The T.H.C. continued to be dominated by the craft unions, represented the artisan viewpoint, showed little interest in the problems of the unskilled worker, and was often contemptuous of the unemployed. When in May 1884 a deputation of unemployed sought assistance, the president and secretary brusquely told them to join unions, rebuked the single men for not having saved, and told them to disperse because marching in procession annoyed the government and brought discredit on the Labour movement and the colony.[39] The Council was, however, cautiously beginning to act on general union matters. It energetically gathered evidence for the Shops and Factories royal commission, took control of major strikes like the Tailoresses', Bootmakers' and Wharf Labourers', and negotiated with employers' representatives. But its inability to impose levies on unions and its puny authority are shown by the secretary's remarks as late as 1888:

> It claims to be consulted through its executive before any dispute reaches an acute stage, to ascertain whether there is just ground for complaint, and whether there is a reasonable prospect of success; and [advises] a course to be pursued, and [requests] that its advice should be acted upon before the assistance of the other trades . . . is asked for.[40]

The central union body in Sydney had long had greater powers. A paid secretary of the Melbourne T.H.C., D. Bennet of the Engineers, was first appointed in 1888 at £4 a week;[41] several unions had had secretaries on similar salaries for some years past. Most of the T.H.C.'s funds were used to help establish the Working Men's College* and to extend the Trades Hall.[42] A proud occasion was the opening in March 1884 of the new Council Chamber, 'the prettiest hall which Melbourne possesses, a chamber which recalls the luxury of a theatre dress circle. It is aesthetically and richly decorated in light green, with upholstery to match, on elegant round-backed white iron seats.' There were portraits of George Higinbotham, Sir Charles Darling ('the people's Governor'), Plimsoll and George Stephenson, and a bust of Ben Douglass (and later of Charles Jardine Don, Wilson Gray and Higinbotham). Douglass was the son of a Quaker chartist, was an eight-hours veteran, formerly a contractor and recently a government inspector of works. As first president of the new T.H.C., he now welcomed his friend, Higinbotham, the leading Liberal members of the government, and Francis Ormond, the philanthropist, as official guests. Higinbotham and Berry were the only speakers. The former dwelt on the past, eulogizing Wilson Gray and Darling; Berry also recalled the saintly Gray, and both of them soft-soaped the assembled artisans and encouraged them in their noble task. Deakin noted in his diary that they were 'splendid speeches'.[43]

In the following month of 1884, that remarkable year of international labour ferment, the second Intercolonial Trade Union Congress met in the new Council Chamber. Fifteen delegates from New South Wales and four from South Australia joined fifty Victorian unionists. W. E. Murphy, the T.H.C. secretary, had organized the meeting, but Douglass, who presided, was out of sympathy with most of the proceedings, for he was a 'moral persuader' who vehemently opposed strikes and political action by unions. Service and Berry addressed the delegates, and again the old radical Berry displayed his oratorical charm:

> You do not want to see the working classes altogether governing the colonies, or that they can do what they like. (Cries of 'No, No.') You do not want to raise up antagonism upon the part of any other class; but you do want to show that there is a very safe element, a very important element. . . . You want them to be fully represented in the councils of the nations, and you cannot express your views better than by using moderate language. . . . Be cautious, be moderate, be determined. . . .[44]

* In starting the movement and providing generously for the Working Men's College, Francis Ormond, the pastoralist, was deliberately trying to break down what ill-feeling there was between the classes. The Trades Hall responded warmly, but Ormond's desire to name the college after Prince Leopold, the Queen's son, and to add his nominees and representatives of the donors to the Council led many at the Trades Hall to believe that they were being patronized. They wanted to control 'their' institution and Higinbotham, who supported them, withdrew from the movement. Nevertheless, the foundation of the college was a remarkable illustration of 'social harmony'. Its success was staggering: more than 2,000 students enrolled in 1887 and 1888. (S. Murray-Smith, 'A History of Technical Education in Australia', ch. 6.)

Cautious, moderate, determined: the words were welcomed, and sum up the union approach of the time. But determination to turn also to political channels and to promote closer union of workingmen colonially and nationally was growing. The agenda included not only old grievances which required legislative redress but also 'amalgamation of trade unions' and 'direct representation of labour'. W. G. Spence moved that the various unions in each trade in each colony amalgamate under a governing body; and that an authority be elected from a conference of these governing bodies with power to act (unlike, presumably, the Melbourne T.H.C.) on matters affecting 'the working classes' generally. He also envisaged, though not at all clearly, an Intercolonial Federal Council of Amalgamated Trades which then 'could really govern this country'. The conference, in some confusion about what exactly was being proposed, supported him unanimously. The conference also agreed that each colonial T.H.C. should elect a parliamentary committee, 'to assist in the passing through Parliament measures for the benefit of labour and, where possible, endeavour to obtain for labour direct representation in Parliament', and that these colonial committees should federate. A committee for Victoria was appointed there and then.[45] Fred Bromley (chairman), Murphy, W. A. Trenwith of the Bootmakers, Boyd of the Ironfounders, and Spence and Williams of the Miners went zealously to work and promised a full report for the next intercolonial congress when, as with the Trades Union Congress in England, their report would be first business.[46] The T.H.C., however, was lukewarm, and within a few months twenty dissatisfied unions were meeting to consider forming a rival Trades and Labour Council to develop political action based on the labouring unions as well as the trades.[47] The movement died, but the parliamentary committee worked vigorously to help achieve trade union legalization in 1884, the Factories Act of 1885 and an attempted Employers' Liability Act. However, after months of excited debate, the T.H.C. resolved late in 1885 not to stand candidates for parliamentary election. Despite this, a bitter feud lasting for two years broke out between the conservative, old-guard Trades Hall trustees, led by Ben Douglass, and the T.H.C. The political activity of the reformers was the root of the conflict. After half a dozen unions had disaffiliated, Murphy had been defeated as secretary in 1886, and Douglass had severed all connections with the T.H.C., reasonable order was restored.

The unions regarded the legal situation as thoroughly unsatisfactory. The old Masters and Servants Act, as amended in 1864, was still in force: employees under written or verbal contract were liable to three months' imprisonment for leaving their job or for misconduct or other offences. In 1874 when striking Castlemaine tanners were imprisoned, protests brought assurances that the law would not again be applied. In the early eighties, however, actions were occasionally brought and light penalties imposed. The *Age* damned the Act as 'more applicable to a community of convicts than of free men and women', and the Intercolonial Congress of 1884 demanded repeal. Later that year the Fitzroy bench imprisoned striking bootmakers for a month. Otherwise the Act remained almost a dead letter; yet there was surprisingly little protest at its occasional use.[48] Trade unions were not even legalized before 1884, and hence could not take legal action, especially to protect their funds against defalcation, but could be proceeded against. South Australia had legislated in 1876, New South Wales in 1881, and Britain as early as 1871. Victoria in 1878 had actually adopted harsher legislation than a British Act of 1875 on conspiracy, by which strikers, and specifically those employed in railways, tramways, gasworks and water-supply, could be coerced. At last in 1882 the Amalgamated Miners put pressure on politicians to introduce a legalization Bill closely modelled on the British Act; it passed the Assembly but the Council held it up. In 1883 similarly, the Bill passed the Assembly on the voices and again the Council threw it out. In 1884 the government adopted the Bill and put it through the Assembly almost without discussion. Dr Hearn now made his contribution to working-class suspicion of university men by leading the Council to amend the Bill, by deleting the clause providing that members of unions, as such, should not be liable to criminal prosecution for conspiracy. The government, although irritated, accepted the amendment to save the Bill. The T.H.C. fruitlessly petitioned the Governor not to assent and, inspired by its angry parliamentary committee, not one union registered under the Act in 1885. In 1886 only the Portland Fishermen's Union and three branches of a farmers' union registered. When in that year an amending Bill to restore the original proposal passed the Assembly, the Council did not oppose it. Most of the unions still refused to register and supply information to the Statist, probably for fear of revealing publicly their limited membership and assets.[49]

The eight-hours movement

Victoria led the world in the achievement of the eight-hour day, and Victorian artisans knew it.[50] The hours question remained the dominant concern of trade unions in the bad days of the sixties, the better days of the seventies and the great days of the eighties. By 1879 sixteen trades, including building craftsmen, gas-stokers, brickmakers, seamen, some metal workers, and many miners, were working only eight hours. The greatest gain—immensely important as an example—was the agreement from 1874 to write the principle into government contracts. Then the Service government included the eight-hours proviso in the Mines Act for underground workers, the Tramway Act and the Harbor Trust Act, and brought pressure on the Railways Commissioners to adopt the principle as much as possible, thus reducing the hours of many thousand workingmen. No minister would dare to alter the eight-hour system for government works, Service told a Trades Hall deputation in April 1883.[51] However, nearly all politicians agreed that it would be foolish to legislate for a common eight-hour day, for it could not be applied in rural industry and would certainly bring about lower wages in sections of industry based on piece-work. At least seven attempts to legislate between 1869 and 1887 failed; a Bill passed the Assembly in a thin house in 1885 but was negatived without a division in the Council.[52] From 1882 many strikes or threatened strikes won the eight hours, especially between 1884 and 1886. The Bakers' was the most extreme case: they were accustomed to work seventy hours or more. 'They who would be free, themselves must strike the blow,' their banner for the eight-hours day procession proclaimed; by negotiation they reduced their hours first to sixty and then in 1884 to forty-eight, without lowered wages or dearer bread. In 1885 the official *Handbook to the Colony of Victoria* listed thirty-seven trades working eight hours. In 1886 the Wharf Labourers led the way for clamant semi-skilled and unskilled labourers. By 1888, masons and bricklayers, though not carpenters, were working a forty-four- or forty-five-hour week, though sometimes with a reduction of wages. By the close of the decade about sixty occupations and perhaps two-thirds of urban wage-earners had won the forty-eight-hour week. The main exceptions were nearly the whole clothing trade, the woollen mills which mostly continued to work for sixty hours, millers, ropemakers, and, of course, shop-assistants and rural labourers.[53]

A variety of local rules confuses calculation of hours habitually worked. The ten-hour day sometimes included two short meal-breaks; the eight-hour day had only one meal-break which was usually not included. The difference between ten and eight hours was not always two. The eight-hour day, when achieved in the past, had usually meant five days of eight and a half or nine hours with a Saturday half-holiday. Now the wide achievement of the principle made a Saturday half-holiday the rule, and gave great stimulus to organized sport. One foreign observer described Saturday in Melbourne as a day of carnival, drinking, sport and wasteful activities generally.[54] Paid annual leave was confined to some salaried workers, including civil servants from the early eighties. The great majority of employees had leave only on public holidays, for which white-collar workers tended to be paid and blue-collar not. Christmas Day and Boxing Day, Good Friday and Easter Monday, the Queen's and the Prince of Wales's birthdays, Constitution Day and Separation Day were the official holidays; Cup Day became effectively a common holiday; and civil servants and other white-collar workers usually celebrated Saints Andrew, David, George and Patrick.[55] Eight-Hours Day was, however, proclaimed a public holiday by the Berry government in 1879. Thousands annually marched on 21 April behind the treasured banner of 1856 in good-humoured amity and spent the day at sober sports meetings and banquets. In 1885 the Governor attended for the first time, and representatives of commerce, manufacturing and the Employers' Union took their places at the official dinner.[56] A year or so later, even the trams stopped for two hours while the celebrants took over the city. In 1888, however, when the day fell on a Saturday, the Eight-Hours Committee was upset by football matches, an intercolonial boat race and the Moonee Valley races being permitted as counter-attractions.[57]

At Ballarat, Bendigo, Bairnsdale and elsewhere, the procession and subsequent sports meetings were annually celebrated without major rival events.*[58]

When Swallow & Ariell's introduced eight hours at their biscuit factory in 1885, F. T. Derham wrote to his co-proprietor:

> Today at 1 p.m. the men mustered of their own accord to thank us and give three hearty cheers. I briefly addressed them to the effect that we expected they would show increased goodwill and energy in their work. Most of them seem thankful and highly pleased, though I fear there are some few quite destitute of right feeling in such matters. However, we are keeping a sharp look out for skulkers and must make short work of them now.[59]

The evidence suggests (at least it was widely believed) that the general effect of reduction of hours was to produce both harder work and more efficient management. Employees were said to be more willing and energetic, and thus almost made up the anticipated loss of productivity from shorter hours. The colonial workman was rarely accused of slacking.

Sweated female and child labour and shop-assistants working up to eighty hours a week were the other side of the picture. The prodigious reforming efforts by Liberals, the *Age* and many minor officials, and their limited success, reveal much about both Victorian radicalism and the strength of barriers to change.

The factory reform and early closing movements; the Tailoresses' strike

Secondary industry was of such recent growth that there had been only limited awareness of black spots, and little demand for factory legislation similar to Britain's. The existing Factory Act of 1873–4, which was the product of a Ballarat campaign led by the *Courier* and W. Collard Smith, brought factories with ten or more employees under supervision of health inspectors, and limited some female factory workers to eight hours, but was largely ineffective. In 1879 an attempt by a group of manufacturers to bring about stringent legislation to protect female and child labour was blocked by wide employer resistance. In September 1880 the Melbourne Typographical Society, alarmed at the exploitation of boy labour and the lack of apprentice-training in the printing industry, and backed by the *Age*, called a public meeting which was attended by Bishop Moorhouse, and Collard Smith and other Liberal politicians.[60] At this stage the printers could rouse little interest in factory reform among other

* The men at the Trades Hall were well aware of the historical significance of their achievement. In 1883 they sponsored an investigation into the history of the local movement. In 1884 more than £500 was raised for James Stephens, the eight-hours veteran, who had been maimed by a fall from scaffolding. In 1885 the Eight Hours Pioneer Association was formed. In 1886 it was found that only about one hundred of those who had marched in 1856 still survived, such was the life-expectation of the artisan of that age. In 1889 the campaign began for the Eight Hours Memorial, which was built south of Parliament House in 1891, completed in 1903, and moved close to the Trades Hall in 1924.

Newly felled tree, Mirboo South

First store at Warragul, 1876

MacRobertson's works, 1887

J. Buncle and Son, works

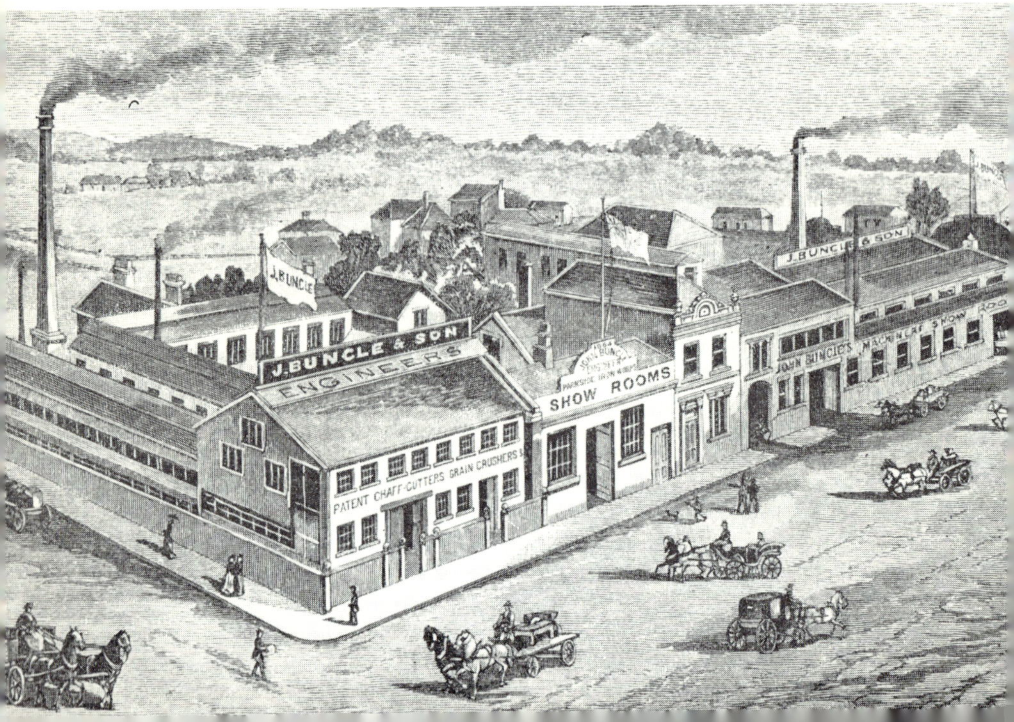

unions. In 1881 the movement changed emphasis when the new Salesmen and Assistants' Union took over the campaign for shorter hours in shops from the lifeless Early Closing Association. Some city stores had adopted six o'clock closing and the Saturday half-holiday, but the great majority of city and suburban shops stayed open every evening and late on Saturday night. Once again the Bishop and other citizens backed by the *Age* met in the Town Hall to protest. A young Liberal member of the Assembly, Jack Gardiner, brought in a Bill to enforce six o'clock closing for shops five nights a week;[61] moral suasion, the reformers now agreed, was not enough. The Bill was referred to a select committee, which in January 1882 was converted to a royal commission with Collard Smith as chairman and Deakin and Gardiner as members. In July the commission requested wider terms of reference to include the 'relations generally of employer and employed', but the O'Loghlen government refused, and the reform movement lost impetus during the political stalemate which followed.[62]

The extraordinary Tailoresses' strike radically altered the political climate. The expanding but highly competitive clothing trade had narrow margins of operation and depended largely on low-paid female labour working very long hours, both in factories and as 'outworkers'. A wage cut by one of the largest firms at last produced a deputation of women, escorted by officials of the Tailors' Union, at the Trades Hall on 10 December 1882. Next night the Trades Hall Committee formed a Tailoresses' Union, with its own executive as office-bearers and a committee of seven women, and brought the 500 female employees of the offending company out on strike.* The *Age* opened a fund for the new union, which received £1,000 in the first week, and shocked readers with its descriptions of sweating in the clothing trade. The Trades Hall drew up a log of claims and Douglass and Murphy negotiated with employers, many of whom agreed to the terms. However, a strike was called, to commence on 15 February 1883 in order to bring dissident employers into line. The union had grown to a militant 2,000 members; Murphy was later to compliment them on carrying out their picketing duties so well. Within a fortnight, nearly all firms had agreed to a mild wage increase, which raised the average rate from 18s a week to 20s, and the remaining firms eventually gave in. Two years later the union log was being paid at all the factories and the union grew to 3,000 members.[63]

The significance of this first major strike was not primarily that it was carried out by a female trade union, or that other unions were encouraged to adopt direct action, or even that the Trades Hall had moved in for the first time to finance and control a strike; but was rather in the impetus given, by the effect of the revelations about working conditions on public opinion, to the anti-sweating, factory-reform and short-hour movement. In May 1883 the Service government, inspired from within by Deakin and Berry, enlarged the Shops' Commission's powers to include investigation of condi-

* There had been a Needlewomen's Union, an offshoot of the Democratic Association of Victoria, in 1872. (F. B. Smith, 'Religion and Free-thought in Melbourne', p. 181.)

tions in factories, and widened its membership to include two radical Liberal members with artisan backgrounds—John Woods, the veteran engineer and inventor of a successful railway brake, and G. W. Hall, former secretary of the Typographical Society and proprietor of the *Benalla Standard*. The commission set to work energetically, investigated forty trades, invited and received evidence from union officials, manufacturers and others, and protected witnesses by withholding their names from reports when necessary. Spurred on by the printers, the Trades Hall set up a committee to give evidence; some conservative unions, like the Bricklayers, walked out in protest at such concern with general working conditions rather than those only of the superior trades. But many union officials saw an opportunity of attacking and eliminating the 'outwork' in the clothing and footwear industries being carried out by non-unionists who greatly weakened the unions in these trades.

The commission's series of reports[64] until June 1884 lifted the lid from 'Marvellous Melbourne'. Conscientious, indignant, fervently moral, the commissioners waxed eloquent. Their reports were a triumph for the *Age*, the Trades Hall, and especially the printers, all of whose recommendations were adopted. Boys and girls of eleven and twelve, who should have been at school, were employed in the tobacco and other industries, were surrounded by evil influences, and were even working dangerous machinery. Apprenticeship was a mockery: 'children were taken on to be taught their trade; were paid nothing, and taught little, and were dropped at the end of their three years' term'.[65] Youths were turfed out when they claimed adult wages. Children of both sexes, without adequate education, starting work young and mixing together in factories, inevitably became larrikins and prostitutes. Many factories were crowded, poorly ventilated and without decent sanitary facilities. Some employers, with 'almost criminal recklessness', exposed their hands to danger from inadequately guarded machinery supervised by unqualified workmen. Sweating was an abomination: many tailoresses had to take work home and work fourteen to sixteen hours a day to earn a living; so long as sub-contracting 'sweating houses' existed, reasonable wages could never be paid in the industry. 'Forced labour' was widespread in the retail trades, where nearly all shop-assistants worked appalling hours; hundreds of young girls attended for ten to fifteen hours daily, notably barmaids (commonly fourteen to sixteen hours), under unhealthy conditions.

The commission demanded an amended Factory Act as an 'imperative necessity' and made thirty-nine recommendations for inclusion. All factories should be registered and inspected by central government officers, who would enforce minimum standards of space, lighting, ventilation and sanitation; boys under thirteen and girls under fourteen must not be employed; apprentices should be paid, legally indentured and limited in number; the eight-hour day should be enforced legally, with special exemptions; machinery should be operated only by technically qualified workmen; sweating and outwork should be abolished; shopping hours should be limited; and many other minor proposals were made.*[66]

The Chamber of Manufactures, which by no means consisted of sweating monsters but predominantly of liberal ex-artisans, was outraged by the commissioners' libellous exaggerations which, they felt, made them out to be swindling scoundrels. Many manufacturers were reformers who wanted protection from unscrupulous rivals and believed efficiency would best be promoted by secure skilled workmen with good conditions of employment. So the Chamber formally approved the recommendations on factory conditions, limitation of hours and child labour, but condemned those on outwork, apprenticeship and rigorous governmental inspection.[67] Immense suspicion had been created of any attempt to legislate, and the more conservative manufacturers helped to found the Liberty and Property Defence League, an odd assortment of factory owners, brewers and shopkeepers. Like the English parent-organization, they advocated 'Individualism as opposed to Socialism' and asserted extreme *laissez-faire* views.[68]

The coalition government, attempting to apply consensus politics, sought approval in principle by the Employers' Union, the Manufacturers and the T.H.C. of a moderate compromise. Deakin, who had dropped off the commission when he joined the government, would certainly have liked to adopt nearly all the commission's proposals. But he could recommend only the less controversial ones on factory conditions, employment of women and children, and early closing. The general eight-hour principle was avoided, except for females and boys; reform of apprenticeship was neglected as it would be too great an interference with industry; and the sweating and outwork problems were too difficult to face, though information would be gathered for future action. The sweating problem was indeed difficult. Perhaps half the manufacture of clothing was done by outwork, which in itself was inoffensive when fair piece-rates were paid either to those working entirely at home or to factory girls taking work home. The problem was rather the desperately low piece-rates offered by the industry. Sweating in the true sense, so common in England, of sub-contractors employing labour in private houses or small workrooms at cut rates, was practised enough by ruthless middlemen to justify much of the protest against exploitation of helpless women and children. The non-unionist outworker was a rival of the factory worker and dragged wages down; one of the results of the Tailoresses' strike was a swing back to outwork. Many young girls were too genteel to take a factory job, or preferred to be 'independent' at lower wages, or were prepared to accept minimal wages while learning the trade (and were sometimes sacked when they had learned it, in favour of fresh recruits to be exploited). But to legislate against out-

* Who was the driving-force of the commission and chief author of the reports? The most likely, Collard Smith, the chairman, would make a fascinating study. The genial Major (later Colonel) of the Volunteers, the masterly opportunist politician who successfully rode the storms of Ballarat politics for twenty-five years, the local entrepreneur, and here the indignant radical reformer, make an odd combination.

work would mean drastic reform of a whole industry. Indeed, probably the only solution was state regulation of wages, which required another decade before becoming politically practicable.[69] Meanwhile, the untouched sweating problem was to remain the chief stimulus to industrial reform.

The government, knowing that chances of immediate success were zero, did not introduce its Bill until 18 November 1884, close to the end of the session, and had to abandon it. The Chamber of Manufactures' annual report took pride in its success in having the Bill postponed because of its 'arbitrary interference with the natural rights of employers'.[70] Next August the T.H.C. organized a Town Hall meeting, at which Prior Butler of the Carmelite Order moved the chief resolution begging the government not to lose heart. Trenwith urged development of the state's role as policeman: 'The more our liberties were infringed by the State, the more freedom we possessed. The greatest liberty we could have was that the whole machinery of the State might be invoked to prevent anyone from injuring us.'[71] Eventually the government again introduced its Bill to regulate factories and shorten hours of trading in shops in October 1885. Two-thirds of the provisions were taken from the consolidated British Act of 1878. But the situation in Victoria was not remotely to be compared with England, Deakin said: there was very little but good to be said of Victorian factories as a whole; the commission had found that only small factories were at fault, that 'the larger the factory, the better the provision for employees'; most employers would be very glad to see the Bill passed. Collard Smith and Woods, as anti-coalition Liberals, were pleased the government had adopted so many of their proposals, but regretted its lack of courage in not tackling sweating. Service, with his customary pungency, remarked that there was no doubt the Bill proposed to interfere with the liberty of the subject, but there was nothing new in that as Parliament was doing it every day; still, the less it did so, the better. The Assembly was content to pass the second reading without dividing; Pearson was prominent in fighting to keep the Bill intact in the committee stages. Opposition was strong only against limitation of shopping hours; Melbourne would be a dismal place in the evening with most of the shops closed, said one aggrieved member. Deakin was stubborn. Ninety-nine out of a hundred retailers, he claimed, were on his side; three shopkeepers were keeping all Chapel Street open at night. Cole's Book Arcade was a rare example of what should become the rule: limited hours of opening and assistants working staggered hours. One shopkeeper had told him:

> Life is not worth living at present: I have no sufficient opportunities of being with my family, no opportunity of study, no opportunity of amusement; I am tied to my counter from morning to night. I cannot afford assistants, and I am bound to keep open, or else my trade would be ruined.

The Bill left the Assembly almost unharmed to face the wild men in the Council. There J. A. Wallace, the mining entrepreneur, objected to making thirteen the minimum age of employment; he had started work himself at the age of ten. 'He believed that the larrikinism in the colony was, to a large extent, due to the Education Act, under which boys were kept at school for a long period, and so trained up in idleness.' The Council proceeded systematically to pass the amendments desired by the Employers' Union. The minimum size of factories coming under the Act was raised to six employees (the Assembly had already raised it from two to four), thus eliminating the tiny workrooms with squalid conditions from supervision by the inspectors. Employers were not to be compelled to provide returns of wages paid, thus making it difficult to gather information on sweating. Penalties were reduced, the procedures for laying charges made more difficult, inspectors were not to be allowed to interview employees alone. The government and Assembly accepted the amendments to save the Bill, after an unsuccessful stand on the size of factories.[72]

Almost all the features of the Bill which went further than British legislation had been removed; but there were substantial gains. An inspectorate was created which gathered information by means of which further reform could be planned and public opinion influenced. Child labour was virtually eliminated. Although few prosecutions were brought on working conditions in the following five years and the law was never enforced to the point where small businesses were severely embarrassed, the inspectorate brought steady pressure to bear to remove blatant abuses, and working conditions did substantially improve. Victorian factories were now under far stricter control than those of any other colony. A standard had been set; New South Wales did not pass its first factory legislation until 1896. The Act did sometimes bring about reduced hours; Swallow & Ariell's introduced eight hours for all its employees because it would have been uneconomic to keep the minority of men at work after women and juveniles had knocked off. But there was probably little change in the hours of women in the clothing trade; on their request the eight-hour clauses were suspended for some time, and permits were later given to work overtime because the piece-rates remained insufficient to enable a reasonable wage to be earned in eight hours. The dangers to workmen from machinery gradually lessened. Some prosecutions were made; an amendment to the Act in 1887, after three unsuccessful bills, provided for certificated control of steam-boilers (for explosions had been a common hazard). And at last in 1886 Wrixon, after six previous attempts had failed, succeeded in persuading the Council to pass an Employers' Liability Act, again copying English legislation, which made it possible for employees, with immense difficulty, to sue employers for negligence when accidents had occurred.[73]

The early closing section of the Act was successful only here and there. The Act laid down 7 p.m. closing and 10 p.m. on Saturdays (except for such shops as cafés, hotels, chemists, fruiterers and tobacconists), but municipalities were given power to vary the hours. So when the early closing provisions were proclaimed early in 1886, the issue had to be fought anew.

Another Shop Employees' Union was formed and affiliated with the T.H.C. with the blessing of the Political Short Hours League in which members of the royal commission and other Liberal veterans were prominent. A Shopkeepers' Union was organized to resist early closing and a Shopkeepers' Early Closing League to support it. Many shopkeepers at first defied the law. There were riots night after night in Smith Street, Collingwood, where crowds of ten or fifteen thousand, a surging mass for hundreds of yards, which scores of police were unable to control, encouraged demonstrating shop-assistants and larrikins to molest defiant proprietors remaining open and sometimes to smash their windows. There were series of demonstrations in Bridge Road, Richmond, in Bourke Street and elsewhere which continued for months, and many recalcitrant shopkeepers were forced to close early. The *Argus* was outraged at the 'reign of terror', but the *Age* contemptuously attacked its rival: 'years and years pass while working people are being forced to toil like galley slaves, and never a word is heard . . . in favour of freedom, but when a little gentle pressure is brought to bear on the employer in the interest of the employed it is denounced as unheard of tyranny'. Municipalities usually imposed fines only of a shilling or so for breaking the law, though the publicity may often have been a considerable penalty. But many suburban municipalities extended the hours, 9 p.m. closing (11 p.m. on Saturdays) remained common, and suburbs varied widely in their practices. Most shop-assistants continued to work sixty or more hours a week, and some as much as eighty, though few employed in the city worked more than fifty. The Shop Assistants' Union—vocal, militant and not at all genteel—continued to protest for many years; in 1889 it formed parliamentary committees to work for friendly candidates in the election. Annual attempts were unsuccessfully made from 1888 by Deakin and others to amend the Act. However, in Bendigo and many country towns, early closing was brought in by mutual agreement; shops shut at 6 p.m. on four days, 10 p.m. on Saturdays, and Wednesday was a half-holiday.[74]

Industrial conflicts: Bootmakers and Wharf Labourers

The 'lockout' in the boot trade from November 1884 to February 1885 was the major industrial conflict of the period; it markedly changed the atmosphere of relations between capital and labour. The industry was highly competitive and there is evidence of ruthless employer policies in the seventies—wage cuts, sacking of 'trouble-makers' and exploitation of juvenile labour. After several attempts, the Operative Bootmakers' Union was formed in 1879; its activities were purely industrial, its fees low, and no provision for benefits was made until 1885. The union grew to a membership of 1,000 by 1882 and presented its log of wages to the employers, who for twelve months refused to confer, and then stated a uniform agreement was impracticable. Throughout 1883 a series of strikes in individual factories continued, by mid-year employers and union were in constant negotiation, and by November the employers had accepted the log and agreed to a standing board of conciliation of fourteen members from each side. The union still had to win the eight-hours principle, but its chief objective was the abolition of outwork and sweating. Most of the 'finishing' in the trade was done outside the factories by hand 'on the last', and some of the sub-contracting outworkers were sweating juveniles and other unskilled assistants.

The union's secretary, appointed full-time in May 1882 as a 'paid agitator', was W. A. Trenwith, who rivalled W. G. Spence as a remarkable Labour organizer. Tasmanian-born of a convict father and without formal education, he had been a prominent pugilist in his youth and, though already half blind, was a determined self-improver. Ultimately he reached the top rank of parliamentarians; on the way, he was to be the stormy centre of the foundation years of the Victorian Labor Party. Even at this stage, he went his organizing rounds of the factories dressed in 'black silk top hat and a sac coat'. 'Good God! Why he looks like a gentleman,' an amazed observer remarked a few years later.[75] He was a slow, stentorian, logical and immensely forceful speaker, whose will was unshakeable; his followers hero-worshipped him. He could and sometimes did lay out opponents with one massive blow. His personality and views, especially his militant atheism, roused hatred and exacerbated the industrial conflict. In December 1883 he was fined for assault and abusive language, but claimed convincingly that an employer had offered £50 to anyone who managed to get him imprisoned; an opponent of the union had followed him for a mile abusing him before being felled. He issued posters listing 'scabs' by name and propounding the definition: 'A scab is to his trade what a traitor is to his country.' He was proceeded against for criminal libel—at the instigation of employers, legend has it—but juries first disagreed, then found him guilty, a decision which was upset on appeal.[76]

In 1884 the Bootmakers widened their ranks to take in semi-skilled men, and in July served notice that from October it would stand firmly on the principle that outwork be abolished. The employers at first agreed, but when two or three stood out, 'reverted to the old system'. The sixty members of the Boot Manufacturers' Association then ranged themselves against the 1,400 members of the union, about half the men employed in the factories. Negotiation brought agreement to set up a conciliation committee of nine from each side, but the employers would not accept Trenwith as a member, so deadlock continued. In December the Ballarat bootmakers, who had been supplying funds, were also locked out. The union started co-operative factories at Melbourne and Ballarat. Many employers were confident that the union would be smashed in a few weeks, and others even planned to import 500 or 1,000 bootmakers from England.[77] Moreover, a rival union, which conditionally supported outwork, had been formed. But the T.H.C. took over the strike and raised over £9,000, including large amounts from other colonies, the Miners, and the printers who imposed a 5 per cent levy on wages. The union stood firm: many members accepted private boot-work or took other jobs, handed in their earnings, and got back 15s or 18s strike pay. Clashes occurred between pickets and loyal employees attempting to smuggle supplies and products in and out of factories. After nearly three months the employers began to crack; the T.H.C. and the union came through to a strong bargaining position. A conference between outside employers and T.H.C. delegates, at which Andrew Lyell, the accountant, first emerged as the 'prince of negotiators', ceded the main point to the union on 10 February 1885: after 1885 outwork was to be eliminated except under a strict permit system with safeguards against sweating. However, the union was forced to forgo the 'right' of entry to factories of its representatives.[78] The industry was gravely damaged and was in a sad state when the 1886 recession took its toll. Intercolonial exports had fallen away, some factories closed, and hundreds of bootmakers were unemployed in 1886 when there were further small-scale strikes because of reduced wages. Murphy of the T.H.C. believed the conflict was a disaster, for which both sides shared the blame.[79] Trenwith's condemnation in 1886 of strikes and lockouts as 'cruel and unscientific means' of settling disputes was the product of sad experience. It was 1888 before the industry was said to be back to its pre-strike condition.[80]

The next Melbourne conflict to raise the industrial temperature was the sixteen-day Wharf Labourers' strike of January 1886. Industrial relations on the wharves had long been tense; the shipping trade was highly competitive and not very profitable, and shipowners made few concessions to employees. Attempts to form a union in 1878 and 1883 had failed; a strike of the unorganized men in 1884 was called off on T.H.C. advice.[81] The refusal of the shippers to allow the customary holiday or extra pay on Eight-Hours Day, 1885 precipitated the issue. The Wharf Labourers' Union was formed on 15 May and, cautiously because of previous failures, wrote into its rules that three months' notice of a strike would have to be given. In September the union, under J. B. Tucker's leadership, made its claim of 10s a day for eight hours instead of the prevailing ten, and 15s a night, and gave notice that work would cease on 1 January unless the claims were granted. The shipowners, when their compromise offer was rejected in mid-December, decided to stand fast, 'especially because of the surplus labour to be obtained elsewhere' in a period of fairly high unemployment in other colonies.[82] The union, which had 870 members while 150 refused to join, rejected the advice of Murphy and the T.H.C., and at a mass meeting on 30 December resolved to fight it out, while warning its members against 'rowdyism'.

So on New Year's Day 1886 the union came out, to the plaudits of the *Age* and abuse from the *Argus*; the shipping firms' yardmen and draymen followed, also the Geelong watersiders who proceeded to form a union of their own. The employers used their ships' officers and clerks to unload cargo, laid up vessels and discharged crews, and urgently recruited labour from New Zealand, Adelaide and Sydney where 500 jobs were advertised. Bruce Smith of Howard Smith & Sons, the militant leader of the ship-

The Demands of Labour

WORKINGMAN: The sun must stand still while this procession passes or —

owners, offered permanent employment at 45s a week with the eight-hour day, and attempted to recruit Bendigo miners. Farmers loaded the potatoes they brought to the wharves. On the 7th the Employers' Union stated it was 'the bounden duty of every employer of labour' to support the shipping firms, and brought pressure to bear on John McIlwraith, who had accepted the union's terms because he had urgent coal contracts to fulfil from ships about to arrive. The T.H.C. accepted the challenge; though it believed the strike was unwise, it had to be supported once the Employers' Union had thrown down the gauntlet. It called for intercolonial support, but told Smith that the dispute should be referred to the proposed Board of Conciliation. The union at first succeeded in dissuading the free labourers by agreeing to maintain them; only three of the first forty engaged went to work and nearly all the first two boatloads from Adelaide went over to the union. The employers argued vigorously with the Harbor Trust and the police, contending that the wharves were leased areas and not public thoroughfares, that union pickets should be 'moved on', and that they had the power to fence off the wharves. Non-union labour, 'the scum of other colonies' according to Murphy, gradually increased.

On the 11th the Adelaide Steamship Co. gave in, and on the same day the Seamen's Union, especially hostile to Howard Smith's, came out in order to cut off the supply of non-union labour. 'We are compelled to take this course', they said, 'owing to the struggle having assumed a new phase, viz: Capital vs. Labour.' The Newcastle miners had refused to supply coal for Melbourne, supplies were dwindling, and the Gas Stokers' Society was considering stopping work. 'Social revolution was pending,' wrote Murphy in retrospect, rather obscurely. Bruce Smith replied to the T.H.C. that the shipowners had agreed to submit the dispute to conciliation, but now would not act under duress from the Seamen. His father, W. Howard Smith, remarked privately that the Seamen's move was not an 'unmixed evil'; their tyranny 'had become unbearable', and he welcomed the opportunity of a showdown. However, the Employers' Union was now prepared to negotiate and Andrew Lyell and Murphy conferred; members of the Employers' Union actually attended the T.H.C. to encourage it to agree to terms for a conference. Lyell later claimed that he 'almost single-handed, induced the parties to agree to resume work' on 18 January.[83] Public opinion was strongly for negotiation; and the shipping firms were perhaps unwilling to bear responsibility for the wide unemployment which would follow if they continued the fight. There is also evidence that Howard Smith's had reached an agreement with the Seamen's Union to their mutual advantage. Hence, a fortnight later, five representatives each from the Employers' Union and the T.H.C. met with Professor W. C. Kernot, the engineer, as an independent chairman, heard sworn evidence about working conditions, and eight days later after a final meeting of thirteen hours reached amicable agreement. The union was granted the eight-hour day and slightly lower wages than it had sought. Both sides claimed a victory, abided by the award for many years, and were full of praise for Kernot. Tense scenes followed on the wharves between unionists and non-unionists, and wage disputes between shipowners and seamen were soon to become savage. But although two wharfies were fined for assault and bad language, the *Bulletin* properly congratulated the men on their behaviour.[84] The most serious threat there had yet been to the harmony of capital and labour had been triumphantly removed by voluntary arbitration.[85]

Miners', Shearers' and transport unions

The creation of the Amalgamated Miners' Association was a remarkable feat. Independent small-investing miners were not easily organized, even when by the seventies such a large majority were employed as wage hands; mining unions remained numerically weak till about 1880. In 1872, unions at Bendigo and Stawell successfully negotiated the eight-hour day and wage increases. In 1874 the A.M.A. was formed with 12 branches and 1,832 members, but the federation collapsed and two or three years later only three branches totalling 250 members were affiliated. The revival came from Creswick in 1878 where, after resistance to a wage cut and an attempt to lease a mine to a group of Chinese, a union was formed. John Sampson, Sir Robert Menzies's grandfather, as president and William Guthrie Spence as secretary led 600 men into the A.M.A. Several strikes at Creswick followed, but in 1882 agreement was reached on wages ranging from 33s to 48s and a forty-five-hour week, and Creswick and Allendale, uniquely, became 'union towns', closed shops. Here and elsewhere, union officials and those attempting to form unions, including Sampson and Spence, had been dismissed and blacklisted; even in 1889 many of Alex. Peacock's supporters against the mineowners' candidate for the Assembly seat were victimized.[86] By 1881 Creswick and Ballarat had 2,600 members of the A.M.A.; Bendigo with 2,000 reaffiliated in 1882, when Spence became general secretary. In 1883 and 1884 and for the rest of the decade there were 7,000 to 8,000 members—by far the largest union in Victoria, but still no more than one-third of European goldminers.

The mining industry was dangerous and the union's mutual insurance function was attractive. Creswick became a closed shop because the union succeeded in capturing the accident funds which the companies had organized according to the usual custom. Mining legislation was strict, partly because of union pressure: Angus Mackay's Regulation of Mines Act of 1873, which Blainey describes as 'one of the most advanced social laws in the English-speaking world', was tightened in 1877 and 1883. There was to be no answer in this generation to the silicosis and tuberculosis caused by dust, which crippled so many men in middle age and led to so many early deaths from 'Miners' Complaint'. Deaths from accidents averaged more than twenty-five a year. In the Creswick branch alone, in ten years, more than 3,000 injuries occurred and forty-four men were killed, including twenty-two in the disaster of December 1882. When the New Australasian Company's workings were flooded, twenty-seven men were trapped in water up to their necks, in darkness with the air giving out. It was two and a half days before rescuers freed the five survivors, while thousands waited above. The terrible scenes of grief, the tales of bravery and mateship, of hymn singing and last messages scratched on billies, deeply stirred all Australasia.[87]

Under Spence's leadership the A.M.A. was moderate and conciliatory but firm on fundamentals. Most of the twenty-nine strikes before 1890 were in defence of the right to establish the union or in opposition to wage cuts. Spence claimed that the union never refused a conference and then never failed to settle the issue amicably. Strikes had to be approved by head office; compulsory levies for strike pay and fear of frittering away benefit funds tempered branches' militancy. In fact the union had quickly won major gains and was wise enough not to press further wage demands when the industry was in decline. By 1886 a joint conciliation board had been formed by mineowners and union. The longest conflict was for ten weeks in 1885 at Bethanga with J. A. Wallace, the mining king of the north-east. When a branch of the A.M.A. was formed, Wallace sacked the unionists who then by picketing prevented non-unionists from working. Wallace threatened and raged but eventually had to submit. One of the shareholders of his company, David Syme, had unsuccessfully opposed Wallace's policy at the half-yearly meeting. Wallace had also persuaded H. M. Chomley, the Chief Commissioner of Police, to proceed against Spence by criminal summons for intimidation. Berry discovered the matter in time to prevent action, dressed Chomley down, and threatened Wallace with cancellation of his leases.[88] By 1884 Spence had succeeded, after years of pleading, in persuading his union to join with coalminers and others elsewhere in the colonies including New Zealand; a sprawling amalgamation was made, and the union's name changed to the A.M.A. of Australasia. The Australasian membership rose towards 30,000, but the intercolonial branches retained near-complete freedom of action. Nevertheless, in the major coal strike in New South Wales in 1888, the Victorian branch levied 1s a week from its members; an Allendale meeting of the union asserted in solidarity that 'Britons never shall be slaves'.[89] Spence similarly worked for closer relations with the Melbourne T.H.C. and was intent on turning his union towards political organization, but it appears he could not carry the Victorian members with him. In the long run they remained aloof from the political wing of the Labour movement and renounced their alliance with miners of 'inferior' kinds.[90]

Spence, of whom so tantalizingly little is known, was a man of genius in his organizing and negotiating skills, whatever might be said about his catastrophic failure of 1890. He was born in Orkney in 1846 of a stonemason father who migrated in 1853, was working on the diggings at the age of nine and earning a man's wage when twelve. He had continued to work as a miner and occasionally as a shearer for twenty years, had suffered from silicosis, and was thus fortunate in finding a new vocation while young. He was deeply religious and was secretary and Sunday School superintendent of the Creswick Presbyterian church; in the eighties, while achieving fame as a union organizer, he became even more evangelical and preached often with the Primitive Methodists and Bible Christians. He was also a representative local man—a member of the militia, a leader of the temperance movement, prominent in the town's debating society which sometimes met at 5.30 a.m., a borough councillor from 1884 and a justice of the peace from 1888. He read and knew his Blatchford, Bellamy, Ruskin and Morris and at an early stage proclaimed himself a gradualist socialist. His remarkable chapter 32 of *Australia's Awakening* reveals the essence of his strength as a negotiator and is useful reading still, not only for trade union officials but for any aspiring committeeman. Genial and quite imperturbable, he stands out as the most remarkable man in the remarkable town of Creswick in the eighties.[91]

Twenty years afterwards, Spence told his story of how the Shearers' Union was founded. A young Creswick shearer and miner named David Temple, who had for long been talking about the need for a union, was protesting at home about a local reduction in the price for shearing. His mother replied, 'Why don't you go to Mr. Spence?' He did so and, said Spence, 'we talked matters over until I got a grip of things, and then we made a start'. Spence wrote announcing his intention to the Ballarat *Courier* on 27 May 1886; Bateman, the editor, wrote a 'slashing article' in support; a founding meeting was held at Ballarat on 14 June and Spence and Temple were elected president and secretary. Only thirty men attended and only thirteen joined; fifteen were present at the second meeting. Temple 'took a run round the western parts of Victoria, but did not meet with much encouragement', but he and several other organizers travelled Victoria and the Riverina and then New Zealand for the rest of the year enrolling members. Spence addressed meetings at Penshurst, Camperdown, Kyneton and Winchelsea. By January 1887, when unions based on Wagga and Bourke (which had been founded later in 1886) amalgamated with Creswick, several thousand shearers were on the books.[92]

There had been many earlier attempts to found a union. The response now was so warm that it appears that only ability to master the difficulties of organizing an itinerant horde had previously been lacking. The pastoralist was the traditional enemy of the landless, and his control of workmen was often in the spirit of the Masters and Servants Acts framed for his benefit. Spence's accounts of working conditions are extreme and no doubt exaggerated. It is impossible to judge how frequently pay was withdrawn or reduced unfairly for unsatisfactory shearing—on some stations, at least, the rule was that the local hospital received the proceeds instead of the shearer—or whether accommodation was frequently as 'shocking' and 'awful' as he claimed. One has only to read Furphy's *Such Is Life* with its rich gallery of squatting types to realize how much conditions must have varied. But Spence claimed, and most shearers agreed, that the 'great body' of the squatters acted unfairly and hence deserved no consideration in return. The rate of pay in Victoria (which, unlike New

South Wales where the prevailing rate was £1, included rations) varied from 8s to 15s a hundred sheep; Spence claimed 11s was the average—perhaps it was a little higher. Spence stated flatly that wage cuts announced in the Riverina and Victoria were the direct cause of the union's foundation; wages were certainly the chief issue in the early years of conflict. From the start, Spence aimed at an intercolonial union—naturally so, for the main body of shearers were professionals who followed the seasons south and often across to New Zealand. Few of them, however, took in Victoria where most shearers were local seasonal workers—farmers and their sons, miners, tanners and millers. The union was confined to shearers and cooks after an unsuccessful attempt at the start to recruit shed-hands. The fees were very low—only 2s 6d entrance and 5s a year at first—with no attempt to provide benefits or strike pay, except rations. Policy-making was unusually democratic with frequent use of the referendum as a substitute for mass meetings.[93]

The union had settled its policy by its first conference in January 1887, with 15s laid down as the wage, a considerable increase. Then, said Spence, 'in 1887 we commenced to force it'. Yet he claimed that 'the policy of the Union from its inception was conciliation. Copies of our rules and proposed agreement were sent to pastoralists a season ahead . . . and they were asked to meet us or suggest amendment.' The *Shearers' Record* constantly preached the harmony of interests between employer and employee and stated the union's mission to be 'one of peace and good-will towards men'.[94] Squatters were even invited to attend annual conferences of the union. Relatively few replied or entered into consultation, though one of the original rules was altered after discussion to give the employer complete control in the shed. The union had one valuable advantage: its policy of supplying labour only through the union office was much more convenient than the cumbersome, unreliable method of individual engagement by mail; and many squatters who submitted to union rules were happy in this regard.[95] Most, however, were prepared to fight and did so, but usually had to give in when the unionists persuaded the rest of the shearers to join them and retire to a camp while grass-seeds got into the wool, or coerced those unwilling to join by 'immersion for scab' or other drastic methods. When union strength became overwhelming, recalcitrants were sometimes 'fined' the dues they would have paid if they had joined the union in 1886.

The Victorian Western District proved to be the most difficult area the union had to face, largely because of the ready availability of casual labour from the farms. There were many incidents in November 1887—free fights between unionists and non-unionists near Branxholme and Warrnambool, rumours that non-unionists near Mortlake were armed with revolvers, and a serious disturbance at Ware's 'Barwidgee' near Caramut where, the *Argus* alleged, the unionists were flying the red flag. Non-unionists were protected by police at the homestead, but four were captured and carried off to the camp; some of the union men were prosecuted and heavily fined.[96] In March 1888 a Western District Sheep Farmers' Association was formed at Hamilton; the prevailing feeling was that the union should be conciliated, but it was agreed to stand on a wage of 12s to 14s.[97] In June and July 'very harmonious' conferences with Spence and Temple, at which sincere attempts to reach agreement were made, broke down only on the wage issue; the pastoralists were objecting to a uniform rate, regardless of size and breed of sheep, as well as the amount.[98] Battle was joined in the spring when the union had twenty-two organizers on the job in Victoria. According to the Creswick branch's annual report, advice of strikes 'began to reach the office of the branch from all parts of the colony. The war between the sheepowners and members now commenced in real earnest. . . . Camps were formed by the union, and its members supplied with rations until the owners of the sheds gave in, and the camps disbanded.'[99] Spence claimed they won 'Union rates over all the country covered by our operations. It was a splendid result for two years' fighting with undisciplined troops.'[1] The claim appears to be largely correct; certainly in 1889, according to lists in the *Shearers' Record*, nearly 400 Victorian sheds 'shore union'. There were, however, several nasty incidents late in 1888, despite Spence's instructions that there must on no account be any violence. The *Argus* featured 'Union Outrages' in almost unprecedented capitalized headlines. Camperdown was said to be in turmoil with many ugly scenes occurring. An 'assault on a station'—'Woodlands', near Koroit—when the owner was 'seriously maltreated', the homestead defenders were disarmed, and nine non-unionists captured, resulted in prolonged court cases; offenders were given severe sentences of imprisonment which were upset on appeal. The *Argus* discerned a link with the Kellys and a reaping of the fruits of the land laws.[2] There were isolated cases of prosecution and conviction for conspiracy, despite the Trade Union Act. Yet the features to be noticed, despite the scale of the confrontation, are how few serious conflicts there were, how well the union controlled its members, and how rarely the law was used, as Spence claimed it was, as a capitalist class-instrument.

Transport unions had a difficult time. A Railways Employees' Association, which was little more than a benefit society, had existed since about 1870. However, governments held strict views on the impropriety of public servants in public utilities pressing industrial demands. After a secret attempt to organize a new railwaymen's union about 1880, the ringleaders were dismissed. When the Commission was set up in 1884, J. J. Longmore was prominent in organizing a new union, the Victorian Railways Service Employees Mutual Association. By 1886 it had 4,000 members out of a possible 9,000 but had neither won permission to affiliate with the T.H.C. nor to represent individual employees before the Commission. There had been talk late in 1885 about crushing the union and disenfranchising railwaymen. The union trod its dangerous path and maintained good formal relations with the Commissioners; honeyed words were exchanged at the union's annual banquet. But its cause was not helped by close association with the outcast politician, David Gaunson, who habitually viciously attacked Speight.[3]

The Tramway and Omnibus Company stood no nonsense. In 1885 after three dozen bus drivers had been dismissed for their part in forming a union, 193 of 230 employees struck for eight hours. After help from the Sabbatarians, all they gained was every second Sunday off.[4] The company refused to recognize the union and systematically dismissed its members; by March 1886 only 100 of 250 employees were unionists, and the union appears to have gone underground.[5] F. B. Clapp's American style of management was a basic challenge, and a bitter showdown followed early in 1888. The company itself attempted to form a benefit-society-union, to which it contributed substantial funds, and 800 employees joined. But most of them revolted when the company insisted that several inspectors be on the committee, that there be no affiliation with the T.H.C. and that rules be subject to company approval. The rebels gained control and the company reformed the benefit society with the proviso that no member could belong to a trade union. About 600, including at least two-thirds of the tram crews, joined the new union which affiliated with the T.H.C., while about 500 including most of the bus drivers joined the company's benefit society. The company was interpreting the eight hours provision in the Tramways Act as eight hours for seven days a week, was promoting the company union men, and fast recruiting new employees. The union, although discouraged by the pessimistic T.H.C., rashly went on strike in mid-February 1888 with the demand that recruits must join the union, and lost the support of the *Age*. At least 350 obeyed the call; trams still running were hooted by workingmen in the city. The company rejected Lyell's offer of mediation and the T.H.C.'s efforts to submit the dispute to the Board of Conciliation, engaged 200 men locally, and arranged to recruit men from other colonies. Within three days the strike collapsed. L. Searle, the union's president, and the T.H.C. recommended return to work in the hope of preserving the union, but the committee would not submit and a hard core of 200 men lost their jobs. This was the most bitter strike of all. Eighteen months later the company gave a bonus of a week's wages to its loyal employees from its enormous profits.[6]

Harmony of interests; the Board of Conciliation

Despite the number of strikes, which although novel were after all not very numerous, the dominant tone of the unionists—bootmakers, wharf labourers, miners and shearers alike—was one of sweet reasonableness, moderation, hope for harmonious relations with employers, and a sense of mutual obligation. There were undoubtedly elements of self-deception in the stress on common interests with employers, their conviction that the 'good employer' would be on their side in bringing the 'bad employer' to see reason, and their regretful resort to the crude, illiberal, uncivilized strike. But the reply to Bruce Smith in 1885 by the Stewards and Cooks' secretary has an honest ring:

William Trenwith, *c.* 1885

Benjamin Douglass, *c.* 1885

Interior of Council Room, Trades Hall

Collins Street East on a Sunday morning

> It is pleasing to know that we are considered 'a powerfully formed organisation', but my executive committee believe that our power is chiefly derived from the fact that we ask for nothing but that we are fairly entitled to; that we treat with employers with a due consideration to mutual benefit, and that we endeavour always to impress upon our members the duty of thoroughly earning the increased money which has been obtained for them.[7]

R. L. Middleton of the printers defined the aim of trade unionism as being 'to bring both employer and employed together for they are friendly not antagonistic forces'.[8] The Miners, supported by the Mineowners' Association, were behind attempts in 1883 and 1884 to introduce voluntary Councils of Conciliation by legislation. The scheme was modelled on English legislation of 1867 but owed much to the long-standing French Conseils des Prud'hommes. Strikes were an evil, there must be machinery to stop them, said R. Richardson, the parliamentary sponsor. The Shops and Factories commission had taken up the proposal, submitted the plan widely to employers and unions, and reported strongly in favour. The Assembly was willing to pass the Bill, but dropped it when the T.H.C. petitioned against it on the ground that disputes were too infrequent to warrant legislation.[9] Very shortly, however, the T.H.C. was to take part in a remarkable attempt to solve the problem of industrial disputes and was to convince itself that the problem had indeed been solved.

As union activity grew, employers were inevitably forced together. The individual employer, however benevolently disposed, was often outraged by a union's challenge to his authority. Formal or informal associations of employers within an industry, despite frequent competitive hostility, were a natural response to union pressure. Employer class-consciousness developed and the gulf between master and man widened, as the number of large factories grew and the intimate relationship of artisan employer with his few hands became less typical. The boot strike was a turning-point. Bruce Smith, Archibald Currie, shipowner and paper-manufacturer, and J. M. Bruce of Flinders Lane were three of the outside employers on the committee which settled that dispute. They were shocked by the boot manufacturers' weak position in the face of a solid union movement financing the employees, and took the lead in forming an Employers' Union. Early in February 1885 a meeting of employers had been held to sympathize with the boot manufacturers in their predicament, and a special meeting of the Chamber of Manufactures recommended a union of employers. 'If the Trades-hall choose to take up such a position,' said Bruce, 'then disputes between capital and labour must be settled in quite a different way.'[10] Bruce Smith wrote an article for the *Victorian Review* titled 'Trades-Unionism in Victoria; or, Who Shall be Master? A Note of Warning to Employers'. The boot dispute marked an epoch, Smith asserted. The greed and steady growth in power and confidence of the working class and their almost perfect organization were startling. The interests and objects of employers and employees were 'antagonistic to one another—the one seeking to obtain the largest amount of labour for the smallest amount of wages; the other, endeavouring to obtain the largest amount of wages for the smallest amount of work'. The employers had to organize in order to take united action against the T.H.C.[11] On 13 March 1885, the Employers' Union was founded. Bruce was in the chair and Bruce Smith the chief speaker. The employers were being defeated in every dispute which arose, he said; in the shipping industry, cooks and stewards were being paid as much as mates. Bruce and Smith were careful to assert their approval of unions—up to a point—and their friendliness to the workingman; but Smith later recalled that he was in a 'savage' condition of mind, especially because of union aggression in the maritime industry. The *Age* was not hoodwinked, and warned the Trades Hall that the agitating employers were putting up a make-believe philanthropic front for workmen whom they intended to put in their proper place.[12]

1890 had almost arrived. Bruce and other employers, however, could see the advantages of direct negotiation between central bodies of employers and unions. They took up the Shops and Factories commission's suggestion of a central council of employers and employees, and on 3 November 1885 requested the T.H.C. to consider establishing a Board of Conciliation to handle future disputes. The T.H.C. immediately agreed, and rather prematurely nominated members.[13] The wharf strike intervened, but the board of arbitration which settled that dispute was a useful model for what was being planned. Bruce Smith, the 'heart and soul' of the Employers' Union, underwent a miraculous conversion. The constant meetings over the strike, he said, 'generated an amount of good feeling, and disclosed on the Trades-Hall side a readiness to co-operate in endeavours to settle disputes upon amicable and reasonable conditions which had not previously been supposed to exist'. So he who had begun as a soldier became a peacemaker. 'I frankly confess that the altered attitude and demeanour which the working classes have assumed, since our two associations came into closer communion, have led me to considerably modify my former opinions as to their judgment.' The T.H.C. leaders were men of 'exceptional intelligence . . . certainly in most cases taking a class view of things, but, on the whole, cool-headed, exceedingly amenable to reason, and evincing every desire to be fair and equitable'.[14] Delegates from both sides settled down to the long process of drawing up a detailed constitution for the Board of Conciliation. Meanwhile, they were called on to act in half-a-dozen minor disputes in 1886, all of which they settled successfully.[15] For months the delegates met night after night, and by August 1886 had agreed on a draft constitution. The parties agreed from the start to avoid the 'freedom of contract' question: employers would recognize unions, unionists would work with non-unionists. Employers and unions were to pledge themselves not to resort to strikes or lockouts until the dispute had firstly been referred to the secretaries of the T.H.C. and the Employers' Union, then if necessary to a joint committee of the two bodies, then finally to the full Board of eighteen whose decision would be final. But it was September

1887 before the constitution was finally accepted by both sides with the government's blessing, and then individual unions and trade organizations of employers had to be persuaded to accept it—a slow process.[16]

Harmony was abruptly shattered by the tram strike of February 1888 when the company was not interested in conciliation. In the same month, however, the Board had a triumph when it settled a dispute in the iron trade. Relations continued to be amicable and both sides prided themselves on their unique Board. The Employers' Union, with 500 firms now members, certainly saw it as a protective device against ruinous strikes. The T.H.C. leaders were also immensely proud of the achievement, boasted at intercolonial congresses about the happy state of industrial relations, and even looked forward to the day when there would be no more strikes.*[17] Sadly, however, the experiment was never really tested—for the best of reasons: the general absence of industrial conflict (with the notable exceptions of the pastoral industry, the iron trades and the tramways) in 1887, 1888 and 1889. Prosperous conditions account for much, but the efforts of organized capital and labour must be held to count for something. However, only twenty-three unions agreed to bring themselves under the Board, while fifty-one refused, perhaps as much from apathy as suspicion or hostility. A four-month strike for higher wages late in 1888 by the Ironworkers, who refused to accept the Board, was eventually informally arbitrated by Lyell and leading employer and unionist members of the Board.[18] The test when it came in 1890 was impossible to meet, but at least there were many on both sides in Melbourne, even then, who worked for moderation and conciliation.

The unions and politics

The movement for direct representation of Labour in Parliament made little headway. The growth of unions had made workingmen much more aware of political issues directly affecting them and of the possibilities of specific reform; but it was a long step still to think in terms of a trade union political party—indeed, it was almost unimaginable. The reformers hoped for no more than a few trade union members speaking for the movement. Charles Jardine Don, M.L.A. from 1859 to 1864, was the only Victorian precedent, and Henry Taylor's attempt to win Creswick and Clunes in 1880, when secretary of the Miners, was a recent isolated example of candidature. The two or three former trade unionists in the Assembly were not direct representatives and had lost touch with the movement. The extreme assertion of the T.H.C. parliamentary committee in 1885 was almost freakish: 'The opinions, needs and rights of those who live by manual labour never can be as fruitfully represented by other classes as by their own. . . . Class questions require class knowledge to state them,

* A Capital and Labour Federation League, formed to diminish friction, increase harmony and engender mutual confidence, was active in 1889; a prominent member was Benjamin Cowderoy, secretary of the Melbourne Chamber of Commerce, who was an enthusiast for profit-sharing. Congregationalists and other churchmen sometimes preached on these lines, e.g. *Victorian Independent*, Oct. 1886, edit.

and class sympathies to fight for them.'[19] Land, Commerce and Capital were all well represented in Parliament; why not Labour? However logical, the notion was alien, for the myth that a parliamentarian represented all his constituents and the community at large held sway among workingmen as much as elsewhere. The very notion of fixed classes was repugnant still to most migrants, especially miners and artisans, who had hoped to escape such categorization. The *Age* deplored the prospect of the Trades Hall standing candidates; the interests of all classes were identical, men and women had to be represented, not sections.[20] John Woods, the veteran engineer-politician, was indignant: 'He served his seven years to his trade, and if he did not represent labour he did not represent anything. If there was one thing they want to get rid of in Victoria it was class representation.'[21]

The parliamentary committee was enlarged in 1885 to include five from the Melbourne trades, one each from Ballarat and Bendigo, and two from the Miners. When Bromley, Murphy and Trenwith, probably aided by Spence, made their move late in 1885, the omens appeared favourable. The English Trades Union Congress had an active parliamentary committee and eleven workingmen had just been returned to the House of Commons. The T.H.C. had fallen out with Berry who was about to leave politics and was freely speaking his mind. The government's tardiness over the Factories Bill led some T.H.C. men to refer to Berry as a fraud, a renegade, and an old humbug, and to deplore the sorry state of the Liberal party.[32] Yet the proposal to stand six candidates in the union interest, when referred to individual unions, won little interest or support. The cost—£1,500 was suggested—was a demoralizing difficulty. Many feared alienating the government's friendship which had led to so many valuable gains. 'Friends of the workers' like Hall, Woods and Gardiner were good enough representatives. The parliamentary committee had been successful in lobbying; its influence might be lost if it was converted to a party. Some favoured the proposal in principle, but realistically pointed to the low proportion of workmen unionized and feared that political defeat would diminish the unions' influence. Some were suspicious of the parliamentary committee's private ambitions. So the proposal was voted down by the T.H.C., and the appearance of an impertinent Workingmen's Political Reform Association with 100 members, which also proposed to run candidates, was treated with hilarity.[23] Bromley, Murphy and Trenwith decided to go it alone, allied themselves with the dissident National Liberal League, and stood as 'Labour candidates'. The T.H.C. ignored their formal request for support, but they managed to stage a 'mass-meeting of the working class' in the yard of the Trades Hall. Bromley ran on the same ticket as Mirams in Collingwood and was soundly beaten, but Murphy and Trenwith in Melbourne North and Richmond were only a few hundred votes short of success.[24] The pattern was similar at the 1889 election.*

The *Age*'s influence is seen most strikingly in the attitudes of the

* See p. 324.

T.H.C. Protection in a crude form was an unchallengeable article of faith; protection, the union leaders (and many manufacturers, too) believed, maintained high wages and steady employment and made the Victorian workingman the most prosperous in the world.[25] The artisan unions which dominated the T.H.C. were not fully representative of the Labour movement; the Miners, Shearers, Wharf Labourers, Seamen and labourers in general had no vested interest in protection, but the Melbourne T.H.C. had the ear of government and was the formal representative of Labour. The other cardinal point of dogma was resistance to assisted immigration. It was held so widely and vehemently that migrants depressed wages and caused unemployment that no government for thirty years dared to raise the question.[26] The T.H.C. even opposed the Centennial Exhibition on the grounds that it would attract to the colony foreign workmen who would be content with low wages.[27] The T.H.C. at least knew that protection meant little without strong unionism. It required a later generation to realize that strong unionism was not enough to guarantee a share in protection's benefits. The *Age* was well to the left of the Labour movement on innumerable specific reforms which it preached to no avail. But Syme's quack nostrum of protection misled and unwittingly pacified the Labour movement in Victoria for a generation. Direct taxation proposals in the seventies were defeated largely because the *Age* persuaded workingmen that the object was to reduce the level of protection. It was a radical Liberal parliamentarian, A. L. Tucker, who asked the fundamental question in 1888: 'How long is the wealth of this country to escape taxation? Are we to continue to raise £2 million through the Customs, and only about £200,000 from realised wealth?'[28] Some workingmen gained from protection, but all paid for it. Syme, his colleagues and his followers unintentionally worked against their own objectives of a more equal distribution of wealth by supporting an ideology which tended to inhibit fundamental reform.

There is little evidence of any ferment of ideas or desire to overturn capitalism in the ranks of Victorian Labour before 1890. In 1884 there was passing interest in the formation of co-operative societies; (the co-operative movement was frequently confused in debate with co-operation between capital and labour). W. Nuttall, who had had thirty years' experience with English co-operatives, had succeeded in establishing the Equitable Co-operative Society with a large city store. His paper to the Intercolonial Congress of 1884 was well received and the Society later entertained the delegates to dinner.[29] The *Age* repeatedly recommended co-operation as the next step forward for the trade union movement, as a means of distributing wealth more evenly, of workers freeing themselves from capitalist exploitation, and as perhaps the only alternative to communism or 'despotism of the State' in some form.[30] But the unions showed little interest. In 1887 the Equitable was on its last legs, though in 1888 a co-operative boot factory still survived and a labourers' co-operative had been formed to tender for public works.[31] The left-wing movement was pitifully weak and lagged far behind Brisbane and Sydney. On May Day 1886 an Anarchists' Club was formed with about twenty members; in 1887 it issued a journal, *Honesty*, and collaborated with some of the Secularists in forming the Melbourne Democratic Club, with facilities for cards, chess, draughts and light refreshments.[32] A small refugee group of German social democrats met regularly. Henry George had certainly been widely read and discussed, but his ideas had tended to reinforce, rather than to capture, the land nationalization and land taxation movements. Despite the votes of their leaders at intercolonial congresses, Victorian unionists were too staunchly protectionist to regard him as anything more than an ally, let alone a saviour. There is little evidence that Bellamy, Blatchford, Morris or Marx were read by many other than the tiny left-wing fringe or that the union movement was in contact with socialist ideas. The Secularists were a far more important radical force than the socialists.

Summing-up

Workingmen were justified in looking back on the eighties as 'the good times'. Real wages increased and unemployment was minimal in a period of general labour shortage. It might even be suggested that the working-class as a whole was not more prosperous for another sixty years. 'At no time and in no place probably was the working man supposed to be more completely master of the situation,' wrote Pember Reeves.[33] Men dreamed of Australia showing the world how to achieve modest affluence for all citizens. Yet, as we have seen, a large minority did not share in the prevailing prosperity and, despite the close alliance between the T.H.C. and the Liberal party which was effective especially in largely bringing in the eight-hour day, most attempted legislation in the union interest was cut to ribbons. And in the economic circumstances the union demands had been limited and remarkably restrained. The union movement had grown several times over; craft unions were gradually relaxing their exclusiveness, major semi-skilled unions had been formed, and partly successful attempts had been made to organize the unskilled, so that a large step towards mass unionism had been made. Although possibly no other country in the world had a higher proportion of trade unionists, perhaps only about one-quarter of the possible membership had been enrolled. Potential strike-breakers abounded and many artisans and labourers were actively hostile to unions. These 'master's men' tended to blame their own incapacity for their lack of success, or believed their hard work must ultimately be rewarded; society was in no way at fault. Others feared they might lose their jobs if they appeared to stand out against their employers, while the high fees of some unions deterred other workingmen. There had been a marked development of loyalty—from loyalty to the union only, to loyalty to the union movement as a whole. Working-class-consciousness and perception of class-differentiation were growing, though the gulf between artisan and labourer was still wide, and the concept of class remained distasteful to most old migrants. There were more unions, more affiliated with the T.H.C., and more working eight hours than in New South Wales, but the Melbourne T.H.C. had much less authority than its Sydney equivalent and was more conciliatory and much less interested in political representation.[34] Nearly all the T.H.C. men spoke the language of pure liberalism and no other. Although the growth of unionism had closely reflected the English trends of organization of semi-skilled and unskilled workers and development of class-consciousness, there was astonishingly little reflection of contemporary English trade union interest in socialism and political activity,* although Bromley, Spence and Trenwith would have liked to keep up. Similarly, the Melbourne Trades Hall seemingly displayed none of the nationalist stirrings of the later eighties. Almost to a man, they were ageing artisan migrants, of an earlier generation than the recent migrants—many of them assisted—who were giving fire and life to the Labour movement in New South Wales and Queensland. Above all, they believed in the harmony of interests of employer and employed and, unaware of the extent to which tolerance was made possible by prosperity or of the magnitude of the challenge they were making by such large-scale organization, assumed that their notions of what was fair and reasonable must prevail.

* Should we make anything of the fact (*Argus*, 24 Apr. 1888, p. 5) that, at the eight-hours celebrations in 1888, the toast 'Success to Trades Unionism' was drunk to the tune of the famous popular song?:

> Work, boys, work and be contented,
> As long as you've enough to buy a meal;
> The man you may rely, will be wealthy by-and-bye,
> If he'll only put his shoulder to the wheel.

Religion

4

The Churches under Stress

The challenge to faith

'Let me tell you', Bishop Moorhouse admonished the people of Manchester in 1888, that the churches in Victoria 'are much better attended than our churches here, a great deal.'[1] Moorhouse was correct. However, after the churches had firmly established themselves in the immediate post-goldrush period, the Protestant churches had had to face, and for the most part retreat in disorder from, the criticisms and doubts of many of their best-informed members and a few others who had lost all faith in Christianity. Just as Victoria, having been overwhelmingly populated by the church- and chapel-going classes, had by far the highest relative church membership of any colony except perhaps South Australia, so the freethinking and doubting movement became stronger than anywhere else in Australia. In England the seventies, when the new spirit of enquiry had trickled through to a semi-popular level, were the crucial years of challenge to the churches from the new scientific knowledge. In Victoria, as usual, the time-lag of ideas ran half a decade or more behind; the early eighties were the years of tense excitement when men and women debated theology as never before or since.

The novelty and enormity of the challenge to faith compelled a whole generation of those with any intellectual integrity to face the issues and take their stand, as the evidence from diverse fields of study accumulated. Darwin destroyed Bible chronology and threw doubt on the account of the Creation; geologists, archaeologists and anthropologists provided evidence of the antiquity of man; Old Testament and Gospel criticism and the study of primitive and comparative religions raised innumerable doubts; and the philosophers and psychologists also had their say. The principles of evolution were applied to all things in heaven and on earth, and the cult of rationalistic science, as the solution for human misery, arose. Herbert Spencer built his entire philosophical system on the application of the laws of natural science to society, and his supreme law was the law of evolutionary progress.

Rationalists were early at work in Melbourne; H. K. Rusden was writing atheistic pamphlets in the mid-sixties and E. W. Cole, the bookseller, published his *Real Place in History of Jesus and Paul* in 1867. The

Eclectic Society, which included many of the sceptical intellectual élite, continually debated religious topics from its foundation in 1867, and from 1870 the Sunday Free Discussion Society formed a rationalist nucleus.[2] Spencer was all the rage at the University in Deakin's time in the mid-seventies; in 1876 the debating club voted its belief in the possibility that life might have evolved from matter.[3] The atheist secularist movement grew slowly and did not become a force till the eighties. The Unitarian answer to orthodox Christianity was confined to a tiny respectable sect with Martha Turner (Webster), Gyles Turner's sister, as preacher; her impressive addresses were surprising in their time and place (and, *pace* Dr Johnson, they were done well).[4] The strongest organized anti-Christian deviation of the time, which attracted several hundred followers, was the Victorian Association of Progressive Spiritualists, founded in 1870 by W. H. Terry and denounced by Bishop Perry as a 'revival of heathen magic and idolatry'. Seeking verification of immortality which they had refused to accept by Christian argument, they recorded their séances as scientific experiments. Inevitably, they were frequently duped by charlatans, and the movement was beset by squabbles and splits.[5] The chief movement of reaction, however—the moderate movement of doubt among professing Christians wishing to liberalize their creeds and reject doubtful or untenable dogmas—did not fully develop till the eighties.

After successful consolidation, the churches were in a transitional period and on the defensive. The extreme secular solution to the education problem had left them divided, uneasy, and discredited because of their lamentable failure to compromise constructively. Withdrawal of the general subsidy to religion had aggravated financial problems, in a period of expansion in new farming areas and later in the new suburbs of Melbourne. The clergy was ageing, and arrangements for training colonial recruits were rudimentary. The Church of England and the Presbyterians were also uncommonly evangelical in tone. The prevalence of sin and the redeeming individual struggle for salvation, the literal inspiration of the Bible and the prime duty to read it constantly, and the certainty of the existence of Heaven and Hell and the conviction that life in this world was merely a preparation for eternity—these were the cardinal beliefs.[6] Evangelical dominance meant that there were few clergy intellectually equipped and eager to carry on rational debate. The tone was set by Perry's early reaction that the Bible had nothing to fear from science and his public arguments with Dr J. E. Bromby, headmaster of Melbourne Grammar School and later canon of St Paul's, who was willing and able to modify his position. Alexander Gosman, the Congregationalist, was another who kept up with the trend of thought. But few clergymen could budge from their fundamentalism and belief in the Bible as God's inspired word; most either lashed out rancorously in reply to the unorthodox, or derided them. Militant critics accused them of ignorance, bigotry or hypocrisy, and of stiffling truth, and renewed their missionary zeal to expose them.[7]

Some devout people were not going to church because they were fed up with the constant accusation that they were miserable sinners.[8] Others reacted against the harsh, joyless Almighty presented by the evangelicals, and rejected what they came to see as a discipline based on fear. Dr Bromby might believe in 'painless non-existence' for the ungodly after death, but 11,000 English clergymen had declared that eternal punishment awaited the wicked. A son of a Methodist minister, Henry Bournes Higgins, wrote of the period when he was emancipating himself:

> The doctrines current as to hell—doctrines which seemed to have become current in all the Christian churches as to the eternal torture of the wicked, of those, indeed, who had not 'accepted Christ'—had from childhood, oppressed me like a nightmare. It was the eternal, never-ending pain, the hopelessness of any limit to the pain even after thousands and millions of millions of years, that affected my mind the most. 'That way lies madness', I thought, 'and certainly God does not want me to become mad.' So I plunged deeply into the work that was before me. It was the horror of what was in store for the majority of our race, that haunted me. . . . In the seventies, there appeared in the newspapers a story of a man who had killed his children from love of them, in order that they might, by dying before they became responsible, avoid the possibility of such a penalty. [I wrote to the newspapers] pointing out that that man . . . was not mad, that he was doing the best thing for them if he accepted the dogma.[9]

If God's purpose could be achieved only by dint of inflicting such suffering then such a theology was simply unacceptable.

Most of the faithful of the older generation were immune to the slightest doubt. David Blair, *littérateur* and sometime Presbyterian minister, wrote in old age:

> As to the 'weir' just ahead of me: a longing to pass it, swiftly and quietly, at any moment the Divine will appoints, confidently certain that in the illimitable Beyond there is an appointed place, and employment befitting, and infinite happiness and in the company of all I have ever loved on earth.[10]

But the shock of challenging ideas demanded a response; people variously resisted, absorbed, or were carried away by them. In her novel, *The Three Miss Kings,* Ada Cambridge excellently creates the atmosphere. The young Elizabeth meets Mr Yelverton, who tells her: ' "I think if I had to label my religous faith . . ., I should say I was a Humanitarian".' ' "A Humanitarian!", she ejaculated with a cold and sinking heart. "Is that all?" To her . . . it was but another word for an infidel.' Elizabeth's friend, Mrs Duff-Scott, advises her:

> 'My dear, whatever you do, you *must* not begin to ask questions of that sort. We can never find out the answers, and it leads to endless trouble. God's ways are not as our ways—we are not in the secrets of His providence. It is for us to trust Him to know what is best. If you admit one doubt, Elizabeth, you will see that everything will go.'

Mr Yelverton tells her: ' "I am not a churchman—I would be if I could, it is not my fault—but if I can't accept those tests, which revolt the reason and consciousness of a thinking man, am I therefore irreligious? *Am* I, Elizabeth?" "You bewilder me", she said; "I have never made these distinctions. I have been taught in the Church—I have found comfort there and help. I am afraid to begin to question the things that I have been taught—I should get lost altogether, trying to find a new way".'[11]

The census of 1881 shows the small number of those who at this stage were willing to declare themselves non-Christian. Over 900 described themselves as freethinkers, some 850 as spiritualists, 69 as Deists, 53 Agnostics, 37 atheists and 24 materialists.* Few conclusions about lack of faith can be drawn from the several thousand who returned themselves under the headings, 'No Denomination' or 'No Religion', nor could the census distinguish those whose faith was in jeopardy but who continued to describe themselves under a denomination. The extent of agnosticism and anticlericalism which had developed among the more educated classes may, however, be deduced from the tone of the *Age* and the *Argus*—outwardly Christian, but under the thin veneer the true opinions of editors and many contributors could easily be seen. A high proportion of leading citizens, though usually religiously inclined, were not good churchmen and were unorthodox in various ways. These include Service, Berry, Gillies, Deakin and Pearson among the leading politicians, Syme and Haddon, Judges Higinbotham and Hartley Williams, and Gyles Turner. Pearson could find no one to answer satisfactorily the theological doubts of the age: 'The only thing, it seems to me, is to do one's duty day by day, and to leave the rest to God.' Syme was an agnostic with 'an almost tender inclination to adore his God if he could only find Him'. Deakin, rare among the native-born, was a mystic, an 'incorrigibly eclectic' amateur theologian whom no church could contain.[12]

Moorhouse and Strong; theological conflicts; the denominations

The sharpening crisis of faith was not dramatically revealed until 1879 when the *Victorian Review* published Marcus Clarke's sceptical 'Civilization without Delusion'; the issue sold 10,000 copies. Bishop Moorhouse replied sharply, Clarke made a scathing rejoinder, and controversy in the journals warmed up.[13] The major crisis, however, was delayed until August 1883 when Higinbotham gave a grave, anguished, lucid, utterly honest and reverent lecture on 'Science and Religion'. He said nothing new, but it was a precise statement of the problems which were worrying a multitude of laymen and, said Higinbotham, 'inducing mental paralysis . . . extending rapidly to all classes'. However, having denounced the clergy for ignorance, and dogmatic theology for impeding Christian practice, he called on the laity to abandon the churches and the supernatural and

* There were apparently few humourists in Victoria, but three described their religion as L.S.D., one as Sun worshipper, and one as Free Trade.

The 'Christian' of Today

'The chaos of creeds and the babble of strong tongues . . . compel every thinking layman to set out alone and unaided on the perilous path of inquiry': Mr Justice Higinbotham

> to meet on the high central platform of thought– . . . God, revealed anew to the intellect, and also to the responsive human heart, as the Father, the Friend, the Guide, and the Support of our race, and every member of it, in the simple but profound philosophy, and also in the sublimest life, of Jesus of Nazareth, the Light of the World.[14]

Higinbotham had moved on from his failure to reconcile church and state in the education crisis of the sixties when he had regretfully adopted the secular position. Since the churches seemed incapable of reforming themselves, he was now recommending going outside them in order to practise Christianity without creeds.

The lecture brought uproar in the religious press–'scandalous vituperation', Gyles Turner protested[15]–and was the immediate cause of Presbyterian schism. An answer had to be made, and only Bishop Moorhouse could make it; he was truly the defender of the faith, though of a broad faith. He replied obliquely in his treatment of the Galatian Lapse in his current series of lectures. Then at the diocesan annual assembly a few weeks later, he shocked many of his audience by stating his deep gratitude for plain speaking, which had clarified the issues, from a noble man who was 'clear of that paralysing agnosticism' which was spiritual death, who was a brother still by virtue of his love for Christ. Moorhouse went on to defend the clergy as teachers, to indicate how science and religion could be reconciled, and to deny the possibility of a Christianity without creeds. His speech was a well-mannered, 'perfect model of polemical theology'.[16] Again, in 1885, when Judge Hartley Williams published *Religion without Superstition*, which quickly ran into three editions, Moorhouse immediately published a reply, though this time he was less polite.[17]

Moorhouse, now in his late fifties, had been bishop of Melbourne since 1876. Son of a Sheffield cutlery manufacturer, he had been to a local private school, become a hearty boxer, cricketer and footballer, gone on to Cambridge for ordination, and won prominence as a celebrated London preacher. He had found the Melbourne diocese drifting, having been three years without a bishop (Samuel Thornton had been appointed to the new see of Ballarat in 1875). The clergy appointed by Perry were mostly markedly evangelical and were regarded (Moorhouse himself said) with 'a popular distrust which identified them with the party of privilege and reaction'.[18] Although 35 per cent of the population were nominally Anglican, the church ran a bad fourth in active adherents. At least one observer believed the church's support was confined to the upper and lower classes and that many low churchmen preferred going to chapel where they heard better sermons and could be hailfellow with the pastor.*[19]

* A clergyman's wife, Mrs Cross (Ada Cambridge), found it strange to come straight from 'our dignified Cathedral life, with its high and mighty Church-and-State tradition, into this democratic Salem-chapel-like atmosphere', but she greatly appreciated the welcome they received. Her visiting sister-in-law, however, was staggered by the 'insolence' of parishioners, when she bestowed 'old clothes and kitchen scraps' on them and had to learn that in Australia parishioners gave presents to the penurious vicar. (*Thirty Years in Australia*, pp. 43-4.)

Moorhouse was firstly a new energetic broom. He reformed the training of clergy by insisting on three years at Trinity College and a degree if possible, instead of a one-year course at the Sydney theological college. He started, at last, the fund-raising for and building of St Paul's Cathedral. He founded the Bishop of Melbourne's Fund for home missions, established a Sunday School Association and the Diocesan Mission to the Streets and Lanes (Community of the Holy Name), and prodded the laity into activity.

His refreshing broadmindedness was novel among colonial clergy. When the government asked the churches to pray for rain in 1882, he refused, though he did not actually say, as was widely believed, 'Don't pray for rain, dam it!'; he regretted he had not had the wit to think of it. Wesleyans and Catholics condemned him for denying the efficacy of prayer; finding himself embarrassingly leading the Secularists on an issue getting out of control, he gave way verbally, but the furthest he would go was to recommend the prayer: 'O Almighty God, we humbly beseech Thee to pardon us for our sinful waste and neglect of Thy bountiful supply of rain and waters, and give us grace to make better use of these Thy precious gifts in the years that are to come.'[20] He was shocked by the extent of sectarianism and worked vigorously to combat it: 'The hatred of Rome here is incredible.' 'Nothing will induce me to join in the bigoted howl.' He had better things to do, he said, than 'wrangling with Dissenters'.[21] He told his Assembly in 1883 that miserable sectarian differences were largely responsible for the absence of the Bible in state schools, the poverty of the rural clergy and the weakness of the defence against the Secularists—it was stupid, mad, wicked.[22] He formed the Pastoral Aid Society to encourage inter-denominational co-operation in rural areas, and some Presbyterians agreed to share pulpits. But he had little success in promoting exchanges with the nonconformists and had to suffer a demonstration in St Paul's by the high-inclined Reverend J. H. Gregory and supporters when Bromby and Charles Strong of Scots Church set a precedent in February 1883.[23] At least he succeeded in persuading Dean Macartney and Dr Cairns, the 'Presbyterian Pope', to visit Bishopscourt to hear the actor, William Creswick, read Shakespeare, but the evangelicals could not tolerate his lending his name to a charity theatre-performance.[24]

Above all, Moorhouse gave reassurance and confidence again to his church. The fervour and glow of his passionate eloquence inspired his laymen; his lunchtime talks to businessmen and annual theological lectures in the Town Hall attracted full houses. His brand of progressive orthodoxy—'admitting everything, conceding nothing'—largely satisfied all but the sceptics and the fanatics. However, the *Age* declared him uncertain of his ground on questions of modern controversy and unwilling to face many of the conclusions of science, while Professor Macdonald of Ormond College condemned him as a mere disciple of Jowett on the Atonement.[25] But he could state disagreeable truths with the minimum of offence and could charm almost any company with his tolerance and good humour; occasionally he made popular appearances, with bulldog and pipe, at football matches on Saturdays, a day normally spent in the study. He had to fight on many fronts and was respected by most of the irreconcilable groups he had to handle, though the rumbles of evangelical discontent occasionally belched forth. There were limitations: his conventional conservative views reduced his understanding of colonial politics and he had little inkling of the environmental contribution to man's turpitude. But when he accepted Salisbury's offer of Manchester in 1885 (after he had agreed to accept an English see from Gladstone in 1883),[26] Melbourne knew it was losing a remarkable man. It was probably true, as he hoped it was, that by then scepticism was 'more hesitating and respectful'. As one of his clergy said, he 'found the Church in Victoria at a low ebb. He left us cheered, inspired, strengthened to a degree no one would have thought possible in so short a time.'[27]

Melbourne's other leading preacher was Charles Strong, much younger than Moorhouse, who had arrived in 1875 to minister at Scots Church, the 'Cathedral' church of Presbyterianism where, according to 'The Vagabond', 'the beauty, fashion, wealth, and talent' of Melbourne were well represented.[28] Moncure Conway, a distinguished visiting ethical Deist, thought Moorhouse and Strong the ablest men in the Australian pulpit. 'They were "broad" in their views and managed to get gibbeted together as "pals" propagating infidelity.' Both of them asked Conway home; he 'found them cheerful martyrs, quite able to appreciate the amusing features of the combination of Scotch Presbyterians and English Hard-churchmen by whom they were pelted'. Strong's offences were manifold: 'He never preached dogmas; he introduced Emerson's essays into a class of young people [and] he was too eloquent.'[29] However, Strong was broader than Conway implied. From the start, though always quite uncombatively, he had acknowledged textual errors in the Bible, stated his belief in evolution and the antiquity of man, and referred to Genesis as a 'Creation myth'.[30] He was the first Victorian Presbyterian to introduce the anthem into the service; he wrote his own *Primer of Religion* for children in which he did not include the Shorter Catechism; and while rousing his congregation to their duties to the poor was welcomed affectionately in the slums. Strong was a product of the liberal movement in the Church of Scotland associated with Principal Edward Caird of Glasgow University. He was by no means the only such minister in Victoria—'Willie' Henderson at Ballarat, for example, was much loved, while notoriously liberal in theology—but because of his central position, because his congregation was so important, and despite his moderation, Strong became the storm-centre.

The Presbyterian church was powerful in Victoria.* It included many old pastoral and mercantile families—Toorak was 'the Highlands of Scotland', the local Anglican minister lamented—and had more regular

* But although there were four successive 'Presbyterian' Premiers between 1883 and 1893, only one of them was a good churchman.

worshippers than the Catholics and almost as many as the Methodists. Yet it was peculiarly vulnerable to the subversive new thought, for a large proportion of the clergy were rigid, hard-line Scottish (and Northern Irish) Calvinists and the basis of the faith was the Westminster Confession of 1643, 'the most formal and historically conditioned creed'.[31] The first official move against Strong followed an article he contributed, on request, to the *Victorian Review* in 1880 on the doctrine of the Atonement. It was an objective historical treatment with no attempt to state the Presbyterian viewpoint, although it was announced as such by the editor. The offending article was discussed by the local presbytery of ministers, and a committee eventually reported that nothing in the article was directly contradictory to the Confession but it was marked throughout by a spirit of compromise. The presbytery after three days' debate resolved only to exhort Strong to lay proper emphasis on the evangelical doctrines of the faith. Strong had already had enough, and in August 1881 announced his decision to resign: 'This Presbyterian Church has alienated my sympathies,' he wrote to a supporter, referring several times to his 'liberal' position and the 'liberal party' in the Church which supported him.[32] Now, however, the Scots congregation swung into full support; it was led by J. C. Stewart, an elder and the Assembly's Law Agent who became mayor of Melbourne in 1885. In defending Strong against allegations of hypocrisy for having signed the Westminster Confession, Stewart and others threw the charge back at all the clergy of holding to a document which was obviously in several respects anachronistic and supported by no one. Scores of lengthy letters crammed the newspapers; the *Argus* even ran the Confession as a three-day serial. The Assembly faced the charge squarely, and in 1882 passed a novel Declaratory Act stating the sense in which the four points of dogma under particular attack were to be understood. The modification of dogma was perhaps taken by the conservatives as the furthest compromise they could make; the men of the old kirk now proposed, having cleared the ground, to stand firm. Meanwhile, Strong had been persuaded by his congregation not to resign, but to return after spending part of 1882 on leave at home.

The explosion came soon after his return. Despite his presbytery's rigid view, Strong took a leading part in the campaign from April 1883 to open the Public Library and Gallery on Sundays; the presbytery noted its extreme regret at his behaviour.[33] The Higinbotham lecture was the final straw. Strong's assistant had asked Higinbotham to address the Scots Church Literary Society; on request, Strong had suggested the topic of science and religion, had chaired the meeting, and had not there and then disavowed the speaker's views (though he did later reply in a sermon). Public controversy was intense: the *Age* and *Argus* both printed the full text of the lecture and wrote leaders in support of Strong and Higinbotham, while the *Telegraph* and the *Southern Cross*, an interdenominational evangelical weekly, reviled them. The presbytery was appalled; one member described the lecture as 'a dastardly attack on Christianity'.[34]

The Reverend Duncan McEachran, a Highland Calvinist, was reported as saying of Strong:

> Ever since he came among us he has not ceased to attack those standards which are dear to us, and which he himself has signed. . . . He has always been the first to begin the strife. We have never touched him till he has touched that truth which is dearer to us than life. We have never gone a hunting for heresy; but in the most uncalled-for way he has flaunted before us views which, in faithfulness to God and our Church, we could not allow to pass without notice.[35]

Strong replied:

> I am only one of many Presbyterians who are convinced that if our church is to be a living power in the nation . . . there must be some measure of reform in the direction of wider intellectual freedom, adaptation of our forms of worship to the wants of a new country and a new age, together with a wider human sympathy. . . . Mr McEachran must know that there is at present much lamentable and alarming alienation from and indifference to the Church. . . . It seems to me a dreadful, dangerous, and anti-protestant tyranny which Mr McEachran wishes to establish in the Church.[36]

McEachran then wrote formally to Strong to inform him that at the next presbytery,

> I shall charge you with promulgating and publishing heretical and unsound doctrine both by your action in connection with the recent lecture of Mr Justice Higinbotham and otherwise, also with being guilty of teaching and conduct tending to destroy the order, unity, and peace of the church, also with failure to assert, maintain and defend the doctrine of the church when it was in your power to do so, and, further, with failure to comply with the instructions of the Presbytery to give prominence in your teaching to the incarnation, the atoning life and death and the resurrection and ascension of our Lord.[37]

Strong had already decided finally to resign and go home again. He wrote to Pearson:

> With the absolute and arbitrary powers of our own Church Courts, the ignorance of the clergy, and their virulent fanaticism, I could see no practical result flowing from a struggle with such men. It seems to me that if the laity are convinced that our present systems are hurtful to religion and morality, and if they desire a freer and truer interpretation of Christianity, they must take the matter into their own hands and demand reform. . . . There seems to be no way but for me to go. Whether I shall come back again is an open question.[38]

Strong did in fact stand aside and allow the laity to fight the battle which he and they regarded as basically about the infallibility of the Scriptures. The Scots congregation included several parliamentarians and leading pastoralists such as James Lorimer, J. Orkney, J. S. Johnston (the old *Argus*

The case of the Rev. Charles Strong before the Presbyterian Assembly

demagogue), William Cumming, Archibald Fisken, William McCulloch and Robert Simson, most of whom held conservative political views. They now began to plan secession 'on the basis of adherence to the standards of the Church of Scotland'. The Scots Church District Social Society produced a petition from the 'inhabitants of the lowest lanes and alleys of the city'.

> Many of us had sunk very low in vice, misery and crime when Mr Strong found us out. No city missionary or minister of religion ever visited our dwellings. . . . We never heard any Christian teaching until Mr Strong came to our homes himself and brought his friends to help us.[39]

The presbytery continued to meet and wrangle, and eventually referred the heresy charge to the full Assembly.

14 November 1883 was an extraordinary day in the history of Presbyterianism in Victoria. Debate in the Assembly, which had begun on a civilized plane, was resumed on the motion that Strong, who was departing next day, be invited to attend to 'disavow all complicity with the erroneous doctrines of Mr Justice Higinbotham's lecture, and also declare his faith in the true Deity of the Lord Jesus Christ, the propitiatory character of His death, and the real resurrection of His body from the dead'. Strong's supporters and those who thought it best to drop the matter were borne down by increasingly malicious assertions, and shortly after three o'clock the motion was carried by 143 votes to 42. Strong was summoned for six o'clock or later; but he could not be found. Meanwhile a huge gathering of his supporters and friends was assembling at the Town Hall down the street, to hear emotional, fighting speeches by Johnston, Lorimer and others. Higinbotham asked:

> What shall we say of the people of Victoria when an insignificant ecclesiastical minority—(loud and prolonged cheers)—is able to drive from our shores a man, a fellow-clergyman, because he has been able to draw to himself the admiration and affectionate regard of all the thinking men and women in the community?

J. G. Francis presented an address from the Church of England and Dr Bromby also spoke. A cheque for £3,000 and presents from ladies and children were handed to Strong. He spoke simply and unpretentiously in reply, saying he had been working for unity with the Church of England and that wider tolerance, liberty and charity were what Victoria needed. Strong did not receive the summons until after nine o'clock and promised a reply by ten. Meanwhile the Assembly had been grimly waiting; shortly after eleven o'clock a motion of contempt was moved and then, just as it was being put, Strong's reply was handed in. It was as dignified and courteous as all his conduct had been, and was greeted with tremendous cheering by his supporters: he refused to attend, as he could see no point in further arguing the issues and he regarded the charges as unconstitutional.[40] The Assembly adjourned and next morning, while Strong and his family were steaming down Port Phillip Bay, appointed a committee to consider the situation. That night, an ambiguous motion which was intended to be a compromise was passed, 'disjoining' Strong as a minister.[41]

The Presbyterians were riven asunder. The proceedings of Assembly and presbytery were open to press and public; disgraceful rows were reported verbatim, a few clergy jostled each other, while Strong's supporters in the gallery had frequently to be called to order. Dr Alexander Morrison, headmaster of Scotch College, whom Strong regarded as an old friend who had conspired against him and betrayed him,[42] was hissed one day by the Scots congregation in church. The *Argus* and *Age* revelled in reporting the presbytery's 'wrangles, its fierce hatreds, its inquisitorial spirit, its violent outrages on modesty of language and equity of procedure. . . . Scenes of strife belonging to the days of Luther mingle with the sound of harsh Scotch voices scraping out points of order.'[43] Many of the clergy believed they were being martyred by a prejudiced press and public and grimly stood by their conviction that their faith was in peril. They were surely correct in their accusation that there was little Presbyterian in Strong's teaching. It is more doubtful whether, at this stage, Strong could be said to have abandoned the basic doctrines of Christianity; and even more doubtful whether, as later apologists claimed, assurance of 'sincere attachment to the supernatural in Christianity and in the person of Christ' was all his opponents were demanding. They feared especially 'that dry rot of Unitarianism which is the spiritual disease to which the Christian faith in Presbyterian Churches has been most exposed'.[44] The large number of ministers of Free Church background tended to make their stand more rigid; the Scots congregation certainly saw itself as defending the Church of Scotland tradition. The conservatives were also sustained by the mass of evangelicals in the community who were less articulate than their critics.

Month after month, year after year, the ferocious disputes dragged on in full public view. Early in 1884 the Scots congregation tried to pass a bill through Parliament which would enable them to retain the church property if they separated. The other denominations rallied in alarmed support of the Presbyterians, Robert Harper handled their case cleverly, and most politicians wanted to avoid intervention and were doubtful of Parliament's rights: the bill was dropped.[45] Peacemakers like James MacBain tried to reconcile congregation and Assembly, but later in the year the breach was widened when Strong was refused the certificate which passed a minister from one presbytery to another; despite vigorous protests by the Reverend J. Hay and others, the Assembly agreed to supply only an extract of minutes showing how Strong had left. There was talk of a dozen more congregations considering breaking away. Late in 1885 the Reverend Robert Scott of Chalmers Church, who had been a prominent Glasgow churchman, resigned in protest at his presbytery's behaviour. A memorial to him from Strong's supporters was signed among others by Service, M. H. Davies, and the businessmen, Samuel Amess and John Blyth. Amess suggested asking the Church of Scotland to send out missionaries to convert the Melbourne presbytery.[46] Then the worst case of all raged through 1886. The Reverend George Dods had been acting as minister at Scots since Strong's resignation. Late in 1885 the congregation, from which the militant minority had just seceded to form the Australian Church, called him as their minister. Alexander Morrison appealed on the ground that his doctrines were unsound, and the presbytery ordered Dods to produce his sermons for examination. Dods refused on constitutional grounds, and was declared guilty of contumacy; the Assembly confirmed the verdict.[47] It was widely believed that Dods's only crime was to have remained neutral through the Strong conflict. Again the *Age* and *Argus* fought the battle of enlightenment with ruthless invective:

> As for Dr Rentoul, a lady, . . . when he rose, shuddered, and asked who he was, and declared that from his face he was capable of sacrificing everything to be on the winning side. . . . when he finished his speech she exclaimed, is that a Christian professor? . . . Such a speech as his should never be tolerated. It imputed motives, misrepresented acts. . . . Mr Yule got pathetic at the finish. He anticipated the verdict of the public. The accusations of tyranny, narrowness, bigotry, suspicion—his voice reached a whine. Water came to his eyes. He protested that it was truth and truth only for which he and his followers cared. So protested the Pharisees and the inquisitionists, and so have all those who did injustice and broke the laws of charity in every age.[48]

Rentoul's behaviour was indeed abominable; his assertion that the contest was 'between Christian righteousness on the one hand and looseness of living on the other' (he claimed to have been misreported) caused further uproar.[49] Dods left the colony saying the church in Victoria was a 'miserable farce' and that most of its clergy were uneducated and not gentlemen. The Church of Scotland accepted him as a minister without enquiry and was consequently bitterly attacked by the Victorian Assembly.[50]

Peace eventually came to Scots Church after a succession of tactful appointments from Scotland. But Victorian Presbyterianism had suffered great damage to its prestige and influence. Agonized laymen acknowledged that 'the teachings of our Divine Master' had been turned into a 'burlesque'. The Melbourne presbytery had made it 'a sort of disgrace to be known as a Presbyterian'; one was continually met by fellow-citizens with jeers, jibes and badinage.[51] Despite the large growth of population in the eighties, fewer Presbyterian adults were attending services at the close of the decade than at the beginning. Nevertheless, a Church Jubilee Fund of £40,000 was raised (with another £20,000 promised) between 1887 and 1889 to celebrate fifty years' work in the colony. Slowly, the moderate men began to rebuild the wreckage, erring brethren were tolerated more readily, and perhaps the newer generation of clergy was not so turbulent.[52]

Strong was offered a charge in Scotland, but returned to Melbourne early in 1885. He had been thinking of opening a girls' school, but his staunch supporters had other ideas. On 5 October the foundation of the

Australian Church was announced and its aims stated as follows:

> Believing that theology is a progressive science, that genuine religion is confined to no one form of belief, and that to fetter the minds and bind the consciences of ministers or people is not only a ridiculous folly, but a sin, in this 19th Century . . . the promoters of the Australian Church have sought to found a Society which while reverencing whatever is venerable in the past, will ever be avowedly open to any new light of God, and which may unite men of many shades of opinion in the unity of the religious spirit and of practical Christianity.[53]

Strong accepted the invitation to become minister, and preached Jesus as the model for humanity and God as Infinite Thought, Ideal Goodness, Ultimate Reality and the Living Father;[54] all literature was searched for impressive forms of prayer. Strong always claimed not to have founded the Australian Church: he had agreed to advise, and to become minister if it was founded. William McCulloch was chairman of the organizing committee which, like the nucleus of the first congregation of about one thousand, was formed from the diehard Scots supporters.

The Australian Church, it has been remarked,* was the colonial dream translated to religion. Strong explicitly held the hope of a 'new faith in a new world'. The utopian hopes which were so prevalent, of a better society in which men might be brothers, were almost invariably based on Christian foundations. A better form of Christianity might be found which rejected the divisive creeds with their arguable dogmas, returned to fundamentals by stripping off the ecclesiastical accretions of centuries, took into account modern discoveries about the universe, and was intellectually more coherent and responsive to social needs. The Australian Church, however, was only to have limited short-term success and was to divide among itself. It was far easier to criticize existing forms of religion than to agree on a new one. Some of the intellectually discontented were attracted by the Unitarian, the Reverend George Walters. At the opening of his new church in 1887, Higinbotham made a comparatively intemperate attack on the orthodox.[55] Many others were more or less satisfied by seeking and finding a 'broad' minister within the Anglican, Presbyterian or Congregational churches. And, perhaps, too few of the younger generation were deeply enough involved. Although for more than half a century Strong was to continue to make a notable contribution to Melbourne life, it was as a social worker rather than as a priest, and his church died soon after he did.

The Presbyterian deputies at the Wesleyan Methodist conference in 1887 told their hosts that they had been 'fighting for purity of doctrine and purity of worship' and thanked them for sympathy throughout their ordeal. The Reverend J. Watsford replied, congratulating the visitors 'on having so bravely fought the fight for an honest pulpit'; their victory might

* By Miss Jill Roe, on whose excellent article, 'Challenge and Response: Religious Life in Melbourne, 1876-1886', *Journal of Religious History*, vol. 5, no. 2, Dec. 1968, I have heavily drawn. My other major guide for this chapter has been Dr F. B. Smith's notable unpublished M.A. thesis, 'Religion and Freethought in Melbourne, 1870 to 1890'.

save the Wesleyans from similar conflict.[56] The Wesleyans stood in the old paths, for the time being intellectually immune; their belief in the literal reading of the Bible and the inevitability of eternal punishment for sinners was hardly shaken. Few ministers or laymen were highly educated or widely read; whereas the Presbyterians required a B.A. degree from their apprentice clergy before they began theological training, the Wesleyans did not demand even matriculation. Most were bewildered by the controversies of the day and managed largely to ignore them. When their leading publicist, the Reverend W. H. Fitchett, headmaster of the Methodist Ladies' College, editor of the *Southern Cross* and prominent in the counsels of the *Spectator* and the *Daily Telegraph*, expressed limited support for evolutionary doctrine, his co-brethren were gravely alarmed.

In the early eighties about 13 per cent of the population were Methodists—about 100,000 Wesleyans and another 20,000 Primitive Methodists, Bible Christians, Free Church, and New Connection Methodists, all of whom were to reunite with the main branch in 1902. In the gold towns one person in five (in some towns three in ten) was a Methodist, in Melbourne one in ten. After immense success in the gold-rush period, the seventies had been disappointing, but in the eighties the Wesleyans more than held their own in nominal membership and new building at least. Massive red-brick churches were built at Essendon, Toorak and Auburn. The church remained predominantly lower middle class in membership, strong among small suburban businessmen and artisans, while its limited appeal to the working class gradually declined. As Fitzroy became more working class in character, so the Methodist church there weakened. Methodists were classically 'upwards socially mobile'; their thrift, perseverance and desire to 'improve' themselves made frequent rise of station possible. Edwin Moran believed his change of occupation from carriage-maker to grocer had been divinely guided; in 1881 he invited his cousin, Fred Cato, to join him and nine years later their shops had increased from two to forty. It may be, however, that economic success and the diversions of city life tended to induce a decline in pietistic religion. By about 1880 there was sharp controversy within the church over the need for regular attendance at the weekly class meeting, as a 'means of grace' and evidence of 'a sincere desire to flee from the wrath to come', as the test for full membership. The conservatives won for the time being, but it seemed that many of the younger generation wanted to modify the 'rigid, soul-searching and fearful religion of their fathers'. Nevertheless most of the old revivalist enthusiasm was maintained: as a result of W. H. Edgar's work in Ballarat, Geelong and Port Melbourne,

> Drunkards were reclaimed, unhappy hearts and homes were changed, prodigals returned to the father's home. Sleeping Christians were awakened, careless and indifferent sinners were aroused and convicted of their sin. Numbers who were outside the fellowship of the Church were brought into it, and inactive members became 'zealous of good works'.[57]

However, there was growing awareness in the eighties that the artisan class was lapsing. E. H. Sugden's 'People's Services' at Wesley Church late in the decade were a forerunner of later sustained efforts to win back the working classes. The dual tradition within Wesleyanism continued to produce tension: on the one hand the withdrawal from society of pietistic groups, on the other the active liberal urge to reform secular society. The Methodists had few able representatives in Parliament, but were frequently influential at the local level in forming opinion. Wesleyan small businessmen dominated suburban councils like Camberwell and St Kilda as well as local strongholds like Ballarat West.*[58]

The energy and vitality of lay evangelical activity needs special remark. The thousands of Protestant lay preachers, elders and committeemen, the Sunday School teachers nearing 20,000 in number, the tens of thousands who belonged to mutual improvement, young people's and church sporting clubs, indicate the pervasive influence of the churches in determining conduct of life. James Balfour, merchant and Legislative Councillor for nearly forty years—member for 'the Aborigines, the Chinese and the South Sea Islanders'[59]—was the 'complete Elder' and lay preacher and had a profound influence, especially through his Bible classes. Even in terms of the day it might be said that he was something of a philistine and theologically conservative, but in his personal rectitude and decency he represented standards of life which were still dominant.

Such was its self-contained frame of reference and authority over its flock, the Roman Church could disregard the new learning, apart from an occasional contemptuous reference to 'monkeyism';[60] the *Syllabus of Errors* and other encyclicals had said the last word. The more important corrupting influence was Protestantism, which led inevitably to infidelity (Cardinal Newman had said), as there was no logical standpoint between Rome and atheism. The venerable Dr Goold, Bishop of Melbourne since 1848 and Archbishop since 1874, was weakening in his grip and was in bad health (especially since the attempt on his life at Brighton in 1882 by the crazed brother of the O'Farrell who had almost assassinated the Duke of Edinburgh in 1868); but he was still successfully resisting attempts to appoint a coadjutor. By now he was an irascible, impatient authoritarian, quick to criticize his subordinates; some of his successors doubted his competence.[61] Since 1874 bishops at Ballarat and Bendigo, and from 1885 at Sale, had taken over large areas of authority. From the late sixties, the Jesuit order had been responsible for the eastern suburbs of Melbourne. The Catholic population declined slightly in the eighties, in relative terms,

* The other main Protestant denominations were the Congregationalists (19,878 at the 1881 census), Baptists (20,373), Lutherans (11,149), and Church of Christ (4,859). There were also 4,330 Jews and 11,159 'Pagans', all but twenty of whom were Chinese.

Congregationalism, despite the presence of able clergy like Gosman, J. J. Halley, and Llewelyn D. Bevan from 1886, failed to increase its strength in the eighties in proportion to the population-rise. This is odd, perhaps, in view of its relative absence of creeds, awareness of the doctrinal issues of the day, favourable attitude to the liberal state and social concern.

For histories of minor denominations, see note 58.

mainly because a smaller proportion was migrating from Ireland, but remained more than one-fifth of the population; however, a notable increase in church attendance occurred. The Catholic flock, so overwhelmingly Irish in origin, adored and venerated the Pope much more than the Queen; Goold like the other Australian bishops had been zealous in supporting the proclamation of the Pope's infallibility. Cardinal Cullen had held sway as much in Victoria as elsewhere in Australia, and three-quarters of the priests were products of All Hallows College, Dublin.[62] The first signs of native Irish-Australian restlessness were appearing, however, despite the formation in 1881 of the Catholic Young Men's Societies 'to create and foster a spirit of union and co-operation among Catholic young men'.[63] Goold himself was warning that some of the Irish priests were rather rough in manners and inadequately educated for Victorian conditions: 'the people here are very smart—especially the Colonial born'.[64] But in this most obedient of the colonies of Rome there was no hint of the 'liberal Catholicism' which was rife in Europe. Intellectually sterile and passive, the Church in Victoria was almost totally preoccupied still with the pioneering task of building churches and creating the separate educational system at all speed—disciplining the flock into it and desperately striving to attract teaching orders. Despite the 'great educational injustice', suspicion of masonic conspiracy, and the backwash of Irish Home Rule protest, the Church appreciated the religious liberty and equality which prevailed in the colony. Its few well-qualified spokesmen like Dr Brownless, W. H. Archer and the Duffys were over-worked in fulfilling their representative functions in secular society. When Goold died in 1886, Archbishop Thomas Carr, Bishop of Galway and formerly vice-principal of Maynooth, brought new vigour to the task.

The Secularists

In the mid-eighties militant atheism made a sustained challenge. Through the seventies the Sunday Free Discussion Society, founded by Robert Service and H. K. Rusden, had nurtured a small group of dissidents of varying viewpoints; Trenwith, the bootmaker, was a frequent speaker. On 17 July 1882 the 'materialist' section of the society joined with a minority atheist and agnostic group in the Victorian Association of Spiritualists to form the Australasian Secular Association. The society was a reflection of Bradlaugh's National Secular Society founded in 1862, whose rules it closely followed. The objective was 'to maintain the principles and rights of free thought and their application to the secular improvement of mankind'; secularism 'declares that the promotion of human improvement and happiness is the highest duty and that the test of morality is utility'. By science and by science alone, human misery could be eliminated.[65] Thomas Walker, a twenty-four year old, who had been in the colony only for a year, was elected president. He had been a trance-medium since he was a boy and was the Spiritualists' star lecturer, until in the midst of a performance he denounced spiritualism as fraudulent and declared his conversion to atheism.[66] Other prominent founders were H. K. Rusden, James Donovan and Monty Miller, the Eureka veteran. Early in 1883 Walker was appointed as lecturer, and his witty, rude and crude attacks on the churches and the prominence of the society in the campaign to open the Public Library and Gallery on Sundays helped to attract 600 members within a year. In August, after an intercolonial conference, branches were formed in Sydney, Newcastle, Adelaide and Dunedin. In September, however, when the Spiritualists revealed details of Walker's murky past in Toronto, he left hurriedly for Sydney; he returned briefly in January 1884 for a three-night debate with David Blair who was defending the Christian position.[67] He had lost the support of the society, however, which wrote to Bradlaugh asking him to send out a lecturer.

Bradlaugh sent one of his vice-presidents, Joseph Symes, who arrived in February 1884. A former Wesleyan minister now in his forties, tall and erect, dark and dressed in black, wearing gold-rimmed eyeglasses, he was an impressive lecturer.[68] His audience in the Hall of Science was equally sober: respectable, grave, attentive, mostly well-dressed shopkeepers and artisans, husbands and wives frequently, many of them from nonconformist backgrounds.[69] Among the leading members, recent migrants and native Australians were at least as prominent as old settlers.* Symes immediately launched into a programme of frenetic activity. Debates, a Sunday morning social 'service' (songs, recitations and short talks on science, religion or current affairs), a secular Sunday school and a mutual improvement class were added to the weekly lecture. On 1 June appeared the first issue of the threepenny weekly *Liberator* which Symes largely wrote himself. He defined Christianity as 'a set of fables and falsehoods . . . immoral and debasing in its teaching and effects'; secularism was 'the best of everything in civilisation'. Taunting letters to Moorhouse in the first few issues and repeated challenges to debate demanded a reply. Moorhouse would not so demean himself as to appear with a representative of those who were 'lower than the beasts', but put up two of his clergy to debate with Symes in July. In August Symes was debating with H. J. Browne, the spiritualist. Membership had now risen to 843 and audiences at lectures were often 1,000 and more. The *Liberator* at its peak in 1886 had twenty pages, a circulation of several thousands and for a time was sold on the streets. Determined to force a confrontation and attract maximum publicity for the cause, Symes used all his ingenuity to mock and blaspheme as offensively as possible—parodying the Church of England litany and publishing caricatures of God, Jesus and the Virgin Mary. The Secularists' forays out of Melbourne displayed him pioneering under adverse conditions. Ballarat was 'extremely pious' and the bigots had such strength that a hall was

* Other than the many testimonies in the *Liberator*, the best description of an individual conversion to secularism is in Victor Kennedy and Nettie Palmer, *Bernard O'Dowd*, chs 3-4. O'Dowd edited the Association's *Lyceum Tutor* (Melb., 1888), an extraordinary document.

difficult to find. At Daylesford tar-barrels were prepared for Symes if he came, and at Woodend a mob assaulted him with the approval of the local policemen (who were reprimanded).[70] Societies were formed at all three centres, however, and at Briagolong where much local strife followed. Supporters in other rural centres formed debating societies in which they could spread the good word, and lonely secularist prophets became the butts of many townships.

In the week the *Liberator* was first published, Customs officers broke into the Hall of Science and burned copies of the English *Freethinker* as blasphemous. Under constant pressure from the *Daily Telegraph* and the evangelicals to shut Symes up, the government had to take decisive action if it could. Any prosecution under the ancient common law crime of blasphemy would be unlikely to succeed. The government chose to act in October 1884 at the instigation of the Sunday Observance Society under an English Act of 1771 on the charge of 'keeping a disorderly house', that is charging for admission to a public entertainment on Sundays; the laws prohibiting Sunday meetings had not been enforced in England since the fifties. Symes objected on the ground that the Act did not apply in Victoria and fought the case through for eleven months until the Full Supreme Court decided the Act did apply. Meanwhile the government had brought a charge under another near-obsolete Act which required the proprietor of a journal to give sureties against blasphemy and sedition; most publishers did not observe this law. Symes was found guilty in the Supreme Court in August 1885, but was fined the minimum and continued to refuse to pay sureties. The crisis came in October when the government prosecuted again on the disorderly house charge after extreme, offensive performances by Symes in September. In a three-hour address to the jury, Symes's chief point was that the Secular Association was a denomination as entitled to hold Sunday meetings as any other. Higinbotham advised the jury that this was the crux, but reminded it of Symes's 'gross and outrageous insults upon the faith of a large section of the community'; the relevant lecture 'as an intellectual performance . . . was beneath contempt'. The jury could not reach a decision; in November a second jury could not agree; the Attorney-General abandoned the case. Symes had triumphed. The government dropped its persecution apart from banning the *Liberator* from the mails for six months in 1886, although nothing was done to prevent its distribution by rail. The evangelicals stormed and fumed; an Anti-Atheist Society demanded repression.[71] Late in 1886 Deakin said, perhaps not entirely sincerely for his conscience must have been strained, that the government was still trying to devise means of suppressing the *Liberator*.[72] Symes, who was not lacking in that fanatical self-righteousness and self-dramatization of which many martyrs are made, had been perfectly prepared to go to gaol. 'Without a god', he wrote, 'with no hope of heaven or fear of hell, without hope of reward in this world or any other, the Editor plies his task, being fully assured that mankind will reap the full benefit of the work he is doing.'[73] Under great strain, he lapsed into indiscriminate abuse and crude blasphemy, as when he described Victorian politicians as mostly vermin, few of whom would not disgrace any Assembly in the world, and published his comparison of Christianity to phallic worship.

When he had found his feet in the colony, Symes launched out on an iconoclastic political programme in the *Liberator*, which had announced its policy as 'Republican and Atheistic'. As her Jubilee approached, the Queen or 'Mrs Brown' came in for sustained abuse, the jingo-imperialists and General Gordon were scarified, and the government's preoccupation with New Guinea and the New Hebrides mocked. The *Liberator* attacked the squatters for their treatment of shearers–'God and Mammon work hand in hand',[74] recommended land nationalization, supported Irish Home Rule, harked back to Eureka as a noble tradition, and opposed persecution of the Chinese. The Secularists, though they had little contact with the Trades Hall, were a nursery for the extreme left. However, by 1886 internal political divisions were beginning to destroy the movement, whose influence was already past its peak. Symes's extreme methods had alienated some of his supporters who pleaded with him to moderate his language. For most of the atheists were as respectable as the pious churchmen they mirrored. In 1888 the Association lapsed into factious discord, partly the result of Symes's personality and partly of major political disagreements, and was never again to be an important force.[75] The Victorian Association of Spiritualists also had fallen away to about one hundred members and by 1887 was almost dormant.

The Salvation Army

At the other extreme, far more prominent in the public eye than the Secularists, was the Salvation Army. Four years after General Booth began dressing his missioners in uniform (and two years after the Army opened fire in South Australia), Major and Mrs James Barker and five officers arrived from England, founded the first corps at North Melbourne in December 1882, and made Collingwood Flat their first major battleground. Within a few months, corps had been founded in other working-class suburbs and successful attacks made on Ballarat, Bendigo and Geelong. In Victoria, as elsewhere, dissatisfied Methodists and members of other sects rallied to join the disciplined organization preaching the simplest revivalist evangelicalism: 'Come to Jesus!' Reformed criminals, alcoholics, blasphemers, larrikins, even an occasional secularist, testified with the ecstasy of spiritual drunkards to a running accompaniment of 'Hallelujah!' and 'Praise God!'; penitents wended their ways to the platform to make public confession of their sins. The 'swing and precision' of the Army bands (the better ones) were 'incalculably effective as a stimulant'.[76] Part of the secret of the Army's success was that women could share equally in the work; the most famous Hallelujah lasses were 'Happy Dinah' and Mrs Captain Piper, 'the Victorian Larrikiness'.

The Army based its campaign on shock tactics and the belief that all publicity was good for the cause, and thereby roused great resentment. Horses bolted at the thump of the drum or the sound of Army lasses running down the street dragging kerosene tins to attract attention to a meeting. The sheer noise at night grossly disturbed suburban peace. Moreover, larrikin gangs formed 'skeleton armies' and took riotous licence. In North Melbourne once, an Army contingent was pelted with stones, rotten eggs, dead cats, red ochre and flour; in South Melbourne a gang of 300 was prevented by police from rushing a hall where the Army was holding a service, and resorted to ribald songs, raucous shouting and improper language. In Bendigo, it was alleged, publicans incited the roughs to break up meetings, and at Williamstown the police were said to be in league with the larrikins.[77] Some policemen were infuriated by threats from zealous privates that God would strike them down for their interference. Property-owners near Army barracks petitioned that they could not get tenants because of the noise and disturbance. Magistrates and municipal councils cracked down hard, using their by-laws against unauthorized processions; the city magistrates led the way in April 1883 by a decision which encouraged the police to attempt to disperse and to proceed against the nightly bands.[78] Nearly all the suburban councils followed suit; angered by the Army's self-righteousness, Prahran councillors described them as arrogant, defiant and a public nuisance. But the Army marched on, and refused to pay fines; several officers went to gaol. In August 1884, on appeal, the Supreme Court backed the municipal authorities. Gradually, however, the Army and the councils arrived at compromise arrangements for limited activities.[79]

After twelve months' operations the Army gathered 10,000 people for a celebration at the Exhibition building: twelve corps had been formed, the South Melbourne barracks was now the Australasian headquarters, many other barracks were being built, and the *War Cry* was being distributed in tens of thousands. At Bendigo, 'the whole city for months, seemed to be moved, and thousands professed to find the Saviour'.[80] The campaigning continued. In February 1884 the Army 'opened fire' at Maryborough and 'after a desperate charge, six surrendered, and pleaded for mercy'; Castlemaine, it was claimed, became 'a law-abiding, God-fearing locality' to the great detriment of its drinking-saloons and dancing-dens. 'The sweets of experience' had come even to 'the onion-growers of Drysdale'.[81] In July the Collingwood brigade, followed by a crowd of 5,000, led the way to a demonstration in the Melbourne Town Hall. In August another mass meeting welcomed Colonel Ballington Booth, the 'Marshal for the Colonies'. On New Year's Eve, after a march through the city, 20,000 people were said to have gathered in Albert Park, and on Cup Day 1885, 10,000 in Royal Park.[82] The Army claimed 30,000 were attending its Sunday services.

Nearly all the churches and newspapers were at first outraged by such 'antics in the sacred name of religion' and 'irreligious burlesques' by these 'mad sensationalists'. The Catholic *Advocate* continuously condemned

Bishop Moorhouse

Rev. Charles Strong, 1881

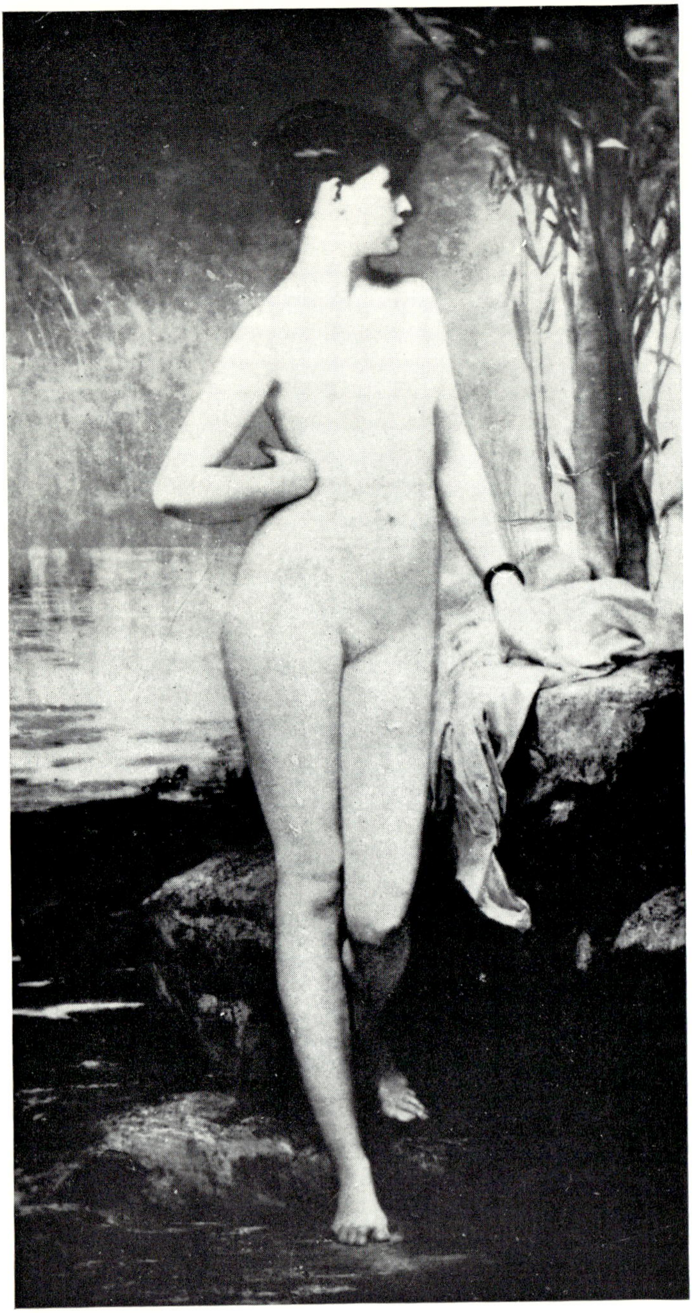

Chloë

these 'outrageously grotesque and ludicrous' buffoons. From the pulpit of St Patrick's, Dean Donaghy attacked 'proselytising agencies for the conversion of Catholic children to Protestantism, craftily conducted under the cloak of philanthropy'. Anglican clergy predicted that this epidemic of vulgarity would be a passing craze, and warned against susceptibility to such 'unhealthy excitement'.[83] Nearly all the Protestant churches were worried by the drain on their congregations from the recruiting tactics of these 'freebooters' and the interruptions to services from their parades. Moorhouse, however, partially came round. In 1882 he had condemned the Army's unscriptural doctrines and wild dances and wilder cries bordering on profanity. But in September 1884 he told his startled Assembly that although he could not believe 'its religious patois, its military ritualism, its noise and disconcerting familiarity can ever be made tolerable to men of thought, culture, and largely developed religious reverence', yet his heart went out to them in love and admiration, they were God's children. 'If the Master were here I am sure that He would own them and honour them above me.'[84] James Munro, the Presbyterian, and James Campbell, the Wesleyan Postmaster-General, spoke at Ballington Booth's welcome. Graham Berry opened the Brunswick barracks in the same month and claimed the Army was 'exercising a great influence for good'.[85] Though most church papers continued to attack, the *Telegraph* and *Southern Cross* gave qualified support.[86]

The Army's social work was bringing it increasing respect. 'The "Harmy" ', originally a term of contempt for lower class illiteracy, was coming to be used in grudging admiration. 'Go for souls and go for the worst,' was the General's routine order. The Army's belief that only simple workingmen and women could talk to the poor and outcast was being justified in its work among alcoholics, criminals and prostitutes. Dr John Singleton turned his reclamation organization over to them. Torchlight processions routed out the drunkards from the pubs. The Prison-Gate Brigade met nearly every man leaving gaol, took him to an Army house in Carlton for a meal, and kept in touch. The police approved; from early 1884 the Army was being given custody of first offenders and from 1886 the government allowed a small grant for the prison-gate work. A Fallen Sisters' Home was established late in 1883 and 400 women passed through it in a little over a year. In 1885 a Rescue Home in Brunswick was established for venereal disease cases, against opposition from Catholics and Methodists who declared that it pandered to vice.[87] By this time a general inclination was growing to leave such unpleasant problems to the Army, just as it later saved government the embarrassment of setting up a labour bureau for the unemployed.[88]

The force of the Army's impact is difficult to gauge. By the close of the eighties its barracks could accommodate as many worshippers as the Presbyterian churches and its Sunday attendances were asserted to be more than half any denomination's. In 1885 it claimed 8,000 members; 13,500 proclaimed themselves at the 1891 census—not one-quarter of those said to be attending services. The huge crowds which welcomed General Booth in 1891 indicate lasting strength, but we may be sure that most of the members were transfers from the sects rather than converted sinners. The Army's lasting success was the tacit acknowledgment by the Protestant churches of its efficacy among the 'irreclaimable working class' and of its mastery in humane social work.[89]

Reassessment

The years 1883 to 1885, when Presbyterians were at each others' throats, when Moorhouse's dynamic influence was at its zenith, and when the Secularists and the Salvation Army were campaigning at their peak, were a period of shock and new departures. The later eighties was a cooling-off time of reassessment, for none of these movements went as far as had appeared likely. While zealots of the Australian Church like John Blyth snorted still about the 'priestly tyranny' and 'absurd dogmatism' of the old denominations,[90] the fact remained that the movement for Christianity without creeds had produced only Strong's congregation of about one thousand and an expanded Unitarian congregation. The Church of England sagged in enthusiasm and morale when Moorhouse, who had done so much to present Christianity in reputable intellectual terms and so much to restore the prestige of the clergy, was succeeded by the pious Field Flowers Goe who, inevitably, suffered sadly in comparison. The Secularist Association declined into factional squabbling and made no more headway; between the censuses of 1881 and 1891 the number of those declaring no religion or no denomination or who did not specify their beliefs increased from about 14,000 only to 25,700. The Salvation Army was being accepted as just another important sect. Anticlerical sentiment remained strong; it was based on lack of respect for the intellectual quality of the clergy as a whole—Deakin, a prejudiced witness, certainly, thought them 'pathetic'—and to some extent on the political Toryism and remoteness from burning social issues of most Anglican and Presbyterian ministers.[91] Pearson was not unduly unfair when he contemptuously asked: 'Who has ever heard a clergyman denounce the greed of house owners, which has led them to convert whole streets of our populous city into rookeries . . . ? Has any one in Victoria ever heard a clergyman denounce dummying, or speak of salted invoices and other tricks of trade?'[92] Concern with the elements of theology remained almost as keen as ever: R. W. Dale, the eminent visiting Congregationalist, noticed the keen excitement (in contrast to other colonies) when he touched on matters of dogmatic controversy in his sermons.[93] Prominent clergy and unorthodox laymen met privately to discuss 'thoroughly, but amicably, the interrelations between religion, science and philosophy' in the Philosophical Society of Victoria in 1886 and its successor, the Victoria Society, in 1887.[94] Service, Deakin and leading scientists took part in the performance in the Town Hall by Stuart Cumberland, the world-famous thought-reader; a huge crowd followed him and marvelled when he located a pin hidden in a near-by street.[95] It may be that the shocks of controversy ultimately induced some relaxation of rigid stances and more tolerance. Francis Anderson (who was briefly Strong's assistant before becoming professor of philosophy at the University of Sydney) and the Reverend J. Hay were claiming in 1888, perhaps justly, that many sermons and lectures being given in the orthodox churches would have been denounced as heretical three or four years earlier.[96] The churches' response to fundamental criticism was beginning to emerge: not a new religion but the right kind of clergy, not no creeds but reformulated ones.[97]

The churches' 'social cement' function remained as important as ever. The new migrant found the familiar atmosphere of his old church a welcome aid to easy settlement and social absorption. In outer suburbs and rural areas especially, the churches were community centres where groups of friends formed and a sense of local cohesiveness naturally grew. The weekly service in a country township was often the only time of social gathering, when heads of families gravely discussed the weather, crops, prices and local government (and sometimes made preliminary moves for business deals); when their wives exchanged recipes, organized aid for those in distress or merely gossiped; and when the young laid the basis for future courting.[98] Support for the existing denominations remained very solid, in contrast to the United States. Revivalists had moderate success from time to time in the gold towns, but even there the purer evangelical sects did not grow very much and no new groups of saints held together for long. The 'Nunawading Messiah', James Fisher, with his tiny zealous following, was a rare phenomenon; so were J. A. Dowie and G. M. Stephen, the faith-healers. Despite the number of volatile evangelicals, there were few branchings from well-trodden paths.

On the face of it, the Christian faith of the masses was hardly shaken at all by the intellectual movements of the day, whose filtering effects were delayed for a decade or more. At the close of the eighties as at the beginning, on any Sabbath almost exactly half the population of Victoria was at church or Sunday school. Less than a quarter of the population, probably, never went to church. The statistics are remarkable (although not entirely trustworthy) when infants, the sick, and others unable to attend are taken into account, also the difficulty the churches had had in keeping up with the pace of outer suburban development. Dale estimated that three out of five adults who could possibly attend—half as many again as in New South Wales—were worshipping every Sunday and over 70 per cent of those between six and fifteen were at Sunday school. The Methodists and the Salvation Army had carried out remarkable building programmes, and all the churches had developed their social and charitable work. Only the Catholics managed to increase their proportion of regular worshippers to nominal adherents. The Presbyterians and Methodists lost ground—the former presumably mainly because of internal strife, the latter from the Army's inroads. It seemed that the evangelical grip was hardly shaken and that church-going habits remained unimpaired. But statistics alone tell nothing about the inroads of creeping doubt; or the degree to which materialist assumptions and secular notions about the pursuit of happiness in this world were reducing religious fervour; or whether the rising generation, though schooled into church, would retain their faith or as active a faith.

	Number of clergy		*Adherents at census 'ooos*				*Average attendance principal service 'ooos*				*Church accommodation 'ooos*	
	1881	*1889*	*1881*	*% pop'n*	*1891*	*% pop'n*	*1881*	*% adhnts*	*1889*	*% approx. adhnts*	*1881*	*1889*
Church of England	174	217	300	35	402	35	49	16	60	16	85	114
Presbyterian	170	218	133	15	167	15	73	55	70	44	83	97
Methodist	175	258	115	13	158	14	85?	74?	86	57	122	191
Roman Catholic	104	167	203	24	249	22	71	35	108	46	104	115
Salvation Army	—	368	—	—	14	1	—	—	64?	—	—	96
Other Protestants	144	184	78	9	97	8	25	—	35	—	—	—

The Free Church of England and the Free Presbyterian Church of Victoria are included under C. of E. and Presbyterian.

All the Methodist sects, including the Bible Christians, are included under Methodist.

'Protestants', included in the censuses under C. of E., are under Other Protestants.

The population increased between 1881 and 1889 by 28 per cent and by 30 per cent between 1881 and 1891.

The Methodist figures for attendance were obviously inflated by enthusiastic ministers, especially of the sects.

About 60 per cent of the population were aged 15 or more. Figures for Sunday school attendance are not included above.

5

Evangelicals in Action

These godly people would forbid the ball,
The races, theatres, and briefly all
That's cheer'd existence since the Human Fall![1]

In 1888 the Reverend E. H. Sugden, a young Yorkshire Methodist, arrived to become first Master of Queen's College at the University of Melbourne. He wrote home recording his first impressions:

> The religious people here have a good deal more influence on politics than in England. They have succeeded in almost abolishing Sunday trains. . . . Sunday is the more strictly observed, teetotalism is almost universal: there is very little smoking, the theatre is a horror to them. In the families where we have been out to tea they play bagatelle: they sing 'Resignation', 'He wipes the tear from every eye', 'The sweet bye and bye', and the like. I confess it was rather dull.[2]

'Wowserism' looms large in the history of Victoria and Melbourne; an examination of its effectiveness at a crucial stage will be a useful test of its traditional importance.

About one-third of Victorians in the eighties were Presbyterians and nonconformists, almost as large a proportion as in South Australia and half as many again as in New South Wales. Support by the evangelical wing of the Church of England and, sometimes the very straight-laced Catholic church, made a decisive majority on some social questions. In the absence of mass political parties or many organized pressure groups, the churches were potentially a strong political force. The numerous Presbyterians in Parliament, led by James Munro, Robert Harper and James Balfour, were backed by Methodists, such as James Campbell, and Independents like James Mirams. The Presbyterians were deeply divided on conservative-radical lines but made a formidable striking-force on social issues. Balfour, Matthew Davies and Harper had founded the weekly *Southern Cross* in 1874. They remained appalled that the 'agnostic popular science of the day had a base for aggressive warfare in every newspaper office in Melbourne' and in 1883 bought out the *Daily Telegraph* and *Weekly Times* to represent the views of the 'vast majority' against the 'doubts of the noisy minority' expressed in the other dailies. Balfour, Davies, James McKinley and four other evangelicals put up £5,000 each for 'a task planned, undertaken, and carried out to advance the Kingdom of Christ amongst men'.[3] The *Telegraph* led the 'holy howlers' on innumerable issues, reported the races but did not give betting details, and managed to produce its Monday issue without Sunday work.

Secular education

The evangelicals were entirely unsuccessful in their campaign to restore the Bible to the state schools. The Education Act of 1872 had not provided for religious instruction, but it had empowered local boards of advice 'to recommend what use shall be made of school buildings after the children are dismissed from school'. When some boards had recommended unsectarian religious instruction, Ministers of Public Instruction had given permission, provided teachers took no part and individual parents gave consent. About one-tenth of state school children were attending such classes and churchmen found the situation highly unsatisfactory. There were not enough clergymen to act as regular teachers and few laymen were available during the afternoon; children resented having to stay after school and discipline was hard to maintain.[4] Moreover, secular purity had been taken to extreme lengths. After the Jews had objected in 1876 to references to Christ in the Irish National Readers in use, the Minister, Robert Ramsay, had ordered their replacement by the Nelson 'Royal' Readers, which were then edited to remove all mention of Christianity. Much material suitable for incidental moral and broad religious teaching, a 'thin theism', remained, but the secular 'bowdlerizing' had been taken to ludicrous lengths. The evangelicals were appalled: their more unscrupulous controversialists, like the Reverend Andrew Harper, referred to a 'terrorist secularism' unparalleled save in France at its worst periods.[5] On this issue they were for once united with Bishop Moorhouse who became president of the interdenominational Bible in State Schools League, formed in 1882. Parliamentary spokesmen regularly pleaded for the Bible in schools, and also argued for decentralization of the state system on the assumption that local bodies would be more inclined than Parliament and the Department to favour religious instruction.[6] The Bible League campaigned for boards of advice having the power to prescribe readings of scriptural extracts by teachers in the Department, within the ordinary curriculum if possible, or at least before or after normal school hours, with conscience provisions for teachers and parents. Another organization, the Undenominational Education League, with Dr Singleton as president, was formed in 1886 to fight the losing battle.[7]

Inevitably the cause was tangled with Catholic claims and thereby discredited. The carefully chosen royal commission on education, which the O'Loghlen government had set up as a sop to the Catholics, issued a dual report in 1884. The predominantly Catholic half recommended state support for Catholic schools and religious teaching in the state schools; the Protestant half wanted to restore the Bible to the state schools, but observed that giving the Catholics an educational grant was 'tantamount to endowment by the State of that particular form of religion'.[8] Fanatically obsessed by their educational predicament, the Catholics were playing their hand very badly. Perhaps their range of thought was so enclosed that they meant what they said, but the *Advocate* of 1883 makes appalling reading. 'The State School Leprosy' was the heading of one editorial; the state schools were 'hotbeds of vice and irreligion', in which 'gross immorality' flourished. J. F. Hogan later asserted that public money was 'literally thrown away on a vain attempt to de-Christianize the rising generation'.[9] Some of the evangelicals were equally credulous in their assumption that the absence of religious teaching inevitably led to iniquity: a nasty rumour that eleven pupils at a mixed state school had been treated for venereal disease was widely believed.[10] The malicious anti-Catholics replied in kind, and futile argument went on and on about the behaviour of state and Catholic schoolchildren. Sir Archibald Michie remarked that it would be fair enough to give the Catholics their education grant if they would pay the relatively higher costs of their criminals and paupers. The *Age*, also using the Statistician's figures on religion and crime, remarked that 'if those who parade their peculiar holiness can keep their sect free of the police and free of the gallows, the State may consider it advisable to organise its schools in accordance with the Church's recommendations'. The *Leader* claimed that police records showed that nearly all the larrikins were products of Catholic schools.[11]

A crucial factor was that about half the Catholic children were still attending state schools (in which one-quarter of the teachers were Catholics).[12] The bishops preferred the state system to remain entirely secular, would accept no form of undenominational religious teaching—not even Bible reading—and suspected the Bible in Schools League was a Protestant plot to corrupt Catholic children. Late in 1884 Bishop Moore threatened that, if the Bible was introduced, the state schools would become 'proselytising establishments' and every Catholic child would be immediately withdrawn.[13] When W. H. Archer and other laymen formed the Education Union League early in 1885 (with lukewarm support from the clergy), they hoped to gain support from the Bible League for a grant to Catholic schools in return for support of the introduction of the Bible into state schools—a bargain which Moorhouse favoured. It is not surprising that they made no impact.[14]

The government ignored the report of the royal commission and made only the slightest of concessions to the Bible League. Service wanted to aid the existing practice of after-hours instruction and permitted teachers to stay, if they wished, to keep order, but he refused to allow instruction before school (which was contrary to the Act).[15] In 1886 Cabinet was willing to sanction the introduction of the Lord's Prayer into the classroom, until the churches began to quarrel about which version should be adopted.[16] In 1889 the National Scripture Education League (the Bible League's successor) launched another parliamentary campaign which was quickly voted down.[17] Defence of the Education Act had been one of the bases of the anti-Catholic coalition. It is clear from the nervous behaviour of politicians that the Act had been generally accepted by the public as sacrosanct. Sugden put his finger on one important aspect when he remarked: 'the working people are afraid that if the Bible were introduced, the Romanists would at once agitate for grants . . . and perhaps smash up the whole State School system and with it the *free* education which is what the working man wants.'[18] But the fact that so many Catholic children were still attending state schools was vital; and it was assumed that the Catholics were unlikely to succeed in building a comprehensive system. 'To protestantize' the state schools would be a gross injustice to Catholics, who would then really have cause for complaint and might precipitate a major crisis by ordering their children to be withdrawn. In short, it was widely believed, as Alexander Sutherland, the teacher-scholar, put it, that 'the smallest deviation or concession will cast the education of our young into the arena to be struggled for and mangled by bitterly-contending factions'.[19] The evangelicals, moreover, were not united. Some believed that only dogmatic instruction of religion was worthwhile and were indifferent about the teaching of pallid 'common Christianity', while staunch voluntarists continued to believe that religion in state schools did more harm than good. R. W. Dale remarked that if he were an enemy of the Christian faith he would recommend that teachers in state schools be required to teach religion.[20] Thus governments remained convinced that the fairest and most peaceable solution was to leave all the religious parties (except the voluntarists) out in the cold.

Sabbatarianism

To keep the Sabbath holy was a prime article of the Presbyterian and Methodist faiths. Sunday must be kept as a day, wrote Fitchett, 'whose quiet hours are filled with rest; with closer home life; with worship; with meditation; with social intercourse; with Christian work'. Rentoul believed that 'England's strength of moral manhood, the iron of the nation's moral blood, has been intermixed for more than the last two hundred years with the faith, worship, reverence, home-memories, and religious sanctions of the British Lord's Day.'[21] The holy Sabbath was a Divine Law; and, in practical terms, any distractions would diminish church attendances. The Sabbath in Victoria had long been brought under order. Sunday trading was eliminated under the Police Offences Act; few other than church trains were permitted to run in Melbourne and none in the country, and no public buildings were open. (In Sydney, in contrast, some shops and the Public Library, Gallery and Museums were open, and concerts and a variety of other entertainments were allowed.) A Presbyterian 'front' organization, the Lord's Day Observance Society, had for long protested at every breach—hectoring the Governor for travelling on Sunday, bringing the government to order when railway employees were allowed to go by train to their annual picnic, condemning Sunday excursions by paddle-steamer down the Bay. In 1884 the Society had 1,900 members, but not enough of them attended the annual meeting, for after Francis Ormond had delivered a tirade against the 'Continental Sunday' from the chair, the Secularists took over proceedings, the lights were put out and the meeting ended in uproar.[22]

In 1883 the Sabbatarians were challenged on fundamentals: a major controversy arose over the opening of the National Gallery on Sunday afternoons. A loose alliance of liberal intellectuals, sceptics, leading Anglicans and Catholics, and of course the *Age* and the *Argus*, attracted massive public support against the Sabbatarians; obviously this minor issue was used as a symbolic protest. A minority of trustees had previously failed several times to have the institutions opened; Charles Strong had met with presbyterial disapproval for supporting opening the Library in a sermon in November 1882.[23] A letter to the friendly *Argus* by one Horatio Beauchamp on 12 April 1883 was the spark, several bitter letters followed, and on the 19th Gyles Turner presided at a meeting convened by Beauchamp to form a Sunday Liberation Society. On the 23rd, at a small meeting of the trustees, Professor H. A. Strong carried a motion that it was desirable for the Library and Gallery to be open on Sundays. The Sabbatarians sprang into action with a meeting convened by Dean Macartney at the Y.M.C.A., at which it was resolved to form a Working-Men's Lord's Day Rest Association. At a meeting of the 'openers' on the 27th Charles Strong, supported by Dr Bromby and the Reverend H. F. Tucker of Christ Church, South Yarra, came out militantly: 'We have the right on our side and in the end the right will win.' The reforming trustees decided to fight it out: on the 30th Edward Langton and Pearson carried a motion to open the Gallery and the Technological Museum on Sundays; they had found that opening the Library was ruled out by a specific order-in-council. On 3 May a mass meeting, largely of young people, crammed the Town Hall, voted Higinbotham to the chair, and excitedly supported Bromby's motion in support of opening.* The Presbyterian Assembly was in session, however, and that day had organized 'a very large deputation' of clergy and citizens to call on Service to stop the rot. Against his own opinion but under pressure, Service wrote to the trustees to request them to revoke their decision until Parliament assembled. The trustees met next day, and, led by Pearson, refused to comply by a majority of one. On Sunday the 6th no fewer than 5,752 citizens passed through the turnstiles to the Gallery and Museum; according to a detective on duty, they were 'nearly all of the working classes, mechanics, labourers, drapers' assistants, bank clerks etc., all of whom seemed very much pleased with what they had seen'.[24] There were more than 4,000 visitors, largely young working people, on each of the next three Sundays.

* Those prominent at this meeting and on other occasions, other than those already mentioned, included Sir Archibald Michie, Judge Holroyd, Woods M.L.A. and Shiels M.L.A., Cahill S.J. and Daly S.J., Bromley and Trenwith of the Trades Hall, Professors Elkington and Nanson, Purves Q.C., Mullen the bookseller, and Browne the spiritualist.
On the other side the familiar names of Balfour, Fitchett, Mirams, Nimmo, Ham, Davies, Harper, Munro, Wrixon and Vale stand out.

Meeting and counter-meeting continued and both sides began to whip up petitions; Sunday School children were mobilized to doorknock for signatures, and no doubt the other side canvassed the hotels and football grounds. The newspapers carried page after page of correspondence. The Lord's Day Observance Society concluded its manifesto: 'We assert the supreme majesty of God's Sabbath law against its violators, nation or individual. We will fight to the death for Sunday for every toiler of the nation.' Bishop Moorhouse announced that he personally was in favour of opening, but felt 'deep regret and shame at much of the fierce and uncharitable language which is being used'. He struck hard at the Sabbatarians when he said: 'We have a day of rest set apart . . . , but we have no explicit directions for the observance of that day. The enlightened conscience must decide for itself.'[25] The *Melbourne Review* ran a symposium on the theology of the matter. The Sabbatarians' best argument was the right of every working man to complete Sunday rest; to which it was replied that the harm to the few who would have to officer the institutions (who, anyway, had volunteered) was far less than the benefit to a much larger number from improving use of their leisure, and that the Sabbatarians were inconsistent in that they allowed church trains and no doubt worked their servants on Sundays. The Trades Hall in fact was divided on the issue; it eventually voted in favour of opening in 1888. Why, said the 'openers', should nearly every other city in Australia have institutions open on Sunday and not Melbourne, why should Mechanics' Institutes in country towns be open on Sundays and not Melbourne's Library, and why should the Zoo and Botanic Gardens be allowed to open? To which the Sabbatarians replied that several wrongs did not make a right, that the imperial Parliament refused to open the British Museum on Sundays, and that the Zoo did not charge for admission. But the most cogent plea of the 'openers' was the argument from democratic rights against restrictions by a tyrannical minority, or even a majority, on the way in which a large number of people wanted to spend their leisure, and in public institutions at that.

The Sabbatarians, however, had the numbers in Parliament. Although the number of petitioners for opening (38,000) far exceeded those for closing, the latter were drawn from constituencies all over the colony. Mirams cleverly organized his party to spring a surprise vote on 4 July while many of the 'openers' were absent and, despite fine filibustering speeches by Shiels and Pearson, carried his motion to close the Gallery and Museum on Sundays. 'It is Brummagen philanthropy', said Shiels, 'that spares the Museum attendant and slaves the cook and table-maid. To prate of Sunday rest, and overwork and underpay the factory-hand, the clerk, the shopman, is . . . shoddy Christianity.'[26] But as many subsequent attempts in Parliament to reverse the vote showed, most members were unwilling to offend the evangelicals. In 1889 and 1890 the issue was still emotionally charged, in and out of Parliament; the 'openers' packed the Town Hall and howled down Bishop Goe when he attempted to move contrary amendments.[27] Parliament eventually gave way in 1904 and allowed the opening of Library, Gallery and Museums. It is said that Melbourne was the last city in the Empire to receive this privilege.[28]

Poor 'Chloe' had been at the centre of the controversy, to the vast amusement of the uncommitted public. Lefebvre's painting of the romantic nude was a serious work of art which had been awarded the Grand Medal of Honour at the Paris Salon in 1876 and had also won the gold medal for paintings shown at the Melbourne Exhibition of 1880–1. Dr (Sir) Thomas Fitzgerald bought it, and lent it to the National Gallery for further public display in 1882. As usual, however, the Presbyterians were alert. The Committee on the State of Religion and the Sabbath reported to the Assembly on 2 May 1883 that 'the recent introduction of a certain French picture into the Gallery' and some of the statues there were 'likely to suggest impure ideas'. In discussion on the report, Dr Rentoul said that the statues were unobjectionable but 'representations of the nude in colour' were improper. There were laughter and hisses when one clergyman made light of the fuss: 'It was well known that the sons and daughters of elders and ministers of the church visited the art galleries of Europe, where the pictures were said to be incomparably worse than those in the gallery of Melbourne.' James Balfour asked 'what consolation to souls to which eternity seemed very near were pictures and statues?'[29] Realization of the moral dangers of visiting the Gallery on any day of the week increased the determination to keep it shut on Sundays. 'Chloe' now became the subject of heated controversy in the press. One John Russell demanded the removal of the 'indecent picture of a naked woman'. 'Would any of the gentlemen trustees permit a nude picture of their daughter or sister, to be hung there; and if not, why anyone else's daughter?' A reply came next day from Fred McCubbin, John Longstaff and six other artists defending 'a work so pure and elevating in sentiment and masterly in execution' and claiming that the only indecency was in the mind of John Russell.* Correspondence raged for weeks. One objected that 'Chloe' broke up family parties which could not possibly look at her in company; another suggested a separate room for such works of art with different visiting-hours for males and females. One jester defended the painting for 'its positively moral tendency': if anything could 'induce a young man to go straightway and commit matrimony, it is the sight of Chloe'.[30] Such publicity made 'Chloe' the centre of attention of the Sunday crowds and Fitzgerald soon requested the return of his painting. 'Chloe' had been immortalized. But Melbourne being Melbourne, she was captured finally as a battle-trophy by the anti-wowsers, to be ogled as a naughty nude rather than a reputable work of art by the patrons of Young and Jackson's Hotel.[31]

In 1884 the Sabbatarians suffered a notable defeat on the Sunday trains issue. They had succeeded in having a clause inserted in the Railways

* Perhaps it should be remarked, for the benefit of lynx-eyed scholars, that John Russell, the artist, was in Europe at the time. The correspondence appears to be serious and not a put-up job.

Construction Act which prevented the Commissioners authorizing Sunday trains on the new lines. But in December, to strengthen the government's hand, the Assembly resolved that it was desirable that the Commissioners should run Sunday trains on all lines at their discretion. The attraction of additional revenue was paramount, perhaps, but the line drawn by the Sabbatarians and by existing custom was so illogical that faint-hearted liberals found courage. Church trains already ran and grain trains in season, and cabs and omnibuses were permitted. Trains ran on the Brighton line but not to Mordialloc, to Essendon but not to Coburg. Why should it be made difficult to visit friends and family, and why should not excursion trains be run after church? Moreover, Sunday trains were general practice in England.[32] The *Argus* was delighted that a burning question was doused, but the Sabbatarians fought back hard. The Commissioners were discreet but, when in 1888 they proposed to run trains to Dandenong, Frankston and Lilydale, Balfour led a deputation of churchmen, including Bishop Goe, to Gillies and threatened to deploy all their political influence. The government weakly compromised and ordered the Commissioners not to run trains to Dandenong and Lilydale.[33] In 1889 the Sabbatarians won again when the Sunday Newspapers Act, which was to remain law for eighty years, was passed. A Sunday Times Publishing Company had been formed, but it suffered from some of its supporters like Gaunson, and naturally was opposed by the existing newspapers. Nevertheless, a full Town Hall meeting, at which members of the Australian Church were prominent, assembled; but its arguments that every large city in the world had Sunday papers, that Sydney had them, that London had twenty, were of no avail.[34]

Temperance

The wowsers had a better case in seeking to reform the liquor laws and drinking habits of the people of Victoria. Consumption of alcohol was not as high as in Britain and Western European countries, even at the height of the boom, but Victorians drank more per head (spirits especially) than New South Welshmen and South Australians, and more than Americans.* Liquor was dearer than in England, and Victorians spent a slightly higher proportion of their incomes on it than New South Welshmen or Englishmen. If we assume, as we conservatively may, that one-quarter of the men in the colony were abstainers or almost so, the average consumption of the majority was very heavy. In 1885 there was one public-house or beer-shop for every 225 people, relatively nine times as many as today—384 pubs in Melbourne City and Carlton alone; moreover, grocers' licences were almost unrestricted. Public-house licences had been stabilized since legislation in 1876; the number remained almost stationary although the population had increased by one-fifth by the mid-eighties.

* Consumption of beer per head was not surpassed until the nineteen-fifties, but modern Victorians consume relatively less than half the amount of spirits, while wine-consumption is similar.

Hotel hours were 6 a.m. to midnight, and the law which had banned Sunday trading in 1854 was honoured more in the breach than in the observance. Arrests for drunkenness rose from 10,000 in 1880 to 18,500 in 1890 and the rate of convictions was slightly higher than in England.[35] Twopeny asserted that, unlike England, it was not just the lower classes who got drunk, but everyone who drank; and drunkards were only pitied, not blamed.[36] Deakin wrote from California that 'alcohol is not used to such an excess as with us. Men here can actually meet, talk, do business, call, and part, without drinking.'[37] Publicans were strong on the Melbourne City Council, and packed the bench as magistrates when their interests were at stake.[38] On the other hand, popular festivals like Eight-Hours Day and Cup Day were relatively sober. 'The Vagabond' once wrote of the Eight-Hours festival: 'Above all there is no drunkenness. People in Australia can be jolly and lively without getting drunk. At a similar gathering in England some would be intoxicated before they arrived, and few would be sober when the time came to go home.'[39] But in general, the traditions of the goldfields slygrogger, the fleecing bush-publican and 'work and burst' prevailed.

Resistance to liquor reform was remarkably strong. The more extreme reformers, though their tactical objectives were usually limited, roused much oppositon because of the fanaticism of their crusade against alcohol as an evil. They were fighting a phenomenon of which they had little understanding. In the nineteenth century over much of the world, secure tenure of long-term employment was uncommon, the state did not provide social services to cushion the impact of mishaps, and life expectancy was shorter and medical protection against disease uncertain. Hence, in their anxiety and insecurity, men more frequently resorted to the stupifying release and temporary escape which alcohol allowed. Some of these factors applied less in the colonies, perhaps, than elsewhere; on the other hand, higher living standards gave the opportunity to drink as never before to the many who knew no better way of using their money. The extreme liquor reformers, whether strong enough to do without alcohol or so warped that they could not enjoy the pleasures of its temperate use, were appalled by the waste of human beings, and especially by their inability to better themselves and attain some security by saving. Such men had to be rescued from their incapacity to think in other than mere subsistence terms. For one of the dominant assumptions of the Victorian age was that workingmen had it in their power to raise themselves to respectability, a higher social class, a higher level of existence, by means of hard work, thrift and abstinence. The alternative, the 'improvers' usually assumed, was further degradation by means of sloth and alcohol.

The temperance and gospel temperance movements were a phenomenon of the United States and Britain in the second half and especially the last quarter of the nineteenth century. Temperance was then used in its correct sense, meaning temperate men, who usually were but were not necessarily total abstainers, desiring to restrict the liquor traffic rather than to prohibit it. By the eighties there was a wealth of temperance organizations in Victoria. The Independent Order of Rechabites, with more than 6,000 members, was the most famous. The Australasian Temperance and General Mutual Life Assurance Society, an offshoot of the Rechabites, had 8,000 policy-holders in Victoria. The oldest educational-propagandist societies were the Melbourne Total Abstinence Society and the Catholic Father Mathew Society, both founded in the early forties. The prohibitionist Good Templars, formed in 1872, were strong, while the Bands of Hope, of Yorkshire origin, dated back to the fifties in Victoria. The Band of Hope Union crusaded for temperance education in the state schools and won some success in legislation of 1889; many an innocent child was coerced into signing the pledge. The most powerful gospel temperance agency was the Blue Ribbon movement which reached Victoria from the United States via England in 1882. Two American evangelists packed the Exhibition building for three weeks in 1884 and a vigorous campaign followed in the suburbs and country towns. 2,000 attended at Ballarat to hear T. W. Glover and the Blue Ribbon Mission Choir; 372 took the pledge and 500 ribbons were distributed, while at Creswick hundreds were crowded out of the meeting.[40] In 1887 another American body was reproduced; the Women's Christian Temperance Union had several branches within the year and went on to a formidable career as guardian of public morals. In 1881, following discussions at an International Temperance Conference held during the 1880–1 Exhibition, the Victorian Alliance for the Suppression of the Liquor Traffic was formed, on the model of Sir Wilfred Lawson's United Kingdom Alliance which had succeeded in bringing in local option in 1880. James Munro was elected president when Higinbotham, who was fully in support and gave regular financial assistance, refused nomination. John Vale was appointed secretary of this federation of temperance bodies, which became a mighty political machine.[41]

Munro was to become almost the representative man of the decade. The son of a tenant farmer, he was born in the Highlands in 1832, became a printer in Edinburgh and migrated in 1858. The iniquity of the clearances of the crofters by the Dukes of Sutherland and Argyle was deeply embedded in his memory. After following his trade in Melbourne for seven years, he launched out to found the Victoria Permanent Building Society, which he managed for sixteen years and nursed into the largest building society in Melbourne. In 1874 he won the Melbourne North seat in the Assembly, was briefly Minister of Public Instruction, and in 1877 defeated the publicans' candidate in his Carlton stronghold. Munro had uncommon energy and vitality, was a consistent democrat and protectionist, and, while making a bid to take over from Berry as popular leader, was organizing the temperance movement which became his political base. In the early eighties he was president of the Alliance, the Total Abstinence Society and the Caledonian Society, and was on the committees of the Rechabites, the Good Templars and the Toorak Presbyterian church. Meanwhile he was founding the Federal Bank (whose notes publicans were instructed not to accept) and beginning the wild land and other speculations which were to ruin him and give him claims to be the most irresponsible boomer of them all. In 1885 he visited Britain for business and health reasons and to study Lawson's methods at the general election; he also urged Lord Derby to introduce total prohibition into New Guinea. When he returned home he campaigned against the sale of wines and spirits at the Centennial Exhibition.[42] This fiery, determined and unscrupulous future Premier never had any doubts of his own moral virtue.[43]

All the churches firmed in active support of the temperance cause in the eighties, when the movement increasingly took on a religious rather than a moral tone. No denomination, however, except the Salvation Army, came out directly to say that alcohol was an unmitigated evil. The Wesleyans were the most firm and far more rigid on this question than in England. From 1874 when a temperance committee of the Wesleyan Conference was formed, the church was solidly united, but after tending towards prohibition moved back to a local-option-temperance position.[44] Presbyterian hostility to the drink traffic grew from 1878 when a temperance committee of the church was established, but the tradition of the dram was strong and many a minister refused to abandon his temperate drop or deny it to his guests. A Ministers' and Elders' Total Abstainers' Society was formed, but most of the clergy would not join.[45] The Anglicans as a body gave less enthusiastic support, and the Catholics less still; however, Cardinal Manning's League of the Cross was reproduced in Victoria in 1888, enrolled 15,000 young Catholics within a year,[46] and went on in the nineties to gather about one-third of the Catholic adherents. Arguments about sacramental wine raged through the eighties, but the use of unfermented wine for communion became general.[47]

Two particular movements stood out in the general anti-liquor crusade. The first was the campaign against the belief of most of the medical profession in alcohol as food and stimulant, especially for fevers, pneumonia, septic diseases and in operation cases. Vast quantities of brandy, wine and stout were habitually prescribed in the hospitals, and some erring souls tended to look on out-patients' departments as free grog-shops. Dr Singleton was the pioneer in opposing the practice and was decried by the whole profession; it appears he was right, though probably for the wrong reasons. By 1880 opinions were changing and, following overseas experience, prescribing of alcohol declined sharply. Singleton and his allies fought hard to set up a temperance hospital from 1883 but, sad to say, the funds they raised were eventually lost in Munro's Federal Bank.[48] The other cause close to the heart was the coffee-tavern and coffee-palace movement. As in England, this was a deliberate, moralistic attempt to provide an alternative to the public-house as the accepted social centre where friends gathered to yarn. In 1878 William McLean, the Baptist ironmonger, J. A. Kitchen, M. H. Davies and others founded the Coffee Taverns Company and opened 'snack bars' at which coffee, tea, cocoa and milk were served. The company did not flourish: only three taverns were operating in 1883.[49] Moorhouse and Higinbotham were similarly hoping to keep workingmen out of the pubs when they sponsored the Workingmen's Clubs movement in 1883. They hoped men would meet in them in a Christian and temperate atmosphere, but the one club which was founded was wound up in 1887 as a lamentable failure.*[50] There was nothing very new about coffee-palaces; Melbourne had had many temperance hotels. What was new was their number and size. The city needed new large hotels, and financiers like Munro and Mirams were quick to anticipate highly profitable business. As Munro put it, 'philanthropy and ten per cent made a very good combination.'[51] The Victoria in Collins Street, accommodating 300 people, was ready for the 1880 Exhibition and the Melbourne (later the Australian) in Bourke Street, holding 250, in 1882. Many more, often of three or four stories, followed in the suburbs and provincial cities; by 1888 there were fifty in Melbourne alone. Many well-to-do non-drinkers moved to live in them for long periods, and others entertained there in luxurious surroundings free from the foulness of alcohol. In 1886, with Balfour, W. L. Baillieu and others, Munro floated a company with £250,000 nominal capital to buy out the recently built Grand (Windsor) Hotel in Spring Street. Legend has it that Munro presided over the opening celebrations and, to abstemious cheers, dramatically set fire to the useless liquor licence. Munro, Mirams and John Nimmo went on to build greater follies: the Federal in Collins Street, the largest of them all, was completed in time for the 1888 Exhibition.[52]

After the formation of the Victorian Alliance the campaign for liquor reform steadily accelerated, with the Wesleyans as mass activists. The press was mostly in support. The *Age*, for once in line with the *Telegraph*, hit hard as always: unless two-thirds of the liquor shops were closed, 'prostitution and the crimes of violence which arise from excess in drink cannot be diminished. So many bars cannot possibly thrive except on the moral ruin of society.' The *Argus* was flippant in support of the liquor interest on general *laissez-faire* grounds: 'It is a matter of dispute whether total abstinence would lead to a social amelioration or universal dyspepsia.'[53] The *Alliance Record* and several minor temperance publications were chock-full of instructive verses and stories detailing the dreadful fate in store for those who fell victims to the demon drink. The temperance cause excelled in producing rollicking songs for its campaign meetings and weekly entertainments in the Temperance Hall. John Vale's lyric to the tune of 'Men of Harlech' concluded:

> See the havoc drink is working,
> Everywhere the danger lurking;
> Shout, your duty never shirking,
> Alcohol shall fail![54]

* The movement was launched at a meeting in the Town Hall of 2,000 people, who were addressed by Moorhouse, Higinbotham, Strong, Berry, Turner, Bromby, Ormond, Coppin, and Bromley and Douglass from the Trades Hall. It was a classic example of Melbourne high-mindedness. The workingmen's clubs in England were fairly successful, possibly because they were often linked with political parties.

The Victorian Navy

Headquarters Staff, Victorian Military Forces, 1884

Governor Sir Henry Loch, family and staff, *c.* 1885

Watsford, the Methodist cleric, wrote 'The Victor's Song':

Shout, Soldiers! Shout the victory!
The day is surely ours,
The Drink Fiend flies before us,
With all his hellish powers.
Now forward, fellow-soldiers,
Nor trust in spears or swords;
All heaven is fighting for us—
The battle is the Lord's.[55]

More ambitious versifiers had their opportunities. The inaugural ode at the 1888 Temperance Conference ran:

Free were these lands from Bacchus power,
Free from the drunkard's loathsome vice
Till Britain's sons in evil hour
Brought in the liquors that entice.
Thence came the dark and saddening strain
Thence came Australia's fatal bane.

Arise, arise, let every state
That bears the one Australian name
Unite with mind and heart elate
To extirpate Australia's shame.
Australia's sons and daughters rise,
Press on the Temperance enterprise.[56]

Extremists in positions of authority did their best to help the cause. Nimmo, as Harbor Trust Commissioner, tried to persuade his colleagues that all applicants for jobs be required to produce the pledge.[57] Nimmo was a devotee of 'Rabbie' Burns: the Legislative Assembly used to wait anxiously to see whether he could, and roar with delight when he did, quote Burns in support of Sabbatarianism and temperance.

At the 1883 election, the Alliance's organization was still relatively ineffectual, though it had many supporters in the Liberal party. By 1886 it was far more formidable, and twenty-nine of the forty-three candidates it backed to the hilt were returned to the Assembly, although hardly any of them stood primarily in the temperance interest.[58] After the 1889 election there were fifty-four reliable supporters of local option, including twenty total abstainers.* From early in the eighties, ministers were regularly beleagured by deputations complaining about the police and magistrates, pleading for enforcement of the Sunday trading law and for legislation for local option; a resolution in favour of local option first passed the Assembly in 1882.[59] In 1884 Deakin and Berry were on the platform,

* The leading parliamentary supporters in the eighties included: Munro, W. Anderson, R. Baker, Balfour, Deakin, Dow, Gordon, Hall, C. J. Ham, D. Ham, J. James, Longmore, Mirams, Nimmo, Outtrim, Richardson, Rose, J. Russell, T. Smith, Williams. The most prominent defenders of the liquor interest were the brewers, Carter and Fitzgerald, and Bailes and Gaunson.

moving resolutions, at the Alliance's annual meeting, and members of the government refused invitations to the annual dinner of the Licensed Victuallers' Association.[60] At last, in 1885 the government was prepared to face the mammoth task of recasting liquor legislation; in the end it took almost the whole parliamentary year to do it.[61] Nearly 600 petitions poured in; Deakin and Nimmo presented one, 1,800 feet long, from 44,501 women who regarded 'the liquor traffic as the most prolific source of broken hearts, ruined homes, and blighted lives, and their sex as the greatest sufferers by these misfortunes'.[62] The *Temperance News* intemperately described licensed victuallers as 'self-poisoning scorpions, vicious venomous snakes, ruffians and rogues'.[63] The watch committee of the Licensed Victuallers' met daily; their friends (or hirelings, it was sometimes alleged) broke up many a temperance meeting.

The Act was far from satisfactory to the Alliance, but put the liquor industry well on the defensive. Hours were shortened only from midnight to 11.30 p.m., but a statutory number of hotels* was fixed, which effectively reduced the number, and a complicated scheme of local option allowed for further reduction with compensation. Hotels could be abolished if one-fifth of the electors petitioned for a poll and a simple majority voted for reduction, provided one-third of the electors voted. Sunday trading was now policed more effectively; fifty-six city publicans were charged on one day in 1887. Deakin wrote prohibition into his legislation for Mildura. The local campaigns proved disastrous for the reformers, for the one-third vote was very difficult to attain, when rolls were inaccurate and the liquor interest advised its supporters to abstain and sometimes intimidated those attempting to vote. In 1887 Parliament once again had to go through long and bitter wrangling—especially between Munro and Carter in the Assembly and Balfour and Nicholas Fitzgerald in the Council—before the one-third clause was revoked.[64] The campaigns began again. At Port Melbourne the crusading Methodist, A. R. Edgar, and his supporters were pelted at open-air meetings by the publican party with flour-bombs, dirt, stones and rotten eggs, and their speeches were drowned by hearty choruses of 'Here's to the good old beer! Drink it down'; but they reduced the number of hotels from forty-eight to twenty-four. At Ballarat East a large majority was found to eliminate forty-five pubs and leave only twenty-seven. At the declaration of the poll the victors fervently sang the Doxology and the National Anthem. The temperance men won five and lost six contests up to September 1888.[65] But even when defeated, the liquor interest often found technical loopholes in the law relating to compensation, and many condemned hotels continued in business. Within a few years the Alliance was abandoning local option polls and campaigning again for drastic reform.[66] In this conflict of extremes, there was no inkling on either side that it was possible and desirable to make the pub a respectable, comfortable, cheery and fairly sober place.

* One to 250 people in a district for the first thousand people, and one per 500 thereafter.

Morals

Prostitution, or 'the social evil' as it was almost invariably termed, was too bewildering and embarrassing a phenomenon for most of the evangelicals to face. In the seventies Melbourne was still, as George Meudell put it, a roughish town, 'wide open and frankly immoral' with blatant and largely uncontrolled prostitution.[67] One of the bars at the Theatre Royal, the 'Saddling Paddock', was notorious, as was Stephen Street and the 'back slums' around it; Stephen Street was cleaned up in 1879–80 and had its name changed, because it was the main way to the Exhibition. The top of Lonsdale Street became the next centre, and although police applied some coercion in 1883 there were still said to be forty brothels in the one block in 1884. The number of prostitutes was somewhere between the 400 (and 69 brothels) known to the police in 1884 and the 2,000 asserted by Methodist spokesmen. The figure of 597 stated in the *Victorian Year Book* was an outrageously smug or dishonest attempt to suggest that Melbourne's rate of prostitution was lower than that in the other capital cities. The extent was not in the least remarkable in terms of London, Paris or American cities, but it may well have been greater than anywhere else in Australia. The number of prostitutes openly soliciting in the main streets at night was the most conspicuous feature. Collins, Bourke and Flinders Streets and Victoria Parade were all mentioned as especially notorious.[68] Some of the Wesley Church congregation would not attend evening service for fear of being offended in the area. There were occasional moves to expose the owners or landlords of brothels. In 1883 some Methodists proposed to nail up the names of relevant property-owners on every church door; in 1884 Nimmo called for penal provisions against notorious landlords who rode to church in their carriages. Later, Randolph Bedford was instructed by his newspaper to list the owners of brothels, but was called off 'because a shining light of Reform, who was also a Cabinet Minister' was heavily involved.[69] From December 1883 to February 1884 the *Herald* exposed the workings of the profession in lurid detail, while sanctimoniously protesting its moral highmindedness. It did name a few entrepreneurs, at least one of whom was subsequently charged and gaoled. Moreover, the *Herald*'s publicity and support from the evangelicals led the police temporarily to toughen their attitudes.[70]

The evangelicals did not campaign consistently on the 'social evil', although the Wesleyan *Spectator* had much to say about it. Some Protestant ladies started refuges for their fallen sisters, but in this field the Salvation Army, Dr Singleton, and the nuns of the Good Shepherd Convent at Abbotsford stood out.[71] No change was made in the law, and brothels and prostitutes were probably no fewer at the close of the eighties. The police policy had been to remove as many prostitutes as possible from the main streets, not to allow any new houses to be opened, and to suppress the most disorderly.[72] There is little doubt that the problem was much less obtrusive in the late eighties; one visitor who found Melbourne an 'openly and flagrantly immoral city' in 1875 was surprised by how orderly it was when he returned in 1886. In 1887 the Congregational Union's Morality Committee believed that Melbourne was moral compared to European and American cities.[73] But when in May 1889 the famous Madame Brussells was charged with keeping a house of ill fame, she escaped conviction, even though her only defence was that her house was well conducted.[74] The worldly view, that men being what they were there was nothing to be done about prostitution except to prevent it becoming too obvious, had prevailed.*[75]

The reputation of barmaids suffered most in the wowser agitations of the eighties. The royal commissioners on conditions in shops and factories were nearly all temperance men who after superficial enquiry reached damning conclusions implying that the worst conditions in hotels were standard. Many girls of a superior class, they reported, became barmaids because the pay was slightly better than in factories or domestic service. But hotel conditions were disastrous, many hotels were fronts for brothels, and the prostitute class was largely recruited from barmaids. A city missionary had told them:

> As soon as a girl gets rather faded in one house she goes to a house of a lower grade, and down and down, until no publican will have her. The next time you will find her knocking about Lonsdale Street or Little Bourke Street. Then she goes amongst the Chinamen; from thence to the hospital, and then into the grave.[76]

Moorhouse led a deputation to the Chief Secretary, lamenting that girls were used as decoys in the foul atmosphere of bars to induce susceptible men to drink. The Victorian Alliance got up a monster women's petition calling for abolition of the profession. The government submitted, and included a clause in the liquor Bill of 1885 which forbade further engagement of barmaids. After fierce debate the clause was passed, but later after even fiercer argument it was defeated by one vote. However, the reputation of barmaids had been almost irretrievably ruined. The issue remained alive for years, while the churches continued to condemn the employment of women in such conditions and the Women's Christian Temperance Union sought out individuals and implored them to change their calling.[77]

Another great cause which came to nothing was protection of women from 'seducers'. Throughout the early eighties there was sporadic agitation, reflecting the English movement, to make 'seduction'—getting young un-

* The Public Health Conservation Act of 1878 was an ineffective attempt to compel prostitutes suffering from venereal diseases to undergo medical treatment. But a combination of squeamishness, vindictiveness to sinners, and old-fashioned views on the liberty of the subject prevented any further state action to control venereal diseases. Despite pressure from the Central Board of Health, the police and the *Age*, the government would not set up a Lock Hospital in 1885, but tried to pass the matter to the Salvation Army. The *Age* courageously and sensibly argued that it was a question of public health and not of morals (21 Feb. 1885, edit.).

married women or girls pregnant—a criminal offence. Apart from resentment at the natural injustice of males escaping the consequences, it was widely assumed that the victims, being ruined, commonly became prostitutes. The press gave full sensational details of cases of suicide, infanticide and concealment of birth. In Ballarat early in 1884 more than one thousand married men met, following the suicide of a pregnant girl, to demand legislation against seduction and abduction; Bishop Thornton detected a 'growth of seduction in the colonies'.[78] Later in 1884 Moorhouse led one of several deputations requesting a raising of the age of consent from twelve to fifteen or sixteen. The Congregationalists, backed by the *Telegraph*, wanted to raise the age to eighteen, or twenty-one in the case of domestic servants or other employees seduced by a master, and also recommended making brothel-keeping and soliciting criminal offences.[79] The government was not eager to enter so controversial a field, but in 1885 prepared a Bill which was based on current English proposals and a recently passed Act in South Australia. It still might not have moved, but for the coup of W. T. Stead in England who, to force action, purchased a girl of thirteen from her mother for £5, kept her overnight (unharmed), and shipped her to the Continent (actually to a Salvation Army officer). Although he was imprisoned, he roused such an outcry that an Act was quickly passed raising the age of consent from thirteen to sixteen and making it an offence to procure a girl under twenty-one. Stead's sympathizers, led by the Salvation Army, thronged the Melbourne Town Hall to send a message of sympathy.[80] Under pressure from most of the churches and the Society for the Promotion of Morality, the government proceeded with its Bill which was introduced in the Council by James Campbell, the Methodist Postmaster-General who had chaired the Town Hall meeting. The Bill provided for raising of the age of consent to sixteen, penalized brothel-keepers, and attempted to define seduction. The Council passed an amended version of the Bill, but it was too late in the year for the Assembly to deal with it.[81] The Gillies-Deakin government dodged the issue in the following four years, although legislation was passed in most of the other colonies, and it was not until 1891 that the age of consent was raised to sixteen. Some members of the Council had found the Bill 'vile, unwholesome, or suggestive'[82] and, indeed, many moralists were convinced that, in this as in other fields, to draw attention to immorality would only increase it.[83]

Moorhouse, especially, was perturbed by the moral dangers in cities: Melbourne was particularly dangerous because so many were living away from home. Immorality was an even greater danger than drunkenness, largely because of the 'warmer sun', the 'southern climate', and the accessibility of 'lonely forests'.* The struggle for purity was the great struggle of the day. He was appalled by French decadence, exemplified in Zola's novels—'indulgence of animal passion and the glorification of carnal luxury'. The 'fleshly school', 'an aestheticism which has for its heart the

* Did he know his Byron?, one wonders: 'What men call gallantry, and gods adultery, / Is much more common where the climate's sultry.'

heart of a beast', was making an impact in England and some of its apostles had visited Australia. In a public lecture in 1883 he appealed to his audience:

> Oh, Christian men and women, do your best to help and protect our young men of all classes who are subjected in this city to temptations which are well-nigh intolerable. Make your homes bright. Give your sons amusements there in which they can ask the steady youths and pure maidens of their acquaintance to partake. Frown down the evil where-ever you see it, and refuse to tolerate those who notoriously commit it. Create clubs for young men who have got no homes. . . . Cleaner homes, larger homes, homes which belong to those who dwell in them; let us do our utmost to multiply these. . . . Such homes, with the truth of God to lighten, and the love of Christ to warm them, will do more than anything else to preserve this great city, so justly dear to many of us, from the fate of Great Babylon, with her grandeur and her pauperism, her cultivation and her immorality, her pride and her ruin.

Moorhouse believed in frankness, in organizing resistance to evil, and fighting it back. In being so frank, he may have done something to break down the conspiracy of silence on any discussion of sex. In 1884 he followed the British example of the previous year by founding the White Cross Union for young men of his church. A member was required to promise that he would

> treat all women with respect, that he will frown down on all obscene conversation, that he will never defile his eyes with foul pictures or literature, that like a knight and hero he will defend the weak and ignorant, at personal risk if need be, from the attacks of villains formidable for their craft or wealth.

'Fight down the ape within you,' Moorhouse exhorted his young knights.[84]

On few subjects, obviously, has the historian less evidence on which to build. It may be, however, that Moorhouse was rather alarmist, as he sometimes was. Archibald Forbes, a famous visiting journalist, found the 'decorum of social life' to be 'marked and beautiful'; 'the tone of conventional decency' was 'rigidly accentuated'. There were few domestic scandals, and they rarely reached the light of day, and there was little dirty-mindedness among the men. No man wanting to keep a place in Society would dare to flaunt a mistress, and ladies did not discuss scandal in their drawing-rooms. Henry Handel Richardson recalled that in her youth 'a nice woman was forbidden even to damp down the shine on her nose'. Deakin was shocked by the profligacy of English high society and was probably glad that Australia had no aristocracy to set a bad example.[85] There are occasional hints of domestic irregularities among public men, and, of course, there were thousands of men and women who defied the code. *Table Talk* deplored the fact that 'a good many females of doubtful character—or rather of no character at all—were among the guests at the Jubilee Ball at Government House'.[86] The illegitimacy rate of 5 per cent of all births was lower than in Britain and broadly similar to most periods of the twentieth century. In view of the near-impossibility of divorce, the several thousand women whom the census-takers found living in concubinage are no cause for surprise. The tiny numbers of those arrested for 'unnatural offences', or intention to commit, are not significant.

We may assume that the sexual *mores* of middle class England and Catholic Ireland broadly applied: sex was an embarrassing, taboo subject upon which many youths and most girls ventured in practice in near-total ignorance, and the code forbade a decent man to lay a hand upon a decent woman unless with matrimonial intent. The middle class custom of men delaying marriage until they could keep their brides in the circumstances to which they were accustomed made extreme demands on continence. The extent of the legendary manifestations of prudery may be questioned. But public statues were disfigured with plastic fig-leaves, 'Kiss in the Ring' was banned at some church picnics, euphemisms were sometimes used for the inflammatory words, 'leg' or 'bed'. It was widely understood that women were not expected to gain pleasure from the sexual act, and many probably did not. Some people also believed that sex for pleasure, other than for procreation, was wrong: but when Mrs Harrison (Bessie) Lee, the Colonial Evangelist of the Women's Christian Temperance Union, created a sensation by writing to the *Herald* to proclaim this belief (admittedly in extreme terms), her employers were forced to part with her.* The extent of prostitution in the Victorian era was in part a reflection both of the frequent dissatisfaction of the marriage-bed and the demands of continence made upon youth. Yet it is impossible to believe, of this period when the family was sacrosanct and often very happy and when married love was never held in such high honour, that instinct did not frequently triumph over ignorance, prudery and the conspiracy of silence. The unregenerate working class, moreover, was to some extent immune from the *Zeitgeist*, for servant-girls, it appears, were not infrequently the willing victims of the 'master' or the 'young master', and part of the objection to larrikins was how often they could be 'seen sitting with girls in the gardens in a way that should not be allowed for a moment'.[87] Chaperonage was not the common rule, as the number of 'sweethearts' promenading in the weekends clearly showed.[88]

The evangelicals, especially the Methodists, would allow no compromise on dancing or the theatre. Dean Macartney asserted in 1888: 'Skating

* 'Fearlessly do I declare that what is a sin before marriage, is still a sin after Christ's words have bound a man and maid together, and that the Divine Command, "Increase and multiply", should be divinely regarded and obeyed, but not made the excuse of marital sin. It is utterly out of all human or divine reasoning to believe that a man and woman must be spotless and pure up to the day of their marriage, that then the words so grand and beautiful, binding them together in holy companionship for mutual help and love, at once opens the way for unbridled liberty. Impossible!' (*One of Australia's Daughters*, p. 119.) Her book, *Marriage and Heredity* (Melb., 1894) sold many thousand copies.

rinks were a curse. They combined all the abominations of the theatres, ball rooms, and low music halls. As to dancing, Herod's daughter was bad enough, but she did not dance with a man's arm around her waist.'[89] The Methodist press, month after month, declared that dancing was worldly, non-Christian, involved discreditable handling of ladies, was performed to vulgar music, led to temptation to indulge in intoxicants, made its devotees unfit to discharge their duties next day, and was often the origin of the ruination for life of virtuous young females.[90] Many Methodist and Presbyterian clergy similarly fought last-ditch stands against the evil influence of the theatre and its sexual excitement:

> It is wrong to cross the threshold of an institution three-quarters of whose influence is pernicious and poisonous. Its very advertisements are an appeal to lust. What is the idea of exhibiting young women, not only improperly but indecently clothed—so clad to the eye of the audience they seem, and are meant to seem, almost naked? Does anyone need to be told why? Simply to breed lust and furnish candidates for the brothel.[91]

The bigots were regrettably incapable of making any distinction between the art of the theatre and the cruder displays of vaudeville and the music-halls.

The cause of sexual enlightenment was left almost entirely to Symes and the Secularists. Since they saw the moral code as a simple reflection of Christianity, they attacked existing assumptions more in passing than directly; in so far as they considered sexual ethics, their chief plea was for honest and open study and discussion in place of inhibited secrecy. Compared with Bradlaugh, Symes did not pay much attention to birth control, although he lectured on it occasionally, and the *Liberator* was almost the only journal which printed the basic texts and advertisements for contraceptive devices. In 1888 Symes published a local edition of Knowlton's *Fruits of Philosophy*, no doubt in the hope that he would be prosecuted like Bradlaugh. It is not possible to make any more than the broadest conjecture about the development of that great furtive movement. It is probable that the spread of knowledge was very slow and perhaps twenty years or more behind England or the United States; no effect on the Victorian birth-rate can be discerned before 1900. Serious discussion of sexual matters was almost non-existent. One rare exception was an *Argus* editorial of 1884 which attacked the conspiracy of silence:

> In our anxiety to be decorous . . . children grow up to puberty in complete ignorance of subjects affecting their future health, character and welfare; and our ethical codes are incomplete as regards precepts and counsel adapted to strengthen the foundations of morality where all experience proves them to be weakest. . . .[92]

But the taboo prevented further discussion. All the daily press, in varying degree, knew that immorality was news and exploited the subject sensationally, printing full gory details of divorces, sexual assaults and girls in distress, while preserving in most cases a hyprocritical tut-tutting façade. Only the *Liberator*, the Melbourne correspondents of the Sydney *Bulletin*, and inferior journals like the *Melbourne Bulletin* (1880–6) and *Truth* (1884) ridiculed the respectable pious on matters relating to sex.[93]

The puritans paid surprisingly little attention to book censorship. A Victorian version of Lord Campbell's Obscene Publications Act of 1857 was adopted in 1876 to counter a 'police budget' type of publication and was adequate to check cheap smut. For the rest, it seemed sufficient to rely on the good taste of publishers, booksellers, librarians and the general reader. The challenge of French naturalistic writing, however, was too much; encouraged by successful prosecutions in London, deputations waited on the government in the mid-eighties. Early in 1887 Customs seized some Zola novels, and for once *Age* and *Argus* agreed with the *Telegraph* that it was right to prohibit such filth. When the Brighton Free Library was opened, Higinbotham advised excluding realistic French novels, and Maurice Brodzky, editor of *Table Talk*, observed that 'the undisguised obscenity of Emile Zola and Paul de Koch simply disgusts the robust morality which is generally inseparable from the Anglo-Saxon character'.[94] The first of many major debates on censorship in Victoria occurred in 1889 when Patterson, the Minister for Customs, seized 162 volumes of French works which E. W. Cole was importing for sale. When these 'boulevard novels' were sent for advice to Pearson, as Minister for Public Instruction, he passed only Daudet's *Sappho*, and advised that works by de Maupassant, Zola and others were of immoral tendency.[95] No systematic policy was followed out, however, and another forty years were to pass before governments seriously began to protect citizens from literature.[96] Curiously also, there was relatively little campaigning against gambling, which was so to pre-occupy Methodists of the next generation. In 1883 and 1886 laws were passed, first to prohibit advertising of, then to ban entirely, racing and other sweeps. Operators moved to Sydney and flooded the mails. Perhaps there was some conscious recognition that gambling was too far-reaching a question to pursue in this particular period. A final field in which it appears that the law was very active was anti-swearing. George Augustus Sala, a visiting lecturer, wrote to the *Argus* to say it was nonsense to claim that bad language was unduly common in Australia, as he had been told, and that he was staggered by magistrates imposing fines of up to £5 for profane or indecent language. There was little to be said in favour of 'the well meant but unwise attempt violently to coerce human nature into being sober, moral, devout, civilly spoken'.[97]

The extent of wowser influence

The chief agency which attempted to coerce human nature by means of government action was the Society for the Promotion of Morality. The supposed crisis of morals united the Protestant churches at last in common action. The Society had been founded by Bishop Perry in 1869 with

Dr Singleton as secretary, but had become inactive when Perry left. Late in 1882 it was resuscitated with Moorhouse as president, Singleton as secretary again, Dean Macartney and Sir William Stawell as vice-presidents, and Balfour, Bromby and the Baptist and Independent ministers, Chapman and Hamer, on the committee. The Wesleyans, who had formed a committee of public morality at their 1882 conference, were also represented. The Promotion of Morality committee spent many days in January and February 1883 inspecting the 'back slums'; they were shocked especially by the Chinese dens with *de facto* European wives in residence.[98] This activity by the Society perhaps marks a shift of opinion towards recognition that social conditions, as well as inherent human weakness, had something to do with promoting immorality. For the rest of the decade, the committee lobbied the government to request the closing down of brothels, legislation to protect women, policing and reform of the liquor laws, and book censorship. They supported the coffee-tavern and coffee-palace movement, the foundation of workingmen's clubs, improved housing for labourers, and establishment of an 'inebriate retreat for confirmed drunkards of the poorer class'.[99] In 1886 the Victorian Christian Alliance was formed by about twenty clergy and laymen to protect the Sabbath and social purity, to defend the Gospel against enemies, to care for outcasts in the slums, to work for liquor reform and to educate the public to 'regard moral worth as essential' for its political representatives.[1] In 1887 the Y.M.C.A. founded another Association for the Promotion of Morality.[2] The Evangelistic Association, formed in 1883, was yet another interdenominational body, in which Balfour again was prominent; after its first conference, members dispersed into the streets and induced passers-by into the Temperance Hall for a service. Six years later, its annual meeting was told that in the previous year sixty-two missions had been undertaken—to shearers in the Western District, navvies on the waterworks and the Healesville railway, and many more.[3] In 1888 a society was formed to supply a copy of the Bible to every room in every hotel.[4] The Catholics took no part in such activities, but some of their spokesmen were as rigid as any Protestant wowser. J. F. Hogan, the schoolmaster who became an Irish member of the House of Commons, took the firm line that popular tastes had to be corrected: the theatre was licentious and should be censored, football was a brutalizing pastime, and London was a sinful city where the pubs were open on Sundays and women were allowed into bars.[5]

The wowsers' achievements in the eighties were not very extensive. They did not succeed in introducing the Bible into the state schools; they kept the Public Library, Gallery and Museums closed on Sundays, but strict Sabbatarianism was declining; reforms in the liquor laws were limited; they had little effect on prostitution except to make it much less conspicuous. They were to have much more success in the early years of the twentieth century, when the Methodists especially were a more able and vigorous crusading force. They were strong enough to set the tone in politics and the press on moral issues; yet politicians as a whole rejected their notion of the state as a moral being and their attempts to purify and mould public life in their own image. Worldly men doubted the wisdom of attempting to make men moral by Act of Parliament. Like the young Patrick McMahon Glynn, many of them despised the evangelicals' 'shallow prudence and contemptible prurience'[6] and recognized the fear of pleasure which characterized so many of the moralists for what it was—the sad belief that worldly enjoyment was incompatible with spirituality.[7] Nearly all the evangelicals were, indeed, blind and deaf to intellect and the Arts, and in their anti-intellectualism and philistinism they made a notable contribution to Australian history. The *Southern Cross* habitually sneered at 'persons of culchah and advanced opinions'; Nimmo brushed off study as a 'weariness of the flesh'.[8] In their narrow conformism, they reached for their Bibles to refute any serious theological suggestion. With some reason, the liberal Dr Bevan of the Independent Church considered 'thought and its utterances were less free' than in England.[9] Yet they were admirable in their concern to do right, whatever the consequences, and were the mainstay of opposition, for example, to the exploitation of non-European labour. And they were admirable too in the way they gave to charity and gave themselves to those in distress. It may be that because of the relative absence of the destitute and distressed in Victoria, the evangelicals were attracted into the area of reform of public morals rather than the relief of private misfortune. But they were following closely the pattern of their British brethren.[10] In the strength of its wowsers Victoria was more like Britain than other colonies; and if Melbourne gained a unique reputation in Australia for wowserism, the real problem to ponder may be why the evangelicals made less impact in most of the other capital cities and colonies.

Nationality

6

Crisis in the Pacific and the Campaign for Federation, 1883–1887

New Guinea, the New Hebrides and the federal Convention

On 14 June 1883 about one thousand Victorians and New South Welshmen—the Governors, members of Parliament, clergy, judiciary, businessmen and other notables—assembled in the engine-shed at Albury station to celebrate the linking of the two colonies by rail. Edison incandescent lamps dispelled the wintry gloom, flowers covered the pillars and tables, and on high an allegorical painting displayed Victoria and New South Wales clasping hands in unity, while behind them an engine was crossing a bridge. Unfortunately the Victorians wore morning dress and the New South Welshmen evening dress. But there was no confrontation: when each discovered his place at the tables, he found he had representatives of the other colony on either side. Lively chaff about the superiority of one colony over the other and the possibility of federation naturally followed until the speechifying began. Old Sir John Robertson was genially uncompromising: Victoria had separated when she was rich and New South Wales poor, but the mother colony bore no ill-will, would gladly embrace her daughter again, and let bygones be bygones. Alexander Stuart, the Premier, was far more enthusiastic and was heartily cheered when he said he was looking forward to federation. However, Service made the speech of the day, and the Victorians shook the roof when he said:

> We have been long separated, and rivalries and jealousies and ignorance of each other have sprung up in consequence; but now we are looped together with bands of iron. . . . Gentlemen, we want federation and we want it now. . . . I decline to subscribe to the doctrine that I am to die before the grand federation of the Australian colonies. There is no earthly reason why it should not be achieved . . . I tell my honorable friend, the Premier of New South Wales, that at a very early opportunity . . . we intend to test this question. The Government of Victoria have determined to send a message to New South Wales asking them what are the obstacles that stand in the way?[1]

Thus the challenge was made. The fraternal spirit held up well through the fifteen speeches, invitations to new friends were freely made to travel on for a couple of days in Melbourne or Sydney, and Stuart accompanied

Service to Melbourne for further talks about the possibility of federation and the current New Guinea and New Hebrides crises.[2]

When in mid-April the news of Queensland's dramatic annexation of New Guinea had broken, the *Age* exulted:

> The timorous policy which fears any further extension of the British Empire finds no echo here. There is no reason why that large and fertile island should not be made a new field for immigration, or why the great colonising race of Englishmen should be debarred from replenishing this magnificent wilderness. The enterprising spirit of the times of Raleigh, Frobisher and Drake,
>
> Adventurous hearts who bartered bold
> Their English steel for Spanish gold
>
> is not yet dead.[3]

Service immediately wired his Agent-General in London to 'promptly and earnestly support' Queensland's action and urged the other Premiers to do likewise; Stuart acquiesced. It seems that neither Service nor other Australasian Premiers had been consulted by Sir Thomas McIlwraith. Victoria had little direct interest in New Guinea and, although she had joined the other colonies in urging the imperial government to annex Fiji in the early seventies, her politicians had been far less conscious than those of New South Wales of Australia's possible destiny in the Pacific. Melbourne's trade with the Islands was negligible, not one-tenth of Sydney's. When in 1874 and 1875 the Royal Colonial Institute campaigned for annexation of New Guinea and the Colonial Office sounded out the colonies, the Victorian government made no official response, whereas the Robertson ministry in New South Wales urged a wholesale policy of annexation in the Pacific. A few wild men in the business world (including Hugh McColl and Benjamin Dods, the irrigationists) formed a Colonization Company in 1878 and planned to seek a royal charter for settlers to exploit New Guinea's undoubted rich mineral resources and to 'lay out the lands in plantations, farms or stations'. Then, believing that Britain was on the point of annexing eastern New Guinea and handing it over to one of the colonies, they requested Parliament to claim the territory and 'the remaining islands of Australasia' as well, on the grounds of Victoria's relatively small area and large population.[4] However, Berry, as Premier, believed acquisition of New Guinea would be of doubtful value, and enthusiasm died with the failure of the minor gold rush of 1878 and disillusioning reports about the island. Now in mid-1883 there was an attempt to revive the company, and shipping interests and sugar investors with an eye to labour needs were also interested. But such influences on government were unimportant in comparison to the agitation roused by the expansion of German trading interests from Samoa to New Britain and New Ireland and by commercial and journalistic pressure on Bismarck to colonize New Guinea.[5]

While the colonies anxiously waited for the British reaction to Queens-

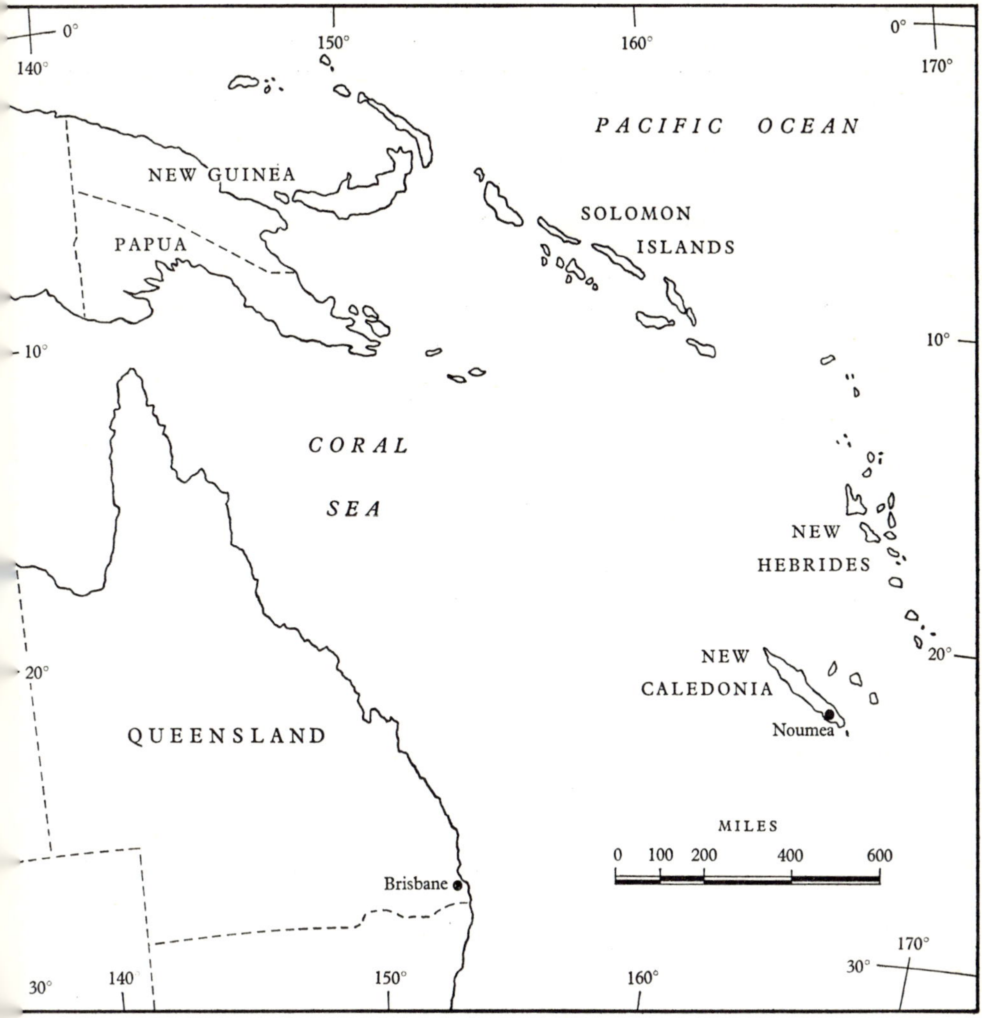
0°
150°
160°
0°
140°
170°
PACIFIC OCEAN
NEW GUINEA
PAPUA
SOLOMON
ISLANDS
10°
10°
CORAL
SEA
NEW
HEBRIDES
NEW
CALEDONIA
20°
20°
Noumea
QUEENSLAND
MILES
0 100 200 400 600
Brisbane
170°
30°
30°
140
150°
160°

land's bold action, a further complication arose: the campaign by the Presbyterian mission to the New Hebrides for British annexation of all South Sea Islands not under foreign control was adopted by the Victorian government. Already on 18 April a Cabinet member had stated the government's intention to work for a British protectorate or at least prevention of French annexation.[6] On 6 June Service received a deputation of leading missionaries, prominent Wesleyans, and Presbyterian and nonconformist parliamentarians. Having been assured that France was on the point of annexing the islands, he quickly persuaded the other Premiers to agree to send a deputation of the Agents-General to the Colonial Office to lobby on both the New Guinea and New Hebrides questions.[7]

The New Hebrides had long been the chief mission-field of the Victorian Presbyterians and since 1857 the headquarters of the Reverend John G. Paton, a saintly and single-minded evangelical with a gift for public relations and fund-raising. By 1871 twelve stations had been established in the island-group. The area was notoriously exploited by 'blackbirders', and the mission had from 1862 petitioned for a British protectorate and whipped up Victorian feeling against the semi-slave trade. The establishment of the Western Pacific High Commission based on Fiji did not satisfy the missionaries, who were becoming alarmed about the threat of French settlers from the neighbouring convict colony, New Caledonia. They petitioned again and again for a British protectorate, and in 1877 convinced Graham Berry of the justice of their case. However, he lost interest when in 1878 the French and British governments agreed in an exchange of notes that neither would annex the islands.[8] In the early eighties arguments sharpened over land-ownership, trading rights and French influence on the natives. Indeed the missionaries had cause to worry, for John Higginson, English-born but a naturalized Frenchman long resident in Noumea, who saw his life's work as the capture of the New Hebrides for France, had gained promises of support from leading French politicians; in 1882 he formed a company in New Caledonia to colonize the New Hebrides.[9] The Presbyterians redoubled their pleas. Service, at least, was now completely convinced: 'politics, religion, commerce, civilization, humanity', all pointed in the same direction.[10] His Governor, Lord Normanby, told him he could give no support; the movement was strategically unnecessary. Meanwhile, as the Agents-General prepared to see Lord Derby at the Colonial Office, news of the 'Australian annexation movement' produced uproar in Noumea, where the Governor was urged to annex the New Hebrides immediately. The men on the spot were beginning to force the hands of the metropolitan powers.

It was by no means certain that Queensland's annexation of New Guinea would be ruled out of order. The Colonial Office, especially the permanent Under-Secretary, Sir Robert Herbert who had been the first Premier of Queensland, had recognized for some time that New Guinea must in the long run be regarded as vital to Australia. For some weeks Derby treated the question as an open one; other Cabinet members—Childers, Dilke and Chamberlain—were inclined to be sympathetic; Queensland had some support in the press and from the Conservative spokesman on colonial affairs, the Earl of Carnarvon; the Royal Colonial Institute lobbied insistently. Assurances were sought and gained from the German and French governments that they had no intentions towards New Guinea. When in May the Italian government intimated that it was considering establishing a penal settlement in New Guinea, it was firmly warned off; fortunately, perhaps, the colonies heard nothing of this. But Gladstone remained obdurate. The colonies were told that annexation was out of the question for the moment, but might be considered if they federated and arranged to cover all costs. Meanwhile, it might be possible to extend the protection of the Western Pacific High Commission to New Guinea by strengthening the naval force on the Australian station. Fears about the New Hebrides were brushed aside, for the agreement with France was regarded as absolutely binding.[11]

Service and McIlwraith and their governments had expected the worst and were ready to move together, not only to try to produce an agreed Australian policy in the Pacific but to make a deliberate attempt to bring about federation. 'I agree with you', Service wired McIlwraith, 'that Imperial proposal is quite inadequate. . . . "Federation and all the islands" should be our watchword.'[12] On 11 July Service gained parliamentary support for his annexationist policy. His authority was such that his resolutions passed both houses without dissent in one evening. It was agreed that 'New Guinea and the Pacific Islands lying between New Guinea and Fiji including the New Hebrides should be annexed to the British Crown or that England should establish a protectorate over them'; and Parliament consented to carry the costs. Service asserted that every man in Australasia had an 'intense desire that this question should once and for all be settled'. 'The islands of Australasia ought to belong to the people of Australasia'; the colonies, having reached the age of puberty though not of manhood, were entitled to ask the mother country to act for them. There was little worry yet about the defence of Australia but they must look to the future and prevent the conversion of the Pacific into another Europe, an armed camp with a 'variety of nationalities . . . each one armed to the teeth against the other'; peace must be assured for future generations. Service was thinking primarily of menace from the French, for he dwelt on the dangers of tolerating convict settlements in the Pacific which might become a 'cesspit' where European nations dumped their 'refuse'. Nor did he overlook potential trade benefits if the islands were under British and not French rule. He was supported in the brief debate mainly by Presbyterians fearing a triumph by their Catholic rivals.[13] A rally in a half-filled Melbourne Town Hall followed on 16 July. The speakers were chiefly Presbyterian and nonconformist politicians and clergy. But George Higinbotham had been captured for the evening to give the main speech supporting annexation; and he dwelt chiefly on the evils of the labour traffic.* He concluded by warning that although the entry of European powers into the Pacific appeared to be damaging to the Empire, the colonies should abandon all agitation if the imperial government decided against an annexationist policy.[14]

A couple of days later, newpaper cables appeared which raised agitation to a new pitch. Vague rumours over the previous months were confirmed: the French government had introduced legislation by which it was proposed to increase the transportation of criminals, especially to New Caledonia. It was suggested that 20,000 of France's worst criminals, officially described as 'dangerous, steeped in vice, debauchery and crime', should be transported there for life in the next four years. Some speakers had wanted the New Hebrides to be annexed and convicts sent there also.[15]

Few things could have provoked the colonies more. Escaped convicts from New Caledonia had been a growing irritation; since 1874 the colonial governments had made regular complaints to the Colonial Office. 250 had been located by the colonial police forces (only 33 in Victoria), hundreds more were believed to be undetected, and the New Caledonian administration had refused all requests for extradition and was believed to encourage emigration to Australia. A magistrate had claimed, unbelievably, that one-sixth of Melbourne's criminal population were Frenchmen from New Caledonia; worse still, some of them had been transported as communists.[16] The question was central to what little national tradition the colonies had. Migrant colonists were acutely sensitive to Englishmen's doubts about their background, were subject from time to time to the sneers of the ignorant and imagined them even when not present. The worst legacy of the convict system was the lasting contamination of the social relationships of Englishmen and Australians.† Determination to cleanse the colonies' reputation had produced major movements of protest. The sustained campaign of the late forties, the Victorian defiance of the imperial veto on legislation to arrest Tasmanian emancipists and

* There was a lively public opinion in Melbourne against the labour traffic, produced partly by Paton's agitation and partly by revelations in the *Age* by young Ernest ('Chinese') Morrison, son of the headmaster of the Presbyterian Geelong College, who had sailed on a blackbirding expedition from Mackay to the New Hebrides. He denounced the trade as slavery and wrote: 'Three of our boys were hauled dead out of the hold with a rope around their neck, within the first thirty-six hours, and four more were flung overboard before the end of the voyage. . . . A nice pretty chaste girl leaves for Queensland, and a year or two later she is sent back to her home an ugly, wrinkled, diseased hag. When a number of women are recruited by a vessel the ship becomes a brothel.' (*Age*, 9 May 1883, p. 7.)

The *Age* from time to time attacked the Queensland government for sanctioning murder and man-stealing. In mid-1883 Syme sent Morrison on an exploring expedition into New Guinea. The *Argus* replied by sending Captain Armit to New Guinea and Stanley James ('The Vagabond') to the New Hebrides.

† Cf. Higinbotham: old colonists 'were made in various ways to feel what the effects of coming to a convict continent were in English opinion. Englishmen looked down upon us; that is, having done us a wrong they really were disposed to despise us for coming to live in contiguity with a community that was criminal.' (*Argus*, 17 July 1883, p. 7.) And Shiels: 'We know how our sensibilities have quivered under the stupid ignorance of our countrymen at home in thinking of us, and in sometimes saying and writing of us, that we are the descendants of convicts.' (*P.D.*, vol. 45, p. 361.)

'bolters', and the campaign led by Victoria in the sixties to abolish transportation to Western Australia were proud features of colonial history.[17] Thus there was now an outraged reaction, and the annexationist movement was greatly strengthened.

On 24 July Service cabled Robert Murray Smith, the Agent-General: 'England must act promptly and firmly. Latest news Noumea shows great danger. Intense indignation here if France is allowed to make New Hebrides cesspool for convicts. Consider this crisis Australian history.'[18] In Parliament he hoped that England would now be roused to a sense of duty. On the 27th he pleaded to the Colonial Office for reconsideration of the whole question of annexation.[19] 'It appears to us incredible', thundered the *Argus*, 'that British statesmen and British philanthropists should stand by and allow these virgin territories—christianised by our martyr missionaries—to be violated by ruffianage from France.'[20] Scores of public meetings throughout the colony and resolutions of local councils, nearly all stressing the convict menace, vehemently assented. Paton stumped the colony for most of the next six months. The press, the Chamber of Manufactures, the Congregational and Baptist churches and, later, the Intercolonial Trade Union Congress, all gave staunch support. It is difficult to judge how much grass-roots enthusiasm there was: government supporters were put to work to produce adulatory local resolutions. But the Governor confessed he had 'never known any question in Victoria which has commanded such universal support'.[21]

The Colonial Office regarded the new French policy on transportation as a matter of serious concern and in August the imperial government made representations to the French government. The immediate consequence, however, was confirmation on 30 August of the agreement that neither power would annex the New Hebrides. Despite the flurry of deputations from and correspondence with the Agents-General, they were not consulted; nor were they or the Premiers informed of the reaffirmation of the agreement for some time. On 31 August the Colonial Office sent a temperate and reasoned reply to the case for wholesale annexation; privately Derby considered the annexationists to be madmen. By now, however, the Colonial Office at least knew from consular and Admiralty advice that the missionaries' reports on local French activities were fairly accurate. Official policy was now to try to induce the French to abandon or modify their convict bill, which had been delayed.[22]

Meanwhile, with great difficulty, Service had been arranging a 'federal convention'. For tactical reasons, he had been happy for McIlwraith to approach the other governments in July. But McIlwraith then had to fight an election which he lost to Griffith, so Service had to make the running. At the Victorian election early in 1883 almost every successful candidate had pledged himself to support federation. The new government immediately decided to adopt the cause and to prepare the ground as much as possible. One of Service's first actions, before the storms broke in the Pacific, was to create a Premier's Department to handle relations with other colonies, the Governor and the Colonial Office, and the Agent-General.[23] Most politicians agreed that Victoria's recent protectionist excesses and especially the behaviour of its delegates at the 1880–1 intercolonial conference, when they had led the opposition to Parkes's proposal for a Federal Council, had been narrowly provincial; the time had come to think in national terms.[24] Previous intercolonial conferences had been largely futile: Service once remarked that of twenty-three subjects dealt with in ten conferences over twenty years only three had been effectively settled, and not one agreement for uniform legislation had been carried out.[25] In May, however, a postal conference in Sydney had been successful; despite immense suspicion, Berry had carried the Victorian government's proposals. Crisis in the Pacific now appeared to make a fruitful move possible.

The other colonies agreed to confer with varying enthusiasm. When Service announced that at McIlwraith's request he was proposing to convene a conference and suggested 25 September in Melbourne, Stuart replied that the time was inconvenient. When Service suggested October or November, he replied with calculated aloofness that his pending land Bill made it difficult for him to agree to any date. Surely, wrote Service, the matter was so important that parliaments should be adjourned. Stuart answered that his government did not feel that federation was as urgent as did Victoria and Queensland, but he had no desire to prevent discussion and would be happy to meet in Sydney. It had been quite evident, retorted Service, and it was surprising, that New South Wales was lukewarm:

> I could understand it so long as we were not threatened with annexation by France of some of the most important of the islands, and with the avowed intention of making them the receptacle for the moral filth of that country; but that any Australian can coolly contemplate an irruption of people into these parts, in comparison with whom the Goths and Vandals were civilised races, is to me quite incomprehensible. But for these two dangers, . . . we might have contented ourselves with nudging the old folks at home. . . . The people of England are at our back. If we are prompt and resolute, the battle is as good as won; if we are cool, or hesitating, or indifferent, I believe the New Hebrides, and probably some of the other groups, will be lost to us.

Stuart, a Gladstonian with no jingoist feeling and not subject to local pressure on the issue, now revealed his position. He was not indifferent to the activities of foreign powers or to the convict threat, but he disagreed basically on methods. He believed that urging annexation of the New Hebrides and violation of the agreement would only encourage France and give her some justification to annex the New Hebrides herself. The best solution would be a British protectorate over New Guinea and a joint protectorate with France over the New Hebrides. Annexation would be costly and contrary to free-trade principles; they would do best to work for a general policy of non-annexation.[26]

The Victorian campaign for annexation of the New Hebrides was stymied when on 17 September the New South Wales government formally dissociated itself. It was clear, also, that the New South Wales government had no intention of federating at this stage and that there was little point in meeting for that purpose. In October Stuart told Service that the meeting would really be just an intercolonial 'conference' and not a 'Convention': 'the Colonies here have not unanimously expressed an opinion that the time has arrived. We have all more or less expressed our opinion that the time will come; but there has been, so far as I can judge, no general consensus of opinion that the time has arrived.' Service must by now have realized that the 'Convention' could not be one of Founding Fathers. He replied that 'the Colonies have already approved of the principle of Federation, and that the business of the Convention will be to discover how far and on what points Federal action can be carried out at present'. At least they could create an organization, with legislative and executive powers to deal with pressing questions, which could develop into a full union.[27] But Service knew that there was no immediate hope of tariff union and recognized that the question could not even be raised.[28] The Victorian government nevertheless believed that external dangers justified and were sufficient to bring about confederation or a limited federation. The government of New South Wales did not.

Delegates from all the colonies' governments, including New Zealand and Fiji, met in Sydney on 28 November for the 'anti-convict' or 'annexation' Convention. On arrival, Service and his fellow delegates, Berry and G. B. Kerferd, and accompanying pressmen were appalled at the lack of interest of the Sydney politicians and press; they and other delegates were not even met at the station. Service tactfully arranged that Stuart, who throughout was to be moderate and conciliatory, should preside over the proceedings. The other New South Wales delegates, W. B. Dalley and George Dibbs, were at first frankly hostile to the purposes of the conference. The Victorians had to be persuaded not to reply to Dibbs's opening speech which seemed to be deliberately provocative. The conference proceeded to discuss rival sets of resolutions by Service and Griffith. Several colonies supported the Victorian policy of wholesale annexation of the Islands by Britain, but the balance of opinion favoured Griffith's view that New Guinea was far more important than the New Hebrides and that the agreement with France must be respected. Nearly all delegates were firmly impressed with the danger of German or French annexations and with the French convict menace, especially the immediate question of escaped convicts reaching the colonies. Hence, while a firm recommendation was made to Britain to annex eastern New Guinea and a crucial guarantee was made to bear 'such share of the cost . . . as Her Majesty's Government . . . may deem fair and reasonable', Britain was urged only to work for control of the New Hebrides. Nevertheless, a resounding declaration was made against any foreign annexations in the Pacific south of the Equator, in the confidence that the imperial government would 'promptly adopt the wisest and most effective measures' to ensure this. Moreover, a firm protest was made against French convict transportation and agreement reached to pass uniform legislation to forbid escapees or time-expired convicts landing in Australia.

The Victorians were half expecting the New South Welshmen to withdraw when the time came to discuss federation, but cordiality was growing, especially between Service and Stuart. Service's remarks, it was said, were sprinkled with 'apposite quotations from Scripture' and 'occasional Scotticisms . . . unintelligible to all but Mr. Stuart who relished them immensely'.[29] And at a Sunday picnic Service made a happy speech, with appropriate praise of the harbour he had seen for the first time and recognition of Port Phillip Bay's inferiority. Service, with Griffith's general support, wanted a true federal government if he could get it, though he said he was asking for no more than a beginning, 'a slight attachment' which would develop into a closer union. No delegate imagined that anything more was possible. Griffith's resolution in favour of a Federal Council similar to that proposed by Parkes three years earlier was agreed to, but when a draft Bill was discussed the proposals were diluted to the point of futility. The vehement protests of Sir John Robertson and others against the creation of any federal body persuaded the New South Wales delegates to hold out against any but the most sketchy arrangements, and even they were hard-won. In the end the Council was to have no executive powers and no revenue. Legislative powers were to cover relations with the Pacific Islands and 'prevention of the influx of criminals', also 'fisheries in Australasian waters outside territorial limits, the service of civil processes beyond the limits of a colony, the enforcement of judgments and of criminal process beyond the limits of a colony, the extradition of offenders, and the custody of offenders on Government ships beyond territorial limits'.*[30] The colonies were to have equal representation, Victoria having led the way in abandoning any claim for greater representation on grounds of population. Before the Council could be formed, the imperial government would have to legislate and at least four colonies pass enabling Acts. Service offered to call a special session of the Victorian Parliament to adopt the Bill as quickly as possible, but deferred to Stuart when he argued that it would be preferable for his government to make the first move. Having agreed that Service should act as executive chairman in any necessary consultation, the Convention amicably dispersed.[31]

Sir William Des Voeux, Governor of Fiji and a delegate, was highly impressed with the 'very great ability' of most of the Convention's mem-

* Many other matters (defence, etc.) could be dealt with if two colonies referred them. Many of the delegates must have been uncertain about how they expected the Council to operate. Service probably thought the most important probable gain was a regular conference at which informal agreement on common action might be reached. In April 1884 he remarked: 'We have no intention that the Federal Council should originate one single law or measure of its own accord.' Despite the lack of executive power he said the intention was to make it an executive body for carrying out laws passed by colonial parliaments. (*Argus*, 24 April 1884, p. 9.)

bers: Australasia 'had reason to be proud of its democratic selection'.[32] Yet, while Service's partial success speaks volumes for his enthusiasm and force of character, the proposed Federal Council was, as Herbert commented in the Colonial Office, a 'very rudimentary and lax arrangement'.[33] Victorian allies like Pearson and John Quick were highly dubious; Deakin in retrospect justly considered it all 'a doubtful gain'.[34] But the Victorian government had now committed its prestige and grimly settled down to fight the issue out.

Berry stayed on in Sydney for a few days and was present at the Speaker's dinner; when asked to speak, he let loose. The way in which the Convention had been spoken of in Sydney over the last fortnight was disgraceful. So was the attitude of the local speakers that night, in their lack of recognition that recent events amounted to 'the greatest work done since Captain Cook discovered the land!' Overriding dissent, Berry went on to make a rousing plea for federation and was loudly cheered at the close of his speech.[35] At another banquet in Melbourne, Service was being characteristically forthright and tactless: 'We felt really as if we were about to perform a great work, and that all the world was looking on. . . . But to our astonishment, when we got to Sydney, we found our friends there fast asleep.' There was 'complete oblivion', 'ignorance' of the fact that a convention was being held to eliminate the possibility of future generations of Australians having 'an enemy dwelling on their borders'. 'I found what I had often heard of . . . and could not have believed without having experienced it, namely, the most intense jealousy on the part of Sydney in respect to Melbourne. . . . We had to do the best we could.' Robertson was warm, earnest, kind-hearted, but antiquated in his ideas with 'curious delusions' about Victorian motives; Dibbs was 'really the greatest enemy we had at the beginning'; Dalley was 'cold' at first; but eventually the delegates, at least, had become enthusiastic about the Federal Council. As was his habit, he concluded by calling for three cheers for friends in New South Wales.[36] Reactions in Sydney were violent: the speech 'almost drove the Sydney people mad', the *Argus* correspondent reported. One parliamentarian announced that New South Wales was as far above Victoria as heaven was above earth, while another spoke of the agreement as a disaster which would have terrible consequences and condemned the 'high treason' of the New South Wales delegates.[37] Deakin in *The Federal Story* refers to this 'one irreparable blunder' by Service which could not be excused:

> a considerable quantity of bitterness was thereafter infused into the always jealous relations of the two colonies. Worst of all, it was made perfectly plain that the Convention . . . had really been Victorian and thus the Federal Council became branded as a Victorian invention. As such it became a point of patriotism with many New South Welshmen to belittle and oppose it.[38]

Deakin was exaggerating, for only those who wanted to be angry were made so; nothing was basically altered.

Victoria and New South Wales

In view of the evident lack of national feeling, Service's campaign of 1883 was obviously premature and ill-prepared. The colonies were still very largely isolated from each other. Certainly, there had been much movement of population from one to another; miners and shearers especially were less prone to take colonial loyalties seriously. Nevertheless, few politicians or businessmen had ever met their equivalents in other colonies, and hardly any knew each other well enough to be friends; Service and Higinbotham set foot in New South Wales for the first time at the Albury celebration in 1883. Few businesses, other than banks, insurance companies and shipping lines, were conducted in more than one colony. The colonial economies were largely insulated from each other; the nationalizing of the Australian economy in the eighties and nineties greatly smoothed the path to federation as the hindrances of colonial borders to day-to-day business became increasingly irritating. Although New South Wales imported much wheat and flour from Victoria and South Australia, and Victoria depended on coal from New South Wales, trading contacts were limited, as the economies were not complementary to any great extent. The sense of intercolonial rivalry, however absurd in retrospect, was keenly felt by politicians, businessmen and press proprietors at least; competition for British capital and migrants left little room for any sense of interests in common. Victoria and New South Wales had not even adopted a common time, which varied by twenty-five minutes. Many New South Welshmen, clutching at pretensions to historical dignity, found it difficult to look calmly on upstart breakaway Victoria whose astonishing progress had rested on the chance presence of gold deposits. Victorians were 'people to be mistrusted', Sir Robert Garran remembered from his childhood.[39] Migrant Victorians knew little and cared less about the supposedly backward 'mother colony';[40] the convict poison operated here too. George Reid recalled in old age that one of the characteristic attitudes of New South Wales politicians

> was the strong suspicion expressed as to the *bona-fides* of Victorian statesmen. . . . The Victorians put our feelings down to jealousy and petty provincialism. But we thought they pushed a proper regard to self-interest to extremes. We used to call our ways British, their style American. As a matter of fact, our 'British' needed quite a lot of their 'American'!

He put the turning-point of rivalry down to the capture by Victoria in 1872 of the P. & O. mail contract which made Melbourne the terminal; after that 'our people cultivated a livelier interest in public affairs'.[41] Robertson was Victoria's most frequent detractor, with his contemptuous references to that 'cabbage-garden' and his paranoid fears that the federal movement was a Victorian plot to capture part of the territory of New South Wales. However, he had some small justification, for Syme was prone to argue in the *Age* that a precondition of federation must be a readjustment of colonial boundaries so that Victoria might regain its lost territory of the Riverina.*[42] The *Age* also sometimes asserted that New South Wales was favoured by the Colonial Office because of its free-trade policy and more compliant loyalty. Social climbers in both colonies were from time to time aggrieved at the distribution of honours to one colony rather than the other. Governments even suspected that their loan prospects in London were sometimes sabotaged by their rivals.[43]

The ideological clash over protection was entering its most intense period. Protection against the other colonies had not originally been envisaged, and until Berry's tariffs of the late seventies there was hope for reconciliation. By now, however, in freetraders' eyes Victoria had made the Murray 'a barrier as effective as the great wall of China to the elevating influences of civilising commerce'.[44] For Robertson, federation meant 'marrying our living free trade to the dead carcase of the protection of Victoria'.[45] Rabid Victorian protectionists would only consider federation with protection as the agreed national policy. The *Age* occasionally showed its true feelings. In its editorial of 30 November 1883, surprisingly written by Pearson,[46] it found 'a natural division' between Victoria and South Australia on the one hand and New South Wales and Queensland on the other:

> A great part of their populations grew up in the days when education was not enforced by the State, and their disadvantage in this respect has placed them at the mercy of the squatters and importers, who together control the legislatures of Sydney and Brisbane. The growth of the sugar plantations in both colonies has promoted the introduction of colored labor, and the lavish expenditure on assisted immigration has introduced a large class of voters who have no knowledge of democratic institutions, and no proper feeling of loyalty to their adopted countries. The proportion of Catholics to Protestants is also larger. . . . Our natural ally would seem to be South Australia. . . . We can . . . develop our own resources without troubling ourselves about our neighbours. In time of peace we have no great need of them, and in time of war it is they who will need to be supported by our arms, fed by our corn, and clothed by our manufacturers.

Such madness and arrogance was, however, hardly typical.

The battle for the Riverina predated the ideological conflict over protection. The Riverina was predominantly settled by Victorians, both squatters and selectors; Victorian governments made every effort to exploit this natural geographic sphere of influence whose boundaries are still

* Syme never gave up. Under his pressure, in 1906 and 1908 the Victorian government took the matter up, and in 1911 made a formal claim on the New South Wales government to the area between the Murray and the Murrumbidgee. The case was extremely weak; the Australian Colonies Government Act (1850) defined the boundary as 'from Cape *Howe* to the nearest source of the River *Murray*, and thence by the Course of that river to the eastern boundary' (of South Australia). A source of the Murrumbidgee is closer to Cape Howe than any of the Murray's sources. See The Claim of the Government of Victoria to the Territory . . . [Riverina]. Report by the Solicitor-General of New South Wales (Ferguson Coll., NL); Syme to H. B. Higgins, 4 Oct. 1905, Higgins Papers.

defined by the predominance of brand of beer and code of football. Control of Riverina trade, it was believed, meant more business done in Melbourne and greater status and prosperity for the colony. So the first major trunk railway out from Melbourne was extended on from Bendigo to reach Echuca in 1864, and the north-east line was hurried on to reach Wodonga in 1873. Victorian capitalists were even permitted to construct a Victorian-gauge line from Moama to Deniliquin. The New South Wales counter-attack began from the mid-seventies; the main line slowly snaked down to reach Albury in 1881 and the branch to Hay was opened in 1882. Meanwhile both colonies adopted a policy of differential freight rates; Victoria charged half or less the standard rates on Riverina wool coming down to Melbourne and on commodities consigned to north of the Murray.[47] Victoria pressed on with new lines to the Murray. In 1886 New South Wales began running early newspaper-trains to the Riverina at considerable financial loss to combat the insidious influence of the Melbourne papers.[48] So the wasteful competition, which had such serious financial implications, proceeded.[49]

Perhaps the greatest irritant of all was the tax on stock brought into Victoria. The motivation of the tax which Berry imposed in 1877 was devious and largely to be explained in terms of internal politics, but it was also the most conspicuous act of aggression in a series of ruthless retaliatory moves following the breakdown of the 'free border' agreement between the two colonies, which had lasted from 1867 to 1873. When a Victorian minister visited Sydney in 1879 in the hope of patching up a new agreement, Parkes insisted that first the stock tax be repealed; negotiations broke down.[50] Then at the 1880–1 intercolonial conference, the Victorians brushed aside Parkes's proposal for a Federal Council.

There was some reason why many in Sydney reacted with surprise and suspicion to the Victorian initiative of 1883. The Victorian government nevertheless had had a change of heart and its motives were relatively pure. It resolved at least not to aggravate the problem of diverging tariffs, but despite its apparent assured control of Parliament, it was constantly threatened by the demands of extreme protectionists, farming representatives and the *Age*. Much though it would have liked to eliminate protectionist excesses which were irritating to other colonies, it was in no position politically to do so. It was known that smuggling was rife; the barbarous searching of travellers at Wodonga or Spencer Street station was bad publicity for the colony.[51] Hostility in the Riverina because of the stock tax was producing commercial retaliation; yet even when the protectionist-dominated royal commission on the tariff recommended abolition of the stock tax in 1883, the government took no action for fear of rural interests. Nevertheless the Service ministry, despite constant pressure, refused to adopt any tariff increase.

It was supported throughout in its policy of intercolonial pacification by the Chambers of Manufactures and Commerce. Protection was all very well, but those manufacturers well established behind tariff walls were finding that it had its confining aspects. They were looking now more and more to an Australia-wide market, especially to New South Wales; but very often the Victorians could not compete for price with overseas manufactures in that colony. So their objective became intercolonial free trade behind a national tariff wall. The freetraders in the Chamber of Commerce naturally supported the principle of intercolonial free trade for, even if a national protective policy were adopted, the immediate area of free trade would be widened. Moreover Victorian protection kept out some products of other colonies. For example, in so far as Victorian farmers were protected, Tasmanian and South Australian primary producers were harmed; their governments were tending to impose retaliatory tariffs which hurt Victorian manufacturers. From about 1879 the Chamber of Manufactures had begun spasmodically to press for federation, or intercolonial free trade as a step to that end. As early as 1882 a prominent businessman remarked that 'It is an undisputed fact . . . that the employers of labour have arrived at the conclusion that federation, or some system of intercolonial free trade, is necessary for the proper carrying on of the industries of the colony.' By 1883 the two Chambers were conferring regularly and, although there was violent disagreement over what the national tariff policy should be, both came out strongly for federation and immediate intercolonial free trade with, for the moment, separate colonial tariffs against the world.[52] Business interests were beginning to lend strong support to the federal cause, which nevertheless was being pursued by Service and his colleagues primarily in order to bring about a national foreign policy.

1884: the New Guinea crisis

At a dinner in honour of the Earl of Rosebery on 9 January 1884, Service claimed that the colonies had no lust for territory as such, but wanted to establish 'a Greater Britain in these southern seas'. The islands must be annexed to prevent them becoming sinks of pollution. Britain's 'providential mission' was to exterminate 'moral and material evils' such as convict transportation and blackbirding; that odious and wicked trade must be policed from the colonies. But Britain must pay attention to the views of the colonists, for in fifty years' time Australia's population would be larger than Britain's and she would be ready to relieve the mother country of the task of governing India. Would the Earl of Rosebery be so kind as to tell Mr Gladstone that he might spare some sympathy for three million of his own flesh and blood and not just for Italians, Greeks and Bulgarians? And would he tell the French ambassador that if the convict policy was continued, Australians would come to hate Frenchmen, whom they would know only as convicts and burglars? Berry, in his speech, remarked that Australians were waking to the fact that they had a foreign policy. Victoria was the smallest colony but it had a mission: 'within her territory might spring up a matured public opinion that would govern the whole of the Australian colonies. She might be to Australia what the New

England States were to the United States of America . . . great in ideas.'[53]

Such pretty conceits were only exaggerated expressions of a world-view which was coming to be overwhelmingly accepted in Victoria, with mounting enthusiasm and almost without dissent. Some indication of the order of priorities may be gained from the report of part of Service's speech. He wished to tell Rosebery that they wanted federation (cheers), prevention of 'further foreign domination in the islands of the Pacific' (loud cheers), and 'annihilation of the introduction of convicts into the Pacific' (continuous cheering). The convict threat was to become the major unifying aspect of the Pacific question everywhere in Australia, but nowhere more so than in Victoria. The strength of the Presbyterian interest helps to explain the peculiar Victorian emphasis on the New Hebrides, and especially such aspects as the warm support for Griffith's humane Kanaka policy in Queensland* and the strait-laced tone of attacks on the 'immoral' and 'licentious' French.[54] Service was also expressing part of the Australian dream when he spoke of the need to keep old-world imperialistic conflicts out of the Pacific so that Australia might be free to work out its ideal society; soon this was to become a claim that Australia's destiny was to rule the Pacific. Central to the argument, also, was the assertion of jingo-imperialism, of the need to forestall and resist rival empires, and of the contribution the colonies might make to imperial unity and strength. But the 'antiquated autocracy or bureaucracy' which was the Empire must be reformed. Colonial governments had no representation in the imperial system, were 'outside petitioners to the Colonial Office with scarcely more influence than a county member of the House of Commons'. As things stood, colonists were patronized, humiliated, treated like children; they wanted to be received in England 'as simple citizens, and on a footing of perfect equality'.[55] Federation hence was the necessary course, so that the colonies could reach a united view on Pacific and imperial questions and present them to the imperial government; thus the Empire would be strengthened and an Australian nation formed. Members of the government were convinced of the virtuousness of their stand. They had no need to create a political diversion, as a few parliamentary critics and the exasperated men in the Colonial Office sometimes asserted; nor were motives of economic interest significant. As yet, though all expressed opinion seemed unanimous and there was a 'curious obliteration of party lines',[56] the movement was largely confined to the government circle, the Presbyterians and the newspapers. There was a slight air of spuriousness about the public campaign of 1883 with its half-filled halls and whipped-up petitions. But overwhelming support was to grow, both from the old gold

* Service meant well with regard to Australia's mission in the South Seas: 'Too often the contact of civilisation with savagery has been not only the destruction of savagery but of the savages too. There is room yet for a great and noble experiment: it remains for Australasia to see whether the inferior races cannot be befriended as well as employed, at once utilised and elevated.' (Western Pacific High Commission. Correspondence, *P.P.*, 1884, vol. 4, no. 57, p. 8.)

migrants and, with only the slightest variation of emphasis, from their children.

1884 was a very bad year for the cause: the convict threat worsened, no progress was made with the Federal Council, and the Germans occupied north-eastern New Guinea. There was a curious lull for the first half of the year. The imperial government was unwilling to take seriously the possibility that either Germany or France had annexationist intentions. Derby was appalled at the 'mere raving' of the Sydney Convention in laying down a Monroe Doctrine for the Pacific and Gladstone thought the proposals preposterous.[57] Pressure was, however, kept up quietly on France on the convict question; the Bill was still delayed in the French Senate.[58] Service, fretting at the delay, kept up pressure as best he could. Murray Smith created a precedent by interviewing the French ambassador in London and consulting the British ambassador in Paris. On 17 April he telegraphed Service to suggest 'fresh united pressure' on the convict question, for speeches by Rosebery and a campaign in *The Times* were rousing interest. Service wrote to the Premiers in April suggesting a meeting. Stuart would not agree but concurred in a unanimous telegram requesting the imperial government to protest emphatically to the French government about the convict Bill.[59] When Parliament met in June, Service was warmly supported. The Convention resolutions were passed without a division and the proposed Federal Council was approved by fifty-four votes to five and unanimously in the Council.[60]

At last in mid-June the colonies received Derby's formal response to the Convention. He unkindly pointed out that none of the Parliaments had adopted the Convention proposals, or provided the funds for extension of the activity of the Western Pacific High Commission in the New Guinea area which he had suggested a year before. The colonies must combine and cover costs before action could be taken. Service, of course, had been only too willing to act, but it had been agreed to wait on New South Wales. He now quickly won the consent of the Premiers to provide the necessary annual £15,000. Victoria and Queensland agreed to guarantee the sum together in case there was a hitch, and prepared identical legislation.[61]

In June Bismarck clearly signalled a change to an active colonial policy and forced the British government's hand. In response, the Colonial Office advised an immediate protectorate over all eastern New Guinea; the Cabinet agreed early in August. But after a German declaration of interest the protectorate was confined to the south-eastern shores. The need to conciliate Germany prevailed over colonial interests. The protectorate was declared early in October; but Germany had decided in August to annex the north-east.[62]

Meanwhile Service was very much in the dark. The cabled news of the intended protectorate, which was assumed to cover all eastern New Guinea, was welcome, but there was no news yet of imperial legislation to establish the Federal Council, and the French convict Bill was still under discussion. Then, early in August, the New South Wales government asked the imperial government to delay the Federal Council legislation until its Parliament had expressed an opinion. Service reacted angrily. 'Is Sydney to dominate Australia?,' he asked when cabling the news to Murray Smith. He now unwisely, quite impractically, decided to reopen the campaign on the wide annexation question. He wired again: 'Can you get Derby to promise annexation Islands when the Federal Council constituted? That I think would fetch Sydney. . . . I trust New Guinea may be deemed secure . . . the position of the other islands is critical in the extreme.'[63] Then in mid-September Murray Smith reported rumours of an arrangement with Germany to partition New Guinea. Service sprang into action and cabled the Premiers to urge again annexation of New Guinea and a protectorate over all available islands. This was too much for Stuart and Dalley. Even Griffith thought it better to confine the issue to New Guinea, though the other colonies gave Service general support. Service pleaded with Stuart, to no avail, for help in resistance to European annexation: 'nothing but continual knocking at the door will arouse the Imperial government to action'. Eventually all the Agents-General but New South Wales's joined in a strong letter to Derby on New Guinea. Murray Smith wired that the New South Wales attitude was doing infinite mischief in weakening the Australian case. To his dying day, Service never forgave Stuart and, quite erroneously, attributed to this 'betrayal' the failure to annex north-eastern New Guinea before Germany.[64]

When the limitation of the protectorate was revealed, there were disgusted reactions in Parliament. 'Everybody disappointed by piddling policy,' Service wired Murray Smith.[65] But meanwhile a great campaign, led by the Australian Natives' Association, was developing. The A.N.A. organized major public demonstrations at Ballarat on 23 August, and then on 22 September in the Melbourne Town Hall. It was appalling, said Deakin, so to confine the New Guinea protectorate because of 'some conjectural fear of offending Germany or Russia'; and he quoted:

> We don't want to fight,
> But, by Jingo, if we do;
> We've got the ships, we've got the men,
> And we've got the money too.

Australia's duty was to point out the errors in British colonial policy and 'to revive the colonial policy of the days of Raleigh and Drake, and the traditions of Sir Henry Lawrence in India, and of General Gordon, alone to-day in Khartoum'.[66] Tension grew when a German man-of-war was observed passing Port Phillip Bay and Port Jackson. 'Altogether things look ugly and demand prompt action,' Service cabled. McColl called on the Victorian government to annex north-eastern New Guinea itself.[67] Then on 30 October, the Federal Council proposals were defeated in the New South Wales Assembly by one vote. The imperial government, preoccupied with its proposed reform of the franchise, was only too glad to drop the enabling legislation for that year.

A patriotic meeting, 1885

'At last the end has come,' Service cabled Murray Smith on 20 December:

> Information received reliable source that Germany has hoisted flag on New Britain, New Ireland, and north coast of New Guinea. The exasperation here is boundless. I protest in the name of the present and future of Australia. If England does not yet save us from the danger and disgrace, as far at least as New Guinea is concerned, the bitterness of the feeling towards her will not die out in this generation.[68]

Derby was 'unpatriotic and coward-hearted', fumed the *Argus*; the colonies should petition for his dismissal. The *Age* threatened separation.[69] The A.N.A. called a great protest meeting at which the speakers represented as many sections of the public as possible. 'Now is the crisis in our national existence,' cried Sir Archibald Michie who moved the chief resolution; New Guinea was as much a part of Australia as the Isle of Wight was of Britain. A roar of cheering and waving of hats responded to John Woods's determination to make New Guinea part of Australia. Nicholas Fitzgerald, the leading Irish Catholic orator, announced amid enthusiasm that 'the day had gone for ever when the colonists would tolerate being treated as children. . . . Australasia was rising into the dignity of a nation. . . . if we were now a united people . . . even great Bismarck dare not act in defiance of us.' At Ballarat the same night a meeting of thousands heard a youth declare that the protest they would send home 'would show England that Ballarat remembered the Eureka'.[70] Scores of meetings followed, and indignant outraged letters poured in to the newspapers; a 'Colonist of the Fifties' called on the colonies together simply to take possession of New Guinea—'Have we leaders to give us the word?'[71] Derby was burnt in effigy here and there.

Service tried and again failed to convene a meeting of Premiers; once again New South Wales did not co-operate. Dalley, the acting Premier, went so far as to welcome the German annexation and to claim it was impudent and absurd to protest and embarrass the imperial government. There was little Service and his government could do. They had considered sending an embassy of protest to Britain, but only Queensland and New Zealand could be relied on to join. 'The difficulty of the position from the first', he wrote privately,

> has been that the colonies have not been perfectly united even in saying what they wanted. N.S. Wales' back-draft ruined the annexation question, and left us at the mercy of Lord Derby—who seems as blind as a mole, and as cold as an icicle. And the more vigorous we are, the more sulky New South Wales appears to become. Action therefore which seems obviously right on the face of it, is rendered impossible—or if not impossible, almost useless, because what Victoria feels to be of national importance is regarded as the result of provincial arrogance and self assertion.[72]

There was nothing to be done but to protest: under instructions, Murray Smith bombarded the Colonial Office with requests that the annexation be not recognized. 'New Guinea must be got back,' wired Service,[73] in total ignorance of the diplomatic context which made it essential for the imperial government to submit, despite the humiliation which Bismarck's deception had brought. Ultimately Service could only call on posterity, his conviction that Australians would never recognize any German right of occupation and would one day take the island back. It was

> one of the most melancholy and marvellous illustrations of political imbecility that has ever been recorded in history. . . . a story to be told in time to our children and our children's children—this story of the fight to get New Guinea and the islands, and how they were lost in the most miserable style.[74]

J. A. Froude, the visiting historian, remarked that it was just as well that Australia was not federated, with its own Navy, or these 'hot-headed men' might have 'sent their ships round to warn the Germans off'. 'Young nations', he concluded, 'are like young men, sensitive and passionate; and even their most experienced statesmen do not escape the contagion.'[75]

General Gordon, defence and imminent war, 1885

The long-drawn-out siege of General Gordon in Khartoum had roused deep emotion. When the news of his heroic death arrived early in February 1885, 'most of the people seemed to run mad . . . and were red hot for revenge', one citizen wrote home;[76] indignation meetings hooted Gladstone's name and called for his removal from office. There was great excitement when it was heard that Dalley had offered a New South Wales contingent for service in the Sudan. Victoria hastened to follow suit, planned to send a naval brigade and mounted infantry, and began recruiting. Service hoped that a joint contingent from the colonies might be arranged in order to boost the federal cause, and wired Griffith to express his hope that the event would 'draw us closer together by shewing Victoria will follow as well as lead and has no desire for special pre-eminence in things national'. But the New South Wales offer was accepted by a surprised imperial government and the Victorian (and Canadian) offers declined for the time being; Dalley suavely rejected the suggestion of a national contingent on the ground that it would mean delay.[77] Service kept a stiff upper lip, but there was special cause for rancour, for only twelve months before, his offer of two new Victorian gunboats, on their way out through the Suez Canal, for use in the campaign had been rudely snubbed by Derby, because of their dubious legal status.[78] Service genuinely admired Dalley's coup and believed it had 'precipitated Australia in one short week from a geographical expression to a nation'; 'while we have a man, a ship, or a shilling, England shall never want assistance' in time of peril.[79] He sent warm fraternal greetings to the contingent on its departure. The *Argus*, however, remarked that New South Wales had been favoured as the most subservient colony; acceptance of Dalley's offer was a 'reward for his desertion of the Australian cause' over New Guinea. And later it pointed out that in fact Victoria had been the first colony to have military or naval assistance accepted by the mother country when in 1860 H.M.S. *Victoria* served in the New Zealand wars![80]

Yet public opinion cooled rapidly. As early as 19 February Service cabled Murray Smith: 'Public opinion H.M.G. do not require assistance. Reuter's telegram that offer declined has been received with satisfaction on the part of many. . . . not desirable to press offer.' The *Age* had assumed there was overwhelming support for sending a contingent, but was now swinging round to opposition. The A.N.A. at its annual conference had unanimously supported sending troops, but several branches and many members were now having second thoughts. The subsequent parliamentary debate in June revealed a fairly even division between those who blindly supported sending a contingent as a gesture of loyalty and demonstration of colonial adulthood, and those who opposed or had grave doubts—either because it set a precedent for colonial military support for Britain in any circumstances, or because of fear of foreign raids on Australia in the absence of many of its troops, or because of disapproval in principle of the Sudan war. It was a 'grand thing', said one supporter; 'the greatest historical event in the history of Australia', said another. Conscious now of the remarkable effect the enterprise had had on British and world opinion, Service remained as enthusiastic as ever. The glory was shared by all of us; the New South Wales gesture had 'fused these colonies into one, and welded the Empire together'. Service was buttering up the Sydney government, but his sentiments were honest. Many members like Pearson and W. F. Walker, while they deplored imperial policy in the Sudan and sympathized with 'brave men fighting for their liberty', believed the Empire had to be supported, right or wrong. Moreover, said Walker, 'nothing that has ever happened . . . has done more . . . to make Australia known as . . . a nation, and certainly nothing has done us more benefit in the eyes of the world.' James Mirams alone was totally opposed: it was a 'time of rampant "Jingoism" and militarism run mad', it was a 'disgrace to this country . . . that our first effort in warfare, our first plunge into foreign politics' should be this mean, miserable, contemptible fight in the Sudan.[81] Mirams's most notable supporter was Gyles Turner who in a scathing article in the *Melbourne Review* placed the Sudan venture in the context of other recent British colonial wars:

> the whole business in Egypt has been a purposeless and inconsequential muddle. . . . To call it . . . going to the assistance of the mother country in her hour of peril is simply ludicrous. . . . the whole thing was a bold and costly piece of political claptrap, which brought New South Wales to the front with a bound. . . . To claim patriotic virtue for the men who are ready to shoot Arabs, negroes, Abyssinians or Egyptians indifferently at 5s. a day is a miserable prostitution of terms.

But of course if England were really threatened, Victoria would spring to her aid without question.[82]

General Gordon's 'pure and noble life' was an inspiration to the whole Empire; his self-martyrdom was a high point of agony of the Victorian age and a crucial incident in the rise of the new imperialism. Nowhere, perhaps, was the emotional response greater than among right-thinking people in Victoria. A memorial fund was opened to which nearly 50,000 people subscribed; the *Argus*'s suggestion of a statue was adopted, and a replica bought of the one ordered by the House of Commons to be built in Trafalgar Square.[83] 'He is accepted by people of all classes and creeds as the type of those qualities that make the men of Britain great. . . . His private letters . . . are gems in Christian literature, . . . [He is] the most heroic of modern Englishmen,' ran the Fund's circular.[84] The cream of Melbourne packed a fund-raising meeting in the Town Hall. The Governor, Sir Henry Loch who had been a friend of Gordon, was in the chair; the ladies wore mourning and the 'Dead March in Saul' was played; Moorhouse made one of his great emotional speeches eulogizing the 'perfect knight', the 'modern Bayard'; honest Ben Douglass pledged the trade unionists to contribute; speakers' references to the 'shame' of Gordon's death brought hysterical weeping. It was a great anti-Gladstonian demonstration.*[85] 'We believe that many an Australian school-boy of to-day already begins to ask himself, "What would General Gordon have done in my place?" ' wrote George Gordon McCrae, the poet:

> His statue shall never need an inscription, for his deeds are written on the hearts of this people. . . . It may be, even in ages yet to come, that someone . . . on the very verge of a contemplated crime shall, in passing this statue . . . cast his glances upwards, and there and then, smitten to the soul by the sight of the noble type before him, turn away repentant. . . .[86]

Four years later the statue was unveiled in Spring Street before a crowd of thousands.[87] Meanwhile a shire, a torpedo-boat, the new Geelong technical college, a lodging-house in Little Bourke Street, and innumerable babies had been named after Gordon.†

Early in March the imperial government indicated that a Victorian force might well be welcome later in the year for service in the Sudan. But the proposal was ignored in the following months of crisis when it was believed that war with Russia was almost inevitable. Victoria was carrying out an armament programme which was far in advance of any other Australian colony. After early enthusiasm in the fifties and sixties, colonial defences had been allowed to deteriorate. The colonial Navy—the

* Cf. the poem on Gordon's death by 'McC., Castlemaine' (Rev. A. R. B. McCay?), which concluded:

> Curse on the laggard statecraft that palsied England's might!
> And trebly cursed the treason that turned her day to night!
> A martyr's death, full glorious, has crowned her Gordon's story,
> But crimson are the bloodstains that dim her Gladstone's glory.

(*Once a Month*, 15 Mar. 1885.)

† And, in 1894, Robert Gordon Menzies.

ironclad *Nelson* and *Cerberus*—was 'an utter and entire sham', the Governor reported in 1880. The two hundred and fifty men

> cannot be really effective sailors for they never go to sea from one year's end to another and the boilers of both ships are in such a state that it would hardly be safe to send either outside the Heads. . . . as fighting ships they are useless as they can neither of them go more than about seven knots. . . .[88]

After the departure of the last imperial troops in 1870, the colony relied only on its Volunteer Forces on which a royal commission in 1875 had reported scathingly. However, in 1877 Major-General Sir William Jervois and Major P. H. Scratchley were appointed by the imperial government to report on the defence of the Australian colonies, and over the following six years they produced comprehensive findings. The growing imperial consciousness of danger, especially from Russia, and the need for preparedness for major war was strikingly reflected in the colonies. The assumption was that the main danger in time of war would be a running attack by enemy cruisers, which might destroy shipping, hold Melbourne to ransom, and retire. In 1878 at the time of the Russo-Turkish crisis, the imperial government issued a general warning to all colonies to be on guard against raids by enemy squadrons if war broke out.[89] Theoretically, the development of the steam-driven, armour-plated man-of-war and the rifled gun decreased distance and made a major attack on Australia possible. It must have been wildly improbable, given the difficulties of coaling. However, there is inconclusive evidence from an intelligence report that about 1878 the Russians were considering, in the event of war with Britain, attacking Newcastle (in order to coal their ships), Sydney and Melbourne with five cruisers, and exacting bullion. The information became known late in 1884, to the alarm of the Victorian government which was already suspicious of the activities of visiting friendly Russian vessels and of alleged private visits by Russian naval officers.*[90] Certainly *The Battle of the Yarra*, a pamphlet of 1883 by 'An Old Colonist' arguing the urgency of federation, envisaged a Russian invading force of 3,000 men storming the Heads, landing at Port Melbourne, and after a sharp fight for the bridges over the Yarra, exacting a ransom of £3 million![91]

In 1882 the O'Loghlen government had acted on the Jervois-Scratchley reports by voting £140,000 for torpedo-boats and gunboats. The Service ministry, driven on by Frederick T. Sargood, a zealous major in the Volunteers, brought about sweeping changes. A Department of Defence, with Sargood as first minister from November 1883, and a Council of Defence were created. Small permanent forces of artillery and engineers were formed, the Volunteers were disbanded and a paid militia was recruited,

* After a visit by a Russian squadron in 1882, there was an extraordinary scare when the *Age* was hoaxed by information given about an alleged forthcoming attack, by H. Bryant (or de Beaumont), supposedly a former Russian agent. See Verity Fitzhardinge, 'Russian Naval Visitors to Australia', *Journal of the Royal Australian Historical Society*, vol. 52, pt 2, June 1966, pp. 148-52.

and rifle clubs and school cadet corps were encouraged. Colonel T. R. Disney, R.A. and three other imperial army officers arrived late in November 1883 to take command. Extensive fortifications were begun at Port Phillip Heads. Land batteries, mines, torpedoes from two shoal-forts, a fast gunboat outside the Heads; and the *Cerberus*, torpedo-boats and gunboats inside, would make things hot for any attacking force. Batteries were also to be emplaced at Portland, Port Fairy and Warrnambool. All were to be financed from a vote of £550,000 over five years.[92] The government proudly proceeded with its programme, conscious that it was doing its duty in so handsomely providing for local defence and adding to the might of the Empire. *Brassey's Naval Annual* of 1884 reported the Victorian Navy to be a 'formidable flotilla'. A modern naval historian describes the gunboats, *Victoria* and *Albert*, as 'fearful and wonderful specimens of the naval architects' art . . . these lilliputian over-gunned hulks . . . exhibited the sea-going qualities of half-tide rocks.'[93]

On 5 March 1885 Murray Smith cabled: 'We have reason to believe war Russia not probable but possible. Advise preparations but quietly as possible.' Successive telegrams over the next seven weeks concluded with one which regarded war, arising out of a clash on the Afghan frontier, as inevitable.[94] On 18 March, partly in order to allay public alarm, the Governor held a Council of Ministers together with Jervois, Scratchley and Rear-Admiral G. Tryon, the Pacific Fleet commander, all of whom happened to be in Melbourne. The Governor reported home that the forts were not yet capable of preventing the entrance of a hostile squadron; in three or four weeks, work would have proceeded far enough to stop vessels forcing an entrance, and two months would be enough to shut out any conceivable opposing force, despite a shortage of torpedoes. Meanwhile the channel through the Heads was being mined and, possibly in response to vague reports from Singapore about the movements of Russian naval vessels, a proclamation was issued on 28 March forbidding any foreign ship to enter the Heads after sunset. The Melbourne Coal Company sold several hulks to the government for sinking at the Heads if necessary.[95] As the news became graver, Cabinet met on 11 April and again on the 13th to hear Colonel Disney and Captain A. B. Thomas, R.N. report on what they were doing 'to prepare the colony against an invasion'. Advice from home was urgently sought on what should be done if a Russian man-of-war sought entry to the port before war was declared. Meanwhile the populace became more and more belligerent: the Melbourne City Council carried unanimously a proposal to arm and drill the whole male population; loyal meetings worked up the jingo spirit; volunteers clamoured to be enrolled; Germans, Irish and native-born began movements to form national regiments; elderly ladies withdrew their deposits in gold from bank branches 'for fear of the Russians'.[96] Then on 30 April Tryon ordered the Victorian fleet to the Heads, and Naval Reserves were commanded to hold themselves in readiness.

The diplomatic settlement early in May was a deflating anticlimax.

Melbourne's assumption that, if there had been war, it would have been a prime objective of the Russians, despite its remoteness and the fact that there was only one Russian armoured cruiser in eastern seas, is a classic example of its pride and self-regard. Yet the insecurity of isolation, even in a period of overwhelming British naval supremacy, is a constant thread in Australian history. For years yet, newspapers and armchair strategists would argue that it would be an intolerable menace to Australia if the Russians reached the Indian shores and that the first line of Australian defence was in Afghanistan.[97]

The Federal Council established

Such threats, real or supposed, from Germany, France and Russia in turn must surely, thought Service, build up enthusiasm for federation; but there was little response in New South Wales. Despite much shilly-shallying, the senior colony would not join the Federal Council, even when early in 1885 Derby proposed an amendment to the draft enabling Act which would give any member colony the right to withdraw from the Council once established. The Victorian government dickered, but eventually agreed with Queensland, South Australia and Tasmania—the four governments now described themselves as those 'prepared to confederate' —to oppose the proposal strongly. They had been prepared to agree if it would mean that New South Wales (or New Zealand) would join, but as even this proposal appeared to be insufficient to satisfy New South Wales the objection was maintained.[98] Nevertheless Derby introduced the Federal Council of Australasia Bill in April with the offending clause and other minor amendments still included. Then in July, too late, Stuart asked for delay as he might have further proposals to make. After consultation, the other Premiers, suspicious that this was an attempt to shelve the Bill, agreed that it must proceed: 'all attempts to meet Sydney seem fruitless', Service remarked. When the Bill was passed on 14 August, Stuart said that now there was no chance of New South Wales joining.[99] The Sydney *Bulletin* had no doubts about what had happened. While it deplored Service's imperialism, it despised the 'deep-rooted suspicion of every project emanating from Victoria' which characterized New South Wales politicians: 'From the beginning, their object appeared to be not only to stand aside themselves, but to prevent the other provinces from coming together.'[1] Queensland, Tasmania, Western Australia and Fiji quickly passed adopting Acts, and Victoria in October with a roar of 'Aye' and cheering.[2] Then the forlorn cause seemed almost lost, for South Australia would not proceed, and Service almost abandoned the whole enterprise. He consulted Murray Smith: was it worthwhile, if less than half the population of Australasia was to be represented? 'What do you think? You can imagine my chagrin should it fail.' Murray Smith advised perseverance. But although Service 'wined Downer', Adelaide stayed out, and the Federal Council when it first met in January 1886 was a poor puny infant.[3]

Victoria's federal campaign had gone badly astray. The ricketty Federal

Council, in the absence of New South Wales and South Australia, met only once before 1888. Victoria and New South Wales continued to differ widely on imperial and foreign questions. No progress was made towards intercolonial free trade. The Victorians had been alarmed by the no doubt half serious and tactical discussion by some members of the 1883 Convention of the possibility of a customs union excluding Victoria.[4] As the largest exporter, Victoria had to placate the other colonies and go on to capture wider markets; it would be disastrous if protection against Victoria developed further. Those colonies which joined the Federal Council would at least consider a customs union. The Tasmanian government in mid-1883 had once again suggested, as they had from the late sixties, a reciprocity treaty. Late in 1884 the Victorians responded, and at a conference in January 1885 both governments agreed harmoniously to a near-complete customs union for a three-year trial period, subject to parliamentary ratification. The *Age*, the *Argus* and both Chambers (which continued jointly to lobby the government in favour of intercolonial free trade) warmly approved. Berry, who had negotiated the agreement, was sharp with protesting delegations of primary producers: it was ridiculous to regard Tasmanians as foreigners or to claim the treaty was inconsistent with a standing policy of protection. But opposition grew, not merely from sawmillers, hop growers, oats and barley producers, orchardists and berry growers, potato farmers and jam manufacturers (and Tasmanian manufacturers), but also from doctrinaire protectionists led by Mirams, and, even more serious, from the dogmatic Trades Hall Council which seemed to be guided more by protectionist theory than the immediate interests of its constituents. Late in 1885, when the government proposed ratification, the Opposition scented a useful election issue and was hostile. The government caved in and dropped the measure. Although Service in later years was to refer to his own humiliation and his ministry's great failure, it is difficult to believe that the government could not have rallied its ranks. Adye Douglas of Tasmania believed his colony had been sold: once they had agreed to join the Federal Council, no more was heard of the reciprocity treaty. But the probable explanation is to be found in a remark by Deakin nearly two years later: the treaty was abandoned because it was considered unfriendly by another colony—was it New South Wales or South Australia?[5] Negotiations for a limited reciprocity treaty with Queensland in 1886 failed to get far. The Chambers of Commerce and Manufactures drew up proposals, while Melbourne investors in Queensland sugar busily lobbied the government. On 9 August, F. T. Derham, himself deeply involved in sugar, raised the question in Cabinet. On 21 August Gillies wrote to Griffith to suggest that, in order to combat the dumping of subsidized European sugar, they should discuss the possibility of Victorian tariff preference to Queensland sugar and Queensland preference to Victorian agricultural products. Alarmed Tasmanians angrily considered ways and means of retaliation. But Queensland did not respond.[6] In the same period there was a strong movement in Fiji for tariff reciprocity, even amalgamation, with Victoria. In October 1887 Gillies indicated that there was no point in further lobbying.[7]

The strength so early of support for federation in Victoria may partly be explained by Melbourne's comparatively extensive intercolonial interests. Victorian businessmen's investments in the other colonies made them much more accustomed than businessmen elsewhere to think in intercolonial or national terms. The need to widen markets for industrial and agricultural products became increasingly important through the decade. Yet motives of economic advantage for Victoria are obviously minor in explaining the government's campaign from 1883, when compared to fear of the European powers in the Pacific, imperial zeal, and the call of national destiny.

The New Hebrides crisis, 1886–7, and the Colonial Conference

While the New Guinea protectorate was being established in 1885, the colonial and imperial governments exchanged some acrimonious correspondence. Sir Peter Scratchley had been appointed as Special Commissioner in charge, and when he arrived in Australia early in the year he was instructed to confer about the boundary with Germany which should be sought. In high disdain, Service stated that his government was unwilling to offer advice because by all reports the British and German governments had already agreed. 'Mr Service seems to be almost a monomaniac upon New Guinea,' remarked Bramston of the Colonial Office. 'It is a bit of temper,' Derby minuted.[8] An unseemly squabble then followed over provision of finance. The colonies had offered their 'share' of the costs in 1883, and had agreed in 1884 to Derby's suggestion of £15,000 a year. In November 1884 Derby had intimated that more would be necessary; the colonial governments, because of the limitation of the protectorate, brusquely refused to contribute more. Anger grew when it became clear that the imperial government had no intention of itself contributing at all. Service protested at the 'shabby way' in which the colonies had been coerced. But he was eventually praised by Bramston for his 'moderate and practical' contribution to settling the argument.[9]

Tension was lessening over the New Hebrides. The French Senate modified the terms of the 'Relapsed Criminals Bill' and, as promulgated in May 1885, the number proposed to be transported was greatly reduced; it was understood that no more than 2,000 would be sent to the Pacific. The Victorian government regarded this as at least a negative victory. There was little point now in passing the prepared quarantine legislation against French convicts, especially as New South Wales had shown so little interest.[10] Moreover in May Derby made the crucial promise that no French proposal to annex the New Hebrides would be considered without consultation with the colonies and the securing of satisfactory conditions.[11] In fact, however, the annexation movement was growing stronger in France. New Caledonian lobbyists were pressing their case that the colony needed both convict and New Hebridean labour and newspapers were whipping up resistance to the provocation of the Australian colonies.

Early in 1886 the storm broke. While the Federal Council was meeting for the first time at Hobart, news arrived that Germany and France had reached an agreement whereby Germany would not object to French annexation of the New Hebrides. Service and Griffith rallied the Council and produced a flurry of resolutions and telegrams. In Melbourne Duncan Gillies, who had just succeeded Service as Premier, set about mobilizing the other colonies. For once all the colonies did act together. On 23 February the Agents-General met Earl Granville, the new Colonial Secretary, to urge prevention of convict transportation and protection of the *status quo* in the New Hebrides. But Granville now told them that France had proposed that she be allowed to annex the New Hebrides in return for abandonment of transportation. In line with Derby's promise, he formally asked the colonies for their opinions, but gave a cautiously favourable response to the French initiative and then cabled the colonial governments urging acceptance. With the Foreign Office, the Colonial Office and several of the Agents-General in agreement, the matter appeared to be all over bar the recriminations.[12]

When the news became public on 12 March, the pressure groups swung into action again and Gillies was 'daily besieged' by deputations; the clamour was sustained at high pitch for months. Every manse became a hive of activity again; in high agony Paton spoke and wrote constantly: 'My heart weeps for the oppression and destruction of my spiritual children on the islands, and the evils to Australia sure to follow, if France is allowed to annex the New Hebrides. Let us protest and oppose to the last, and God may avert this calamity.'[13] The A.N.A. organized public meetings all over the colony; at its Melbourne mass meeting speakers were all native-born, but on the platform were representatives of the clergy, the Royal Society, the Chamber of Manufactures, the Medical Society, the Imperial Federation League, the Geographical Society and the Railways Union, and 200 university students lent support. The New Hebrides were an Australian heritage, it was proclaimed; Australia would eventually tell the French and the Germans to 'Get up and get.'[14] The *Age* bombastically attacked Gladstone: 'The recovery of the islands would be the dominant purpose of our national life and we should not be satisfied till the flag of Australia floated over the entire Southern Polynese'.[15] A united press and the great majority of politicians drove the government on to a last-ditch stand.* Service appealed privately to Rosebery, now Foreign Secretary: 'We are sick and wounded at heart that Home Government does not recognize our interests and protect them. Our hope now rests on you.'[16] Gillies was proving to be an apt pupil; he cabled Murray Smith: 'What would be

* The Catholics and the Secularists tended to be cool or hostile; see *Advocate* and *Liberator*, *passim*. The *Imperial Review*, an independent liberal occasional journal, also described it as a hollow, upper-class agitation with 'the working class not caring two straws' (Oct. 1886, p. 65).

use speaking of Imperial Federation in face of an act which would proclaim stronger than any language contemptuous indifference for our wishes and future prospects? Should English Ministers give away or allow to be taken New Hebrides today, Australia will assuredly take them back when able.'[17] In forwarding the cable to the Colonial Office as instructed, Murray Smith lost his sense of duty and wrote that he was ashamed of the tone of the message, and that he believed the French proposal would be 'a splendid bargain for Australia'. Herbert sourly noted that the cable was 'no doubt instigated by Mr Service and prompted by his disgust at finding that the more loyal Colonies are assisting and not impeding Her Majesty's Government in the attempt to carry out the wish of Australia that transportation may be finally ended.' 'The more loyal Colonies' were New South Wales and New Zealand.[18]

Gillies and Griffith were in constant communication. By 12 March they had agreed on a draft protest by members of the Federal Council, who all agreed within a few days, and South Australia too. Support from Sir John Thurston, Governor of Fiji and a respected expert on Pacific affairs, was especially welcome. Gillies released Thurston's secret memorandum which had a marked impact in England; Herbert angrily noted that the Victorian government was 'absolutely untrustworthy'.[19] Still, despite prompting, no reply to Gillies came from New South Wales. But on the 22nd Sir Patrick Jennings, the new Premier, cabled home that his government favoured the French proposal. When on the 29th the decision was made public, Gillies angrily wired: 'This dissension between the Colonies may, I fear, breed serious disaster in the future. Cannot we act together for once?'[20] Griffith bitingly rebuked New South Wales for always isolating herself. The *Bulletin* supported Jennings, deploring the 'parsonical land grab' of the 'holy howlers' and applauding England's indifference to 'the ravings of Paton and the cocoa-nut-oil party'.[21] On 22 April the Colonial Office sent another firm memorandum urging acceptance.[22] But the tide was beginning to turn. Lieut.-General Sir Andrew Clarke—a staunch Liberal Party candidate, old Victorian colonist and former colonial Governor—was now acting as Victorian Agent-General and threw himself into the fray. On 30 April he addressed an emotional, yet formidably competent statement to the Colonial Office: throughout the Pacific 'manifest destiny impels and spreads the expeditions, the evangelisation, the settlements of our own people'. Herbert dismissed it as 'preposterous' and deplorable as coming from an imperial officer.[23] On 7 May Clarke sent Gillies a report—it turned out to be a false alarm—that a French ship was proceeding to occupy the New Hebrides, and suggested that the senior naval officer should be persuaded to send ships. Rear-Admiral Tryon told Gillies that he could obey only the Admiralty. Clarke then succeeded in seeing Gladstone himself—in the midst of the Home Rule crisis! Berry then arrived to take over as Agent-General and proceeded to lobby forcefully as only he could. Hugh Childers, too, from within the government had been urging the claims of his old colonial associates on a not entirely unsympathetic Rosebery. But the decisive event was that New Zealand finally came down on the Victorian side. Its government had been inclined to accept the French proposal; a ferocious campaign by the Presbyterians, however, had so roused opinion that in mid-May it announced a change of policy.[24] New South Wales was now isolated. Rosebery and Granville accepted the verdict, and on 19 May Berry proudly cabled that the French ambassador had been informed that there was no prospect of British assent. Melbourne rejoiced: the right of consultation had been established, colonial advice had been accepted, the Federal Council had got off to a great start.[25]

The triumph was brief. Early in June, 400 French marines from New Caledonia occupied the New Hebrides. There is doubt to this day about whether the coup was ordered from Paris or was an initiative of the militant local commandant. Whatever the truth, the French government skilfully exploited the situation, claiming that the troops were sent to protect French settlers from native outrages and that there was no act of annexation. Alarm in Victoria was intense. Gillies suggested to Tryon that he strengthen his forces in the area and offered the Victorian gunboats; Tryon did quickly move H.M.S. *Diamond* to the scene. A. T. Clark, the member for Williamstown, wanted to send off a colonial force: the government 'ought to adopt a manly course . . . let Downing-street do what it likes. . . . I undertake to say that there are quite enough Australians to hold the islands against all the combined powers of the world. (Laughter.)' He was supported by the *National Australian*, the A.N.A.'s journal.[26] The English reaction was reassuring: 'Press, Parliament, Government unanimous defending Australian interests. . . . Public opinion excellent,' Berry cabled Gillies. Rosebery was indeed very angry, protested strongly several times, and dismissed finally the original French offer for a settlement. The senior Colonial Office men no longer wrote sneering comments on despatches from Victoria about Pacific questions. In Australia, Gillies and Griffith continued to use the Federal Council as the channel for their protests. Despite strong local pressure, Jennings refused to co-operate, but was eventually forced by public opinion to protest at the continued French occupation, though he still continued to support the original French offer.[27]

It was a stalemate, and negotiations dragged on and on. France, while denying its intention of annexing the New Hebrides, used the occupation as a bargaining counter in a series of British-French differences in the Pacific and North Africa of which the most important was over Suez.[28] In this frustrating situation, public fervour inevitably fell away, although the Presbyterians kept up their campaign with remarkable stamina. Agonizing reports of the consolidation of French interests continued to spur the government, but Gillies was floundering far out of his depth, as his letters to Berry show.[29] His main recommendation was to send a rival British force to occupy parts of the islands. He later developed a more sophisticated view: that because of the touchiness of French public opinion, Britain should secretly seek French agreement to sending a British force, and that then both would withdraw by agreement, thus preserving each other's dignity. In the long run, he agreed with Service, the only answer probably was to buy the French out of the Pacific.[30] Occasionally he and Berry dropped clumsy hints, which may have had some substance, that Victoria was seriously considering 'going it alone' and sending a force to occupy, or rather to take by force, the New Hebrides. Deakin wrote later that 'Australians had grown tired of appealing and protesting and were determined to act for themselves on behalf of the Empire should the necessity arise.'*

By the close of 1886 the outlines of a probable settlement appeared clear. The Foreign Office, the Colonial Office and the Agents-General all took the view that, after French withdrawal, a system of joint Anglo-French control of the New Hebrides might be devised—if possible with a French guarantee to abandon transportation. The Victorian government considered not inviting France to take part in the Centennial Exhibition. Meanwhile the first conference of British colonies, which was chiefly to discuss defence, was preparing to assemble in London in April 1887. Gillies stayed home, while Deakin was to lead the Victorian delegation whose other members were Berry, Service and James Lorimer. Early indications boded ill for Australian unity. On board ship Deakin found Downer of South Australia and Griffith full of self-will, undecided about what should be attempted at the conference yet anxious to assert their individuality, and jealous of Victoria and New South Wales.[31] In London Berry was thinking much the same thing: 'Each colony has an axe to grind and all join in bitter jealousy of Victoria.'[32] However, Gillies had been in touch with Parkes, who had recently become Premier and seemed to be willing to co-operate.[33]

On the opening day of the conference Deakin, alone of the colonial spokesmen, went beyond polite formalities. He spoke of the immense difficulty the colonies had in making their views known to the Colonial Office; it was even more difficult to reach the Foreign Office, let alone the Cabinet. He would not admit any distinction between imperial and colonial interests:

> We cannot imagine any description of circumstances by which the Colonies should be humiliated or weakened, or their power lessened, under which the Empire would not be itself humiliated, weakened, and lessened. And we are unable to conceive any circumstances under which the wealth or status of the Colonies could be increased, which would not increase in the same degree the wealth and status of the Empire.

* In this mysterious passage in *The Federal Story* (pp. 24-5), Deakin refers to a plan of the Victorian inner Cabinet, in 1888 or 1889, to send a detachment of the Victorian forces to the New Hebrides in a privately chartered steamer to hoist the British flag. The plan was called off on the eve of execution when it was heard the French did not have designs.

The Defence and Premier's Archives disclose nothing on this matter. If there was such a plan, early September 1889 appears to be a likely time, but 1886 remains a possibility. Deakin never revised his manuscript, and his memory of the 1887 Colonial Conference is so faulty that it is possible he greatly exaggerated what may well have been discussed as a possibility by the inner Cabinet and also misdated the incident.

He hoped Britain would develop 'a spirited colonial policy' similar to France's and Germany's. The despatches received by the colonies on the New Guinea and New Hebrides questions

> exhibited only the disdain and indifference with which English enterprise was treated in the Colonial Office, . . . we hope that from this time forward, Colonial policy will be considered Imperial policy; that Colonial interests will be considered and felt to be Imperial interests; that they will be carefully studied, and that when once they are understood, they will be most determinedly upheld.[34]

Discussions on the New Hebrides did not occur for another three weeks. Sir Henry Holland (Lord Knutsford) asked the Prime Minister to attend and to tell the colonials—he certainly had the Victorians most in mind—that they must not try to set up a Monroe doctrine over all the Pacific Islands.[35]

The confrontation which followed had an accidental quality. Salisbury was worried about broad serious problems in dispute with France, was not well informed on the history of the New Hebrides dispute, and became impatient with the discussion as it proceeded. By the most likely account,[36] Wisdom of New South Wales, Service and Downer had all stated their determination that France should not have the New Hebrides, and no doubt Service had pressed again for British annexation. Salisbury then condescendingly derided the idiocy of quarrelling with France about so trivial a matter, and saw no reason why France should not retain possession if she would abandon transportation. His speech was either a poorly judged piece of bullying or, more likely perhaps, an uncalculated loss of temper. But in effect this was a return to the French proposals of 1885 which had been rejected before the French occupation, and a reversal of the line of British negotiation over the previous ten months. No wonder there was consternation among the delegates! Berry replied immediately—'one of the best and smartest speeches' he ever made, according to Service.[37] Then Griffith made his protest, though more temperately, and Deakin made his famous speech. According to his own account,

> He broke quite new ground not only with unrestrained vigour and enthusiasm on the general question as his colleagues had before him, but because he did so in a more spirited manner, challenging Lord Salisbury's arguments one by one and mercilessly analysing the inconsistencies of his speech. . . . Deakin went on to declare in an impassioned manner that the people of Victoria would never consent to any cession of the islands on any terms and that the Australian-born who had made this question their own would forever resent the humiliation of a surrender which would immensely weaken their confidence in an Empire to which hitherto they had been proud to belong.
>
> The effect of such a bold protest was electrical. Lord Salisbury several times stared at the speaker, as well he might, in considerable amazement at his plain speaking. . . .[38]

Then followed Jennings of New South Wales to deny that there was Australian unanimity, as a large party in his colony was still prepared to accept the French offer; but if that was to be rejected, New South Wales would act in co-operation with the other colonies. Salisbury was not impressed by the protests; in reply to a note next day from Holland saying that the delegates were 'very sore indeed', he remarked: 'They want us to incur all the bloodshed and the dangers, and the stupendous cost of a war with France . . . for a group of islands which to us are as valueless as the South Pole—and to which they are only attached by a debating-club sentiment.'[39] The delegates demanded further discussion on the 28th when Service, who led off, was supported by all the other Australian colonies. Service subsequently often referred to the striking unanimity of the Australian delegates over the New Hebrides issue which had great effect on the imperial statesmen; and he gave credit to Parkes for his support.[40] Certainly Deakin, Berry and Service, no doubt on the basis of private assurances, were all convinced that their defiance had produced a firmer imperial stand against France.[41]

All the delegates seemed to regard the conference as having been highly successful. But still, although agreement had been reached in principle, the French government stalled, while Gillies niggled away at the Colonial Office and the Presbyterians complained about harassing of their missions. Late in August Gillies pressed for an ultimatum, and, failing action, the landing of a military force.[42] At the end of September Paton called a meeting which almost filled the Town Hall; some A.N.A. members still were foolishly crying that they wanted the New Hebrides and would have them.[43] At last, late in October, the agreement for an Anglo-French joint naval commission and French evacuation was reached. Yet it appears that imperial agreement was not a foregone conclusion, for Salisbury remarked: 'I have assented to these proposals, as it seemed to be the feeling of the Cabinet that the New Hebrides convention must somehow be obtained: but it has a bad effect on my liver to think how those Australian colonies put upon us.'[44] Berry wrote exultantly to Gillies: 'At length our time has come.'[45] It was of course only a negative victory which left the Presbyterians aggrieved, but still a famous victory. Within a few weeks there was a flurry when it was heard that France was sending convicts to New Caledonia again, but the issue petered out, although echoes were to be heard again and again in subsequent years, and Deakin and several Commonwealth governments were to find it a constant problem.[46]

Naval defence

The major question settled at the Colonial Conference had been naval defence. As international tensions grew, proposals to reinforce the Royal Navy's Pacific squadron had been discussed. The intercolonial conference of 1881 had recommended additions paid by Britain while the colonies built up their local defences. The Earl of Carnarvon's royal commission of 1882 had firmly recommended that the colonies contribute to the cost of reinforcing the Pacific Fleet. The Admiralty became concerned about

Land sale, 1888

Matthew Davies, 1887

James Mirams, *c.* 1887

James Munro

Tommy Bent

the growth of colonial navies for local defence which were outside its control; it also infuriated colonial sailors by refusing to allow the Victorian Navy to fly the royal flag. When Tryon took charge of the Australian station, he was instructed to attempt to negotiate an agreement whereby the colonies would agree to pay for a British-built and British-manned auxiliary cruiser squadron, and allow their navies to be brought under his command. Tryon quickly found there was no chance of agreement to the latter point; moreover he found that the Victorian government, broadly supported by Queensland, wanted a 'fleet built, manned, and owned by Australia itself'.[47] Throughout, however, the government of New South Wales broadly accepted the Admiralty's proposals. Ultimately, Victoria and Queensland did not press their plan for a national fleet or even insist on opportunities for colonial sailors in the Royal Navy, and agreed in principle to a financial contribution. The major difficulty was the amount; the discussion provided many opportunities for argument about what was proposed to be protected–British investments and shipping, or Australian interests. When Derby complained that the British Fleet on the Australian station was costing £157,000 a year, the *Argus* retorted that this 'insurance payment is not 1s. per £100 on the British capital invested in Australia'.[48] Late in 1885 the Admiralty ceded the point about local control of colonial navies and guaranteed that the auxiliary squadron would be confined to Australasian waters. Tryon patiently negotiated, but many details remained at issue; Victoria, especially, was holding out for a smaller contribution to the new squadron, chiefly because of its greater expenditure on its own navy and some feeling that Australia was being singled out from the rest of the Empire for discriminatory treatment.[49]

The details were settled by compromise at the Colonial Conference.[50] Late in 1887 the Victorian Parliament, in the presence of the Earl of Carnarvon and the Marquis of Drogheda, made the passing of the Australasian Naval Force Bill an imperial occasion. Gillies reviewed the history of the negotiations and proudly claimed the agreement was a federal triumph; he also significantly remarked that, though it would have been desirable, it would have cost twice as much to provide entirely for Australia's own naval defence. Only three others spoke, and the Bill was carried *nem. con.* Gravely, nineteen Councillors spoke in agreement. Sir James Lorimer believed that the debate in this and other colonies was being

> watched by the great foreign powers of the world with the utmost anxiety. . . . By carrying the Bill honorable members will show to the world the determination of the Victorian people to stick, whatever happens, to the grand old nation from whence they have sprung, and to be prepared to protect their joint interests, not only with their money, but also with their blood, if necessary.

Proceedings in the upper house concluded with three cheers and one cheer more for the Empire, and a unanimous vote.[51] In retrospect Deakin believed the agreement was 'a final reply to those who were clamouring for a step towards separation', and a massive demonstration for imperial union.[52] In New South Wales Parkes carried the proposals, but Queensland delayed provision of the five new cruisers, for it did not ratify the agreement until 1891. The brave little colonial navies, ignored by the Royal Navy, went into decline.

Victorian diplomacy and the imperial response

Over four years of disagreement, the British officials—patiently on the whole—had tried to restrain these wild colonial boys. With ineffable tact the Earl of Carnarvon reiterated the facts of life in Melbourne in November 1887:

> Whilst we are bound to the best of our power to reduce such a nuisance and to safeguard your interests, on the other hand, let us count upon your patience, your support, your forbearance, very often in difficult matters. In dealing with great nations we cannot always invoke the mere engines of force. Diplomacy is the sole treatment. European diplomacy, as you well know, is a very complex matter....[53]

Of course Britain could not partition the Pacific at her pleasure, was trying to delay the partition process in other parts of the world as well, and believed that the colonial policy of bold annexation would create more diplomatic difficulties than maintaining the *status quo*. When the process was forced on Britain from 1884 to 1886, she was not in a strong bargaining position. France was hostile to British policy in Egypt, and Russia was threatening on the Indian border, so Germany had to be conciliated. There could be no strong protest at the German annexation in New Guinea or any firm stand when settling the demarcation of the boundary; Gladstone saw it as urgent to wind up 'these small colonial controversies', to get 'out of the way the bar to the Egyptian settlement'.[54] Similarly the New Hebrides was one minor issue among several in dispute with France which were settled together in 1887.

In this situation the Victorians must be seen as elephantine blunderers. It is almost certainly true, as many in the Colonial Office and local critics like Higinbotham believed,[55] that the antagonism they created in Berlin and Paris spurred the continental powers on towards annexation. On the other hand, it is possible to argue that the German and French governments, under pressure themselves, would have annexed anyway; and that Victoria, by rousing the imperial government barely in time, at least gained compromise solutions instead of total losses. In calmer moments the Victorian leaders recognized their ignorance of the wider diplomatic situation, but defended their behaviour on the grounds that the imperial government refused to take them into its confidence and was blind to colonial interests unless they were forcibly brought to its attention. The 1885 promise that the colonies would be consulted in future on matters directly affecting their interests, was a significant breakthrough. The Agents-General were consulted more and more, less important confidential information was revealed to them, and they partly replaced the Governors as channels of communication.[56] Service for one believed by 1888 that there had been a basic change in attitude, and that relations between colonies and mother country were highly satisfactory.[57] Rosebery's behaviour over the New Hebrides, Lord Knutsford's conciliatory attitude as Secretary of State, and the success of the Colonial Conference were evidence of the change. In 1888 the imperial government treated the colonies most considerately and tactfully, as we shall see, over the Chinese crisis. But no other external issues, which might have revealed divergent imperial and colonial interests, were to arise for many years.

7

Migrants, Native-born and Irish-Australians

Imperial loyalty and migrant patriotism

Midway through 1885, Robert Harper, a maverick conservative politician, attacked the Victorian government. It seemed that 'the men who rule in Melbourne thought they ought to rule the universe'; leading men in New South Wales were asking, 'Has your Premier lost his head? Are the people in Melbourne mad?'[1] Not for another thirty years, until the era of W. M. Hughes, was an Australian government so to assert itself internationally. In order to explain the ardent unanimity of Service, Deakin, Gillies, Berry and the mass of politicians, press proprietors, the A.N.A., Protestant clergy, leading trade unionists and so many others on imperial and Pacific questions, we need to examine the pattern of imperial, national and local colonial loyalties, and the problem of Australia's future in the Empire.

James Anthony Froude, historian and imperialist, visited Australia in 1884–5 and found the 'great, modern, progressive, middle-class community' of Victoria to be all and more than he had hoped. The colonists were more English than the English themselves, 'as if at the circumference the patriotic spirit was more alive than at the centre'. It 'was English life over again: nothing strange, nothing exotic, nothing new or original. . . . All was the same—dress, manners, talk, appearance.' There was not the 'slightest symptom of a separate provincial originality either formed or forming'.[2] Froude's book is a classic case of myopia; he faithfully reflected the views and hopes of those he met at Government House, the Melbourne Club, 'Ercildoune' and Sir William Clarke's Sunbury estate. He was not wildly astray, however, if we confine his generalizations only to English and Scottish migrants. In a thousand ways, as one visitor after another noted, the institutions and customs of England and Scotland were reproduced and mimicked. 'The first thing that strikes one is that people are so intensely English,' remarked the second Earl Brassey.[3] The 'steady, somewhat narrow, conventional decorum of the middle classes',[4] the earnest statement of new five-year old ideas from home, the style of the newspapers and the theatres, the eating and drinking habits, the pride and joy of suburbanites in their English gardens and the oaks and elms in the parks, all bore provincial witness. Despite the efforts of Governors to induce more suitable fashions, the superior set persisted in wearing heavy frock coats and 'toppers' to the races, even in sweltering weather; evening dress was worn on semi-formal occasions more frequently than in London; 'full side-face whiskers, which of late are becoming old-fogeyish at home' remained common in the eighties. The Mayor of Melbourne provided his annual banquet—turtle soup and all—on the same day as the Lord Mayor of London.[5] G. A. Sala remarked that his hosts preserved intact 'a large number of old English customs and usages, which we at home . . . have long since discarded as coarse and inelegant'.[6]

The migrant colonists' touching and pathetic loyalty to the Crown, much more evident than in England itself, long predated the wars and rumours of wars of this period. Victoria was the Queen's own colony; almost every speech, it seemed, had its inflated loyal reference; statues, busts and prints of the Queen bestrewed public parks, buildings and private houses. Her birthday was devotedly celebrated, and the Prince of Wales' birthday had also long been a public holiday. The Governors were revered as the Queen's and old England's* representatives. When Sir Henry Loch arrived in July 1884, the streets from Port Melbourne to the city were densely crowded all the way; more than 5,000 citizens put their names down at Government House.[7] Visitors and colonists returning from a trip 'Home' were rushed for the latest first-hand news of the old country. Storms of applause greeted Garnet Walch's 'Lions' Cubs' when sung in the music-halls:

> There is not a strong right hand
> Through all this Southern Land
> But would draw a sword in dear old England's cause;
> Our numbers may be few,
> But we've loyal hearts and true,
> And the Lion's cubs have got the Lion's claws![8]

Many an ageing migrant grew increasingly nostalgic for 'Home', which he knew he would never see again; the song, 'Home, Sweet Home', with transposed meaning, always deeply moved colonial audiences. Absence at such a distance certainly made most hearts grow fonder. Several observers remarked that Victoria was more fervently and unitedly loyal than any of the other colonies,[9] but some also noticed the oppressive aspect of this loyal fervour; 'Intolerance comes of it; it frowns down liberty of speech.'[10]

Even the most loyal migrants, however, were strained in their relationships with Englishmen. Cabinet ministers resented being treated with indifference, almost as strangers and nuisances, as though sentiment and the blood relationship counted for nothing. On the individual social level, Englishmen's ignorance about the Empire and their patronizing of 'colon-

* 'Britain' was hardly used except by a few Scots. In 1885 the Caledonian Society protested against the 'anglicising tendency at present at work in the Colony'—the constant use of 'England' and 'English' instead of 'Britain' and 'British'. In 1887, after protests, 'England' was changed to 'Britain' in the illuminations of Parliament House for the Queen's birthday. (A. H. Chisholm, *Scots Wha Hae. History of the Royal Caledonian Society of Melbourne* (Sydney, 1950), pp. 19, 23.)

ials' as somehow inferior beings, were infuriating.[11] Sensitive colonials eagerly read the numerous books by visiting Englishmen about Australia, but usually found them to be teeming with errors and misunderstandings, while the occasional tagging of colonists as 'inferior English' or 'inferior Scotch' was outrageous.* The behaviour of upper-class English black sheep, who were shipped out on remittance to redeem themselves in the belief that anyone could make good in the colonies, was a constant irritation; their frequent insufferable snobbery and decline into alcoholic cadgers made them a by-word of reproach.[12] Australians in England were often regarded as curiosities and not socially acceptable; the convict-poison was the chief reason. The colonial, contrary to the popular assumption in Britain, claimed he was a member, not a subject, of the Empire or of the 'English' nation, and that his colony was a part and not a possession of the realm.[13] Chafing under his dependent status, he needed praise for his achievements and, lacking it, was often boastful.[14] The history of Victoria was a triumph of material and moral achievement; its wealthy capital city needed relatively only half the policemen London required. Australia would be another United States with a population of fifty million in another fifty years and perhaps one hundred million by the 1980s.[15] Victoria was peopled by a superior sample of the population of the British Isles, men and women who had shared the great experience of striking out and fending for themselves, and had come through in good order and learned a lot in the process.

Even those conservatives who had never reconciled themselves to colonial democracy, who were still brooding on being exiles, sometimes felt the need to justify their failure to return home permanently. Those who did retire home were sometimes grievously disappointed; Gyles Turner believed that as many as nine out of ten decided to return to Victoria. Childhood friends were scattered and changed, the climate was unpleasant, they even tired of the idealized lush landscape; and they often met social difficulties in a society in which wealth did not open all doors. 'Richard Mahony' found his corner of rural England a 'stiff, uncharitable little world', and recalled that his colonial associates had not only been warm-hearted and generous, but had also displayed 'a certain breadth of view'.[16] Unaccustomed direct taxation was outrageously oppressive. And the colonial conservative even found himself shocked by the extent of poverty—'the all-pervading sense of helpless mendicancy that obtrudes upon you in all large towns'.[17] Victoria was not just a more pleasant place in which to live but also, he sometimes conceded, a juster society. Squatters' sons at Cambridge discovered themselves to be Australian patriots. Some con-

* Froude's *Oceana* may have been ridiculous in some ways, but its message that the colonies were marvellous places, tremendously valuable assets to the Empire and 'part of England', and that colonial opinion must be given more weight, struck home with the 75,000 purchasers of the book. Several other books (e.g. J. E. Taylor, *Our Island Continent* (London, 1886), p. 255) stated the same case. Leaving aside Twopeny, who was a migrant, none of the 'visitors' impressions' of the eighties rivalled Trollope's *Australia and New Zealand* of 1873; Dale's *Impressions of Australia* was perhaps the best.

servatives remained maladjusted to colonial society and pessimistic about its future, but most had some rudiments of patriotic and nationalist sentiment, based on pride in material pioneering achievement.

Radical migrants' patterns of loyalty are difficult to define. The colony for them was not so much a place of exile as a field of liberty and opportunity, where they might build another, better England, the England that might have been.* They had made their choice, had half-rejected England and, however nostalgic, most had fared well enough to be fervently optimistic about the future of Victoria as their and their children's permanent home. 'Are we not ourselves the realization of More's *Utopia*?', asked one enthusiast.[18] Whether so complacent or not, the old migrants of the fifties had set a determinedly egalitarian tone to the colony. The 'class-system' and old-world privilege were not to be tolerated; small-man antagonism to aggrandisement in any form remained potent. The theme of Victoria as a juster society than Britain and free of class oppression continually recurs. 'Do we not know', asked J. L. Dow,

> that the existing social system at home is one very largely made up of highly paid revenue-consuming aristocrats, while the common people are oppressed by heavy taxes . . .? . . . we in this part of the world have a right to be prouder of the country we are in than of that from which we are derived. . . .[19]

Even 'Jingo' Patterson laid it down that 'It is not the dukes and earls and rubbish of that kind—for whom I have a complete contempt—who have made old England at all; it is the great middle class'.[20] When, in 1887, there was a betting dispute between a visiting peer and a bookmaker, and the magistrates found in favour of the former, the Trades Hall led the outcry of 'Privilege!'[21] Public opinion disapproved of the judiciously distributed imperial honours. C.M.G.s were derided as 'colonial-made gentlemen'; Francis, Higinbotham, Lalor, Deakin, Gillies and Murray Smith all refused the offer of knighthoods. John Woods denounced the 'rotten titles [whose] relative baseness . . . even the College of Heralds could not declare . . . The Jingoes in England want subordinate Jingoes here.'†[22]

* George Cockerill reports the following conversation:
'I am tired of this damned country. I hope to go back soon to a land where life is worth living. . . .'
'I'll wager that until you came to this land of full and plenty you did in the Old Country much the same as I did—kicked the snow off a bloody turnip to get your breakfast.' (*Scribblers and Statesmen*, p. 23.)

† It was well recognized, however, that a knightage was a political handicap. Chief Justices, Speakers, Presidents of the Legislative Council and Agents-General were automatically offered knighthoods. Puisne judges were borderline cases. There were few others apart from these. In the early to mid-seventies knighthoods were granted to Duffy, McCulloch, O'Shanassy and Sladen, but there were no other political awards until Lorimer was honoured during the 1887 Colonial Conference. The eighties was a lean period for all the colonies.

W. J. Clarke (the only Victorian created a baronet) and Samuel Wilson (who owned more sheep, possibly, than anyone in the world and had an annual income approaching £100,000) were the only philanthropists honoured, although Francis Ormond was about to be knighted when he died. It was clearly understood that a wealthy man of good

On such matters the *Age* and the *Leader* spoke for the masses. They attacked the honours system, sniped at the Governors both as imperial watchdogs and the focus of the upper class, deplored the 'uncontrolled wantonness of blue-blooded profligates' when Stead made his disclosures in 1885, and seized with glee on the summonsing of another visiting peer for not paying his hotel bill. They even attacked the Prince of Wales for discreditable behaviour.[23] It may be that, in his earlier period, Syme was more anti-monarchical and separatist than he allowed his editors to reveal. He consistently backed the Higinbotham campaign against the Colonial Office. The assumption that protection was essential to enable some local control of the shape of the economy, a bitter dislike for English capitalists' exploitation of their workmen, and a determination to build a modern industrial society based on comparatively egalitarian principles, were all basic to Syme's creed.

Nevertheless, although we may have reservations about Syme, none of these radical attitudes were necessarily inconsistent with profound imperial loyalty. The aristocracy might be corrupt and oppressive; governments and the Colonial Office might be blind and neglectful; but the Queen and old England and the Empire still retained all their sentimental attraction. Higinbotham's combination of militant defence of the right to complete colonial self-government and fervent imperial loyalty was only an extreme example of the typical;* and the *Age* came down on the jingo side in the eighties.

A limited migrant patriotism—hardly yet a nationalism—was developing. It was based on shared pioneer experience and a sense of difference as a community, on gratitude to the adopted country, pride in material achievement and craving for recognition of it, and some growing sense of destiny—the probability that Australia would become 'as great a nation as any on the face of the earth'.[24] Few events in Victorian history were notable or distant enough yet to be used as the core of a tradition, although the struggles against transportation† lay close to the surface of memory and a few radicals would proudly hark back to Eureka from time to time.[25] A substantial minority, most of whom were politically conservative, remained contemptuous of the colony and of themselves for having settled for a second-rate colonial life. As Gyles Turner once protested, they scoffed

---

character and manners could buy an honour by endowing educational or charitable institutions. Ferdinand Mueller had been knighted in 1879, but no one in education, science or the arts was honoured in the eighties. Berry's elevation in 1886 was widely regarded as an offence against democratic propriety, on which the comment was made: 'Yes, his offence is rank.' (*Leader*, 17 July 1886, p. 26.)

* Higinbotham's influence was vast but we need not accept Deakin's flamboyant exaggeration that 'None of the other colonies exhibited just the same firm alliance between radicalism and loyalty to the mother country because no other colony had a Higinbotham.' (*Federal Story*, p. 9.)

† There were a few kindly references in Parliament once to convicts being more sinned against than sinners, in line with the *Bulletin* myth. But two of the three speakers were former New South Welshmen. (*P.D.*, vol. 45, p. 64.)

at everything colonial from wine to tweeds.*[26] No doubt those who automatically cringed were often correct in their judgment on colonial products, but the assumption of necessary inferiority was pathetic. There is, however, a modification to be noted of the standard identification of political conservatism with truckling to Britain and decrying Australia: the successful man with property to conserve was often properly grateful and loyal to his adopted home. Colonial loyalty to Victoria as against Australia had never been clearly defined (except in rare cases like Syme), but the Victorian loyalty had been more explicit, and simple prejudice against the other colonies had abounded. However, by the eighties the sense of vague Australian nationality and the obvious need, sooner or later, for political union were growing fast. To hazard a guess, most Victorian migrants would have found it almost impossible to decide whether they regarded themselves first and foremost as Victorian, British or Australian. Perhaps most would have said Victorian. Their children's answers are just as difficult to guess.

The future of the imperial relationship; Imperial Federation

The problem of the future relationship between Australia and Britain tortured this generation of migrants. The double loyalty already existed—the consciousness of being as British as ever and loyal to Crown and Empire, and also the sense of belonging to a community which must become a mighty nation. But all historical precedents seemed to lead to the view that the two loyalties could not co-exist indefinitely, that dependent colonies would inevitably grow into independence, that imperial control and colonial liberty were irreconcilable. Not that imperial control was irksome. Since the sixties the Colonial Office had been very careful not to interfere, or to give any appearance of interfering, in domestic colonial matters. Memories of former conflicts remained, but hardly any one but Higinbotham regarded clarification of colonial rights to self-government as urgent. However, the Colonial Office and Liberal opinion in England appeared to expect the colonies to separate in the normal course of events. New generations of native-born Australians would inevitably feel less closely attached to the mother country by bonds of sentiment, and the keeping of the British connection would 'become merely a question of advantage and opportunity'.[27] Some time in the future, colonial self-interest must inevitably clash with loyalty to Britain. In a moment of pessimism in October 1885, Deakin noted in his diary: 'Second reading of Federal Bill. Probably the beginning

* 'A wealthy man will never give you colonial wine, not because it is necessarily worse than the imported stuff on his table, but because it is colonial' (Twopeny, *Town Life*, p. 67). Hubert de Castella, the vigneron, lamented that many men in the highest positions drank local wines 'only en famille and with intimate friends'; it was not done to offer them to guests (*John Bull's Vineyard*, p. 150).

The Tariff royal commission complained of 'widespread and deep-seated prejudice' against colonial manufactures and the foolish notion that it was 'unfashionable and a sign of meanness or poverty to purchase colonial-made goods' (Report, p. lxxvii). Free trade sentiment had a lot to do with this.

of Separation.'[28] Certainly there was no immediate danger; the only likely crisis was Britain's involvement in an unpopular war which would strain colonial loyalties. (The *Age* had long supported Gavan Duffy's claim to the right of colonial neutrality on these grounds.) Many colonists thus distractedly debated the theoretical question of closer union with Britain by formal links, versus separation and subsequent free alliance on a basis of independence.[29]

The question was nothing like as serious in Victoria as elsewhere, for genuine separatist sentiment was to remain very weak. As Wrixon remarked in 1882: 'No one can pretend that any considerable collection of men in this colony [would be found sympathizing] with any proposal to dismember the grand old British Empire. A few harmless political lunatics might indulge in such an idea'.[30] The possibility of separation in the shorter run was raised only in moments of stress in relations with the imperial government. In September 1883 a rural member of parliament remarked that, unless the imperial government improved its behaviour on Pacific issues, the colonies would most reluctantly be compelled to consider separation. The *Hansard* reporter noted there was a 'Sensation', members leapt up to declare that not a man in their constituency wanted to 'cut the painter', and the poor man had to withdraw and protest his loyalty.[31] His threat was to be a political commonplace in 1884 and 1885. The *Age* quite often hinted darkly at the desirability of separation, but in calmer moments it would dismiss the question, as the *Argus* did consistently, as one suitable only for debating clubs.[32] Dr Hearn denied the basis of the argument, that 'perfect political maturity' was unattainable without independence. The colonies were as much part of England as any part of England was: 'There is nothing, absolutely nothing, in the colonial relation to imply as a natural event separation.' Nothing except their own will would make them cease to be part of the great English nation.[33] The native-born Tommy Bent also refused to recognize any problem: 'Some persons talk about "cutting the painter". But how can that come to pass, seeing that we are English—that we are of the same flesh and blood, and that we are as loyal as people in England?'[34] As so often, Pearson saw the essence of the matter:

> There is not one of us who wishes to separate from England, but what attaches us to England is our feeling of loyalty to our Sovereign, the sentiment of nationality, the feeling that we belong to the great English race—that wherever the English arms have planted the flag of victory, and wherever English thought has made its mark in literature, we have a part in it. Beyond that we have the enormous bond of self-interest . . . it is of the last importance to us, who are going to be an Asiatic power also, that England, and no one else, should hold India and Singapore. That being the case, there is not the least danger that the bond between England and this country will ever be relaxed in its intensity.[35]

It was Salisbury who made the point at the 1887 Colonial Conference that because of the new expansionist tendencies of European powers the colonies would have to remain within the Empire to be safe.

The force of the fallacious argument that the only alternative to separation was closer formal union of the Empire lured some Victorian loyalists into the blind alley of Imperial Federation. The idea was not new. William Westgarth and Edward Wilson, the old Victorian radicals of the fifties, had preached the doctrine in London before and after the foundation of the Royal Colonial Institute in 1868. Despite all the talk in the seventies about imminent dissolution of the Empire, the idea of formal union was gaining strength as the Tories laid increasing stress on the imperial mission, as the propaganda of Froude, Dilke, W. E. Forster and others made headway, and as pressure grew from the European powers. By 1884 the stage was set. In February Murray Smith told a meeting of the Royal Colonial Institute:

> Two paths are open before the statesmen of Great Britain, one leading to Federation, the other to—what shall I call it?—disintegration. If they select the latter, their country, in the narrowest sense, may—although I doubt it—be prosperous, it may even be happy, but it will not, I fear, be great. . . . But if they choose the former path, 'she may renew her youth like the eagles', she may hold the Empire in her grasp justly, gloriously, and safely.[36]

Three former Victorians—Westgarth, Francis Labilliere and J. Dennistoun Wood—were on the preparatory committee of six, prior to the foundation of the Imperial Federation League later in the year. Service instructed Murray Smith to represent the colony at the founding conference and to give general support to the idea of Imperial Federation, 'guarding, of course, our local self government'.[37] From the first, the League disclaimed any intention of reducing colonial rights of self-government; its purpose was to gain colonial representation in the supreme imperial policy-making body. But its title was unfortunate, for many of its supporters, although they wanted closer union for purposes of defence or economic policy, did not agree that federation was the answer. From the start the League in England was plagued with disputes about the best method of colonial representation and the relative merits of a *Kriegsverein* or a *Zollverein*, and eventually broke up into dissident groups in 1894.

On 5 June 1885 an enthusiastic full house at the Town Hall founded the Victorian branch of the League—long before any other colony responded. G. D. Carter, the Mayor, E. G. Fitzgibbon, the Town Clerk, Professor E. E. Morris and William Ievers jun. had been the prime movers. Judge Holroyd regarded defence as the overriding motive, Murphy of the Trades Hall believed Imperial Federation should precede Australian federation, but it was Bishop Moorhouse who brought the audience to its feet: 'we are a great people, born to lead, born to teach . . . we are the fittest race to fill the vacant spaces of the world; fittest to help, to protect, and to guide the backward races of mankind.' The *Age* summed up the speech as 'one of the most painful extravagances of Jingoism ever exhibited by an ecclesiastical descendant of the Apostles'.[38] At a later meeting Moorhouse was to say:

> If I thought that Imperial Federation meant the smallest interference with the absolute liberty of local legislation in Australia, I would not touch it with one end of my finger. . . . What I want Imperial Federation for is to give Australia some voice in the decision of questions materially affecting her which she does not at present possess. . . . England has no business to govern us and use us as she pleases. We have a right to a voice in the great empire of which we are part.[39]

Professor J. S. Elkington also ranted about those

> Whelps of that lion whose terrible might
> E'er guarded the weak, and defended the right.[40]

More than one thousand members were quickly enrolled, local mayors were organized to call meetings, and a panel of lecturers went the rounds.

Within a few months the League had almost collapsed. There had been an accidental quality about its foundation at a time of tension and excitement. The inaugural meeting took place a few days after the Gordon memorial meeting, after long weeks' expectation of war with Russia. It was, above all, a demonstration of imperial loyalty consciously aiming to display Victorians' true affections, as a counterweight to all the recent harsh words over events in New Guinea and the New Hebrides. Some may also have felt that the New South Wales gesture over the Sudan called for a special Victorian demonstration. But it amounted to little more than this. As Governor Loch reported, there was an 'elastic character' about the term Imperial Federation and 'varied interpretations' of what it meant.[41] People joined the League in the belief that it was a movement for closer imperial union, to keep the colonies within the Empire. But any plan for closer formal union—an imperial assembly, colonial members of the House of Commons, colonial representation in Cabinet—hardly bore a moment's examination. No scheme appeared remotely practical; moreover, popular sentiment, not so much in Victoria as elsewhere in Australia, would not possibly tolerate any diminution of the powers of self-government or the abandonment of eventual full Australian nationhood. Imperial Federation would inevitably mean free trade within the Empire, the abolition of colonial protection. It is no wonder that the League became inactive almost immediately; in 1886 it did little, except to promote essays in support of the cause. 'Imperial Federation is a myth,' said Walker, the Customs Minister, in July 1887. 'It is utterly impossible. I do not know what it means. I have never heard anyone attempt to define it.' 'We are going on well enough as we are,' said Patterson.[42] Hardly one politician took it seriously as a practical proposition. The measure of the movement's strength was the small reaction it produced; though this is a measure also of the weakness of republicanism in Victoria. In New South Wales and Queensland, the Imperial Federationists were a devilish bogy.[43]

Victoria, of all the British colonies, most welcomed the signs of new interest in Empire at home, was most aware of the growing threats to the Empire, and responded most enthusiastically to the rising tide of jingoism

The Old Story

LITTLE RED RIDING HOOD: What great teeth you have, grandmamma!
WOLF: All the better to eat you with, my little colonial dear!

and the calls for a no-nonsense imperial policy. Disraeli had had no more passionate admirers than in Victoria, when he began to bang the drum and assert British might in foreign fields, and contained Russia so brilliantly in 1878.[44] These migrants of the fifties of the Crimea period had gloried in their youth in Palmerston's exploits. They now found in the new imperial movement a noble cause which seemed both to justify their own achievements as civilizers of the wilds and to glorify the notion of 'fighting a righteous war in the name of civilisation'.[45] J. R. Seeley's *The Expansion of England* (1883) and Froude's *Oceana* (1884), and the fervour of the Royal Colonial Institute and the Imperial Federation League in London, gave assurance that the Manchester Liberals' determination to slough off the colonies and the Colonial Office's tendency to accept the inevitability of separation were no longer dominant beliefs. The Earl of Rosebery's visit in 1883–4 and his message that the Empire was 'the greatest secular agency for good that the world has even seen' also built up faith:

> I say that these are no longer colonies in the ordinary sense of the term, but I claim that this is a nation—a nation not in aspiration or in the future, but in performance and fact. . . . Does this . . . imply separation from the Empire? God forbid! There is no need for any nation, however great, leaving the Empire, because the Empire is a Commonwealth of Nations.[46]

Gladstone's unhappy policy in Africa roused frantic resentment at 'poor old England' being 'dragged through the mire';[47] his Home Rule Bill seemed to amount to deliberate dismemberment of the Empire. Conservative electoral victories brought rejoicings in Victoria. The successful Colonial and Indian Exhibition in London in 1886, for which Tennyson wrote his thrilling ode, was further encouragement:

> Sharers of our glorious past,
> Brothers must we part at last?
> Shall we not thro' good and ill
> Cleave to one another still?
> Britain's myriad voices call
> 'Sons, be welded each and all,
> Into one imperial whole,
> One with Britain heart and soul!
> One life, one flag, one fleet, one Throne.'
> Britons, hold your own![48]

The Queen's golden jubilee and the first Colonial Conference in 1887 appeared to indicate that the Empire had been saved from dissolution.

Anxiety about the Empire predisposed Victorians to be super-sensitive to imperial policy in the Australian region. Service was an extreme fervent imperialist who wanted to help revitalize the Empire and who agonized over the shameful weakness of Gladstone's policy. England, in the Pacific and elsewhere, was so often giving way 'instead of taking her stand upon the ground that if a thing is right we must *insist* on it'. 'Is this generation going to be looked back upon by its descendants as [the one which] destroyed the fabric of the greatest Empire which the world has ever seen?' Again and again he stressed the love and affection of Victorians for the mother country: 'We cling to the idea of the Unity of the Empire. We do not wish to see anything of estrangement between Young Australia and Great Britain. We want our sons and daughters to grow up to love the Old Country.'[49] Service and his colleagues also had a developed sense of national interests, the interests of all the Australian colonies which they took to be identical with imperial interests, being threatened by the European powers. The neglect of these interests by the imperial government, the 'air of icy superiority'[50] of the Colonial Office,* which treated colonial governments like children, was maddening. Not many politicians talked yet in terms of an Australian nation, though Service did:

> As far as France is concerned, Australia is simply a geographical expression. But we want to make it more than that; we want to make ourselves a nation, a united people . . . who are able to command respect. . . . Everyone of us must feel our hearts beat strong and more strong when we think of ourselves not merely as Victorians, or New South Welshmen, . . . but as Australians.[51]

The question of who would govern Pacific territories when annexed—Britain directly or a colony or colonies on her behalf?—was secondary, but a small minority of extremists were genuine Australian imperialists. Even Deakin could say that 'we intend to be masters of the Pacific by and by', and use the specious argument of Victoria's confined territory as a justification for colonization in the Pacific.[52]

Possibly the clearest statement of the Victorian case was made by Berry in an address to the Royal Colonial Institute in 1886 in London. The great strength of the Empire was the fond sentiment of the colonies towards Britain—'affection . . . solidified by mutual interest'. The great problem of the Empire was how to mobilize its potential strength and increase its coherence. The Australian colonies had reached the stage of recognizing, as well as their rights, their responsibility to help bear the burdens of Empire. But they were also beginning to distinguish Australian regional interests and to develop a foreign policy: 'A feeling of nationality is arising in Australia quite consistent with loyalty to the Crown, but which takes cognizance of Australian interests even in the distant future; which feels legitimate pride in the progress of the country, and which links indissolubly Australian sentiments with its loyalty.' The more the Colonial Office had withdrawn its supervision, the stronger the imperial link had become. But the imperial system was urgently in need of reform so that the colonies might have a voice in imperial affairs: 'The change in the centre of gravity of the Empire has not been sufficiently realised. The growth in wealth and

* The Colonial Office's insensitivity and patronizing contempt for the opinions of colonial politicians possibly displayed attitudes to people of 'inferior' social class as much as to colonists as such.

population of the Colonies has scarcely yet been adequately reckoned with.' The argument so far was faultless: it was only when Berry went on to the implied claim that the policy of a colony on a regional problem should automatically become imperial policy—that imperial unity would best be achieved and colonial connections preserved by militantly protecting the extremities equally with the heart from all injury and insult—that the great problem of possibly diverging imperial and colonial interests became evident.[53]

It was beginning to be recognized that Australian national objectives might continue to develop within a framework of imperial loyalty. Service, who at first had been strongly attracted to Imperial Federation, and Deakin too, by 1887 were both disputing the view that it was the only alternative to separation. They recognized that Imperial Federation must mean a loss of self-government, could only become a possibility when Australia itself had federated and had grown closer to equality in power with Britain, and looked forward to it only as a desirable, far-distant goal.[54] They agreed with Sir George Bowen:

> all we should do at present is to stimulate and organize public opinion both at home and in the colonies with a view to some future arrangement for (1) common Defence, and (2) a joint Foreign Policy, which would save the Colonies from being dragged into Foreign Wars without their own consent.[55]

They were certain that the imperial government and Colonial Office had had a change of heart, had recognized the colonies as parts of the realm, and had pledged themselves not 'to do anything which would affect the interests of the colonies without consulting them'.[56] The situation had indeed greatly changed. Englishmen were becoming much more racially exuberant and proud of their colonial cousins; a twenty-year period of ecstatic jingoism had just begun. The Salisbury government was fully conscious now of the power which the colonies contributed to the Empire, had made important steps towards their military organization, and by calling the Colonial Conference had made the first long step towards admitting the colonies to political partnership. Victorians were beginning to believe that nationalism and imperialism might after all be reconciled, and were looking forward to the era of consultation and co-operation which was ultimately to come in the nineteen-twenties. It remained to be seen how the next generation would behave when it came to power, and whether the growth of an exclusive Australian nationalism, especially in reaction to the excesses of jingo imperialism, could be so lightly dismissed.

Native-born Australians; the A.N.A. to 1887

As the number of adult native-born swelled in the eighties, the old migrants—three-quarters still of those over thirty were migrants—fretted over how the younger generation would handle their inheritance. *Would*

Federal Hotel,
Collins Street, 1888

E.S. & A. Bank, 1887

Kamesburgh, Brighton

Goodrest, South Yarra
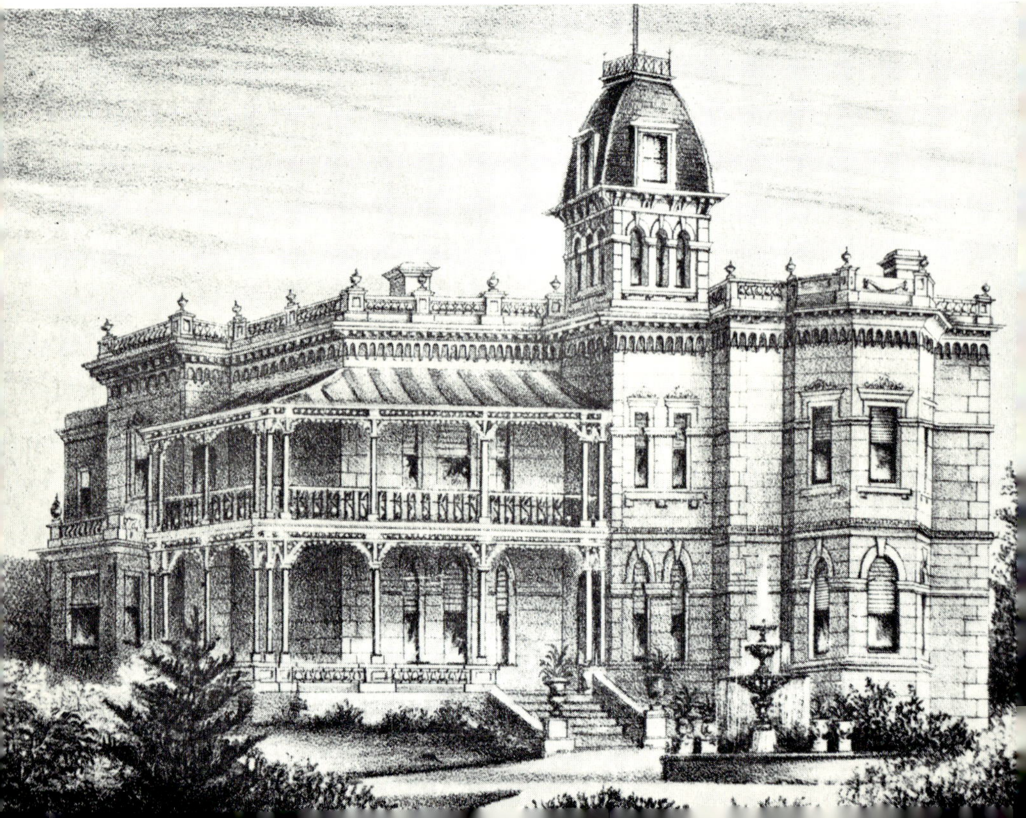

the race degenerate? Surely the British heritage was strong enough to prevail; surely the superior stock which had peopled Victoria, and had largely cleansed it of convict traces, had bred an equally fine strain. Yet as Marcus Clarke assumed in his flippant 'The Future Australian Race',[57] climate must obviously cause fundamental modifications; possibly the Australians would become something like the Greeks. And the younger generation lacked so many advantages—direct old-world associations and the discipline and hardships which their parents had undergone in making their mark. Educationally, they had been well provided for in the modern, free and compulsory state system. But they took the benefits of an affluent society so much for granted, so lacked gratitude, and were so self-satisfied. Need the Australian race necessarily be very different to the British, anything other than an improved version? What would happen when the younger generation took control, as it must in the next ten and twenty years, when 'the larrikin comes on the stage' as Robert Lowe had remarked ominously to Gavan Duffy?[58] Above all, would the young Australians retain their loyalty to the Crown and glorious old England?

In Parliament the native-born had been slow to make their mark. In 1856 only one had been elected to the Assembly. In 1883 there were still only 12 out of 86, in 1886 17, and in 1889 22 out of 95, but by 1894 there were to be 37. The first generation of children of the forties and early fifties were numerically swamped; very few of them, like the lawyers, J. L. Purves and Hartley Williams, became prominent citizens. Of the twenty-six members of the coalition ministries of the eighties, only A. L. Tucker, J. F. Levien, and M. H. Davies, all born in the forties, and Deakin, were natives. The younger generation had got off to a bad start: two of the earliest members had been conduced straight from Parliament to Pentridge. However, J. A. MacPherson, born near Canberra in 1833, had briefly been Premier in 1869-70. Gaunson and Bent, the two lairs, were now the twin terrors of the House; another, Jack Gardiner, had been elected on his merits as a Carlton footballer. But there was also now 'a band of modest, clever, capable young men . . . not the hope but the pride of the Assembly'[59] —among them Deakin, M. H. Davies, J. J. Madden and John Murray. There was little tension between the generations here; the paternal elders freely encouraged their juniors. It might even have been helpful to Deakin and Davies, when they stood for the Liberal leadership and for Speaker, that they were natives. It was noticed that the young Australians ranged themselves instinctively against 'the promoters of old-world quarrels'.[60]

Naturally enough, no clear picture emerges of the rising generation from the welter of superficial and contradictory observations by visitors and the older generation. Surprisingly, many believed that the sons were more sober in their habits than the fathers. The foreman of the Australian Glass Company told the Shops and Factories commission that, although his was a thirsty trade, more than half the colonial hands were teetotallers. He found 'the colonial youth generally intelligent, expert, and steady'.[61] On the other hand, gambling and betting were all too common—'a natural development', wrote one visitor, 'of the risky occupation of the gold miner and mining speculator, from whom a reckless fatalism has been inherited by a large proportion'.[62] The larrikins distressed many elders, who recognized neither how universal they were nor how small a minority. Charles Clark, the eminent public lecturer, was disgusted by some of his experiences: 'As to oratory in these parts: well, Young Australia shouts "Yah!" "Shut up!" "Gammon!" and makes vulgar signals at the bare mention of splendid sentiments clothed in splendid language. "My word! Don't the old bloke blow?" A detestable race!' The explanation of such behaviour, he believed, was hereditary convictism, low-bred natural viciousness and sordid money-worship.[63] J. F. Hogan, schoolmaster and Catholic spokesman, defined the three chief characteristics of colonial youth as inordinate love of sport, disinclination to accept the authority of parents and superiors, and dislike of mental effort; there was not nearly enough flogging in the schools. 'The coming inhabitant of the southern continent', he concluded, 'will be peaceably disposed and sportively inclined; rather selfish in conduct and secular in practice; contented and easy going, but non-intellectual and tasteless.'[64] Francis Adams found young Victorians self-confident, ignorant, indifferent to religion, history and the outside world,* yet 'wonderfully free from cant' and naturally friendly. Gyles Turner deplored the 'superior complacency' of the natives about their own status; and the well-spoken were grieved by their children's 'slovenly articulation and nasal twang'.[65] Major-General Tulloch, however, enthused over his volunteer militiamen:

> Better stuff, or men more amenable to discipline by those who know how to deal with them, do not exist. The well-to-do, comfortable existence . . . seems to resuscitate the old yeoman spirit and self-consciousness of power which made the England of the middle ages so formidable. . . . Better circumstances bring out the old fighting strain in the blood, and make the men instinctively turn towards soldiering.[66]

Polished young Englishmen like Adams, Harold Finch-Hatton and Twopeny tended to find better-class Australian girls, in contrast to English girls, frank, free and easy, unaffected, comradely and not prudish.†[67] Thus local youth was anxiously measured—on the one hand Samuel Alexander's triumphs at Oxford or the casual fortitude of the twenty-year-

* P. A. Jacobs (*A Lawyer Tells* (Melb., 1949), pp. 113-14) tells of a fellow student who, when asked whether he would like to see the world, replied: 'No. I guess there are sheep round about Coleraine and Harrow as good as you'll get anywhere in the world.'

† Harold Finch-Hatton (*Advance Australia!*, p. 320) wrote: 'The frank demeanour and the entire absence of affectation that makes an Australian girl such a pleasant companion after ten minutes' acquaintance, would in England, of course, be set down to fastness, if to nothing worse. . . . it is infamous to say that the absence of reserve . . . argues the slightest inferiority of moral principles to those who have been brought up to consider that purity can only be preserved in ice.' Cf. The Lady Casey on her parents' generation (*An Australian Story*, pp. 34-5): 'The young women of the eighteen eighties and nineties were affected by the windy climate and sense of space in the same way that the larrikins were, they were high-spirited, independent, capable of improvisation, aware of the Australian code of mateship'.

old Ernest Morrison's stroll from the Gulf of Carpentaria to Melbourne, on the other the latest larrikin excess or irresponsible student 'rag'.

The older generation apprehensively watched the emergence of the Australian Natives' Association from 1883. It had been founded in 1871 as the Friendly Society of Victorian Natives by a group in which J. F. Levien and S. V. Winter of the *Herald* were prominent; A. L. Tucker and George Turner were also original members. The name was quickly changed, in 1872, and eligibility widened to include all native Australians. The old-world mumbo-jumbo of most friendly societies was rejected from the start: no secret signs, grips or passwords were used, there was no regalia, and meetings were open to the public. Mutual insurance was the society's prime purpose, although honorary members, who perhaps already belonged to other friendly societies, were permitted to join.

Progress was slow: by 1880 there were only 235 members in half a dozen branches. Ballarat had become the headquarters in 1879 and for the next few years the society grew mainly in the gold towns, while the Melbourne branch stagnated. An Irish-Catholic element, which perhaps saw the A.N.A. as a means of breaking away from the confining attitudes of their church and tribe, remained a fairly strong minority, while other pockets of strength developed, like the Geelong football team who were members almost to a man. From the early eighties, the high birth rate of the sixties made massive recruitment possible; membership rose from 645 in 14 branches in 1882, to 1,554 in 21 branches in 1884 (when the Ballarat branch had 500 members), to 4,414 in 58 branches in 1886.[68] The rise in the number of native-born and the gulf between the generations were so noticeable that it was perhaps natural for the natives to join together in organizations, and may partially explain why the A.N.A. 'took' in Victoria more than elsewhere. There were handicaps to organization, however. The name itself—'Natives' was an American usage—was odd and ambiguous and provoked comment. The rigid rule confining membership to the native-born was difficult to justify logically, and could be defended only by the argument that drawing the line at a particular age of migration was even less satisfactory. John Quick, who had migrated at the age of two and was a leading spokesman for the younger generation, was granted honorary membership of the Bendigo A.N.A., but many other child-migrants must have been resentful. Several attempts within the society to modify the rule were defeated.

Judging by the absence of references in the metropolitan press, the A.N.A. was an insignificant body before late 1883. Yet it was clearly a nursery of striking talent. Its first law, that it was an association for 'moral, social and intellectual improvement', had encouraged its ambitious young members—the best the gold towns could produce—to read and to speak in public, though on topics which as yet hardly varied from those common to any church debating or mutual improvement society, in England or Australia. However, the A.N.A. was increasingly becoming a political training-ground, the great events of the day were commonly discussed informally, many members were becoming local councillors and some, like R. H. Hart,* the chief president in 1883, were even standing for Parliament. From 1882 a monthly journal was produced—successively the *Native,* the *Australian Native,* the *National Australian* and the *Australian,* all edited from Ballarat. But those members who wanted the society to develop a political role were held back by the rule which forbade adoption of party political causes—necessarily, since the raising of divisive issues would threaten the insurance-benefit basis of membership. The board of directors tirelessly refuted the popular belief that the A.N.A. was a political organization, and dissociated themselves from the numerous Natives' Democratic societies which the Liberal party had fostered in the 1880 and 1883 elections. The fact was, however, that the A.N.A. was radically oriented, and their elders knew it; many of them were frightened of its potential as an extreme democratic movement. The young men of Ballarat, among whom Hart was most prominent, were indeed urging Deakin in 1884 to proclaim himself leader of a new Liberal party, based on the gold towns, which they would organize; many of them were land nationalizers.[69]

For many years the A.N.A. remained modest and deferential to the older generation. One of its members, however, was a notable exception. George Meudell, son of the general manager of the Bank of Victoria and author late in life of an autobiography which exposed the shady side of the land boom, remained a classical Australian nationalist and *enfant terrible* all his life. In 1882 (when he was twenty-two, not fifteen as he claimed in *Pleasant Career of a Spendthrift*) the *Melbourne Review* published his brash, clever, partly tongue-in-cheek 'Australia for the Australians' (the slogan which, on Meudell's suggestion, the *Bulletin* adopted in 1888).[70] In a sense the article was an unexpected climax to sporadic conjectures in print about the 'future Australian race'. Meudell simply stood previous assumptions on their heads by claiming that the Australian environment was so much better than the English that a far superior race was developing. It was not perfect yet, because young Australians had been led astray by their bigoted elders, who in many respects were ignorant and prejudiced, especially in their sectarianism. 'Here Democracy is in its prime; in England, in its infancy', he wrote in a later article, and gleefully quoted:

> Crabbed age and youth cannot live together....
> Youth is hot and bold, age is weak and cold....

The English were foreigners, Australia would not be well governed until the native-born took over and declared an independent United States of Australia. Meudell was aiming to raise a 'Young Australia' party, but the political programme he outlined was conventional and uninspiring.[71]

In 1882 such American-style 'nativism'—antagonism to foreigners and

* R. H. Hart (1854-84), son of a Methodist minister, educated Wesley College, schoolmaster there and elsewhere, established Ellerslie Girls' School 1878-82, beaten by John Woods for Stawell in 1881, Berryite and anti-Catholic. Deakin thought the world of him (*Federal Story*, p. 9). See T. Williams, *Assiduity: being a Memoir of the late Richard H. Hart* (Ballarat, 1886).

assertion of superiority of the native-born—won little or no support in the A.N.A. 'It is not fair to judge the race', wrote O. E. Wilson, editor of the *Native*, 'by the noisy obstructionists and windy orators who . . . boast of their being Australian Natives. . . . Nowhere is the contempt for such asses stronger than amongst their fellow countrymen.' He rejected the slogan 'Australia for the Australians' and apologetically hoped the native-born would emulate their fathers.[72] Yet the number of politically conscious members was quickly growing and discussion on the potential role of the native-born was becoming keener. Wilson himself, who became chief president in 1884, was encouraging literary contributions to the journal on Australian history and geography, and as early as March 1883 recommended adopting federation as the A.N.A.'s particular cause. New Guinea and the New Hebrides provided the rallying issue for the activists: Ballarat held the first important A.N.A. public meeting in September 1883 in support of annexation.[73] In August a Clunes member exhorted his local branch:

> What grander theme can we have than the contemplation of Federal Australia? Stretching from the equator to the 44th degree of latitude, from New Guinea to Tasmania, from Western Australia to New Zealand and the New Hebrides. A territory comprising some of the fairest portions of the earth's surface, comprising almost all degrees of climate, of territory unlimited, mineral and agricultural resources, and favoured by nature with everything the heart can wish for.[74]

By August and September 1884, when the Ballarat and Melbourne branches held ambitious demonstrations, Service was using the A.N.A. as the driving-force of the annexation movement. Federation, however, could not be explicitly supported because it was politically controversial, especially in relation to the divisive protection issue. It is striking indication of public unanimity on the Pacific question that it was not considered to be political in the same sense.

1885 to 1887 were remarkable years of expansion under the presidency of Alexander Peacock, a Creswick legal manager of mines, and Thomas Jefferson Connelly,* a Bendigo solicitor and university graduate; the Association now formed many branches in the Melbourne suburbs. Peacock even led an expedition to Sydney and after a stormy reception—Sir John Robertson accused him of fomenting racial rivalry—succeeded in forming a branch there. By this time members were absorbed in trying to define their sense of distinctiveness as young Australians and the proper objectives for the emerging nation. In the branches, the political or literary subject-matter of the debates, discussions, informal speeches, songs, poetry readings or recitations which followed formal business was coming to be predominantly Australian. The heady wine of nationalism, historically so attractive to the young, inflamed a growing minority to accept utopian

* T. J. Connelly (1858-92), Bendigo-born and mayor of that city, according to Deakin was of 'uncommon mental capacity, great force of character' and intellectual energy (*Federal Story*, p. 6). See Leavitt and Lilburn, *Jubilee History*, vol. 2, pt 4, p. 31.

notions of their superiority as a new breed of man, especially in the Melbourne branch which had been rejuvenated by the arrival of Meudell and others from the gold towns who were inclined totally to reject the old world. The board of directors remained cautious and moderate, but Peacock was putting more emphasis than his predecessors on development of a national purpose: 'We aim at supporting national claims and interests [and] developing a broad and enlightened national opinion and sentiment.'[75] Connelly, in his first editorial for the *National Australian* on 13 November 1885, argued that the great task was 'to join and fuse the separate communities [of Australia] into one great state, and their peoples into one great race, [and to] develop a deep and strong race sentiment'. The A.N.A. could best contribute to this by encouraging its members to involve themselves to their utmost in public issues, but the A.N.A. itself must not be involved in party politics. Migrant pressmen grew increasingly indignant at belittling of the older generation's achievement and claims by the native-born of a higher right to the title 'Australian', and made merry at the expense of the more callow and naïve nativist boasting. The *Age*, with justification, could defend its own idealism and social conscience in comparison with the natives'. The migrant generation had 'the points of the Charter graven upon their minds' and had created a society in which the younger generation could not find glaring wrongs to be redressed.[76]

Bickering between the generations inevitably grew; there were many footling disputes between local A.N.A. branches and the Old Colonists' Association and other pioneer bodies. George Cockerill, the *Age* journalist, grew up in Bendigo in the eighties and recalled the division between youth and age:

> The good Britishers who represented the elders, retained a love for their homeland so active and complete, that to them, by comparison, Australia and every other land on earth were inferior. They extolled the fields, the woods, the fruits, the flowers and all the natural loveliness of the Old Country, and laughed at the suggestion of Australian fertility and beauty. The apples here did not taste the same; Australian peaches were coarse and tasteless; the English peaches delicate and luscious. . . . To these fine old British patriots Australia compared even more unfavourably with Great Britain in production of men and women. Every virtue, every capacity, every achievement laid to the credit of an Australian-born youth could be overmatched by youth 'at Home'.[77]

Increasingly the young, with sarcastic references to ' 'ome', guyed their elders.[78] Connelly had the capacity to understand the nature of the tensions between the generations—the references on the one hand to 'bumptious young fools' and 'ungrateful young wretches' and the inability of youth to understand why they were so irritating: 'And so the wretched business proceeds, engendering mutual ill-will.'[79] In 1886 Bella Guerin, the 'first sweet girl graduate' of the University of Melbourne, wrote a tactful article on 'The Development of National Character' for the *Argus*. She admitted that the natives lacked idealism, high aims, and reverence for greatness.

The older generation usually attributed this to want of old associations, but the natives could not revere 'the associations which our parents possess' because of divided loyalty and 'double allegiance'; inevitably the local bonds were stronger. 'We elect to stand apart from old associations, and thoughtlessly strive to lessen that dignity which we refuse to share', or else stay silent and refuse just praise to the generation which had made Victoria, because of a sense of 'jealous nationality'. 'We fully realise all the advantages of the home countries, but we mentally decide that it is all very well for people who claim their superior lands as *their* homes to call upon us to join in admiring these advantages, [and] we will not oblige them—certainly not without personal experience of the British Isles.'[80] Such rebelliousness by ardent young Australians was natural but, as always between youth and age, appeared more serious and likely to be more lasting than it turned out to be.

Even the old colonists who were most proud of the colony lapsed all too easily into sentimentality about the old country and found it difficult to admit that their children could possibly improve on their achievement. 'Young Australia indeed' growled old Sir John O'Shanassy, when defeated for Parliament by J. J. Madden in 1883; 'time enough for young Australia to speak in twenty years' time.'[81] The best of the young revolted against their complacency, and challenged their assumptions about the twin superiority of Britain and Victoria. Why, some began to ask, were Australian history and geography not taught in the schools; why were Leichhardt, Sturt and Burke and Wills not eulogized as Mungo Park and Livingstone were? 'I do not wish to praise anything because it is Australian,' one of them reasonably remarked, 'but because an idea is colonial it is not therefore shoddy. The same battle was fought in America.'[82] If the migrant achievement was so great, if the stock was so superior, and if they had provided such fine education for their children, then surely their children's patriotic hopes deserved more serious attention. Some of the young Australians who went overseas had already developed classical attitudes. Ethel F. (Henry Handel) Richardson arrived in England in 1887 at the age of seventeen, she says, 'a sturdy young radical, convinced that one man was as good as another', who detested English snobbishness and reverence for titles, and found the frank and informal Americans much more like Australians.[83] Susie, the heroine of Francis Adams's delightful novel, *The Melbournians*, was appalled by the 'servility of the ordinary English' and exclaims:

> 'Oh *I* would talk any amount of disloyalty! You don't know how I detest England. It is so wretchedly old and corrupt, and all its ways disgust me. We should sever from it, or be able to treat with it equally, and not as—as inferiors. . . .'
>
> 'I don't see why Australians shouldn't be proud of being Australians, and not to be ashamed of owning it, as they are in England. One woman asked me once if I wasn't a *Kaw-lonial,* just as if you'd be asked if you weren't a *Haw-tentot* or an *Esquim-maw.* I said no; I was an *Aw-stralian.*'[84]

Even the youngish Deakin, plain living and high thinking, was scathing about the royal family, the immoral aristocracy, and the snobbishness, 'insincerities and formalities' which pervaded English life.[85]

Late in 1886 A. S. Bailes, an 'almost native' publican recently elected to the Assembly for Bendigo, remarked in debate that while he had nothing against the Queen he hoped the monarchy would be extinguished when she died. 'Moreover the character of the Prince of Wales was not obviously high. [He had] always been mixed up with scandal wherever he had gone.' Loyal members were horrified and Gillies administered a dressing-down. Bailes later apologized to the Assembly and his constituents. In Melbourne he received an anonymous challenge to a duel (pistols or foils) with the warning that refusal would bring a horsewhipping. There was uproar in Bendigo. A meeting of about five thousand people broke up in disorder, after rival renditions of 'God Save the Queen' and 'The Bonny Flag of Australia', and cheers, boos and groans for Bailes and the Prince of Wales had prevented any speaker being heard. The local youths had turned out in force to wreck the demonstration against Bailes; most of them no doubt were only in it for a lark, to tease and shock their migrant parents. Their elders were shocked indeed, not only by the fact that one-third or more of the meeting had supported Bailes but also by the number of letters to the press in his support, from old residents as well as natives. The next Sunday most congregations demonstratively roared the National Anthem.[86]

Such incidents were rare, and the A.N.A. leadership deplored them. Although nativist sentiment was growing, only a handful as yet were dubious about loyalty to the Empire. The board of directors and the annual conference approved of sending troops to the Sudan, adopted a complimentary address to Dalley, and disavowed rebel members of the Melbourne branch. The Association was the chief driving-force in the renewed agitation over the New Hebrides in 1886. Meudell was recommending application for American assistance; he now had a vision of a Western Hemisphere alliance embracing the Americas, Australia and the ocean between.[87] A Bendigo member wanted to plant 'the Union Jack with the Southern Cross upon it on these islands' and to leave Britain to fight it out with France.[88] It appears that such views were not confined to militant extremists, for the *National Australian* in August 1886 supported Victorian occupation of an island in the group. Service continued to look to the A.N.A. as his chief allies, and when he retired as Premier made a point of passing the banner to them as leaders of the national cause at the annual conference banquet in February 1886.[89] The rise of the Imperial Federation movement forced on the process of defining loyalties. A dozen extremists from the Melbourne branch formed a dissenting minority at the foundation meeting of the League, and they and others attacked it bitterly in letters to the press. The movement, however, was long and earnestly discussed in A.N.A. branches, for it did provide a superficially attractive formula whereby Australia could not only have its voice heard but also share in the making of imperial policy, though abandoning all aspirations to independent policy. In the end, Imperial Federation gained few supporters in the A.N.A. and Calder Smith's view remained dominant:

> As an Australian, I would protest against the servile homage which would surrender our rights and our independence, and extinguish our aspirations without questioning. . . . The masses of the people in the colony are satisfied to continue their relations with the old country. . . . Notwithstanding the irritating political relations with the mother country, we can continue as at present in close alliance with her, and leave to the future the work of determining the mutual relations.[90]

When eventually it was realized that the Colonial Office was consulting the government on Pacific issues, the A.N.A. leadership was broadly content, especially when Deakin, their pride and joy, returned as a hero from the Colonial Conference in 1887.

So far, then, apart from a small republican minority, the native-born seemed likely to accept their heritage, to acknowledge their fathers' achievement and to remain loyal to Britain. Although numerically only a small fraction, the A.N.A. may be assumed to be representative of the better educated and politically conscious native-born; few natives who were not members were becoming prominent in public life. To this stage at least, it was predominantly an urban movement based on the gold towns, made up roughly equally of artisans, labourers and men of the middle class, and led by young businessmen. Radical though its political tone was, it was no more than a reflection of the current advanced thinking of liberal groups, and there was minimal contact with the trade union movement. The A.N.A.'s most prominent virtues—not negligible in their effect on public opinion—were rejection of intercolonial prejudice, and determination to combat or scorn sectarianism. By 1887 it had become a major political force whose ultimate contribution remained unpredictable, for the full flowering of nativism and the crisis of loyalties were still to come.[91]

Irish-Australians; the Home Rule movement

In front of St Patrick's Cathedral one statue stands alone: that of Daniel O'Connell, the 'Irish Liberator'.* One-fifth of the colony's population, whose religion and patriotism intertwined, had very different problems of nationality from the rest. Educationally and economically, Irish Catholic migrants as a whole were worse off than other migrant Victorians; yet they had reason to be proud of their record. J. F. Hogan's book, *The Irish in Australia* (1887), claimed to be a demonstration of what the Irish could achieve when given a chance. Though slightly ludicrous in its inclusion of every notable English migrant with Irish links, the book was an important essay in public relations which was also intended to boost Irish Catholic

* The movement to erect the statue began in 1871; in 1888 the statue, which cost £1,800, arrived from London; it was unveiled on 30 May 1891. (W. A. Ebsworth, *St. Patrick's Cathedral 1839-1939* (Melb., 1939), p. 54.)

morale; it ran through three editions in four months.[92] The grand strategy of the Church, led by Bishop Goold and Sir John O'Shanassy, as a minority group at odds with many of the majority assumptions, had been to consolidate its position and to defend the civil and religious liberty which it so appreciated. It recognized that forcing the Irish issue too far would antagonize the Protestant majority; and attempted to coerce its more undisciplined members in areas like the Kelly country into realization that old traditions of resistance to government, landlord and parson were largely irrelevant in the colonial context.* However, the Education Act could not be accepted, and from the late seventies O'Shanassy and the Catholic parliamentarians gave and withdrew support to ministries simply on the basis of their attitude to redress of the educational grievance.[93] The anti-Catholic reaction was violent, and as events in Ireland again reached crisis-pitch the eighties saw the worst period of sectarian antagonism until 1916.

The Home Rule movement was revivified with the foundation of the Irish National Land League in 1879; Victorian branches were formed in 1881 and set about gathering funds. 1882 was the centenary of Grattan's declaration of independence, and early in the year the militants drew up an 'Address of the Irish in Victoria to the Irish in Ireland' which included reference to a 'foreign despotism' and an 'alien parliament' ruling Ireland. The Protestant Francis Longmore and John Gavan Duffy and three other Irish Catholic politicians signed the document, some of them without reading it closely. Then occurred the outrageous murders of the Chief Secretary for Ireland and the Under-Secretary in Phoenix Park, Dublin. Building on inflamed public opinion, Patterson, the Orangemen and the *Age* raised the contrived cry of treason and sedition against the Grattan signatories. Liberal Orangemen saw an opportunity of driving a wedge between the Constitutionalists and O'Loghlen's ministry, and hoped to expel the signatories from Parliament. After three evenings of bitter debate and several protests against such display of old-world prejudices, the Assembly carried on party lines a mild motion of censure moved by J. G. Francis, the Constitutionalist leader. No more was heard of a Liberal motion, which had been tabled by A. T. Clark and Deakin, calling for Home Rule for Ireland, in line with a resolution recently carried by the Canadian lower house. The Liberal Orange faction had found the issue which might win an election. 'We are Englishmen, and this is an English colony', screamed the *Age*. '... we do not intend to let a handful of "foreigners", if they will have themselves so, impugn our loyalty to the hard-won traditions of race.'[94]

The cry was inadequate to bring the Liberals to power. But militant Protestantism was a major factor in promoting the eventual coalition government and in dismissing about half the Catholic M.P.s, including

* Old traditions died hard. As late as the nineties, 'jovial good-natured Irishmen' back of Warrnambool, aided by a 'wonderful system of bush telegraphy and espionage', were distilling huge quantities of whisky on Crown land, for fun and from tradition rather than for profit. (H. W. Osborne, *Memories* (Terang, 1939) , pp. 12-13; *The Reminiscences of Detective Inspector Christie* (Melb., 1913), chs 14-15.)

O'Loghlen and O'Shanassy. Tension increased immediately after the election, for in March 1883 the Phoenix Park murderers were rounded up and Fenian dynamite explosions rocked London. That St Patrick's Day saw a defiant mass parade of the green; 'no old colonist could remember that such a proud avowel of nationality had ever before been made in Melbourne by the sons and daughters of ever beloved Erin', the *Advocate* reported.[95] A further crisis was at hand: Parnell had sent out the brilliant John and William Redmond, one an M.P. at the age of twenty-five, the other twenty-one and soon to be elected, to win support and raise funds for the Irish National League (the new name for the Land League which had been banned in 1881 and reformed). After some months in the other colonies, they arrived late in May to spend two months in Victoria rousing demonstrations, while the government and Protestant leaders were preoccupied with the Albury celebrations and the New Hebrides and federation campaign. The local leaders of the League strove desperately to refute the popular assumption, viciously promoted by the *Age*, that the Redmonds were to be identified with assassins and dynamiters, but the City Council and municipalities combined in refusing them use of public halls.[96] Warned by their friends of the state of public opinion, the Redmonds spoke more moderately than usual; their meetings concluded with the National Anthem. Even so, there was some rioting, and the press largely ignored their speeches, though editorial vilification continued. The clergy turned out massively in support, despite papal disapproval of the League; but Archbishop Goold, alarmed by the Protestant reaction, wrote home angrily: 'Keep your red hot politicians in Ireland where they are much needed.'[97] Some of the more wealthy and influential Catholics were opposed to the League's attack on property rights, and withheld support. Not one of the remaining Catholic politicians—not even O'Loghlen, an old family friend of the Redmonds—would mount the platform for fear of destroying their political careers. William Redmond condemned these 'cowardly Irishmen—(loud groans)—who hadn't the common manliness to stand by their side and adhere to the principles which in secret they professed to hold'.[98] At another meeting two nights later, however, Frank Gavan Duffy, who forty-seven years later was to become Chief Justice of the High Court of Australia, pointed out that following one's conscience meant the sacrifice of friendships with Protestants who genuinely believed the League was seditious and who detested the introduction of Irish politics into Australia. Under these circumstances he could understand men saying, 'we sympathise with the Land League, but in this distant Victoria our first duty is to Victoria'. The meeting was outraged and broke up in embarrassed confusion.*[99]

* The Protestant Henry Bournes Higgins dined that night with Duffy and 'bemoaned our fate, for our conduct in defying the strong public feeling [against Home Rule] would very probably ruin our careers at the Bar. Solicitors, who distribute the briefs, are usually bitter reactionaries'. But the worst that happened to Higgins was that he was refused membership of the Melbourne Club. (MS. Autobiography, Higgins Papers, pp. 83, 86-7.)

In July there was an odd conclusion to the long-drawn-out story of the Phoenix Park murders and the subsequent manhunt which the press had so exploited. Two of the criminals, who had been pardoned when they turned informer, arrived in the colony with the encouragement of the Irish authorities. All sides were angered by this renewed dumping of convicts. Service refused to have 'rubbish shot upon us' and would not allow them to land; the imperial authorities arranged for their return home, and the Colonial Office expressed regret for the mishap.[1] Tension remained high. Patterson and the Orangemen persuaded the Mayor not to allow C. H. Bromby, son of the former Anglican Bishop of Tasmania and nephew of Canon Bromby of St Paul's Cathedral, to speak in the Town Hall in support of Home Rule.[2] The government refused, because of public feeling, to support a proposal to build a monument to O'Shanassy, who had died in May.[3] Some militants urged the government to ban the Irish Australian Convention planned for November with the object of establishing the National League on a federal basis. But the Convention, when it met for a day on 7 November under the presidency of the old rebel, Kevin O'Doherty of Queensland, was carefully decorous. About three-quarters of the 150 delegates were Victorian; the clergy had been so disciplined that only one was present as a delegate, but John Redmond declared that the Bishops and priests had given him 'practically unanimous support'. A cable from Parnell was greeted with 'prolonged and enthusiastic cheering'. Longmore's resolution supported Home Rule on the grounds that 'we Australasian colonists experience great benefits from self-government, and our enjoyment of that privilege strengthens our attachment to the Crown'. The *Age* sourly commented that if they were plotting treason and disintegration they had no right to complain if they were treated as 'traitors and aliens'.[4]

The roots of disharmony between English and Scottish Protestants and Irish Catholics sank deep. More than 300 years of English history had not allayed suspicion of Catholic subversion. The recent papal assaults on liberalism, and local Catholic attacks on the secular state bred new fears of a disloyal, unassimilable minority owing allegiance to a foreign power. Migrants had brought to the colony their guilt towards poverty-stricken Ireland and their fear of competition from cheap Irish labour. To agree that Ireland had wrongs, was to admit that she was oppressed by Englishmen and Scots. The Kellys and their sympathizers—a black mark of crime and ignorance—had only recently been suppressed. An educated man like Patchett Martin could say, 'we are veritably two races'[5]—a view with which no doubt most Irishmen agreed. Horrified by an agrarian outrage—an Irish tenant had shot his landlord attempting to evict him—the government had recently hanged the criminal while an appeal to the Privy Council was pending.[6] Hayter, the statistician, was recording a disproportionate amount of crime by Irish Victorians, who included relatively more illiterates. The *Advocate* was reprinting the propaganda of the more extreme Irish-American agitators. Catholic gatherings toasted the Pope before the Queen (although this was the common practice of English Catholics, and the National League and the St Patrick's Society were scrupulously undenominational in their formal procedures).[7] The barrage of press propaganda allowed small prospect for rational judgment; the reader was not to know that even the London *Times*'s widely reprinted reports were written by one of Dublin's leading Orangemen. Above all, the Irish activity was seen as disloyal and dangerous to imperial unity. To the argument that what was good for Australia would be good for Ireland, it was replied that it was outrageously impertinent to intervene in British politics.

A few thousand members of the Loyal Orange Institution, 'a purely religious organisation' to 'defend the Protestant religion and the connexion of the colonies with the Empire', stoked the sectarian fires. Their task, as they saw it, was to resist Catholic 'encroachments on civil and religious liberty', while observing the principles of toleration.[8] Their slogan was 'Home Rule equals Rome Rule'; no other group sang the National Anthem with quite such fervour. Their strength lay among the Presbyterian Ulster migrants and the nonconformist sects; although Dean Macartney appeared on the platform at the Protestant Hall, the Church of England was not strongly represented. The Orangemen were usually sound Sabbatarians and temperance advocates; their membership largely overlapped with that of the Protestant Alliance Friendly Society, whose *Victorian Standard* was yet another vehicle for anti-Catholic propaganda. They used the occasion of the four hundredth anniversary of the birth of Luther for a sustained counter-demonstration against the Irish Convention in November 1883. The Orangemen were numerous enough to make up a potent political organization; members were pledged to vote only for Orange or other Protestant candidates, never to refrain from voting, and always to support candidates adopted by the Institution.[9] They claimed much of the credit for bringing about the coalition ministry and exulted over the election results of 1883. 'They had stifled treason on the threshold', claimed Patterson, who was in effect the Orange political leader though he said he was not a member.[10] The successive grandmasters, R. Richardson of Creswick and Simon Fraser, were handily placed in Parliament to exert pressure, while Ballarat frequently returned Orangemen.* Their great grievance was their inability to parade, which was forbidden under the Party Processions Act. Service refused to amend the Act in 1883 and was warmly supported by most parliamentarians. Bent remarked that 'as Australians we don't want to have anything to do with' Orange versus Green, while the *Argus* (in contrast to the *Age*) condemned their 'evil' methods which tended only to drive the Irish back into the clerical fold.[11] So the annual celebrations of the Battle of the Boyne had to be confined to indoor meetings. The Catholic clergy drilled their flocks to stay at home on those days and nights.[12] Church policy was similarly to ignore the Orange-sponsored public lectures in 1887 of the 'Escaped Nun', Biddy O'Gorman.[13]

* Others returned in 1883 who were either members or closely associated were Baker, Bell, W. M. Clark, James, McColl, Nimmo, Russell, Uren.

Irish affairs were relatively quiet in 1884 and 1885 but, with Gladstone's conversion to Home Rule, mass demonstrations were renewed. Reflecting changing English opinion, a few more Protestants appeared on the Irish platforms at the great meetings in the following agonizing years; Dr Strong and Dr Bevan, whom the *Argus* dubbed 'meddlesome sentimentalists',[14] and the politicians Mirams, Gaunson and John Murray joined the staunch H. B. Higgins. However, most politicians remained hostile—unlike New South Wales, where many Gladstonian political leaders came out in support. O'Loghlen and John Gavan Duffy took their places again as tribal leaders, but most of the Catholic politicians still stayed away from meetings. In June 1886 when the Home Rule Bill was being debated, the Melbourne City Council refused to allow the Town Hall to be used for a meeting in support of the policy of the imperial government. Some 7,000 people met in the open at Carlton to thank Gladstone for his wise and generous policy and to sympathize with him over the defeat of the Bill in the Commons.[15] After the great disappointment of Gladstone's electoral defeat, regular meetings of thousands continued through 1887 to protest at the Tory Coercion Bill, to support Parnell against the forgeries published in *The Times*, and to sympathize with evicted tenants.[16]

The discipline and peacefulness of the Irish Catholics at this time of provocation is impressive, in view of their scapegoat role as an ethnically distinct and underprivileged group. There was no trace in Victoria of the Irish-American dynamite party, nor any notable deviation from British constitutional procedures; anti-British feeling was held firmly in check by the clergy and lay leaders. They felt themselves, with some justification, to be persecuted; and they were indeed isolated on the Irish question, apart from the support of a handful of Protestant home rulers and the unwelcome Secularists. The *Advocate* fairly claimed that Melbourne was exceptional, that 'just and liberal views' prevailed 'in other capital or large Australian cities'.[17] The Catholic community was largely united on the issue. Lalor and O'Shanassy in their last days were notable exceptions (though O'Shanassy's son-in-law, Nicholas Fitzgerald who succeeded him as the most prominent spokesman, was militant); other non-participants, like the Madden brothers, may have feared that the more the Irish issue was pressed, the more the cause would suffer. The rank-and-file bitterly resented defections by Catholics in higher social positions. Archbishop Goold did not commit himself, but Archbishop Carr, the bishops of Ballarat and Bendigo and the mass of clergy left no doubt about where they stood. The tens of thousands of pounds contributed to the Home Rule cause made a remarkable sum, when the financial demands of the Church and the relative poverty of the Irish are taken into account. The *Advocate*, the only Irish Catholic journal, whose proprietor, Joseph Winter, was the key figure of the Home Rule movement in Victoria, devoted much more of its space to Irish than to Australian news. Its editorials were vehement on education and Home Rule; it has been remarked that its arguments ranged from pointing to the practical benefits to England of a happy Ireland to threats of Divine punishment of England for its sinful oppression.[18] It habitually broadsided the *Age* for being the 'organ of the Orange conspirators' and for its 'horrible ungodliness'.[19] Otherwise it was cautious and mealy-mouthed on public issues, and avoided controversy in order not to expose Catholics to further hostility and to give the impression of Irish Catholic unanimity. It was coolly hostile both to the coalition government and to the Trades Hall where, since few Irish migrants had artisan backgrounds, the Catholics were weakly represented.

The *Advocate*'s lack of attention to the Pacific-imperial issues, the federal movement and problems of Australian nationality indicate that the Irish Catholic minority may have been largely divorced from current trends of thought. The journal occasionally praised Service for his efforts to bring about federation, though in November 1883 it claimed that the Irish-Australian Convention dwarfed the Federal Convention in importance.[20] There was occasional sniping on the New Hebrides issue, which was probably based more on antagonism to the local Presbyterians than sympathy for French Catholic influence in the islands.[21] Editorials often avowed Irish Catholic loyalty to Queen and Empire, but derided the grovelling of super-loyal imperialists: 'Some people would have Australians sing "God Save the Queen" morning, noon, and night.'[22] When the Queen's Jubilee coincided with the Coercion Bill, overt attacks on Her Majesty appeared, especially for her personal attitude towards Ireland. It is unlikely that many Catholics contributed to the Jubilee charity-funds or took part in the celebrations.[23] In May 1887 the *Advocate*, in reaction to the Colonial Conference and its 'militarist' decisions, made a rare comment on Australia's future (which was possibly a contrived reaction to coercion of Ireland by the imperial government):

> [The native-born Australian's] first duty is to the land of his birth, and he should not allow an inherited sentiment to interfere with his performance of that duty. . . . Great Britain has neither hold nor claim on us . . . for anything the parent state has done for us she has been amply repaid. Our hands are perfectly free. . . .

The time had come for serious consideration of separation.[24] Later it claimed that separation 'at no very distant date' was inevitable; but on another occasion it approved of the naval agreement, since for better or worse Australia would inevitably be involved in Britain's wars.[25]

The *Advocate*'s uncertainty and caution reflected the divided or unformulated views of its readers. Nearly all of them, if Home Rule had been granted, would have been content to be loyal to Crown and Empire. Only so long as the Irish injustice remained would they tend towards separation, and continue to curse the 'foreign despotism'. They were keenly aware of the extent of liberty and equality (apart from the Education Act) they had in a home-rule situation in a British colony; and rejoiced that, given opportunities lacking in Ireland, they had been able to contribute so much to community development.[26] Their loyalty to Australia as part of the Empire, though not to Tory England, was frequently felt strongly. In the nineties Michael Davitt found it strange that many houses, especially those of the clergy, displayed pictures of the Queen, flanked by Gladstone and often Parnell or Dillon, and that the Queen was toasted at formal Irish gatherings.[27] A proposal to recruit an Irish-Australian force for service in the Sudan won some support.[28] An interesting question, on which there is almost no evidence, is to what extent the native-born Irish-Australians were developing an Australian patriotism and rejecting their parents' preoccupation with Erin. There were more of them in the A.N.A. than in the Catholic Young Men's Societies, which were disappointing to their sponsors.[29] For a long time yet, the Irish issue was to continue to distract them, and also to encourage development of an anti-English Australian patriotism. The overriding tension of the Home Rule question in the eighties tended to isolate all the Irish—Catholic or Orange, migrant or native-born—from the rest of the community, and to inhibit and delay their contributions to the formulation of national attitudes.[30]

The High Boom Years

R

8

Fools' Paradise, 1887–1888

> If you succeed your profits are stupendous,
> And if you fail, pop goes your eighteen pence.
>
> W. S. Gilbert[1]

The land boom develops

The Australia-wide recession of 1886 affected Victoria less than the other colonies. The slump in wool and wheat prices reduced export income by a quarter, and land speculation almost ceased. Nevertheless, although money was very tight and the banks were 'scouring up everybody',[2] land prices did not fall and the rate of house-building continued to grow. Heavy pastoral investment continued; in October David Carson and others formed the Victorian Squatting Company to take up five million acres on Cambridge Gulf in Western Australia—an enterprise outstripped only by the earlier flotation of more than £500,000 of the Australian Mutual Pastoral Company, to acquire C. B. Fisher's Northern Territory leases totalling 34,000 square miles.[3] In 1887 full boom conditions developed again and 1888 was to be an insane miraculous year, which began with wild speculation in Broken Hill silver and carried on to extreme follies of land speculation. The combination of unlimited access to British capital, large government spending, heavy immigration, and a massive building programme gave Victoria (but not the other colonies) an outlandish boom which is not paralleled in any period of Australian history. The trade deficit, covered in a sense by the enormous import of capital, grew wider every year. For the four years 1882 to 1885 the gap between imports and exports was less than £10 million; for the four following years it amounted to £36 million, and in 1889 exports were barely half the value of imports. In the second half of the decade over £50 million of British capital, more than to the rest of Australia, poured in to Victoria. Most of it was private capital which was applied to rebuilding the city of Melbourne and extending its suburbs, to land speculation, conspicuous consumption of largely fictitious profits from investment companies, and hardly at all to productive industries. Government meanwhile carried out extensions of railways (which accounted for three-quarters of Victoria's public indebtedness) and irrigation and water supply and other public works, especially local government works in the newly-settled suburbs.

Until the mid-eighties, Melbourne's increasing building-rate and rising land values were very similar in scale to Sydney's. The steady land boom was based on quickly expanding demand for housing, deriving from increasing immigration and growing numbers of young married couples. Then in the three years 1886 to 1888 Victoria's population increased by about 10 per cent—by immigration alone. In 1888 there was a net gain of 40,000 people through the ports. These new residents were attracted to Melbourne, rather than to Victoria: the stagnant or declining possibilities of wool and gold and the difficulties of farming development enforced a further spurt of metropolitan growth. The phenomenal rate of home-building which followed was entirely justified until at least 1889. Similarly, the rise in land values was not inordinate before 1887, in view of the growth in the city's scale. The new factor in the later eighties was the importation of capital on a scale which was relatively several times greater than in modern boom Australia. For the first time, Australia had become the favourite foreign field for British investors, to whom the Victorian government, municipalities, banks, pastoral and mining companies, building societies and land finance companies offered apparently safe returns at unusually high rates of interest. Even the most cautious British investors, like large assurance companies, succumbed. Moreover, during the decade, the Savings Banks and the Post Office Savings Banks trebled both the number of accounts and their deposits. The rising real incomes of the early boom years had created a new class of investors. These people tended either to leave their modest savings in a bank, or, following folk tradition, to take the supposedly safe course of buying land, rather than to venture on speculative forms of investment through the Stock Exchanges. Millions of pounds of borrowed money seeking outlet, in addition to the steady demand for building-sites and land for investment, drove the price of suburban land sky-high.[4]

The co-operative building societies, which financed most house-building, were lending more than £2 million annually from 1885 to 1887; in 1888 they advanced more than £4 million. Many of their clients now were speculative builders, rather than owner-occupiers or landlords. And most of the societies had added the function of deposit-banks to their basic activities and competed seriously with the banks; Mirams's Premier Permanent Building Society had added 'Savings Bank' to its title. By 1887 the building societies held more deposits than the Savings Banks, which had been forced to raise interest rates. A minority of the societies took advantage of the Building Societies Act of 1874, which varied from the English model to allow societies 'to buy and sell or mortgage freehold or leasehold estate', and were tempted into real estate transactions; many of their subdivisions were highly successful. However, most of them eschewed speculation and, with notable exceptions like the Premier Permanent, had no direct part in encouraging the land boom.[5]

The major speculative force was the motley assortment—'cancerous growths' in reputable bankers' eyes—of land investment companies and mortgage banks. The oldest of any importance was the Land Mortgage Bank of Victoria (1864), which was followed in the seventies and early eighties by a dozen more institutions whose names combined variously the terms, Land, Property, Investment, Realization, Freehold, Estate, Mortgage and Banking.[6] Many more were formed at the height of the boom. They took some part in financing housing but their chief interest was dealing in urban real estate. They were the main channel of imported capital used for urban land speculation, much of it raised directly in Britain as capital, debentures and deposits; they also attracted large local deposits by offering high interest and often allowed customers to operate cheque accounts. The outstanding operator in this field was the native-born Matthew Davies, Geelong's gift to Melbourne, who as a young solicitor was associated with C. H. James, the pioneer suburban subdivider of the late seventies. Davies reached the top of his switchback career by becoming Speaker of the Assembly and a knight by the time he was forty. Fourth of five brothers, grandson of an Independent pastor, son of a tanner, president of the Y.M.C.A., pillar of the Presbyterian church and married to a minister's daughter, Davies had a glorious vision of the immensely prosperous Victoria, which might be developed by intelligent application. A generous man of uncommon charm, he formed the Colonial Investment Co. in 1880 to borrow money and buy and sell land, the Freehold Investment & Banking Co. in 1882 (with his brother, J. B., as managing director), Henry Arnold & Co. in 1884, the Australian Deposit & Mortgage Bank (with his brother, G. S., as manager), the Country Estates Co. and several other ventures for land speculation; ultimately he became the key man in more than thirty companies. In addition, in 1885 he entered the true banking field when he took over the small-scale Australian Economic Bank and converted it into the Mercantile Bank with £1 million capital, £400,000 paid up. Meanwhile he built a splendid mansion on the corner of St George's and Lansell Roads, Toorak, and presided in Parliament and in Collins Street over the boom which some said he had invented.[7]

James Munro, the political leader of the temperance men and powerful dissident Liberal, was another early systematic boomer. In 1882 he resigned his building society managership to found the Federal Bank, with the backing of J. B. Watson, the Bendigo millionaire, John Robb, a contractor, and William McLean, an ironmonger. £500,000 capital was quickly subscribed and along with deposits was smartly lent out to the directors and their friends. Associated with the bank was the Federal Building Society, of which Alexander, one of Munro's sons, was secretary. Another son, Donald, joined up with W. L. Baillieu, twenty-six years old and fresh from the country, as estate agents in 1885; two years later they were selling more land even than C. J. and T. Ham. James Munro launched into huge land dealing in the suburbs, purchase of pastoral properties and leases in Western Australia and Queensland, and financing of coffee-palaces. In 1887, in order to rationalize his miscellaneous investments, he founded the Real Estate Bank 'for the purpose of enabling the industrial and thrifty

Henry Gyles Turner, 1886

classes to participate in the distribution of real estate, or secure a large portion of the large profits which are made by purchasing land in large quantities and selling the same in moderate-sized farms or allotments'.[8] Gyles Turner, as historian many years later, splenetically described such institutions as 'the swarm of land-jobbing, financial and mortgage agencies and property investment companies, which, by the misleading use of the word bank in their titles, made a large haul of borrowed wealth, and upset all business calculations by their prodigal expenditure of it'.[9] But part of the trouble was that some of the banks themselves—Davies's Mercantile, Munro's Federal and the Commercial Bank of Australia, which Turner himself managed—were prodigal in their policies and implored their customers to accept large loans. Turner was a key figure in the boom and almost the last of the reputable bankers to scent danger. Amateur actor, chief founder of the *Melbourne Review*, patron of writers, office-holder and sponsor of many cultural societies, and as a Unitarian a leading defender of liberal clergy, this tall, lean and genial banker had built up the Commercial since 1870 into almost the busiest bank in Victoria. Twice he tried to resign—in 1884 and 1887—but was persuaded to continue the good work after taking long leave. He was overseas for most of 1888 when it is said the Commercial accepted much bad business; if so, it was no change of policy.[10]

The banks were being driven to compete with the land banks in making advances on the 'security' of urban land. They had for long been breaking away from English practice and finding ways round their out-dated charters which forbade lending on land. As Turner smugly put it in 1888: 'animated by that fertility of resource which is the secret of the success of British colonisation, they rose above the conservative traditions of Lombard-street and became an important factor in national development. . . . And the end has certainly justified the means.'[11] Many pastoralists, merchants and struggling farmers had been carried, but urban real estate was becoming an increasingly important form of security. The older Anglo-Australian banks had concentrated their business in pastoralism where the dangers were real enough; C. B. Fisher's overdraft approaching £500,000 caused his bank great anxiety. They watched with concern the increasing involvement of the Commercial and most of the younger local banks in Melbourne land speculation. E. S. Parkes of the Australasia regarded Turner's rate of increase of advances in 1886 as 'evidence of very bad banking'.[12] Francis Grey Smith of the National was shocked in 1887 by the ease with which the Federal, the Mercantile and the City of Melbourne were gathering deposits in England and Scotland and by the degree to which they were channelling them into real estate. 'The speculation in City and Suburban property just now exceeds anything of the kind ever known in Australia. We are keeping well out of it!'[13]

In 1887 Gillies set up a royal commission on banking and chose as its chairman the supreme financier, Matthew Davies, and Turner as representative of the senior bankers. The chief reason for the commission was the wide feeling, after the failure of the Oriental Bank in 1884, that redemption of bank notes should be made the first charge on assets; the commission so recommended. Its report was highly complacent. Turner claimed that it 'demonstrated the groundlessness of much idle talk about dangerous irregularities in banking practice, and proved the general soundness and safety with which the vast financial operations of the colony were conducted'.[14] It recommended abolition of remaining restrictions in banks' charters on lending on land; for land was always marketable, there was no better security in Australia. It called for one minor reform: financial institutions should be prevented from making misleading statements and be compelled in advertising to distinguish clearly between subscribed and paid-up capital. Parkes, in giving evidence, had attacked the pseudo banks:

> You so often see now, 'Subscribed, £2,000,000'. I saw it the other day without the slightest reference to how much has been paid up. . . . I passed an institution [which] has a name in front as a permanent building association; but on the wall I see written, 'Deposit Bank and Savings Bank'. I have no doubt that Government might prosecute that institution, but they do not. There, you see, there is, in bold letters, something put up which is not the title of the company, and we know it is going

> on, and high rates are paid. Several are paying $7\frac{1}{2}$ per cent now, while the banks are paying 5. It must mean disaster to somebody.[15]

Other evidence brought out the dangers of the banks' prevailing low coin reserves; the reserve ratios of nearly all the banks rose after the commission. The government in 1888 passed legislation which followed the commission's scanty proposals.[16]

In the suburbs the men who bought by the acre and sold by the foot began spruiking again when, after the check of 1886, the second stage of the suburban boom began. The spread of suburban railways had given major stimulus to subdivisional sales along the new tracks, notably the Caulfield-Oakleigh and Camberwell-Box Hill lines. The construction of the tramway network from 1885 now again brought major shifts in relative values. In the spring of 1887, when prospective buyers were less likely to be put off by mud or dust, the huckstering resumed once more as a Saturday attraction. Masters of the puffer's art composed double-column advertisements which featured misleading maps and subdivisional plans, terms of small deposit and generous time, and free rail passes for special trains; drags and carriages cut short the distance from station to site and a free lunch with whisky or champagne, in gay marquees with brass band blasting, sapped the resistance of the crowd of would-be purchasers. Then the grandiloquent auctioneer summoned all his resources of poetry and prose to perform his time-dishonoured art of describing the glorious views, the salubrious neighbourhood, the certainty of improvements, and the inevitability of rising values. A few dummy bidders to set inflated standards for the early lots, and the sale was away to a good start. The carving down and slicing into small lots of most of the large estates of Brighton, Malvern, Toorak, Essendon, Hawthorn and Kew continued. The subdivision of suburbs such as Camberwell, Caulfield and Northcote was almost completed; the sales moved on to Coburg, Preston, Heidelberg, Balwyn, Glen Iris, and in 1888 went far beyond.[17] Market values of outer suburban lands rose five, ten, in some cases twenty times, in five years; but these fictitious values were rarely tested in terms of income derived from the property. Transactions increasingly were merely on paper, as more and more business fell to large-scale speculators who had no intention of paying until they had resold at a profit. Nevertheless, the extent of small investment was such that possibly every third man in Melbourne bought a suburban block of land.

In the city, land values roughly trebled in three years from 1885 (almost without a check in 1886) and the inner city was largely rebuilt over a slightly longer period. A major technological innovation—hydraulic elevators—intensified existing boom pressures. Melbourne had in fact been lagging behind Sydney in introducing both mechanical and hydraulic passenger lifts. By chance, a vice-president of the American Otis company, which had been manufacturing lifts for thirty years, visited Melbourne on holiday in 1884, was struck by business opportunity, and persuaded

F. W. Prell to raise his new building at 15 Queen Street from four storeys to six with an elevator. Prell went on to erect three nine-storey buildings in the same street. Values soared when it was recognized that return from rents could be doubled on the same site, and owners of small buildings returning only 2 per cent or so on current values rushed to pull them down and reconstruct. The engineering firm of P. Johns & Co., which had long been installing goods lifts, profited greatly in 1886 and 1887. Meanwhile the ubiquitous B. J. Fink amalgamated the new Austral Otis company with the flourishing engineering firm of Hughes, Page and Rigby (at a personal profit of at least £40,000), and from 1887 the four-acre South Melbourne works of the Austral Otis Elevator and Engineering Co. held 300 employees. In 1888 the English firm of Waygood's formed a local company, which eventually amalgamated with Johns'. Hydraulic equipment had to be installed in each building until the Melbourne Hydraulic Power Company was floated, with George Swinburne as manager; it won a concession from the government to lay seven miles of high pressure mains through the streets and from 1889 connected up with most of the lift installations. Building was usually confined to about one hundred feet in height, partly because of the limitations of hydraulic power but chiefly because construction in brick required such sturdy and widespread foundations. Yet by the late eighties Melbourne's skyscrapers were as lofty as any except those in New York and Chicago. The tallest, the Australian Property and Investment Company on the corner of Elizabeth Street and Flinders Lane, was of twelve storeys and over 150 feet—about the height of Nelson's Column in London, the *Argus* boasted.[18] Crowds daily gathered to watch this wonder of the Southern Hemisphere ascend to the heavens. Elevators were the chief marvel of the day, but the adventurous public which flocked to ride for novelty's sake in the ornate carriages with uniformed conductors felt some justified sense of danger, for accidents were not uncommon. The high buildings were not an unqualified commercial success, for many businessmen deplored the disadvantage of not being able to advertise themselves in first or second storey windows, while some of their customers disliked travelling so far into the skies to do business. Moreover, the fire brigades were equipped only to reach two storeys up and special precautions had to be taken.[19]

One adventurous boom scheme did not come off. A royal commission was set up in 1887 to report on a proposal to move Spencer Street station 'to allow of the extension of Melbourne westward'. The City Council had recommended moving the station several hundreds yards to the north so that Collins and Bourke Streets could be carried through to the new docks. The majority report followed the views of the Railways and Harbor Trust Commissioners and regarded the future needs of the Railways as paramount. Barely £1 million would be gained by selling the land made available, the main station would be less accessible and it would be far more difficult to make the connection with the Flinders Street station. The majority recommended extending Flinders Street to the new docks and building a viaduct over the railway yards at La Trobe Street. The minority argued that the proposal was worthwhile, as it would require moving the station only to the north side of Bourke Street. In Parliament the plans of the 'boomers' were revealed: they had their eyes not merely on the station area but on the West Melbourne swamp. There was an 'untold amount of wealth in the swamp,' claimed G. D. Carter, 'sufficient to pay off our national debt'. Bent deplored the sacrifice of a splendid piece of land, a 'grand heritage', which would raise at least £3 million and possibly £20 million. The government, with great difficulty, forced through a Bill to provide for railway development in the area, but not without a terrible scene between Gillies and Bent when the Premier made a remark about the activities of land syndicates.[20]

Peak of the boom

In September 1887 the *Argus* was delighting in the 'biggest boom we have ever seen';[21] mining speculation all over Australia was lending a new massive boost. The Broken Hill Proprietary had been registered as a company in August 1885, and henceforth was directed from Melbourne. The silver bars from the first smelting at Spotswood, when displayed in the City of Melbourne Bank, roused speculative ardour. B.H.P. was largely owned by Melbourne investors and the huge dividends in the following years became a major factor in the Victorian economy. In 1886 its shares rose from £15 to £83; by the end of 1887 they were up to £174 and everyone was talking Broken Hill. One visitor remarked that 'an extraordinary number of quiet people, who, in England, would never touch speculations of the sort, held shares in it.'[22] The new year opened with a silver-mining boom which was far wilder than any previous gold boom. Announcement of a successful government loan early in January increased the jubilation. The volume of trading on the Stock Exchange was three times higher than ever before; led by the Governor, speculators kept brokers' offices open late at night and sometimes all night; on 20 January 1888 transactions passed the £2 million mark. B.H.P. shares topped £400 in February (and even then were actually under-valued). B.H.P. itself sold off more than half its ground to three new companies it floated. Other Broken Hill companies rose with the leader and new concerns were floated for country thirty miles around Broken Hill—nearly all of them worthless ramps. Eighteen new silver companies were formed in eighteen days.

> You only had to issue a prospectus which contained the magic words Broken Hill, . . . and an eager frantic public was ready to subscribe £50,000 or £100,000 in half an hour; and next morning the stock was launched upon the market and snapped up at 100, or even 500, per cent premium.[23]

At Easter, at the end of March, the brokers declared a twelve-day break for recuperation, and on resumption share prices fell away; however, although £9 million was taken off Broken Hill shares, the market did not collapse.

'The age of romance is by no means over in Australia,' the *Argus* remarked.[24] Huge fortunes had been won and thrown away, and enormous prices paid for non-existent mines. The *Age* was disturbed by the 'mysterious fluctuations' of share prices and the 'facilities for swindling' within the system, demanded legislation to separate 'jobbing' from broking, and frowned on the Melbourne Stock Exchange which was less reputable than the Stock Exchange of Melbourne.[25] Several short-lived rival exchanges were founded in the following months.

The torrent of speculation had been checked, only to break out into a new channel. April to June 1888 was the peak period of formation of the myriad land banks and land finance companies. Soon twenty-eight such companies, half of them calling themselves banks, listing £24 million subscribed capital with £7 million said to be paid up, were being quoted on the Stock Exchanges under 'Banking and Financial Institutions'. The banks, in self-defence, began publishing advertisements which listed their authorized and paid-up capital and that of the imposters.[26] Among the new foundations was the Royal Bank of Australasia, which was formed for legitimate banking, not land business, and which was to survive the depression without reconstruction.*[27] All told, in 1888 150 new land and property companies were registered, of which at least a dozen had authorized capital of £1 million or more.[28] In the twelve months to the end of June companies with capital of £52 million were floated, including several land companies launched in England. In one month the public agreed to pay £2,700,000 to new companies and more again in future calls.[29] There seemed to be no limit to the amount of capital which could be raised. One promoter remarked that he found little difficulty in making £100,000 in an afternoon.[30] 'The more risky and uncertain the speculation,' commented the *Age*, 'the bigger is the amount of nominal capital . . . in the expectation that the public will be attracted by nothing mean and small.'[31] Some of these companies were declaring 50 per cent dividends within a couple of months of starting business. In fact, they were buying land at peak prices and were nearly all doomed. The ultimate was reached with the formation of the Great Centennial Land Distribution Company, promoted by sons of Sir John O'Shanassy and 'Money' Miller, which proposed to distribute its purchases by public lottery.[32]

More than 80 per cent of the nominal capital of new companies formed in the high boom was in land and finance and trading companies which added nothing productive to the economy. However, 1888 was also a peak year for the transformation of private into public companies. Until 1887 the banks and mining companies distributed by far the greater part of dividends of public companies; from now on, the range was to be much more diverse. Some of the large conversions were of breweries and other

* Authorized capital was £3 million; £750,000 was immediately subscribed, of which £300,000 was called and paid by mid-1889. The directorate (F. T. Derham (chairman), D. Beath, C. Campbell, F. S. Grimwade, J. A. Kitchen, Charles Smith) is interesting in that five were manufacturers. Does this indicate dissatisfaction with the other banks' attitudes to manufacturers?

manufactories such as Swallow & Ariell and P. Johns & Co. Peter Johns and others of the gold generation were ageing and willing to forgo personal control.[33] The speculative public largely neglected the shares of these reputable productive concerns in favour of the flashy lures of the property companies. One interesting new enterprise floated in Melbourne, whose shares were not all taken up despite a 10 per cent guarantee for four years, was the Kauri Timber Company, which ultimately became one of New Zealand's largest enterprises.[34]

In July 1888 share prices levelled out and then began to fall back, while the volume of transactions declined. Now, while the Centennial Exhibition was drawing huge crowds, the last follies of the boom began, as investors moved from share to land speculation. The building trade had never been so active; there was hardly any of the normal winter slackening. Advances from many banks and land banks and finance companies were available for the taking; a man worth £2,000 had little trouble in raising £40,000 or £50,000 for land purchases.[35] The best city land climbed to £1,500 to £2,000 a foot; a corner of Collins and Elizabeth Streets sold for £2,300 a foot. A visiting English banker concluded that city properties were 'eight times as high as any well managed insurance company would advance on them. Nearly the whole community considered these prices based upon actual values.'[36] Modern Melbourne has five times the population of 1888 and the real value of its city land is about half the prices then reached.[37] In August the City and Suburban Investment and Banking Company, the largest of them all, was floated with a nominal capital of £3,500,000 and a first issue of £500,000—so large that the market could not quite meet it. Land had been changing hands so rapidly that sometimes there was a chain of four or five vendors between the still unpaid holder of the title and the latest purchaser.[38] Melbourne speculators, not content with local opportunities, were dabbling in Sydney and Brisbane lands. An offer of £300,000 was made for St Paul's Cathedral which was more than half built; yet, after agonized debate, the proposal was rejected by only one committeeman's vote. 'Business men', said one, 'will remember bitterly in the future, when funds are scarce, that the sale of the cathedral would have represented a perpetual income of £15,000 to £20,000 a year.'[39] £140,000 was offered for St Francis's Church, but although tempted to use the money to build a university college, Archbishop Carr would not accede.[40]

Spring brought the marketing of many of the suburban properties bought by the new land companies. Multi-column advertisements in new lavish form covered three and four pages of the *Argus*. Munro and Baillieu offered abundant hospitality at their sales in Moonee Ponds, Coburg and Elsternwick. In one week there were more than thirty subdivisional sales; fifty special trains ran one Saturday. Ringwood, Dandenong, Frankston and Mordialloc came under the hammer; land ten miles out fetched up to £1,000 an acre, twenty-five miles out brought £100 to £250 an acre. Twenty-five acres at Ascot Vale in 127 lots were sold for £83,517. O'Shanassy's 'Tara' estate brought £25 a foot for blocks on Burke Road, Camberwell.[41] The highest price paid outside the city was £306 a foot in Prahran. Less than an acre on a corner of Burwood and Auburn Roads, Hawthorn brought over £30,000 and the mayor paid £180 a foot for the first block; the ruling price in Burwood Road in 1885 had been £8 to £12 a foot.[42] A syndicate built a private tramway from Clifton Hill to Preston, while another established the first electric tramway in Australia from Box Hill to Doncaster. The Coburg and Somerton Junction Estate Co. employed a florid 'puffer':

> The people are alive to the great benefits of possessing land, and when the land is the birthright of a people depend upon it the people are free and independent. The old country is hampered by traditions, heredity, primogeniture, and a thousand effete and worn out associations, sapping the prosperity and warping the independence of an otherwise industrious shrewd and hardy race. Here we are under more favourable auspices and every thrifty man and woman can, if they choose, become a landowner. 'The possession of land is a people's greatness'.[43]

Altona was 'the Margate of Australia', confessed the promoters of the Altona Bay Estate; water, gas, the railway and steamers to the city were imminently expected. Land fever infected Werribee and speculation ocurred six miles out of Geelong.[44] The Wesleyans floated a subdivision at Ocean Grove (named after an evangelical settlement in New Jersey) with a covenant on titles prohibiting sale of liquor.[45] £50,000 was paid for 500 acres of poor soil twenty-six miles from Melbourne. *The Times* remarked that such a sum would buy in England an estate of 1,550 acres 'with a really grand old mansion built by an eminent historical personage, a deer park, walled gardens, lawns, terraces, cedars, and six park lodges, one mile and a half from a railway station, and within thirty miles of London'.[46] In the first nine months of 1888 land sales totalled more than £13 million.[47] The *Argus* exulted:

> And possibly in describing what we are now doing—when the twentieth century journalist or historian refers to the issue of today's paper as we today refer curiously to old Sydney gazettes—he will hold it to be not the least of the merits of the men of 1888 that they had a profound belief in the Australian future.[48]

But Michael Cannon has summed up for posterity: 'The big speculators were selling to the medium speculators, the medium speculators were selling to the small speculators, and madness was in the air.'[49]

On 22 October 1888 the Associated Banks, after some disagreement, broke the speculative land boom by agreeing to refuse further overdraft extensions for land purchases and by raising interest rates by 1 per cent. The recent rapid increases in advances without more than a slight rise in deposits, and three insolvencies of notorious speculators which totalled over £1 million, had encouraged action. Suburban land sales almost ceased and many contracts of sales were renegotiated; not a few purchasers had to forfeit their deposits, and some of those who believed they had made fortunes found that they still had their land to sell. By December the value of shares of land and land-finance companies had fallen by about half. About a dozen of them failed; and early in 1889 the *Age* carried almost daily reports of angry shareholders' meetings under the unwontedly flippant heading, 'Reminiscences of the Land Boom'.[50] However, after this sickening lurch, the economy resumed its headlong progress. The boom was only checked and not deflated.

Government, politicians and the boom; boom morality

Duncan Gillies, as Premier and Treasurer, had modestly introduced his Budget in July 1888, claiming no credit for the largest surplus ever and the enormous prosperity of the people. There was not the slightest need to fear for the future; there was 'every reasonable prospect of natural causes working satisfactorily, so as to secure the best possible results to individuals and to the community'. Munro, emerging as main challenger to the throne, agreed, but triumphantly announced that the real cause of so much prosperity was Protection![51] The government's lavish borrowing and public works policies were giving massive backing to the boom. Yet to this stage the railway-building programme might be defended as justifiable, although Speight's extravagances in detail and his ready compliance with politicians' private pressure were not. The rate of increase of population, especially by immigration, made huge spending on school-building and local works inevitable, though municipal competition in grandiose town halls was a conspicuous extravagance. Luxuries such as the Centennial Exhibition and the west front of Parliament House were excusable at this time, if ever. The problem is to estimate the degree to which Gillies and the government believed themselves to be in control of the economy, or indeed the degree to which they believed themselves to be responsible for it. There is an extreme contrast between the unusual development of governmental responsibility in particular fields—provision of public works for general benefit, nurture of agricultural development in diverse ways, care to foster manufacturers by protective tariffs—and refusal to accept responsibility for control of the *general* health of the economy. There was a marked hangover of *laissez-faire* assumptions, as indicated by Gillies's trust in 'natural causes'. Government certainly acknowledged the banks' prior duty to control investment in the private sector, and hardly seemed aware of the banks' loss of control when the land-finance companies ran amuck. Senior civil servants were apparently of little importance as advisers.* Developmental policies in colonial economies have historically proved very difficult to control, but there is at least a prima facie case that Gillies was unusually uncomprehending. The best evidence is the insane financial policy of 1890, by which time the local correspondent of the London *Economist* was assert-

* What was the role of E. S. Symonds, Under-Treasurer from 1857 to 1887? A glance at the Archives has not shown that his advice was of any significance, but little work on the history of the Victorian civil service has been done.

ing that the finances had been conducted incompetently and indolently and that hardly one politician had a firm grasp of finance.[52]

We may indeed predicate insanity as characterizing politicians, businessmen and the whole populace; our task will be to find explanations. At this stage, the curiously assorted honour-roll of the clearsighted who were not taken in needs to be listed. The most competent of the bankers and the most sceptical about the soundness of the boom in its early days was E. S. Parkes of the Australasia; he was tragically killed in a railway accident in May 1887, but his successors, John Sawers, D. Finlayson of the Union, and Grey Smith of the National were wise Jeremiahs who followed sound conservative policies. Nearly all the general managers and directors of the other banks participated in the rush to be rich. The colony's most famous economist, Edward Hearn, had been condemning from his seat in the Council the scale of borrowing and railway extension,[53] but he was a sick man in 1887 and died in April 1888. His protégé and student, however, William Shiels, was the one parliamentarian who regularly and consistently cried havoc. This brilliant young Irish-born barrister, with nearly all the gifts except good health, was the classic intellectual with at this stage a much firmer grasp of basic values than Deakin. In April 1888 he was calling for husbanding of resources and preparation for the inevitable depression; there could be no justification for the 'mad whirl of speculation', certainly there had been no increase in production. Later he was to deplore Service's retirement, for Gillies was so imprudent and inexperienced in finance.[54] Shiels was supported by the editor of the A.N.A. journal, the *Australian,* who wrote in August 1888:

> we regard the period from 1889 to 1892 (without knowing at which end to expect the great crisis) as about to inaugurate one of the most dangerous and misery-stricken seasons within the memory of the bulk of Australian Natives. If they are wise they will prepare for the contingency as best they may.[55]

Joseph Symes in the *Liberator* was not likely to be taken in, and occasionally foretold doom. In 1885 he was writing: 'The future prospects of the colony are mortgaged to meet the present demands; all the people seem eager to pile up the agony and prepare for a universal smash.'[56] Ultimately he was to exult over exposures of the evangelical boomers. There was little criticism of the boom in the press. The *Insurance and Banking Record* occasionally called for caution, but for the most part was happy to marvel. Maurice Brodzky, who had founded *Table Talk* as a society weekly in 1885, expressed occasional misgivings about the number of suburban allotments being sold or about over-building in the city, and dropped asides about prevalent low commercial morality, but he did not begin his scourging role until early 1889.[57] All the daily papers were complacently cocksure about Victoria's immediate economic future. The *Telegraph,* in which Matthew Davies had a large say, was zealous in its booming propaganda, while Syme's two chief protectionist lieutenants were Munro and Mirams!

The histories of the country towns and shires have little mention of any boom in 1888. Provincial and rural areas shared in the handouts for railways and municipal improvements; however, wool prices had fallen, gold was declining, and fluctuating wheat prices remained far lower than a decade before. Geelong, Ballarat and Bendigo were no places for land speculators, and no other towns had sufficient prospects of quick growth to attract them seriously. The Melbourne boom accelerated the rate of departure of young men from the mining towns, while the farmers canalized their resentment as being left out of the boom into more systematic political organization.

Government took no action to check the shady activities of the boomers (except for the penalties, imposed after the land boom was over, on misleading advertisement of capital by banking companies).* Land banks, building societies and finance companies were allowed to advertise themselves on their windows and in the press as 'banks' without legislative curb, while the false pretences of many land syndicates and companies continued unchecked. Robert Reid, the softgoods importer and president of the Chamber of Commerce, became the most notable champion of business rectitude. At the peak of the boom in spring 1888, he warned the Auctioneers' Association to abandon fictitious reports of sales and acceptance of 'dummy' bids, and early in 1889 publicly condemned the promoters of 'wicked schemes' and the extent of forgery which was occurring. 'To such an extent did men who were called smart carry on their nefarious practices that they endangered the whole character of this colony. . . . In all large banking and commercial institutions they had not gone on the old-fashioned lines of the British merchant sufficiently.'[58]

H. B. Higgins recalled that

> nothing was more common than for Smith to secure a piece of land say for £1,000 and then to go round to his friends and acquaintances and say 'I am forming a syndicate to buy this land for £1,800. I am taking a share for myself, as it is a very good thing: shall I put your name down for a share, I want to give you an opportunity of making a little money?' The point is, that Smith does not disclose that he is the vendor. Now for a long time most of the men of business to whom the transaction became known could not see anything wrong in it. It was a 'smart' thing, a clever thing, perhaps a thing which Smith ought not to do to his intimate friends; but business is business, and if you are willing to buy at a given price, why, that is your look out.[59]

No wonder 'syndicate' became a very dirty word. A. L. Tucker, Minister for Lands in the Service government, crusaded in 1888 for a commission to investigate reform of the company laws in order to protect investors:

* 'Banking companies' were not defined. What was the intended meaning? The Bill was rushed through in suspicious circumstances, late at night after a member who had been waiting to make exposures had gone home. The government presumably wanted to avoid adverse publicity for the colony. (*Argus*, 19, 21 Dec. 1888.)

> Four or five men would become interested in a large block of land, and one of them would remain in the background, and be apparently the sole vendor, while the names of the others would appear in a prospectus as provisional directors of a public company proposed to be established to purchase the land, although they were really partners with the vendor, and secretly received profit out of the sale of the land to the company. The public . . . rushed to take shares in the company on the strength of the names of those persons and others, including many members of this House, appearing on the list of directors.

The House shuddered when Tucker threatened to mention names. Bent thought it a most improper reflection on members, while Gillies promised to consider the matter.[60] The practice had also become common of persuading politicians and other prominent men to lend their names, with no other commitment, as provisional directors of companies in return for a parcel of shares.[61] 'Experts', as was so common in mining prospectuses, gave reassurance about the value of the company's property. Theodore Fink recalled that solicitors were kept busy giving advice on prospectuses, and how difficult it was 'to get over-astute company promoters and their clever and over-zealous officers to keep to the straight line'; the art of company-mongering or fleecing people by means of their own cupidity, he remarked, was finely developed.[62]

The Companies Act of 1864 laid down a minimum of control or protection to investors. To obtain incorporation and limited liability, more than seven people had to be involved, a memorandum of association defining the rules of the organization had to be drawn up and registered, and annual reports had to be submitted, but no prescribed form for accounts was demanded. Until December 1888 the government was not even policing the Act, for many companies were not supplying required information to the Registrar.[63] In April 1888 the *Insurance and Banking Record* made an appeal (which it did not follow up) for revision of the Act. It was objecting especially to the frequency with which private businesses, recently converted to companies, were being bought by syndicates which were reselling to the hapless public at huge profit. Either the vendor was getting too little or the public was paying too much, certainly the syndicates were making unjustifiable killings; the *Record* demanded that the original price paid be a required statement in prospectuses.[64] In 1889 and 1890 the government, in line with current English reforms, considered making directors liable for false statements in prospectuses and reports, but still took no action. Similarly a bill prepared on the advice of the Chamber of Commerce and the Associated Banks to regulate the procedures of bankrupts' trustees was dropped by the government.[65]

In 1888 the trickery and deception of estate agents and syndicates became widely known, but no major scandal or other evidence of criminal business activity disturbed public confidence; nor were there to be many cases in 1889. Here we need to take account of the evidence presented by Michael Cannon, who in his swingeing book, *The Land Boomers*, has meted out justice to many a rogue, implied the worst of many an innocent fool, and condemned Parliament and much of the business community of wholesale corruption. His descriptions of the major scandals and nearly all his detailed researches stand as accurate. Not so, perhaps, some of his conclusions and particular inferences; and his account of general corruption needs extensive qualification. The great majority of criminal or totally unethical actions occurred in the early nineties when men were desperately struggling to preserve solvency and save what they could from the wreckage. Nor does business failure or bankruptcy necessarily imply dishonesty. However, as Cannon demonstrates, the rot had certainly set in by 1888. At least four building societies were being bled by their secretaries. Managers and some directors of the Land Credit Bank (founded 1876) and the British Bank of Australia, Ltd (1888) were practising frauds and were eventually gaoled. The Imperial Banking Company (1886) and the Metropolitan Bank (1887) were swindles, though the former may have been within the law, and several more of the financial foundations of 1888 were probably fraudulent from start to finish. In the case of the fourteen associated banks, the general manager of the City of Melbourne Bank was behaving criminally, and Munro's Federal and Davies's Mercantile Banks were involved in activities which were probably criminal. In addition, the general manager of the Colonial Bank and high executives of the Commercial were speculating wildly themselves; their ultimate downfall was gravely to damage their banks.[66] In no case did the real state of affairs become clear before 1890.

The three most dashing speculators of 1888 were B. J. Fink, James Mirams and Thomas Bent. Benjamin Josman Fink was a boy of fourteen when he migrated from England in 1861. He made his way to New Zealand in 1863 and after three years returned to Melbourne, became a clerk in Wallach's furniture store and in 1874 was joint owner. By 1884 he had bought out his partner, expanded to Sydney, purchased W. H. Rocke's furniture business and largely controlled the trade. In 1880 and shortly after, he had founded the Joint Stock Bank of Ballarat, bought and sold a coal mine at Newcastle, invested in gold mines at Creswick and Maryborough and been elected to the Assembly by the latter town. He proceeded to amalgamate the Ballarat bank with the City of Melbourne Bank, keep the Maryborough mines alive (to the miners' undying gratitude) and, despite his considerable wealth, plunge into manic speculation. The Mercantile Finance Company (which paid 40 and 50 per cent), the Austral Otis Elevator Company, the ten-storey Fink's buildings on the corner of Flinders and Elizabeth Streets, extensive hotel interests, flotation of McCracken's Brewery, purchase of pastoral properties, and sale of his land to the Stock Exchange of Melbourne for their new building, were some of his subsequent ventures. George Meudell, his employee, described his high finance as 'pure grotesquerie';[67] the Mercantile Finance Company was to lose almost £1 million. A master of the art of guaranteeing himself, this madman or conscienceless gambler on an unparalleled scale was to go bankrupt with

B. J. Fink, 1888

debts of about £2 million—no mean achievement. He used Parliament only for convenience; he was known to have spoken in committee. The intellectual power his brother Theodore displayed, as a legal manipulator, patron of the arts, education reformer and newspaper entrepreneur, indicates the quality of the great gifts which the brothers at this time so misapplied.[68]

Jimmy Mirams was a diminutive man with a flowing beard, famous for his umbrella and bantam-cock strut. Born in London in 1839, he had migrated when eighteen with his father, a Congregational minister. After teaching for a time and farming unsuccessfully, Mirams became a newsagent in Smith Street, Collingwood until 1874, when he founded the Premier Permanent Building Association which for many years he managed very successfully. One of the leading organizers of the National Reform and Protection League, he was elected for Collingwood in 1876 and for a decade was perhaps the most principled and consistent radical democrat in Parliament, a firm protectionist who supported land leasing and creation of a national bank of issue. At the same time this man of extraordinary vitality (with fourteen children) became the archetypal wowser of the day; always prominent in the Congregational church, he was a rigid Sabbatarian and Rechabite. Mirams's self-confidence was enormous.

He was convinced he was a statesman destined to became a great popular premier, but his political career went wildly astray. Despite his knowledge, integrity and application, he was difficult to take seriously, if only because he spoke at such length and volume that his speeches were almost impossible to bear. He fell out with Berry, who he believed had wrecked the National Reform and Protection League. His achievement as chairman of the royal commission on the tariff was remarkable, but Berry took his co-member for Collingwood, George Langridge, as Minister for Customs in 1883 and the great report was entirely ignored. Then in 1886, after allying himself with the Trades Hall candidates, he lost his seat and all prospect of leadership of the Liberal party. It may be that he reacted extremely from such crushing rebuffs by taking up wild speculation. Turner dated the birth of the boom as the day in 1885 when Mirams paid £700 a foot for a corner of Collins and Elizabeth Streets.[69] The Premier Permanent became the most notorious building society and attracted huge deposits in 1887 and 1888, though Mirams no longer gave much time to it. He joined Munro in promoting the Federal Coffee Palace, the most ambitious of all, invested hugely in country and suburban lands, borrowed all round the town, kept a stable with a dozen horses at his Caulfield mansion, built another one in East Melbourne, and drove down Collins Street daily in coach-and-four with two flunkies in bright buttons. Then he floated his Freehold Farms Company and Essendon Land and Tramway Company for £1 million each. When the land boom broke, he was immediately in grave trouble. Freehold Farms had to be wound up, and he was forced by the directors to resign his secretaryship of the Premier Permanent because his private business activities were harming the society.[70]

The bluff and burly Tommy Bent was a formidable bully. Born near Sydney in 1838, he became rate-collector for Brighton in 1861, then local member and somehow a large landowner in the seventies, and dominated the Brighton and Moorabbin councils. He made the first of his fortunes by subdivision in the early eighties. He was a man of tremendous force, a master of the craft of binding men and manipulating them, a master of intrigue, a master of log-rolling. He was coarse, vulgar, unscrupulous, cunning, a liar and a larrikin, from one point of view; he was also a cheery good fellow with some comic gifts, generous, loyal, and widely popular among his fellow-politicians. Theodore Fink thought him 'a marvellous man . . . like a composite portrait of Don Quixote, Sancho Panza and Henry VIII'.[71] He was not entirely self-seeking and not entirely a political charlatan, it has been remarked. He had no political beliefs except devotion to progress and development, and conviction that what was good for Tommy Bent was good for Brighton and Victoria, but he was a hard-working and able administrator in office. He was Deakin's pet aversion, but Deakin thought him only 'probably' corrupt; scandal hung around him but he kept within the law. In the mid-eighties he moved on from his Brighton killings to become the director of innumerable suburban land syndicates and speculative companies. In 1888 he achieved the acme of cheek by forming the Thomas Bent Land Company, and thereby attracted investors to in effect buy from him ninety-five acres at Ringwood. He had ready access to the banks, especially the Commercial; his interviews with Turner, with whom he had little in common but faith in the boom, were probably brief and to the point.*[72]

These three of the most prominent boomers, and Matthew Davies and Munro were all members of the Legislative Assembly. Davies was Speaker; Munro and Bent were leaders of the Opposition; Munro was to become the next Premier, Bent the next Speaker and eventually Premier. There seems good prima facie backing for Cannon's view that 'Parliament became a sort of land speculators' club', where the most blatant use of political power for private gain became commonplace. 'A rich State was plundered by the very men who had been elected to advance its interests.'[73] On the other hand Dilke concluded at the time that bribery and corruption were almost unknown: 'The *Argus* is as proud of the financial purity of the Victorian Assembly as is the democratic *Age*, and it is a fact that since payment of members was introduced parliamentary money scandals have been all but unknown.'[74]

A balanced judgment, if it were possible to make one, would be complex but, leaving aside the half-dozen leading boomers as special cases, the truth would be not nearly as deplorable as Cannon asserts. Bribery and corruption in the narrow sense *were* rare: no doubt a member's vote was occasionally bought, but the newspapers' zeal to expose anything to the discredit of politicians of whom they disapproved at least made any venal members very careful indeed. The borderlines of political corruption are never easy to define. Many men went into politics primarily or partly to gain profitable tips or advance knowledge of developments which might be turned to private profit, or to put themselves in a strategic position to influence events to their pecuniary advantage. Acquisition of inside knowledge early is the immemorial privilege of those at the centre of the business and political worlds. Desirable though it might be, it is unreasonable to expect back-bench politicians to refrain entirely from investing in business areas affected by political decisions. In the late nineteenth century the ethics of using political knowledge for private gain were looser than they were to become in the twentieth century. Yet the area of potentially profitable operation was not extensive. A politician had to be very ruthless and very clever to arrange for a railway line which was not an obvious extension of the network, or to divert its route through or near to his land. The accusation was sometimes made that many politicians so

* A publican's classic epitaph on Bent bears repeating: 'Say what they like about Sir Thomas Bent, but he was a man. He mightn't have much honesty, if there was big money to be got, and he liked his gin and tonic strong an' fraquint, an' [he had] a rovin' eye for wimmen, but outside them matters he was as pure as the drivellin' snow.' (Randolph Bedford, *Naught to Thirty-Three*, p. 330.)

Another story which has a genuine ring is Bent's reported appeal to a journalist: 'I know what you're going to say against me, Mr Carey. You are going to say that I have a wife and family in every suburb and that I neglect them. I *don't* neglect them, Mr Carey.'

behaved.[75] But the 1884 Act was in public gestation for years and almost every constituency gained its new line. Some politicians owned land along the new lines, but they had had only a marginal advantage over other investors in acquiring it. Interested politicians operated more in the shady area of influencing the Commissioners on the precise route of a line, location of a station, frequency of trains and possibly the priorities of construction;[76] and they probably had considerable influence on Commissioners anxious not to offend powerful friends. There is little doubt that most politicians, like most of the community, speculated in land. Davies, Bent and Munro pulled many of their political associates into their ventures; most of them were only too grateful to be let in on a good thing. Davies and A. C. Groom apparently formed the Country Estates Company as a subdivisional racket dependent on the appropriate siting of a railway station.[77] Bent bought C. B. Fisher's Maribyrnong River estate for subdivision, formed a company largely of his parliamentary friends, and sold at great profit; C. E. Jones was secretary and liquidator. (But the purchaser could not pay, the politicians were very angry indeed, and Theodore Fink had to wangle them out of trouble.)[78] The old radical, John Woods, was entangled in the Munro net. But because a politician speculated or lent his name as a director does not necessarily imply shady dealings or participation in the operation of a company. A diligent research student might ultimately conclude that most of the politicians were directors of companies of which relatively few were improperly operated; and of those which were, relatively few of the politician-directors were aware of what was being done, though some probably connived.

The government was partly invaded by the boomers. It is noteworthy that Service's men from 1883 to 1886, with marginal exceptions, later steered clear of boom activities, while several of Gillies's men were tainted. Yet there is no doubt that most of them were thoroughly honest, upright men. Gillies himself, however foolish his policy, practised very proper views about the duty of a Premier not to be involved in private business. Several of his businessmen colleagues—Cuthbert, Lorimer and Walker—were men of established wealth and spotless reputation who probably took no part in current speculation. It is not possible that the three intellectuals—Deakin, Pearson and Wrixon—could have held any but the most conventionally moral views on any shady suggestion. While Deakin and Pearson at least were profoundly antipathetic to the values of the market-place, all were probably too deferential to the businessmen on economic policy. Deakin lost his inheritance and his own savings by his investments, and was foolishly persuaded to lend his name to many enterprises.* Pearson, who

* At various times he was chairman of the Australian City and Suburban Investment and Banking Co., the City of Melbourne Building Society (succeeding M. Davies), Robison Bros, Campbell, Sloss & Co. and the Australasian Natives Executors and Agency Co., and a director of Austral Otis Ltd, J. A. Kitchen & Sons, Wright & Edwards Ltd, the Australian Natives Building Society and the Australian Property and Investment Co. (Munro). Deakin referred once to 'the hardness, the keen selfishness and the merciless push of successful business men' (Deakin Papers, 1540/20/279/234). His friendships with

had as his private Eighth Commandment, 'Eschew the practice of the Stock Exchange', and lost his little money on suburban land investment, may have been more aware of the economic dangers.[79] Wrixon had married wealth, remained uninvolved, and was unconscious of any need to worry about the state of the economy. Of the remainder, Dow was in debt throughout his great term as Minister of Agriculture and was a business innocent, foolish enough to become a silent partner in several building societies and land syndicates. Nimmo was involved probably as a cipher with Munro and Mirams in the Premier Permanent and the Federal Coffee Palace. Derham was in grave financial trouble throughout his ministry, sought and gathered overdrafts from several banks and eventually went smash for £500,000. Matthew Davies was a member of the ministry only until October 1887, and James Bell, the grain merchant, as a director of the Mercantile Bank was sucked into the Davies whirlpool.* In addition, Berry, the Agent-General, was a London director of the Mercantile Bank. It is likely that the boomers inside the Cabinet were influential enough to dissuade their colleagues from tightening the Companies Act.

The outstanding exponents of the great game of 'Grab' tended to be relatively young; to be 'new men' on the way up and not from established business backgrounds, and to be Presbyterians or nonconformists. Munro, the working printer, was the oldest of them, one of the gold generation who had migrated in his twenties. Mirams, the minister's son, migrated in his teens in the fifties, and the Finks migrated as boys in 1861 with their small-draper father. Of the native-born, Matthew Davies was born in 1850, the son of a small tanner; Bent in 1838, the son of a hotel keeper and market gardener; W. L. Baillieu in 1859, the son of a boatman and lighthouse keeper at Queenscliff. C. H. James had been a suburban grocer. The old squatting-mercantile-financier group of leading businessmen had little to do with the land and building boom; neither did many of the rising manufacturers who, like Alfred Felton and F. S. Grimwade, were determined to finance their own growth. The new men, however, who in their meteoric rise had acquired little in the way of conventional financial training or much grasp, sometimes, of standard business ethics, rashly applied their little dangerous knowledge. James Munro, the Davies brothers, and David Munro, the machinery manufacturer and contractor, were Presbyterians; McLean, the ironmonger, was a Baptist; Mirams, C. J. Ham, the auctioneer, and G. W. Taylor, the suburban speculator, were Congregationalists; the Finks and other boomers like Joseph Woolf and Abraham Kozminsky were Jewish. On the other hand, the Derham, Kitchen and McKinley families, many of them notorious dabblers, were Anglican. Methodists,

---

Derham and Theodore Fink were part of his undoing. His chief losses were in the Pyramid sugar company (Derham paid some of his calls for him) and the Premier Permanent Building Society. He was an innocent abroad—as yet without very firm principles.

* Pearson, writing to Deakin in 1893, hoped Bell would be found 'not guilty' in the Mercantile Bank case, while he thought Davies and Munro should be gaoled (Deakin Correspondence).

oddly perhaps, and Catholics seem to have been absent from the top rank of speculators.*

On the face of it we have more confirmatory evidence of a connection between Calvinism and capitalism. Margaret Kiddle suggested in *Men of Yesterday* that some of the Scottish squatters were encouraged by their religion to believe that their riches were the product of thrift and hard work and thereby a sign of Divine favour and a proof of virtue.[80] Can we see a parallel in Munro and Matthew Davies finding assurance in material success as proof of moral superiority and religious sanctity? While glorifying God by financial support of their church, they became Mammon-worshippers—but only in the face of traditional warnings from the pulpit of the terrible dangers of wealth and the sin of acquiring money for its own sake. Perhaps the incitement to hard work and austerity of a standard Calvinist upbringing induced capitalist zeal more than any specifically doctrinal teaching.[81] We have no intimate biographical knowledge of the devout Davies, Munro or Mirams which would provide, as we have in the case of Niel Black, the squatter, any evidence of tortured doubt. At least we know that, somehow, they managed to ignore the Proverbial warning that he that maketh haste to be rich shall not be innocent. These were the men who inspired the *Bulletin* (following Marcus Clarke) to predict that the future Australian religion would be Presbyterianism tempered by the rate of exchange.[82] Somehow, also, we know, they and many thousands more persuaded themselves that there was no parallel between playing cards for money or taking a ticket in a sweep, and speculating in land or on the Stock Exchange. The historical connection between Wesleyan zeal and 'gainful enterprise' is well established; Wesleyan conferences were well aware of a problem and varied in their advice. They warned once against 'undue ardour in matters of commercial enterprise' and enjoined caution and benevolence, but on another occasion laid it down that 'neither the seeking of this world's goods nor the possession of them is inconsistent with true piety. To be "diligent in business" is the duty of all who engage in it.'[83] Perhaps Wesleyans were not so prone to gamble in business, although Fitchett, their leading spokesman, was a medium-scale speculator.[84] The boomers come out badly by the test of philanthropy. Matthew Davies was generous to a variety of good causes and G. W. Taylor wanted to found a Congregational university college, but otherwise the boomers are not to be found among the few notable benefactors of the period who, like Wilson, Ormond, Clarke, Grice and Wyselaskie, were nearly all from the 'landed gentry'.

The churches in the boom years sadly lacked outstanding leaders to make a strong public stand on traditional grounds. There was a little justice—but only a little—in the subsequent plaint that the churches had been lacking in guidance which might have prevented destruction. Some of the clergy, perhaps, gave in too easily to the spirit of the day and thanked the

* It is dangerous to generalize so without more biographical work, but these trends do extend down some distance among the top few dozen boomers.

good Lord for bestowing so many benefits on the colony.[85] Strong, at least, who in the late eighties was the best-known and most popular clergyman, did not tire in his attacks on materialism:

> We are fond of show and luxury and pleasure, and for the higher or deeper aspects of life have little taste. The pursuit of money becomes all absorbing, and the great question comes to be, not how can we make money honestly and what good end we can devote money to when we have made it, but [how much] have we managed to amass, and how can we invest at the highest rate of interest? We are a gambling society. . . .[86]

Other clergymen were occasionally scathing. According to J. F. Fitzgerald, a Catholic priest:

> Nothing in Victorian society was more conspicuous than the homage paid to mere wealth in the person of its possessor. Men were heard boasting or congratulating themselves on the honour, as they called it, of being spoken to or shaken by the hand by some individual who was known to possess immense wealth. No man who thus elevated gold into the position of the idol of his heart had any right or title to the name of Christian.[87]

The *Victorian Independent* found the eager struggle to be rich was the greatest curse of the colony and warned of the fearful desolation which must fall on a people that would be rich at any cost.[88] The eminent Congregationalist theologian, R. W. Dale, did not like what he saw on his visit in 1887. He advised the Congregationalist young men to

> create a public sentiment that shall discourage ostentation and luxury, and shall make the ideal of social life plain living and high thinking. . . . Brand with your fiercest disapproval gambling of all kinds—in land, in wool, in mining shares. . . . Let it be said, in future ages, that the young men of this generation in Australia rose above the base attractions of material prosperity.

Those so eager to find a short cut to wealth might find themselves on the broad way to damnation.[89] Australia needed 'a religious faith of exceptional vigour' to combat moral sickness and to lead men to attempt to apply the teaching of the Sermon on the Mount.[90]

Many other visitors deplored Melbourne's money-grubbing tone.[91] An old Harrovian wrote home devastatingly:

> I don't much care for Melbourne Society: they are a very young growth, having made heaps of money very fast. [At the Melbourne Club] they stink of money. They dress 'loud' talk 'loud' bet and play very high and can drink nothing but champagne. . . . In a London Club half the men would be 'barred' and nearly half the rest would be considered 'bad style'.[92]

There were few in the colony who were not dazzled. Fundamental criticisms were rare, and confined almost to Shiels's remonstrances, the reports of a few sermons, the sniping of the Secularists and an occasional worried plaint from a young native;[93] the old aristocracy appears to have been largely silent. James Smith, the art and literary critic, was not deceived:

> There are few cities or communities which afford greater scope for the censor and the satirist than our own; its vices, its religious hypocrisies, its political follies, its social shams, its abject worship of money and what money can buy, its low standard of commercial morality, its debased and debasing taste in the matter of literature, art, and music, all invite the lash.[94]

There was, also, a local Juvenal who gently scourged:

> Hear Melbourne's voice: 'Get money, money still,
> And then let Virtue follow if she will. . . .'
> Go to a dinner, and the talk is still
> Of how your pockets you may quickly fill;
> Nay, at a ball itself they talk finance,
> Sandwich'd between flirtation and a dance.

And chiding the sweet girls who married Presbyterian businessmen:

> Before fat Mammon Love and Honor pale,
> And Money wins where Birth and Merit fail.[95]

To some extent Victorian bourgeois materialism and speculative excess reflected trends elsewhere. The English middle class was 'drugged with business', according to Matthew Arnold.[96] Trollope wrote *The Way We Live Now* partly to attack the 'commercial profligacy' of the age and the rise to power and social esteem of a new class of financial manipulators. Shiels was typical of the English intelligentsia who stood against the flood of money, the snobbery of wealth, the new rapacious materialism and riotous, graceless display.[97] There are also American parallels in the lesser 'robber barons' of the 'Gilded Age', Chicago's boom and bust and the land speculators of golden San Francisco. About the same time as Melbourne, Rome suffered similarly at the hands of company promoters, land speculators and jerry-builders. If individualism—every man following his own interests as he saw fit—had been the dynamic of English economic life, then Sidney Webb's shrewd observation of Victoria in 1898 hits the centre of the target: 'The trouble is that the people are an exceptionally Individualist graft from our Individualist epoch (1840–1870); and they are all of them gambling profit-makers, keen on realising the Individualist ideals of the lower Middle Class of 1840–70.'[98] As John Morley remarked, 'belief in progress had become the basis of social thought'.[99] Material progress had come to be seen as automatic, almost an inevitable law; colonists' confident assumptions about the inevitability of progress were only mild variants on the English. The colonial Philistine may have been the rankest flowering of Arnold's type, but he was the same vulgar boor for whom culture was nothing but frill and ornament, and education was little more worthy of respect.

However, without doubt, the colonial experience encouraged blatant materialism and super-optimism. What justifications in personal terms of migration were there other than material success; and how better could colony stand proudly before mother country than by displaying its material achievement? What other than land and wealth was Sir Samuel Wilson thinking of when he referred to 'those hopes of success in obtaining the rich prizes of life which are the principal motives leading to the successful colonization of new countries'?[1] James Moloney, who was regarded as a cultivated man, could say: 'Wealth was necessarily and properly an object of respect here because it was the main feature to denote a man's success in his efforts to advance.'[2] The symbol of the age, perhaps, was 'Money' Miller in his dotage, playing with sovereigns.[3] This was the first golden age of the colonial bourgeoisie, constantly being reinforced by new successful recruits, revelling in their riches, preaching the gospel of wealth, and by implication equating it with happiness as the noble end of striving. Those wishing to emulate them were encouraged to believe that 'luck and pluck', rather than traditional industry, patience and intelligence, was the right approach.[4] The Davies and Munros justified themselves by claiming in all sincerity to be public benefactors who were carrying the populace with them to greater happiness. But their assumption that what was good for business, what was in their interest, was good for the country, led them all too easily to justify risks and devious practices—and perhaps worse—in terms of public benefit. The local experience of mass participation in the gold lottery, the widespread abandonment of respect for law and morality in the struggle for land, even the common practice of presenting fake invoices to Customs officers which a protective system cultivated,[5] encouraged a permissive commercial ethic. When the temptations of fleecing a credulous public became irresistible in the eighties, business morals deteriorated further. A prominent lawyer had to remind businessmen that 'It is a curious fact . . . that there are many transactions which the Courts strongly reprehend as fraudulent and visit with civil consequences, but which you ordinary men of business treat as legitimate.'[6]

There is a touching innocence about the public's gullible faith in 'those dignified personages with frock coats and white waistcoats, spade beards and polished chimney-pot hats, who promoted their alluring companies'. Not only old maids, widows, parsons and school-marms but also steady clerks and artisans walked into the 'traps, baited with the names of men in high positions, notorious for piety, respectability, and business acumen',[7] and handed over their savings—not as a rule expecting to make a fortune, often merely hoping to secure their old age. A baffling problem of the boom period is why the skilled businessmen were so credulous, when the financial structure became so crazy. Shrewd and simple alike were bemused by the notion of the inevitability of progress, by the illusion of Victoria's predestined right to ever increasing prosperity, and by the last long-delayed chance to make the golden pile for which they had migrated.

9

'Marvellous Melbourne', 1887–1888

Boom Melbourne described; style of life

Many visitors to Melbourne agreed—often grudgingly, in the face of so much skiting about the 'city which untravelled colonists deemed the finest in the world'[1]—that it had to be described as phenomenal, marvellous, magnificent, noble. They were usually surprised, first, at the vast panorama seen from the Bay; then, after a deflating railway trip through dowdy suburbs or a voyage up the stinking river, came the revelation of a spacious city with stately public buildings and broad streets crammed with traffic, a city which was unquestionably a metropolis. 'I don't think people at home have the least idea of its magnificence and extent,' wrote E. H. Sugden. 'It is a world's wonder.'[2]

According to some Americans and globetrotters, the grid-plan of the city, the style of architecture and the ugly telegraph and telephone poles gave Melbourne an American look; Chicago, Philadelphia, San Francisco, and even New York, were named as parallels.[3] British migrants and visitors were, however, reassured by its familiar appearance. Liverpool came to mind most readily, Edinburgh New Town sometimes—'Glasgow, with the sky of Alexandria' was perhaps the most imaginative reaction.[4] Similarities to London were noted, for example the resemblance of Collins and Bourke Streets to Bond and Oxford Streets.* Likenesses were found with Paris and even Rome. Francis Adams found Melbourne's attraction to be that there was 'something of London in her, something of Paris, something of New York, and something of her own'. The city had the metropolitan tone, the metropolitan look; it expressed movement, progress, conscious power.[5]

The high-flown parallels are comprehensible, for Melbourne was now touching half a million in population, was about thirtieth city of the world by the test of numbers, (and no doubt, as was claimed, could be ranked much higher in terms of wealth). It was catching Buenos Aires as the most populous city of the Southern Hemisphere, was larger than Birmingham, Boston and most European capitals, and was the seventh city of the Em-

* James Smith (Garnet Walch, *Victoria in 1880*, pp. 165-6) made a detailed tally of the repetition of London's features. Bourke Street was High Holborn with a difference; Fitzroy Gardens and East Melbourne were Kensington in the bud; Chapel Street, Prahran, was like Tottenham Court Road; St Kilda was a highly genteel Gravesend; Hawthorn and Kew were like Highgate and Hampstead, etc.

pire, behind London, Bombay, Calcutta, Glasgow, Liverpool and Manchester.[6] Marvellous Melbourne, the Metropolis of the Southern Hemisphere, the Chicago of the South, the Paris of the Antipodes! Its delighted citizens (but not the dwindling majority of Victorians) exulted.

Sydney and Adelaide were provincial cities, wrote Twopeny; Melbourne was 'quasi-metropolitan'. Contemporary opinions on the characteristics of Melbourne and Sydney are strange in the light of standard twentieth-century views. Melbourne was an American city, Sydney English; Melbourne was like New York, Sydney like London; Melbourne had style, Sydney was solid; Melbourne was flashy, Sydney was slow; money was made in Melbourne, in Sydney it grew.[7] 'Sydney gives the impression of beauty, of soundness, and of home; Melbourne of progress, of courage, of success, and of expansion.'[8] Francis Adams remarked that

> The men and women of Sydney do not live so fast mentally as the men and women of Melbourne: they give more free play to their emotional passions. As we say, they 'take things easier'. They cling to the past which Melbourne throws away: they consider the present, which Melbourne has very little time for.[9]

Twopeny concluded that Melbourne 'people dress better, talk better, think better, are better, if we accept Herbert Spencer's definition of Progress. There is far more "go" and far more "life" . . . to be found in Melbourne [where there is] the fullest development of Australasian civilization.'[10]

The broad streets and the verandahs, which some said were like those in Bologna or the Rue de Rivoli in Paris, were often praised.[11] Many visitors were delighted, too, by the pure, smokeless air and noticed how clean the buildings were, that it was a city where ladies could wear white dresses and men white coats and waistcoats.[12] But the dust and flies were abominable in the summer. Suburban developers' systematic stripping of trees had made the dust worse, but it was not so bad in the city itself since the paving of most of the streets with wood blocks. Many of the broad footpaths were asphalted, and the perils of wet-weather navigation were only a memory since the recent substitution of underground drains for the wide and deep gutters with their picturesque bridges. St Kilda Road had recently been planted with trees but was still, like most of the main suburban roads, very rough to drive on. Collins Street was the pride of the city: 'Between the elm trees that rustle on either side of the street we look down on a noble avenue, with lofty buildings on either hand.' Looking back from the far end, facing away from the corrugated-iron expanse of Spencer Street station, which was such a shabby anticlimax to a noble boulevard,

> The eye is delighted with the extent and liveliness of the scene as it follows the rows of buildings, their domes, and turrets, and spires, growing ever apparently closer to each other, and dimmer and more airy looking till they terminate in the far-off Treasury Buildings, now a mile away.

In the central area between, where the design of the city tended to concentrate traffic, was a 'dense congregation of business, bustle and enterprise; [a] teeming area of scheming brains and active hands'.[13]

> Hansom cabs rattled about . . . ; four-wheeled vehicles of an inexcusably awkward style, also for hire, abounded; messenger-boys . . . hurried hither and thither; high-hung omnibuses with three horses abreast, like those of Paris and Naples, dashed rapidly along, well filled with passengers; men galloped through the crowd upon small horses, carrying big baskets of provisions on their arms; dog-carts driven by smart young fellows, with a flunky behind in gaudy livery, cut in and out among the vehicles; powerful draught-horses stamped along the way, drawing heavily loaded drays; . . . light and neat American wagonettes glided along among less attractive vehicles.[14]

The traffic demanded 'enterprising pedestrianism', but the police rigorously compelled drivers to observe the 'Walk over Crossing' signs at intersections.[15] Every evening, crowds of clerks and shop-assistants surged down Swanston and Elizabeth Streets to Flinders Street station, from which by 1888 300 trains a day left for the southern and eastern suburbs.

From late 1885 the cable trams were Melbourne's pride and joy—delightful toys and a most efficient and unusual form of transport. Frederick Cowen, the musician, was 'much fascinated by . . . the first horseless vehicles [other than trains] I had ever seen'.[16] They were elegant and quiet (except for the ceaseless underground rumble) and each did the work of three lumbering omnibuses. 'These luxurious aristocratic trams give the finishing touch to Melbourne polish,' enthused a journalist in 1888.[17] No generation enjoyed more than the first the delight, especially on summer nights, of riding on the open dummy.[18] Sydney had had steam trams from the early eighties, but Melbourne profited by being late in the field. Very soon the trams were applauded as 'safe, clean, and punctual as the town clock'.[19] They maintained eight miles an hour, including stops; the high flat fare of threepence, except for workmen's trams, demonstrated the traffic the boom would bear. In the first eighteen months, however, the silent and speedy vehicles were involved in thirty accidents, with seven fatalities.

No British city outside London could boast of as many large public buildings or, Twopeny for one asserted, as fine ones.[20] Government House was larger than the residences of the Viceroy of India and the Lord Lieutenant of Ireland; its ballroom was eighteen feet longer than the State ballroom at Buckingham Palace, someone told the visiting princes in 1881. St Patrick's—almost finished but for the spires—was claimed to be the largest cathedral in the Southern Hemisphere. There was no rival in scale anywhere in the Empire to Parliament House, whose crowning cupola was never, however, to be built. The visitor in the late eighties saw much evidence of further improvement. The west front of Parliament House, the third storey and tower of the General Post Office and several buildings like the Working Men's College were nearing completion. After the removal of the reef, more bridges over the Yarra were being built and the new Prince's Bridge was opened in 1888; Sir John Coode's deep-cut canal and the Victoria Dock system were well advanced. There was one common criticism, however. Melbourne city had a gawky, higgledy-piggledy look because of the wildly irregular building heights and the broken continuity of the verandahs; noble buildings stood next to structures which were little better than shanties or sheds. The rebuilding of the later eighties tended to increase incongruity. William Westgarth the financier, back in Melbourne after thirty years' absence, wrote to the mayor to suggest enforcing some degree of symmetry, while retaining variety. The reply, of course, implied that any such restriction on 'progress' would be intolerable.[21] There were also many protests at the unsightly cluttering of the streets with telegraph and telephone wires and poles; in 1886 the government considered running the wires underground but regretfully decided it was not feasible.[22]

Trams, verandahs and public buildings gave Melbourne an individual character. So did the parks and gardens which were one of La Trobe's great legacies, especially the Botanic Gardens which W. R. Guilfoyle was landscaping into lasting beauty. So did Chinatown round little Bourke Street, Cole's Book Arcade, and the Public Library which was one of the great libraries of the world and the centre of a network of more local public libraries than existed in the United Kingdom: five or six hundred artisans and workmen crowded the reading-rooms on Saturday afternoons. George Augustus Sala, the visiting lecturer-journalist, who coined or popularized the 'Marvellous Melbourne' slogan, remarked that he knew no streets in the world more interesting and amusing that Collins and Bourke.[23] On Saturday mornings, as a matter of course, most of fashionable Melbourne 'did the Block'. Ladies showed off their dresses, gentlemen bowed to friends and cut their enemies, the young lingered to flirt. *Table Talk* deplored the growing number of offensive 'mashers' and their 'amatory leering and ogling'.*[24] Bourke Street on Saturday night, always crowded and raucous, was the equivalent proletarian parade.[25]

Melbourne was undergoing convulsive growth as its population increased by about three-quarters in eight years; at the end of the decade almost every second house was new. The old inner suburbs were nearly built up and reached their ultimate stable populations; South Melbourne with 42,000 led the way, followed by Prahran and Richmond. In 1889 the inner suburbs—16 per cent of the defined area of Melbourne—still held 70 per cent of the population. Brunswick and Footscray each climbed in the decade from about six to twenty thousand people. Suburbs like Hawthorn and Essendon were half occupied, while extensive building-up began in

* Old Robert Russell thought the 'crowd of faultlessly-attired, eye-glassed exquisites' were 'mostly loafers from the old country, or lads not yet fledged.' Hume Nisbet refers to ladies 'whose equals for physical beauty, stature, and grace of carriage are nowhere else to be seen in the world; they all look goddesses as they glide along' (*A Colonial Tramp*, vol. i, pp. 88-91).

areas still further out like Coburg, Camberwell and Caulfield (all six to eight thousand). The proud suburban 'cities' raised grandiloquent town halls as evidence of their importance; Emerald Hill's (1880) was unexcelled even by Collingwood's (1887). In the newer suburbs, terraces were rarely built; the single-storeyed house with garden front and back, on rectangular strips of about one-sixth of an acre, became standard. Then as now, newcomers and homecomers from Europe noticed the flat openness of the suburbs and the expanse of sky which wide streets and low buildings revealed. Wooden houses with corrugated iron roofs predominated, especially in the northern and western suburbs; the south and east had relatively many more of brick and slate. The division between working-class north of the river and better-off south and east was sharpening. As transport improved and numbers grew, the middle and further-out suburbs lost most of their village community atmosphere and sense of individuality, when their residents became predominantly commuters to work elsewhere and uniform housing blotted out peculiarities of landscape. On the other hand suburban shopping-centres like Chapel Street, Prahran, and Smith Street, Collingwood, were taking trade away from the city. Between 1883 and 1887 Emerald Hill, Sandridge and Hotham altered their names to South, Port and North Melbourne partly to cash in on the city's reputation.

During a practice of forty years, Joseph Reed designed most of Melbourne's major public buildings in any and every historic style.*[26] His 'hybrid Florentine-French' Exhibition Building of the late seventies encouraged an orgy of decoration and display in the business palaces and suburban mansions of the boom years. Already the banks and other major commercial firms, recognizing that lavish building was an economical form of advertising, had spent enormous sums on their Collins Street headquarters. Then in the eighties, Melbourne's business centre was further rebuilt on a scale which was to suffice for the next half-century. The several dozen new multi-storey buildings were constructed in a wild variety of styles, of which Gothic Revival variants were the most conspicuous. Most of them reflected the self-confident brash ostentatiousness of the day in their attempts to assert the eminent achievement of the proprietors and their clients. Towers, spires, domes and turrets reared to the skies; exteriors and interiors were cluttered with decorative flora, fruit and shells, as architects revelled in the new mass production of plaster ornament. Colour in patterned brick and marble became progressively more riotous as the decade passed. The hotels and coffee palaces, constructed to cater for the large increase in transient population and visitors to the Centennial Exhibition, were extravanganzas of lavishness. The Federal Coffee Palace, built between 1886 and 1888 at a cost of more than £150,000, was the triumph of the day. A bewildered contemporary found its style difficult to define: 'It comprises a little of everything—Corinthian, Ionic, Doric,

* Reed was the architect of among others, the Town Hall, Public Library, the Scots, Independent and Wesley churches, the Trades Hall, Ormond College, Wilson Hall and the A.N.Z. Bank.

early English, late English, Queen Anne, Elizabethan, Australian—in fact, it may be called the last.'[27] Of seven storeys and with more than 500 rooms, the Federal had six Waygood lifts, an ice-plant, electric bells and cash registers; its dining-room was, of course, 'the largest and most magnificent room south of the equator'. Entry was made under an arcaded loggia of fourteen Ionic columns, which led through an inner hall to a great hall, all paved with black, white and red marble. The whole building was smothered with plaster decoration; out of the central pediment rose 'Venus, a nude figure of full life size, drawn on the waters in a cloud chariot by four sea horses and accompanied by several other figures, the whole representing the Aurora Australis'.[28]

Only once, perhaps, extravagant boom ideas produced an aesthetic triumph. Sir George Verdon, Inspector-General of the E. S. & A. Bank, employed his friend, William Wardell, architect of the Catholic cathedrals of Melbourne and Sydney; both of them had known Pugin. The new E. S. & A. office completed in 1886 had a Venetian Gothic exterior in red sandstone with pointed tower on the corner, and a glorious interior with light blue ceiling, exposed steel supports, and gold leafing running wild.[29] The most prominent Gothic revivalist was William Pitt, who was responsible for the highly embroidered and colourful Italian Gothic Stock Exchange, Rialto and Olderfleet buildings, all in Collins Street. He also had a hand in the Federal and rebuilt the Princess Theatre voluptuously, with opening roof and ceiling. New trends were exemplified in the amazing twelve-storey Australian Property and Investment Company building which was described as being in a rather late Queen Anne style. The most notable new addition to public buildings was St Paul's Cathedral, designed from afar by the distinguished William Butterfield; when he fell out with his clients, Joseph Reed was at hand to complete the task faithfully. Overall, however, as an architectural historian has remarked, Melbourne city's new buildings gave the impression of 'a Renaissance gone wrong'.[30]

The new business tycoon had to build or buy a 10- to 30-acre suburban mansion and estate, imposing enough to provide conclusive evidence of great worldly success. The boom-mansions tended to follow the pattern of the earlier great houses of the sixties and seventies in their mixture of Classical and Italianate styles and confusion of period, although occasional Spanish, Moorish, Oriental and other exotic influences appeared. The typical massive, unbalanced, two-storeyed mansion had a sombre grey-stuccoed exterior, almost inevitably a tower and flagpole, and arcaded, mosaic-tiled, cast-iron-festooned verandahs. It had two or three halls, drawing, dining, breakfast and morning rooms, several bedrooms upstairs, a 'nursery suite', and servants' bedrooms along the back passage with separate sewing-room and bathroom; the kitchen was as far to the back as possible through a baize swing door, near pantries, scullery, store-room, laundry and maids' sitting-room; across the yard were meathouse, dairy, stables, coach-house and woodshed.[31] The complete mansion needed a ballroom, a banquet-hall, a billiard-room (with a local Alcock table—the finest in the world) and a picture-gallery. The ballroom at F. T. Sargood's 60-acre Rippon Lea seated three hundred, had a stage for amateur theatricals, and was used for fencing and glee-club meetings.[32] Gardens, surrounded by high iron fences, were planted with English trees and often a few pines, palms and Moreton Bay figs and, as contemporary prints show, remained exposed and scrawny for several years. Buffalo-grass lawns, rose-gardens, shrubberies, winding paths with archways, fern-houses, conservatories, statues and fountains, croquet-lawn and lawn-tennis-court completed the lay-out. Small-scale farming was still frequently practised on the larger estates. The huge squat bulk of Cliveden in East Melbourne—Janet, Lady Clarke's town-house and social headquarters—was one of three notable late boom excesses. Mark Moss built Norwood or 'The Castle', a 34-room red-brick and yellow-stucco fantasy, on the Brighton Esplanade.[33] In East Malvern J. M. Davies raised a huge folly (later Malvern Grammar School), whose fifty-feet-high hall or internal courtyard, ringed with balconies and with allegedly the largest parquet floor in the Southern Hemisphere, had 'something of the internal spatial atmosphere of an eighteenth-century central-European church'.[34] Davies's occupancy in full splendour was brief.

Immense sums were spent on furnishing and interior decoration; several migrant professional decorators shared fully in the profits of the boom. Painted and gold-leafed walls, ceilings and cornices tended to replace wall-paper. William Greenlaw's Villa Alba at Studley Park (1884) had a frieze and panels in the dining-room depicting scenes from Scott's novels, while panoramic views of Edinburgh and Sydney Harbour adorned the main corridor.[35] Bold colours were popular—increasingly harsh reds, blues and purples, especially when stained glass became the rage. 'It seems that in no way can one obtain the same amount of beauty for so small an expenditure as in stained glass,' the *Builder and Contractors' News* remarked in 1888.[36] Over-stuffed and antimacassared furniture from Rocke's (another of B. J. Fink's services) and miscellaneous bric-à-brac cluttered the drawing-room-museums. Vases, statuettes, cut glass, porcelain, aspidistras, waxed fruit, ebony elephants from Ceylon and other knick-knacks loaded every table, mantelpiece and shelf. Steel engravings, paintings, water-colours, painted fans, photographs and mirrors covered almost every square inch of wall within reach. Venetian blinds hung wherever the forbidden sun might intrude. The new aristocrats discovered and displayed armorial bearings and family trees; shields, coats of mail and bizarre weapons lined their hall-ways. A retinue of indoor servants was needed to maintain such establishments; a trained manservant was a great prize. Gyles Turner remarked that liveried indoor servants, previously almost unknown, became common enough to be taken for granted; he deplored 'this servile copying of an older social system [which] was prejudicial to the manly independence and healthy simplicity associated with the idea of colonial life'.[37] The style of carriage and horses was all-important. Proud, disciplined, sixteen-hand thoroughbreds were groomed and cosseted like racehorses. New-model carriages came on the market almost monthly; glossy custom-built vehicles were painted fifteen times perhaps, had 1½-inch thick hippopotamus-hide for brake-blocks, tiger-skin rug, and silk linings and tassels to the upholstery. Imported English broughams cost as much as £360 and wives were quick to persuade husbands to trade in at the first sign of shabbiness. Dignified coachmen wore tight white breeches, black polished boots, cut-away coat, white cravat, top-hat and gloves.[38]

A boom style of middle class housing emerged in the late eighties. The symmetrical plan of the standard Italianate Georgian house was broken more frequently by the projection forward of one of the front rooms in a semi-octagonal bulge. A heavily ornamented parapet-façade—so symbolic of boom pretensions—hid most of the slate roof, while the festooning ironwork round the verandah became even more elaborate. New brick-making processes allowed production of a variety of reds, creams, browns and greys, and the Australian invention in the mid-eighties of the cavity-wall encouraged the abandoning of plaster-stucco exteriors and the display of patterned coloured brick. Front doors were edged with side and top panels of vivid stained glass, and fireplaces with coloured-tile panels. 1886 saw a most significant innovation when Marseilles tiles were first imported in quantity; they were welcomed as being colourful, and cooler and more durable than slates. Considerable overlap of styles remained: the simple straight-fronted, verandahed box pattern was still being used for substantial brick houses in 1890 and remained the standard design for poorer dwellings, whose timber-fronts were often mass-produced to give the appearance of stone. The workingman's double-fronted detachment and his garden-plot, even in Footscray and Brunswick, was good evidence of his relative prosperity.[39]

The seamy side: the stench; larrikins

Ludicrously, Melbourne's splendour had one terrible flaw: the city often stank to high heaven. The Yarra was a 'common sewer'[40]—inky black with foul gases emanating from it; the Liffey in Dublin was said to be sweet by comparison. A Governor had formally protested to his ministry about the 'disgusting smell' which made it 'constantly impossible to open any of the windows'.[41] Tobacco was a necessity for those who worked on, or whose business took them to the wharves. Liquid refuse from kitchens, baths and laundries, factories, stables and public urinals drained into open street channels and thence into almost every watercourse or lagoon in the metropolitan area. In many suburbs, the channels were unmade, but in the inner suburbs and city they ran into underground drains. Every night the noisome nightcarts went about their homely tasks; hundreds clanked down St Kilda and Punt Roads making for their disposal points in the sand-belt; municipalities warred with each other in their attempts to delimit trade.[42] The *Bulletin* gleefully began to refer to 'Marvellous Smelbourne'.

The 'filth diseases'—typhoid and diphtheria—grew worse year by year.

Melbourne's death-rate from typhoid was five times worse than London's, and the country towns were almost as bad. In 1889 there were 910 deaths from typhoid in Victoria (558 in Melbourne), a mortality-rate of over 10 per cent; in the 'season' from February to May, patients were carted round from one hospital to another, seeking admission. The number of typhoid and diphtheria cases varied greatly from suburb to suburb; it became very clear that the rate was closely connected with local drainage conditions. In February 1888 an angry doctor suggested hanging a mayor for criminal neglect whenever a typhoid case occurred.[43]

There appear to be few mitigating factors to qualify a verdict of extraordinary neglect. A detailed contour-study for a deep drainage scheme had been made as early as 1854; it was found that Melbourne's topography would, compared to most cities, make a comprehensive scheme of sewerage difficult and expensive. Meanwhile surface drainage was cheap and the Yarra convenient. But Adelaide made the big step in 1878 and Sydney in 1880; by the late eighties Adelaide's sewerage system was almost completed and Sydney's was well advanced. The Melbourne City Council, suburban municipalities and Parliament continued to blame each other for the lamentable lack of action. The stopgap 1883 Public Health Act was largely ineffective, for it gave the Central Board of Health inadequate power and left crucial authority to careless municipalities.[44] By 1887 the scandal was so desperate that the legislative machine was forced to lumber into action. A conference of municipalities accepted the need for fundamental reform, and the government in 1888 appointed a royal commission, chaired by a medical professor, H. B. Allen, on the Sanitary Condition of Melbourne. The commission soon began producing reports with a tone reminiscent of Edwin Chadwick in England fifty years before.[45] The sanitary reformers used the Intercolonial Medical Congress of January 1889 as a platform, where Pearson displayed his gifts of irony and sarcasm:

> We valued so highly our constitutional rights—the right of a man to pollute running water; the right of a man to spread contagious diseases descending even to the third generation; the right of a man in every possible way to poison the life of the members of the community—that many of us would oppose to the death any interference with these privileges. . . . the vested right of every Englishman to carry death into his neighbour's household.

He was sure that most of the press would denounce any comprehensive control of public health as 'grandmotherly legislation'.[46] Meanwhile correspondents in the press used heightened language to bring home to Melbourne its disgrace. Cosmo Newbery, the scientist, thought Port Said was a legitimate comparison: 'dirty tins, papers, broken bottles . . . disease-disseminating, old, dirty, encrusted pans' littered vacant allotments in rich and poor suburbs alike. 'I never saw a dirtier city than Melbourne, not even among the Heathen Chinee,' wrote another. Others demanded flogging or ten years' imprisonment for the many nightcartmen who were cutting their journeys short by depositing their loads in the streets.[47]

The vital decisions were taken in 1889. The government followed the precedent of Sir John Coode and the harbour works in seeking and paying appropriately for the best English expert. James Mansergh, the distinguished sanitary engineer, was brought out to advise on a deep-sewerage scheme. When he reported in August 1890, he endorsed the Sanitary Commission's condemnations and believed even stronger language was called for:

> People who have never known what it is to live unsurrounded by cesspits, privies, night-soil pails, or ill-kept earth-closets, or other of the vile appliances I saw in Melbourne, will wonder how they could have existed under such conditions when these things have been swept away, and decent water-closets have taken their place.*[48]

Late in 1889 the government anticipated his report by forcing through a Public Health Act,[49] which established a ministry and gave teeth to the Central Board of Health. With the appointment of Dr D. A. Gresswell, and the formation of the Melbourne and Metropolitan Board of Works to carry out Mansergh's plan, Melbourne began to be cleaned up from 1890.

Melbourne was a metropolis and had a criminal class but, although the back lanes of the city appear to have been 'squalid haunts of vice and crime', the number of habitual criminals was not large enough to give the police many problems. Most of the blatant prostitutes were forced back out of sight. The most obvious disgraceful nuisance was larrikinism. Loutish behaviour, verging on criminality, by gangs of unskilled, culturally isolated working-class youths from inner suburban tenements was a problem of many of the world's industrial cities. The problem, and the word,† had first been noticed in the sixties. The incidence now of these youths' insulting behaviour, obscene language, hustling and jeering of passers-by, pelting with bluestone, vandalism, intimidation of publicans to provide free drinks, assaults on police and lone citizens at night, and petty robberies appeared to be increasing. Well-dressed gentlemen were special targets of abuse because of their top-hats, white waistcoats and gloves. By some accounts, the larrikin was usually weedy, undersized and slouching, but wiry and active.[50] In the mid-eighties his fashion of dress appears to have been all-black—short, tight coat and bell-bottomed trousers, neat high-heeled boots and wide-brimmed dark felt hat. The Kellys had been their heroes and, as inheritors of one strong Australian tradition, their hatred for the police was virulent. The Salvation Army and the Chinese were obvious butts: two hundred or more tormentors once mocked a Chinese funeral ceremony at the cemetery, laughing and jeering and trampling on

* Mansergh was, however, impressed by 'the almost universal and very free use of baths' for which he had to make special allowance in his planning.

† Dr Noel McLachlan's explanation of the origin of the word—that it derives from the Yorkshire 'larack' and/or the London usage of 'leary' ('leary kid' being a term in use in the sixties)—is far more convincing than the traditional story of police-sergeant Dalton referring to youths 'larkin'' about ('Larrikinism: an Interpretation', pp. 9–16).

graves.[51] Nat Gould, the popular writer, defined Collingwood roughs as 'about the worst specimens of human brutes on earth. They are savage and cruel, and delight in kicking a man until he is well-nigh dead.'[52] This was possibly a rash generalization from a few cases, but according to Francis Adams 'the street-riots of the Melbourne "larrikin" are as different as can be from the "rows" of the London or Birmingham "rough". It is the difference of tigers and bears at angry play.'[53] Perhaps there were only about one thousand of them and only a couple of the highly organized fraternal 'pushes' which were to become so dangerous in the nineties. But the problem was approaching its most serious stage.

Senior citizens and police were gravely alarmed and floundered in search of explanations. Dr Youl told the commission on shops and factories:

> If you go about the place, and notice the conduct of the factory boys and girls standing at the corner of the street at night, smoking and talking and larking, the language is very disgraceful, and there is a demoralization going on which is utterly destroying the whole community. . . . I was driving down Rathdowne Street, and there was a little fellow standing there about fourteen years of age, smoking a pipe. The cabman knew him, and he said, 'Billy, I will tell your father of you;' and he said, 'I do not care a d— if you do, I can earn more wages than he can.'[54]

Some explained the larrikin as the product of inherent depravity of convict children or of the conspicuous lack of discipline applied by colonial parents; others wondered whether early maturing in a warm climate or the availability of cheap meat were relevant. In October 1883 the Melbourne magistrates held a special meeting to consider the problem[55] and by 1887 had succeeded in promoting legislation authorizing flogging for some juvenile crimes. W. M. Forster founded his Try Excelsior classes (of which the City Newsboys' Society was an offshoot) to provide clubs and trade-training, as a more constructive answer to juvenile delinquency. The inadequacy of apprenticeship-systems may have been related to the problem, but it is doubtful whether it can be argued that economic deprivation was very relevant in a period of unparalleled rewards for unskilled labour. Anything peculiarly Australian about the larrikin may possibly be explained by the pervasive sense of democratic equality, which mildly eroded respect for authority, and by the faint traces in Victoria of the convict tradition.[56]

There was some abject poverty in boom Melbourne, but it was dismissed as the product of moral weakness and improvidence and largely ignored, with that singular lack of pity, the heartlessness amid all the benevolence, which characterized the age.[57] Many a new migrant was penniless and stranded until he found his feet. Seasonal unemployment was as bad in 1887, though perhaps not in 1888, as ever. And they were cruel days for widowed or deserted working-class women, for the chronically afflicted, for the defeated and incapacitated. The charitably inclined were often unaware that the boom reached only a certain distance down and tended to neglect their duty to the poor.

The Queen's Jubilee, the Centennial Exhibition, culture, sport, and incidents of the day

In June 1887 Melbourne and Victoria demonstratively celebrated the Queen's Jubilee. Parliament met to adopt a loyal address and adjourned for a fortnight. A two-days' holiday was proclaimed; the city was decked with flags and bunting and illuminated at night; great crowds ranged the streets singing 'Rule Britannia' and other patriotic songs. There was a naval and military tournament, a musical festival and a monster demonstration by the Salvation Army. At a concert at the Exhibition, Amy Sherwin sang 'Home, Sweet Home', 'The Harp that once in Tara's Halls' and 'Edinburgh Town'. Beethoven's Ninth was the main item at the concert given at Sunbury by the Clarkes to 7,000 guests, mainly Freemasons.[58] The Governor held a fancy-dress ball for 4,000 prominent citizens; Lady Loch appeared as Queen Elizabeth, Lady Clarke as a French Countess, Mrs Cain, the mayoress, as Rubens's wife, and Mrs Thomas Bent as an Indian princess.

> Happiness and eagerness to do honour to the occasion were depicted on every face, and it was impossible to avoid the conclusion that no more loyal subjects of Her Majesty had ever gathered together in the British Empire. Not a hitch occurred to mar the harmony of this magnificent tribute to Victorian loyalty.*[59]

A charity dinner for 1,100 people was provided at the Temperance Hall; the first course consisted of the surplus from the Mayor's dinner. The Wesleyans named their University college after Her Majesty. A rather meagre £5,400 was raised as a Jubilee contribution to the Imperial Institute in London. Lady Loch sponsored a Queen's fund for Victorian women in need.[60] The *Argus* published two special supplements and featured Alexander Sutherland's poem, 'The Empire and the Queen'.[61] Elsewhere Sutherland noted an extraordinary coincidence:

> It was on the 20th of June 1837 that Her Majesty commenced that long and eventful reign which makes so wonderful an era in the history of human kind. The first land sale of Melbourne had taken place twenty days before, and we may well suppose that it was just about the time when the girl Queen was roused from her slumbers at break of day to be informed of her uncle's death that the pioneers of Melbourne . . . began to lay the foundations . . . of what is now so handsome a city. . . . it has been a great and goodly work. . . .[62]

'We have no minority here!', the *Argus* exulted and joined *Table Talk* in condemning the 'treasonous bombast' of the Sydney *Bulletin*: in New

* The writer was Maurice Brodzky in *Table Talk*. The following week, however, in his role as spokesman for High Society, he deplored the laxness with which the invitation list had been made up. 'Many guests were present whom no respectable man would ever dream of introducing to his wife or daughters. . . . A very large proportion of provincial mayors and shire presidents would be far more at home in the servants' hall than in the yellow drawing-room.' (*Table Talk*, 1 July 1887.)

South Wales Messrs Walker, Norton and Traill had managed 'to diffuse the poison of their anarchical doctrines among the dregs of the masses, and disloyalty, turbulence, and outrage are the outcome'.[63] Indeed, there were few signs of disloyalty in Melbourne. It is true that the *Age*, 'while yielding to none' in loyalty, deplored all the 'grovelling gush'. Was it possible that 'loyalty is nearly allied to madness, and that the Queen's Jubilee will eventuate in an emotional epidemic like that which produced the Ecstatics and Convulsionaires of the Middle Ages?'[64] George Elmslie, a future Labor Premier, was quoted as saying at the Trades Hall that 'he thought people were Jubilee run mad. He had actually heard of a proposal to illuminate the cattle yards and abattoirs at Flemington. . . . It would not surprise him if a proposal were next made to illuminate the corporation tip and the night carts.'[65] But really disloyal Victorians were hard to find. Symes, of course, continued to abuse the Queen and opened a Republican and Atheistic Jubilee Fund; the proprietor of the *Williamstown Advertiser* was horsewhipped for a reference to the Queen as 'an obese old woman fond of whiskey'; and the young anarchist, 'Chummy' Fleming, won the support of a large meeting on the wharf for the proposition that starving men should not celebrate the Jubilee.[66] English visitors were greatly moved by the enthusiasm:

> The outburst of loyalty during the Jubilee at Melbourne will never be forgotten by those who saw it. I wish we could take a lesson from them; I wish we in the old country had a little more of that independent spirit and confidence in ourselves which now chiefly characterise our countrymen beyond the seas.[67]

One of Melbourne's historians has remarked that 'the enthusiasm was greater, and the celebrations more costly, than in any other part of the Empire'.[68]

1887 and 1888, the Centennial Year, were carnival days when the wealthy indulged themselves in luxurious excess. Balls, dinners, theatre parties and other entertainments followed each other in weekly profusion. Liquor consumption possibly broke all colonial records.* At the fashionable balls, Herr Plock's band swung into the Lancers, Quadrilles, waltzes, polkas, Varsovianas and Schottisches. Colonial young ladies were usually judged to be accomplished dancers; certainly they had practice enough, for weekly dances in private homes were customary. For the 'starched and whaleboned women' (the description is Ada Cambridge's), life was 'one long scurry of cards and calls'.[69] On fine afternoons the fashionable drove in their carriages round Albert Park Lake, a 'kind of Rotten-Row' where Herr Plock's band again added 'tone'. Lady Loch, Lady Clarke and their children had their portraits painted by Herr Kahler; no one, however, could rival Simon Fraser's triumph of having his portrait done by Sir John Millais for 3,000 guineas.[70] Immortality could also be bought in the 'puff'

* For 1888, £5 15s 5d per head (N.S.W. £4 9s 9d, England £3 6s 8d). (*Age*, 6 July 1889, p. 14.)

biographical compilations—*Victoria and its Metropolis* which included more than 6,000 'biographies' of pledged purchasers at six guineas for the two volumes (in 1889 the courts were cluttered with cases against those who had not paid up), and *Australian Representative Men* (ten guineas an entry).[71] The trade unions, also, indulged in encyclopaedic publication: *The History of Capital and Labour in all Lands and Ages* gloried in the fact that the working classes were making history, especially in Australia, and canonized Captain Cook as the saviour of society.[72] Only a handful of carping intellectuals were not carried away. Shiels growled: 'I don't think that lavish entertainments, sumptuous hospitalities, and the vulgar ostentatious extravagance of wealth raises a community. . . . [We are] setting up here a plutocracy of the very worst American character.'[73] (Shiels was described as young and inexperienced.) Ada Cambridge was to look back on 'the "good times", when we were rich and dishonest and mercenary and vulgar'.[74]

The Centennial International Exhibition—immensely exciting to those who took part—was the culmination. The Victorian government, knowing that New South Wales lacked an Exhibition Building and had left it too late to organize an Exhibition as part of its centennial celebrations, brought off a prestige-building coup with the utmost tact, and also persuaded itself that it was carrying out a major essay in intercolonial goodwill. Gillies suggested to the New South Wales Premier in 1886 that Melbourne might mount an Exhibition late in 1888, after Sydney's celebrations were over: it would be 'a public occasion which not only sums up the past, but also prognosticates the future of Australian achievement', it would 'tell of the bounty of nature and the perseverance of man'. 'Without a "World's Fair" in which should be displayed the results of the industrial progress of the colonies since their foundation, the celebration of Australia's centenary would be lamentably incomplete.'[75] The suggestion was accepted by Sydney with moderate enthusiasm. The Prince of Wales was invited to open proceedings. There was no chance of that, but against all English predictions, Deakin succeeded in persuading him, as a special favour to Victoria, to head the English commission.[76] Every government of the civilized world was asked to take part; most agreed, and several sent dignified commissioners to preside over their exhibits. The government initially budgeted for £25,000, but as the boom developed it grandly waived charges to exhibitors for rent and power, extended the building to meet demand for space, and determined to put on a show which would rival Chicago and Paris. Higinbotham, who had been presiding over the planning, resigned in protest at such wanton extravagance and F. T. Sargood assumed chief executive authority.[77] In the end, the Exhibition cost more than £250,000—a shocking amount, it was generally agreed. Against this sum, however, must be placed some of the money spent by visitors, increased Customs and railways revenue, and additions to the Exhibition building. Modern governments would regard an equivalent sum as well spent on a promotional exercise.

The opening on 1 August 1888, declared a public holiday, was very grand. The procession through an immense crowd in the streets was the finest attempt at pomp and pageantry yet made in the colonies; nearly one thousand visiting seamen from foreign warships added colour and dash. The 10,000 assembled within the Exhibition building included most of the leading men of the colonies. Only a disagreement between the Chief Justice and the Speaker about precedence marred the day; Higinbotham absented himself on principle. Otherwise all was geniality and harmony: when the detachment of the St Patrick's Society came abreast of the Protestant Alliance group, the latter, instead of jeering, gave three cheers which were heartily returned.[78] In the next fortnight the distinguished guests submitted to a 'ceaseless routine' of banquets, balls and receptions; pioneers of Port Phillip like Francis Henty and William Westgarth were honoured and revered. The Clarkes, as was their custom in Cup Week, hired the Town Hall for a lavish ball. The colonial Chief Justices met to discuss their common problems and the shape of federal courts of the future. The populace delighted in the modern marvels displayed in the extensive acres of the Exhibition, and were very impressed by the brilliant electric lighting at night and Mr Edison's phonograph. More than two million people passed through the turnstiles in the six months of opening. Earnest clerks and artisans agreed that it was a 'free education worth years of school'. But as the mocking *Bulletin* and *Punch* well knew, the didactic purpose was secondary to pompous self-display, proud assertion of achievement, and glorification of progress and development. The Exhibition announced that Victoria was taking its place among the nations; it was also sincerely felt to be an acknowledgment and 'summing-up of the work of the pioneers'.[79]

In contrast to the previous Exhibition in 1880, the Centennial included, as a major aspect, a cultural celebration. The music festival was an astonishing achievement. Twopeny had remarked, probably fairly accurately, that in few parts of the world was so much music to be heard, and in no part so much bad music.[80] Strumming the piano and vocal harmonizing were extraordinarily popular, even by the fashions of the period. A core of competent professionals in Melbourne, many of them German, provided instrumental and vocal concerts of fairly high standard, but orchestral work was almost unknown. The South Street contests in Ballarat had begun in 1879, Nellie Mitchell (Melba) had won a fine reputation before going overseas in 1886, and Francis Ormond had founded a chair of music at the University in 1887. The Exhibition Commissioners were determined to have the best, and approached the distinguished English conductor, Frederick Cowen, who named a fee of £5,000 for a six months' engagement. To his surprise the Commissioners did not demur. Cowen brought with him fifteen orchestral players as a nucleus, combined them with local instrumentalists, and drilled the orchestra and a combined amateur choir of 708 singers for a month. They then launched on an astonishing programme, which may never have been equalled anywhere, of more than

260 concerts, averaging ten concerts and three or four rehearsals a week, and covering the whole standard repertoire. About 11,000 people attended every Saturday; the Beethoven symphonies and Wagner became immensely popular. A popular plebiscite declared the order of preference to be: Beethoven's Pastoral Symphony, the overture to *Tannhaüser*, Handel's 'Largo', Liszt's 'Hungarian Rhapsody Number 1', and the overture to Wagner's *Rienzi*—not an ultra-modern choice, said Cowen, but one which would do credit to any community. He thought the soloists and choir excellent, while the orchestra, though patchy in quality, showed great 'precision of ensemble and technique'. There was a moving demonstration at the final concert; flowers showered down from the balconies, the ladies in the choir waved their scarves and 'Auld Lang Syne' was tearfully sung. Such an advance of proficiency and taste could not be allowed to wither away. An attempt was made to found a permanent orchestra; a government subsidy and private subscriptions enabled another English appointment, but the promised quality was lacking and the venture died.[81]

Most of the 2,000 paintings which were hung in the Exhibition galleries were collections on loan from Britain, France, Germany, Belgium, Austro-Hungary and elsewhere. The British collection alone numbered more than 500 items and, although representative of Royal Academy taste, included works by Constable, Turner, Millais and Holman Hunt. The best of the Old World, it was believed, had been gathered for the edification of young Australia. Inevitably there were protests about the obscene nudes in the French court. One visitor delighted in

> Frith's telling series of the career of the mining swindler, like Hogarth's 'Rake's Progress'; that splendid picture of the glowing red fires in the dark Hawaiian crater; then that other one, of the sick and dying King Edward the Sixth; the waves and sea gulls under a lofty Scotch cliff; . . . 'Circe' turning her admirers into pigs, was a comic picture, and I liked that little etching of 'Stoke Poges' Church.[82]

Dominant taste of the day insisted that every picture should tell a moral story or at least stimulate the 'moral and spiritual faculties' and cultivate a sense of beauty. John Longstaff's *Breaking the News*, based on a mining disaster at Clunes, had recently won the first travelling scholarship awarded by the National Gallery. The Trustees purchased from the overseas works on sale two sculptures—one of them, *St George and the Dragon* by J. E. Boehm, signifying the triumph of good over evil, is familiar to those who visit the State Library—and three paintings by forgotten artists, one of which depicted a dying martyr-gladiator scratching a cross on the ground. Two major paintings were also purchased in 1888: Alma Tadema's *The Vintage Festival in Ancient Rome*, said to be his finest work, for 4,000 guineas, and Watts's portrait of Tennyson for 600 guineas.[83]

At the same time, in protest at such standards, what was to become a national school of painting was being formed by young Melbourne rebels. The National Gallery School under Eugene von Guerard, Thomas Clark and George Folingsby and suburban schools of design had long been training young artists. Louis Buvelot had pioneered painting the suburban bush. Several British and continental artists were attracted to Melbourne by the possibility of commissions from the wealthy and the regular work available in the illustrated journals. Julian Ashton and others painted in the open; Ashton also encouraged young artists like Fred McCubbin to paint the life around them, rather than continue the tradition of academic studio-painting. In 1884 a Bohemian Sketching Club was formed, from which developed the Box Hill camp in blue-gum country within a mile of the station. Tom Roberts, just back from some years' painting in Europe, and McCubbin were the nucleus, and in 1886 were joined by the young lithographer, Arthur Streeton—'He is the genius,' Charles Conder remarked. Roberts first met Streeton by chance at Mentone: 'He was standing out on the wet rocks, painting there, and I saw that his work was full of light and air. We asked him to join us'.[84] The association was momentous, and memories of the Box Hill and the later Eaglemont camp were unforgettable. Streeton wrote in 1902:

> every detail and trifle is ingrained in my brain for life—the Houstons [at Box Hill], the creek, the horehound patch, the black wattle, the messmate, the long open space up to the road, the hurrying up the hill on Sunday with the Proff [McCubbin] well to the fore: Heidelberg, the she-oak and sienna dust over all; the straw-brown hills; pale Dandenongs; the Old England [hotel], college, tennis; pines and coppery light; hazels, japonica; Impressionist exhibition; gorse up the drive; girls; the picnics in the twilight, and all the loveliness....[85]

Here in their impressionistic sketches of local scenes, they began solving the problems of Australian light, heat, distance and, especially, colour. Streeton settled his blue-gold palette, the instrument which made him 'the discoverer, the first to look into the heart of our landscape'.[86] Here, too, they discussed the problems of depicting Australian history and life. Some of the results were Roberts's *Coming South* (1886), an essay on the hopes and fears of various types of migrants, and *Shearing the Rams* (1889–90), McCubbin's *Lost Child* (1886), depicting one of the standard tragedies of bush life, and *Down on his Luck* (1889), and Streeton's *Selector's Hut* (1888–9). In 1888 the arrival from Sydney of Charles Conder introduced new influences, for Conder was not only a genuine Bohemian dandy, but was linked with the aesthetic movement in England and was influenced especially by Whistler. He immediately became associated with the novelists, the Mannington Caffyns, who in their Brighton salon were lonely pioneers of Ibsen, Zola and other radical realists and closely in touch with modern movements in the arts. Roberts led a breakaway from the Victorian Academy of Arts to form the Australian Artists' Association in 1886, but by 1888 the two factions were reconciled in the Victorian Artists' Society. The Impressionists exhibited in the Society's shows early in 1889, but the Ruskinite art patron and *Argus* critic, James Smith, recognized a

Catalogue of the Impression Exhibition

dangerously subversive movement and began to attack the 'fad of Impressionism'. The famous 9″ x 5″ exhibition of 153 cigar-box sketches by Roberts, Streeton, McCubbin and Conder (and a few by three others) followed in August. Conder sketched an *art nouveau* cover for the catalogue and the paintings were hung amid draped silks, fans, screens and *japanoiserie*. The catalogue note, Smith's savage review and the artists' reply are among the leading documents in Australian art history. Something like four-fifths of the sketches were a pain to the eye, grotesque and meaningless, said Smith. This critic appears to have been representative of both refined and popular taste, for two of the classic works of Australian painting—Roberts's *Bourke Street* (1885–6) and Streeton's *Golden Summer* (1889)—were not sold when exhibited. Theodore Fink was one of a very few discriminating patrons. These *avant-garde* modern artists, imbued with vague nationalistic yearnings and determination to paint the typical life of Australia and the real countryside, were also in contact with the Sydney *Bulletin* and the Labour movement. Their joy in the sun, as a symbol of Australian hope and optimism, came slowly to be accepted by a later generation.[87]

The theatre in the eighties, as elsewhere, had made a big stride towards show-business, while serious drama was at a low ebb. Melbourne, said one much-travelled observer, was the 'greatest theatre-going place in the world for its population'.[88] The new firm of J. C. Williamson, Garner and Musgrove presented the brilliant and rather naughty Offenbach operettas; the versatile and greatly-loved Nellie Stewart starred in the wildly popular Gilbert and Sullivan operas; from 1886 the Brough and Boucicault Comedy Company began its run of highly polished performances. In 1888 Alfred Dampier's fruity melodrama, 'Marvellous Melbourne',[89] with topical scenes at Spencer Street station, Toorak, country homesteads, the wharves and Chinese dens, was immensely popular. However, in September 1889—the same year as it was first staged in London and five years before Paris—Janet Achurch played the lead in Ibsen's revolutionary *A Doll's House*; violent controversy ensued about women's rights and the new naturalistic drama. 'The Bard' was not neglected: in 1884 Professor E. E. Morris founded the Shakespeare Society and the classicist, Professor Samuel Way, became its 'heart and soul'. The monthly meetings usually attracted an audience of two hundred, often including Deakin, Sir George Verdon, and James Smith and David Blair, the senior critics; about one thousand devotees, 'all in full dress', attended an anniversary meeting in 1888 at the Athenaeum Hall.[90] George Meredith and Thomas Hardy were the current literary giants, while Robert Louis Stevenson, Conan Doyle and Rider Haggard were becoming popular; *Plain Tales from the Hills* by a young writer named Kipling was the latest success. 'The poet Gordon' was widely popular, the *Australasian* was running serials by Ada Cambridge, and Rolf Boldrewood's *Robbery Under Arms* (serialized in the *Sydney Mail* in 1882–3) won a Melbourne audience when published in 1888. Dr S. Mannington Caffyn was writing his *Miss Milne and I* (1889) and in Brussels

Jessie Couvreur ('Tasma') was writing her notable Melbourne novel, *Uncle Piper of Piper's Hill* (1889). The greatest literary success was Fergus Hume's pioneer detective-story, *The Mystery of a Hansom Cab*, which was redolent of Melbourne of the period. Published in 1886, it ran through 20,000 copies in three editions, and was then issued in England in 1887–8 in 175,000 copies.[91] Meanwhile a parliamentary majority of the 'unco' guid', 'wealthy lower orders', Catholics and Jews, all of whom the author had offended, refused a pension to Marcus Clarke's impoverished widow.[92] Of the native-born literary giants of the future, 'Henry Handel Richardson' had left in 1887 for the Leipzig Conservatorium; Bernard O'Dowd was working in the Supreme Court Library, was taking second year Arts at the University, and was prominent in the Secularists' Lyceum. Henry Lawson late in 1887 was attending the Eye and Ear Hospital as an out-patient, in hope of a cure for his deafness, and working as a coach-painter and as a toucher-up of photographs; his first contributions were published in the Christmas issue of the *Bulletin* that year.[93] The sixteen-year-old Shaw Neilson, out in 'the poor, poor country' of the West Wimmera, was helping his father on a fencing contract on which they nearly perished, and struggling for a meagre living on a selection.[94] And Joseph Furphy, after years of battling, was now working in his brother's agricultural implement works at Shepparton, slaving away at nights in his outhouse, and snatching hours in the Public Library on his visits to Melbourne to collect goods or as delegate to Church of Christ conferences; an avid *Bulletin* reader, he made his first contribution in 1889.[95]

By the late eighties, organized sport—both as pastime and spectacle—had become a distinguishing feature of Australian urban life. Rising prosperity, the Saturday half-holiday and adequate parklands helped its growth. Cricket and football had established themselves as the national games. There was immense public excitement over test matches with England—but not in the 1887–8 season for because of Sydney-Melbourne disagreement, two English teams were touring the colonies. Claims were already being made about the superiority of the Australian code of football; Twopeny thought the leading Melbourne teams showed far more ability and style than the best English rugby clubs.[96] However, H. C. A. Harrison failed in an attempt in 1884 to introduce the game in England. New South Wales had been colonized in 1880, a N.S.W. team played South Melbourne in 1883, and an intercolonial conference of 1885 made important changes in the rules. In its primitive state the game was for iron men only and the 'barracker', 'fluent in oath and objurgation, cursing like an inmate of the pit', was already a conspicuous part of the game.[97] Lawn-tennis was becoming fashionable with men and women alike. 'Penny-farthing' cycling was very popular; the first ride from Sydney to Melbourne was made in 1884 and the Melbourne Bicycle Club, in their uniform of myrtle-green coat, knickerbockers, stockings, cap and silver badge, had regular jaunts.[98] Roller-skating was a craze in 1888; there were eight suburban rinks where lads and lasses, hand in hand, gyrated and pirouetted.[99]

Racing was the great popular sport where the classes and the masses mingled; the Irish and the squatters lent fervent support. Cup week was High Society's chief festival period; the Governors of the other colonies attended and ships of the Royal Navy were usually in port; it was almost impossible to get any business done. Lord Rosebery had described the Cup as a garden-party with a race thrown in; other visitors defined it as a 'gigantic national picnic' and commented on the cleanness of the sport and the sober behaviour of the crowd, in contrast to English racing crowds.[1] The largest number of visitors Melbourne had ever had was in town for the Exhibition and the Centennial Cup. It had been raining on the Monday but the holiday was fine and about 100,000 people made their way to Flemington. Eighty-four trains ran from Spencer Street and the prosperity of the time was reflected by the 'new drags, broughams, barouches, and all manner of stylish equipages in the inner enclosure'. Foreigners, including turbaned Indians and Chinese and Burmese, added colour to the stands; countrymen, worried by the dry season and poor prices, were making the best of their holiday; as usual, all was fun and frolic on the Flat and the Hill. This year the fashions of the gorgeous promenaders on the lawns were notably restrained; white linen dresses and pale-shaded costumes prevailed, though some crimson and purple gowns made striking contrasts. Both Lady Loch and Mrs Charles Ryan wore green with black lace; Figaro jackets were very popular. The vice-regal party in landau and drag were welcomed by the V.R.C. committee amid cheers from the crowd; Signor Zelman's Australian Military Band played the National Anthem. The cup was won by Mentor (Mr D. S. Wallace owner, Michael O'Brien up) carrying 8 stone 3 lbs in the fair time of 3.30¾. Two horses ran into the fence and had to be shot. Meanwhile thousands were attending the Salvation Army's picnic in Royal Park, while the Y.M.C.A. was voyaging down the Bay. At the theatres that night, *The Mikado* was playing at the Princess, Simonsen's Italian Opera Company was performing *Carmen*, the Brough and Boucicault Company was presenting *Sophia*, and Mr Dampier's company was appearing in *The World Against Her*. There was a minstrel and variety company at the Hibernian Hall and Jem Mace's variety hall was open as usual. Wirth's circus was performing near Swanston Street north, there were fireworks in the Friendly Societies' Gardens, and numerous dance-halls were packed.[2]

In these years, as always, the public was vicariously moved by the tragic sensations of the day. On 11 May 1887, in the twilight about a quarter to six o'clock, the 5.30 train from Flinders Street to Elsternwick was halted by a signal in the cutting between Prahran and Windsor stations. The signal changed, but the train could not start for the brakes had jammed on. Guard and driver located the fault and began to repair it. Through the Prahran station at a rattling pace came the crowded 5.40 express to Brighton and was given the all clear. Under High Street and round the curve it dashed. Driver Maskell saw the stationary train less than one hundred yards ahead. He stayed at his post for the few seconds of life

Elizabeth Street and Collins Street, 1889

Opening of the Centennial Exhibition

remaining to him, braked as best he could and screamed his whistle. The express ploughed through the guard's van and rear carriage, and its engine and front three carriages were smashed; the wreckage extended over one hundred yards. The terrible noise of impact and the succeeding shouting, screaming and moaning brought ten thousand local residents running to aid and hinder. A cloud of scalding steam was eventually doused by the Prahran Fire Brigade; fires were kindled to light the rescue work. Amazingly, only six were killed, while about 250 were injured. The mangled body of E. S. Parkes of the Bank of Australasia was pulled from the wreckage by W. K. Thomson of McEwan's whose overdraft had been one of Parkes's chief worries. Passengers on the express included Speight and a fellow Commissioner. A memorial to driver and fireman stands near their home depot at Port Melbourne.[3]

Shortly after eight o'clock on the night of Wednesday 31 August 1887, Laura Swain and her fiancé, Captain Moore of the *Sarah Grice*, were seen talking on Victoria Bridge. Did she jump, did she fall or was she pushed? Moore claimed that he turned away briefly to light his pipe, she said 'Good-bye', and jumped over. He rushed to the bank, but in his haste fell and hurt his back badly, so that he was unable to attempt to save her from drowning. The river was dragged for four days. On the Sunday afternoon 20,000 or 30,000 people from all parts of the city and suburbs streamed to view the scene. The crush on the bridge was so great that the police feared it might give way, while the crowd lining the Hawthorn bank was said to have been larger than that on 'The Hill' on an important Flemington race-day. Pleasure-boats followed the police-boats engaged on their task. Then the body was found, midway between Victoria and Hawthorn bridges. Police had to force a path through the huge crowd massed at the landing-place. Ten thousand men, women and children, behaving more like savages than Christians it was said, followed the corpse to the Bridge Hotel. The inquest sat for seven days and the *Herald* broke its circulation record. According to one commentator, the Crown Prosecutor was compelled to act the bloodhound, 'all the women of Victoria being ready to hang Moore, without judge or jury'. The examining doctor told the coroner that Miss Swain had not 'lived virtuously'; it emerged that both Miss Swain and Captain Moore used to drink heavily and quarrel violently. Witnesses, who had been some distance from the scene, gave conflicting evidence. The jury, after five and a half hours, returned an open verdict, and no further proceedings were taken.[4]

Drift to the city

'Marvellous Melbourne', 'loud voiced and reckless' Melbourne to Kipling,[5] was irresistibly attractive to the young men in the country towns who could see no prospects there to fit their talents. The gold towns declined in population in the eighties; Creswick, like others, was a 'town of old men' by 1890, after its youth had departed for Broken Hill, Western

Australia, Gippsland and Melbourne. Many of the bright young men of the A.N.A. branches in the gold towns were prominent in new branches in the Melbourne suburbs in the later eighties. The new migrants from overseas stayed in Melbourne: there was not much else open to them. Melbourne had the employment opportunities; men could earn much more there, take advantage of ever-opening opportunities, and enjoy the wide range of cultural and recreational pursuits. Meanwhile, as the city's proportion of the colony's population, running neck-and-neck with Adelaide, climbed over 40 per cent, parliamentarians and editorialists lamented the rise of the 'great wen', a 'huge magnet which attracts to itself not only the wealth, but the energy, and a very great deal of the enterprise of the colony'. No metropolis in Europe, Asia or America held anything like such an unhealthily high proportion of its community.[6] The critics had little inkling of the basic reasons—notably the low labour requirements for the Australian wool and wheat rural economy—why Melbourne was advancing so fast. But the farmers were beginning to organize in protest against Melbourne control and Melbourne wealth, and were ultimately to exact their revenge. Everything—politics, the banks, schools, land administration, the police—was centralized. While wool and wheat prices declined, a bitter anti-metropolitan creed aimed at city capitalist and trade unionist alike began to take shape.

10

National Issues, 1888

The Chinese 'menace'

Chinese immigration provided the major crisis of 1888. The number of Chinese in the colony had been steadily declining since the peak of the gold rushes. In the mid-eighties there remained few more than 10,000—roughly the same number as in both New South Wales and Queensland. Nearly all of them were Cantonese adult males of whom a few hundred had European wives; only about fifty Chinese women lived in the colony. More than half the Chinese had been described in the 1881 census as miners; they were excluded from company mines so there must have been large parties still, dwindling year by year, fossicking round abandoned fields. All the larger gold towns had their camps of a few hundred Chinese,[1] while only a thousand or so were in Melbourne. Some 1,500 were market gardeners; almost every township had its vegetable grower, and Chinese gardens were scattered round the city's outer suburbs and along the river. 'John' at the back door was a welcome visitor to most housewives. Grubbing parties were sometimes employed to clear land, a few were employed as station cooks and in isolated cases as shearers and station hands, some grew tobacco along the Ovens and King rivers, some were hawkers, others made furniture, and a sizeable minority were traders within the largely self-contained national community. The most serious attempt to employ cheap non-European labour was by a group of pastoralists and farmers near Warrnambool, who in 1883 and 1884 employed, not Chinese, but a group of Indians whom they had imported; the experiment failed dismally.[2] A handful of merchants like Kong Meng and Louis Ah Mouy (who was also a mining entrepreneur and land speculator) had won wide respect.

Following a major shipping strike in protest against the use of Chinese seamen at cheap rates, restrictions on Chinese immigration had been reimposed after intercolonial conferences of 1880 and 1881. Numbers entering were restricted to one to every hundred tons of ship's burthen and a poll-tax of £10 was levied. Yet most people showed little hostility to the Chinese. Their New Year processions, with gorgeous costumes, dragons, and crackers to dispel evil spirits, delighted local communities.[3] Little Bourke Street was often denounced as 'a hotbed of crime and vice of the most revolting description'.[4] But many would argue in defence that the

Chinese crime rate was much lower than the rest of the community's; houses in the Little Bourke area were less crowded than the colonial average; and opium-smoking and fan-tan were no more reprehensible than drunkenness or betting on horse racing; prostitution in the Chinese quarters was no more extensive than elsewhere; and nearly all the Chinese spent only limited time in the colony and usually felt bound by religious and traditional ties to return to their homeland. The fear that they might become a problem like the Negro in America could be met until the mid-eighties by the simple answer of steadily dwindling numbers.[5] The miners and the trade unions were the main hostile groups. By the mid-eighties several hundred Chinese, by dint of long hours and low wages, had largely captured the cheap furniture trade. At the intercolonial trade union conferences of 1884, 1885 and 1886, H. A. Harwood and other officers of the Furniture Trade Society gave papers attacking the Chinese menace. They also revived the Anti-Chinese Committee of the late seventies which now again became a lively centre of propaganda. In 1885 the Assembly provided for the stamping of Chinese-made furniture, in order to guide purchasers wishing to buy European-made goods, but the Council refused to permit it.[6] Inspectors under the Factories Act had difficulty in explaining to Chinese and enforcing the laws on working conditions. Under the Act, a factory was defined as a workplace employing six or more workmen; in 1887 Parliament passed a discriminatory amendment which defined one Chinaman working as a factory. 'If we save one conquered trade', said Deakin, 'and prevent the Chinese from conquering others, we shall have accomplished a great good.' Once again, however, the Council refused to allow stamping of Chinese-made furniture.[7]

In May 1887 General Wong Yung Ho and other commissioners visited Victoria on behalf of the Imperial Chinese government, as part of their tour of the Pacific and Indian Oceans to investigate the treatment of overseas Chinese. Local Chinese leaders presented to them a petition which objected to the poll tax, the taxation of Chinese moving from one colony to another and the 'unprovoked and cowardly assaults' on tea and vegetable sellers by 'the young and the simple'.[8] The commissioners were treated with the greatest respect and hospitality. They judged the Melbourne Benevolent Asylum, which had twelve Chinese inmates, to be an honour to mankind. The one objection they openly stated was to the poll tax, since it was imposed only on Chinese, and they warned that retaliation might be necessary.[9] The visit coincided with an outburst of sustained agitation by the Anti-Chinese Committee (Harwood was now T.H.C. president) and the *Age*, partly in the belief that the visitors would encourage further migration. One English sinophil observer referred to the 'European carpenters of Melbourne who started the outcry taken up so rashly and unjustly by the Sydney masses'.[10] The Anti-Chinese Committee now began holding protest meetings in middle-class as well as working-class suburbs, to demand abolition or the tightest possible restriction of immigration. The *Age* thought it a 'life and death' matter to the workers and feared a

'Conservative plot for doing away with strikes'.[11] In July 1887 the Amalgamated Miners were outraged by employment of Chinese at a mine at Bonang. The Chinese community took pains to provide a spectacular carnival as their contribution to the Jubilee celebrations.[12] In September a conference of delegates from the T.H.C., the Miners and Cheltenham market gardeners called urgently for legislation. The A.N.A. had withdrawn from the conference, as its current policy called for a royal commission, but within five months it also was recommending stringent restriction.[13] Thirty-three unions were now represented on the Anti-Chinese Committee; deputations pestered Gillies and Deakin; the Timber Yard Employees were excited by the opening of a Chinese timber yard; some grocers began to complain about competition; John Norton wrote to the T.H.C. to say an Anti-Chinese League had been formed in Sydney; 1,100 citizens met at Collingwood and 450 at Richmond to protest at the government's inactivity; a movement to boycott Chinese tradesmen began to develop. The mild, scholarly Anglican missionary, Cheong Cheok Hong, tried to refute popular misconceptions in a lecture at the Freemasons' Hall.[14] In Parliament Gaunson posed what he saw as the real question: were they strong enough to force Britain to make a treaty with China which would eliminate migration? He succeeded in carrying a resolution that restriction should be much tighter.[15]

The government fully intended to act, but once again wanted to take a national approach. It was more worried about the influx into the Northern Territory and possible overland immigration than with conjectural consequences of the commissioners' visit. After long years of decline, the Chinese population was slightly increasing in the mid-eighties in both Australia and Victoria. Moreover in 1886 the government, to its annoyance, had discovered that the shipping companies, the Hong Kong recruiters of migrants and many Chinese in the colony were engaged in a systematic racket in naturalization papers, in order to evade the poll tax. In the four years to 1881 only 28 Chinese had been naturalized; in the four following years 2,862 became British citizens. Only a few entrants were paying the poll tax and there was a remarkable correlation between the figures of naturalization one year and of immigrants the next. Papers were being sent to Hong Kong, or sold by returning migrants.*[16] A complicating problem was that a few migrants were genuine British subjects from Hong Kong. In January 1886 sixty migrants on the *Afghan* were detected with false papers; the captain was fined £100 and sternly warned. The government cut down severely on naturalization which had ceased altogether by October 1887. Customs officers, who had been making secret marks on natural-

*	*Chinese Naturalizations*	*Chinese Immigrants*
1883	519	433
1884	601	557
1885	1,178	670
1886	173	1,108

ization papers, were instructed in November 1887 not to allow entry by naturalization papers if in doubt about identity, and public warning was given on 5 December.[17] On 3 November Gillies, seeking a united approach, wired the premiers: 'Do you propose to legislate on Chinese question this session? If so can we come to an understanding . . . as to proposals?' Parkes replied next day, agreeing that all should legislate in the same terms. On the 19th Gillies urged a conference before anyone took action. However, at this moment, Parkes was in conflict with him over other matters, and on the 26th he threatened to proceed unilaterally. On the 30th Gillies pleaded with him to confine any action for the moment to 'temporary expedients', and made suggestions about how existing legislation might be brought into conformity. It was too late in the year now, however, for legislation to be possible.

In December 1887, following the report of their commissioners, the Chinese government protested formally to the British government about the discriminatory poll tax legislation in the Australian colonies, which was inconsistent with British-Chinese treaty obligations, and requested its repeal. In January Lord Knutsford asked the colonial governments for their comments. Before replying, Gillies again circularized the premiers on 22 March, suggesting a joint answer to the effect that while all agreed that further restriction of immigration—'even to prohibition'—was necessary, it would be better to seek a treaty with China through the British government than to legislate. 'Thus might be accomplished inoffensively—through the means of diplomacy—all that we desire, while legislative measures . . . might engender an international bitterness.' Gillies was earnestly seeking the course which would least embarrass the imperial government, and had noted the recent negotiation of a treaty (which in the end was not ratified) between China and the United States by which Chinese labourers were to be excluded. All the governments favoured the attempt at a treaty, but Queensland believed it urgent to pass immediate legislation and the New South Wales government would not discuss the matter. It got in first with a strong telegram to Knutsford on 31 March recommending treaty negotiations, and suggested the other colonies should lend support.

On 27 April the *Afghan* arrived at Port Melbourne with between 250 and 300 Chinese on board; most of them were new migrants as their dress, long pigtails and shaven heads showed. It is not clear whether the government had premeditated action. The Trades Hall Council called an emergency meeting and orators recalled the tradition of resistance to convicts landing. A deputation led by Harwood and Trenwith hurried round to see Gillies, and Trenwith warned that violence was likely. Gillies suspended action over the weekend, while police guarded the ship and a crowd—described in a Chinese petition as a 'body of murderous ruffians'—gathered on the wharf. The captain proposed to land fourteen passengers by poll tax and fifty-three by naturalization papers. On the Monday, Musgrove of the Customs Department, with the help of Ah Mouy and a representative of Grice, Sumner, the agents, inspected the sixty-seven for several hours. He judged that a dozen of the naturalization papers were genuine and the rest fictitious. The government arranged with the agents that the substantial fines would be remitted if no passengers at all were landed. (A few days later Gillies cabled the Colonial Office: 'Chinese immigrants entitled to land on payment of poll tax have not been refused. Captain did not insist on landing them.') The ship sailed three days later, to the lamentations of the passengers. Meanwhile a Town Hall meeting, crowded with workingmen, heard Munro compare Chinese to scabby sheep and convicts, while J. L. Purves spoke for the A.N.A. Five thousand attended a Ballarat meeting where the A.N.A. was again prominent. A few days later, the government demonstrated another method of asserting power to exclude. After the *Burrumbete* had been passed by the quarantine officers down the Bay, the yellow flag was hoisted at Williamstown on the issue of an Order-in-Council declaring Hong Kong, Singapore and other eastern ports to be infected. The passengers were quickly released and a few were allowed to land according to strict interpretation of the immigration laws, which were applied to later ships.

Apart from pandering to public opinion, the government, however clumsily, was trying to establish a major constitutional point: that the colony, irrespective of particular immigration laws, had the power to exclude undesirable aliens by executive action on the ground of public safety, as it had done in the case of the Irish informers in 1883 and as it would do with a shipload of convicts. In doing so, it was trying to demonstrate to the public and the other colonies that new offensive restrictive legislation was not necessary while an attempt to negotiate a treaty was made. Though it chose a demonstrable case of blatant attempt to evade the law on which to take action, it did not anticipate the consequences. The *Afghan* case started a chain of anti-Chinese demonstrations round Australia. The Governor warned that the law was being seriously strained. The Chinese government began a series of embarrassingly strong protests and the Governor of Hong Kong was outraged. The government was denounced by the *Argus* and the *Telegraph* and widely among the middle classes which objected to the Trades Hall leading them by the nose. The Public Questions Committee of the Presbyterian Church was severely critical, though the Methodists meeting in Australasian conference temporized when the Victorian delegates warned that the church was already seriously alienated from the working class.[18] Gillies issued angry press statements in reply to the Presbyterians and the Chinese leaders, whose deputations he refused to receive.

The *Afghan* attempted to land its passengers at Sydney, but it had arrived in the same week as several other vessels carrying Chinese which had been diverted from Darwin after the South Australian government had imposed immigration restrictions on the Territory. The mass outcry in Sydney was far more vehement than in Melbourne, Parkes was faced with a major crisis, and resorted both to exclusion by executive action and harsh legislation which passed the Assembly in one day. The South Australian government had already called urgently for a conference and now with Queensland appealed to Parkes to delay introduction of the Bill to his Legislative Council before a conference. The Victorians were furious with Parkes and asked the Colonial Office to veto his Bill if it passed before a conference was held. The Foreign Office complained that the proposed legislation would make negotiation of a treaty almost impossible. The intercolonial conference met in Sydney in mid-June and no doubt there was some plain speaking. The Victorians had been doubtful whether it was worth proceeding, but considerable agreement was reached. The imperial government's proposal for a general immigration law to put all nations on the same footing, and thus remove apparent discrimination against the Chinese, received short shrift. But it was agreed to encourage the imperial government still to negotiate a treaty and, to aid the objective, to abolish the poll taxes. It was also agreed to pass uniform restrictive legislation based on the formula of one migrant to 500 tons; Victoria unwillingly concurred only for the sake of unity and New South Wales flatly refused to abandon its Bill imposing a £100 poll tax (which was ultimately passed) until the other colonies had legislated. In spite of everything, the imperial diplomatists succeeded in agreeing on draft terms of settlement with the Chinese government. On 14 September the colonial governments were formally asked whether the moderate proposals were satisfactory. The main points were abolition of the poll tax, restriction of entry of Chinese labourers to one to 300 tons, free entry for merchants, travellers, officials and students, and rights for Chinese already in Australia to leave and return. The Victorians were very happy to agree, hoping as they were for a diplomatic triumph and proud of their statesmanship and co-operation with the imperial government. The other colonies also eventually agreed—except New South Wales which, despite repeated reminders, did not reply to the despatch. The proposed treaty was abandoned in 1892.[19]

Nearly all the politicians, except a few Councillors, now agreed that immigration of Chinese labourers must be eliminated, or almost so. But many deplored the 'panic' measures of April-May 1888 and the injustices to individual Chinese. Opposition spokesmen, of whom at least Shiels and Harper were sincere, waxed hot and strong over such un-British procedures, hoping as they were at the time to rally the farmers to overturn the government.[20] Sargood, the militiaman, was worried that a potential ally against Russia might be offended.[21] Many zealots strongly supported the government, however, though the most rabid of them, R. T. Vale, was howled down for what was widely regarded as a 'cowardly' attempt to debar Chinese from being licensed as 'bottle-ohs' and garbage gatherers.[22] Late in the year the government brought in the Bill which had been agreed to at the intercolonial conference. It still hoped that a treaty might be arranged, feared that new legislation might jeopardize negotiations, but fulfilled its obligation after Queensland and South Australia had put the Bill through. The poll tax was abolished, but immigration (apart from visiting merchants and other unobjectionable categories) was restricted to one to

500 tons, which would allow only the merest trickle. Naturalized Chinese were to come under the quota. Nearly every member agreed with such drastic restriction, but the provisions for an internal pass system, whereby a permit would be necessary to move from one colony to another, roused strong opposition. The restriction aimed at preventing entry from the Northern Territory, but provided for imprisonment and made a felon of any Chinese crossing a border without a permit. Old-fashioned liberals like Shiels were appalled and joined with Service in the Council to make a last-ditch stand against such monstrous and tyrannical legislation. A meeting of local Chinese protested at the proposed 'ticket of leave' system and the virtual prohibition of further migration and of visiting China on business.[23] A few churchmen and the Secularists and Spiritualists supported them. The Council adopted a South Australian amendment which provided that the permit system should not operate except when an emergency was proclaimed, removed naturalized Chinese from its provisions and substituted fines for imprisonment. The government and the Assembly stood firm—for the agreed intercolonial Bill and against Council interference—but had to submit on the last day of the session.[24]

Meanwhile the Chinese community had challenged the procedures used on the *Afghan* passengers. Ah Toy had been prepared to pay the poll tax but was refused entry, and a case was brought on his behalf. In September a four to two majority of the Supreme Court awarded him damages. Judge Hartley Williams remarked on the 'most unpleasant and invidious position, that we are at present without the *legal* means of preventing the scum or desperadoes of alien nationalities from landing on our territory'.[25] Higinbotham used his dissenting judgment to state his general interpretation of the powers of the Victorian government. The government was determined to test its claim to exclude aliens by executive action, and decided to appeal to the Privy Council for a decision, as Attorney-General Wrixon put it, on whether the colony had the 'right to protect itself against the irruption of dangerous foreigners'.[26] Pearson was a more vehement spokesman: 'We are really fighting again that battle which Chief Justice Higinbotham began—for the right of this people to govern themselves—and we intend to vindicate that right as an integral part of our liberties.' The government was not setting aside the law: 'in cases where the law does not apply, and where the public safety requires it, we may act on our view of the public safety and may come afterwards to Parliament for our indemnity.'[27] More than two years later the Privy Council reversed the Supreme Court judgment, but refused to consider the broader constitutional issues. Deakin, however, considered Wrixon's appearance had educated English legal opinion on the self-governing rights of colonies.[28]

The crisis had effectively ended Chinese immigration. The imperial government conceded the issue and the Governor of Hong Kong was ordered to abolish the British shipping companies' recruiting trade.[29] Victoria came through its crisis without the minor cases of violence against

Chinese which disgraced Sydney and Brisbane, and without the anti-imperial demonstrations which were almost totally unjustified. The Melbourne trade unionists, fearful of economic competition, had inspired and led the campaign. But they were not quite as extreme as their colleagues elsewhere in demanding total prohibition, nor was there any equivalent to the diatribes of William Lane in the *Boomerang*. Nevertheless the issue ran very deep. The *Argus* observed that 'The Chinese question never fails. At every meeting somebody in the hall has a word to say in regard to it, and visions of countless millions of the barbarians swooping upon the colony in a solid body rise on the mental horizon of every man present.'[30] Instinctively middle-class spokesmen supported severe restriction of alien immigration in order to safeguard national homogeneity, but few could formulate their principles explicitly. Chinese were 'inferior', they knew, to Europeans in terms of their current civilization; the composition of the Australian colonies had to be safeguarded to ensure their continued development on the lines laid down; a 'helot' class would strike at the fundamentals of Australian democracy. But only Pearson had the intellectual clarity, which he was to display in his *National Life and Character* (1893), to define the basis of educated Australian opinion on non-European immigration. As chosen specimens of a naturally selected higher race, Australians were 'guarding the last part of the world, in which the higher races can live and increase freely, for the higher civilisation'.[31]

The formal imperial relationship

For all practical purposes Victoria was entirely self-governing in domestic affairs. Governors did not reserve any legislation of solely internal relevance, nor did the Colonial Office veto any. Determined resistance to imperial interference, deriving from the anti-transportation campaigns of the fifties and sixties and the Governor Darling crisis, made the Colonial Office very careful to avoid conflict. The Governor had important powers as head of state in interpreting the constitution and in granting or withholding dissolutions to ministers; but, so long as it was lawful, he otherwise followed the advice of his ministers on internal matters. In this field, the Governor was no more than and perhaps less than the monarch; for it appears that, unlike the practice between Queen and Prime Minister in Britain, little trouble was taken to consult him, except formally in the Executive Council, or to keep him well informed. Sir Henry Loch occasionally protested to his ministers that statements on important matters were made before he knew of them, that he was not given time to make enquiries about candidates proposed for major appointments, and that lesser appointments were announced before they had been submitted to him in the Executive Council.[32] Governors arrived with inflated ideas of their powers and possible sphere of influence and were surprised to find that by local custom they were little more than figureheads. They were not even expected to take lone responsibility for the prerogative of pardon in capital cases;

hence there was no conflict on this matter from the mid-seventies. Normanby and Loch made few attempts to report to the Colonial Office on domestic affairs, and when they did their comments were superficial and largely derived from newspapers. The Lochs, however, unlike the Bowens and Normanbys, made Government House neutral political ground and were deservedly among the most popular vice-regal couples Victoria has known.

Higinbotham's influence and inspiration had schooled a generation of Victorian politicians to stand firm on their domestic rights. The Colonial Office 'interfered' no longer in local matters. But Higinbotham's continued vendetta against the Colonial Office, and reaffirmation of his views on the constitution when Chief Justice from 1886, were largely irrelevant and an embarrassment to the political leaders. By his almost unique interpretation of the constitution, the Governor's Instructions were not just outdated but were illegal, as was any correspondence on domestic matters between Governor and Colonial Office. For in his eyes the Governor was the Queen's representative, he had all the powers and prerogatives of the Crown vested in him by statute, and he was 'legally independent of all external influence and authority, and [on local matters could] be lawfully guided only by the advice of his responsible ministers.'[33] Whether or not such an interpretation of the written constitution was legitimate, this was certainly not the intention of the drafters in the fifties or the general understanding. In law, the imperial government, if it chose to exercise it, had entire power of veto over all classes of colonial legislation; the Governor could reserve any Bill for consideration at home. The matter came to a head when Higinbotham, as Chief Justice, was expected to become Lieutenant-Governor. Agitated negotiations followed in order to ascertain whether he would abide by the rules if he were to become Acting Governor. He most certainly would not; rather he would 'use the increased power and possible large opportunities of that position to secure the independence of the Queen's representative in the colony, and to expose and resist the illegal interference of the Colonial Office in our domestic affairs'.[34] He wrote to Sir Henry Holland (Lord Knutsford), explaining his view of the constitution and referring to 'the sinister and clandestine policy which the office over which you preside has successfully pursued for the third part of a century'.[35] Other Lieutenant-Governors were appointed from time to time. The press suppressed any reference to an outburst by Higinbotham at a banquet to the Earl of Carnarvon late in 1887.[36] However, his protests led directly to the revision of the Governor's Instructions, which were archaic. They had not been revised in 1855, and the Canadian Instructions had recently been brought up to date. The Colonial Office was caught out in neglect, and after consulting Wrixon, who remarked that the Instructions were drawn up as if 'in oblivion of the actual facts of our daily government', referred the question to the Crown Law officers late in 1887. They replied remarkably quickly in January 1888 recommending drastic revision, and a draft was made. Gillies, Deakin and Wrixon, however, advised against immediate action, for if they had to advise formally, questions would be raised which were better avoided. The Liberals included amendment of the Instructions in their 1889 election policy. The revised Instructions to Australasian Governors were eventually issued in 1892, shortly before Higinbotham died.[37] The Law Officers, like the men in the Colonial Office, brushed aside Higinbotham's view that it was illegal for Governors to correspond on local matters with the Secretary of State. Higinbotham was asked whether he would accept their view and become Acting Governor in the period between Loch's departure and Hopetoun's arrival. He refused, protested at the appointment of Sir William Robinson and, to the anger of the Colonial Office, released the correspondence to the press. Only a few lawyers were capable of judging the abstruse issues of constitutional interpretation. Sir Archibald Michie denounced in the *Argus* the 'ludicrous impertinence' of Higinbotham's attacks on the Colonial Office. The senior officials there looked forward with delight to the Privy Council's judgment on *Musgrove* v. *Toy* and were disappointed that the issue was avoided. And yet, whatever Higinbotham's legal eccentricity, his view of what should be the case in domestic self-government had history on its side.[38]

Colonial claims for expansion of self-government were occurring not in the purely domestic but in the 'imperial' field, over such matters as external relations and foreign immigration. Here Higinbotham was even more of an embarrassment, for this staunch imperial patriot and rigid legalist read the constitution so as to exclude any colonial rights. He insisted on attempting to draw a sharp line, which could not be clear as the constitution-makers had well known,[39] between 'domestic' and 'imperial' powers. He encouraged the imperial government to warn off the colonies 'by refusing to recognise or permit any direct interference with international questions'.* Service, Berry, Deakin and Gillies had fought for and won the right to warn, advise and be consulted on foreign-imperial issues in the Australian region. The imperial government had behaved impeccably in accepting and defending Australian policies on Chinese immigration. From 1888 Berry and Gillies were opening the negotiations which eventually, after imperial legislation in 1895, would allow the colonies to make commercial treaties with foreign countries.[40] In 1884 there had been a major conflict between Sargood, the Minister of Defence, and Disney, the Military Commandant. The ministry had been created in 1883, but Disney believed he was responsible only to the Governor, and Loch agreed with him. Sargood carried out a master-stroke by appointing a retired Major-General, M. F. Downes, as secretary of the department, and the Colonial Office eventually agreed to permit local political control of local defence.[41]

* These remarks on Higinbotham's constitutional views are unorthodox. A full-scale re-examination by a legal historian is urgently needed, for the matter is biographically crucial. It is not possible that Higinbotham could have propounded legal conclusions, of which he was not intellectually convinced, to suit his political views. But it is possible that his passions dominated his intellect. Frank Gavan Duffy possibly had the *Musgrove* v. *Toy* case in mind when he made his famous criticism of Higinbotham: 'In laboured judgments lucidly obscure,/Perspicuously wrong'. ('A Dream of Fair Judges', *Australian Law Journal*, vol. 19, June 1945, p. 43.)

From time to time, as the need occurred, imperial legislation had been passed to extend colonial control on such matters as local defence, merchant shipping, naturalization and extradition. The only cases of the imperial veto being applied to legislation were on broad matters where consultation to ensure uniformity was desirable; one rare example was the Marine Board Bill which, after reservation and agreed suggested amendments, was made law in 1888. The expansion of self-government into areas with foreign-imperial implications occurred naturally; as the case was made, the ground was usually yielded without friction. For ultimately, of course, the colonies had to be given their head, since there was no way of stopping them except by risking their resignation from the Empire.

One extreme case of imperial resistance was over divorce. In 1860 the Colonial Office had vetoed a Victorian Bill and insisted on legislation identical with recent English amendments. Divorce was so difficult and allowed on so few grounds that there were only about twenty a year in the eighties. In view of the variation between English and Scottish law, the case for imperial uniformity was weak. When New South Wales passed a Bill in 1887, Salisbury bowed to clerical pressure, took the matter to Cabinet and, against Knutsford's advice, vetoed the Bill. However, a hint was given that another Bill passed in the next parliament might be tolerated if the other colonies legislated similarly. A remarkable display of intercolonial cooperation followed. In 1889 divorce Bills with identical (good Scottish) grounds, supported by the chief justices and nearly all the newspapers and leading politicians, were presented to the Parliaments of Victoria, New South Wales and South Australia. Shiels made one of his great speeches in introducing the Bill, attacking on behalf of liberalism 'the forces of sacerdotalism, and the stupid mole-blind conservatism that so often aids and abets it in its arbitrary and reactionary policy'. Wrixon, the High Church Attorney-General, spoke for most of the churches in reply, but the Protestants were divided. The Bill passed the Assembly by large majorities, met with no resistance in the Council, and was reserved by the Acting Governor. The *Age* was now whipping up public opinion; it had become a matter of principle to fight the imperial government. The new Governor, Lord Hopetoun, was alarmed and wrote privately to Knutsford:

> It is impossible for you to conceive the amount of excitement which the question of the Divorce Bill is causing amongst all classes. . . . it would be a great misfortune if you [vetoed it. It] would create much irritation amongst the loyal part of the population, it would give a great impetus to the *small* but noisy section who profess themselves opposed to the British connection.

The government adopted the Bill and Gillies supported it in the strongest terms, using the tried technique of writing to his Agent-General in the knowledge that he would forward the letter to the Colonial Office; thereby he could use forceful undiplomatic language. If the Bill was vetoed, it would be resubmitted year after year:

> How infinitely preferable to do at once with a good grace what must inevitably be done otherwise later on. . . . The Colonies as you know are most jealous of their powers of legislation being interfered with and it may be difficult to foresee the result, should the idea get abroad that those powers are being unnecessarily restricted.

Knutsford took the letter to Cabinet, several of whose members had been lobbied by Shiels who had journeyed to England for the purpose. The Agents-General joined him in a united deputation. The imperial power bowed.[42]

In theory the Governor was expected to be very active as imperial agent, intermediary and channel of communication on matters of concern to the imperial government. However, the Victorian government deliberately built up the ambassadorial function of its Agent-General in London.* Loch protested in 1884 that he was being continually by-passed in negotiations over the New Hebrides and New Guinea and asked that the Agent-General's authority be curtailed. However, the Colonial Office recognized that once again the Canadians had set a precedent, and could insist only that governors be given full information.[43] Loch complained again in 1886 that the Colonial Office was using the Agent-General as the channel of communication, and again in 1888, although efforts had been made to supply him with information by earlier mails than the Agent-General could use.[44] However, the negotiations over Chinese immigration were carried out through the Governor. But in no sense did the Governor, on this matter or the Pacific questions, join with his ministers in formulation of policy. When Loch indicated to Gillies that he considered the law was being strained over the *Afghan* case and that he might take action in the future, Gillies's reply was cold and firm: 'Your Excellency is quite in error' on several points, he wrote.[45] Loch was more active and useful in the negotiations over the naval agreement in 1885–7. He several times suggested conferences of governors, or of governors and premiers, to formulate policy on national matters, and even proposed a Council of Advice of governors and representatives of governments and parliaments, instead of the Federal Council. The Colonial Office was sensible enough to recognize that the period when such paternalism might have been acceptable was long over.[46]

An Australian governor once remarked that the colonists regarded the Colonial Office much as the Irish did Dublin Castle.[47] Despite all suspicion, Victorian governments had come to a reasonably good understanding with Downing Street after the stormy conflicts over the Pacific. Knutsford was recognized as more able and considerate than any of his recent predecessors. But Deakin told Dilke that the Colonial Office blundered continually, especially on minor matters like award of honours.[48] The conscientious officials defended colonial interests more frequently and ably than Deakin and other politicians knew. Yet the sporadic attention which could be

* The Agents-General sometimes called on Hugh Childers for help; he has been termed the greatest patron of the colonies since Banks (Atkins, 'Representation of Australia in England', p. 241).

given to any one problem inevitably led to many mistakes and misjudgments. Herbert and his colleagues did not and could not know the men they were dealing with, let alone understand them. They regarded Higinbotham, for example, as a bad lawyer, a crank and a demagogue, and had no inkling of his stature. Herbert understood the Victorians so little that he did not include them among the 'more friendly' Australasian colonies in 1888,[49] presumably because they had been less subservient. Yet the Victorians were much less inclined than Parkes and McIlwraith for example, at least from 1887, to win cheap political capital by whipping up campaigns against imperial misrule. They did, however, constantly use the threat of alienation of sympathy if their advice was not followed; the Colonial Office must have become heartily sick of the warnings about encouraging separatist leanings. But Victorian governments were broadly satisfied with the imperial relationship, once the right to consultation had been recognized and the colonies' value as parts of the Empire had been appreciated by British public opinion. They knew that in practice there was nothing to stop them being as self-governing and independent as they liked.

Towards a decision on nationality; the A.N.A.

On one notable occasion Victoria, in contrast to the other colonies, stood proudly loyal to Britain and the Colonial Office. In 1888 the governments of New South Wales and South Australia, but not of Victoria, requested the right of consultation over the appointment of governors, and Queensland protested at the appointment of Sir Henry Blake, partly because of his record as an imperial officer in Ireland.[50] Gillies rounded off a brief discussion in the Assembly on 15 November by declaring that Victoria 'has no desire to appoint its Governor, has no desire to veto the appointment of any Governor, but feels perfectly confident' of imperial judgment.[51] The matter had occasionally been raised before. Shiels, for example, who detested the snobbery associated with Government House, had referred to the 'broken-down noblemen' and drunkards, 'far beneath some of the common labouring men in this community for honour and honesty', who had been governors of some colonies, and had urged the right of consultation.[52] Perhaps between a quarter and a half of the Assembly would have agreed if a serious vote had been taken. But when on 28 November Sir Bryan O'Loghlen, objecting to Gillies's statement, moved support for the other colonies, the occasion was used for a demonstration against the Irish Catholics, who were currently holding mass meetings in defence of Parnell.[53] The more free the colonies were, said O'Loghlen, the fewer causes of friction there were, the more loyal they were. This was a case where true zeal for federation could be shown by supporting the other colonies. This was said to be an Irish cry, but he was not aware that Parkes, Playford or McIlwraith had Irish axes to grind. The *Age*, he claimed, was strongly opposed to the system of appointing governors and had recently been inclined to support Sir George Grey's proposal that governors be elected.[54] Old radicals like Collard Smith and McLellan leapt in to protest the perfection of the existing system; they owed all they had to the imperial government. Gillies was in his element: he produced sound practical reasons for the *status quo*, quoted Higinbotham's view that the appointment of governors by the Queen was the most important constitutional tie of all, then asked with a wealth of meaning, 'Why is this issue with the Imperial Government raised?' His audience, venomously anticipating the slaughter, roared in response. O'Loghlen replied weakly and was defeated by fifty-nine votes to three. Only John Murray, the one classical nationalist in the House, and one Catholic supported him; most of the Catholics and others who agreed 'squibbed the vote'. There was a shout of 'No!' when the vote was taken and three backbenchers led the House in the National Anthem and three cheers for the Queen.[55] The Governor's proroguing speech written for him a few days later stated that

> A happy accident gave the Legislative Assembly an occasion of testifying its loyalty to the Crown.... The enthusiasm with which the news of this debate was received in the House of Commons is a significant proof that these communities were never more closely linked or dearer to England than they are now, when they are practically free to determine their own destinies.[56]

O'Loghlen wrote to the Governor to protest, especially at the National Anthem being 'degraded into a party emblem'.[57] The imperial government was encouraged to give a firm answer to the other colonies, rejecting outright their request for consultation.[58] Elsewhere in Australia, radical nationalists increasingly suspected that Victoria sought federation as a step towards Imperial Federation.

This demonstration was in part a reaction to the seemingly dangerous republican, nationalist movement which had developed in New South Wales and Queensland and to its mild reflection in Victoria in 1888.[59] George Black's visit from Sydney in April to form a branch of the Republican League had failed dismally. The meeting (whose numbers were calculated at twenty-five or more than one hundred according to the bias of the reporter) appointed a committee of four, including Bernard O'Dowd, to draft a constitution for an Australian Democratic Federation or National League; the feebleness of the A.N.A. was said to be one motive. However, the movement was abandoned at the next meeting, for lack of support.[60]

The battle in Victoria was to be fought out largely within the A.N.A. During 1887 there had been a surge of nativism and growing criticism of the imperial relationship. Although at the time of the Jubilee the *Australian* eulogized the Queen and dismissed the grumblers as a futile minority, the natives' loyal celebrations were clearly not as fervid as their elders'. The Chinese question, especially, led some dissidents like Wilson to lay all Australia's troubles at Britain's door. Speakers at branch meetings sometimes derided royalty, the aristocracy and the established church, and even

Collins Street, looking east, 1886

Sturt Street, Ballarat

defended the founding convicts against the monsters who had convicted them.[61] Newton Wanliss, who had recently returned from an English university, denounced Imperial Federation as a means of using 'Australian blood and treasure to uphold imperial jingoism'.[62] The decisive change came at the annual conference early in 1888 when the Melbourne branches successfully ran J. L. Purves for president against the goldfields junta; the outgoing executive was appalled. Purves was a leading barrister of squatting background, an all-round sportsman and *bon viveur*, and a failed politician on the conservative side who made many enemies. He had been an A.N.A. member since 1874, but never active. He was rather a bully in court and prone to use the bludgeon, but his power in cross-examination and his histrionic ability made him very successful with juries. In contrast to his worthy provincial predecessors, he was a well-known man of striking personality who sought publicity by controversy. 'The Emperor', as he was sometimes known, now attempted to turn the A.N.A. into a nationalist pressure-group. His nativism was genuine, but his ambiguous statements on separatism and imperial loyalty were to induce more heat than light.[63]

On 26 April 1888 the Melbourne branch of the A.N.A. held its annual banquet; five senior members, including Wilson, with others sympathizing, remained seated while the loyal toast was drunk. Purves, the main speaker, did not repudiate them. The dissident republicans were deliberately trying to bring the loyalty issue to a head. As expected, the *Argus* reacted wildly, called either for a purge or the withdrawal of respectable men from the A.N.A., and made space for many letters from loyal natives. 'I am a native of Australia', wrote one, 'as was my father before me. I come of one of the oldest colonial families, and I am proud of being an Australian, but I glory, too, that I am an Englishman.' The Minister of Defence instructed militia officers who were A.N.A. members to 'discourage and discountenance' the republican peril. Many branches were gravely upset by the incident, passed loyal motions, and put pressure on the directors to take action. However, their neutralist stance was supported by a conference late in May which also gave Purves a unanimous vote of confidence. Only a few resignations followed.[64] The next scandal was a series of separatist statements by Judge Hartley Williams, a native. Separation would come 'as surely as the sun will rise tomorrow': Australia was not yet ready, for it lacked the dignity and dimensions of a nation; but the sooner Australia grew to adequate stature and separation came about the better. Hostile criticism in the *Argus* was venomous; for very many people, any criticism of the imperial connection was intolerable, and outrageous when it came from such a source.[65] The newspapers set out to discredit the A.N.A. The *Age* used the weapon of mockery: 'For the life of us we have never been able to thoroughly understand what the Cause is which the Natives' Association represents.' The *Argus* resorted rather to misrepresentation and abuse of 'political puppyhood' and the 'juvenile ferment of ideas'.[66] At this time Deakin spoke frequently at local meetings to boost the A.N.A., and Higinbotham once supported him at Eaglehawk.[67] *Young Australia*, a monthly owned and edited by Lieutenant M. J. O'Farrell, set out to become a rival journal to the *Australian*. It had begun in March 1887 as the *Australasian Naval and Military Gazette* and in December 1888 became the official organ of the Imperial Federation League. The journal was highly conservative, federationist, anti-Chinese and anti-semitic, and consistently sniped at the A.N.A. as not representing one in twenty of native youth. Harry Armytage became a leading native spokesman against the A.N.A. The ultimate indication of the A.N.A.'s disgrace was the Presbyterian Assembly making it the subject of special prayer.[68]

Much of the argument was a misunderstanding. The A.N.A. republicans were a tiny minority, and the much larger number who discussed separation were only considering what appeared to be an inescapable problem. Purves certainly was ambivalent and inconsistent, but he was usually saying that separation was inevitable in the fairly short run, should not be unduly hurried, but should be prepared for; it was absurd to think that when Australia had fifty million people the existing relationship would suffice.[69] Some were thinking in terms of separation followed by close alliance. Usually no basic hostility to Britain was implied, merely a recognition of inevitability; an answer had to be found to the problem of the conflict between authority and liberty. In reply to charges of disloyalty, Field Barrett wrote: 'Some like myself, think and hope that in the fullness of time there will be an Australian republic allied, not hostile, to the mother country, but forming with her and "the States", a great syndicate of the English-speaking people'.[70] In the meantime most were coming to believe that the question was not immediately relevant, that separation might occur in the very long run but not for fifty or a hundred years. The A.N.A. leadership and the large majority of members were accepting the view of their hero, Deakin, that the answer was neither separation nor Imperial Federation but co-operation within the Empire—Australian federation before an attempt to unify the Empire, Australian interests first and imperial interests a close second.[71]

Mid-1888, when it was shown that even in the A.N.A. the republican minority was tiny, appears to have been a decisive period. It was now coming to be generally accepted that separation was not inevitable in the short run, that there need be no vital conflict between Australian and imperial interests, and that liberty and Empire were not necessarily opposed.[72] The *Age*, which had long been fearful of the iniquitous wars into which Britain might drag the colony, was becoming more conventionally imperialist. Purves was talking much less about separation. Late in the year, however, he supported the movement for consultation on appointment of governors, but the issue threw the Melbourne branch into wild conflict and the directors decided to remain neutral.[73] In 1889 the A.N.A. was quiet on the national-imperial issue, though many remained doubtful and official policy statements on the glories of Empire were cool compared to the white heat of most public pronouncements. By this time separatists were fairly described as 'an obscure and unimportant fraction'.[74] Australian nationalism meant so little to the *Argus* that it used the term with reference to the federationists.[75] Many of the public continued to believe the A.N.A. was basically anti-British, just as many people today judge university students or policemen in the light of the behaviour of small minorities. The *Age* busily circulated the view that Irish Catholics controlled the A.N.A.*[76] But in all essentials it had adopted the views of the older generation.

From 1886 A.N.A. branches more frequently discussed 'political' controversial matters such as labour relations and land nationalization. Many members were becoming local mayors and councillors, and branches were taking increasingly direct action in local politics. Even federation, however, could be accepted as an objective only in the broadest terms: a motion at the 1887 conference for intercolonial free trade and national protection was ruled out of order as too controversial.[77] In 1888, although conference agreed to push the federal cause, little action followed. Similarly, policy on Chinese immigration developed slowly; although the directors supported further restriction and Barrett especially was fanatical, they proceeded very cautiously. Antarctic exploration was adopted as a worthy objective, but not the controversial Chaffey irrigation schemes. Henry d'Esterre Taylor, a leading spokesman for Imperial Federation, was campaigning from within to eliminate all but benefit activities, and unsuccessfully appealed to the Registrar of Friendly Societies to ban all political activity. Immediately on election, Purves led an embassy of twenty members to Sydney to attempt again to form a branch there. He faced a huge left-wing meeting which he had to chair himself and had a lively time; a branch was ultimately formed with very different rules.[78] Ballarat migrants were more successful in forming branches at Charters Towers and in Western Australia. Purves had a vision of the A.N.A. as the driving-force of a native-born political party ruling the country.[79] The *Age* was highly suspicious of 'the new generation banded together for the purpose of removing the elders from the control of public affairs'.[80] But the directors, ever wary of the dangers of deep political divisions to the benefit basis, held Purves in check. Without doubt, many prominent members were using the A.N.A. as a stepping-stone; of twenty-five who stood at the 1889 election, twelve were returned. But although membership was steadily growing, the A.N.A. was losing some impetus; the *Australian* had to be closed down for financial reasons late in 1888.

By 1887 many of the young zealots in the A.N.A. had come fully to

* In 1888 the A.N.A. was under continual Orange attack. In December Purves rejected an invitation to speak at Ballarat on behalf of the Parnell Fund and took care to publicize his refusal. The A.N.A. maintained its extraordinary capacity to override sectarianism, however. Irish Catholics were well but not prominently represented.

It is odd how few Irish-Australian nationalists emerged in Victoria compared to the northern colonies. One delightful example was William Ievers, junior: 'Great Britain should cut herself off from Europe and its cut-throat politics, throw herself into the arms of her colonial offspring, and plant her seat of government here, . . . where a new and lasting Empire of Peace might be founded, that would realise Plato's dream of a Republic and More's vision of "Utopia". . . . Here we should look for the perfect fusion of the Celtic and Saxon races.'

accept their distinctiveness—even their superiority—as Australians, and were groping to find ways and means of expressing their Australianism. They were certain of their destiny: the editor of the *Australian* wrote of 'the mass of young life advancing gladly and confidently on the great problems before it, the development of a continent, the evolution of a nation. Surely there is something in the order of Spring time in humanity here.'[81] A heavily Australian 'literary' emphasis appeared in the journal and in branch readings: jingling patriotic verses, long stories deriving from the melodramatic English serials which covered so many columns in the weeklies, didactic essays on nativist beliefs, and discussions of Kendall and 'our Australian poet', Gordon. The Southern Cross was hymned again and again as the symbol signifying national aspirations and freedom. Little talent emerged, although Bernard O'Dowd was a member and John Shaw Neilson was entering the literary competitions. During the Exhibition Dr McInerney organized a grand native concert in the Town Hall, with exclusively Australian compositions and performers.[82] Branch socials frequently featured all-Australian programmes, and ballrooms were decorated with wattle blossom, gum-tips, wild-flowers, ferns, Australian flags, and occasionally aboriginal relics. Branches discussed the possibility of an Australian anthem to replace 'The Queen'.[83] Meudell had the idea of making 26 January the national holiday; the directors approached Gillies who won intercolonial agreement.*[84] The public zestfully celebrated the first Australia Day in the centenary year, though with some puzzlement over what it was all about, but the A.N.A. failed to find any appropriate Australian festive form. The metropolitan committee's ideas were thwarted by the directors, and excursions were the only outcome; in Ballarat a sports-meeting and a moonlight concert on Lake Wendouree were all that were attempted.[85] In 1888 the A.N.A. sent a deputation to Pearson to urge the teaching of Australian history in schools; Pearson was sympathetic, ordered additions to the Royal Readers, and gave an interesting appraisal of the sort of Australian history which might be taught.[86] But in general the A.N.A. had difficulty in finding suitable traditions in Australian history, perhaps because of the identification of what there was with their migrant parents. Curiously little reference was made to Eureka which in other quarters was being increasingly recalled with affection. There is little evidence that many A.N.A. men were influenced by the Sydney *Bulletin* which, indeed, probably had a very small circulation in Victoria.†

Almost invariably, the tone of pronouncement on Australia's achievement and future was super-confident. William Ievers junior asserted that

* It is ironical that the Sydney *Bulletin* was campaigning for commemoration of Eureka instead of 26 January (21 Jan. and 21 May 1888).

The government had already in 1883 abolished Separation Day as a public service holiday, as out of keeping with the spirit of the times, but it still remained a bank holiday.

† Meudell and John Murray, the two public men most in sympathy with the *Bulletin* approach, both grew up with J. F. Archibald in Warrnambool and kept up their friendship. Archibald also knew Tom Roberts and Brodzky.

Australia had had superior migrants to the United States and must continue to reject foreign rubbish. Frank Stuart claimed as Australia's special virtue that 'the rich were poorer, and the poor were richer here than in any other part of the globe'.[87] Meudell continued to affirm that Australian men were the strongest, women the most dazzling, children the healthiest and best educated, and scenery the most beautiful in the world; while the chief drawbacks were the Queen, Governors, awards of titles and kowtowing to 'Home'.[88] In Parliament the natives constantly stood out against perpetuation of old-world feuds.[89] But McInerney indicated the growing reconciliation with the older generation when he argued that 'the most advanced civilisation which the world has beheld' was mainly the product of

> enterprising, resourceful men from Europe, who came here in search of gold, . . . men of all creeds [who] met around the camp fire, and found that they could fraternise in spite of the differences in their belief. . . . If, however, any attempt were made to govern Australia by British opinion a flame would be kindled which would never be extinguished.[90]

And R. W. Best wanted Australia to 'be one great nation—a part and parcel of the good mother country'.[91] It is some indication of Charles Strong's stature that, almost uniquely among the migrants, he could support the growth of 'an Australian individuality' and 'a national personality' and the discarding of claptrap about the honour and glory of Britain, but warned: 'The most fatal enemy to Australian and every nationality is *nationalism*.'[92]

The federal campaign bogged down

Parkes's electoral victory early in 1887 had raised the Victorian government's hopes for federation. He visited Melbourne in February and met Gillies who wrote to Berry:

> he speaks (tall) of all the Colonies being federated—but while this is all very well in its way; to strain after the unattainable and pass by the attainable . . . I hope that he will give practical effect to his general opinion as often expressed and join us: if he does we will be at one on this continent.[93]

Parkes's co-operation over the Colonial Conference in London was highly encouraging and for some time no intercolonial tiffs occurred. Parkes and Gillies conferred again in September.

However, the centennial year was to mark the low point in relations between the colonies. The issue which led to the widening of the breach was ludicrous—Parkes's serious attempt to alter the name of New South Wales to Australia. When his Assembly supported him by a large majority, the *Bulletin* despaired over such a 'narrow parochial policy of intercolonial hatred and distrust' and seriously predicted ultimate civil war.[94] The rest of Australia reacted with mingled mirth and anger. The *Australasian* unkindly suggested that the appropriate name for New South Wales was 'Convictoria'. The Victorian government moved quickly and jointly protested with Queensland and South Australia. Berry rushed round to the Colonial Office to see the Secretary of State and publicized the assurances he was given. Herbert had no doubt that any bill passed would be disallowed.[95] No more was heard of the proposal beyond an angry, sarcastic and patronizing public letter from Parkes to Gillies.[96] Unfortunately, this was the very time when Gillies was trying to arrange for joint action on the Chinese problem. He also, undiplomatically, soon afterwards proposed a conference to aim at ending the railways war by eliminating differential rates for goods. The South Australian government was willing, but Parkes replied with a vague letter which probably led Gillies to believe that there was no point in pressing him.[97] In December also, Gillies took up a proposal which, on Victoria's initiative, had been discussed at the Colonial Conference and later with Parkes; that the colonies should jointly request that a general officer inspect the colonial troops and advise on planning for 'united defence in case of an invasion'. It was hoped that Lord Wolseley himself would be made available. Parkes delayed a decision, but after Gillies had pressed him twice in March 1888, rejected the proposal. Gillies wrote again at length, but Parkes did not reply.[98] Another Victorian plan, backed by the Federal Council, was to establish a federal ammunition factory. Negotiations were opened with an English firm, which chose a factory site on the Maribyrnong River. When it was suggested that New South Wales might purchase its ammunition from the factory and share in any necessary subsidy, Parkes began a long stalling operation, pressing for a site on the border. The Victorian government eventually lost patience and the Colonial Ammunition Factory, from which the munitions industry was to grow, was established at Maribyrnong.[99] Most important of all, Parkes proceeded independently on the Chinese question throughout 1888. The Victorian government, not surprisingly, lost heart.

On the economic front, progress was mixed: urban businessmen firmed in support of federation, while the farmers played up. In 1887 the Chamber of Manufactures became very active under the leadership of Emanuel Steinfeld, a furniture manufacturer. It arranged a conference of the three Australian Chambers at Adelaide in October when Steinfeld called for an end to the tariff war. It would be sinful and criminal to delay union; limited markets had caused many manufacturers to fail and had deterred investment; if operations could be enlarged beyond one colony plenty of capital would become available. 'Base insinuations are promulgated that Victoria wants to fatten into prosperity at the expense of the other colonies. This is false. The people of Victoria are animated by a sincere desire to unite the Australian colonies, to prosper with, and through, each other.' Anyway, he continued, Victoria had an unfavourable trade balance with New South Wales and Queensland, and manufacturers in other colonies would always be protected to some extent from the Victorians by transport costs. Some South Australian delegates, for fear of Victoria, opposed intercolonial free trade; but the New South Welshmen, who believed they had more to gain from national protection than to lose from Victorian competition, were enthusiastic. The conference formed an Australian Federal Union—'really the first practical step towards the Federation of the Colonies', said Steinfeld—and broke up with great fraternal backslapping.[1] A few months later a joint conference with Chambers of Commerce was held at Sydney, but the local Chamber of Commerce boycotted it. The Sydney and Melbourne manufacturers were still working closely together and won unanimous agreement to a resolution in favour of intercolonial free trade and a uniform national tariff, on the understanding that the motion did not imply that the tariff was necessarily to be protective. The conference also agreed that it was desirable to negotiate intercolonial reciprocal treaties immediately. But the Victorian protectionists ran into some strong criticism. Douglas of Tasmania believed Victoria was only trying to serve its own purposes: 'The greatest enemy Tasmania had had was her child Victoria, for when Victoria grew up she did all she could to cripple Tasmania.' A commercial Victorian delegate remarked that if he were a New South Welshman he would take no part in the conference: 'It was all very well for Victoria . . . to say to her neighbours, "Pull down your fences, and we shall have a fair fight".' Other Victorian delegates, in sorrow rather than in anger, denied that they were wolves in sheep's clothing.[2]

More significant still, at the first congress of Chambers of Commerce in Melbourne late in 1888 there were strong demands for uniform legislation on such common interests as the estates of deceased persons, insolvency, recovery of debts, partnerships, patents, trade marks, insurance, and other matters. In introducing the federal question, the president, Melbourne merchant Robert Reid, deplored the 'great darkness which still prevails in Victoria' on fiscal matters. Yet Edward Pulsford, the Sydney free trade propagandist, had difficulty in carrying a motion in favour of unrestricted free trade in all aspects. Steinfeld had been invited to join the Melbourne delegation and to read a paper; his motion for a customs union with a uniform tariff was carried against the Sydney delegates, who were prepared to support a customs union only if each colony could retain its own tariff against the world outside Australia. Then, after a rip-roaring speech by Service, a resolution in favour of all colonies joining the Federal Council was carried unanimously.[3]

Proceedings at these conferences show to what extent businessmen in all the colonies, with the notable exception of the Sydney merchants, were recognizing the need for federation. In this regard the movement was gathering strength. But from 1887 the Victorian government was faced by the serious challenge of the Farmers' Protection Association which came close to wrecking its federal policy.* As the government well knew, the stock tax was the standing evidence of Victorian selfishness and determination to get the better of her neighbours. It was hurled in their faces again and again by the Sydneysiders; as late as January 1889 Parkes bluntly

* See chapter 11.

said in Melbourne that 'so long as Victoria indulged in the pastime of this most barbaric tax it was useless to ask the other colonies for federation'.[4] There was even talk of New South Wales imposing an export duty on wool bound for Port Melbourne. In 1888 the government did not waver; Deakin warned that the New South Wales protectionists had told him that, if they came to power, they would try to shape a tariff which would not injure Victoria, but if Victoria meanwhile unsheathed the sword these assurances could not hold.[5]

The other curb to the government was the *Age*. Syme's attitude to federation over the years was invariably suspicious, and fluctuated according to immediate tactical estimates of the prospects for protection and the maintenance of his paper's influence under federation. He retained his obsession about the colony's limited territory and resources which might in the long run mean being a comparatively junior partner in a federation; in 1886 he recommended amalgamation of Victoria and South Australia as the latter's answer to its current depression. He regularly attacked the New South Wales statisticians for allegedly misleading compilations, and suspected that federation was a free-trade plot, especially when Parkes came to power and held private discussions with Gillies. He feared that in the long run the national tariff would be a free-trade one; in the short run moves for higher protection in Victoria were inhibited.[6] By 1888 he was openly sabotaging the government's policy. He was basing his hopes now mainly on the growth of protectionist parties in the other colonies. Protective policies by one colony against another would assure a national protective policy and were probably the quickest road to federation. He supported the farmers' case for a higher stock tax: 'It is time enough to ask Victorian producers to make sacrifices for a national object when there is some immediate prospect of that object being attained.' Syme's mischief-making went further: he set out deliberately to rouse intercolonial hostility. There was no need to worry about reprisals from New South Wales to protective increases in Victoria, he asserted. To make reprisals they would have to go protectionist and whether they did or not, they would be forced for many years to buy Victoria's surplus manufactures and agricultural produce. The merchants who dominated the colony's politics used as their tools men of 'inferior intellectual calibre' like Parkes, Robertson and Jennings.[7] In reply to such abuse, the infuriated Robertson denounced the rascality of Victorians at length in the Sydney press. Syme was Victoria's Robertson, the ultra-provincialist, the classic 'Victorian nationalist' even.

Things were not altogether easy for the Victorian government in its policy of intercolonial pacification. The approach via the Federal Council seemed to have worked out badly; Quick and others were deploring it as a most unfortunate miscalculation.[8] In 1887 the government seriously considered abandoning it, if South Australia could not be persuaded to join. No meeting was held in 1887 and little could be done at the January 1888 session. The basic difficulty was intercolonial scepticism about Victorian intentions. Victoria was morally compromised, having been the economic aggressor and remaining so despite all good intentions. Honest as always, Service summed up late in 1888:

> From the first to the last the Victorian policy has been a selfish one, and it is a selfish policy now. People say that when it suited Victorians to establish protection the protectionists were supported by a great many of those identical gentlemen who are now crying out for intercolonial free-trade. It is to our political advantage now, they say, that we should have this intercolonial free-trade. The feeling in the other colonies is that this is but another movement in favour of our noble selves. It is very natural that they should have this feeling, and it is no use shutting our eyes to the fact. What we in Victoria have to do is to join with the other colonies rather than endeavour to take the lead. Let the Sydney people lead, and let us follow them.[9]

Service was now very pessimistic: it would be years before federation could be won, but meanwhile the Federal Council was potentially useful.[10] Gillies agreed that Victoria could not make any new major initiative, and he, too, resorted to flattery and cajolery of Parkes, appeals to him to get on with the great work:

> We did not desire unnecessarily to press for the lead in this matter. Victoria has offered to assist New South Wales, as it was its place to take the initiative. Victoria has offered, if New South Wales will take the lead, to follow. We have no pride except the pride of duty, and we are willing to follow.

Privately, he was writing tactful, chummy notes to Parkes, urging him to visit the Exhibition.[11]

11

Close of an Era, 1888–1889

Political development; dissident farmers

In 1888 and at the election early in 1889, the angry farmers made the first serious challenge in five years to the coalition government. An internal break-up was threatened, for nearly all the rural members were attached, more or less firmly, to either the Constitutionalists or the Liberals. Gillies and Deakin had almost equal numbers of firm supporters who made a bare majority of the Assembly;[1] a dozen more usually toed the line. As in the previous Parliament, the remaining third of the Assembly formed a motley Opposition—old members of the O'Loghlen ministry, high protectionist Liberals who had fallen out with Berry and Deakin, a handful of wayward 'Conservatives', most of the Catholics, and some pastoralists.* The *Age* was cool towards the coalition, but could see no workable alternative. The Catholic group lacked ability and welcomed O'Loghlen's return in 1888; the able young Allan McLean was behaving more like a stock and station agent than a Catholic in politics. The religious issue was still so explosive that Pearson, as Minister, abandoned attempts to amend the Education Act in 1886 and 1887.

Under Bent's leadership, the Opposition was not a serious threat to the government. In 1887 a weak no-confidence motion on the Budget, based on 'tinkering with the tariff' and the current troubles of the woollen mills, was defeated by forty-four votes to eighteen; the minority included most of the Geelong, Ballarat and Bendigo members.[2] But the Opposition certainly opposed effectively. Bent's chief wrecking agents were his 'bodyguard', David Gaunson—the agitator for the Kellys, the publicans' puppet and later John Wren's legal 'fixer', who appears at this time almost to have been mentally deranged—and C. E. Jones, making a comeback after his iniquitous political career in the sixties. The Assembly had abandoned the 'gag' after the unhappy experiences of the seventies and now lacked any effective check on stonewalling or means to enforce priority of government business. In contrast to the massive achievement of the previous Parliament, this ministry had to abandon much of its proposed legislation and many bills were rushed through by hook or by crook and barely discussed. Even

* 'O'Loghlenites' were Bent, Gaunson, Graves, C. Young and L. L. Smith; dissident Liberals included Munro, Patterson, Quick, W. C. Smith, Vale, Woods and C. E. Jones; dissident 'Conservatives' included Harper, McIntyre and Shiels.

the iron Speaker, Peter Lalor, sometimes failed to keep order; when he retired in ill-health in 1887, Bent stood in his place and the proceedings by which he was defeated by M. H. Davies by one vote and the aftermath were disgraceful.[3] Nevertheless Willoughby of the *Argus* remarked, 'If no House has had worse members, yet few Houses have had a larger proportion of decent, steady, estimable men.'[4] Davies used his conciliatory gifts to keep good order, but the irresponsible sabotage within the rules was so damaging that the government made a major election issue of it in 1889. Bent, whose friends disqualified him as a potential Premier, was put out of action by a serious accident in 1888, then by financial troubles. Munro steadily emerged as the alternative Premier.

The farmers' protest movement developed gradually. Scattered selectors' associations and farmers' unions had long existed. In 1879 and 1880 many of them had joined in the Victorian Farmers' Union which began to organize politically; however, regional differences and disputes about protection and free trade brought quick collapse. In 1886, the representatives of farming constituencies began to meet as a group which excluded only Melbourne, Ballarat, Bendigo and Geelong members; Walter Madden, G. W. Hall and George Graham were the leading spokesmen. However, this country faction broke up between August and October 1886 after a running dispute on the inescapable protection issue.[5] The lively arguments reflected the respective needs of established farmers, who were confident in the open market and hoped to develop intercolonial markets, and their struggling insecure brothers in newer areas. The vital new departure came in August 1887 with the formation at Tallygaroopna near Shepparton of the Victorian Farmers' Protection Association, inspired by James Coldwell who proved to be a first-rate political organizer. At a November conference the policy was laid down: increased duties on nearly all crops and dairy produce, an export bounty for wheat, a large increase of the stock tax and lower freight charges.[6] By March 1888 the V.F.P.A. had come to terms with Hall and Graham, the Liberal protectionists.[7] By its second convention in April 1888 it had twenty-seven branches (mostly previously existing farmers' organizations); twenty-nine shire councils, and agricultural societies and other groups also sent delegates. Its hostility to financiers and middlemen was shown in discussion of the possibilities of a state bank and co-operative export marketing.[8] Coldwell went on during that boom winter to organize the wheat-farmers and Gippsland graziers. 'When this agricultural protection movement is completed', he told a Horsham audience, 'we could form a Country Party. . . . The Government and its officials will then be our servants instead of masters.'[9] By August there were 200 branches averaging fifty members.[10] At a conference that month a delegate urged them to aim at becoming 'like the Trades Hall Council, a great power, which could dictate to the Government; so strong that the trades should be glad to claim them as partners; so powerful that the Trades Hall would not be able to dictate to them.'[11] Clearly, there was a new power in the land. The awkward insistent question was posed: why should the only direct taxation be on rural land, while urban property escaped? The assertion was made that because farmers were not sharing in the boom they were being treated unfairly by the state, in comparison to the parasitic protected Melbourne manufacturers and their molly-coddled eight-hour workmen.

Many Wimmera wheat-growers and South Gippslanders were certainly ailing. Local wheat prices had fallen from an average of 4s 5d a bushel in 1879–83 to 3s 7d in 1884–8. In June 1888 Madden, who was member for the Wimmera, made a major statement which was depressing and alarming. Because of dry seasons, all-time low prices and rabbits, Wimmera farmers were overwhelmed with debt and were selling out in hundreds. There were immediate protests that Madden had misrepresented the position of farmers in general, for land in the north had recently risen sharply in value; there were hundreds of selectors in the Goulburn Valley now with properties worth £10,000 to £20,000, and some of them even had sons at Cambridge.[12] The government was well aware that the wheat industry's future was uncertain, and for years had been planning ways and means of diversifying agriculture. Major investment was being made in irrigation and water-supply works whose benefits would be slow to emerge. John Lamont Dow, the Minister for Agriculture, was expert and energetic. In his youth this Scottish Methodist had been a farmer, miner, shearer, and explorer of the Gulf country in Queensland, before settling down as agricultural editor of the *Leader* for a dozen years. A great raconteur and something of a showman, he had been a famous lecturer on land reform in the seventies. Now, as Minister, he founded a Department of Forests and reserved Wilson's Promontory. But his major task was to develop dairying into an export trade—which involved education and supervision of farmers. The first Swedish Laval separator had been imported in 1884 and displayed widely at shows in 1885, and the first co-operative butter factories on the American and Scandinavian models were established at Cobden and Warrnambool in 1887 and 1888. In 1888 a government model dairy was on show at the Exhibition and then began to tour farming areas. Sheds at 170 railway stations were equipped for reception of dairy produce, a coolstore for free storage in Melbourne was established, and the Department arranged a large overseas shipment; supervision began of quality, packing and grading. Danish migrants helped to introduce appropriate techniques, and the groundwork was laid for the highly successful development of the next decade.[13] Government had also long been subsidizing rural areas by means of uneconomic freight rates, relatively high subsidies to rural shires, and removal of duties (unlike New South Wales) on corrugated iron and fencing wire.

Although Gillies knew he was facing a crisis, his Budget of July 1888 was flatly federationist. He would not increase the stock tax, and he was revising the tariff to eliminate or reduce duties on many products of other colonies. To avoid the rural backlash, he proposed to spend £250,000 from the budget surplus of 1887–8 on bonuses (for the best samples of primary exports, the best packing of dairy produce and fruit, and inventions of agricultural machinery), subsidies (to butter and cheese factories and canneries and fruit-drying plants), and agricultural education. Furthermore, terms of irrigation finance would be eased, freights for primary produce would be reduced again, and grants to shires increased.[14] The following night Gillies rallied the coalition by brazenly and blatantly raising the sectarian issue. His reference to Catholic demands 'set the House on fire, and Sir Bryan O'Loghlen . . . stood with his right arm bared half way to the elbow, his first closed tightly and yelled, "and we mean to get them—and justice of the colony will give them to us".'[15] The country members, meanwhile, were meeting again in two groups, one led by Madden, the other by Rees, Hall and Graham, closely reflecting nominal party affiliations.[16] The Farmers' Protection Association was now seeking support from the protectionist manufacturers and trade unions. They got no change from Emanuel Steinfeld, president of the Chamber of Manufactures, who believed farmers were already 'the most favoured class in the community', that their demands would endanger federation, and that no support could be given to a policy which would increase the price of bread and meat.[17] The Trades Hall Council, however, resolved to help, for it recognized the justice of the case for protection, though it disapproved of an export bonus for wheat. Some leaders on both sides had grand plans: Trenwith of the T.H.C. was hoping that 'the trades and farmers could go to the next election a solid phalanx, and crush into powder any opposition to their interests'. But when the V.F.P.A. moved to support reintroduction of assisted immigration, the T.H.C. threatened to withdraw support for agricultural protection. Moreover, some V.F.P.A. branches disaffiliated in protest against flirting with the unions.[18]

The Opposition moved its inevitable no-confidence motion in August 1888, hoping to snare some of the country members by basing it on higher agricultural protection. None of Munro, Mirams and Shiels had previously supported the stock tax, but they now made its increase their central point. They might have succeeded, if the V.F.P.A. had not changed its mind and agreed with the two 'country parties' that there was more to be gained by continuing to support the government. Hardly any of the rural members defected, and the motion was lost by twenty-five votes to fifty-one.[19] The government, however, was forced to allow free votes on the items of the Budget and the Assembly divided almost evenly, now one way now another, when it came to voting on the stock tax and other items of agricultural protection. On 18 September the government called a halt, announced it would fight an election on its policy (it could not immediately go to the country as redistribution was necessary), and opened negotiations with its rural supporters.[20] Gillies broadly got his way: the new agricultural bonuses and subsidies were eventually passed, but the stock tax was not increased. Madden, who had been offered a Cabinet post by the Opposition, held his support, and the government lasted out the year with about fifty-four supporters to twenty-nine opposed.[21]

Some farmers were sensible enough to realize that, at best, further agricultural protection could be only marginally helpful and might be highly damaging. Camperdown graziers opposed the stock tax because it raised prices to the consumer, did not add to the value of local stock, taxed Riverina men who were mostly Victorians, and provoked other colonies to retaliate.[22] Increasing the tax would be of benefit mainly to large landowning graziers. Yet the low stock tax became the symbol of the farmer's wrongs (and eventually in 1892 it was greatly increased). Munro and the other opportunists seeking power may possibly have agreed with the *Age*, though it is unlikely, that the best way to promote federation was by a tariff war. Deakin told Dilke that he was 'at issue with a large section of my own party . . . because while they believe Federation to be distant and of doubtful advantage I believe it to be of vital and immediate importance and am prepared to go out of public life altogether rather than be responsible for an internecine war of tariffs throughout Australia.'[23] A system of protection which was protective only against other Australians was contemptible, he told the Assembly.[24] The government stuck to its guns for another year.

The three-year Parliament was drawing to its close and the government had urgently to redistribute seats; the 1876 boundaries still applied. Ominously, one of the 'country parties' resolved in July 1888, that, despite Melbourne's growth, the existing ratio of seats between Melbourne and the rest should be retained. Despite his tactically weak position, Gillies carried out a fair and reasonably democratic redistribution. The Assembly was enlarged by eight members and Melbourne gained six (or seven, depending on definition) of the new seats. The Council offered unusually little opposition. With about 40 per cent of the population, Melbourne now had 31 per cent of the seats—by far the nearest to proper representation it was to have for another sixty years, for the early twentieth-century conservative-rural alliance of gerrymanderers were anything but democrats.*[25]

Late in the session, perhaps as a gesture insisted on by the Liberals, the government attempted to abolish plural voting for the Assembly. The right to vote in any electorate where property was owned possibly resulted in the return of conservatives instead of radicals in three or four constituencies. Munro confessed that he had a vote in twenty-three electorates and had voted as many as fifteen times.[26] A large majority of the Assembly professed to favour abolition; the Opposition tried to get in first with its own Bill. Deakin made a fine second-reading speech: 'If it be admitted that in no country of the world is there so general a distribution of property, so wide a diffusion of intelligence and of education, as in this, surely in no country of the world is there so strong a case . . . for the equalization of political privileges.' Property had more than adequate representation in the Council. There was no principle behind the existing plural vote: 'It offers a premium, not for education, intelligence, or even for the possession of wealth or landed property, but a premium for land-jobbing, for allot-

* As proposed in the Bill, 128 Melbourne votes = 112 in provincial cities and towns = 97 in rural areas; the final result varied little from this.

ment-dividing among different constituencies.'[27] In reply, the conservatives suggested that no man should have more than two votes, the proposal on which they were to stand and fight in the great contest for 'one man, one vote' in the nineties. The Council, led by Service against his old colleagues, brusquely defended plural voting for the other house, and the government had to submit on the last day of the session in order to save the rest of the Bill which included a variety of electoral matters.[28] After twice previously refusing it, the Council agreed to give policemen the vote,[29] but was not called on to reject either compulsory voting, which the government had seriously considered proposing, or the vote for women. Although a Women's Suffrage Society had been agitating for four years with the support of the *Age*, the female franchise was not yet practical politics.[30]

The eighties was a relatively peaceful period in relations between the Houses. Few radical bills were produced for the Council to savage, and for the sake of peace it even allowed payment of members of the Assembly to be made permanent in 1886. The Council's main conservative gestures had been to maim the Factories Bill and to maintain plural voting. In the late eighties, however, clashes were becoming more frequent and some Council firebrands, like W. A. Zeal, were militantly proclaiming their co-equal rights.[31] Since the widening of its franchise in 1881 the Council felt itself to be more popular, and gained in confidence; a wider variety of businessmen became members, although nearly half still were pastoralists and graziers. Deakin summed up fairly when he said nine-tenths of the Council were Conservatives, whereas almost seven-tenths of the Assembly were Liberals.[32] Most Council elections—twenty-one of thirty-six between 1881 and 1887—were settled without a poll. To save expense, a candidate arranged for supporters to requisition him and by display of strength to warn off possible opponents; in 1886 almost a full-page newspaper advertisement listed about 4,000 electors requesting Simon Fraser to represent them.[33] In 1888, in line with the Assembly, the Council was increased from forty-two to forty-eight members. A select committee recommended three new members from Melbourne and three from the country, but Melbourne was reduced to two—the northern Melbourne area naturally being the victim.[34] The Liberals knew they would eventually have to mount a major campaign to clip the Council's near-absolute powers, which alone made a mockery of any claims to the existence of democracy in the colony.[35]

The government courageously fought and triumphantly won the March 1889 election on the issue of federation versus higher agricultural protection. This was the parting of the ways, said Gillies and Deakin: were protection and national feeling to be Australian or Victorian? The *Argus* referred to the contest between 'Nationalists and provincialists' over 'whether we are to conciliate or to incense our Australian neighbours'.[36] The *Age* strongly supported an increased stock tax; Deakin, as a former editor, resented the consistent misrepresentations of the *Leader*.[37] At conferences in November and February the Farmers' Protection Association settled its manifesto of a 25 per cent stock tax and accompanying cash benefits for farmers, organized its 200 branches by electorates, and pledged candidates. Hall and Graham resigned from the Liberal party. Were the Chamber of Manufactures to become the gods of the colony, and to crush the farmers, and to make serfs and slaves of them? howled a delegate from Echuca.[38] The cause was not helped by the case of one grazier on a deputation arguing for an increased stock tax, who was making £3,500 a year from his cattle, having paid £1,000 in instalments for a selection now worth £30,000.[39] The case was very different with the Gippslanders struggling to establish themselves. And although, on the face of it, wheat-farmers had little to gain from higher protection, some of them who were running stock were attracted by the V.F.P.A. case. The president of the V.F.P.A. argued bluntly that 'the farmers have nothing to do with "sentiment", but have to think only of their pockets'[40]—thus demonstrating that narrow preoccupation with self-interest, to the exclusion of national needs, which came to characterize the Country Party. But in 1889 farmers were still too divided in interest and in interpretation of interest, and not convinced enough that a party rather than a faction was required to represent their interests, to be fully effective.[41] After its defeat, the V.F.P.A. declined as a force and died after a few years.

Once again the Liberal Oppositionists—Munro, Collard Smith, Woods and others—although backed by the *Age* as well as many at the Trades Hall, failed to build a wide electoral organization or win much support.[42] The Catholics altered their tactics, and, while claiming state aid, usually did not attack the state system of education. They remained entirely isolated, and the *Age* was as vicious as ever in its attacks.[43] The Trades Hall Council adopted a political programme at the last minute and attempted to persuade candidates to support it, but would not sponsor Labour candidates. The parliamentary committee had lapsed in 1886, but was reformed in August 1888. Bromley and Trenwith had been engrossed in creating the Board of Conciliation—which indicates that those most interested in parliamentary representation were not necessarily class-conscious militants. Trenwith, however, again stood informally for Richmond as a 'Labour' candidate, and this time was returned, but other independent union men were unsuccessful. Whatever the case in New South Wales after 1889, payment of members, which made a Labor Party possible, had had no effect in Victoria. In the second half of the decade, the Labour movement in Victoria did not advance rapidly, if at all, towards the creation of a political party.[44]

Two-thirds of the successful candidates supported the coalition, and the Liberals gained several seats.[45] More than one-third of the Assembly were new members. Among them were a dozen Liberal A.N.A. men, including the three future knights, George Turner, Alex. Peacock and Robert Best, who in the mid-nineties were to inherit the whirlwind. The native-born also included Trenwith and two others who were to be returned as

Labour candidates at the next election.* Deakin was delighted at his success, but had to withstand Collard Smith's demand for a Liberal government. He wrote in self-defence to Berry in London:

> I have had some trouble with the Liberal party but so far have managed to keep them pretty well together. . . . The coalition is popular as keeping peace and prosperity or being supposed to do so but a good many Liberals chafe at Conservative association. Gillies has liberalised wonderfully and it is only Cuthbert and Lorimer that resist—Wrixon and Derham are more than half with us. I do not despair of seeing the coalition thoroughly Liberal but for its Upper House men and with good fortune it may yet last a long time—aspirants for office are numerous and my task is by no means pleasant in meeting them. . . . The Age wants a change just for excitement sake and is much annoyed with me for refusing to head a revolt but I know their fluctuations of old and besides found that after the land boom people of all classes deprecated any fierce party struggle. Besides the trouble is where to find a casus belli if we wanted one.[46]

Service remarked on how solidly fused the two parties were and how the attempt of the dissident Liberals to revive old distinctions had utterly failed; everyone in the Assembly, he exaggerated, called himself a liberal, and the Opposition consisted simply of the 'outs'.[47] Minor adjustments to the ministry were made. In place of Walker who wanted to retire, Gillies brought in Patterson, the ambitious old Berryite who had long been deviously scheming against the coalition and trying to build support round himself.[48] Deakin retained the eminent Pearson and the successful Dow, and replaced the unhappy Nimmo with D. M. Davies.[49] The Opposition front bench remained much as it was, but Munro was elected as leader in place of Bent whose business affairs were now in chaos.[50] One of the election's happy results was the dismissal of Gaunson and C. E. Jones. At the beginning of the session, with the Opposition's co-operation, the Assembly spent a week discussing reforms in procedure. Extensive revisions were made in order to avoid renewal of wrecking tactics, but the government finally withdrew its recommendation for a ruthless technique of closing debate. Nevertheless the 1889 session was conducted with more speed and efficiency than any for many years. The *Argus* was not entirely dissatisfied with the colony's politicians: culture and ability were largely excluded, 'we have dropped permanently down to a vestry standard', but 'we have to be thankful for shrewdness, integrity and good behaviour.'[51]

Despite its electoral victory, the government eventually had to make major concessions to the provincialist protectionists. Gillies introduced a 'prosperity' Budget and declared a sensational accumulated surplus of £1.7 million. He also stated a new determination to use revenue and not loan money for non-productive public works. Penny postage was at last to be introduced. He did not now intend completely to revise and consolidate the

* Dr William Maloney (West Melbourne) and W. T. Carter (Williamstown). John Murray (Warrnambool since 1884) was also returned as a Labour man in 1892.

tariff, which he had attempted and not been permitted to carry out in 1888; but he proposed some protective increases, with no revenue intent, and abolition or heavy reduction of duties on tea, coffee, cocoa, kerosene and safety matches. A variety of bonuses and subsidies was to be provided for the farmer on the lines of the previous year, and duties were to be abolished on some kinds of agricultural machinery.[52]

When Allan McLean, who was now sometimes called the leader of the country party, moved for a high stock tax and higher duties on grain, the government made it an issue of confidence and knocked out the proposal by a majority of two to one.[53] But the battle had barely begun: this was the most strongly protectionist Assembly there had been. Munro actually claimed that eighty out of ninety-five members were protectionist, but only three of the eleven members of the ministry.[54] The Trades Hall Council was now demanding prohibition rather than protection over a wide range. Encouraged by Munro and other extreme Opposition protectionists, the trade unions and the Farmers' Protection Association were again trying to negotiate a common programme of mutual high protection. Berry's ancient protectionist-farmer alliance was showing new life. 'Who are the backbone of protection but the farmers? Who initiated it?' he later asserted.[55] The government only just carried the general principle of bonuses for farmers, which true protectionists regarded as anathema, and the temperance lobby joined the doctrinaires to defeat bonuses for wine producers.[56] When the government made a present of jewellery to the departing Lady Loch, the protectionists objected not only that the gems were bought in London but that no duty was paid on them, and nearly won their point.[57] Munro won increased protection for the woollen manufacturing industry, and a variety of duties were raised 5 and 10 per cent up to 30 and 35 per cent. These were the greatest protectionist increases for a decade. In addition, duties were imposed or increased on eggs, fruits, grains, jams, malt, preserved milk, oatmeal, peas and beans and sauces. Many of them could have made little practical difference, and were proposed by the government as a sop to the farmers. They were 'driven into these concessions to avoid others', Deakin explained to Dilke.[58] But there were hostile reactions in South Australia and Tasmania, and the *Argus* regarded it as a despicable betrayal of the federal cause.[59]

Clinging to power, and frightened of offending the Trades Hall, the manufacturers or the farmers, the government was demonstrating its tiredness. Little major legislation was passed in the session. The Public Health Act and planning of the Metropolitan Board of Works were major preoccupations. Amendments were made to the terms of land tenure in the Mallee, and money was poured into a massive attack on the rabbits, notably by means of interest-free loans to landholders for wire-netting.[60] Royal commissions were set to work on the goldfields and coalfields, and administration of the civil service was overhauled. Francis Adams summed up: 'The political soul of Victoria at the present moment seems dead . . . the huge system of political rule by loaves and fishes for the constituencies, and sops to the Democratic Cerberus when he grew cross, and growled and showed his teeth, still working triumphantly.'[61]

On the face of it, the achievements of the Liberals within the coalition governments were thin. Deakin was coming under attack for lacking solid purpose and succumbing to the influence of the wealthy; he was certainly lacking in ideological determination. His continuation of the alliance, whose wisdom he frequently doubted, always had as a possible alternative a Liberal-protectionist compact with some country members, backed by the *Age*. Deakin justified his policy by the overriding importance of federation, the increasing prosperity of the workingman, and the absence of a strong popular radical movement. But minimal progress was made towards the long-term objectives which Pearson had defined in the late seventies: labour legislation, state provision for the sick and aged, free education through grammar school to university, and direct taxation as a means of redistributing income. Pearson, as Minister, made great advances in technical education and increased the number of scholarships for secondary schools, but his plan to found state high schools did not succeed.[62] Taxation of wealth was being postponed until the money was needed, Deakin said in 1888.[63] Few assaults were made and no victories won in the campaign to democratize the constitution in order to clear the path for future reforms. Some small gains had been made in factory legislation, but little effort was made to renew the fight. Extensive though it was, state action still aimed to assist the entrepreneur rather than the employee.[64] Most of the new developments in state assistance to the farmers, however, were a progressive response in an area of urgent need. The strongest defence of Deakin's and Pearson's quietism may be that the radical forces, especially the *Age* and the Trades Hall, were so imbued with the cure-all propensities of extreme protectionism that it was futile to turn to the offensive. Deakin and others, beginning to fumble towards a refined protectionist creed, had not yet found a coherent radical programme and meanwhile failed to recognize the economic follies of the day.

The boom, 1889

The pricking of the land-bubble late in 1888 had caught a few large operators like Mirams and Bent, caused large losses to shareholders in the minority of land-finance companies which collapsed, and wiped out most of the paper gains of thousands of speculators. However, the impact was scattered and selective. Land sales and speculation were cut off for the moment, but land values were broadly maintained. After a slight down-turn in February, the economy quickly stabilized again in high boom conditions; full employment remained and there were no credit restrictions on normal business. The many remaining land banks and finance companies and some of the building societies took themselves to London, formed impressive English boards of well-known citizens, raked in deposits, and resumed their lavish distribution of advances and 'profits'. By March 1889 suburban sales were again a weekend attraction.[65] Building remained brisk late in 1888, fell off slightly in the summer, then kept up right through the year; 1889 was the record year for brick production.

1889 was also probably the peak year of import of British capital for, as well as the gathering of deposits by finance companies, government investment was maintained at a very high rate and many other companies were actively borrowing.[66] A rally in wool prices in 1888 helped prosperity; then, after a bad harvest, the drought broke early in 1889. In the second quarter of the year the stockmarket began to boom again; mining was very lively and Tram shares soared almost to £9. Manufacturing employment was increasing in nearly every trade. Most of the coffee houses, however, were barely paying their way, for accommodation needs had been grossly overestimated; the directors of the Federal were considering renting some of their rooms as offices and even feared they might have to apply for a liquor licence.[67] Winter unemployment was worse than for several years; about two thousand men were out of work. Nearly one thousand accepted free rail passes to seek work in the country, while the government arranged work for others with the Harbor Trust (on murderous piece-rates). Gillies and many others were almost incapable of recognizing that there could be so many genuine unemployed. A capable committee of the workless, aided by Dr Singleton, produced irrefutable evidence, but few were still out of work by the spring.[68] The London *Statist* was foretelling a crash in a series of articles through the year,[69] while Brodzky was campaigning in *Table Talk* for reform of company law to protect investors, and anticipating future revelations of fraud.

Gillies proudly carried over a huge surplus into the new Budget. Shiels preached another jeremiad, rightly stressing the decline in exports and the adverse balance of payments, the misapplication of loan moneys, and the lack of growth of productive enterprises. To approve of recent developments was 'like mistaking the flush on the cheek of a man who had just swallowed a pint of brandy for an indication of health and strength'.[70] But businessmen, politicians and public, basking in the Indian summer of the boom, ignored him.

Imperial relations and defence

1889 was a quiet year in imperial relations; correspondence with the Colonial Office and the Agent-General dwindled away. Although widely suspected as disloyal, the A.N.A. was going quietly, and any other possible centres of an exclusive Australian nationalism were insignificant. There was general agreement to let the imperial association alone and to ignore the theoretical question of the inevitability either of separation or closer union. Opinion had consolidated firmly against Imperial Federation as a practical solution; so long as its exponents confined themselves to the promotion of a united imperial sentiment, they were regarded as harmless. When George Parkin, the famous Canadian exponent of the cause, visited

Australia in 1889, he found he was far more sympathetically received in Victoria and South Australia than in the north-eastern colonies. The local members of the League thought him an immense success and persuaded him to stay for longer than he had intended. But the emphasis of Parkin's stirring addresses was all on imperial unity rather than on any scheme of union in the near future. He so irritated the *Age* that it reverted to its opinions of former years which recently it had been forgetting. Ultimate separation was unavoidable, it was inevitable that the interests of Britain and Australia would diverge, and the desire for a distinctive Australian nationality was growing. 'By leaving matters as they are we can render separation easy and of a friendly character, whereas the Imperial Federationists . . . would bind us to the mother land by ties which could not be ruptured without throwing the whole of the Imperial machinery out of gear.' This was virtually an A.N.A. position, though many in the A.N.A. now believed that neither separation nor closer union was inevitable. The argument went round and round, Parkin's visit produced only a mild revival of interest, and the local branch of the Imperial Federation League lapsed once more into virtual inactivity for several years.[71]

The Irish question boiled up again in April 1889 when three envoys—John Dillon, who had just been released from gaol, Sir Thomas Esmonde and John Deasy—visited the colony. They had been warned that Melbourne would be the only city in Australia where they would not get fair play; sure enough the press was, if anything, more venomous than it had been towards the Redmonds. Huge meetings of the faithful, with isolated Protestant supporters, contributed generously to funds for evicted tenants and the National League. The Pope had recently condemned the Plan of Campaign and the boycott movement which the League supported; there was much less protest at this depressing development by Victorian than by New South Wales Catholics. But Carr and the other bishops gave entire support to the envoys, donating money and sometimes chairing meetings, while the Catholic politicians rallied almost to a man. Another convention of the local National League was held in September, to help Dillon plan future activities.[72] But enthusiasm for what was little more than a fund-raising organization waned when he left the colony, and the Parnell-O'Shea divorce scandal in 1890 reduced the movement to wreckage.

Victoria's armed forces were in fine shape and the fervently loyal militia officers were lusting for battle in the imperial cause. By 1889 the scheme of local defence had been virtually completed and the colony, as the Governor said in his speech to Parliament, was in a position absolutely to defy insult or attack.[73] A modern Zalinski dynamite gun had been ordered from New York. When on the death of the German Emperor the government asked whether salutes should be fired, it was remarked in the Colonial Office that the Victorians were itching to try out their new big guns.[74] Major Tom Price commanded the Victorian Mounted Rifles, one of whose two battalions was based at Ballarat; members supplied their own horses. Sir William Clarke at Sunbury and Andrew Chirnside at Werribee Park maintained troops of horse-artillery. New employees of the Harbor Trust had to enrol either in the Naval Reserve or the Artillery.[75] Nearly 5,000 children, mostly twelve- to fourteen-year-olds, were in school cadet corps. This movement was far more advanced than in England and was widely held to have produced a marked improvement in behaviour and to be an excellent answer to larrikinism.[76] In addition, well over 10,000 state school children were being instructed in military drill. Inch-to-the-mile military mapping of the colony was proceeding.[77]

Imperial statesmen were lavish in praise. Knutsford was proud that the defences of Port Phillip (and Port Jackson) were 'among the strongest in the world'.[78] Dilke considered the 'Victorian army is a model army for colonial defence, and an admirable nucleus for the Australian federal defence army of the future.'[79] The Earl of Carnarvon found it difficult to praise adequately: 'The contrast, indeed, between our practice and that of Victoria in these questions of national defence is remarkable, and not to our credit'.[80] When Major-General Tulloch took command in 1889 he was 'fairly startled at the fine well-drilled battalions and batteries which I saw turned out for my inspection'.[81] The government had co-operated enthusiastically with the (imperial) Colonial Defence Committee since its establishment in 1885 under G. S. Clarke (a future Governor). When the committee reported favourably in 1889 on the Victorian scheme of defence, Tulloch and Bell, the Defence minister, commented that they believed the dangers of the Chinese and Japanese navies and of New Caledonia as a hostile base had been underestimated. Clarke noted: 'Much of this is the wildest rubbish. . . . The idea of raising a scare about the New Caledonian convicts, and the Chinese navy, is simply ludicrous.'[82] The colonists were also very lax about security. The Colonial Office was shocked when in 1887 Lorimer, the Defence minister, gave the press a report on the Port defences: 'Every word of this Report has before now been studied in Russia and France,' Herbert minuted. The following year the Governor was reprimanded when reports by the naval and military commandants on combined manoeuvres were published in *Young Australia*.[83] In 1889 the government brought in an Official Secrets Bill, but dropped it when it became clear that the imperial Act must apply in the colony; one intention had been to reduce some of the drastic punishments prescribed.[84]

The Russians remained the chief bogy, but almost any power was suspect. A sketch in the *Argus* in 1887 described how a combined French-Russian squadron stormed the defences at the Heads, sank the shipping in the Bay, but was finally beaten off by the *Cerberus*![85] The anonymous *The Battle of Mordialloc* (1888) envisaged, a decade ahead, a crisis over Chinese immigration, an imperial veto of colonial prohibitive legislation, an Australian Declaration of Independence, and subsequent war between Britain and Russia. The Russians cut the cables, and at the close of the Melbourne Cup meeting news was heard of a huge fleet bearing down and of a secret treaty between Russia and China to partition Australia. The invaders landed at Western Port and advanced on Melbourne, and the Victorian army was slaughtered after magnificent resistance. After larrikins had plundered the city, it was burned by the Chinese. Britain sent an expedition to reconquer the country. The pamphleteer was obviously inspired by the events of the day, for on 30 June 1888 both submarine cables by chance were out of action, and Gillies and Lorimer decided to carry out a test mobilization. It is possible that they believed the cables might have been cut by a hostile force and that they played safe. The batteries at the Heads were manned, the *Cerberus* and the gunboats were sent down the Bay, and the naval reserves and the artillery were called up. The *Age* was taken in, and came out with headlines in unprecedented size:

ALARMING WAR SCARE
GUNBOAT ALBERT SENT TO THE HEADS
VICTORIAN FLEET READY FOR ANY EMERGENCY

In the confusion, many of the populace believed that war had been declared and a sharp watch was kept for hostile cruisers. Portland and Warrnambool were gravely worried about their inadequate defences.[86]

Early in 1889 the imperial government offered to order Major-General J. Bevan Edwards to report on the colonies' defences; Parkes now concurred. Edwards was highly complimentary about Victoria's forces and fortifications, but his main task was to draw up a series of recommendations for federation of the colonial forces and other joint defensive activities. As a minor point he remarked that federal organization would prevent 'the unseemly scares which take place whenever the relations of the mother country with a foreign power are somewhat strained; the mere fracture of the cable between Darwin and Batavia, which recently took place, was sufficient to cause uneasiness throughout all the Colonies'.[87] The colonies at last agreed, as Victoria had for years been pressing, to make joint provision for the defence of Albany and Thursday Island. But none of Edwards's basic recommendations were to be carried out until after federation.

Towards federation

The Victorians had deliberately used the gathering of intercolonial leaders at the opening of the Exhibition to discuss informally the prospects of federation. They were also bringing tactical pressure to bear on New South Wales through the Federal Council. In 1888 the governments of Victoria and South Australia were in close contact and both were delighted when late in the year the Bill to join the Council passed the South Australian Parliament. When in January 1889 Parkes came to Melbourne to speak at a medical congress and to see the Exhibition, there was some sort of reconciliation with the Victorian leaders after a year of disharmony. They discussed federation privately; Deakin saw the old man at least twice.[88] Nevertheless it was disappointing that the New South Wales protectionists failed to win the election a few weeks later. The Federal

Council meeting in January-February was harmonious. C. C. Kingston of South Australia went out of his way to praise the Victorians' handling of Council affairs and their 'spirit of liberality in dealing with the smaller colonies'.[89] The Council agreed to enlarge its membership from each colony and then, at its next meeting, formally to consider the question of federation. As Deakin subsequently wrote, the Council 'became influential by the excitement it occasioned around Port Jackson'.[90]

There were many other powerful reasons why Parkes made his move in 1889—especially local political factors and consciousness of how little time he had remaining to earn the plaudits of posterity. On 15 June, after boasting to Lord Carrington that he 'could confederate these colonies in twelve months',[91] he opened negotiations with Gillies, intimating his intention to call together a convention representing the colonial governments, if Victoria and one other colony approved. Gillies replied briefly on the 21st, querying whether this was the right moment.[92] Deakin was probably reflecting governmental scepticism about Parkes's motives when on 5 July he wrote to Dilke: 'Parkes has recently made *private* overtures but as he wishes it accomplished only in such a manner as will recognise the hegemony of N.S.W. and put all the rest of us in the position of penitents it is not likely to lead to much.'[93] The Victorians suspected that Parkes was disloyal to the Empire, and feared that the radical nationalists might be influencing him.[94] But they were also embarrassed by their weakening internal authority and the provincialist challenge of the farmers and the *Age*. Gillies eventually wrote at length on 12 August to say that he believed there was no chance of achieving full federation at the moment, and appealed to Parkes to join the Federal Council. There was no reply from Sydney.

Parkes's next move was to make an outcry about the Murray waters. It was perhaps both a protest against the trend of the current Victorian Budget discussions and a crude attempt to coerce Gillies to submit to his federal proposal. Parkes wildly accused Victoria of draining the Murray and jeopardizing future navigation, and threatened to 'assert the right' of New South Wales to control the river, by stopping Victorian irrigation works and by giving the Chaffeys notice that they were trespassing in their use of water. The basis of his claim was the odd fact that the bed of the river was New South Wales territory. When the Victorian government began to plan its major irrigation works in 1886, it sought a treaty with New South Wales over use of the Murray waters, but negotiations had broken down, partly because of South Australian hostility. The Victorians claimed that, as by far the greater part of the water in the river came from Victorian streams, they were entitled to take a large quantity out. 'We shall not surrender our rights even if we have to dig another river in our own territory to carry all our streams,' Deakin remarked. The obvious answer, recommended by the Victorian government and many New South Wales parliamentarians, was an intercolonial authority. On this occasion, the Victorian government took no notice of Parkes's provocation.[95]

Six days after the release of General Edwards's report, Parkes telegraphed the Premiers on 15 October to suggest a conference to consider the implications; the second instalment began of the long-drawn-out correspondence with Gillies. Parkes made his premeditated move to Brisbane to consult with the Queensland government, and on the way back on the 24th made his call to the nation at Tenterfield, and thus forced the issue. Ultimately, after much correspondence in which the Governors took a part, the other Premiers unitedly forced Parkes to agree, not to the convention he had suggested, but to a meeting of members of the New South Wales government with the Federal Council to discuss his proposal, with the face-saving compromise that they would meet as 'representative public men'.[96] There was much prestige at stake. Despite their calls to Parkes to take the lead, when it came to the point the Victorians found it intolerable that the Federal Council should be bypassed. They had been long-suffering, had kept their tempers continually in the face of provocation by the man who, they believed, had wrecked almost every recent attempt at intercolonial co-operation. Their dignity could not be outraged to this extent. All this understood, it has also to be acknowledged that Gillies believed what he said when he argued that the immediate prospects for federation were hopeless, but that confederation in a reformed Federal Council was attainable; his letter of 12 August rings true. Ironically, the government was now much more pessimistic than the A.N.A. and the Chamber of Manufactures. Despite the potential benefits of intercolonial free trade, it had come round to the view that the recent history of intercolonial relations, the evident balance of opinion in New South Wales and their own local difficulties put agreement on full federation out of the question for the time being. Gillies's case for confederation at this time is not strong, perhaps, but deserves more attention than it is commonly given. The entry of New South Wales and an increase in powers might have made the Federal Council a suitable body to handle matters of defence and foreign policy for an interim period. It happened that these questions were to be not nearly as urgent in the nineties as in the eighties. And Gillies's case lost all force when South Australia failed to legislate to enlarge the Council in 1889 and then resigned its membership. But Gillies was at least correct in his assessment of the immediate possibility of federation.

The Victorian government entered pessimistically on the preparations for the conference. South Australia and Tasmania had been hurt by the protectionist excesses in the Budget, and South Australia was further insulted by the narrow defeat of the government when it moved to submit an old dispute about the precise borderline between the colonies for adjudication by the Privy Council.[97] The enthusiastic co-operation by the Sydney branch of the A.N.A. in 'promoting federal sentiment' and a joint meeting of the residents of Echuca and Moama calling for immediate federation were inadequate signs of the times.[98] There were many lions still to be slain on the way.

Economic doubts, late 1889; Labour and the London dock strike

Late in the year there were signs of a break in business confidence. Gyles Turner, when he returned from overseas leave, was gravely worried by the rash advances made by the Commercial Bank during his absence, but was slowly reassured by the continuing volume of business. There were more share market transactions in 1889 than in 1888; in November a burst of speculation, even larger than in early 1888, broke out in Broken Hill silver.[99] But government finances were showing signs of strain. Unexpectedly, Gillies announced in October that there could be no new railways approved in 1889.[1] In November, he made it known that the government was seeking a new £4 million loan in London. What has happened to the budget surplus? was the cry. Gillies revealed that nearly half of it, £750,000, had gone on underestimated railway expenditure, mainly land purchases. Murray Smith attacked Gillies for his reckless financial policy: 'Victoria will not be ruined, but she will be landed in very serious embarrassment and distress, and will pay the penalty for her previous extravagance in years of depression'. He would not enjoy being proved right. Service joined him in criticizing his old colleagues for their reckless borrowing: a huge number of workmen were dependent on public works; what would become of them if there was a slackening?[2] The *Argus* became alarmed, began to make serious financial investigations, and lost confidence in Gillies. The *Age*, which had long been sniping at Gillies's railway administration,[3] also began to consider the general finances. The writing was on the wall for the coalition. The final shock for the year was the collapse of the Premier Permanent Building Society, to the undisguised satisfaction of reputable building societies which regarded its speculative activities as disgraceful.[4] Yet it was reasonably argued then, and has been since, that the Victorian economy was basically sound.[5] The public debt per head was still lower than in all the Australasian colonies except Western Australia. Over the ten years 1881–90 Victorian governments borrowed £26.6 million compared to New South Wales's £32.3 million.[6] If future borrowings were confined and land speculation held in check, the economy might be brought on to an even keel and bad times avoided. So argued the optimists, who had never known really hard times and did not realize how vulnerable the Victorian economy was to overseas events.

1889 was a very peaceful year in relations between Capital and Labour; there was little work for the Board of Conciliation, and even in the Western District the Shearers met little resistance. The Trades Hall Council was preoccupied with absorbing newly formed unions; affiliations were now about seventy in number. The Trades Hall leaders remained moderate and conciliatory; they voted £51 in support of the New South Wales coalminers' strike in August 1888, but also suggested to the Employers' Union that they jointly attempt to mediate. Melbourne commercial circles regarded the Newcastle miners' telegram, that 'the gist of the whole question in dispute was the unequal distribution of wealth', as 'promulgation of communistic ideas'.[7] The T.H.C. disdained the weekly *Trades Hall Gazette*, published by the politician, J. H. Graves, from July 1888 to June 1889, but was incapable of sponsoring any journal of its own. The left wing was weakly stirring. Early in 1889 a branch of the Australian Socialist League (founded in Sydney in 1887 as an offshoot of William Morris's Socialist League) was formed, but it broke up in discord after six months. Its attempts to agitate on behalf of the unemployed led the *Argus* to bring heavy invective guns to bear:

> long-haired, uncollared people, heavy-jowled men with strong moustachios; old fellows with the appearance of professional beggars; black-bearded, bright-eyed, quick-witted little devils . . . ; chinless wretches with sunken eyes and receding foreheads, such as you may find by scores in the wards of our lunatic asylums; and the old Australian loafer, with the beard and the shirt and the coat and the boots, and the dirt and the discontent he has carried about for years. . . .

They smelled of tobacco, onions and beer; the main thing they needed was soap.[8] In March 1889 a gathering of forty people celebrated the eighteenth anniversary of the Paris Commune, and a tiny group of Communists had recently seceded from the Melbourne Anarchists' Club.[9] Formation of a branch of the American Knights of Labor demonstrated a very different foreign influence. In July S. A. Rosa and others founded a Social Democratic League. But the emergence of significant left wing thought or of a politically oriented trade union movement appeared to be wildly remote possibilities in 1889.

In August 1889 the London dockers struck for sixpence an hour. Remarkable financial backing from Australia, nearly two-thirds of which came from Victoria, was mainly responsible for them winning their battle. The movement of support was largely spontaneous, but the *Age* led the way with its strongly sympathetic editorial of 29 August; cheques began flowing in the next day. The Trades Hall Council opened an appeal that day and called a public meeting, as did the Land Nationalisation League followed quickly by the Socialist League; the Furniture Trade Society met and voted £50. Within a few days the Seamen had donated £300, the Wharf Labourers £500, the Salvation Army £100, the Celtic Club £50, the Chamber of Manufactures £50 as a first donation, and Duncan Gillies £50. Cabinet donated £5 a head and seventy-two members of the Assembly and fifteen Councillors three guineas each. The Chamber of Commerce called a special meeting, and decided to wire its London counterpart for advice before giving support; the reply recommended delay. In response, James Service moved for sympathy with the dockers 'in their efforts to better their condition' and for financial support by the Chamber; it was one of his great emotional speeches. These men were trying to better themselves: 'Generation after generation of these people were being raised, actually apprenticed to misery and villainy', whereas in Australia 'improvement in material condition has been followed by a greater sense of self respect and a general elevation of character.' 'Perish the commerce that cannot stand without trampling underfoot our fellowman', he concluded amid ringing cheers. But the majority, though they voted £500, amended his motion to sympathize merely with the dockers' distress; some were persuaded to give support only by the strength of public opinion and the argument that existing conditions were promoting socialism and anarchy.[10] The Congregational Union and the T.H.C. combined in a crowded Town Hall meeting at which Dr Bevan appealed for aid for the strikers. Their happy collaboration was sealed a month later when Bevan received a presentation at a Trades Hall ceremony and remarked that 'it might be a good thing if a union of parsons could be established, so that a delegate might sit on the Council. It was not to be forgotten that the founder of the Christian religion had been a carpenter, its great expositor a tentmaker, and its early teachers fishermen.'[11] Methodist churches gave willingly, but the Presbyterians were seen in a bad light when the Melbourne North presbytery, while supporting relief, carefully refrained from passing any opinion on the merits of the dispute. One of the majority said the workers' drunkenness was the basis of their distress, while some of the minority deplored the Church's political cowardice.[12] The Melbourne Head-teachers Association agreed to take up collections in their schools; the Carlton and South Melbourne football clubs donated the takings from their match.[13] The Ballarat Trades Hall Council raised nearly £2,000 and hung a portrait of that friend of the dockers, Cardinal Manning, in their council room.[14]

Victoria raised almost £23,000 (approaching $500,000 in today's terms from a community a third the size) of the Australian contribution of about £37,000 and the total from all quarters of about £50,000. Much less than half the Victorian total was from trade unions directly and from workmen on the job. New South Wales, where the campaign began later, raised about £8,000, by far the greater part of which was from the unions. The standard account by Labour historians that the trade unions subscribed £30,000 is wildly astray,[15] for the Victorian middle-class contributed generously. The appeal was couched in terms of humanity, not class, and most of the organizations which contributed were careful not to take sides in the dispute. The *Argus* was trapped; while claiming to support relief of distress, its emphasis on the difficulties of the dock companies and any misbehaviour of the strikers it could find to report earned it the contempt of the rest of the press and most of the public.[16] The Trades Hall took every care to base its moderate appeal on the relief of distress, and even sent the money it collected to *The Times* fund and not to John Burns. By contrast, the militant anti-capitalist views of the New South Wales organizers, their transfer of money to the *Reynolds' News* appeal, and current industrial disputes in the colony partly explain the lack of wide public support there.

The remarkable gesture may, perhaps, defy explanation. It was a demonstration of pride in Victorian achievement and a display of half-convinced belief in the superiority of colonial to home life. It was a justification of migration and a calculated condemnation of the English ruling class. It was a conscientious distribution of largesse from the profits of the boom and a marvellous opportunity, better even than the Exhibition, to advertise Australia. More fundamentally, it was a demonstration of the central colonial conviction of the duty of capital to pay, and of the right of the workingman to receive, a fair wage. Essentially, perhaps, it was a display of loyalty, of the special concern of Victorians with problems at home and with British national life. It could not have happened in any year thereafter.[17]

Conclusion

Peter Lalor, Sir William Stawell and William Westgarth, three heroes of the fifties, died in 1889. The pre-gold settlers were nearly all gone and the gold generation was dying out. The many prosperous elderly men who remained looked back on their work, and knew it was good.

Distinguished visitors recognized that Victoria had claims to have reached a level of civilization which was unparalleled for a colony. The Earl of Carnarvon described it as 'busy, stirring, Imperial England' and remarked on the 'high level of thought', 'great vigour of action', and 'splendid liberality in all the great institutions and manifestations of public life'.[18] Dale, the theologian, explained Victoria's striking character in terms, firstly, of the men of exceptional physical vigour, boldness, force, self-confidence and individualism who were attracted to the diggings; then proceeded to note the high proportion of Scots and Ulstermen, who added elements of industry, fortitude, tenacity, courage, thrift and shrewdness; and suggested finally that a minor American influence helped to explain the colony's 'daemonic energy'.[19] The gold generation's self-regard was endorsed by some of their sons. Deakin regarded the gold migrants as a 'large proportion of the best' of the Australian population; the 'bold, enterprising, active, inventive, effervescing gold settlers' brought about a 'total transformation of the character of our people'. Theodore Fink inherited the opinion that the men who made Victoria were 'some of the most virile advance-guard of Britain and Europe'. And the outrageous George Meudell, despite his keen eye for the absurd, stuck to his view that 'Gold made Victoria, Victoria made Australia, and Australian gold made the present British Empire.'[20]

The Victorian colonists continually confused and contradicted themselves in their determination both to reproduce 'England' and to make of Victoria a better 'England'. Why were they so imitative? James Smith asked:

> Is it the ingrained love of precedent, the deep distrust of innovation, and the profound reverence for authority . . . ? Is it affection for what is old, and familiar, and home-like? Or the want of imaginative and inventive power? . . . Why does society . . . arrange itself in the same

> groups, . . . and adopt the same habits and usages in democratic Victoria as it does in aristocratic England?[21]

Almost every British institution, ancient or novel, was reproduced; legislation was often copied verbatim, and nearly all the current movements, debates and new organizations founded in Britain were faithfully reflected. The colonists also inherited British certainty of racial superiority over lesser breeds. It was Britain of the fifties which was the mould—Britain at the peak of confidence.[22] The relative literacy of these letter-writing and journal-reading migrants of the middling classes kept them closer in touch with 'Home' than other Australian colonists, but the time-lag of ideas grew wider, perhaps, as they aged and, despite all their contacts, tended to drop out of touch. Nevertheless, the level of discussion of religious, philosophical, political, economic and cultural questions in metropolitan, provincial and some rural newspapers, and in journals like the *Melbourne Review*, the *Victorian Review* or the *Insurance and Banking Record*, displayed at the very least good provincial English standards.[23]

Convinced of the superiority of British institutions and the inevitability of material and moral progress, the colonists had applied themselves enthusiastically to the taming and ordering and civilizing of their corner of the new continent. Many of them—explicitly or vaguely—were ambitious to achieve much more. In their 'Centennial Song', Philip Beck and Fergus Hume wrote:

> We have heard not war's harsh trumpet calling to the battle plain,
> Nor have plenteous harvests ripened over men unjustly slain,
> Girdled by our isolation, all the old world fades from view,
> Ancient quarrels are forgotten, we begin the world anew.
> If we learn the bitter lesson, taught so oft in days of yore,
> All those antique dreams Utopian will to us be dreams no more.
> We can realize those visions which the ancient seers foretold,
> Starting thus our new world's history with the wisdom of the old.[24]

By the eighties such sentiments had become clichés. Not all the old world's ancient quarrels had been forgotten or all its bitter lessons learned, and already isolation was being threatened. But optimism and millennial hopes of a heaven on earth in material terms were being justified by achievement of remarkable living standards, relative social justice, and harmony between the classes. So far the drive to create a 'better England', without the poverty and blatant injustices of the old world, had made impressive progress.

There was some reason for the complacency which characterized the period. But such remarkable success was too heady: bombast and rant prevailed. H. B. Higgins, with tongue in cheek, remarked that the active, enterprising spirit of the day

> urges men to the interior for new pastures, to the Pacific for sugar, to the Indies for tin; it floats innumerable bogus companies, patents many bogus inventions, gives bogus values to land. Nothing is impossible to

> us. We are in no way surprised to find that a child is claimed to be a second Mozart, or a youth a second D'Israeli. . . . In the possession of this spirit of hopeful never-tiring enterprise, Australia resembles the England of Elizabeth. . . .[25]

In the boom years, solid provincial virtues were overlaid by shoddy materialism. The 'gambling profit-makers, keen on realising the Individualist ideals of the lower Middle Class'[26] set the tone. The lure of gold, for the second time in this generation, overrode traditional values. The churches, the social reformers, the temperate self-improvers, all lost ground to the smart practical businessmen, who were so certain of their values and so impractically blind to economic reality.

The individual colonies' distinctiveness has hardly been adequately recognized in the writing of late-nineteenth-century Australian history. Some of the major differences between Victoria and New South Wales were the origins of the respective populations, the farming-goldmining-manufacturing emphases of the Victorian economy, and the high proportion of devout Presbyterians and nonconformists in Victoria as against the larger number of Anglicans and Catholics in New South Wales. Victoria had wider intercolonial business links, and its population was more concentrated in the capital and provincial cities (of which Victoria had three with a population of over 20,000 to New South Wales's one). Victorian politics were relatively stable, were based more clearly on 'parties' than factions, and were characterized by a protectionist orthodoxy and a discrediting of free-trade internationalism. The wheatgrower-selector set of values was well developed, while the ideology of the pastoral bush-worker had only a marginal impact. Differences in attitudes were seen most clearly on national-imperial questions, in the near-absence in Victoria of republican or socialist beliefs, and in the relative moderation of her trade union leaders. Federationist sympathy and the urge to unite on national questions were far more evident in Victoria, whose government a score of times took the initiative in seeking agreed policies on issues of common concern, only to be spurned by Sydney. New South Wales was a much more complicated and diverse society.[27] The unity of Victorian opinion is to be explained largely by the homogeneity of its ruling class—politicians, businessmen and other opinion-makers—who were nearly all still the young migrants of the fifties. They were more urban middle class in origin and intellectually more provincially English than the ruling class of any other colony. The society they created was more metropolitan-dominated, more industrially developed, more closely in touch with the currents of English opinion—and hence more sensitive to the rise of the new imperialism and threats to imperial security and less isolationist than other colonies. A mere half-century of history did not allow much deep-rooted provincial loyalty based on long tradition to exist. Victorians were taking the lead in developing that blend of imperial and Australian loyalty which the young men in the A.N.A. branches were thrashing out in their debates, and were groping towards a conception of equal partnership of ex-colonial nations in the British Commonwealth of the far future.

The eighties were a decade of apparently growing dissidence, of conflicts sharpening but then losing their point and dying away. The challenges of trade unionists, nationalists, Irish Catholics, critics of orthodox Christianity, countrymen against the city—even of bohemians and larrikins—were being contained. Harmony prevailed still in labour relations; the native-born were about to take control but did not appear likely, if the A.N.A. was a good guide, to differ widely from their parents; the Irish Catholic issues remained essentially unchanged; secularism and undogmatic Christianity had made only limited impact and widespread loss of faith was not yet evident; rural interests were still incapable of fully mobilizing their potential strength. Victorians believed themselves secure still in all essentials, and remained brashly complacent in their prosperity. But it was the close of an age of harmony and generosity. The years 1890 to 1893 were to be one of the great divides in Australian history. The late eighties were the last, dying days of Australia Felix.

Abbreviations

A.D.B.	*Australian Dictionary of Biography*
A.I.B.R.	*Australasian Insurance and Banking Record*
A.J.P.H.	*Australian Journal of Politics and History*
A.N.A.	Australian Natives' Association
BM	British Museum
CO	Colonial Office
edit.	editorial
Hist. Studies	*Historical Studies*
La Trobe Lib.	La Trobe Library, State Library of Victoria
ML	Mitchell Library, Sydney
NL	National Library of Australia, Canberra
P.D.	Victoria. *Parliamentary Debates*
P.P.	*Votes and Proceedings of the Legislative Assembly with Copies of Various Documents Ordered (by the Assembly) to be Printed* [vol. 1]. *Papers Presented to Parliament* [vol. 2–].
S. of S.	Secretary of State for the Colonies
supp.	supplement
T.H.C.	Trades Hall Council
VA	Archives Division, State Library of Victoria
V.F.P.A.	Victorian Farmers' Protection Association
Vic. Hist. Mag.	*Victorian Historical Magazine*

x

Notes

THE YEARS BETWEEN, 1861-1882

1 John Martineau, *Letters from Australia* (London, 1869), pp. 33-4.
2 Rosamond and Florence Hill, *What We Saw in Australia* (London, 1875), p. 393.
3 J. M. D. Hardwick (ed.), *Emigrant in Motley. The Journey of Charles and Ellen Kean in quest of a theatrical fortune in Australia and America, as told in their hitherto unpublished letters* (London, 1954), p. 138.
4 Coghlan, *Labour and Industry*, vol. 2, p. 903.
5 Martineau, op. cit., p. 56.
6 Charles H. Pearson, *Reviews and Critical Essays* (London, 1896), p. 220.
7 Herbert to Bowen, 23 Nov. 1877, quoted in Bowen to Sir M. Hicks-Beach, 22 Apr. 1880 (Papers of the first Earl St Aldwyn, Witcombe Park, Glos.).
8 Trollope, *Australia and New Zealand*, p. 251.
9 The most illuminating works on the sixties and seventies by contemporaries are E. Carton Booth, *Another England. Life, Living, Homes, and Homemakers in Victoria* (Melb., 1869); Deakin, *Crisis in Victorian Politics*; Charles Wentworth Dilke, *Greater Britain: a Record of Travel in English-speaking Countries during 1866 and 1867* (London, 1868); Sir Charles Gavan Duffy, *My Life in Two Hemispheres* (2 vols, London, 1898); Charles H. Pearson's article, 'Democracy in Victoria'; and Trollope, *Australia and New Zealand*. Useful and detailed later works by contemporaries are Coghlan, *Labour and Industry*; Morris, *George Higinbotham*; and Turner, *History of Victoria*.

The only substantial studies of the period are unpublished theses, of which the most important are Bartlett, 'Political Organization and Society in Victoria'; F. K. Crowley, 'Aspects of the Constitutional Conflicts between the two Houses of the Victorian Legislature, 1864-1868' (M.A., Univ. Melb., 1947); L. C. Duly, 'Land Selection Acts of Victoria, 1859 to 1869' (M.A., Univ. Melb., 1959); Joy E. Parnaby, 'The Economic and Political Development of Victoria, 1877-1881' (Ph.D., Univ. Melb., 1951). Works covering a wider period which are most useful include A. G. Austin, *Australian Education 1788-1900* (Melb., 1961); Blainey, *The Rush that Never Ended*; Butlin, *Investment in Australian Economic Development*; Dow, *George Higinbotham*; Gollan, *Radical and Working Class Politics*; J. S. Gregory, 'Church and State, and Education in Victoria to 1872', E. L. French (ed.), *Melbourne Studies in Education 1958-1959* (Melb., 1960); Hall, *Stock Exchange of Melbourne*; Kiddle, *Men of Yesterday*; and Sayers, *David Syme*. (See Bibliography for works listed without full details.)

1 POLITICAL FRAMEWORK, 1883-1886

1 Deakin, *Crisis in Victorian Politics*, chs 6-8; J. F. Hogan, *A Biographical Sketch of the late most Reverend James Alipius Goold* (Melb., 1886), pp. 10-11; Bartlett, 'Political Organization and Society in Victoria', pt 2, ch. 4; M. Mullaly, 'Aspects of the Catholic Viewpoint on Education and its Political Consequences in Victoria, 1870-1881' (B.A. thesis, Monash Univ., 1966).
2 *Age*, 20 Feb. 1883, p. 4.
3 *Punch*, 15 Feb. 1883, p. 69.
4 *Age*, *Argus*, Feb. 1883, *passim* (*Argus*, 24 Feb., p. 9, lists candidates' affiliations); R. McGhee, 'A Study of the general Election in Victoria 22.2.1883 . . .' (B.A. thesis, Univ. Melb., 1965); Finlayson, 'Groups in Victorian Politics', ch. 1.
5 Pratt, *David Syme*, pp. 172-5; Sayers, *David Syme*, pp. 141-2; *P.D.*, vol. 39, p. 169; *Argus*, 10 Apr. 1883, p. 6.

6 *P.D.*, vol. 42, pp. 28-54; Stebbing, *Charles Henry Pearson*, p. 223; Parkes to Selby, 13, 24 Feb. 1883 (A.N.Z. Bank records).

7 Service newspaper cuttings; Deakin, *Review of Reviews*, Nov., Dec. 1892; Froude, *Oceana*, pp. 104-6.

8 Deakin, *Crisis in Victorian Politics*, ch. 2, *Federal Story*, pp. 12-13; *Imperial Review*, no. 7, June 1882; Geoffrey Bartlett, *A.D.B.*, vol. 3.

9 See the forthcoming *Members of the Victorian Legislature, 1851-1900* by K. Thomson and G. Serle.

10 *Argus*, 1 Dec. 1885, p. 5.

11 *Imperial Review*, no. 10, July 1883.

12 H. J. Wrixon, *Democracy in Australia* . . . (Melb., 1868), pp. 11, 12.

13 *P.D.*, vol. 54, p. 293.

14 Twopeny, *Town Life*, pp. 176-7; *P.D.*, vol. 39, p. 169.

15 *P.D.*, vol. 66, p. 202; Smith, *Liberty and Liberalism*, p. 5.

16 *Democracy in Australia*, pp. 10-11.

17 *Liberty and Liberalism*, p. 10.

18 Goodwin, *Economic Enquiry in Australia*, pp. 325-35.

19 *Australasian*, 20 Sept. 1884, p. 553.

20 Ingham, 'Aspects of Victorian Liberalism', p. 9.

21 *Argus*, 8 Feb. 1883, p. 4.

22 'Democracy in Victoria', p. 696.

23 Ingham, op. cit., pp. 6-20. This section of this chapter owes much to Ingham's pioneering work.

24 'Democracy in Victoria', p. 688.

25 Report of the Royal Commission on the Tariff, *P.P.*, 1883, vol. 4, no. 50; Minutes of Proceedings, *P.P.*, 1884, vol. 2, no. 9.

26 Langridge, *P.D.*, vol. 57, p. 136.

27 Dilke, *Problems of Greater Britain*, p. 118; Goodwin, *Economic Enquiry in Australia*, pp. 321-3.

28 *Outlines of an Industrial Science*, pp. 181-5.

29 *Age*, 24 Apr. 1888, edit. La Nauze (*Political Economy*, p. 132) is probably correct in attributing the leader to Syme.

30 Much in this paragraph derives from La Nauze, op. cit., pp. 98-134.

31 Deakin, *Crisis in Victorian Politics*, pp. 72-3; Sayers, *David Syme*, especially ch. 23; La Nauze, *Alfred Deakin*, vol. 1, pp. 34-7; Deakin's Introduction and Syme's reminiscences are the only valuable sections of Pratt's *David Syme*.

32 Tregenza, *Professor of Democracy*; Stebbing, *Charles Henry Pearson*.

33 *Age*, 19 Feb. 1883, p. 2.

34 David Syme, *Representative Government in England. Its Faults and Failures* (London, 1881), p. 122.

35 Claude McKay, *This Is the Life* (Sydney, 1961), p. 10; Sir Edward Cunningham, *The Victorian Press: a Survey* (Melb., 1936), ch. 1; T. H. G. Esmonde, *Round the World with the Irish Delegates* (Dublin, 1892), pp. 84-5; Deakin, *Crisis in Victorian Politics*, pp. 73, 61.

36 Pratt, *David Syme*, p. 269; cf. Syme's own claims, p. 303.

37 Sayers, *David Syme*, p. 154.

38 Pratt, op. cit., p. xvii.

39 *Intercolonial Free Trade Conference, 1887, Report of the Proceedings*, p. 91.

40 E.g. Bedford, *Naught to Thirty-three*, pp. 256-7. Note Pearson's playing-down of the *Age*'s influence, 20 Oct. 1883, edit.

41 *P.D.*, vol. 44, pp. 1759-60.

42 Esmonde, op. cit., p. 84; Deakin, *Crisis in Victorian Politics*, p. 61. Examples of distortion are the treatment of Woods (exaggerating a good case), 10 July 1883, pp. 7, 10, and of Judge Hartley Williams, 14 Sept., p. 7 and 17 Sept. 1888, p. 8.

43 *Bulletin*, 26 Mar. 1887, p. 5; Stebbing, *Charles Henry Pearson*, p. 266.

44 Twopeny, *Town Life*, p. 222, and pp. 222-31 for further comments; Haddon Papers (La Trobe Lib.); J. S. Johnston Corresp. (Univ. Melb. Archives).

45 Harper, *James Balfour*, pp. 219-24; Hoare, *Looking Back Gaily*, ch. 20.

46 Kimberly, *Ballarat and Vicinity*, pp. 108-9.

47 Cf. *P.D.*, vol. 62, p. 2170.

48 *Argus*, 18 Aug. 1888, p. 5.

49 Cf. Dilke, *Problems of Greater Britain*, p. 121.

50 E. M. Clowes, *On the Wallaby through Victoria* (London, 1911), p. 52.

51 *Argus*, 8 Aug. 1885, p. 5.

52 Quoted by Turner, *History of Victoria*, vol. 2, p. 139.

53 *P.D.*, vol. 71, pp. 3763-4 (Service), 3784-6 (Shiels), 3787 (Maloney); Deakin, *Federal Story*, pp. 9-10; Bedford, *Naught to Thirty-three*, pp. 332-3; Dow, *George Higinbotham*; Morris, *George Higinbotham*.

54 *P.D.*, vol. 43, pp. 286-95, 659-71; 'The Public Service Act', *Melbourne Review*, vol. 9, 1884, pp. 219-25; Pearson, 'Democracy in Victoria', p. 694; Governor Bowen to Carnarvon, 10 July 1876, Carnarvon Papers (Public Record Office, London), PRO 30/6/25, no. 105.

55 *P.D.*, vols 43-4, *passim*, especially vol. 43, pp. 103-22; R. L. Wettenhall, 'Savings Banks, Bureaucracy and the Public Corporation', *A.J.P.H.*, vol. 10, Apr. 1964, pp. 54-69; Wettenhall, *Railway Management*, p. 12 and ch. 3; R. J. Beveridge, 'Victorian Railway Policy: 1850-1883' (M.A., Univ. Melb., 1962).

56 *P.D.*, vol. 48, p. 25; vol. 56, p. 2272; *P.P.*, annual reports of the Public Service Board; Petition, *P.P.*, 1886, vol. 1, E2.

57 Turner, *History of Victoria*, vol. 2, pp. 242-4; *The Speaker* (London), 11 June, 23 July 1892. See also Davison, '"Marvellous Melbourne"', ch. 5, for pioneering work on the Victorian Public Service. I read this admirable thesis (which is to be published by M.U.P.) only when this book was already in the press.

58 Tariff commission report (see note 25); *P.D.*, vol. 45, pp. 110-11, 568-78; *Argus*, 29 July 1887, p. 5.

59 Cf. rival petitions from the South Barwon Shire Council and from Bendigo, *P.P.*, 1883, vol. 1, E3 and 4.

60 J. Wisker, 'The American Railway System and Ours', *Victorian Review*, vol. 9, Nov. 1883, p. 95.

61 *Argus*, 24 Oct., p. 5 and 27 Oct. 1884, p. 6, for entertaining descriptions of the process.

62 *P.D.*, vol. 47, pp. 1650-64; Wettenhall, *Railway Management*, p. 33.

63 Mary Fullerton, MS. Autobiography (Moir Collection, La Trobe Lib.), pp. 178, 185.

64 *P.D.*, vol. 43, pp. 451-61; A. S. Kenyon, 'The Story of the Mallee', *Vic. Hist. Mag.*, no. 14, Dec. 1914, p. 74; no. 15, Mar. 1915, pp. 124-5.

65 *P.D.*, vol. 45, pp. 497-506; William Epps, *Land Systems of Australasia* (London, 1894), pp. 74-7.

66 Pearson, *National Life and Character*, p. 19.

67 Dilke, *Problems of Greater Britain*, p. 117; *P.D.*, vol. 17, pp. 2049-70.

68 La Nauze, *Political Economy*, pp. 128-31; Tregenza, *Professor of Democracy*, pp. 94-104.

69 *Argus*, 19 Jan. 1883, p. 6; *Age*, 30 Apr. 1883, supp. 1; *P.D.*, vol. 42, pp. 76-82, for a Mirams-Quick motion.

70 Richard Hain to Deakin, 28 Apr., 17 May 1884 (Deakin Correspondence).

71 Gollan, *Radical and Working Class Politics*, pp. 120-1.

72 *P.D.*, vol. 47, pp. 2188-524; *Argus*, 12 Dec. 1884, p. 4.

73 Ingham, 'Political Parties', pp. 98-100.

74 *P.D.*, vol. 42, pp. 169-73, 226-31; vol. 52, pp. 1948-2001, 2478-9.

75 *Argus*, 24 Apr. 1883, p. 9; *Age*, 18 Aug. 1883, supp. 1.

76 *Argus*, 18 Apr. 1883, p. 7; Belcher diaries (La Trobe Lib.), *passim*.

77 Quoted in Sayers, *David Syme*, p. 155; *P.D.*, vol. 65, p. 2264; Deakin, *Review of Reviews*, Dec. 1892, p. 127.

78 *Argus*, 16 Mar. 1883, p. 5.

79 *Argus*, 14 June 1884, p. 5.

80 Deakin's diary, 22 Oct., 15, 18 Dec. 1885 (Deakin Papers).

81 Deakin, *Federal Story*, pp. 5, 31; Dilke, *Problems of Greater Britain*, p. 132; *P.D.*, vol. 51, pp. 104-5, 108; *Bulletin*, 23 Jan. 1886, p. 6; *Age*, 17 Dec. 1887, p. 13; *Once a Month*, May 1886.

82 Turner, *History of Victoria*, vol. 2, pp. 249-51.

83 Richard Hain to Deakin, 23, 28 Apr., 9, 17 May 1884 (Deakin Correspondence).

84 Crisp Correspondence.

85 *Argus*, especially 15 Jan., p. 5, and 20 Jan. 1886, and *Age*. For the young Deakin, see La Nauze's masterly biography, chs 1-4.

86 *Argus*, 27 Jan., p. 4; 2 Feb., p. 6; 17 Feb. 1886, p. 6; *Age*, Jan.-Feb. 1886; Ingham, 'Aspects of Victorian Liberalism', pp. 117-20.

87 Quick to Deakin, 7 Feb. 1886 (Deakin Correspondence).

88 *P.D.*, vol. 51, pp. 100-2; vol. 54, p. 101; Jas. Campbell to Deakin, 6 Aug. 1887 (Deakin Correspondence).

89 *P.D.*, vol. 51, p. 179; *Argus*, 6 Oct., edit.; 20 Oct., p. 5; 25 Nov. 1885, p. 8; 6 Mar. 1886, pp. 8-10.

90 *Argus*, 6 Mar. 1886, pp. 8-10; *P.D.*, vol. 51, pp. 6-221.

91 *Argus*, 2 June 1886, p. 5.

92 Parkes to Selby, 21 Jan. 1886 (A.N.Z. Bank records).

2 ECONOMIC SKETCH

1 *Town Life*, pp. 1-3.
2 Butlin, *Investment in Australian Economic Development*, p. 46.
3 Ibid., *passim.*
4 Quoted by Cyril Pearl, *Morrison of Peking* (Sydney, 1967), p. 33.
5 Butlin, op. cit., pp. 187, 238-40; Hall, 'Kinked Age Distribution'.
6 *Victorian Year Book*, 1892, pp. 147-8; *Commonwealth Year Book*, no. 1, 1908, pp. 154, 162-3.
7 J. D. Bailey, *Growth and Depression. Contrasts in the Australian and British Economies 1870-1880* (Canberra, 1956), p. 17.
8 Kiddle, *Men of Yesterday*, pp. 380-1.
9 *Argus*, 8 Sept. 1887, p. 11; Kiddle, op. cit., pp. 320-2.
10 Alan Barnard, *The Australian Wool Market 1840-1900* (Melb., 1958), ch. 7.
11 *Argus*, 22 Sept. 1885, edit.; 20 Apr. 1886, p. 5.
12 *Argus*, 9 May 1885, p. 9; 6 Apr. 1886, p. 9; E. A. Beever, 'A History of the Australian Meat Export Trade, 1865-1939' (Ph.D., Univ. Melb., 1967), pp. 8-21.
13 *Argus*, 1 Dec. 1885, p. 4; J. T. Critchell and J. Raymond, *A History of the Frozen Meat Trade* (London, 1912), pp. 30-4; Kiddle, *Men of Yesterday*, pp. 398-400; Blainey, *Tyranny of Distance*, pp. 271-6; Butlin, *Investment*, pp. 118-19; Beever, op. cit., pp. 28-38.
14 J. D. Bailey, *A Hundred Years of Pastoral Banking. A History of the Australian Land and Finance Company 1863-1963* (Oxford, 1966), p. 74.
15 Butlin, *Investment*, ch. 2; Bailey, *A Hundred Years*, especially pp. 55-6, 74; Franklyn, *A Glance at Australia*, pp. 196-247.
16 *P.D.*, vol. 61, p. 1013.
17 Finch-Hatton, *Advance Australia!*, p. 314.
18 *Argus*, 1 Feb. 1883, p. 5; 5 Jan. 1884, p. 9.
19 *P.D.*, vol. 49, p. 1520; Kiddle, *Men of Yesterday*, p. 470; Dilke, *Problems of Greater Britain*, p. 114; R. V. Billis and A. S. Kenyon, *Pastures New* (Melb., 1930), p. 159.
20 *Argus*, 3 Sept. 1883, p. 9; 6 Jan. 1885, p. 7; 17 Aug. 1886, p. 5; F. T. Derham letter-books; J. L. Parsons, *The Sugar Industry in the Mackay District . . .* (Adelaide, 1883); G. C. Bolton, *A Thousand Miles Away. A History of North Queensland to 1920* (Brisbane, 1963), pp. 136-9; A. G. Lowndes, *South Pacific Enterprise. The Colonial Sugar Refining Company Ltd.* (Sydney, 1956), ch. 1.
21 Lord Casey, *Australian Father and Son* (London, 1966), pp. 75-82.
22 Butlin, *Investment*, pp. 173-80, 418.
23 R. Wallace, *The Rural Economy and Agriculture of Australia and New Zealand* (London, 1891), ch. 5; *Punch*, 21 Jan. 1904, for Walter Manifold's Warrnambool estate.
24 Report for 1888 of 'Proceedings taken under the Provisions of the Land Act 1884 and the Mallee Pastoral Leases Act 1883', *P.P.*, 1889, vol. 3, no. 85.
25 E. Dunsdorfs, *Wheat-growing Industry*, pp. 532-3; Graham, *Formation Australian Country Parties*, p. 33.
26 S. Rinder, 'More about the Northern Farmer', *Melbourne Review*, vol. 9, 1884, pp. 278-9; cf. Dunsdorfs, op. cit., p. 151.
27 Cf. Blainey, *Tyranny of Distance*, pp. 165-6.
28 Priestley, *Warracknabeal*, pp. 39-40; Rinder, op. cit., p. 282.
29 Rinder, op. cit., pp. 279-80.
30 Rinder, 'The Northern Farmer', *Melbourne Review*, vol. 9, 1884, p. 126.
31 Dunsdorfs, op. cit., p. 152. Cf. 'In 1882, the strippers came into general use' near Numurkah (John Sweeney's MS. diary, La Trobe Lib.).
32 Cf. James Cuming, *An Autobiography* (ed. M. A. Cuming, n.p., 1916), p. 58.
33 Rinder, op. cit., pp. 126-7, 129, 276, 287-8. In general for the above, R. H. Stainthorpe, 'The Stainthorpe Story' and Sweeney diary (MS., La Trobe Lib.); Dunsdorfs, *Wheat-growing Industry*, ch. 4; Priestley, *Warracknabeal*, chs 3, 6; Palmer, *Track of the Years* (St Arnaud), chs 15, 19; Sayers, *Shanty at the Bridge* (Donald), chs 13, 15; Forster, *Waranga*; J. E. Robertson, *The Progress of Nhill and District* (Melb., 1918); Blake and Lovett, *Wimmera Shire*, chs 7, 8, 10; W. H. Bossence, *Kyabram* (Melb., 1963), chs 3-5.
34 'Irrigation in Western America. First Progress Report of the Royal Commission on Water Supply', *P.P.*, 1885, vol. 2, no. 19, p. 56.
35 Supply of Water to the Northern Plains, *P.P.*, 1881, vol. 2, no. 18; Irrigation. Supply of Water to the Northern Plains, *P.P.*, 1882-3, vol. 3, no. 74; Reports of the Royal

Commission on Water Supply, *P.P.*, 1885, vol. 2, no. 19, no. 19*; vol. 3, no. 51; *P.D.*, vol. 44, pp. 1386-96; vol. 51, pp. 415-47; Martin, *Irrigation and Closer Settlement*, chs 3-6; J. H. McColl, 'Hugh McColl and the Water Question in Northern Victoria', *Vic. Hist. Mag.*, no. 20, June 1917; La Nauze, *Alfred Deakin*, vol. 1, pp. 84-8; Blake and Lovett, *Wimmera Shire*, p. 93; Forster, *Waranga*, pp. 73-7; Priestley, *Echuca*, pp. 153-8; C. E. Sayers, *Shepherd's Gold. The Story of Stawell* (Melb., 1966), pp. 143-4.

36 *P.D.*, vol. 53, pp. 2701-814 (Waterworks Construction Encouragement Bill).

37 A. Deakin, 'Irrigation in Australia', *Year Book of Australasia*, 1893; J. A. Alexander, *The Life of George Chaffey* (Melb., 1928); Ernestine Hill, *Water into Gold* (Melb., 1937), chs 4-7; J. P. Fogarty, *George Chaffey* (Melb., 1967).

38 A. S. Kenyon, 'The Story of the Mallee', *Vic. Hist. Mag.*, no. 14, Dec. 1914, pp. 73-4; no. 16, June 1915, p. 183.

39 *Argus*, 8 Oct. 1884, p. 7.

40 Kenyon, op. cit.; S. F. Wessels, 'E. H. Lascelles and the Victorian Mallee: a Survey of Settlement 1850-1905' (M.A., Univ. Melb., 1966); Priestley, *Warracknabeal*, pp. 45-52; Dunsdorfs, *Wheat-growing Industry*, pp. 154-61; J. W. McCarty, 'Four Factors in Wimmera Wheat Development to 1890' (unpubl. MS.).

41 B. Collett, 'Land Settlement in the Foster Area, South Gippsland, before 1890' (M.A., Univ. Melb., 1962).

42 *Land of the Lyre Bird*, p. 26.

43 See the two superb chapters by W. H. C. Holmes, 'Scrub Cutting' and 'Picking Up', in *Land of the Lyre Bird*, pp. 54-76; J. W. Eisdell, *Back Country* or *The Cheerful Adventures of a Bush Parson in the Eighties* (London, 1936), ch. 4; Caleb Burchett, 'Early Days of South Gippsland' (MS., La Trobe Lib.); cf. Wilfred Burchett's lyrical description of clearing a block in the 1930s in *Passport* (Melb., 1969), ch. 4.

44 'Victoria', p. 50.

45 Holmes, 'Pack-tracks and Packing'; T. J. Coverdale, 'The Roads and How We Got Them', *Land of the Lyre Bird*, pp. 42-53, 77-86.

46 *Argus*, 7 Oct. 1889, p. 11; also 17 Oct. 1889, p. 5.

47 E.g. *Age*, 27 Feb. 1886, p. 13.

48 Cf. *Argus*, 16 Nov. 1888, p. 7; *Age*, 27 Feb. 1886, p. 13.

49 H. de Castella, 'Victoria as a Wine-producing Country', *Colonial and Indian Exhibition, Handbook* (Melb., 1886); de Castella, *John Bull's Vineyard*, pp. 98-100; Lynnette J. Peel, 'Viticulture at Geelong and Lillydale', *Vic. Hist. Mag.*, no. 142, Nov. 1965.

50 R. H. Stainthorpe, 'The Stainthorpe Story' (MS., La Trobe Lib.).

51 Bossence, *Kyabram*, pp. 44-5; Priestley, *Warracknabeal*, p. 39.

52 E. L. Barnes, 'Shirtsleeves to Shirtsleeves' (MS., La Trobe Lib.), pp. 29-30.

53 Priestley, op. cit., pp. 42-3.

54 E.g. William Hancock's memories of Nathalia; see W. K. Hancock, *Country and Calling* (London, 1954), pp. 11-12.

55 Cf. D. B. Waterson, *Squatter, Selector, and Storekeeper. A History of the Darling Downs 1859-93* (Sydney, 1968), *passim*; Graham, *Formation Australian Country Parties*, p. 39; also Henry Nash Smith, *Virgin Land. The American West as Symbol and Myth* (Cambridge, Mass., 1950), Book 3.

56 Blainey, *The Rush that Never Ended*, p. 61.

57 *Argus*, 1 Jan. 1883, p. 9.

58 Mackay, *History of Bendigo*, pp. 87-94; Blainey, *The Rush that Never Ended*, pp. 73-80.

59 *Argus*, 18 Jan., p. 9; 22 Jan., p. 9; 26 Jan., p. 9; 29 Jan. 1883, p. 9; Withers, *History of Ballarat*, pp. 221-34; Margaret McAleese, 'Creswick in the 1880s' (B.A., Monash Univ., 1968), pp. 2-8.

60 *Argus*, 2 Feb., p. 9; 5 Feb., p. 9; 12 Feb. 1883, p. 9; Sayers, *Shepherd's Gold*, ch. 19.

61 Palmer, *Track of the Years*, pp. 262-4, 268.

62 Raymond Paull, *Old Walhalla. Portrait of a Gold Town* (Melb., 1963), ch. 8.

63 *Age*, 16 Oct. 1888, p. 7; *Argus*, 21 May 1887, p. 13; 14 May 1888, p. 5.

64 Blainey, *The Rush that Never Ended*, pp. 78-9.

65 Hall, *Stock Exchange*, pp. 98-9.

66 Blainey, *Rush*, pp. 100-2.

67 *Argus*, 21 May 1887, p. 13.

68 Progress Report of the Royal Commission on Gold Mining, *P.P.*, 1891, vol. 3, no. 2, p. 6.

69 Hay Kirkwood, *History of the Bendigo Goldfield . . .* (Sandhurst, n.d.), pp. 2-3; cf. Smyth in *Argus*, 1 Jan. 1883, p. 9; Blainey, *Rush*, pp. 97-100; T. A. Rickard, 'The

Bendigo Gold-Field', *Trans. American Institute of Mining Engineers*, vol. 20, 1891, pp. 529-30.

70 Froude, *Oceana*, p. 134.

71 Trollope, *Australia and New Zealand*, p. 276.

72 Parkes to Selby, 20 Dec. 1881, 24 Oct. 1884 (A.N.Z. Bank records).

73 *Town Life*, pp. 188-9. In general on the banks, Butlin, *A.N.Z. Bank*, pp. 231-43; Blainey, *Gold and Paper*, chs 8-9; Franklyn, *A Glance at Australia*, pp. 319-32; Coghlan, *Labour and Industry*, vol. 3, pp. 1683-90.

74 Butlin, *Investment*, pp. 383-9.

75 Parkes to Selby, Confidential letters, 1884-6 (A.N.Z. Bank records); Coghlan, *Labour and Industry*, vol. 3, p. 1690.

76 Butlin, *A.N.Z. Bank*, p. 236; Goodwin, *Economic Enquiry in Australia*, pp. 156-60, 186-90.

77 Franklyn, *A Glance at Australia*, pp. 214-316, *passim*; Sutherland, *Victoria and its Metropolis*, vol. 2, pp. 539-731, *passim*; Davison, ' "Marvellous Melbourne" ', ch. 1.

78 Twopeny, *Town Life*, pp. 199-202, 190-5.

79 Fry, 'Urban Wage Earning Class', pp. 47-52, 537, for an indication of how approximate these figures are.

80 Ibid., pp. 55-63, 541, 556.

81 Report of the Chief Inspector of Factories for 1889, *P.P.*, 1890, vol. 2, no. 22, p. 8.

82 Fry, op. cit., pp. 535-7. Butlin, *Investment*, pp. 201-10, for a general treatment of manufacturing development. Parsons, 'Manufacturing in Melbourne', ch. 3, for analysis of the location of industry.

83 Parsons, op. cit., pp. 324-36.

84 Franklyn, *A Glance at Australia*, pp. 278-81; Swallow & Ariell collection (Univ. Melb.).

85 Franklyn, op. cit., pp. 283-6, 306-9; Withers, *History of Ballarat*, pp. 295-6.

86 George Taylor, *Making it Happen. The Rise of Sir Macpherson Robertson, Kt., F.R.G.S.* (Melb., 1934), pp. 41-7.

87 MS. (typescript) history of Carlton and United Breweries (NL).

88 Ibid.; *P.D.*, vol. 61, pp. 1491-2; *Age*, 11 July 1889, p. 5; Cyril Pearl, *Beer, Glorious Beer!* (Melb., 1969), pp. 53, 57-9; Parsons, 'Manufacturing in Melbourne', pp. 336-50.

89 *Argus*, 18 Apr. 1885, p. 13.

90 Geoffrey Blainey, *One Hundred Years. Johns & Waygood Limited. 1856-1956* (Melb., n.d.), pp. 1-16.

91 For this paragraph, Parsons, 'Manufacturing in Melbourne', chs 2, 3, 6, 9.

92 *Argus*, 14 Apr. 1883, p. 12; *P.D.*, vol. 40, p. 1236; Withers, *History of Ballarat*, p. 293; Parsons, op. cit., pp. 257-91.

93 Helen Hughes, *The Australian Iron and Steel Industry 1848-1962* (Melb., 1964), pp. 16-17; Parsons, op. cit., pp. 350-53.

94 *Argus*, 4 Apr. 1885, p. 13; Leavitt and Lilburn, *Jubilee History*, vol. 2, pt 5.

95 Parsons, op. cit., ch. 7; Hugh Lennon & Co. records (Univ. Melb. Archives).

96 Parsons, op. cit., pp. 319-23; D. W. Meinig, *On the Margins of the Good Earth. The South Australian Wheat Frontier 1869-1884* (London, 1962), ch. 6, especially pp. 106-10.

97 Parsons, op. cit., ch. 10; Michaelis, Hallenstein records (A.N.U. Archives).

98 Fitzgerald, *The Printers of Melbourne*, pp. 62-3.

99 E. H. Sugden and F. W. Eggleston, *George Swinburne. A Biography* (Sydney, 1931), pp. 407-8; Swinburne records (Univ. Melb. Archives).

1 Franklyn, *A Glance at Australia*, pp. 247-9.

2 J. R. Poynter, *Russell Grimwade* (Melb., 1967), ch. 1. In the preceding section on manufacturing, my debt to George Parsons's excellent thesis is obvious. The Report of the Royal Commission on the Tariff of 1882-3 and the evidence presented (see Bibliography) are a mine of information. There are illuminating entries in the *A.D.B.* on many of the people mentioned. See also Davison, ' "Marvellous Melbourne" ', ch. 2.

3 *Argus*, 14 Mar. 1889, p. 11; *P.D.*, vol. 57, *passim*; Final Report of the Royal Commission on Coal, *P.P.*, 1891, vol. 6, no. 178; *Land of the Lyre Bird*, pp. 230-7.

4 Harper, *James Balfour*, p. 99.

5 *P.D.*, vol. 54, p. 669.

6 Report of the Royal Commission on the Tariff, *P.P.*, 1883, vol. 4, no. 50, pp. 341-8; Patterson, *The Tariff in the Australian Colonies*, p. 92.

7 *Argus*, 2 Jan. 1884, p. 5; 26 Mar., p. 9; 1 June, p. 5; 24 July 1886, p. 13; *P.D.*, vols 51-2, *passim*; vol. 60, p. 846; Smith, *Liberty and Liberalism*, p. 343; Parsons, op. cit., ch. 2.

8 *Age*, 1 Feb. 1886, p. 4.

9 *Age*, 16 Aug. 1887, edit.; *Argus*, 17 June 1889, p. 6.

10 Dilke, *Problems of Greater Britain*, p. 113.

11 Parsons, op. cit., chs 4-5, for a very sceptical view of the effects of protection.
12 *Age*, 9 Apr. 1887, p. 4; see also 2, 6 and 7 Apr. for other articles in the series, 'Protection in Victoria versus Free Trade in New South Wales'.
13 E. Pulsford, 'The Australian Lesson', *Nineteenth Century*, vol. 24, Sept. 1888, p. 409.
14 Turner, *History of Victoria*, vol. 2, pp. 350-2.
15 *Argus*, 8 Oct., p. 9; 22 Oct. 1889, p. 5.
16 Reeves, *State Experiments*, vol. 1, pp. 42-4; W. A. Sinclair, 'The Tariff and Manufacturing Employment in Victoria, 1860-1900', *Economic Record*, vol. 31, May 1955, pp. 100-4; D. B. Copland, *W. E. Hearn: First Australian Economist* (Melb., 1935), pp. 68-9; La Nauze, *Alfred Deakin*, vol. 1, p. 38; Patterson, *The Tariff in the Australian Colonies, passim.*
17 Adams, *The Australians*, p. 25.
18 Butlin, *Investment*, ch. 3; Blainey, *Tyranny of Distance*, pp. 264-5; Briggs, *Victorian Cities*, pp. 314-17.
19 Hall, *Stock Exchange*, pp. 50, 52, and 'Kinked Age Distribution', p. 46.
20 Butlin, *Investment*, p. 260; Fry, 'Urban Wage Earning Class', p. 586.
21 Butlin, *Investment*, ch. 4.
22 E.g. Chambers of Commerce and Manufactures, *Argus*, 12 Apr. 1883, p. 11.
23 Butlin, *Investment*, pp. 291-8, 390-404.
24 Geoffrey Blainey, *A History of Camberwell* (Melb., 1964), pp. 50-4.
25 Blainey, *Tyranny of Distance*, p. 237; Priestley, *Warracknabeal*, p. 64; Bossence, *Kyabram*, pp. 61-2.
26 Blainey, *Tyranny of Distance*, pp. 255-6; Wettenhall, *Railway Management*, pp. 31-40; Dilke, *Problems of Greater Britain*, pp. 119-21.
27 Butlin, *Investment*, pp. 368-9, 399, 416-17; Shann, *Economic History*, pp. 295-7, 305-6.
28 Blainey, *Tyranny of Distance*, p. 261.
29 Butlin, *Investment*, pp. 307-14, 402-3; Priestley, *Echuca*, pp. 124, 128-9; Franklyn, *A Glance at Australia*, pp. xxiv, 266-70.
30 *Victorian Year Book*, 1884-5, para. 1087; *Tramway Guide to Melbourne and Suburbs* (Melb., 1894); Moore, 'Marvellous Melbourne', pp. 28-30; Cannon, *Land Boomers*, p. 44; J. D. Keating, *Mind the Curve!* (Melb., 1970); Davison, 'Public Utilities and the Expansion of Melbourne', pp. 180-81.
31 Boyd, *Australia's Home*, pp. 233-4; Davison, op. cit., pp. 185-7.
32 For an entertaining description, Keith Dunstan, *The Paddock that Grew. The Story of the Melbourne Cricket Club* (Melb., 1962), p. 52.
33 *Argus*, 7 Apr. 1883, p. 9; 26 Sept. 1888, p. 9; Butlin, *A.N.Z. Bank*, p. 257.
34 Chamber of Commerce Minute-book, 1888, Annual Report (La Trobe Lib.); *P.D.*, vol. 55, pp. 1117-37; *Argus*, 11 Mar., p. 7; 14 Aug. 1886, p. 9; Boyd, op. cit., pp. 234-5.
35 *Argus*, 26 June 1883, p. 5; *Age*, 20 Aug. 1887, p. 14.
36 Boyd, op. cit., pp. 48, 52.
37 *Argus*, 8 Feb. 1884, p. 10.
38 Brennan to Prof. Kernot, 14 Jan. 1884 (Kernot Papers, La Trobe Lib.); L. Hayward, *The History of Air Cushion Vehicles* (London, 1963), p. 25.
39 Twopeny, *Town Life*, 'Servants'; *Argus*, 5 May 1885, p. 5; *Age*, 4 Apr. 1885, edit.; Butlin, *A.N.Z. Bank*, p. 258.
40 *P.D.*, vol. 42, p. 89.
41 Butlin, *A.N.Z. Bank*, p. 235; Blainey, *Gold and Paper*, p. 127.
42 *A.I.B.R.*, June 1885, p. 315.
43 Parkes to Selby, Confidential letters (A.N.Z. Bank records); *Argus*, 1 Jan. 1885, p. 4; Turner, *History of Victoria*, vol. 2, pp. 248-9; Coghlan, *Labour and Industry*, vol. 3, pp. 1683-90; Butlin, *Investment*, pp. 164-5, 286-7; Hall, *Stock Exchange*, pp. 52, 92-9. Boehm (*Prosperity and Depression*, ch. 3) detects peaks in growth in 1882 and late 1885 and a slight trough in 1884.

3 CLASS AND THE RISE OF LABOUR

1 Cambridge *Thirty Years*, pp. 132-4.
2 Trollope, *Australia and New Zealand*, pp. 304-5.
3 Pearson, 'Democracy in Victoria', p. 690.
4 Cf. Twopeny, *Town Life*, p. 189.
5 'A Few Banking Questions', *Melbourne Review*, vol. 4, 1879, p. 256.
6 Twopeny, op. cit., pp. 105-9.
7 Ada Cambridge, *The Three Miss Kings* (Melb., 1891), pp. 286-7.
8 Twopeny, op. cit., pp. 107-8.

9 Archibald Forbes, 'Some Social Characteristics of Australia', *Contemporary Review*, vol. 44, Oct. 1883, p. 610.
10 Cambridge's *The Three Miss Kings* is excellent for social atmosphere.
11 R. H. Croll, *I Recall. Collections and Recollections* (Melb., 1939), p. 13; cf. N. Lindsay, 'Uncles and Others', *Southerly*, 1955, no. 1, p. 3; M. M. Knowles, *Barbara Halliday* (Melb., n.d.), pp. 46-7.
12 Fry, 'Urban Wage Earning Class', p. 511.
13 Ibid., p. 13.
14 Cambridge, *Thirty Years*, p. 288; Sugden letters (MS., La Trobe Lib.), 10 Feb. 1888; Pelham C. Young Journals (MS., NL); R. C. Seaton, *Six Letters from the Colonies* (Hull, 1886), p. 39.
15 Adams, *Australian Essays*, p. 33.
16 'Tom Collins', 'The Passing of a Pioneer', *Meanjin Papers*, vol. 2, no. 3, Spring 1943, p. 31.
17 Cf. Twopeny, *Town Life*, p. 111.
18 Moorhouse, 'Victoria', p. 55.
19 H. G. Turner, 'Advance Australia', *Melbourne Review*, vol. 7, 1882, pp. 162-5.
20 Twopeny, *Town Life*, pp. 18, 97; Froude, quoted by Waldo Hilary Dunn, *James Anthony Froude. A Biography* (Oxford, 1963), vol. 2, p. 534; John Rae, 'The Eight Hours Day in Victoria', *Economic Journal*, vol. 1, Mar. 1891, p. 41.
21 These comparisons are based on T. A. Coghlan's calculations for the 1890s (*A Statistical Account of the Seven Colonies of Australasia 1897-8* (Sydney, 1898), pp. 352-60). They certainly apply just as strongly to the 1880s.
22 Rae, 'The Eight Hours Day in Victoria', p. 31.
23 Fry, 'Urban Wage Earning Class', pt 3, chs 1-2, and p. 578.
24 Blainey, *Gold and Paper*, p. 219; Butlin, *A.N.Z. Bank*, pp. 260-1; Davison, ' "Marvellous Melbourne" ', appendix 3.
25 Boyd, *Australia's Home*, p. 50; *Australasian Builder and Contractor's News*, 30 Nov. 1889, p. 523.
26 Fry, 'Urban Wage Earning Class', pp. 402ff., for much of the paragraph.
27 John Freeman, *Lights and Shadows of Melbourne Life* (London, 1888), *passim*; Fry, op. cit., pp. 491-7; R. E. Kennedy, 'The Charity Organization Movement in Melbourne' (M.A., Univ. Melb., 1967), *passim*. For living conditions in one of the most depressed areas, see Barrett, 'The Making of an Industrial Environment', pp. 185-95.
28 *Age*, 31 May 1884, p. 10; *Argus*, 21 Aug. 1886, p. 11; *P.D.*, vol. 45, p. 541; vol. 52, pp. 1152-3; vol. 54, p. 358; Fry, op. cit., pt 3, ch. 3, pp. 342ff.; Butlin, *Investment in Australian Economic Development*, pp. 390-1.
29 J. T. Sutcliffe, *A History of Trade Unionism in Australia* (Melb., 1921), pp. 35-6.
30 Norton, *History of Capital and Labour*, p. 150.
31 Coghlan, *Labour and Industry*, vol. 3, p. 1494.
32 Philipp, 'Trade Union Organization', ch. 4; R. N. Ebbels, *The Australian Labour Movement 1850-1907* (Sydney, 1960), pp. 87-92.
33 Fitzgerald, *The Printers of Melbourne*, pp. 46-7; Philipp, op. cit., pp. 165ff.
34 Philipp, op. cit., pp. 60-2, 77-8, for list of unions; Fry, 'Urban Wage Earning Class', pp. 172-3, for 1882-3 campaigns; Gollan, *Radical and Working Class Politics*, p. 89.
35 Fitzgerald, op. cit., pp. 55-62.
36 *Argus*, 15 Feb. 1883, p. 8.
37 Sutcliffe, op. cit., p. 30.
38 *Age*, 28 Apr. 1888, p. 4.
39 *Argus*, 23 May 1884, p. 5.
40 Quoted by Philipp, 'Trade Union Organization', p. 169.
41 *Argus*, 15 Dec. 1888, p. 9.
42 Philipp, op. cit., pp. 165-86.
43 *Argus*, 8 Mar. 1884, p. 10.
44 *Argus*, 24 Apr. 1884, p. 9.
45 *The Second Intercolonial Trades Union Congress. An Official Report of the Debates* (Melb., 1884); Sutcliffe, op. cit., pp. 47-51.
46 *Age*, 16 June, 1884, p. 3.
47 *Argus*, 6 Nov. 1884, p. 5.
48 *Age*, 11 Dec. 1882, edit.; 2 Sept. 1884, p. 6; Coghlan, *Labour and Industry*, vol. 3, p. 1476; Fry, 'Urban Wage Earning Class', pp. 474-81.
49 *P.D.*, vols 40, 43, 47, 51; Annual Reports of the Proceedings of the Government Statist in connexion with Trades Unions, *P.P.*, 1887- ; Fry, op. cit., pp. 487ff.; Sutcliffe, op. cit., pp. 56-9.
50 Fry, op. cit., p. 209.
51 *Argus*, 3 Aug. 1883, p. 3.
52 *P.D.*, vol. 49, pp. 1213-30, 1401-3.
53 John Rae, 'The Eight Hours Day in Victoria', *Economic Journal*, vol. 1, Mar. 1891, pp. 15-42 (pp. 19-20 for the bakers); Fry, op. cit., pt 2, ch. 4.
54 M. M. Ballou, *Travels Under the Southern Cross . . .* (Boston, 1887), pp. 202-3.

55 Gane, *N.S.W. and Victoria*, pp. 149-50; Fry, op. cit., pp. 289-90.
56 *Argus*, 22 Apr. 1885, p. 6. 57 *Argus*, 19 Apr. 1888, p. 7.
58 Clive Turnbull, *Bluestone. The Story of James Stephens* (Melb., 1945); *Recorder* (Melb. branch, Aust. Society for the Study of Labour History), vol. 1, no. 7, June 1965.
59 F. T. Derham to T. Swallow, 16 Nov. 1885 (Derham letter-books, Univ. Melb. Archives).
60 *Age*, 14 Sept. 1880, p. 3. 61 *P.D.*, vol. 37, pp. 436-45.
62 Progress Report of the Commission of Enquiry into the Hours of Employés in Shops, *P.P.*, 1882, vol. 3, no. 43; J. Hagan, 'Employers, Trade Unions and the First Victorian Factory Acts', *Labour History*, no. 7, Nov. 1964; Fry, op. cit., pp. 151ff., 260ff.; Gollan, *Radical and Working Class Politics*, pp. 88-9; Fitzgerald, *The Printers of Melbourne*, pp. 43-6; F. H. Cutler, 'A History of The Anti-Sweating Movement in Victoria 1873-96' (M.A., Univ. Melb., 1956), ch. 1.
63 *Age*, Dec. 1882-Feb. 1883; *Argus*, 13 Feb., p. 8; 22 Feb. 1883, p. 8; 18 Apr. 1885, p. 13; Norton, *History of Capital and Labour*, pp. 168-9; Coghlan, *Labour and Industry*, vol. 3, pp. 1484-5.
64 Second Progress Report, *P.P.*, 1883 (2nd Session), vol. 2, no. 16; On the Operation of the Victorian Factory Act 1874, *P.P.*, 1884, vol. 2, no. 18; On the Employment of Barmaids, ibid., no. 29; Final Report, ibid., vol. 3, no. 39.
65 Reeves, *State Experiments*, vol. 2, pp. 6-7.
66 Fry, op. cit., *passim*, especially pp. 180-1. 67 *Argus*, 1 Apr. 1884, p. 7.
68 *Argus*, 19 Sept., p. 5; 26 Nov. 1884, p. 5; 16 Apr. 1887, p. 5; cf. Smith, *Liberty and Liberalism*, pp. 358-68.
69 Fry, op. cit., pp. 121-47, 386-7. 70 *Argus*, 22 May 1885, p. 6.
71 *Argus*, 24 Aug. 1885, p. 10.
72 *P.D.*, vol. 47, pp. 2167-73; vol. 49, pp. 1438-53; vol. 50, pp. 1756-60 (Deakin), 1871 (Service), 2254 (Wallace); Fry, op. cit., pp. 184ff.; Deakin to Dilke, 30 Aug. 1888 (Dilke Papers).
73 Annual reports of the Chief Inspector of Factories, Workrooms and Shops, *P.P.*, 1887- ; for Employers' Liability, *P.D.*, vols. 43, 45, 47, 49-50, 53; Ingham, 'Aspects of Victorian Liberalism', pp. 98-100.
74 *Argus*, 6 Mar., p. 9; 5 Apr., p. 5; 6 Apr., p. 5; 14 July, p. 7; 5 Aug. 1886, p. 6; 28 Feb. 1887, p. 10; 9 Jan. 1889, p. 5; *Table Talk*, 8 Apr. 1886; Dilke, *Problems of Greater Britain*, pp. 149-51; Reeves, *State Experiments*, vol. 2, pp. 181-91; Fry, op. cit., 266ff.
75 Hume Cook, MS. Autobiography (NL), p. 43; Hoare, *Looking Back Gaily*, p. 142.
76 *Argus*, 1 Dec. 1883, p. 11; 18 Jan., p. 7; 6 Oct. 1884, p. 5; *Outpost*, 25 Aug. 1900, p. 10; Deakin, *Federal Story*, pp. 71-2; Judith L. Watson, 'The Political Career of William Arthur Trenwith' (B.A. thesis, Monash Univ., 1965).
77 *Argus*, 6 Jan. 1885, p. 5.
78 Norton, *History of Capital and Labour*, pp. 158-66; Coghlan, *Labour and Industry*, vol. 4, pp. 2088-9; Sutcliffe, op. cit., pp. 37-9; Ebbels, op. cit., pp. 83-6; Fitzgerald, *The Printers of Melbourne*, pp. 65-6; Cutler, op. cit., pp. 38-42; Fry, op. cit., pp. 131-2.
79 Norton, *History of Capital and Labour*, pp. 166-7.
80 *Argus*, 18 June 1886, p. 5; *Leader*, 12 June 1886, p. 25; Report of the Chief Inspector of Factories, *P.P.*, 1889, vol. 3, no. 30, p. 8.
81 Philipp, 'Trade Union Organization', pp. 79-80. 82 *Argus*, 18 Dec. 1885, p. 5.
83 *Report of Royal Commission on Strikes* (Sydney, 1891), Evidence, p. 305.
84 *Bulletin*, 25 Jan. 1886, p. 4.
85 *Argus* and *Age*, 31 Dec. 1885-18 Jan. 1886; *Argus*, 4 Feb. 1886, p. 4, and following days; Norton, *History of Capital and Labour*, pp. 179-95; Sutcliffe, op. cit., pp. 40-3; G. R. Henning, 'Melbourne Shipowners and their Industrial Relations' (M.A., Univ. Melb., 1969), pp. 11-18.
86 Spence, *Australia's Awakening*, ch. 3; H. H. Pearce, 'The Amalgamated Miners' Association and the Creswick Gold Field', *Recorder*, vol. 3, no. 4, June 1968.
87 *Creswick Advertiser* and *Allendale Telegraph*, Dec. 1882; Blainey, *The Rush that Never Ended*, pp. 297-8.
88 *Age*, 26 Mar.-19 May 1885; Spence, *Australia's Awakening*, pp. 40-2.
89 *Argus*, 7 Sept. 1888, p. 7.
90 Spence, *Australia's Awakening*, pp. 23-52; Spence's evidence to the *Royal Commission on Strikes*, pp. 48-50 and App. 12; Margaret McAleese, 'Creswick in the 1880s' (B.A. thesis, Monash Univ., 1968), *passim*; Philipp, 'Trade Union Organization', ch. 7; Blainey, *The Rush that Never Ended*, pp. 297-301.

91 McAleese, op. cit., *passim*; Coral Lansbury, 'William Guthrie Spence', *Labour History*, no. 13, Nov. 1967.

92 Spence, *Australia's Awakening*, pp. 59-61; W. G. Spence, *History of the A.W.U.* (Sydney, 1961), pp. 15-18; *Shearers' Record*, Feb., Apr. 1889.

93 Spence, *History of the A.W.U.*, chs 1-2; Spence's evidence to the *Royal Commission on Strikes*, p. 54. Cf. E. L. Barnes, 'Shirtsleeves to Shirtsleeves' (MS., La Trobe Lib.), ch. 11, for the impression made on him as a child by the remarkable professional shearers on their annual visit to the Boort district.

94 Spence, *Australia's Awakening*, p. 61; *History of the A.W.U.*, p. 20; *Shearers' Record*, Feb. 1888.

95 Spence's letters to the *Argus*, 1 Sept., p. 8; 7 Sept. 1887, p. 6.

96 *Age* and *Argus*, Oct.-Nov. 1887, especially 30 Nov.; *Argus*, 21 Jan. 1888, p. 11.

97 *Argus*, 3 Mar. 1888, p. 12.

98 *Argus*, 1 June, p. 3; 17 Aug. 1888, p. 8; *Age*, 27 July 1888, p. 5.

99 Quoted by Philipp, 'Trade Union Organization', p. 139; *Age*, 4 Oct. 1888, p. 9.

1 Spence, *History of the A.W.U.*, p. 32.

2 *Argus*, 6 Nov., p. 8; 12 Nov., p. 7; 14 Nov., p. 13; 27 Nov. 1888, p. 7; 19 Mar. 1889, edit.; Spence, *History of the A.W.U.*, pp. 27-9.

3 Almost nothing is known of the early railway unions. The above unreliable account has been put together from Norton, *History of Capital and Labour*, p. 177; *Argus*, 1 Oct. 1883, p. 5; 2 Apr., p. 9; 18 Dec. 1885, p. 7; 26 Mar. 1886, p. 3.

4 *Argus*, 3 Aug., p. 6; 10 Aug. 1885, p. 5.

5 *Argus*, 9 Mar., p. 7; 13 Mar. 1886, p. 13; *Australasian*, 20 Mar. 1886, p. 553.

6 *Age* and *Argus*, 10 Jan.-18 Feb. 1888; *Leader*, 18 Feb. 1888, p. 30; *Argus*, 20 Aug. 1889, p. 5.

7 *Age*, 21 Mar. 1885, p. 4.

8 Fitzgerald, *The Printers of Melbourne*, p. 70.

9 Shop Employés Royal Commission. Final Report. Courts of Conciliation, *P.P.*, 1884, vol. 3, no. 39; *P.D.*, vol. 44, pp. 1513-17; vol. 46, pp. 815-20, 1514-19.

10 *Argus*, 3 Feb. 1885, p. 6.

11 *Victorian Review*, vol. 11, Mar. 1885.

12 *Argus*, 14 Mar. 1885, p. 13; 31 May 1887, p. 8; *Age*, 19 Mar. 1885, edit.

13 *Argus*, 4 Nov. 1885, p. 12.

14 *Argus*, 14 Mar., p. 7; 31 May 1887, p. 8. But cf. Murphy's opinion of Bruce Smith (Norton, *History of Capital and Labour*, p. 180).

15 *Argus*, 4 Aug., p. 7; 6 Aug. 1886, p. 5; 14 Mar. 1887, p. 7.

16 *Argus*, 13 Aug. 1886, p. 5; 15 Jan., p. 9; 21 May, p. 10; 5 Sept., p. 7; 28 Oct., p. 11; 12 Nov. 1887, p. 12; 26 Jan. 1888, p. 13; *Royal Commission on Strikes*, evidence by Lyell, pp. 306, 308.

17 *Argus*, 28 Oct. 1887, p. 11; Bruce Smith, 'Strikes and their Cure', *Centennial Magazine*, Oct. 1888; Rae, 'The Eight Hours Day in Victoria', pp. 29-30; Norton, *History of Capital and Labour*, pp. 195-6.

18 *Trades Hall Gazette*, late 1888. Note the subsequent eight-week strike at the Phoenix Foundry, Ballarat (*Argus*, 27 Apr., p. 10; 29 Apr., p. 6; 3 May, p. 14; 9 May 1889, p. 6).

19 Quoted Gollan, *Radical and Working Class Politics*, p. 85; Norton, *History of Capital and Labour*, p. 174.

20 *Age*, 23 June 1885, edit.; *Bulletin*, 26 Dec. 1885, p. 5.

21 *Argus*, 5 Sept. 1885, p. 10.

22 *Argus*, 5 Sept., p. 10; 14 Nov., p. 11; 25 Nov. 1885, p. 8.

23 *Argus*, 25 Nov., p. 8; 30 Nov., p. 5; 3 Dec., p. 5; 15 Dec. 1885, p. 5; 9 Jan. 1886, p. 10; Fitzgerald, *The Printers of Melbourne*, p. 67.

24 *Argus*, 2 Feb., p. 6; 20 Feb., p. 10; 1 Mar. 1886, p. 4; Ingham, 'Aspects of Victorian Liberalism', pp. 117-20.

25 Report of the Royal Commission on the Tariff, *P.P.*, 1883, vol. 4, no. 50, p. lxxv, and Evidence, *passim*; *Argus*, 8 Oct. 1885, p. 8.

26 See letter by Bennet, *Argus*, 25 May 1883, p. 7, for a good statement of the case. H. H. Hayter's *Handbook to the Colony of Victoria* (Melb., 1884) had glowing descriptions of working conditions which were severely qualified in the 1885 ed. after union protests.

27 *Argus*, 4 Dec. 1886, p. 9.

28 *P.D.*, vol. 57, p. 196.

29 *Age*, 18 June 1884, p. 7; Norton, *History of Capital and Labour*, p. 173. There had been a previous co-operative movement, in which John Ross was prominent, in 1872-4.

30 *Age*, 19 Jan., edit.; 19 Mar. 1885, edit.; 14 Apr. 1887, edit.; 20 Apr. 1888, edit.

31 *Age*, 23 Apr. 1888, p. 5. The Capital and Labour Federation League became the chief co-operative organization from 1889 but had little to do with the unions. B. Cowderoy, *On the Relations of Capital and Labour* (Melb., 1889); B. R. Marshall, 'Co-operation and Political Education', *Hist. Studies*, vol. 4, no. 15, Nov. 1950, p. 257.

32 *Argus*, 23 Dec. 1886, p. 6; 1 Feb. 1887, p. 6; *Liberator*, 1886, *passim*, and 5 June 1887; *Table Talk*, 1 Apr. 1887, p. 2; S. Merrifield, 'The Melbourne Anarchist Club 1886-1891', *Labour History*, no. 3, Nov. 1962.

33 Reeves, *State Experiments*, vol. 2, p. 4.

34 Cf. Philipp, 'Trade Union Organization', pp. 48-9.

4 THE CHURCHES UNDER STRESS

1 Moorhouse, 'Victoria', p. 55.

2 J. S. Gregory, 'Church and State, and Education in Victoria to 1872', E. L. French (ed.), *Melbourne Studies in Education 1958-1959* (Melb., 1960), pp. 67-71.

3 Geoffrey Blainey, *A Centenary History of the University of Melbourne* (Melb., 1957), pp. 47-8.

4 C. H. Spence, *An Autobiography* (Adelaide, 1910), pp. 52-3.

5 F. B. Smith, 'Spiritualism in Victoria in the Nineteenth Century', *Journal of Religious History*, vol. 3, no. 3, June 1965; La Nauze, *Alfred Deakin*, vol. 1, pp. 55-61.

6 Smith, 'Religion and Freethought', pp. 7-8.

7 Ibid., pp. 293-309, for clerical attempts to defend the literal truth of the Bible and for early controversy between churchmen.

8 G. Walters, 'Some Aspects of Religious Thought in Melbourne', *Melbourne Review*, vol. 10, 1885, p. 4.

9 MS. Autobiography (Higgins Papers), pp. 64-5; see also the moving entry for 26 Jan. 1878 in his Note-book. Cf. A. D. Mickle's description of a child's picture of God (*Of Many Things*, Sydney, 1941, pp. 28-9).

10 Blair to Hingston, 23 June 1895 (Blair letters, La Trobe Lib.); cf. Geo. Belcher's simple faith (Belcher diaries, La Trobe Lib.).

11 Ada Cambridge, *The Three Miss Kings* (Melb., 1891), pp. 157, 168, 188-9.

12 Stebbing, *Charles Henry Pearson*, p. 235; Pratt, *David Syme*, p. 258; La Nauze, *Alfred Deakin*, vol. 1, ch. 3.

13 *Victorian Review*, vol. 1, no. 1, 1879, pp. 65-75; Moorhouse, 'Civilization without Delusion: A Reply', ibid., no. 2, 1879, pp. 242-59; Clarke, 'A Letter to his Lordship the Anglican Bishop of Melbourne', *Melbourne Review*, vol. 5, 1880, pp. 103-12.

14 Higinbotham, *Science and Religion* (Melb., 1883), pp. 14-15.

15 Turner, 'Mr Higinbotham on Pulpit Influence', *Melbourne Review*, vol. 8, 1883, p. 383.

16 Turner, ibid.; *Argus*, 25 Sept. 1883, p. 9.

17 *The Bishop of Melbourne in Reply to Judge Williams on Religion without Superstition* (Melb., 1885).

18 *Argus*, 23 Sept. 1884, p. 9.

19 Twopeny, *Town Life*, p. 117.

20 Quoted by Edith C. Rickards, *Bishop Moorhouse of Melbourne and Manchester* (London, 1920), p. 119; Smith, 'Religion and Freethought', pp. 229-30.

21 Rickards, op. cit., pp. 90, 77.

22 *Argus*, 25 Sept. 1883, p. 9.

23 *Argus*, late Feb. 1883, for a tremendous controversy.

24 Dunstan, *Wowsers*, pp. 137-8.

25 *Age*, 1 Oct. 1887, edit.; *Argus*, 31 Mar. 1886, p. 6.

26 Moorhouse to Gladstone, 25 July 1883 (Gladstone Papers, CCCXCVII, BM, Add. MSS. 44482).

27 Bishop Armstrong, quoted by Rickards, op. cit., p. 75. In general for Moorhouse, Rickards, op. cit.; Jill Roe, 'Challenge and Response', pp. 157-60; H. R. Haweis, *Travel and Talk* (London, 1896), vol. 2, pp. 99-101; *Imperial Review*, Jan. and Oct. 1886; *Bulletin*, 23 Jan. 1886, p. 7.

28 John Stanley James, *The Vagabond Papers*, ed. Michael Cannon (Melb., 1969), p. 107; pp. 110-11 for his impressions of Strong as a preacher.

29 Moncure D. Conway, *My Pilgrimage to the Wise Men of the East* (London, 1906), p. 75.

30 Smith, 'Religion and Freethought', p. 310.

31 Roe, 'Challenge and Response', p. 160.

32 Strong to James Lorimer, 28 July 1881 (Strong Papers, La Trobe Lib.).

33 *Argus*, 4 July, edit.; 5 July 1883, p. 7. 34 *Argus*, 8 Aug. 1883, p. 7.
35 *Argus*, 9 Aug. 1883, p. 11. 36 *Argus*, 11 Aug. 1883, p. 5.
37 McEachran to Strong, 28 Aug. 1883 (Strong Papers).
38 Strong to Pearson, 31 Aug., 1 Oct. 1883 (Pearson Papers).
39 *Argus*, 6 Sept. 1883, p. 5. 40 *Argus*, 15 Nov. 1883, p. 5.
41 *Argus*, 16 Nov. 1883, p. 5.
42 Morrison to Strong, 27 Aug. 1883; Strong to Morrison, 6 Sept. 1883 (Strong Papers).
43 *Argus*, 8 Sept., p. 9; 28 Nov. 1883, p. 11.
44 Harper, *James Balfour*, pp. 238, 237.
45 *P.D.*, vol. 45, pp. 515-26; vols 46-7, pp. 703-2126; *Argus*, May 1884.
46 *Argus*, 5 Oct. 1885, p. 5; 18 May, p. 6; 10 June 1886, p. 6.
47 *Age*, *Argus*, throughout Mar. 1886; *Argus*, 12-13 Nov. 1886.
48 *Age*, 20 Mar. 1886, p. 13. 49 *Argus*, 27 Jan., p. 7; 9 Feb. 1887, p. 9.
50 *Age*, 9 Feb. 1887, pp. 5-6; *Argus*, 24 Nov. 1887, p. 8.
51 *Argus*, 24 Sept. 1884, p. 10; 13 Mar. 1886, p. 10.
52 Roe, 'Challenge and Response', pp. 160-6; Aeneas Macdonald, *One Hundred Years of Presbyterianism in Victoria* (Melb., 1937), chs 13-14; *Australian Herald*, Sept. 1889, pp. 18-19; E. Jones, 'The Solitary Bishop' (B.A. thesis, Univ. Melb., 1954); R. White, 'Presbyterian People in Victoria 1880-1900' (B.A. thesis, Univ. Melb., 1964) is a study of Presbyterianism at parish level.
53 C. Strong, *The Broad Church* (Melb., 1889), notice on last page.
54 Roe, 'Challenge and Response', p. 166.
55 *Addresses Delivered in connection with the Opening of the new Unitarian Church* (Melb., 1887); A. W. Gosman, *Mr. Justice Higinbotham on the Orthodox Faith* (Melb., 1887); Roe, op. cit., pp. 156-7.
56 *Argus*, 27 Jan. 1887, p. 7.
57 W. J. Palamountain, *A. R. Edgar: a Methodist Greatheart* (Melb., 1933), p. 91.
58 Renate Howe, 'Social Composition of the Wesleyan Church in Victoria during the Nineteenth Century', *Journal of Religious History*, vol. 4, no. 3, June 1967; Howe, 'The Wesleyan Church in Victoria'; C. I. Benson, *A Century of Victorian Methodism* (Melb., 1935); W. L. Blamires and John B. Smith, *The Early Story of the Wesleyan Methodist Church in Victoria* (Melb., 1886).

Histories of other denominations include: F. J. Wilkin, *Baptists in Victoria. Our First Century* (Melb., 1939); A. W. Stephenson, *One Hundred Years: a Statement of the Development and Accomplishment of Churches of Christ in Australia* (Melb., 1946); L. M. Goldman, *The Jews in Victoria in the Nineteenth Century* (Melb., 1954). See Roe, 'Challenge and Response', pp. 155-6, for comment on the Congregationalists.
59 Harper, *James Balfour*, p. 165.
60 *Advocate*, quoted by Smith, 'Religion and Freethought', p. 332.
61 Patrick O'Farrell, *The Catholic Church in Australia. A Short History: 1788-1967* (Melb., 1968), pp. 139-40; John H. Molony, *The Roman Mould of the Australian Catholic Church* (Melb., 1969), p. 127.
62 T. L. Suttor, *Hierarchy and Democracy in Australia 1788-1870 . . .* (Melb., 1965), p. 217.
63 *Advocate*, 6 Jan. 1883, p. 13. 64 O'Farrell, op. cit., p. 161.
65 *Liberator*, 25 Oct. 1885; Smith 'Religion and Freethought', pp. 186-7.
66 Smith, 'Spiritualism in Victoria' (see note 5), pp. 255-6.
67 *Argus*, 26 Jan. 1884, p. 9. 68 *Liberator*, 15 Jan. 1888.
69 Cambridge, *Thirty Years*, pp. 293-4.
70 *Argus*, 20 Mar. 1886, p. 10; Smith, 'Religion and Freethought', pp. 272-3.
71 *Argus*, 30 Oct. 1886, p. 9. 72 *Liberator*, 26 Dec. 1886.
73 *Liberator*, 23 Nov. 1884. 74 *Liberator*, 16 Nov. 1884.
75 The above is largely based on Smith, 'Religion and Freethought', ch. 5; see also G. Duncan, 'The Wisdom of the Greeks' (B.A. thesis, Univ. Melb., 1957), pp. 22-37.
76 Cambridge, *Thirty Years*, p. 292.
77 *Argus*, 23 July 1883, p. 6; Glenison Alsop, 'The Salvation Army in Melbourne in the 1880s' (B.A. thesis, Monash Univ., 1969), p. 35; J. F. Horsley, *The Victorian Salvation War 1883* (Melb., n.d.), pp. 15-16.
78 *Argus*, 12 Apr. 1883, p. 7. 79 Alsop, op. cit., pp. 35-9.
80 Horsley, op. cit., p. 15.
81 Ballington Booth, *The Salvation War under the Generalship of William Booth; or, how we marched in 1884 through Australasia* (Melb., 1885), pp. 17, 29.

82 *Age*, 23 July 1884, p. 7; *Argus*, 19 Aug. 1884, p. 7; *Age*, 4 Nov. 1885, p. 11.
83 *Argus*, 12 Oct. 1885, p. 5; cf. *Age*, 14 Apr. 1883, supp.; *Advocate*, 15 Dec. 1883, edit.; 17 Oct. 1885; 24 Sept. 1887; Cambridge, *Thirty Years*, p. 287.
84 *Herald*, 12 Sept. 1882, edit.; *Argus*, 23 Sept. 1884, p. 9.
85 Booth, op. cit., p. 28.
86 Alsop, op. cit., ch. 3.
87 Ibid., pp. 65-6.
88 R. Sandell, *The History of the Salvation Army* (London, vol. 3, 1955), ch. 1.
89 In general, Alsop, Booth, Horsley, Sandell, op. cit.; Adams, *Australian Essays; Imperial Review*, no. 13, Apr. 1885; Percival Dale, *Salvation Chariot: a Review of the first seventy-one Years of the Salvation Army in Australia 1880-1951* (Melb., 1952); K. S. Inglis, *Churches and the Working Classes in Victorian England* (London, 1963), ch. 5, for the Army in England.
90 *Argus*, 4 May 1888, p. 8.
91 *Harbinger of Light*, Jan. 1887; *Imperial Review*, no. 17, Jan. 1886, p. 59; Pearson, 'Democracy in Victoria', p. 701; *Age*, 2 June 1883, edit.
92 *Age*, 18 May 1883, edit.
93 Dale, *Impressions of Australia*, pp. 243-4.
94 *Argus*, 6 Aug. 1886, p. 6; 6 Sept. 1887, p. 5.
95 *Argus*, 12 Apr., p. 6; 15 Apr. 1886, p. 7.
96 *Argus*, 3 May, p. 7; 4 May 1888, p. 8; Smith, 'Religion and Freethought', pp. 330-3.
97 Roe, 'Challenge and Response', p. 166.
98 Cf. Louis B. Wright, *Culture on the Moving Frontier* (Harper Torchbooks, 1961), pp. 182-3.

5 EVANGELICALS IN ACTION

1 Lingham, *Juvenal in Melbourne*, p. 20.
2 Sugden letters (La Trobe Lib.), quoted by Howe, 'The Wesleyan Church in Victoria', p. 132.
3 W. H. Fitchett in Harper, *James Balfour*, pp. 219, 220, 223.
4 *Argus*, 23 May 1883, p. 5, for formation of an organization in the Collingwood-Fitzroy area to provide instruction; A. G. Austin, *Australian Education 1788-1900 . . .* (Melb., 1961), pp. 230-2.
5 Harper, *James Balfour*, p. 178.
6 E.g. Robert Harper's 1885 motion, *P.D.*, vol. 49, pp. 1292-311.
7 *Argus*, 19 Mar. 1886, p. 5; Howe, 'The Wesleyan Church in Victoria', pp. 69-71.
8 Report of the Royal Commission on Education, *P.P.*, 1884, vol. 3, no. 47, p. 34.
9 *Advocate*, 3 Mar., 9 June, 20 Oct., 27 Oct. 1883; J. F. Hogan, *The Sister Dominions* (London, 1896), p. 19.
10 *Age*, 30 Oct. 1883, p. 4.
11 Michie, *Observations on the Working of the Victorian Education Act . . .* (Melb., 1885), p. 41; *Age*, 10 Jan. 1887, edit.; 19 Jan., p. 7, for reply by Benjamin Hoare; *Leader*, 6 Oct. 1888, p. 26.
12 Royal commission report, p. 34.
13 *Australasian*, 1 Nov. 1884, p. 881; cf. *Argus*, 28 Apr. 1884, p. 6, for another militant statement.
14 *Argus*, 21 Jan. 1885, p. 9; N. Fitzgerald to W. H. Archer, 1 Jan. 1886; Archbishop Goold to Archer, 26 May 1886 (Archer Papers, Univ. Melb. Archives).
15 *Argus*, 23 May 1883, p. 5; Harper, *James Balfour*, p. 200.
16 C. H. Pearson, *Religious Teaching in Schools* (Melb., 1889), pp. 10-11.
17 *P.D.*, vols. 60-2 (Education Law Further Amendment Bill); *Argus*, 16 July, edit.; 27 July 1889, p. 13; Tregenza, *Professor of Democracy*, pp. 211-14.
18 Sugden letters, 22 Mar. 1889; cf. *Argus*, 18 Sept. 1886, p. 13.
19 A. Sutherland, *Melbourne Review*, vol. 9, 1884, p. 480; *Argus*, 2 Apr. 1885, p. 10, for a defence of the Act by Patterson.
20 Dale, *Impressions of Australia*, p. 235.
21 W. H. Fitchett, 'The Sunday Question', *Melbourne Review*, vol. 8, 1883, p. 348; J. L. Rentoul, ibid., p. 308.
22 *Argus*, 21 Oct. 1884, p. 6.
23 *Argus*, 10 Feb. 1883, p. 9.
24 *P.D.*, vol. 43, p. 176.
25 *Argus*, 17 May 1883, p. 9.
26 *P.D.*, vol. 43, pp. 49-89, 176; vol. 60, p. 116.
27 *Argus*, 31 Oct. 1889, p. 7; *P.D.*, vol. 61, pp. 1457-64; vol. 64, pp. 1411-20; vol. 65, pp. 2104-5.

28 For the above, *Age* and *Argus*, late Apr.-early May 1883; F. B. Smith, 'The Sunday Observance Controversy in Melbourne 1874-1910' (B.A. thesis, Univ. Melb., 1956); Dunstan, *Wowsers*, ch. 2; Tregenza, *Professor of Democracy*, pp. 175-82.
29 *Argus*, 3 May 1883, p. 7.
30 *Argus*, 7, 8, 9, 24, 25 May 1883; cf. *Daily Telegraph*, May 1883; *Herald*, 21 May 1883, p. 2.
31 Smith, 'The Sunday Observance Controversy'; Dunstan, *Wowsers*, pp. 23-7.
32 *Argus*, 5 Dec. 1884, p. 4; *P.D.*, vol. 47, pp. 2417-36.
33 *Argus*, 21 Feb. 1888, p. 7.
34 *P.D.*, vol. 62, pp. 2167-78; *Argus*, 30 Aug., p. 5; 1 Oct. 1889, p. 7.
35 Mitchell, 'Temperance and the Liquor Question', p. 12.
36 Twopeny, *Town Life*, pp. 70-1.
37 Deakin to F. T. Derham, 10 Feb. 1885 (Derham Papers). Punctuation has been supplied.
38 *Imperial Review*, no. 11, Oct. 1883.
39 *Age*, 22 Apr. 1889, p. 5.
40 *Age*, 13 May, p. 5; 9 June 1884, p. 5.
41 Morris, *George Higinbotham*, pp. 275-7; Mitchell, 'Temperance and the Liquor Question', chs 2-3, for details of temperance bodies.
42 *Argus*, 10 Mar. 1885, p. 7; 5 Oct. 1887, p. 7.
43 Deakin, *Federal Story*, p. 33; *P.D.*, vol. 51, p. 713; Ann Mitchell, *A.D.B.*, vol. 5; Cannon, *Land Boomers*, ch. 12; A. D. Milner, 'James Munro. Banker, Boomster, Wowser and Temperant' (B.A. thesis, Monash Univ., 1965).
44 Howe, 'The Wesleyan Church in Victoria', p. 82.
45 *Argus*, 11 May 1886, p. 9; Aeneas Macdonald, *One Hundred Years of Presbyterianism in Victoria* (Melb., 1937), p. 103.
46 *Argus*, 5 Aug. 1889, p. 5.
47 For the above paragraph, Mitchell, op. cit., pp. 90-8.
48 Mitchell, op. cit., pp. 23-40; K. S. Inglis, *Hospital and Community. A History of the Royal Melbourne Hospital* (Melb., 1958), pp. 46-9.
49 *Argus*, 1 June 1883, p. 3.
50 *Argus*, 18 Sept. 1883, p. 6; 22 Sept. 1885, p. 9; 19 Mar. 1887, p. 10.
51 *Argus*, 2 Feb 1887, p. 4.
52 *Age*, 3 Dec. 1887, p. 4; Mitchell, op. cit., pp. 134-52; Dunstan, *Wowsers*, pp. 60-3.
53 *Age*, 5 July 1884, p. 9; *Argus*, 11 May 1886, p. 9.
54 Dunstan, *Wowsers*, p. 100.
55 Mitchell, op. cit., p. 89.
56 *Temperance in Australia. The Memorial Volume of the International Temperance Convention Melbourne 1888* (Melb., 1889), p. 11.
57 *Argus*, 5 Feb. 1885, p. 5.
58 *Argus*, 6 July 1888, p. 7, for membership of the local-option group.
59 *P.D.*, vol. 40, pp. 1175-94; *Argus*, 2 Aug. 1883, p. 11, for description of a typical deputation.
60 *Argus*, 15 July, p. 6; 2 Sept. 1884, p. 5.
61 *P.D.*, vols 48-50, *passim*.
62 *P.P.*, 1885, vol. 1, E8.
63 Quoted *P.D.*, vol. 48, p. 591.
64 *P.D.*, vols 55-6, pp. 1711-2650.
65 *Argus*, 12 Mar., p. 5; 24 Mar. 1888, p. 5; Lee, *One of Australia's Daughters*, chs 15-16; W. J. Palamountain, *A. R. Edgar: a Methodist Greatheart* (Melb., 1933), pp. 85-6.
66 Mitchell, op. cit., chs 4-5; J. S. Meagher, *Licensing Law in Victoria* (Melb., 1908).
67 Meudell, *Pleasant Career*, p. 273.
68 E.g. *Argus*, 21 Feb., p. 7; 26 June 1883, p. 6; 17 Jan. 1884, p. 5; Melbourne United Evangelistic Association, *Melbourne and its Sin* (Melb., 1880), p. 15.
69 *Argus*, 16 Feb. 1883, p. 11; 5 June 1884, p. 9; Bedford, *Naught to Thirty-three*, pp. 132-3.
70 *Herald*, 11 Dec. 1883-5 Feb. 1884; Donald S. Garden, '"Victorian" Sexual Morality in Melbourne in the 1880s' (B.A. thesis, Monash Univ., 1968), pp. 45-6.
71 Garden, op. cit., pp. 47-50.
72 Deakin, *P.D.*, vol. 53, p. 2277.
73 *Federal Gazette*, 17 Nov. 1888, p. 2; H. R. Rae, *Pencilling by Land and Sea* (Hokitika, N.Z., 1887), p. 147; *Victorian Independent*, June 1887, p. 88.
74 *Age*, 9 May 1889, p. 5.
75 *P.D.*, vol. 47, pp. 2463-7; vol. 49, pp. 1200-4; Garden, op. cit., pp. 36-50, 61-5.
76 Royal Commission on Employees in Shops; Report on the Employment of Barmaids, *P.P.*, 1884, vol. 2, no. 29, p. 4.
77 *Argus*, 28 Sept. 1885, p. 6; Mitchell, 'Temperance and the Liquor Question', pp. 221-3; Dunstan, *Wowsers*, pp. 74-8; Garden, op. cit., pp. 54-5.

78 *Argus*, 5 Feb. 1884, p. 6.
79 *Argus*, 5 June 1884, p. 8; Garden, op. cit., pp. 53-4; cf. *Melbourne and its Sin* (note 68).
80 *Argus*, 3 Dec. 1885, edit.
81 *P.D.*, vol. 50, pp. 2138-407.
82 *P.D.*, vol. 50, p. 2140.
83 Garden, op. cit., pp. 51-61.
84 *Argus*, 30 Aug. 1883, p. 11; 23 Sept. 1884, p. 9; 22 Sept. 1885, p. 9.
85 Forbes, 'Some Social Characteristics of Australia', *Contemporary Review*, vol. 44, Oct. 1883, pp. 614-15; Richardson, *Myself When Young* (London, 1964), p. 86; Deakin, *Federal Story*, pp. 168-9.
86 *Table Talk*, 1 July 1887, p. 1.
87 *Melbourne and its Sin* (note 68), p. 10.
88 Sutherland, *Victoria and its Metropolis*, vol. 1, p. 562.
89 *Leader*, 11 Aug. 1888, p. 26.
90 *Spectator*, 28 May 1886; *Herald*, May-June 1884; Garden, op. cit., pp. 34-5; see Alan D. Mickle (*Many a Mickle*, Melb., 1953, p. 102) for a delightful proposal of marriage, provided the beloved agreed to give up dancing.
91 *Spectator*, 13 May 1887; Dunstan, *Wowsers*, ch. 5.
92 *Argus*, 7 June 1884; Garden, op. cit., pp. 71-80, for a general discussion.
93 Garden, op. cit., pp. 20-4.
94 *Table Talk*, 13 May 1887.
95 *Argus*, 21 Sept. 1889, p. 9.
96 Peter Coleman, *Obscenity, Blasphemy, Sedition. Censorship in Australia* (Brisbane, 1962), ch. 1.
97 *Argus*, 28 July 1885, p. 6.
98 *Argus*, Jan.-Feb., especially 13 Feb. 1883, p. 7.
99 *Argus*, 12 Sept. 1884, p. 5; in general, see *Argus*, 20 Nov. 1883, p. 5; 3 Mar. 1887, p. 11; 25 June 1889, p. 9.
1 *Argus*, 14 May 1886, p. 5.
2 *Argus*, 5 Mar. 1887, p. 11.
3 *Argus*, 1 Sept. 1883, p. 9; 17 Mar. 1886, p. 5; 28 June 1889, p. 5.
4 Belcher diary (MS., La Trobe Lib.), 14 Feb. 1889.
5 J. F. Hogan, 'A Plea for a Better Melbourne', *Victorian Review*, vol. 4, Mar. 1882; Hogan, *The Australian in London and America* (London, 1889), pp. 183-9.
6 Glynn diary, 1881 (NL).
7 Howe, 'The Wesleyan Church in Victoria', ch. 4, *passim*.
8 *Southern Cross*, 14 July 1883; *P.D.*, vol. 61, p. 1462 (both quoted by Smith (note 28), p. 18).
9 L. J. Bevan, *The Life and Reminiscences of Llewellyn David Bevan, L.L.B., D.D.* (Melb., 1920), pp. 183-4.
10 For British parallels, see Kathleen Heasman, *Evangelicals in Action. An Appraisal of their Social Work in the Victorian Era* (London, 1962).

6 CRISIS IN THE PACIFIC AND FEDERATION

1 *Argus*, 15 June 1883, p. 6.
2 *Argus*, 16 June, p. 10; 18 June 1883, p. 5; *Age*, 15 June 1883, supp. 1; *Border Post* (Albury), 18 June 1883.
3 *Age*, 21 Apr. 1883, supp. 1.
4 *Votes and Proceedings of the Legislative Assembly*, *P.P.*, 1878, vol. 1, p. 97.
5 Gordon, *Australian Frontier in New Guinea*, pp. 100-13; J. D. Legge, *Australian Colonial Policy* (Sydney, 1956), ch. 2; note the strong interest of the *Argus*, 28 Mar. 1883, edit.
6 *P.D.*, vol. 42, p. 270.
7 Annexation of Islands in the Pacific Ocean, *P.P.*, 1883 (2nd session), vol. 2, no. 23; Australasian Convention, 1883. Report of the Proceedings, *P.P.*, 1884, vol. 2, no. 25, p. 41.
8 CO 881/6, no. 95.
9 W. P. Morrell, *Britain in the Pacific Islands* (Oxford, 1960), pp. 198-200; Thompson, 'Australian Imperialism and the New Hebrides', Part 1.
10 Annexation of Islands in the Pacific Ocean, *P.P.*, 1883 (2nd session), vol. 2, no. 23.
11 Derby to Australian Governors, 11 July 1883, Governors' Inward Despatches (VA); Gordon, op. cit., ch. 7; Paul Knaplund, 'Sir Arthur Gordon on the New Guinea Question 1883', *Hist. Studies*, vol. 7, no. 27, Nov. 1956; Marjorie C. Jacobs, 'The Colonial Office and New Guinea, 1874-84', ibid., vol. 5, no. 18, May 1952.
12 *Argus*, 19 July 1883, p. 7.
13 *P.D.*, vol. 43, pp. 136-45 (Service, pp. 136-8).
14 *Argus*, 17 July 1883, p. 7.
15 Agents-General to CO, 21 July 1883, CO 881/6, no. 96.

16 *P.D.*, vol. 43, p. 132.
17 CO 881/6, no. 96, for résumé of anti-transportation movements.
18 Annexation, Federation and Foreign Convicts. Correspondence, *P.P.*, 1884, vol. 3, no. 38, p. 22.
19 *P.D.*, vol. 43, pp. 320-1; Annexation of Islands in the Pacific Ocean, pp. 9-11.
20 *Argus*, 30 July 1883, edit.
21 Annexation or Protectorate of Islands. Resolutions, *P.P.*, 1883, vol. 3, no. 47; Annexation. Resolutions, *P.P.*, 1884, vol. 2, no. 23; CO 881/6, no. 95.
22 CO 881/6, no. 95; Australasian Convention, 1883. Report of the Proceedings, *P.P.*, 1884, vol. 2, no. 25, p. 122; Gordon, op. cit., ch. 9.
23 Executive Council minute, 29 May 1883; *Argus*, 3 Apr. 1883, p. 5.
24 Note the serious parliamentary debate in Sept. 1882, *P.D.*, vol. 40, pp. 1646-71; vol. 41, pp. 2039-40, 2380-2; *Age*, 12 Nov. 1883, p. 4.
25 *P.D.*, vol. 45, p. 201.
26 Australasian Convention, 1883. Report of the Proceedings, *P.P.*, 1884, vol. 2, no. 25, pp. 44-7; Service to McIlwraith, 10 Sept. 1883 (McIlwraith-Palmer Papers, Oxley Memorial Library, Brisbane).
27 Australasian Convention on Annexation and Federation. Further Correspondence, *P.P.*, 1883, vol. 3, no. 48, pp. 5-6.
28 *P.D.*, vol. 45, p. 202.
29 *Argus*, 10 Dec. 1883, p. 5.
30 J. Quick and R. R. Garran, *The Annotated Constitution of the Australian Commonwealth* (Sydney, 1901), pp. 111-12.
31 Australasian Convention, 1883. Report of the Proceedings, *P.P.*, 1884, vol. 2, no. 25; *Argus*, 30 Nov.-10 Dec. 1883; Deakin, *Federal Story*, pp. 11-16.
32 Sir William Des Voeux, *My Colonial Service* (London, 1903), vol. 2, p. 113.
33 CO 309/129/9.
34 Deakin, *Federal Story*, p. 15.
35 *Argus*, 11 Dec. 1883, p. 8.
36 Ibid., p. 4.
37 *P.D.* (N.S.W.), 11 Dec. 1883, pp. 919-28; *Sydney Morning Herald*, 10 Dec. 1883.
38 Deakin, *Federal Story*, pp. 16-17.
39 R. R. Garran, *Prosper the Commonwealth* (Sydney, 1958), p. 88.
40 *P.D.*, vol. 46, p. 1282; vol. 48, p. 85, for criticisms of attitudes to N.S.W. by Mackay and Harper.
41 Sir George Houston Reid, *My Reminiscences* (London, 1917), p. 52.
42 *Age*, 14 Mar., edit.; 16 June 1883, edit.; *Argus*, 7 July 1883, edit.
43 E.g. *Leader*, 13 June 1885; CO 448/1B/173; Parkes to Selby, 20 Nov. 1884 (A.N.Z. Bank records).
44 Hugh R. Reid, *A Customs Union for Australasia* . . . (Melb., 1883), p. 3; cf. *P.D.*, vol. 45, p. 363.
45 *Argus*, 1 May 1885, p. 3.
46 Dr J. M. Tregenza drew my attention to the notebook in the Pearson Papers which lists Pearson's editorial contributions.
47 *Argus*, 12 Jan. 1883, edit.; 17 June 1886, p. 5.
48 H. Mayer, *The Press in Australia* (Melb., 1964), p. 19.
49 Butlin, *Investment in Australian Economic Development*, pp. 364-9.
50 Joy E. Parnaby, 'The Economic and Political Development of Victoria, 1877-1881' (Ph.D., Univ. Melb., 1951), ch. 6; C. D. Allin, *A History of the Tariff Relations of the Australian Colonies* (Minneapolis, 1918), pp. 165-71; Garran, op. cit., pp. 46-9; *P.D.*, vol. 49, p. 1538.
51 E.g. *Argus*, 2 Feb. 1887, p. 4.
52 W. F. Walker, *P.D.*, vol. 40, p. 1658; *Report of the Delegates representing the Victorian Chamber of Manufactures at the Intercolonial Free-Trade Conference . . . 1887* (Melb., 1887); Reid, op. cit.; H. R. Hogg, *Intercolonial Free Trade in Australia* (Melb., 1883); *Argus*, 26 Sept. 1883, p. 9.
53 *Argus*, 10 Jan. 1884, p. 6.
54 Loch to S. of S., Conf., 4 Sept. 1885, CO 309/121/221; *Argus*, 24 Apr. 1884, p. 9; *P.D.*, vol. 45, p. 62.
55 Service in *Age*, 9 Jan. 1885, p. 6; *Argus*, 24 Apr. 1884, p. 9; 2 May 1887, p. 7.
56 *Age*, 12 Nov. 1883, edit.
57 Derby to Gladstone, 7 Dec. 1883, and Gladstone to Derby, 8 Dec. 1883 (Gladstone Papers, BM); Gordon, op. cit., pp. 195-8.
58 CO 881/6, no. 95; CO 309/126/193; CO 309/128/206-7.
59 CO 309/127/37; CO 309/128/290; Annexation, Federation, and French Convicts, *P.P.*, 1884, vol. 3, no. 38, pp. 89-109.

ORDER NUMBER

PO NYAATP08

BOOK NUMBER

5573814

BAY NUMBER

9020-3

AUTHOR	Serle, Geoffrey
TITLE	The Rush to Be Rich: A History of the Colony

60 *P.D.*, vol. 45, pp. 196-644; *Argus*, 21 June 1884, p. 5.
61 High Commissionership of the Western Pacific, *P.P.*, 1884, vol. 3, no. 44; Protectorate of New Guinea. Correspondence, *P.P.*, 1884, vol. 4, no. 60; *Age*, 20 June 1884, edit.
62 Gladstone Papers, vol. 46 (Childers's letters), v. 560 (Cabinet Papers); CO 881/6, no. 103; Marjorie C. Jacobs, 'Bismarck and the Annexation of New Guinea', *Hist. Studies*, vol. 5, no. 17, Nov. 1951.
63 Vic. Premier's Telegram Book (Tel. Book) (VA), 8, 19, 26 Aug. 1884.
64 Tel. Book, Sept.-Oct. 1884; *Argus*, 14 Jan. 1886, p. 6; Gordon, op. cit., pp. 226-30.
65 Tel. Book, 5 Nov. 1884; *P.D.*, vol. 47, pp. 2300-1. 66 *Argus*, 23 Sept. 1884, p. 6.
67 Tel. Book, 1 Oct. 1884; Loch to S. of S., Conf., 9 Oct. 1884, Vic. Governors' Despatches (VA); *P.D.*, vol. 47, p. 2114.
68 Tel. Book. 69 *Argus*, 20 Dec. 1884, pp. 8-9; *Age*, 29 Dec. 1884, edit.
70 *Argus*, 8 Jan. 1885, p. 6.
71 *Argus*, 7 Jan. 1885, p. 6, where there is also an able article by Howard Willoughby.
72 Service to Crisp, 29 Dec. 1884 (Crisp Corresp.).
73 CO 309/128/365; CO 309/129/320, 321, 326; Tel. Book, 5 Feb. 1885.
74 *P.D.*, vol. 48, p. 214; vol. 50, pp. 2135-6. 75 Froude, *Oceana*, pp. 98-9.
76 Gray Correspondence (La Trobe Lib.), 8 Mar. 1885.
77 CO 309/129/332, 337; *Argus*, 12-19 Feb. 1885; Tel. Book, 13 Feb. 1885.
78 *P.D.*, vol. 68, p. 2496; *Argus*, 15 Feb. 1884, p. 4.
79 *Argus*, 27 Feb., p. 6; 25 Feb. 1885, p. 6.
80 *Argus*, 19 Feb., edit.; 16 Apr. 1885, p. 9.
81 *P.D.*, vol. 48, pp. 225 (Service), 144 (Pearson), 66 (Walker), 130 (Mirams); *Age*, 6 Mar. 1885, p. 6, for letter by Mirams.
82 H. G. Turner, 'Australia Militant', *Melbourne Review*, vol. 10, 1885, pp. 143-54.
83 *Argus*, 3 Feb. 1887, p. 4. 84 Gordon Memorial Fund Circular.
85 *Argus*, 30 May 1885, p. 5.
86 G. G. McCrae, 'Two Great Men of Our Own Time', *Melbourne Review*, vol. 10, 1885, p. 317.
87 *Argus*, 27 June 1889, p. 5.
88 Lord Normanby to Hicks-Beach (St Aldwyn Papers, Witcombe Park, Glos.), 30 Mar. 1880.
89 Richard A. Preston, *Canada and "Imperial Defense"* . . . (Durham, N.C., 1967), p. 96.
90 T. B. Millar, 'History of the Defence Forces of Victoria', pp. 225-8; Preston, op. cit., p. 97.
91 Cf. Anon., *The Battle of Mordialloc* (Melb., 1887); *Argus*, 29 Jan. 1887, p. 4.
92 Defence Re-organization Scheme, *P.P.*, 1883, vol. 2, no. 18; Millar, op. cit.; E. W. Perry, 'The Military Life of Major-General Sir John Charles Hood', *Vic. Hist. Mag.*, no. 115, Aug. 1959, pp. 145-7.
93 H. J. Feakes, *White Ensign–Southern Cross. A Story of the King's Ships of Australia's Navy* (Sydney, 1951), pp. 74, 71.
94 Tel. Book.
95 Loch to S. of S., telegram, 31 Mar. 1885; Secret despatch same date, CO 881/6, no. 108; Loch to Berry, 9 Apr. 1885 (Berry Papers); *Age*, 30 Mar. 1885, p. 4; *Argus*, 31 Mar. 1885, p. 5.
96 *Argus*, 13 Apr. p. 5; 14 Apr., p. 4; 20 Apr. 1885, p. 4; *Age*, 1 Apr. 1885, edit.; *Leader*, 9 May 1885, p. 26; Gray Correspondence (La Trobe Lib.), 18 Apr. 1885; Blainey, *Gold and Paper*, p. 128.
97 E.g. *Age* edit., quoted by George R. Parkin, *Imperial Federation. The Problem of National Unity* (London, 1892), p. 199.
98 *Argus*, 12 Mar., p. 4; 17 Mar. 1885, p. 5.
99 Tel. Book, 17, 20 July 1885; *Age*, 17 July, p. 5; 21 July, 1885, p. 5; *Argus*, 8 Aug. 1885, p. 9; Quick and Garran, op. cit., p. 114; Dilke, *Problems of Greater Britain*, pp. 264-6.
1 *Bulletin*, 29 Aug. 1885, p. 3.
2 *P.D.*, vol. 49, pp. 1513-44; vol. 50, pp. 1587-612.
3 Tel. Book, 18, 20 Nov. 1885; Governors' Papers (VA), Bundle 16, 'Federal Council'.
4 Berry, *P.D.*, vol. 50, p. 1778.
5 Victoria and Tasmania. Treaty for Intercolonial Free Trade, *P.P.*, 1885, vol. 4, no. 85; *P.D.*, vol. 50, pp. 1775-87; vol. 54, p. 680 (Deakin); *Argus*, 29 Jan. 1886, p. 7; *Age*, 13 July 1885, p. 6; *Australasian Commercial Congress, 1888. Report* (Melb., 1889) for Service and Douglas.
6 Gillies to Griffith, 21 Aug., 13 Oct. 1886 (Griffith Papers, Dixson Lib.); Derham to Swallow, 21 Sept. 1885-7 Nov. 1887 (Derham private letterbook).

7 *Argus*, 16 Aug., p. 5; 26 Oct. 1887, p. 11; Minutes of Fiji Annexation Committee (T. H. Prichard Papers, NL).
8 Loch to S. of S., 14 Apr. 1885, CO 309/125/110.
9 CO 309/125/134; *P.D.*, vol. 50, p. 2136; Legge, op. cit., p. 36.
10 *P.D.*, vol. 48, pp. 41, 212-14.
11 Derby to Loch, 18 May 1885 (Vic. Governors' Inward Despatches, VA).
12 CO 881/6/112A; The New Hebrides. Correspondence, *P.P.*, 1886, vol. 2, no. 35; Angus Ross, *New Zealand Aspirations in the Pacific in the Nineteenth Century* (Oxford, 1964), pp. 206-11; McCullough, 'The New Hebrides Crisis', ch. 2. In the next few pages, I owe much to Miss McCullough's unpublished thesis.
13 *Argus*, 1 Sept. 1886, p. 7.
14 *Argus*, 20 Apr. 1886, p. 7.
15 *Age*, 24 Mar. 1886, edit.
16 Tel. Book, 27 Mar. 1886.
17 The New Hebrides. Correspondence, *P.P.*, 1886, vol. 2, no. 35, p. 35.
18 CO 309/130/683.
19 CO 309/130/707.
20 The New Hebrides. Correspondence, p. 38.
21 *Bulletin*, 8, 15 May 1886.
22 CO 881/6/112A.
23 CO 309/130/690.
24 Ross, op. cit., pp. 218-29.
25 McCullough, 'The New Hebrides Crisis', ch. 3.
26 *P.D.*, vol. 51, pp. 148-9; *National Australian*, 9 Aug. 1886.
27 McCullough, chs 4-5; Morrell, op. cit., pp. 200-4; CO 881/7/118; Tel. Book, June-July 1886; Thompson, 'Australian Imperialism and the New Hebrides', part 2, ch. 1.
28 CO 881/7/118; Morrell, op. cit., pp. 200-4; J. M. Ward, *British Policy in the South Pacific, 1786-1893* (Sydney, 1948), pp. 300-2.
29 10 Aug. 1886, 25 Feb. 1887 (Berry Papers); Tel. Book.
30 *P.D.*, vol. 52, pp. 1096-102, 1212-13, 1785-8.
31 Deakin to Pearson, 26 Feb. 1887 (Pearson Papers).
32 Berry to Gillies, 18 Mar. 1887 (Letter-book, Berry Papers); cf. Deakin to Pearson, 31 Mar. 1887 (Pearson Papers).
33 Tel. Book, 24, 28 Mar. 1887.
34 *Proceedings of the Colonial Conference, 1887* (C.5091), pp. 24-5.
35 Holland to Salisbury, 18 Apr. 1887 (Salisbury Papers, Christ Church, Oxford).
36 *Argus*, 28 Apr., p. 5; 9 June 1887, p. 9.
37 *P.D.*, vol. 68, p. 2493; cf. Berry to Gillies, 25 Oct. 1887 (Letter-book, Berry Papers).
38 Deakin, *Federal Story*, pp. 22-3.
39 Salisbury to Holland, 27 Apr. 1887 (Salisbury Papers).
40 *P.D.*, vol. 61, p. 1642; *Imperial Federation* (London), May 1888, p. 96; *Procs Royal Colonial Institute*, 1887-8, p. 343; *Argus*, 10 Feb., p. 4; 15 May 1888, p. 9.
41 Deakin, *Federal Story*, pp. 23-4; Berry to Gillies (note 37); *P.D.*, vol. 54, pp. 262-70.
It will be observed that I have not placed much reliance on Deakin's account (*Federal Story*, pp. 21-3) which is misleading in several particulars. La Nauze's admirable account of the conference (*Alfred Deakin*, vol. 1, pp. 95-104) needs to be modified by Service's evidence (see note 40). Despite Service's statement, English observers did consider Deakin's speech to be the strongest.
42 CO 309/131/282, 290, 297, 317, 659; Gillies to Berry, 6 Sept. 1887 (Berry Papers).
43 *Argus*, 1 Oct. 1887, p. 11.
44 Salisbury to Holland, 16 Oct., 20 Nov. 1887 (Salisbury Papers).
45 Berry to Gillies, 25 Oct. 1887 (Letter-book, Berry Papers).
46 CO 309/131/445-54; CO 309/133/92; CO 309/136/6a; *P.D.*, vol. 56, p. 2543; vol. 64, pp. 1613-26; vol. 65, pp. 2719-28; vol. 62, p. 2468; Tel. Book, 29 Aug. 1893; La Nauze, *Alfred Deakin*, vol. 2, ch. 19.
47 Deakin, *P.D.*, vol. 54, p. 272.
48 *Argus*, 8 Jan. 1885, edit.
49 Preston, op. cit., pp. 98-102; CO 881/7, no. 115; CO 309/129/184; Governors' Papers (VA), Bundle 16, 'Naval Defence'; H. Mortimer-Franklyn, *The Unit of Imperial Federation* (London, 1887), ch. 6; Feakes, op. cit., ch. 16.
50 Feakes, op. cit., ch. 17; G. L. Macandie, *The Genesis of the Royal Australian Navy* (Sydney, 1949), chs 4-5; note Deakin to Derham, 22 Apr. 1887 (Derham Corresp.); note the defence and praise of colonial attitudes by the Fourth Earl Carnarvon, 'Colonial Defence', *Essays, Addresses and Translations*, vol. 3, pp. 150-1, and by Richard Jebb, *The Imperial Conference* (London, 1911), vol. 1, pp. 33-4.
51 *P.D.*, vol. 56, pp. 2186-202, 2254-62.
52 Deakin, *Federal Story*, p. 24.
53 *Argus*, 26 Nov. 1887, p. 13.
54 Morrell, op. cit., pp. 261-2; Jacobs, op. cit. (note 62).
55 Morris, *George Higinbotham*, pp. 205-6.

56 Atkins, 'Representation of Australia in England', pp. 238-49.
57 *Imperial Federation*, May 1887, supp. p. 106; *Argus*, 7 Feb. 1888, p. 8.

7 MIGRANTS, NATIVE-BORN AND IRISH-AUSTRALIANS

1 *P.D.*, vol. 48, pp. 83, 85. 2 Froude, *Oceana*, pp. 106, 151, 103, 156.
3 Frank Partridge, *T.A.B. A Memoir of Thomas Allnutt Second Earl Brassey* (London, 1921), p. 56.
4 Archibald Forbes, 'Some Social Characteristics of Australia', *Contemporary Review*, vol. 44, Oct. 1883, pp. 722-3.
5 'Edward Kinglake', *The Australian at Home . . .* (London, 1892), p. 6; Moncure D. Conway, *My Pilgrimage to the Wise Men of the East* (London, 1906), p. 73.
6 *Argus*, 22 Aug. 1885, p. 5.
7 Loch to S. of S., 17 July 1884 (Governors' Despatches); Governors' letter-books (VA), vol. 5, p. 221.
8 Walch, *Victoria in 1880*, p. 213.
9 E.g. Dilke, *Problems of Greater Britain*, p. 156. 10 Forbes, op. cit., pp. 720-1.
11 Adams, *The Australians*, Pref. and pp. 245-78; Froude, *Oceana*, p. 105; Kinglake, op. cit., pp. 4-9; Martin, *Australia and the Empire*, pp. xiii-xv.
12 E. E. Morris, 'On Sending Out to Australia', *Longman's Magazine*, vol. 2, 1883, pp. 173-85; Gane, *N.S.W. and Victoria*, pp. 141-9; Kinglake, op. cit., ch. 2; J. F. Hogan, *The Australian in London and America* (London, 1889), pp. 193-8.
13 See Dale, *Impressions of Australia*, pp. 170-1, following J. R. Seeley.
14 Cf. Richard Jebb, *Studies in Colonial Nationalism* (London, 1905), p. 103; Froude, *Oceana*, p. 105.
15 Dale, *Impressions of Australia*, pp. 46-7.
16 Henry Handel Richardson, *The Fortunes of Richard Mahony* (London, 1930), pp. 471, 470.
17 H. G. Turner, 'Advance Australia', *Melbourne Review*, vol. 7, 1882, pp. 164-5.
18 Quoted Briggs, *Victorian Cities*, p. 302.
19 *P.D.*, vol. 48, p. 148. 20 *P.D.*, vol. 54, p. 293.
21 *Age*, 14 Mar. 1887, p. 6.
22 *P.D.*, vol. 54, p. 307. CO 448/1-4 for information on awards.
23 E.g. *Age*, 21 May 1884, edit. (honours); 3 Jan. 1885, edit. (Governors); *Leader*, 22 Aug. 1885, p. 26 (profligacy and Prince of Wales); 12 June 1886, p. 26 (hotel bill).
24 J. L. Dow, *P.D.*, vol. 48, p. 146.
25 E.g. *P.D.*, vol. 54, p. 486; vol. 55, pp. 1299, 1424. 26 Turner, op. cit., p. 167.
27 Twopeny, *Town Life*, p. 173. 28 Deakin diaries, 22 Oct. 1885.
29 For the general problem, W. K. Hancock, *Survey of British Commonwealth Affairs*, vol. 1, pp. 13-18. The best case studies are La Nauze's *Alfred Deakin* and Bruce Mansfield, *Australian Democrat. The Career of Edward William O'Sullivan 1846-1910* (Sydney, 1965), pp. 257-73.
30 *P.D.*, vol. 39, p. 543. 31 Cooper, *P.D.*, vol. 44, pp. 1079-82.
32 E.g. *Age*, 26 Aug. 1887, edit.
33 W. E. Hearn, *National Loyalty: or, the Colonies and the Mother Country* (Melb., 1879), pp. 25, 29.
34 *P.D.*, vol. 54, p. 53. 35 *P.D.*, vol. 49, pp. 1526-7.
36 *Procs Royal Colonial Institute*, 1883-4, p. 124. Note the able article in favour of Imperial Federation: 'The Colonial Question', *Melbourne Review*, vol. 1, 1876.
37 Letter of 20 Nov. 1884, *Age*, 9 Jan. 1885, p. 6; Imperial Federation. Correspondence, *P.P.*, 1884, vol. 4, no. 84.
38 *Argus*, 6 June 1885, p. 5; *Age*, 6 June 1885, p. 8.
39 *Argus*, 29 Aug. 1885, p. 5. 40 *Argus*, 12 Sept. 1885, p. 10.
41 Loch to S. of S., 30 June 1885, Conf. (Governors' Despatches, VA).
42 *P.D.*, vol. 54, pp. 484, 290.
43 For Imperial Federation generally, Hancock, op. cit. (note 29), pp. 30-6; Hall, *Australia and England*, ch. 6; H. Mortimer-Franklyn, *The Unit of Imperial Federation* (London, 1887); Blackton, 'The Imperial Federationist Interlude'.
44 Martin, *Australia and the Empire*, ch. 3.
45 Tregenza, *Professor of Democracy*, p. 192, for some suggestive remarks.
46 Quoted by Robert Rhodes James, *Rosebery* (London, 1963), pp. 158, 156.
47 James Graham, private letter-book (Graham Papers, Univ. Melb. Archives).

48 'Opening of the Indian and Colonial Exhibition by the Queen', *The Works of Tennyson* (Eversley edition, London, 1908), vol. 6, pp. 346-7.
49 *Imperial Federation* (London), May 1887, supp. pp. 106-7; *Procs Royal Colonial Institute*, 1886-7, p. 39.
50 Reeves, *State Experiments*, vol. 1, p. 149.
51 *P.D.*, vol. 45, p. 202; *Argus*, 24 Apr. 1884, p. 9.
52 *Argus*, 14 May 1887, p. 13; 10 Apr. 1888, p. 8.
53 Berry, 'The Colonies in Relation to the Empire', pp. 4-29; cf. *P.D.*, vol. 48, p. 107.
54 *Argus*, 12 July 1887, p. 7; 17 May 1888, p. 5; cf. Berry, *Procs R.C.I.*, 1885-6, p. 297.
55 Bowen to Berry, 5 June 1886 (Berry Papers).
56 *P.D.*, vol. 54, p. 284.
57 *The Marcus Clarke Memorial Volume*, ed. Hamilton Mackinnon (Melb., 1884).
58 Charles Gavan Duffy, *My Life in Two Hemispheres* (London, 1898), vol. 2, p. 264.
59 *Argus*, 20 June 1885, p. 5.
60 *Argus*, 27 Oct. 1884, p. 6.
61 Report Royal Commission on Shop Employés, *P.P.*, 1884, vol. 2, no. 18, Evidence, p. 75; H. R. Rae, *Pencilling by Land and Sea* (Hokitika, N.Z., 1887), p. 40; Trollope, *Australia and New Zealand*, p. 255; *Argus*, 28 Aug. 1886, p. 13.
62 Josiah Hughes, *Australia Revisited in 1890 . . .* (London, 1891), p. 241.
63 David Blair to Hingston, 7 Sept. 1896 (Blair letters, La Trobe Lib.).
64 J. F. Hogan, 'The Coming Australian', *Victorian Review*, vol. 3, Nov. 1880, pp. 102-9; see also H. Ling Roth, 'A Few Words in Reply to Mr. Hogan's Coming Australian', ibid., Jan. 1881, pp. 313-15, and H. d'E. Taylor, 'Our Future Rulers', *Melbourne Review*, vol. 7, 1882, pp. 418-36.
65 Adams, *The Australians*, pp. 26-8, 40; Turner, *History of Victoria*, vol. 2, p. 269; *Our Good Words*, Apr. 1889, p. 13.
66 A. B. Tulloch, *Recollections of Forty Years' Service* (Edinburgh, 1903), p. 365.
67 Twopeny, *Town Life*, pp. 83-7; Adams, op. cit., p. 28.
68 *Australian*, Mar. 1887, p. 4.
69 R. E. Hain to Deakin, 23, 28 Apr. 1884 (Deakin Correspondence).
70 Meudell, 'Australia for the Australians', *Melbourne Review*, vol. 7, 1882, pp. 315-24; reply by S. Rinder, 'The "Foreigner" in Australia', ibid., pp. 437-42; Meudell, *Pleasant Career*, p. 237.
71 Meudell, 'An Australian Protest against Imperial Federation', *Melbourne Review*, vol. 10, July 1885, pp. 249, 253, 254.
72 *Australian Native*, Nov. 1883.
73 *Argus*, 24 Sept. 1883, p. 9; Deakin, *Federal Story*, p. 6.
74 *Australian Native*, Sept. 1883.
75 *National Australian*, 13 Nov. 1885.
76 *Age*, 26 Nov. 1885, edit.
77 Cockerill, *Scribblers and Statesmen*, p. 22; see also pp. 41-2.
78 Cf. Adams, *The Australians*, p. 41.
79 *National Australian*, 13 Nov. 1885.
80 *Argus*, 10 July 1886, p. 4.
81 *Koroit Herald*, 19 Feb. 1883, quoted by Stephanie Dew, 'The Belfast Electorate 1863-1883' (B.A. thesis, Monash Univ., 1969), p. 106.
82 ' "Only Colonial" ', *The Catholic Magazine*, Oct. 1888, p. 24.
83 H. H. Richardson, *Myself When Young* (London, 1964), pp. 92-3, 107.
84 Francis Adams, *The Melbournians: a Novel* (London, 1892), pp. 74-5.
85 Deakin, *Federal Story*, pp. 115, 118.
86 *P.D.*, vol. 53, p. 2667; *Argus*, *Bendigo Advertiser*, *Bendigo Independent*, *Bendigo Evening News*, 9-17 Dec. 1886.
87 *Age*, 31 Mar. 1886, p. 5.
88 *National Australian*, Apr. 1886.
89 *National Australian*, Mar. 1886.
90 *Australian*, Feb. 1887.
91 Marian Aveling, 'History of the A.N.A.'. The last few pages owe much to this excellent thesis; most of the quotations have been drawn from it.
92 Note Patchett Martin's debunking (*Australia and the Empire*, chs 5-6).
93 W. H. Archer, 'Sir John O'Shanassy: a Sketch', *Melbourne Review*, vol. 8, 1883, p. 256: see ch. 1, note 1.
94 *Age*, 5 June, edit.; 31 May 1882, edit.; *P.D.*, vol. 39, pp. 203-8, 447-68, 525-61, 592-624.
95 *Advocate*, 24 Mar. 1883, p. 5.
96 *Argus*, 14 Mar., p. 5; 23 Apr. 1883, summary for Europe.
97 Quoted by P. J. O'Farrell, *The Catholic Church. A Short History: 1788-1967* (Melb., 1968), p. 155.
98 *Argus*, 6 June 1883, p. 7.

99 *Advocate,* 16 June 1883, pp. 7-8; *Argus,* 8 June 1883, p. 6. For the Redmonds' visit in general, see John Oldham and Alfred Stirling, *Victorian. A Visitors' Book* (Melb., 1934), pp. 75-81.
1 *P.D.*, vol. 43, pp. 432-3, 488-91; CO 309/126/122, 305.
2 *Argus,* 25 June 1883, p. 3. 3 *P.D.*, vol. 43, pp. 449-50.
4 *Advocate,* 10 Nov. 1883, pp. 5-10; *Argus,* 8 Nov. 1883, p. 5; *Age,* 8 Nov. 1883, edit.
5 Martin, *Australia and the Empire*, p. 160; cf. the racial views of A. M. Topp, 'English Institutions and the Irish Race', *Melbourne Review*, vol. 6, 1881, pp. 9-27.
6 J. A. Gurner, *Life's Panorama . . .* (Melb., 1930), p. 271.
7 E.g. *Advocate,* 24 Mar., p. 6; 10 Nov. 1883, p. 9.
8 *P.D.*, vol. 47, p. 1706; Rev. A. Madsen, *The Loyal Orange Institution: Facts v. Fables* (Melb., 1898).
9 *Argus,* 12 Feb., p. 5; 20 Feb. 1883; H. W. Cleary, *The Orange Society* (3rd ed., Melb., 1897), pp. 130-1.
10 *Argus,* 8 Jan. 1884, p. 6.
11 *P.D.*, vol. 47, pp. 1703-12; vol. 48, pp. 385-6; *Argus,* 17 Apr. 1883, edit.
12 E.g. *Age,* 16 July 1885, p. 5. 13 *Advocate,* 5 Feb. 1887, p. 15.
14 *Argus,* 26 May 1887, p. 7.
15 *Argus,* 1 June, p. 9; 14 June 1886, p. 11; *Advocate,* 5, 12, 19, 26 June 1886; *P.D.*, vol. 51, pp. 386-91.
16 E.g. *Advocate,* 11 June 1887, pp. 6-8; *Argus,* 26 May, p. 7; 6 June, p. 7; 29 Oct., p. 13; 23 Nov. 1887, p. 7.
17 *Advocate,* 16 Apr. 1887, p. 12.
18 Patricia Breen, 'The Reaction to the Irish Question in Victoria 1880-1890' (B.A. thesis, Univ. Melb., 1958), p. 5.
19 *Advocate,* 10 Feb., edit.; 13 Oct. 1883, p. 12; cf. 15 Sept. 1883, p. 14; 28 Nov. 1885, edit.
20 *Advocate,* 31 Oct., edit.; 17 Nov. 1885, edit.; 10 Nov. 1883, p. 12.
21 E.g. 21 July 1883, p. 12; 14 Feb. 1885, p. 17; 29 Jan. 1887, edit.
22 *Advocate,* 5 Feb. 1887, p. 15.
23 Cf. *Advocate,* 19 Mar. edit.; 30 Apr., p. 17; 7 May 1887, pp. 12, 15.
24 *Advocate,* 7 May 1887, edit.
25 *Advocate,* 2 June 1888, edit.; 26 Nov. 1887, edit.
26 Cf. Hogan, *The Irish in Australia, passim.*
27 Michael Davitt, *Life and Progress in Australasia* (London, 1898), pp. 130-1.
28 *Advocate,* 9 May 1885, p. 12.
29 *Austral Light,* Jan. 1892; *Advocate,* 6 Jan. 1883, p. 13.
30 In general for Irish Catholics and the Home Rule movement, see Tobin, 'The Sea-Divided Gael'.

8 FOOLS' PARADISE, 1887-1888

1 W. S. Gilbert, 'Limited Liability', *Utopia Limited; or the Flowers of Progress.*
2 F. T. Derham, private letter-book, 15 May, 7 June 1886 (Derham Papers); cf. Parkes to Selby, 21 Jan., 18 Apr. 1886, 14 Jan. 1887 (A.N.Z. Bank records).
3 *Argus,* 6 Oct. 1886, p. 10; *Leader,* 1 Aug. 1885, supp.
4 Boehm, *Prosperity and Depression*, ch. 3; Hall, *Stock Exchange*, ch. 4, especially the charts, 'Some economic indicators, 1885-93', pp. 115-16; Coghlan, *Labour and Industry*, vol. 3, *passim.*
5 Butlin, *Investment in Australian Economic Development*, pp. 245-66; Beever and Freeman, 'Directors of Disaster?', pp. 123-5.
6 Butlin, op. cit., p. 249n., for a list of the more important ones, also p. 163.
7 Cannon, *Land Boomers*, chs 18-19.
8 Quoted by Coghlan, *Labour and Industry*, vol. 3, p. 1692.
9 Turner, *History of Victoria*, vol. 2, p. 301.
10 Cannon, op. cit., pp. 108-9.
11 Sutherland, *Victoria and its Metropolis*, vol. 2, p. 797; see Shann, *Economic History*, pp. 300-2.
12 Parkes to Selby, 14 Jan. 1887; also 8 Nov. 1886 (A.N.Z. Bank records).
13 Blainey, *Gold and Paper*, pp. 134, 135, ch. 9; Butlin, *A.N.Z. Bank*, pp. 231-2.
14 Sutherland, *Victoria and its Metropolis*, vol. 2, p. 802.
15 Royal Commission on Banking Laws, *P.P.*, 1887, vol. 3, no. 65, Evidence, p. 19.

16 Banks and Currency Law Amendment Act and Banking Companies Registration Act, *P.D.*, vol. 57-9; on the royal commission, Boehm, *Prosperity and Depression*, ch. 8.
17 See, e.g., Geoffrey Blainey, *A History of Camberwell* (Melb., 1964), ch. 5; Bate, *History of Brighton*, pp. 197-200.
18 *Argus*, 14 June 1888, p. 5.
19 *Building and Engineering Journal*, 11 Apr. 1891; *Age*, 20 Aug. 1887, p. 14; Austral Otis records (Univ. Melb. Archives); Swinburne letter-books (Univ. Melb. Archives); Geoffrey Blainey, *One Hundred Years. Johns & Waygood Limited. 1856-1956* (Melb., n.d.), pp. 19-36; Parsons, 'Manufacturing in Melbourne', ch. 10.
20 Report, Royal Commission on the Extension of Melbourne Westward, *P.P.*, 1887, vol. 3, no. 79; *P.D.*, vol. 56, pp. 2658-68.
21 *Argus*, 1 Sept. 1887, p. 8.
22 Dale, *Impressions of Australia*, p. 90.
23 *Illustrated Australian News*, 31 Mar. 1888.
24 *Argus*, 26 May 1888, edit.
25 *Age*, 16 Apr., edit.; 4 June 1888, p. 5; from January to May, editorials warned frequently about the dangers of speculation. In general for the mining boom, Blainey, *The Rush that Never Ended*, pp. 147-52; Hall, *Stock Exchange*, pp. 140-2, 186.
26 E.g. *Age*, 1 Aug. 1888, p. 1; Turner, *History of Victoria*, vol. 2, p. 301.
27 *A.I.B.R.*, 16 Nov. 1888, p. 750.
28 Companies Registered, *P.P.*, 1888, vol. 1, C7; Butlin, *Investment*, p. 413.
29 Turner, *History of Victoria*, vol. 2, p. 303.
30 Theodore Fink, 'Reminiscences'.
31 *Age*, 17 May 1888, edit.; cf. editorials, 31 May, 23 June, 15 Sept. 1888.
32 *Age*, 31 May 1888, edit.
33 Blainey, *Johns & Waygood*, (note 19), pp. 16-17; Hall, *Stock Exchange*, pp. 138, 144-5; note *Argus*, 2 Jan. 1888, p. 9, for analysis of dividends of public companies.
34 Kauri Timber Coy. Records (Univ. Melb. Archives).
35 Fink, 'Reminiscences'.
36 Nathaniel Cork, *The Australian Banking Crisis* (London, 1894), p. 4.
37 Cf. Blainey, *Gold and Paper*, p. 135n.
38 Coghlan, *Labour and Industry*, vol. 3, p. 1701; *A.I.B.R.*, 15 Sept. 1888, p. 582.
39 Cambridge, *Thirty Years*, p. 180; *Argus*, 27 June 1888, pp. 8, 9.
40 *Argus*, 15 Aug. 1888, p. 7; J. Hetherington, *Age*, 30 Oct. 1965.
41 Blainey, *A History of Camberwell*, pp. 55-6.
42 *Argus*, 1 Jan. 1889, p. 7; *The History of Hawthorn to 1895* (Hawthorn, 1896), 'The Building Boom', 'The Land Boom'.
43 *Table Talk*, 5 Oct. 1888, p. 31.
44 *Argus*, 4 Apr. 1888, p. 7; *Age*, 5 June 1888, p. 6.
45 Mitchell, 'Temperance and the Liquor Question', pp. 224-5.
46 *The Times*, 26 Oct. 1888, quoted in *Argus*, 1 Jan. 1889, p. 7.
47 *Age*, 25 Sept. 1888, p. 7.
48 *Argus*, 2 Aug. 1888, edit.; cf. *Age*, 26 Oct. 1888, edit.
49 Cannon, *Land Boomers*, p. 97. In general for the land boom, see Cannon, and Moore, 'Marvellous Melbourne', pp. 33-5.
50 *Age*, 27 Nov., p. 6; 13 Dec. 1888, p. 5; *Argus*, 30 Nov. 1888, p. 7; Higgins, MS. Autobiography, p. 91; Turner, *History of Victoria*, vol. 2, p. 292; Hall, *Stock Exchange*, pp. 131-2.
51 *P.D.*, vol. 57, pp. 518-41, 552.
52 *The Economist*, 31 May, 5 Apr., 13 May 1890.
53 E.g. *P.D.*, vol. 47, pp. 2328-9; D. B. Copland, *W. E. Hearn: First Australian Economist* (Melb., 1935), pp. 52-3.
54 *P.D.*, vol. 57, pp. 278-9; vol. 60, pp. 882-3; *Table Talk*, 22 Mar. 1889, p. 1.
55 *Australian*, Aug. 1888, edit.
56 *Liberator*, 13 Dec. 1885.
57 *Table Talk*, 9 July 1886; 27 May 1887; 29 June 1888.
58 *Argus*, 15 Feb. 1889, p. 9; cf. Meudell, *Pleasant Career*, pp. 256-7.
59 Note-book, box 2, Higgins Papers (unidentified speech).
60 *P.D.*, vol. 58, p. 1077; *Argus*, 3 Oct. 1888, p. 11; cf. Coghlan's description of land companies' operations (*Labour and Industry*, vol. 3, pp. 1704-5).
61 *Table Talk*, 20 July 1888, p. 2.
62 Fink 'Reminiscences'.
63 Hall, *Stock Exchange*, p. 44; *Argus*, 22 Dec. 1888, p. 9.
64 *A.I.B.R.*, 16 Apr. 1888, p. 195.
65 See debate on the Directors Liability Bill, 1891, *P.D.*, vol. 67, pp. 1777-8, 1921-6, 2044; vol. 68, pp. 2953-61; Cannon, *Land Boomers*, pp. 205-6.
66 Cannon, *Land Boomers*, chs 10-11.
67 Meudell, *Pleasant Career*, p. 9.
68 Cannon, op. cit., ch. 17.
69 *A.I.B.R.*, Oct. 1896, p. 732.

70 *Argus*, 27 Feb. 1886, p. 5; *Age*, 26 Oct. 1887, edit.; *Bulletin*, 30 Jan. 1886, p. 7; *Outpost*, 8 Sept. 1900; Deakin Correspondence; Cannon, op. cit., pp. 71-6.
71 Fink, 'Reminiscences'.
72 Deakin, *Crisis in Victorian Politics, passim*; Fink, 'Reminiscences'; *Argus*, 11 May 1888, p. 8; Bedford, *Naught to Thirty-three*, pp. 329-30; Weston Bate, *A.D.B.*, vol. 3, and *History of Brighton, passim*; Cannon, op. cit., ch. 20.
73 Cannon, op. cit., pp. 29-30.
74 Dilke, *Problems of Greater Britain*, p. 122.
75 E.g. *Table Talk*, 24 Sept. 1886, p. 1; *Statist* (London), quoted in *Argus*, 25 Feb. 1889, edit.; *Age*, 9 Oct. 1888, edit.
76 See Cannon's examples, pp. 41-3.
77 Cannon, op. cit., p. 31.
78 Fink, 'Reminiscences'.
79 Stebbing, *Charles Henry Pearson*, p. 320; Tregenza, *Professor of Democracy*, pp. 202-4.
80 Kiddle, *Men of Yesterday*, pp. 502-3.
81 Note the warnings by D. Chambers, 'Capitalists and Calvinists in Colonial Victoria', *Melbourne Historical Journal*, vol. 4, 1964.
82 *Bulletin*, 17 Apr. 1886, p. 6.
83 Howe, 'The Wesleyan Church in Victoria', pp. 26-7.
84 *Table Talk*, 1 June 1888, p. 1.
85 E.g. Rev. W. Allen, *Victorian Independent*, May 1886.
86 *Argus*, 18 May 1883, p. 7; cf. 29 Apr. 1886, p. 6; *Our Good Words*, Jan. 1889, pp. 6-8; *Australian Herald*, Sept. 1889, pp. 18-19.
87 *Argus*, 26 Nov. 1883, p. 5.
88 *Victorian Independent*, Dec. 1887, p. 199.
89 Ibid., Jan. 1888, pp. 6-7.
90 Dale, *Impressions of Australia*, pp. 258-61.
91 E.g. Parker, *Round the Compass*, p. 147.
92 Reginald G. Gallop letter, 8 Mar. 1886 (MS., ML).
93 E.g. A. F. Morrison, *Argus*, 28 Aug. 1886, p. 13. There was an interesting discussion at the Beefsteak Club in 1887 (Deegan, *Chronicles of the Melbourne Beefsteak Club*, pp. 22-4, 120-5).
94 Quoted by Max O'Rell, *John Bull & Co. The Great Colonial Branches of the Firm ...* (London, 1894), p. 68.
95 Lingham, *Juvenal in Melbourne*, pp. 23-4, 32.
96 Helen Merrell Lynd, *England in the Eighteen-Eighties* (London, 1945), p. 62.
97 Cf. N. G. Annan, 'The Intellectual Aristocracy' in J. H. Plumb (ed.), *Studies in Social History* (London, 1955); G. M. Young, *Victorian England. Portrait of an Age* (London, 1953), p. 146.
98 A. G. Austin (ed.), *The Webbs' Australian Diary 1898* (Melb., 1965), p. 115.
99 Quoted by Lynd, op. cit., p. 81.
1 Quoted by Tregenza, *Professor of Democracy*, p. 99.
2 Deegan, *Chronicles of the Melbourne Beefsteak Club*, p. 123.
3 Meudell, *Pleasant Career*, pp. 1-2; cf. *Australasian*, 11 Feb. 1888, p. 313, for an attack on Miller for his meanness; Meudell, op. cit., p. 194, for the incapacity of millionaires to use their wealth.
4 Turner, *A.I.B.R.*, Oct. 1896, p. 731.
5 Twopeny, *Town Life*, pp. 191-3.
6 Note-book, box 2, Higgins Papers (unidentified speech).
7 Cambridge, *Thirty Years*, p. 181.

9 'MARVELLOUS MELBOURNE', 1887-1888

1 Morley Roberts, *Land-Travel and Sea-Faring* (London, 1891), p. 33.
2 Mary Florence Sugden, *Edward H. Sugden* (Melb., 1941), p. 22.
3 Of many which might be cited, Gane, *N.S.W. and Victoria*, pp. 35-6; Lydia Leavitt, *Around the World* (Toronto, n.d.), p. 48; Timothy Coop and Henry Exley, *A Trip around the World* (Cincinnatti, 1882), pp. 78-9; Mark Twain, *More Tramps Abroad* (London, 1897), p. 75.
4 Hume, *Mystery of a Hansom Cab*, p. 99.
5 Adams, *Australian Essays*, pp. 2, 5. David Christie Murray was almost a lone detractor: 'the city is commonplace enough in itself' (*The Cockney Columbus*, London, 1898, p. 184).
6 *Victorian Year Book*, 1892, p. 131.
7 Twopeny, *Town Life*, pp. 73-4; Trollope, *Australia and New Zealand*, p. 228n.; Nat Gould, *Town and Bush* (London, 1896), p. 120; 'E. Kinglake', *The Australian at Home* (London, 1892), p. 137; Finch-Hatton, *Advance Australia!*, chs 19-20; cf. J. F. Hogan, *The Australian in London and America* (London, 1889), pp. 2-5.

8 Parker, *Round the Compass*, p. 100.
9 Adams, *Australian Essays*, p. 52.
10 Twopeny, *Town Life*, p. 3.
11 E.g. M. M. Ballou, *Under the Southern Cross* . . . (Boston, 1888), p. 192.
12 Sugden letters, 13 Jan. 1888.
13 Sutherland, *Victoria and its Metropolis*, vol. 1, pp. 543-5, 558.
14 Ballou, op. cit., pp. 186-7.
15 Hogan, op. cit., pp. 181-2; Froude, *Oceana*, p. 159.
16 Sir Frederic H. Cowen, *My Art and my Friends* (London, 1913), p. 192.
17 *Imperial Review*, July 1888, p. 7.
18 Cf. Casey, *An Australian Story*, pp. 119-20.
19 *Argus*, 12 Mar. 1887, p. 15.
20 Twopeny, *Town Life*, p. 11.
21 Westgarth, *Half a Century of Australasian Progress, A Personal Retrospect* (London, 1889), pp. 82-3.
22 Premiers' Telegram Book, 15, 28 Jan. 1887 (VA); *Age*, 3 Apr. 1889, edit.
23 *Argus*, 15 Aug. 1885, p. 5; 8, 22, 29 Aug. for other articles in his series.
24 *Table Talk*, 16 Nov. 1888, p. 9; cf. Hume, *Mystery of a Hansom Cab*, p. 59; John Freeman, *Lights and Shadows of Melbourne Life* (London, 1888), pp. 78-85.
25 E.g. Hume, op. cit., pp. 98-9.
26 Robin Boyd, *The Australian Ugliness* (Melb., 1960), pp. 39-43.
27 Rev. D. V. Lucas, *Australia and Homeward* (Toronto, 1888), pp. 134-40.
28 *Australasian Builder and Contractor's News*, 27 Aug. 1887, p. 259; Federal Coffee Palace, *Hand Book of Melbourne* (Melb., 1891); J. M. Freeland, *The Australian Pub* (Melb., 1966), pp. 146-8.
29 *Builder and Contractor's News*, 18 June 1887, p. 90; Boyd, op. cit., pp. 47-8; The E. S. & A. Limited, *The Gothic Bank of Collins Street* (roneoed, 1953).
30 Freeland, op. cit., p. 148.
31 Nancy Adams, *Family Fresco* (Melb., 1966), pp. 30-1, for a description of Fanecourt, East Melbourne, *c.* 1890; Maie Casey has an excellent description of Stony Park, Brunswick, *c.* 1886 (*An Australian Story*, pp. 39-45).
32 Dale, *Impressions of Australia*, pp. 20-1; J. T. Goudie, *Notes and Gleanings* (Edinburgh, 1894), pp. 44-5.
33 Bate, *History of Brighton*, p. 332.
34 Boyd, *Australia's Home*, pp. 46-7.
35 *Argus*, 14 Mar. 1884, p. 5.
36 *Builder and Contractor's News*, 28 Apr. 1888, p. 268.
37 Turner, *History of Victoria*, vol. 2, pp. 263-4.
38 *Argus*, 4 Apr. 1885, p. 13; Casey, *An Australian Story*, pp. 57, 63.
39 J. M. Freeland, *Architecture in Australia. A History* (Melb., 1968), ch. 8; Boyd, *Australia's Home*, ch. 5; Butlin, *Investment in Australian Economic Development*, pp. 222-3; J. L. O'Brien, *Domestic Architecture in Victoria 1850-1890* (roneoed, 1959).
40 Sugden letters, 13 Aug. 1888.
41 Lord Normanby, Governors' Minute-book, vol. 2, p. 192, 24 Mar. 1881 (VA).
42 Bate, *History of Brighton*, pp. 212-13.
43 *Leader*, 25 Feb. 1888, p. 27; Progress Report of the Royal Commission upon the Sanitary Condition of Melbourne, *P.P.*, 1889, vol. 2, no. 27; Report of the Board of Public Health 1890-91, *P.P.*, 1891, vol. 6, no. 197; Jacqueline Templeton, *Prince Henry's. The Evolution of a Melbourne Hospital 1869-1969* (Melb., 1969), ch. 10.
44 Cf. *Age*, 12 Jan. 1889, edit.
45 Progress Report (note 43), *P.P.*, 1889, vol. 2, no. 27; vol. 4, nos 103, 112.
46 *Age*, 8 Jan. 1889, p. 6.
47 *Argus*, 21 Jan. 1889, p. 6; *Age*, 10 Apr. 1889, p. 6; *Argus*, Sept. 1888, *passim*; also *Argus*, 23 Feb., p. 13; 24 Feb. 1888, p. 8; 23 Jan., p. 6; 24 Jan. 1889, p. 11.
48 Report on the Sewerage and Sewage Disposal of the Proposed Melbourne Metropolitan District, *P.P.*, 1890, vol. 4, no. 182, p. 13.
49 Deakin's second-reading speech, *P.D.*, vol. 62, pp. 1878-90. In general, see Barrett, 'The Making of an Industrial Environment', pp. 172-86.
50 Briggs, *Victorian Cities*, p. 309; Kinglake, op. cit. (note 7), p. 107; Henry Cornish, *Under the Southern Cross* (Madras, 1879), p. 63.
51 *Argus*, 15 Oct. 1883, p. 5.
52 Gould, op. cit. (note 7), p. 126.
53 Adams, *The Australians*, p. 27.
54 Royal Commission on Shop Employés, *P.P.*, 1884, vol. 2, no. 18, p. 108.
55 *Argus*, 16 Oct. 1883, p. 5; cf. Twopeny, *Town Life*, pp. 98-9.
56 In general, see McLachlan, 'Larrikinism'.
57 Cf. Stephen Murray-Smith, *Australian Book Review*, Nov. 1969, p. 24.

58 *Table Talk*, 29 July 1887, p. 12; for main celebrations, *Argus*, mid- to late-June 1887.
59 *Table Talk*, 24 June 1887, pp. 9-19; *Punch*, 23 June 1887, has a supplement on the ball.
60 Governors' Letter-books, 1887; Morris, *George Higinbotham*, pp. 277-82.
61 *Argus*, 21 June 1887, p. 7.
62 Sutherland, *Victoria and its Metropolis*, vol. 1, p. 490.
63 *Argus*, 20 June 1887, edit.; *Table Talk*, 17 June, p. 8; 24 June 1887, p. 1.
64 *Age*, 5 Feb., edit.; 7 Feb. 1887, p. 4.
65 *Advocate*, 28 May 1887, p. 15.
66 *Liberator*, 8 May, 26 June 1887; *Table Talk*, 2 Dec. 1887. On the extent of poverty, see L. L. Smith, *P.D.*, vol. 54, p. 358.
67 T. Allnutt Brassey, *Sixteen Months Travel 1886-87* (London, 1888), pp. 171, 154.
68 A. S. Kenyon, *The Story of Melbourne* (Melb., 1934), p. 123.
69 Ada Cambridge, *The Three Miss Kings* (Melb., 1891), p. 52; Kiddle, *Men of Yesterday*, p. 346.
70 *Leader*, 21 Feb. 1885, p. 26.
71 Sutherland *et al.*, *Victoria and its Metropolis*; T. W. H. Leavitt, *Australian Representative Men* (Melb., 1887); *Table Talk*, 13 Sept. 1889, p. 3; *Argus*, 10 May 1889, p. 5.
72 Norton, *History of Capital and Labour*, p. v.
73 *P.D.*, vol. 56, pp. 2149-50.
74 Cambridge, *Thirty Years*, p. 188.
75 *Official Record of the Centennial International Exhibition, Melbourne, 1888-1889* (Melb., 1890), pp. 128-9.
76 Premiers' Telegram Book, 1887, *passim*; Deakin to Derham, 15 Apr. 1887 (Derham Papers).
77 Morris, *George Higinbotham*, pp. 282-4.
78 *Australasian*, 11 Aug. 1888, p. 321.
79 *Australasian*, 4 Aug. 1888, p. 265; Cambridge, *Thirty Years*, p. 187; *Argus* weekly supplements, 2 Aug.-25 Sept. 1888; *Argus*, 1 Feb. 1889, p. 8; Westgarth, *Half a Century* (note 21), pp. 57-63; J. R. Thompson, 'The Melbourne Centennial International Exhibition 1888-89' (B.A. thesis, Monash Univ., 1968).
80 Twopeny, *Town Life*, pp. 217-18.
81 Sir Frederic H. Cowen, *My Art and my Friends* (London, 1913), pp. 191-215; Ann K. Wentzel, 'The First Hundred Years of Music in Australia 1788-1888' (M.A., Univ. Sydney, 1963), pt 6, ch. 4; Kenneth Hince, 'Sir Frederic Cowen', *A.D.B.*, vol. 3; A. S. Kenyon, *The Story of Melbourne* (Melb., 1934), pp. 121-3.
82 Nehemiah Bartley, *Opals and Agates . . .* (Brisbane, 1892), p. 263.
83 *Argus*, 6 July 1888, p. 8; 1 Feb. 1888, p. 7; Thompson, op. cit. (note 79), pp. 49-51.
84 R. H. Croll, *Tom Roberts, Father of Australian Landscape Painting* (Melb., 1935), p. 18.
85 Quoted by John Rothenstein, *The Life and Death of Conder* (London, 1938), p. 21.
86 Lionel Lindsay, quoted by Ann Galbally, *Arthur Streeton* (Melb., 1969), p. 1.
87 Bernard Smith, *Australian Painting 1788-1960* (Melb., 1962), ch. 4; Alan McCulloch, *The Golden Age of Australian Painting. Impressionism and the Heidelberg School* (Melb., 1969); Ursula Hoff, *Charles Conder. His Australian Years* (Melb., 1960).
88 Lydia Leavitt, op. cit. (note 3), p. 49.
89 MS., ML.
90 *Argus*, 16 June 1884, p. 5; Sugden letters, 21 Apr. 1888.
91 *Table Talk*, 1 June 1888, p. 2.
92 *P.D.*, vol. 55, pp. 1491-503; vol. 52, pp. 1480-8; Hamilton Mackinnon to Deakin, 8 Sept. 1887 (Deakin Correspondence).
93 Kennedy and Palmer, *Bernard O'Dowd*, pp. 63-76; Denton Prout, *Henry Lawson. The Grey Dreamer* (Adelaide, 1963), pp. 65-8; Colin Roderick (ed.), *Henry Lawson Letters. 1890-1922* (Sydney, 1970), p. 88.
94 L. J. Blake, *Shaw Neilson in the Wimmera* (n.p., n.d.), ch. 2.
95 Miles Franklin, *Joseph Furphy. The Legend of a Man and his Book* (Sydney, 1944), ch. 5.
96 Twopeny, *Town Life*, pp. 207-8.
97 H. C. A. Harrison, *The Story of an Athlete* (Melb., 1923), p. 98; *Argus*, 16 July 1883, p. 8; 5 Nov. 1885, p. 5; Murray, op. cit. (note 5), p. 215. 'The Vagabond', 'Manly Sports' (Michael Cannon (ed.), *The Vagabond Papers*, Melb., 1969) and Steve Fairbairn (*Fairbairn of Jesus . . .*, London, 1931, ch. 6) indicate how rough the game was in the late 1870s at least.
98 *Argus*, 18 Aug. 1884, p. 5; Moore, 'Marvellous Melbourne', pp. 99-100.
99 Sutherland, *Victoria and its Metropolis*, vol. 1, pp. 563-4.
1 E.g. A. B. Tulloch, *Recollections of Forty Years Service* (Edinburgh, 1903), pp. 354-5; Parker, *Round the Compass*, p. 110; Lord Brassey, CO 309/143/542.

2 *Argus*, 7 Nov. 1888.
3 *Age, Argus*, 12-14 May 1887; L. J. Harrigan, *Victorian Railways to '62* (Melb., n.d.), p. 178.
4 *Argus*, 5, 6 Sept. 1887, p. 6; *Australasian*, 3, 10, 17, 24 Sept. 1887; *Imperial Review*, Jan. 1888, pp. 46-8; *Advocate*, 10 Sept. 1887, p. 15.
5 'A Song of the English', *Collected Verse of Rudyard Kipling* (London, 1912), p. 127.
6 Shiels, *P.D.*, vol. 58, p. 1318.

10 NATIONAL ISSUES, 1888

1 E.g. for Creswick, Margaret McAleese, 'Creswick in the 1880s' (B.A. thesis, Monash Univ., 1968), pp. 14-16.
2 *Argus*, 31 Mar., p. 11; 3 Apr., p. 7; 3 May 1883, p. 10; 26 Sept. 1884, p. 5.
3 E.g. *Argus*, 6 Apr. 1888, p. 8; Daryl Lindsay, *The Leafy Tree. My Family* (Melb., 1965), pp. 19-20.
4 E.g. Gane, *N.S.W. and Victoria*, p. 66; cf. Sutherland, *Victoria and its Metropolis*, vol. 1, pp. 557-8.
5 E.g. Turner, *History of Victoria*, vol. 2, pp. 232-6, for a general defence.
6 *P.D.*, vol. 50, pp. 1946-50, 2515-19.
7 *P.D.*, vol. 56, pp. 2562-74, 2635-8; Reports of the Chief Inspector of Factories, *P.P.*, 1888, vol. 2, no. 39; 1889, vol. 3, no. 30; Oddie, 'The Chinese in Victoria', ch. 3.
8 Petition included with Loch to S. of S., 23 June 1887, CO 309/131/170.
9 *Argus*, 28 May 1887, p. 10; *P.D.*, vol. 56, p. 2637; William Westgarth, *Personal Recollections of Early Melbourne & Victoria* (Melb., 1888), p. 161.
10 Report by E. H. Parker of the China Consular Service, CO 881/9/no. 130.
11 *Age*, 2 Jan. 1886, edit.; 14 June, edit.; 8 Aug. 1887, edit.
12 *Argus*, 30 July 1887, pp. 7, 10.
13 *Argus*, 20 Sept. 1887, p. 8; 16 Feb. 1888, p. 5.
14 *Argus*, 22 Sept., p. 11; 27 Oct., p. 5; 6 Dec., p. 7; 15 Dec. 1887, p. 13; 12 Jan. 1888, p. 8; *Australasian*, 24 Dec. 1887, p. 1241.
15 *P.D.*, vol. 56, pp. 2571, 2688-9.
16 Figures in footnote from Willard, *White Australia Policy*, p. 71.
17 Chinese in Victoria, *P.P.*, 1885, vol. 1, C22; Chinese, *P.P.*, 1887, vol. 1, C4; *P.D.*, vol. 54, p. 301; vol. 57, pp. 80-90; *Argus*, 8 Oct. 1887, p. 9; Willard, op. cit., p. 71.
18 *Age*, 22 May 1888, p. 5.
19 CO 881/8, no. 129 and CO 881/9, no. 130 contain the relevant despatches; the terms of the proposed treaty are in Knutsford to Australian Governors, Very Confidential, 14 Sept. 1888; Vic. Premiers' Correspondence and Telegram Books; Chinese Immigration. Papers, *P.P.*, 1888, vol. 1, C20; *Argus*, 1888, *passim*; Willard, op. cit., ch. 4.
20 *P.D.*, vol. 57, pp. 63-295, *passim*.
21 *P.D.*, vol. 56, p. 2637.
22 *Argus*, 20 July 1888, p. 7.
23 *P.D.*, vol. 59, pp. 2360-73, 2524-6, 2642-50.
24 *P.D.*, vol. 59, pp. 2357-695, *passim*.
25 *Musgrove* v. *Toy*. Papers, *P.P.*, 1888, vol. 1, C23; Morris, *George Higinbotham*, pp. 265-8.
26 *P.D.*, vol. 58, p. 1052.
27 *P.D.*, vol. 57, p. 194; vol. 58, pp. 1058-61.
28 *P.D.*, vol. 67, p. 1337; *Musgrove* v. *Toy*. Papers, *P.P.*, 1888, vol. 1, C23.
29 Reeves, *State Experiments*, vol. 2, pp. 339-40; Sir John Pope Hennessy, 'The Chinese in Australia', *Nineteenth Century*, vol. 23, Apr. 1888, pp. 617-19.
30 *Argus*, 10 Mar. 1889, p. 12.
31 Charles H. Pearson, *National Life and Character. A Forecast* (London, 1893), p. 16.
32 Governors' Minute Books, vol. 2, pp. 227, 238, 271 (VA).
33 Higinbotham to Sir Henry Holland, 28 Feb. 1887, in Morris, *George Higinbotham*, p. 214.
34 Quoted by McCormack, 'Victorian Governors and Responsible Government', p. 251.
35 Morris, op. cit., p. 201.
36 *Australian*, Jan. 1888.
37 Loch to S. of S., Conf., 30 Sept. 1886, CO 309/130/293; Loch to S. of S., Conf., 4 Aug. 1887, CO 309/131/230, 726; Loch to S. of S., Secret, 26 Oct. 1888, CO 309/132/517; CO 309/133/369-93 (Law Officers' report); Governors' Minute Books, vol. 2, p. 258; Hopetoun to S. of S., Conf., 3 May 1892, CO 309/137/174; McCormack, 'Victorian Governors and Responsible Government', ch. 10.
38 CO 309/133/431-41; CO 309/134/139; Governors' Papers, Bundle 18, 'Governor and Chief Justice'; *Argus* and *Age*, 16-18 Feb. 1889; *Argus*, 22 Feb. 1889, p. 5 (Michie). Sir Kenneth Bailey's analysis has not been seriously tested in forty years (*Cambridge*

History of the British Empire, vol. 7, pt 1, ch. 14; see also Sir Frederick Eggleston, ibid., pp. 522-8).

39 See Geoffrey Serle, *The Golden Age* . . . (Melb., 1963), pp. 197-8.

40 Renewal of Commercial Treaties, *P.P.*, 1891, vol. 1, C10.

41 *Argus*, 2 Sept. 1885, edit. and p. 10; Richard A. Preston, *Canada and "Imperial Defense"* . . . (Durham, N.C., 1967), p. 225.

42 CO 881/8; CO 309/134/560 (Hopetoun to Knutsford); CO 309/135/508 (Gillies); *P.D.*, vol. 60, pp. 614-34, 815-27; Shiels to Pearson, 18 Feb. 1890 (Pearson Papers); Holland-Salisbury Correspondence (Christ Church).

43 Loch to S. of S., Conf., 31 Dec. 1884, CO 309/127/386.

44 Loch to S. of S., Conf., 3 Mar. 1886, CO 309/130/56; Loch to S. of S., Secret and Conf., 10 Feb. 1888, CO 309/132/65; Governors' Minute Books, vol. 2, p. 218; Atkins, 'Representation of Australia in England', p. 250.

45 Loch to S. of S., Secret and Conf., 10 May and 12 July 1888, CO 881/9, no. 130.

46 E.g. minutes on Loch's confidential despatches of 30 June 1885, CO 309/129/151; 24 June 1886, CO 309/130/18; 6 Jan. 1885, CO 881/8, no. 129.

47 Lord Carrington, quoted by Adams, *The Australians*, p. 268.

48 Deakin to Dilke, 19 June 1890 (Dilke Papers).

49 CO 309/133/77.

50 Hall, *Australia and England*, pp. 203-6.

51 *P.D.*, vol. 59, pp. 1993-2004.

52 *P.D.*, vol. 56, pp. 2147-51.

53 *Advocate*, 3 Nov. 1888, p. 15; *Argus*, 15 Dec. 1888, p. 9.

54 *Age*, 5 Nov. 1887, edit.

55 *P.D.*, vol. 59, pp. 2214-29; *Argus*, 29 Nov., p. 6; 3 Dec. 1888, p. 4.

56 *P.D.*, vol. 59, p. 2699.

57 *P.D.*, vol. 60, p. 15.

58 Knutsford to Australian Governors, 8 July 1889, *P.P.*, 1889, vol. 4, no. 124.

59 Cf. Deakin, *Federal Story*, p. 30.

60 *Liberator*, 6 May 1888, p. 373; *Argus*, 21 Apr. 1888, p. 11; *Recorder*, vol. 2, no. 1, Apr. 1966.

61 *Australian*, July 1887, edit.; Dec. 1887, p. 15; Jan. 1888, p. 17; *Argus*, 24 Mar. 1888, p. 4.

62 *Australian*, Feb. 1888, p. 16.

63 Deakin, *Federal Story*, pp. 6-9; *Table Talk*, 1 Oct. 1886, pp. 2, 4; Theodore Fink, 'Reminiscences'.

64 *Argus*, 27 Apr.-12 May, 26 May-1 June 1888, *passim*; Aveling, 'History of the A.N.A.'.

65 *Age*, 4 June, p. 13; 21 Sept. 1888, p. 7; *Argus*, 15 Sept. 1888 and following days.

66 *Age*, 11 Apr., edit.; 28 Apr. 1888, edit.; *Argus*, 28 May 1888, edit.

67 *Age*, 19 Apr. 1888, p. 5; *Argus*, 10 May 1888, p. 8.

68 *Young Australia*, 1888-9, *passim*; for examples of numerous letters by natives attacking the A.N.A., *Argus*, 11 Aug. 1888, p. 5; 24 Aug. 1889, p. 13; *Table Talk*, 28 Sept. 1888, p. 1.

69 E.g. *Australian*, June 1888, p. 7; Frank Stuart, *Argus*, 3 Oct. 1888, p. 11; Deegan, *Chronicles of the Melbourne Beefsteak Club*, 4 June 1887; Trenwith, *P.D.*, vol. 66, p. 228.

70 *Argus*, 26 Nov. 1889, p. 5.

71 Aveling, 'History of the A.N.A.', ch. 8. In this section, I have again drawn heavily on Mrs Aveling's work.

72 Cf. Hancock, *Survey of British Commonwealth Affairs*, vol. 1, pp. 13-18.

73 *Argus*, 13 Dec. 1888, p. 7; 28 Jan. 1889, p. 5.

74 Dilke, *Problems of Greater Britain*, p. 156.

75 *Argus*, 11 July 1889, edit.

76 E.g. *Age*, 9 Apr., p. 6; 6 May, p. 6; 25 May 1889, p. 3; cf. *Argus*, 7 Dec. 1888, edit. For Purves and the Ballarat invitation, *Argus*, 5 Dec. 1888, p. 8; for a reply to Purves by Marshall Lyle, *Age*, 8 Dec. 1888, p. 4. For Ievers, Deegan, *Chronicles of the Melbourne Beefsteak Club*, p. 87.

77 *Argus*, 18 Feb. 1887, p. 6.

78 *Age*, 21 Apr. 1888, p. 10; *Argus*, 26 May 1888, p. 14; Aveling, op. cit., ch. 8.

79 *Age*, 28 Feb., p. 6; 22 Mar. 1888, p. 5; *Australian*, Mar. 1888, pp. 3-4.

80 *Age*, 3 May 1889, edit.

81 *Australian*, Feb. 1887, p. 3.

82 *Table Talk*, 17 Aug. 1888, p. 1.

83 E.g. Carlton, *Age*, 9 Apr. 1889, p. 6.

84 *Argus*, 10 Mar., p. 7; 16 July 1887, p. 9.

85 Cf. Margaret Gravell, 'Australia Day 1888: a Social Enquiry' (B.A. thesis, Univ. Melb., 1967).

86 *P.D.*, vol. 60, pp. 386-7; C. H. Pearson, *Reviews and Critical Essays* (London, 1896), pp. 215-21; Aveling, op. cit., ch. 7.
87 Deegan, *Chronicles of the Melbourne Beefsteak Club*, p. 89.
88 We may take *The Pleasant Career of a Spendthrift* as representative of his view in the 1880s.
89 E.g. *P.D.*, vol. 60, pp. 143, 183 (W. T. Carter and Maloney).
90 *Argus*, 11 Aug. 1888, p. 14.
91 *P.D.*, vol. 66, p. 214.
92 Lecture at the Working Men's College, *Age*, 22 July 1889, p. 6.
93 Gillies to Berry, 25 Feb. 1887 (Berry Papers).
94 *Bulletin*, 2 Dec. 1887, p. 5.
95 *Australasian*, 3 Dec. 1887, p. 1081; *P.D.*, vol. 56, p. 2211; Premiers' Telegram Book, 25, 29 Nov. 1887; CO 309/131/399, 438.
96 *Argus*, 7 Dec. 1887, p. 5.
97 *Argus*, 14 Dec. 1887, p. 7; *P.D.*, vol. 57, p. 731; Parkes to Gillies, 29 Dec. 1887 (Vic. Premiers' Corr., VA).
98 Inspection of Colonial Forces by an Imperial General Officer. Correspondence, *P.P.*, 1889, vol. 3, no. 57.
99 Parkes to Gillies, 3 Apr., 4 May, 13 Sept. 1888; Gillies to Parkes, 13 Apr., 26 Apr., 29 June 1888 (Vic. Premiers' Corr.); *P.D.*, vol. 59, pp. 2345-7; vol. 62, pp. 2001-3; Priestley, *Echuca*, pp. 137-8; Alan Gross, 'Maribyrnong', *Vic. Hist. Mag.*, no. 86, Sept. 1947, p. 60.
1 *Intercolonial Free Trade Conference, 1887. Report of the Proceedings.*
2 *Argus*, 7 June, p. 5; 8 June 1888, p. 6.
3 *Australasian Commercial Congress, Centennial Year, 1888. Report of the Proceedings of the Congress of Chambers of Commerce* (Melb., 1889).
4 *Age*, 8 Jan. 1889, p. 6.
5 *Argus*, 22 Aug. 1888, p. 7.
6 E.g. *Age*, 20 Aug. 1888, edit.
7 *Age* editorials, 20 Apr., 12 July, 21 Aug., 14 Sept. 1888.
8 E.g. *P.D.*, vol. 51, p. 125; vol. 55, p. 1189.
9 *Australasian Commercial Congress* (note 3), p. 24.
10 Ibid., pp. 50-1; *Argus*, 15 May 1888, p. 9.
11 *Argus*, 12 Nov. 1888, p. 4; Gillies to Parkes (Parkes Correspondence, ML).

11 CLOSE OF AN ERA, 1888-1889

1 Ingham, 'Aspects of Victorian Liberalism', p. 39.
2 *P.D.*, vol. 54, pp. 828-906.
3 *P.D.*, vol. 55, pp. 1161-464.
4 *Argus*, 27 Oct. 1888, p. 11; cf. Pearson, *P.D.*, vol. 60, pp. 167-8; *Argus*, 2 Mar. 1889, p. 13.
5 *P.D.*, vol. 57, pp. 755-6, 841, 864-5, 886; *Argus*, 28 June 1886, p. 10; Graham, *Formation Australian Country Parties*, pp. 67-8.
6 *Argus*, 3 Nov. 1887, p. 7.
7 *Argus*, 12 Mar. 1888, p. 7.
8 Graham, *Formation Australian Country Parties*, p. 48; *Argus*, 5 Apr. 1888, p. 4.
9 Quoted by Graham, op. cit., p. 53.
10 *Age*, 17 Aug. 1888, p. 8.
11 Quoted by Graham, op. cit., p. 50.
12 *P.D.*, vol. 57, pp. 117-21, 148; *Argus*, 10 July, p. 9; 4 Aug. 1888, p. 5.
13 Hume Dow, 'J. L. Dow', *A.D.B.*, vol. 4; J. L. Dow, 'Agriculture', *Colonial and Indian Exhibition, London, 1886. Illustrated Handbook of Victoria, Australia* (London, 1886); Fitzpatrick, *British Empire in Australia*, pp. 173-7; Reeves, *State Experiments*, vol. 1, pp. 372-3.
14 *P.D.*, vol. 57, pp. 518-40.
15 *P.D.*, vol. 57, pp. 570-86, 589-94; *Argus*, 26 July, p. 7; 28 July 1888, p. 4.
16 For composition, *Argus*, 16 Aug. 1888, p. 8.
17 *Argus*, 15 Nov. 1887, p. 5; 3 July 1888, p. 5.
18 *Argus*, 20 June, p. 8; 31 Aug., p. 9; Sept. 1888, *passim*.
19 *P.D.*, vol. 57, pp. 649-1000; *Argus*, 18 Aug., p. 5; 27 Aug., p. 7; 1 Sept. 1888, p. 5.
20 *P.D.*, vol. 58, pp. 1110-85; Deakin to Josiah Royce, 31 Dec. 1888 (Deakin Papers).
21 *Argus*, 17 Dec. 1888, p. 5; *P.D.*, vol. 58, p. 1233.
22 *P.D.*, vol. 58, p. 986; *Argus*, 25 May 1888, p. 7.
23 Deakin to Dilke, 30 Aug. 1888 (Dilke Papers).
24 *P.D.*, vol. 57, pp. 721-44, 538-9 (Gillies).

[25] *P.D.*, vol. 58, pp. 1213-892; vol. 59, pp. 1912-2616; *Argus*, 5 July, p. 7; 22 Oct., p. 10; 3 Nov. 1888, p. 7.
[26] *P.D.*, vol. 59, p. 1967. [27] *P.D.*, vol. 59, pp. 1959-63.
[28] *P.D.*, vol. 59, pp. 1957-2682. [29] *P.D.*, vol. 58, pp. 1599-601; vol. 59, pp. 1893-7.
[30] *Argus*, 27 Apr. 1888, p. 8; *Age*, 30 July, edit.; 6 Dec. 1888, p. 7; *Liberator*, 31 July 1887, p. 155; petition, 'Women's Suffrage', *P.P.*, 1889, vol. 1, E4.
[31] E.g. Duties of Customs Bill 1889, *P.P.*, 1889, vol. 1, C18.
[32] Deakin to James Bryce, 21 Nov. 1892 (Bryce Papers, Bodleian Library, C4).
[33] *Argus*, 14 Aug. 1886, p. 5. [34] *P.D.*, vol. 59, pp. 2314-448.
[35] E.g. Deakin to Dilke, 31 Mar. 1890 (Dilke Papers).
[36] *Argus*, 25 Feb., edit.; 26 Mar. 1889, edit.
[37] *Age*, 22 Mar. 1889, edit.; Deakin to Royce, 22 Apr. 1889 (Deakin Papers).
[38] *Argus*, 7 Feb. 1889, p. 8; 9 Nov. 1888, p. 10.
[39] Dilke, *Problems of Greater Britain*, p. 143. [40] *Argus*, 9 Nov. 1888, p. 10.
[41] Graham, *Formation Australian Country Parties*, pp. 72-3.
[42] *Argus*, 27 Feb. 1889, p. 6; for the Coalition Committee, *Age*, 17 May 1889, p. 6.
[43] E.g. *Age*, 25 Mar. 1889, edit., but cf. *Argus*, 5 Feb., edit.; 6 Feb. 1889, p. 7; *Advocate*, 6 Apr. 1889, pp. 6, 15.
[44] Cf. Gollan, *Radical and Working Class Politics*, p. 98.
[45] *Argus*, 1 Apr. 1889, p. 10; for the election, Dilke, *Problems of Greater Britain*, pp. 138-44; Finlayson, 'Groups in Victorian Politics', ch. 2.
[46] Deakin to Berry, 9 Apr. 1889 (Berry Papers).
[47] *Argus*, 2 May 1889, p. 10. [48] *P.D.*, vol. 63, pp. 258-60, for Bent on Patterson.
[49] *P.D.*, vol. 60, pp. 44-51; Deakin to Crisp, undated (Crisp Correspondence); Deakin Correspondence, 6043, 6931.
[50] *Argus*, 5 June, edit.; 8 June 1889, p. 5.
[51] *P.D.*, vol. 60, pp. 96-257; *Argus*, 25 Nov. 1889, edit. [52] Ibid., pp. 765-83.
[53] *P.D.*, vols 60-1, pp. 1002-143. [54] *P.D.*, vol. 60, p. 846.
[55] *P.D.*, vol. 73, p. 1597. [56] *P.D.*, vol. 62, pp. 1948, 1970.
[57] Ibid., pp. 2266-73.
[58] Patterson, *The Tariff in the Australian Colonies*, pp. 94-6 for details; Deakin to Dilke, 5 Sept. 1889 (Dilke Papers).
[59] *Argus*, 13 Aug., edit.; 14 Aug., edit.; 20 Aug., p. 5; 7 Sept., p. 5; 23 Sept., edit.; 27 Sept., p. 5; 28 Sept. 1889, p. 5.
[60] *P.D.*, vol. 60, pp. 694-7; vols. 60-2 (Rabbits Destruction Act).
[61] Francis Adams, *The Melbournians; a Novel* (London, 1892), pp. 135, 247.
[62] Tregenza, *Professor of Democracy*, pp. 116-19, ch. 11.
[63] Quoted by La Nauze, *Alfred Deakin*, vol. 1, p. 121.
[64] Cf. Fry, 'Urban Wage Earning Class', pp. 515-16.
[65] *Argus*, 20 Mar. 1889, p. 7; Turner, *History of Victoria*, vol. 2, pp. 292, 304; Shann, *Economic History*, p. 312.
[66] Hall, *Stock Exchange*, pp. 148-9.
[67] *Argus*, 14 Sept. 1889, p. 5; *Table Talk*, 15 Nov. 1889, p. 8.
[68] *Argus*, 25 May, p. 10; 29 May 1889, p. 9; *P.D.*, vol. 60, pp. 469-589; 'The Unemployed', petition, *P.P.*, 1889, vol. 1, E2.
[69] *Statist*, from 12 Jan. 1889; cf. John McA. Howden to B. J. Fink, 31 May 1889, Howden letter-book (Univ. Melb. Archives).
[70] *P.D.*, vol. 60, p. 882.
[71] *Age*, 16 Aug. 1889, edit.; Imperial Federation League, Victorian branch, letter-book (NL); George R. Parkin, *Imperial Federation. The Problem of National Unity* (London, 1892), p. 222; Deakin to Berry, 9 Apr. 1889 (Berry Papers).
[72] *Argus*, 27 Apr., edit.; 29 Apr., p. 6; 3 May 1889, p. 6; J. Dillon and others, *The Irish Envoys in Australia* (Melb., 1889); T. H. G. Esmonde, *Round the World with the Irish Delegates* (Dublin, 1892).
[73] *P.D.*, vol. 54, p. 2. [74] CO 309/132/154.
[75] *Argus*, 24 Oct. 1885, p. 13. [76] Dale, *Impressions of Australia*, pp. 271-4.
[77] Millar, 'History of the Defence Forces of Victoria', appendices G and H for statistics; A. B. Tulloch, *Recollections of Forty Years' Service* (Edinburgh, 1903), ch. 25.
[78] Richard Jebb, *The Imperial Conference* (London, 1911), vol. 1, p. 22.
[79] Dilke, *Problems of Greater Britain*, p. 159.
[80] Fourth Earl of Carnarvon, 'Australia in 1888', *Essays, Addresses and Translations* (London, 1896), vol. 3, p. 132.
[81] Tulloch, op. cit., p. 357. [82] CO 309/135/172.

83 CO 309/131/166; CO 309/133/576. 84 *P.D.*, vol. 63, pp. 429-32.
85 H. W., *Argus*, 29 Jan. 1887, p. 4.
86 *Age* and *Argus*, 2, 3 July 1888; *P.D.*, vol. 57, p. 237.
87 Report on the Military Forces and Defences of Victoria, with attached General Report, *P.P.*, 1889, vol. 4, no. 139, p. 6.
88 Deakin diaries, Jan. 1889; La Nauze, *Alfred Deakin*, vol. 1, p. 116.
89 *Federal Council of Australasia. Official Record of Debates* (Hobart, 1889), p. 79.
90 Deakin, *Federal Story*, p. 18.
91 *Sir H. Parkes' Federation Scheme. Extracts from Lord Carrington's Diary* (ML).
92 Vic. Premiers' Secret Files, 89/5 (VA).
93 Deakin to Dilke, 5 July 1889 (Dilke Papers). 94 Deakin, *Federal Story*, p. 30.
95 *P.D.*, vol. 51, p. 474; vol. 55, p. 1046; vol. 59, p. 2327; *Argus*, 4 July, edit.; 9 Sept., edit.; 19 Sept. 1889, edit.; *Age*, 6 Sept., p. 5; 7 Sept. 1889, p. 8; Deakin to Dilke, 5 Sept. 1889 (Dilke Papers).
96 Henry Parkes, *Fifty Years in the Making of Australian History* (London, 1892), pp. 585-603; La Nauze, *Alfred Deakin*, vol. 1, pp. 115-18; D. McR. McCallum, 'Sir Henry Parkes and Federation', *Journal, Royal Aust. Hist. Soc.*, vol. 34, pt 1, 1948; W. G. McMinn, 'Sir Henry Parkes as a Federalist', *Hist. Studies*, vol. 12, no. 47, Oct. 1966.
97 *P.D.*, vol. 62, pp. 2504-14.
98 *Argus*, 11 Nov., p. 7; 19 Nov. 1889, p. 7.
99 Hall, *Stock Exchange*, pp. 122-3, 161, 165; note on p. 169 the table showing stock and share values in 1889.
1 *P.D.*, vol. 61, pp. 1683-91. 2 *Argus*, 30 Nov., p. 10; 9 Dec. 1889, p. 7.
3 E.g. 5 Oct. 1888, edit.
4 *Argus*, 21 Dec. 1889, pp. 9-10; Hall, *Stock Exchange*, p. 164.
5 Hall, op. cit., p. 123.
6 Butlin, *Investment in Australian Economic Development*, p. 338.
7 *Argus*, 27 Aug., p. 8; 29 Sept. 1888, p. 18. 8 *Argus*, 11 Apr. 1889, p. 6.
9 *Age*, 19 Mar. 1889, p. 5. 10 *Argus*, 7 Sept. 1889, p. 10.
11 *Argus*, 9 Sept., p. 5; 12 Oct. 1889, p. 9; L. J. Bevan, *The Life and Reminiscences of Llewellyn David Bevan* (Melb., 1920), pp. 191-3.
12 *Argus*, 4 Sept., pp. 7-8; 7 Sept. 1889, p. 9. 13 *Argus*, 13 Sept. 1889, p. 6.
14 N. W. Saffin, 'The Portrait of Cardinal Manning in Ballarat Trades Hall', *Labour History*, no. 8, May 1965.
15 E.g. Brian Fitzpatrick, *A Short History of the Australian Labour Movement* (Melb., 1968, 1st ed. 1940), p. 111; H. V. Evatt, *Australian Labour Leader. The Story of W. A. Holman and the Labour Movement* (Sydney, 1945), p. 22.
16 E.g. *Table Talk*, 20 Sept. 1889, p. 2.
17 In general, *Argus* and *Age*, late Aug.–mid-Nov. 1889; D. C. Littlewood, 'The Australian Reaction to the London Dock Strike of 1889' (B.A. thesis, Univ. Melb., 1959).
18 Carnarvon, op. cit. (note 80), pp. 101-2; A. Hardinge, *The Life of the Fourth Earl of Carnarvon* (London, 1925), vol. 3, p. 279.
19 Dale, *Impressions of Australia*, pp. 27-31; cf. George R. Parkin, *Imperial Federation. The Problem of National Unity* (London, 1892), p. 222.
20 Deakin quoted by La Nauze, *Alfred Deakin*, vol. 1, pp. 105-6; Fink, 'Reminiscences'; Meudell, *Pleasant Career*, p. 56.
21 Walch, *Victoria in 1880*, pp. 165-6.
22 Cf. Smith, 'Religion and Freethought', p. 343.
23 Cf. La Nauze, *Alfred Deakin*, vol. 1, p. 25; N. G. Butlin, 'Economic Enquiry in Australia', *Aust. Economic History Review*, vol. 7, no. 2, Sept. 1967, pp. 189-90.
24 *Argus*, 26 Jan. 1888.
25 H. B. Higgins, 'The Muses in Australia', *Melbourne University Review*, 24 Dec. 1885, p. 197.
26 Sidney Webb quoted in A. G. Austin (ed.), *The Webbs' Australian Diary 1898* (Melb., 1965), p. 115.
27 See A. W. Martin (ed.), *Essays in Australian Federation* (Melb., 1969), pp. 53-6, for my more detailed comparison.

Bibliography

This is a select bibliography. Many sources, of which only passing use has been made and which are acknowledged in the Notes, have been omitted. The lists are arranged as follows:

I OFFICIAL CONTEMPORARY SOURCES
- A. Manuscript
- B. Printed

II OTHER CONTEMPORARY SOURCES
- A. Manuscript
- B. Newspapers and Periodicals
- C. Books, Pamphlets and Articles

III LATER WORKS
- A. Books and Articles
- B. Unpublished Theses

I OFFICIAL CONTEMPORARY SOURCES

A. MANUSCRIPT

(i) *Archives Division, State Library of Victoria*

Governors' Papers: Despatches to and from the Secretary of State for the Colonies, letter-books, minute-books, Executive Council papers, and papers classified under various headings.

Premier's Department: Telegram Books, Secret Files, and Correspondence (which includes intercolonial communications).

Only occasional use has been made of material in the Chief Secretary's, Treasurer's, Lands' Department, and other files, which remain almost entirely unexplored territory.

(ii) *Colonial Office Papers in the Public Record Office, London*

Series CO 309 contains the Inwards Correspondence to the Secretary of State from Victoria, with minutes and occasional draft replies. Series CO 881/8 and 881/9 cover important general questions, such as Chinese immigration, the Federal Council and divorce.

B. PRINTED

Federal Council of Australasia. *Debates*, 1886-9. 3 vols. Hobart.

Victoria. Acts of Parliament.

Victoria. *Government Gazette.*

Victoria. *Parliamentary Debates.*

Victoria. *Votes and Proceedings of the Legislative Assembly with Copies of Various Documents Ordered (by the Assembly) to be Printed* [v. i]. *Papers Presented to Parliament* [v. ii-].

Note especially, 'Tariff. Report of the Royal Commission together with Appendices and Minutes of Evidence', *P.P.*, 1883, vol. 4, no. 50; and the several reports of the royal commission on Shop Employés, *P.P.*, 1882-3—1884.

Victorian Year Book (annual).

More detailed statistical material is to be found in the Statistical Registers, published annually in *P.P.*, and in the detailed reports of the censuses of 1881 and 1891 published in *P.P.* See also H. H. Hayter, *Census of Victoria, 1881. General Report, with Summary Tables, Diagrams, and Map* (Melb., 1883).

II OTHER CONTEMPORARY SOURCES

A. MANUSCRIPT

Australia and New Zealand Bank records, London (Bank of Australasia records)

Barnes, E. L., 'Shirtsleeves to Shirtsleeves' (La Trobe Lib.)

Berry, (Sir) Graham, Papers (La Trobe Lib.)

Crisp, Christopher, Correspondence (photo-copies, NL)

Deakin, Alfred, Papers (NL)

Derham, F. T., Correspondence (in Swallow & Ariell collection, University of Melbourne Archives)

Dilke, (Sir) Charles, Papers (BM, Add. MSS. 43,877)

Fink, Theodore, Papers, including 'Reminiscences' (University of Melbourne)

Haddon, F. W., Papers (La Trobe Lib.)

Higgins, H. B., Papers (NL)

Imperial Federation League, Victorian branch. Letter-book, 1889-1910 (NL)

Pearson, C. H., Papers (La Trobe Lib.)

Quick, (Sir) John, Papers (NL)

Service, James, Newspaper-cuttings books (La Trobe Lib. and Royal Historical Society of Victoria)

Stainthorpe, R. H., 'The Stainthorpe Story' (La Trobe Lib.)

Strong, (Rev.) Charles, Papers (NL and photo-copies, La Trobe Lib.)

Sugden, (Rev.) E. H., Letters (typescript copies, La Trobe Lib.)

B. NEWSPAPERS AND PERIODICALS

Daily newspapers: The *Age* and *Argus* were used for the whole period, and the *Daily Telegraph* and *Herald* occasionally.

Weeklies: The main weeklies consulted were the *Advocate, Australasian, Bulletin* (Sydney), *Federal Australian, Leader, Liberator* and *Punch.*

Periodicals: The main periodicals used were the *Australasian Insurance and Banking Record, Australasian Sketcher, Australian, Catholic Magazine, Imperial Review, Melbourne Review, Once a Month, Shearers' Record, Trades Hall Gazette, Victorian Review* and *Young Australia.*

C. BOOKS, PAMPHLETS AND ARTICLES

(including books written later by contemporaries)

Adams, Francis, *Australian Essays.* Melbourne, 1886.

—— *The Australians. A Social Sketch.* London, 1893.

Bedford, Randolph, *Naught to Thirty-three.* Sydney, n.d.

Berry, Sir Graham, 'The Colonies in relation to the Empire', *Proceedings, Royal Colonial Institute,* vol. 18, 1886-7.

Cambridge, Ada, *Thirty Years in Australia.* London, 1903.

Castella, Hubert de, *John Bull's Vineyard. Australian Sketches.* Melbourne, 1886.

Cockerill, George, *Scribblers and Statesmen.* Melbourne, n.d.

Dale, R. W., *Impressions of Australia.* London, 1889.

Deakin, Alfred, *The Crisis in Victorian Politics, 1879-1881. A Personal Retrospect* (ed. J. A. La Nauze and R. M. Crawford). Melbourne, 1957.

—— *The Federal Story. The Inner History of the Federal Cause 1880-1900* (ed. J. A. La Nauze). Melbourne, 1963 (1st ed., 1944).

(Deegan, J. F. ed.), *The Chronicles of the Melbourne Beefsteak Club, vol. 1, 1886-1889 by "The Recorder".* Melbourne, 1890.

Dilke, Sir Charles Wentworth, *Problems of Greater Britain.* London, 1890.

Finch-Hatton, Harold, *Advance Australia!* London, 1886.

Franklyn, H. Mortimer, *A Glance at Australia in 1880 . . .* Melbourne, 1881.

Froude, James Anthony, *Oceana or England and her Colonies.* London, 1886.

Gane, Douglas M., *New South Wales and Victoria in 1885.* London, 1886.

Harper, Andrew, *The Honourable James Balfour M.L.C. A Memoir.* Melbourne, 1918.

Higinbotham, George, *Science and Religion or the Relations of Modern Science with the Christian Churches. A Lecture.* Melbourne, 1883.

Hoare, Benjamin, *Looking Back Gaily.* Melbourne, 1927.

Hogan, J. F., *The Irish in Australia.* London, 1887.

Hume, Fergus, *The Mystery of a Hansom Cab.* London, 1959 (1st ed., 1887).

Intercolonial Free Trade Conference of Delegates from the Chambers of Manufactures . . . 1887, Report of the Proceedings of the. Melbourne, 1887.

Kimberly, W. B., *Ballarat and Vicinity. . . .* Ballarat, 1894.

—— *Bendigo and Vicinity.* Ballarat, 1895.

The Land of the Lyre Bird. A Story of Early Settlement in the Great Forest of South Gippsland. . . . Korumburra, 1966 (1st ed., 1920).

Leavitt, T. W. H. and Lilburn, W. D., *The Jubilee History of Victoria and Melbourne*. Melbourne, 1888.

Lee, Mrs Harrison, *One of Australia's Daughters. An Autobiography*. London, 1900.

Lingham, H. C. J., *Juvenal in Melbourne. A Satire*. Melbourne, 1892.

Mackay, George, *The History of Bendigo*. Melbourne, 1891.

Martin, A. Patchett, *Australia and the Empire*. Edinburgh, 1889.

Meudell, George, *The Pleasant Career of a Spendthrift*. London, [1929].

Moorhouse, James, 'Victoria', *The Journal of the Manchester Geographical Society*, vol. 4, 1888.

Morris, E. E., *A Memoir of George Higinbotham*. London, 1895.

Nisbet, Hume, *A Colonial Tramp. Travels and Adventures in Australia and New Guinea*. 2 vols. London, 1891.

(Norton, J. and others), *The History of Capital and Labour in all Lands and Ages*. . . . Sydney and Melbourne, 1888.

Parker, Gilbert, *Round the Compass in Australia*. London, 1892.

Pearson, C. H., 'Democracy in Victoria', *Fortnightly Review*, vol. 31, May 1879.

—— *National Life and Character. A Forecast*. London, 1893.

Reeves, William Pember, *State Experiments in Australia and New Zealand*. 2 vols. London, 1902.

Smith, A. Bruce, *Liberty and Liberalism: a protest against the growing tendency toward undue interference by the State, with individual liberty, private enterprise, and the rights of property*. Melbourne, 1887.

Spence, W. G., *Australia's Awakening. Thirty Years in the Life of an Australian Agitator*. Brisbane, 1942 (1st ed., 1909).

Stebbing, W. (ed.), *Charles Henry Pearson. Fellow of Oriel and Education Minister in Victoria*. London, 1900.

Sutherland, Alexander and others, *Victoria and its Metropolis. Past and Present*. 2 vols. Melbourne, 1888.

Syme, David, *Outlines of an Industrial Science*. London, 1876.

Trollope, Anthony, *Australia and New Zealand*. Melbourne, 1873.

Turner, Henry Gyles, *A History of the Colony of Victoria from its Discovery to its Absorption into the Commonwealth of Australia*. 2 vols. London, 1904.

Twopeny, R. E. N., *Town Life in Australia*. London, 1883.

Walch, Garnet, *Victoria in 1880*. Melbourne, 1881.

Withers, William Bramwell, *The History of Ballarat from the First Pastoral Settlement to the Present Time*. Ballarat, 2nd ed., 1887.

III LATER WORKS

A. BOOKS AND ARTICLES

Australian Dictionary of Biography (ed. Douglas Pike), vols 3-4: 1851-1890. Melbourne, 1969 and 1972.

Bate, Weston, *A History of Brighton*. Melbourne, 1962.

Beever, E. A. and Freeman, R. D., 'Directors of Disaster?', *Economic Record*, vol. 43, March 1967.

Blackton, Charles S., 'Australian Nationality and Nationalism: the Australian Natives' Association, 1885-1901', *Journal of Modern History*, vol. 30, March 1958.

——— 'Australian Nationality and Nationalism: the Imperial Federationist Interlude, 1885-1901', *Hist. Studies*, vol. 7, no. 25, November 1955.

Blainey, Geoffrey, *Gold and Paper. A History of the National Bank of Australasia Limited*. Melbourne, 1958.

——— *The Rush that Never Ended. A History of Australian Mining*. Melbourne, 1963.

——— *The Tyranny of Distance. How Distance Shaped Australia's History*. Melbourne, 1966.

Blake, L. J. and Lovett, K. H., *Wimmera Shire Centenary*. Horsham, 1962.

Boehm, E. A., *Prosperity and Depression in Australia 1887-1897*. Oxford, 1971.

Boyd, Robin, *Australia's Home. Its Origins, Builders and Occupiers*. Melbourne, 1952.

Briggs, Asa, *Victorian Cities*. London, 1963.

Butlin, N. G., *Investment in Australian Economic Development 1861-1900*. Cambridge, 1964.

Butlin, S. J., *Australia and New Zealand Bank. The Bank of Australasia and the Union Bank of Australia Limited 1828-1951*. Melbourne, 1961.

Cannon, Michael, *The Land Boomers*. Melbourne, 1966.

Casey, Maie, *An Australian Story 1837-1907*. London, 1962.

Clark, C. M. H. (ed.), *Select Documents in Australian History 1851-1900*. Sydney, 1955.

Coghlan, T. A., *Labour and Industry in Australia from the first Settlement in 1788 to the Establishment of the Commonwealth in 1901*. 4 vols. Oxford, 1918.

Davison, Graeme, 'Public Utilities and the Expansion of Melbourne in the 1880s', *Aust. Economic History Review*, vol. 10, no. 2, Sept. 1970.

Dow, Gwyneth M., *George Higinbotham: Church and State*. Melbourne, 1964.

Dunsdorfs, E., *The Australian Wheat-growing Industry 1788-1948*. Melbourne, 1956.

Dunstan, Keith, *Wowsers*. Melbourne, 1968.

Fitzgerald, R. T., *The Printers of Melbourne. The History of a Union*. Melbourne, 1967.

Fitzpatrick, Brian, *The British Empire in Australia*. Melbourne, 1949.

Forster, Harley W., *Waranga. 1865-1965*. Melbourne, 1965.

Gollan, Robin, *Radical and Working Class Politics. A Study of Eastern Australia, 1850-1910*. Melbourne, 1960.

Goodwin, Craufurd D. W., *Economic Enquiry in Australia*. Durham, N.C., 1966.

Gordon, Donald Craigie, *The Australian Frontier in New Guinea 1870-1885*. New York, 1951.

Graham, B. D., *The Formation of Australian Country Parties*. Canberra, 1966.

Grant, James and Serle, Geoffrey, *The Melbourne Scene 1803-1956*. Melbourne, 1957.

Hall, A. R., 'Some Long Period Effects of the Kinked Age Distribution of the Population of Australia 1861-1961', *Economic Record*, vol. 39, March 1963.

—— *The Stock Exchange of Melbourne, and the Victorian Economy 1852-1900*. Canberra, 1968.

Hall, Henry L., *Australia and England. A Study in Imperial Relations*. London, 1934.

—— *Victoria's Part in the Australian Federation Movement*. London, 1931.

Hancock, W. K., *Survey of British Commonwealth Affairs. Vol. 1. Problems of Nationality 1918-1936*. Oxford, 1937.

Ingham, S. M., 'Political Parties in the Victorian Legislative Assembly 1880-1900', Margot Beever and F. B. Smith (eds), *Historical Studies. Selected Articles. Second Series*. Melbourne, 1967.

Kennedy, Victor and Palmer, Nettie, *Bernard O'Dowd*. Melbourne, 1954.

Kiddle, Margaret, *Men of Yesterday. A Social History of the Western District of Victoria 1834-1890*. Melbourne, 1961.

La Nauze, J. A., *Alfred Deakin. A Biography*. 2 vols. Melbourne, 1965.

—— *Political Economy in Australia. Historical Studies*. Melbourne, 1949.

Martin, Colin Swinburne, *Irrigation and Closer Settlement in the Shepparton District 1836-1906*. Melbourne, 1955.

Palmer, Nettie, *Henry Bournes Higgins*. London, 1931.

Palmer, Vance, *The Legend of the Nineties*. Melbourne, 1954.

Palmer, Yvonne S., *Track of the Years. The Story of St. Arnaud*. Melbourne, 1955.

Patterson, G. D., *The Tariff in the Australian Colonies 1856-1900*. Melbourne, 1968.

Pratt, Ambrose, *David Syme. The Father of Protection in Australia*. Melbourne, 1908.

Priestley, Susan, *Echuca. A Centenary History*. Melbourne, 1965.

—— *Warracknabeal. A Wimmera Centenary*. Brisbane, 1967.

Roe, Jill, 'Challenge and Response: Religious Life in Melbourne, 1876-1886', *The Journal of Religious History*, vol. 5, no. 2, December 1968.

Sayers, C. E., *David Syme. A Life*. Melbourne, 1965.

—— *Shanty at the Bridge. The Story of Donald*. Donald, 1963.

Shann, Edward, *An Economic History of Australia*. Cambridge, 1948 (1st ed., 1930).

Tregenza, John, *Professor of Democracy. The Life of Charles Henry Pearson, 1830-1894. Oxford Don and Australian Radical.* Melbourne, 1968.

Wettenhall, R. L., *Railway Management and Politics in Victoria 1856-1906.* Canberra, 1961.

Willard, Myra, *History of the White Australia Policy.* Melbourne, 1923.

B. UNPUBLISHED THESES

(University of Melbourne, unless otherwise stated)

Atkins, Barbara R., 'The Problem of the Representation of Australia in England: the Origins and Development of the Australian Agencies-General during the Nineteenth Century', M.A., 1959.

Aveling, Marian, 'A History of the Australian Natives' Association 1871-1900', Ph.D., Monash University, 1970.

Barrett, A. H. B., 'The Making of an Industrial Environment: Collingwood, Victoria, 1851-91', M.A., 1970.

Bartlett, G. R., 'Political Organization and Society in Victoria, 1864-1883', Ph.D., A.N.U., 1965.

Davison, Graeme, 'The Rise and Fall of "Marvellous Melbourne" 1880-1895', Ph.D., A.N.U., 1969.

Finlayson, M. G., 'Groups in Victorian Politics, 1889-1894', M.A., 1963.

Fry, E. C., 'The Condition of the Urban Wage Earning Class in Australia in the 1880's', Ph.D., A.N.U., 1956.

Howe, Renate, 'The Wesleyan Church in Victoria, 1855-1901: its Ministry and Membership', M.A., 1965.

Ingham, S. M., 'Some Aspects of Victorian Liberalism, 1880-1900', M.A., 1949.

McCormack, G. P., 'Victorian Governors and Responsible Government', M.A., 1962.

McCullough, Judith, 'The Australian Reaction to the New Hebrides Crisis of 1886: a Study in Australian Nationalism', M.A., 1956.

McLachlan, N. D., 'Larrikinism: an Interpretation', M.A., 1950.

Millar, T. B., 'The History of the Defence Forces of the Port Phillip District and Colony of Victoria, 1836-1900', M.A., 1957.

Mitchell, Ann M., 'Temperance and the Liquor Question in Later Nineteenth Century Victoria', M.A., 1966.

Moore, R. J., ' "Marvellous Melbourne": a social history of Melbourne in the 'eighties', M.A., 1958.

Murray-Smith, S., 'A History of Technical Education in Australia with special reference to the period before 1914', Ph.D., 1966.

Oddie, G. A., 'The Chinese in Victoria, 1870-1890', M.A., 1959.

Parsons, T. G., 'Some Aspects of the Development of Manufacturing in Melbourne, 1870-1890', Ph.D., Monash University, 1970.

Philipp, J., 'Trade Union Organization in New South Wales and Victoria, 1870-1890', M.A., 1953.

Roe, Jillian I., 'A Decade of Assessment. Being a study in the intellectual life of the city of Melbourne between 1876 and 1886', M.A., A.N.U., 1965.

Smith, F. B., 'Religion and Freethought in Melbourne, 1870 to 1890', M.A., 1960.

Thompson, Roger C., 'Australian Imperialism and the New Hebrides, 1862-1922', Ph.D., A.N.U., 1970.

Tobin, G. M., 'The Sea-Divided Gael: a study of the Irish Home Rule Movement in Victoria and New South Wales, 1880-1916', M.A., A.N.U., 1969.

Index

Abbott, J. H., 42
Achurch, Janet, 290
Accountants and Clerks' Association, 94
Adams, Francis: cited, 78, 89, 230, 235, 272, 273, 282, 326-7
Adelaide Steamship Co., 110
Advocate, 31, 148, 155, 207n., 239, 240; policy, 242-4
Agnosticism, *see* Secularism
Age: history, 26-30; and protection, 7-8, 25, 76-7, 192, 323; political policies, 10, 18, 22, 39, 40-2, 55, 120, 220, 318, 323-4, 334; social policies, 92, 97, 100-1, 106, 108, 116, 118, 120-1, 335; sectarianism, 17-18, 155, 238, 241, 243; religious scepticism, 130-40 *passim*; moral and cultural policies, 157, 164, 173; Pacific policy, 180, 184n., 198, 207; federation, 190-2, 205, 316, 322, 323-4; on imperial relations, 200, 220, 222, 223, 284, 305, 307, 310, 329, 335; and war scares, 202n., 331; and A.N.A., 234, 311; and Chinese, 296-7; and boom speculation, 255, 258, 259, 265
Agricultural Implement Makers' Union, 93
Agriculture: expansion 1860-80, 4-5; development in 80s, 36-8, 50-63 *passim*, 320; agricultural colleges, 38, 53, 321; machinery and methods, 52-3, 57-61, 83, 320-1; societies, 54, 63, 205; *see also* Dairying; Irrigation; Land Acts; Victorian Farmers' Protection Association; Wheat industry; Winegrowing
Ah Toy, 301, 304
Ah Mouy, Louis, 295, 298
Albion Woollen Mills, 75
Alcock, A. U., 83
Alexander, Samuel, 230
Allan, G. L., 68
Allen, Professor H. B., 280
Allendale, 64, 111
Alston & Brown, 68
Altson, David, 75
Amalgamated Miners' Association, 95, 98, 117, 119, 121, 297; history, 111-12
Amalgamated Society of Carpenters and Joiners, 94
Amalgamated Society of Engineers, 94
Amess, Samuel, 139-40
Anarchists' Club, 122
Anderson, Francis, 151
Anderson, R. S., 20n.
Anderson, W., 165n.
Anderson's Inlet, 60
Annexation in the Pacific, 13, 179-89, 193-9, 204, 206-12, 214-15, 224-8
Apollo Stearine Candle Co., 74
Ararat, 3
Archer, W. H., 144, 155
Architecture, Melbourne and suburbs, 276-9; *see also* Building industry
Argus, 40, 55, 73, 114, 201, 265, 325, 334; quality, 28, 30-3; political and social policies, 7-8, 10, 23, 25, 30, 76, 90, 106, 108, 115, 335, 336; religious scepticism, 130, 135, 139, 140; moral and cultural policies, 157, 160, 164, 172, 173; imperial, federal and Pacific policy, 184n., 185, 198, 199, 205, 213, 222, 283, 323, 326; sectarianism, 241-2; and the boom, 253, 255, 257; and Chinese crisis 1888, 229, 302
Armytage, Harry, 310
Arnold, Matthew, 270
Arnold, Henry, & Co., 249
Art, *see* Culture
Artisans: social status, 88-90; wages, 91; housing, 91-2, 276, 279; Methodism and, 142-3
Ashton, Julian, 288
Atheism, *see* Secularism
Australasian, 31, 54, 290, 313-14
Australasian Mortgage & Agency Co., 48-9
Australasian Secular Association, 144-7
Australasian Temperance & General Mutual Life Assurance Soc., 69n., 162
Australian Artists' Association, 288
Australian Church, 150, 160; foundation, 140-1; *see also* Strong, Dr Charles
Australian Deposit & Mortgage Bank, 249
Australian Estates Ltd, 49n.
Australian Federal Union (1887), 315

Australian Frozen Meat Export Co., 48
Australian Mortgage (Mercantile) Land & Finance Co., 49
Australian Mutual Pastoral Co., 247
Australian Mutual Provident Soc., 69n.
Australian Natives' Association: general survey, 231-7, 308-13; Pacific policy, 196-8, 207, 209, 212, 216, 233, 236-7; and Sudan war, 200, 236; and nativism, 232-7, 311-13; and Chinese, 297, 299; and republicanism-separatism, 308-13, 328-9; and federal movement, 311, 333; and 'political' questions, 311; members in parliament, 324
Australian Property & Investment Co., 253
Australian Paper Mills, 74
Austral Otis Elevator & Engineering Co., 252-3, 262

Bailes, A. S., 165n., 236
Baillieu, W. L., 164, 249, 256, 267
Bairnsdale, 5, 100
Baker, R., 165n., 241n.
Balfour, James, 31, 68, 153-4, 157n., 159, 164, 165n., 166, 174; summing-up, 143
Ball & Welch, 68
Ballarat, 41, 63-4, 72-3, 100, 111, 196, 198, 231; about 1880, 2-3; religion and morals, 42-3, 145, 147, 162, 166, 169; *see also Courier*
Banking, 65-7, 84, 247-60 *passim*; royal commission, 251-2; Associated Banks, 67, 257; *see also* Land Banks; names of individual banks
Bank of Australasia, 65-6, 83; *see also* Parkes, E. S.
Bank of New South Wales, 66
Bank of Victoria, 66
Baptist Church, 143n., 185
Barker, Major and Mrs James, 147
Barmaids, 168
Barrett, Field, 310
Barrett, Herbert, 311
Bateman, E. J., 31, 113
Beath, D., 255n.
Beauchamp, Horatio, 157
Bedford, Randolph, 33, 167
Bedggood, J. C., 72
Beechworth, 3
Bell, James, 42, 241n., 267
Bendigo, 42, 61, 72, 73, 100, 111, 143, 147-8, 192, 234, 236; about 1880, 2-3; chief mining town, 63-5
Bendigo Rolling Stock Works, 73
Bennet, David, 96
Bent, 'Tommy': as Minister for Railways, 17, 33, 36; as Opposition Leader, 39, 42, 318; on Separation, 222, 229; as speculator, 254, 261, 266, 267, 327; biog. sketch, 264-5
Berry, Sir Graham, 27, 37, 40, 96, 101, 112, 130, 149, 264, 267, 318, 325, 326; 1877-80 ministry, 8-9; formation coalition, 17-20; biog. sketch, 20; and temperance, 164n., 165; annexation, 180, 182, 193, 208-12, 216; federation, 186, 189, 205; stock tax, 192; knighthood, 220n.; on imperial relations, 227-8, 304
Berry, Henry, 68, 74
Best, R. W., 313, 324
Bevan, Rev. Dr Llewelyn D., 143n., 175, 242, 336
Bible in State Schools League, 154-6
Birchip, 58
Black, Alexander, 54-5
Black, George, 308
Blainey, Geoffrey, 52n., 81, 111
Blair, David, 129, 145, 290
Bleasdale, Rev. J. J., 61
Blyth, John, 139, 150
'Boldrewood, Rolf' (T. A. Browne), 86, 290
Boot and shoe industry, 71-2, 76, 106-8
Booth, Colonel Ballington, 148-9
Booth, General William, 147, 150
Boot Manufacturers' Association, 106-8
Bosisto, James, 74
Bourgeoisie: social attitudes, 87-8; and the boom, 270-1, 338-9; housing, 275-9 *passim*; and London dock strike, 336-7
Bowen, Governor Sir George, 9, 228
Box Hill, 80, 257, 288
Boyd, Martin, 86
Bradlaugh, C., 145, 172
Branxholme, 114
Brennan, Louis, 83
Brewing industry, 71
Briagolong, 146
Brighton, 252, 264
British & Australasian Trust & Agency Co., 49n.
British Bank of Australasia, Ltd, 262
Brodzky, Maurice, 173, 259, 283n., 328
Broken Hill Proprietary Co., 254-5
Bromby, C. H., 240
Bromby, Rev. Dr J. E., 10, 128, 129, 133, 138, 157, 164n., 174
Bromley, Fred., 97, 119-20, 123, 157n., 164n., 324
Brookes, William, 74
Browne, H. J., 145, 157n.
Brownless, (Sir) Dr A. C., 144
Bruce, J. M., 117-19
Brunswick, 78, 275, 279
Brunton, Thomas, 70
Brussells, Madame, 168
Buckley & Nunn, 68
Building industry, 78-9, 247-58, 274-9, 327-8
Building societies, 78-9, 91-2, 248; *see also* Premier Permanent Building Soc.
Bulletin (Sydney), 173, 232, 283, 286, 291; cited, 111, 268, 279, 313; on Federal Council, 204; on Pacific annexation, 208; and the Impressionists, 290; influence in Victoria, 312

Buncle, John, 73
Bury, Thomas, 31
Butler, Prior, 104
Butterfield, William, 277
Buvelot, Louis, 288

Caffyn, Dr S. M., 288, 290
Caird, Principal Edward, 134
Cairns, Dr Adam, 133
Calvinism and capitalism, 268
Camberwell, 78, 143, 252, 256-7, 276
Cambridge, Ada, 290; cited, 86, 87n., 88, 89, 129-30, 132n., 285
Campbell, James, 20n., 149, 153, 169
Camperdown, 47, 113, 115, 322
Cannon, Michael, 257, 261-2, 265
Capital and Labour Federation League, 119n.
Capital: investment and accumulation, 45-50 *passim*, 84, 247-51; investment N.S.W. and Q., 49-50; required for farming, 52; in mining, 64-5; bank control of investment policy, 67; public sector, 79; speculation, 248-57
Carlton, 6, 160
Carlton Brewery, 71
Carnarvon, 4th Earl, 213, 214, 303, 330, 337
Carr, Archbishop Thomas, 144, 242, 256, 329
Carrington, Lord, 332
Carson, David, 247
Carter, G. D., 71, 165n., 166, 223, 254
Carter, W. T., 325n.
Casey, R. G., snr, 50
Castlemaine, 3, 64, 148
Catholic, *see* Roman Catholic
Catholic Education Defence Association, 17
Catholic Young Men's Societies, 144, 244
Cato, Fred, 142
Caulfield, 78, 252, 276
Censorship of books, 173
Chaffey, George and William B., 56
Charities, public and private, 92, 282, 283
Cheong Cheok Hong, 297
Childers, Hugh, 208, 306n.
Chinese, 143, 168, 174, 275, 281; situation in Vic., 295-302; Chinese Commissioners, 296-7
Chirnside, Andrew, 329
'Chloë', 159
Church of Christ, 143n.
Church of England, 9-10, 128-30, 132-4, 150, 163
City and Suburban Investment & Banking Co., 256
City of Melbourne Bank, 66, 251, 254, 262
Civil Service, 33-5
Clapp, F. B., 82, 116
Clark, A. T., 209, 238
Clark, Charles, 230
Clark, Thomas, 287
Clark, W. M., 241n.
Clarke, Lieutenant-General Sir Andrew, 208
Clarke, (Sir) G. S., 330
Clarke, Marcus, 10, 130, 229, 268, 291
Clarke, Sir W. J., 51, 66, 216, 219n., 283, 286, 329; Cliveden, 278
Clarke, W. J. T. ('Big'), 4
Classes and class relations, 6-7, 86-90; *see also* Artisans; Bourgeoisie; Commercial classes; Farmers; Gold miners; Labourers; Manufacturers; Pastoralists; Selectors
Clothing industry, 71-2
Clunes, 3, 64
Coal industry, 74-5
Cobb & Co., 81
Cobden, 320
Coburg, 78, 80, 252, 256, 257, 276
Coburg and Somerton Junction Estate Co., 257
Cockerill, George: cited, 90n., 219n., 234
Coffee taverns, 163-4; *see also* Federal Coffee Palace
Coghlan, Sir Timothy, 94
Coldwell, James, 319
Cole, E. W. and Cole's Book Arcade, 68, 104, 127, 173, 275
Collingwood, 6, 106, 120, 264, 276, 297
Colonial Ammunition Factory, 314
Colonial and Indian Exhibition (London), 226
Colonial Bank, 66, 262
Colonial Conference (London) 1887, 210-13, 228, 237, 243, 313, 314
Colonial Gas Association, 74
Colonial Investment Co., 249
Colonial Mutual Life Assurance Soc., 69n.
Colonial Office, 11-12, ch. 6 *passim*, 220-8, 237-40, 302-7, 314, 328-31; *see also* Imperial relations
Colonial Sugar Refining Co., 50
Commerce, Chamber of (Melb.), 40, 42, 119n.; and federation, 192-3, 205, 314-15; and the boom, 260, 261; and London dock strike, 335-6
Commercial classes: social status, 87-8; wages, 91; and the boom, 267, 269-71; *see also* Artisans; Bourgeoisie, etc.
Commercial Bank of Australia, 19, 66, 250-1, 262, 265, 334
Companies Act, 261, 267
Conciliation, Board of, 116-19, 324, 334
Conder, Charles, 76, 288-90
Congregational Union, 143n., 168, 169, 185, 267, 269, 336
Connell, John, & Co., 68
Connelly, Thomas Jefferson, 233
'Conservative' party, *see* Constitutionalist party
Constitutionalist party, ch. 1 *passim*, 318-25 *passim*

Convicts: heritage, 184-5, 218, 220; French, in Pacific, ch. 6 *passim*; Irish informers, 240
Coode, Sir John, 274-5, 281
Co-operative societies, 121
Coppin, George, 164n.
Couchman, Thomas, 34
Country Estates Co., 249, 266
Courier (Ballarat), 31, 40, 113
Couvreur, Jessie ('Tasma'), 87n., 291
Cowderoy, Benjamin, 119n.
Cowen, Frederick, 274, 286-7
Craig, Williamson & Thomas, 68
Creswick, 3, 63-5, 86n., 111-15, 119, 162, 293-4
Creswick, William, 133
Crisp, Christopher, 31
Culture, 286-91; A.N.A.'s efforts, 312; *see also* Public Library and National Gallery
Cumberland, Stuart, 150-1
Cumming, William, 138
Cunningham, Edward, 55
Currie, Archibald, 48, 74, 117
Currie, John Lang, 47-8
Cuthbert, Henry, 41-2, 266, 325

Daily Telegraph, 31, 135, 142, 146, 149, 153-4, 164, 169, 173, 259, 299
Dairying, 51, 60, 320
Dale, Rev. R. W., 218n.; cited, 150, 151, 156, 337; on the boom, 269
Dalgety & Co., 48
Dalley, W. B., 187-98 *passim*, 236
Dampier, Alfred, 290, 292
Dandenong, 160, 256
Danks, John, 72
Darling, Sir Charles, 8, 96, 302
Davies, D. M., 41n., 325
Davies, J. M., 278
Davies, Sir Matthew, 42, 139, 153, 157n., 163, 229, 259, 262, 265-8; biog. sketch, 249; banking royal commission, 251-2; elected Speaker, 319
Davitt, Michael, 244
Daylesford, 3, 146
Deakin, Alfred, 20n., 22, 27, 33, 37, 170, 219, 229, 232n., 259, 322-3, 337; cited, 19-20, 27, 29, 30, 161, 189, 264; relations with Syme, 27; biog. sketch, 40-1; coalition with Gillies, 40-2, 318-27; irrigation, 55-7; factory and early closing reform, 100-6; religion, 128, 130, 150; moral and cultural attitudes, 165, 166, 290; Pacific policy, 196, 210, 211; 1887 Colonial Conference, 210-12, 237; and imperial relations, 220n., 221-2, 227, 228, 236, 238, 301, 304, 306; and boom morality, 266; and Chinese agitation, 296-300; and A.N.A., 309-10; on federation and protection, 316, 322-6, 331-3; and Liberal non-achievement, 327
Deasy, John, 329
Decentralization League, 42
Defence forces, 201-3, 329-31; 1887 naval agreement, 212-14; argument over control, 304; and federation, 314, 331; *see also* Colonial Ammunition Factory
Derby, Earl, ch. 6 *passim*
Derham, F. T., 38, 42, 50, 68, 71, 100, 205, 266-7n., 267, 325
Derry, J. D., 54, 55
Des Voeux, Sir William, 188-9
Dibbs, George, 187, 189
Dilke, Sir Charles, 22, 26, 182, 223, 265, 306, 322, 330
Dillon, John, 329
Disney, Colonel T. R., 203, 304
Divorce law, 305-6
Dods, B. H., 54, 180
Dods, Rev. George, 140
Donald, 54
Don, C. J., 96, 119
Donovan, James, 145
Douglas, Adye, 205, 315
Douglass, Ben, 33, 96, 97, 101, 164n., 201
Dow, John Lamont, 41, 55, 165n., 219; and the boom, 267; biog, sketch, 320; as Agriculture Minister, 325
Dow, T. K., 55
Dowie, J. A., 151
Downes, Major-General M. F., 304
Downer, Sir John, 204, 210-11
Drift to the city, 293-4
Drinking habits, 160-1, 229, 284
Drouin, 60
Drysdale, 148
Duffy, Charles Gavan, 12, 219n., 222, 229; Duffy family, 144
Duffy, Frank Gavan, 239, 304n.
Duffy, John Gavan, 238, 242
Duncan, G. S., 82

Eaglehawk, 63, 65
Early-closing movement, 100-6
Echuca, 55, 80, 192, 324, 333
Eclectic Society, 128
Economic conditions, 2-6, ch. 2, ch. 8 *passim*, 327-8; standard of living, 90-3; *see also* Agriculture; Banking, etc.
Edgar, A. R., 166
Edgar, W. A., 142
Education: 1872 Act, 10-11; women teachers, 84; teachers' salaries, 91; attacks on Act, 154-6; royal commission, 154-5; question of Australian content, 235, 312; attempted amendment of Act, 318; state in 1889, 327
Education Union League, 155
Edwards, Major-General J. Bevan, 331, 333
Eight-hours movement, 98-100
Elections: 1883, 17-18, 185; 1886, 42; 1889, 323-5
Elkington, Professor J. S., 157n., 224
Elmslie, George, 284
Employers' Liability Act, 105
Employers' Union, 99, 103-5, 110; foundation and Board of Conciliation, 117-19

English, Scottish & Australian Bank, 66, 277
Esmonde, Sir Thomas, 28-9, 329
Essendon, 78, 252, 275
Essendon Land & Tramway Co., 264
Eureka tradition, 220, 312, 312n.
Evangelism, 128-9, 143, ch. 5 *passim*
Evangelistic Association, 174
Excelsior Woollen Mills, 75
Exhibition, Centennial, 163, 210, 256, 258, 283, 285-7; building, 276
Exports, *see* Trade and Commerce

Factory legislation, 39, 75, 97, 100-5, 120, 296; *see also* Shops and Factories Commission
Fairbairn, George, 49
Fanning, Nankivell & Co., 68
Farmers and selectors, 88; farming conditions, 50-4, 58-60, 61-3; as political force, 205, 319-24
Federal Bank, 66, 162-3, 249, 250, 251, 262
Federal Coffee Palace, 164, 264, 267, 276-7, 328
Federal Council: proposed by Parkes, 186, 192; 1883 proposal, 188-9, 195-6; established, 204-6, 207-9, 313-17, 331-3 *passim*
Federal movement: before 1883, 12-13; campaign, ch. 6 *passim*, 313-17, 331-3
Felton, Alfred, 267
Felton & Grimwade, 68, 74, 267
Ferguson, Mephan, 72
Finance, government, 35, 42, 46, 67, 79-82, 247, 258-9, 328, 334
Finch-Hatton, Harold, 230
Fink, B. J., 64, 253, 267, 278; biog. sketch, 262-3
Fink, Theodore, 260-8 *passim*, 337; described, 263
Finlayson, D., 259
Fisher, C. B., 247, 251, 266
Fisher, James, 151
Fisken, Archibald, 138
Fitchett, Rev. W. H., 31, 142, 156, 157n., 268
Fitzgerald, Rev. J. F., 269
Fitzgerald, Nicholas, 71, 165n., 166, 198, 242
Fitzgerald, Dr Thomas, 159
Fitzgibbon, E. G., 223
Fleming, 'Chummy', 284
Folingsby, George, 288
Food and drink manufacturers, 70-1
Football, 291
Footscray, 78, 92, 275, 279
Forster, W. M., 282
Foster, W. M. and R., 71
Francis, J. G., 138, 219, 238
Frankston, 80, 160, 256
Fraser, Simon, 18, 49, 241, 284, 323; biog. sketch, 49n.
Free Trade: political principle, 7, 19; and conservatism, 23-4; Syme's attack, 26; intercolonial, 192-3, 205-6, 314-16, 320-2
Freehold Farms Co., 264
Freehold Investment & Banking Co., 249
Froude, J. A., 216, 218n., 223, 226; cited, 20, 65, 90, 199
Fruitgrowing, 51, 55-6
Fry, James, 68, 70
Furniture trade, 278, 296; Furniture Trade Society, 296, 335
Furphy, Joseph, 113, 291; cited, 89

Gambling, 173, 229-30
Gardiner, Jack, 101, 120, 229
Gas and electricity, 74, 82-3
Gaunson, David, 39, 116, 160, 165n., 229, 242, 297, 318, 325
Geelong, 6, 48, 61, 87n., 142, 147, 249, 257
George, Henry, 25, 37, 122
Gibbs, Bright & Co., 68
Gillies, Duncan, 20n., 24, 42, 130, 205, 219, 236, 266, 285, 304-35 *passim*; biog. sketch, 40; and federation, 313-17, 331-3
Gillies ministry: foundation and 1886 election, 40-2; and boom economy, 247, 251-2, 258-61; personal involvement in boom, 265-7; and Chinese crisis, 295-302; and imperial relations, 302-7 *passim*; and federation, 313-17, 331-3; opposition to farming protection, 314-17, 320-6 *passim*; composition, stability, 1889 election, etc., ch. 11 *passim*
Gippsland, 5, 74, 80, 294, 320, 324; settlement South Gippsland, 58-60
Gladstone, W. E., 183, 195, 201, 207, 208, 226, 242, 244
Glass, Hugh, 4, 49n.
Glen, W. H., 68
Goe, Bishop Field Flowers, 150, 158, 160
Gold industry, 2, 63-5, 111-12; *see also* Gold miners
Gold miners: legend of, 1, 337; morals of, 64-5; status, 88-90; Chinese, 295; *see also* Amalgamated Miners' Association
Goldsbrough, Mort, 48
Goold, Archbishop J. A., 143-4, 238, 239, 242
Gordon, Adam Lindsay, 290, 312
Gordon, General Charles G., 199-201, 224
Gordon, George, 54-5
Gosman, Rev. A., 128, 143n.
Goulburn valley, 5, 55, 82, 320
Gould, Nat, 282
Graham, George, 319, 321, 324
Granville, Earl, 207, 209
Graves, J. H., 318n., 335
Gray, M. Wilson, 96
Great Centennial Land Distribution Co., 255
Great Morwell Brown Coal Mining Co., 74
Greenlaw, William, 278
Gregory, Rev. J. H., 133

Gresham, W. H., 37
Gresswell, Dr D. A., 281
Grey, Sir George, 307
Grice, R., 268
Griffith, Samuel W., 185-211 *passim*
Grimwade, F. S., 74, 255n., 267; *see also* Felton & Grimwade
Groom, A. C., 266
Guerard, Eugene von, 287
Guerin, Bella, 234-5

Haddon, Frederick W., 29, 30, 130
Hall, G. W., 102, 120, 165n., 319, 321, 324
Ham, C. J., 157n., 165n., 249, 267
Hamilton, 115
Harbor Trust (Melbourne), 98, 110, 328, 330
Harkness & Co., 72
Harper, Rev. Andrew, 154
Harper, Robert, 39, 42, 139, 153, 157n., 216, 300, 318n.
Hart, R. H., 232
Harwood, H. A., 296-8
Hawthorn, 78, 252, 257, 275
Hay, Rev. J., 139, 151
Hayter, H. H., 47n., 240
Health, 168n., 279-81, 326
Hearn, Dr W. E., 23, 26, 38, 98, 222, 259
Henderson, Rev. W., 134
Heidelberg, 80, 252, 288
Henty, Francis, 286
Herald, 31, 167, 293
Herbert, Sir Robert, 12, 182, 189, 208, 306-7, 314
Higgins, Henry Bournes, 33, 129, 239n., 242, 260, 338-9
Higginson, John, 182
Higinbotham, Mr Justice George, 27, 37, 96, 96n., 157, 173, 184n., 190, 219, 285-6, 308, 309; as politician in 60s-70s, 7, 8, 12; and religion, 13, 130-2, 147; biog. sketch, 32-3; and temperance, 162, 164; and Pacific annexation, 183-4, 214; and imperial loyalty, 220; constitutional views, 301, 303-4; Herbert's opinion, 307
Hogan, J. F., 155, 174, 230, 237-8
Holroyd, Mr Justice E. D., 157n., 223
Honours, imperial, 219, 219n., 306
Hopetoun, Lord, 304, 305
Horsham, 5
Howard Smith, William, & Sons, 82, 94, 108-10
Huddart, Parker & Co., 82
Hughes, Page and Rigby, 253
Hume, Fergus, 291

Ievers, William, jun., 223, 311n., 312-13
Immigration, 8, 35, 46-7, 79, 121, 190; lasting link, 2; during boom, 247-8; Chinese, 295-302
Imperial Banking Co., 262
Imperial Federation League (Vic. branch), 223-8; and A.N.A., 236-7, 309-11; Parkin visit, 328-9
Imperial loyalty: re Pacific events, 193-9; on Gordon's death, 199-201; and colonial defence, 201-4, 329-30; of migrants, 216-21, 283-4, 307-8, 336-7, 337-8; of native-born, 236-7, 308-11; of Irish Catholics, 243-4
Imperial relations: attitude to self-government, 11-12, 302-6; Pacific question, ch. 6 *passim*; reaction to Gordon's death, 199-201; and colonial defence, 201-4, 329-31; 1887 Colonial conference, 210-13; new understood relationship, 214-15; English attitudes to Australia, 217-18, 226, 228; future relationship and Imperial Federation, 221-8; Chinese crisis, 295-302, 304; Governor's function, Higinbotham and the Colonial Office, 302-7; divorce, 305-6; appointment of Governors, 307-8; nationality 1888-9, 308-13, 328-31; *see also* Australian Natives' Association; Colonial Office; Imperial loyalty; Nationalism; Republicanism; Separatism
Imports, *see* Trade and commerce
Industrial relations, 93-123 *passim*
Investment, *see* Capital
Irish Australians, 237-44
Irish Home Rule movement, 17, 237-44, 311n., 329
Irrigation, 38, 54-7
Irvine, W. H., 33
Irving, Professor M. H., 34

James, C. H., 249, 267
James, John, 42, 165n., 241n.
Jennings, Sir Patrick, 208, 209, 211, 316
Jeparit, 58
Jervois, Major-General Sir William, 202
Jewish religion, 143n., 154
Johns, P. (& Co.), 72, 253, 256
Johnston, J. S., 136, 138
Jones, C. E., 266, 318, 325
Journalism, 26-31; *see also* names of individual newspapers

Kahler, Herr, 284
Kauri Timber Co., 256
Kelly gang, 11, 73, 238, 240, 281, 318
Kendall, Henry, 312
Kerang, 55
Kerferd, G. B., 20n., 24, 40, 187
Kernot, Professor W. C., 110
Kiddle, Margaret, 268
Kingston, C. C., 332
Kipling, Rudyard, 290, 293
Kirkwood, Hay, 65
Kitchen, J. A., 163, 255n., 267
Knights of Labor, 335
Knutsford, Lord (Sir Henry Holland), 211, 215, 298, 303, 305, 306, 330
Kong Meng, Lowe, 295
Koo-wee-rup, 37

Korumburra, 60, 75
Kozminsky, Abraham, 267
Kyneton, 113

Labilliere, Francis, 223
Labour movement: *see* Artisans; Labourers; Trades Hall Council; Trade unions
Labourers: status, 89-90; wages, 91-3; housing, 91-2; sweated conditions, 102-3
Lal Lal Iron Mining Co., 73
Lalor, Peter, 219, 242, 319, 337
Land Acts: effects 1860-80, 3-5; 1883-4, 36-8; operation selection mid-80s, 50-4; *see also* Agriculture
Land banks, 248-9, 251, 255-8, 327
Land Credit Bank, 262
Land Mortgage Bank of Victoria, 249
Land reform movements, 37, 335
Land settlement, *see* Agriculture; Wheat industry
Lane, William, 93, 302
Langlands' Foundry, 70, 72
Langridge, G. D., 20n., 264
Langton, Edward, 23, 157
Lansell, George, 64
Larrikins, 281-2
Lascelles, E. H., 57
Latham, Edward, 71
Lawson, Henry, 291
Leader, 27, 28, 54, 155, 220, 320, 323
Lee, Bessie, 171
Legislative Assembly, 8, 324-5; members' composition and beliefs 1883, 20-1, 22-6; electoral qualifications, 38, 322-3; native-born members, 229, 324-5; members' behaviour during boom, 265-7; 1889 redistribution, 322
Legislative Council: relations between Houses, Council obstructionism, 7-9, 38-9, 323; conservatives in Council, 23-4; and Chinese question, 296, 301
Lennon, Hugh, 73
Leongatha, 60
Levien, J. F., 20n., 56, 229, 231
Liberal 'party': in 60s and 70s, 8-9; 1883-6, 17-18; principles, 24-6; Higinbotham influence, 32-3; land question, 37; 1886 dilemma, 39-42; Liberals outside coalition, 39-41, 318, 324-5; and T.H.C., 120, 122; and parliamentary reform, 322-3; and 1889 election, 324-5; achievement within coalition, 327
Liberator, 145-7, 172, 207n.
Liberty and Property Defence League, 103
Licensed Victuallers' Association, 166
Lifts, 252-3
Lincoln, Stuart, & Co., 71
Lindsay, Norman, 86
Literature, *see* Culture
Loch, Sir Henry and Lady, 201, 203, 217, 224, 283, 302-6 *passim*, 326
London Chartered Bank, 66
London dock strike, 335-7
Longmore, Francis, 165n., 238, 240
Longmore, J. J., 115
Longstaff, John, 159, 287
Lorimer, Sir James, 38, 42, 136, 138, 213, 219, 266, 325; as Minister for Defence, 330-1
Lutheran Church, 143n.
Lyell, Andrew, 108, 110, 116, 119
Lysaght & Co., 68

Macartney, Rev. H. B., 133, 157, 171-2, 174, 241
MacBain, Sir James, 139
McColl, Hugh, 54-5, 180, 241n.
McCrae, George Gordon, 201
McCubbin, Frederick, 159, 288-90
McCulloch, William, 82, 138, 141
Macdonald, Professor Murdoch, 133
McEachran, Rev. Duncan, 136
McEwan, James, & Co., 68
McIlwraith, Andrew, 48
McIlwraith, John, 72, 110
McIlwraith, Sir Thomas, 180, 183, 185, 307
McInerney, Dr T. P., 312, 313
McIntyre, John, 23, 39, 41n., 42, 318n.
Mackay, Angas, 30, 111
McKay, H. V., 73-4
McKinley, James, 153, 267
McLean, Allan, 318, 326
McLean Bros & Rigg, 68
McLean, William, 163, 249, 267
McLellan, W., 308
MacPherson, J. A., 229
Madden, J. J., 229, 235
Madden, Walter, 242, 319-21
Maffra, 58
Maldon, 3
Mallee, 36-7, 48, 49, 54; settlement in, 57-8
Maloney, Dr William, 33, 325n.
Malvern, 78, 252
Manning, Cardinal, 163, 336
Mansergh, James, 281
Manufactures, Chamber of, 40, 42, 103-4, 117, 185, 207, 335; and federation, 193-4, 205-6, 314-15, 321, 324, 333
Manufacturers: social status, 88; and the boom, 255n., 267
Manufacturing, 5-6, 69-77; *see also* names of individual industries
Martin, A. Patchett, 240
Maryborough, 3, 63-4, 148
Masters and Servants Act, 97, 113
Mechanics' Institutes, 158
Melba (Mitchell), Nellie, 286
Melbourne: expansion, 6, 77-9; as metropolis and financial centre, 2, 45, 48, ch. 9 *passim*; growth during boom, 247-58; general description, life-style, problems of growth, culture, ch. 9
Melbourne and Metropolitan Board of Works, 281, 326

Melbourne City Council, 161, 203, 239, 242, 253, 280
Melbourne Club, 216, 269
Melbourne Coal Co., 203
Melbourne Glass Bottle Works, 74
Melbourne Hydraulic Power Co., 253
Melbourne Iron Works, 72
Melbourne Lead Works, 72
Melbourne Mackay Sugar Co., 50
Melbourne Meat Preserving Co., 48
Melbourne Review, 158, 250, 338
Melbourne Steamship Co., 82
Melbourne Typographical Society, 94, 100, 102
Melbourne Woollen Mill Co., 75
Menzies, Sir Robert, 111, 201n.
Mercantile Bank, 66, 249, 251, 262, 267; *see also* Sir Matthew Davies
Mercantile Finance Co., 262
Metals and machinery industries, 72-3
Methodist churches, 21, 65, 149, 151, 182, 257, 299, 336; general description, 141-3; and social questions, 156-75 *passim*; and the boom, 267-8
Metropolitan Bank, 262
Meudell, George, 167, 262; as a nativist, 232-3, 234, 236, 312-13, 337
Michaelis, Hallenstein, 74
Michie, Sir Archibald, 155, 157n., 198, 304
Middleton, R. L., 117
Migrants: 'Englishness', 216-17, 219-20; patriotism, 220-1; imperialism, 217, 220; sectarianism, 240-1; Irish, (problems) 237-8, (restraint) 242, (attitude to Empire) 243-4
Mildura, 56-7, 166
Miller, Henry 'Money', 35, 271
Miller, Monty, 145
Mining, *see* Gold industry; Gold miners
Mirams, James, 35, 39, 42, 120, 153, 157n., 158, 164, 165n., 200, 205, 242, 259, 267, 321, 327; biog. sketch, 263-4; *see also* Tariff commission
Mitchell, Sir William, 38
Modern Permanent Building and Investment Society, 79
Moe, 37
Moloney, James, 271
Moore, Bishop J., 155
Moorhouse, Bishop James, 54, 59, 90, 100, 127, 145, 149, 150, 154, 155, 158, 163-4; on scepticism, 130-2; biog. sketch, 132-4; and morality, 167-74 *passim*; and imperialism, 201, 223-4
Mooroopna, 55
Moran, Edward, 142
Morris, Professor E. E., 223, 290
Morrison, Dr Alexander, 139, 140
Morrison, Ernest ('Chinese'), 184n., 230-1
Morrow, James, 73-4
Mortlake, 114
Morwell, 60
Moss, Mark, 278
Mount, L., 74
Mueller, Sir Ferdinand, 220n.
Mullen, Samuel, 68, 157n.
Munro, David, 29-30, 72, 267
Munro, James, 41, 42, 75, 149, 153, 157n., 166, 259, 267, 299; biog. sketch, 162-3; and coffee palaces, 162-3; business dealings during boom, 249-50, 265-6; challenge for premiership, 258, 318n., 319; and farming protection, 321-2, 326; *see also* Federal Bank
Murphy, W. E., 96, 97, 101, 108, 110, 120, 223
Murray, John, 229, 242, 308, 312n., 325n.
Murray, Stuart, 55
Murtoa, 53
Music, *see* Culture

Nagambie, 55
National Bank, 66, 84, 91, 251
National Gallery, *see* Public Library and National Gallery
National Liberal League, 41, 42, 120
National Mutual Life Association, 69n.
National Reform and Protection League, 8, 22, 41, 93, 263, 264
National Scripture Education League, *see* Bible in State Schools League
National Trustees Executors & Agency Co., 69n.
Nationalism: migrant patriotism, 217-21; Australian imperialism, 226-8; nativism, 232-7, 310-13; Irish Catholic, 243-4; and Impressionists, 290; and racialism, 301-2; and republicanism, 308-10; *see also* Australian Natives' Association; Native-born
Native-born: alleged characteristics, 228-31; nativism, 232-7; in Parliament, 229, 324
Naval defences, *see* Defence forces
Neilson, John Shaw, 291, 312
Newbery, Cosmo, 280
New Guinea, 163, 180-8, 193-9, 206
New Hebrides, 182-9, 193-9, 206-12
New Zealand Loan & Mercantile Agency, 49n.
Nhill, 57
Nicholson & Co., 68
Nimmo, John, 41n., 42, 157n., 164, 165, 165n., 166, 167, 175, 241n., 267, 325
Normanby, Lord, 17, 182, 303
Northcote, 78, 252
North Melbourne, 6, 147
Nuttall, W., 121

Oakleigh, 80, 252
O'Brien, Michael, 292
O'Connell, Daniel, 237
O'Dowd, Bernard, 145, 291, 308, 312
O'Farrell, M. J., 309-10
O'Loghlen, Sir Bryan, 9, 17-18, 154, 202, 239, 242, 307-8, 318, 321

Operative Bootmakers' Union, 93, 95, 106-8
Orange Institution, Loyal, 241-2, 311n.; Orangemen in politics, 17-18, 25, 49n., 238, 241-2
Oriental Bank, 66, 84, 251
Orkney, J., 136
Ormond, Francis, 96, 96n., 157, 164n., 219n., 286
Ormond College, 133, 276n.
O'Shanassy, Sir John, 17, 219n., 235, 238, 239, 240, 242, 256

Parkes, E. S., 66, 251, 259, 293
Parkes, Sir Henry, 12, 20, 192, 210, 212, 316; and anti-Chinese agitation, 298, 299; and intercolonial relations, 313-17 *passim*, 331-3
Parkin, George, 328-9
Parliamentary reform, 38-9, 322-3, 325, 327; *see also* Legislative Assembly; Legislative Council; Payment of members
Parnell, C. S., 239, 240, 242, 244, 307, 329
Pastoral Aid Society, 133
Pastoral industry, 3-4, 47-50, 57, 328; pastoralists as class, 86-7; *see also* Shearers
Paterson, Laing & Bruce, 68
Paton, Rev. J. G., 182, 184n., 185, 207, 208, 212
Patterson, J. B., 17-18, 22, 39, 42, 173, 219, 224, 238, 240, 241, 318n., 325
Payment of members, 32, 323, 324
Peacock, Alex. J., 111, 233-4, 324
Pearson, Charles Henry, 25, 30, 37, 41, 104, 130, 136, 173, 189, 200, 312; cited, 7, 18, 24, 87, 150, 191, 280; biog. sketch, 27; and Sunday opening of Gallery, 157-8; and imperial relations, 222, 301; and the boom, 266-7; on the 'higher civilization', 302; as Education Minister, 318, 325, 327
Peninsula and Orient S.N. Co., 82
Penshurst, 113
Permewan Wright, 82
Perry, Bishop Charles, 10, 128, 173, 174
Philosophical Society of Victoria, 150
Phoenix Foundry, 72-3, 80
Pickles, G. F., 73
Pitt, William, 277
Police, 167-8, 281-2, 323
Political development: *see* Gillies ministry; Liberal party; Protection; Service ministry, etc.
Poowong, 58
Population balance, 1-2, 46-7; *see also* Immigration
Portland, 54, 331
Port Melbourne, 142, 166, 217, 293
Poverty, 92-3, 282; *see also* Unemployment
Prahran, 6, 148, 257, 275
Prell, F. W., 252-3
Premier Permanent Building Society, 248, 263, 267, 334
Presbyterian Churches, 9, 128, 150, 151, 299, 310, 336; schism 1883, 134-40; sabbatarianism and other social issues, ch. 5 *passim*; and the New Hebrides, 182-5, 207-9, 212; and the boom, 267-70
Presbyterians in politics, 153, 158, 159-60, 183
Preston, 78, 80, 252, 257
Price, Major Tom, 329
Prostitution, 167-8, 281
Printers' Union, *see* Melbourne Typographical Society
Protection, 5-6; as political ideology, 7-9, 25-6; general effects, 75-7; *Age* and, 120-1; as intercolonial problem, 191-3, 204-6, 314-17; and farmers, 316, 319-22, 323-6; *see also* Free trade
Protestant Alliance Friendly Society, 241, 286
Public Library and National Gallery, 83, 275, 291; Sunday opening, 13, 135, 145, 156-9; Gallery, 287-8
Public Service Association, 34-5
Public Service Board, 34-5
Pulsford, Edward, 77, 315
Punch, Melbourne, 18, 31, 90, 286
Purves, J. L., 157n., 229, 299; biog. sketch, 309; as A.N.A. president, 309-12
Pyramid Co., 50

Quick, John, 37, 42, 90n., 189, 231, 316, 318n.

Rabbits, 48, 50, 53, 57, 326
Railways, 5, 49n., 52, 72-3, 78, 98, 115-16, 158, 159-60, 252, 253-4, 334; reform 1883, 33-4; construction and administration, 35-6, 38, 79-81
Railways Employees' Association, 115-16, 207
Ramsay, Robert, 154
Rationalism, 127-8, 151
Real Estate Bank, 249-50
Red Cross Preserving Co., 71
Redmond, John and William, 239
Reed, Joseph, 276-7
Rees, John, 321
Reid, Robert, 68, 260, 315
Reeves, W. Pember, 122
Religion: 9-10, ch. 4; and social questions, ch. 5 *passim*; and the boom, 268-70; *see also* Church of England; Rationalism, etc.
Rentoul, Rev. Dr L., 140, 156, 159
Republicanism, 147, 224, 232, 236, 283-4, 308, 309-10
Richardson, Ethel F. ('Henry Handel'), 170, 218, 235, 291
Richardson, R., 117, 165n., 241
Richmond, 6, 106, 120, 275, 297
Ritchie, S. S., 48
Riverina, 3, 47, 49, 86, 113, 190-2, 322

Robb, John, 249
Roberts, Tom, 288-90
Robertson, George, 68
Robertson, Sir John, 179, 188-91, 233, 316
Robertson, Macpherson, 71
Robinson, A. B., 27
Robinson, Sir William, 304
Rocke, W. H. & Co., 68
Roman Catholic Church, 148, 149, 163, 174, 207n.; general condition, 9-11, 143-4, 151; and education, 9-11, 154-6; and Irish question, 237-44
Roman Catholics in politics, 17-18, 39, 40, 42, 154-5, 237-44, 307-8, 318, 321
Rosa, S. A., 335
Rose, Dr J. Marmaduke, 41n., 165n.
Rosebery, Earl of, 193-5, 207, 209, 215, 226, 292
Rowlands, Evan, 71
Royal Bank of Australasia, 255
Royal Colonial Institute, 180, 183, 223, 226-8
Royal family, 12, 217, 220, 236, 243-4, 283-4, 285, 308
Rusden, H. K., 127, 144
Russell, James, 165n., 241n.
Rutherglen, 61

Sabbatarianism, 116, 146, 156-60, 241, 263; *see also* Public Library and National Gallery
St Arnaud, 3, 5, 54, 64
St Patrick's Cathedral, 274
St Patrick's Society, 241, 286
St Paul's Cathedral, 133, 256, 277
Sala, G. A.: cited, 173, 217, 275
Sale, 5, 143
Salisbury, Marquess of, 211, 212, 222, 228, 305
Salvation Army, 13, 147-50, 151, 163, 167, 169, 281, 283, 292, 335
Sampson, John, 111
Sands & McDougall, 74
Sargood, F. T., 20n., 68, 202, 278, 285, 300, 304
Savings banks, 248
Sawers, John, 259
Scots Church, 134-40, 276n.
Scott, Rev. Robert, 139
Scratchley, Major-General Sir Peter, 202, 203, 206
Seamen's Union, 95, 110, 121, 335
Searle, L., 116
Secularism, 122, 144-7, 150-1, 172, 207n., 242, 270, 301
Sectarianism, 13, 17-18, 133, 144, 154-6, 311, 318, 321; Irish question, 28-9, 237-44, 329
Separatism: English opinion, 221; in Vic., 222, 236-7, 243-4, 306-7, 308-11, 329; *see also* Republicanism
Servants, domestic, 83-4, 88n.
Service, James, 18, 24, 33, 40, 42, 77, 96, 98, 104, 240, 241, 301, 323, 325, 334; biog. sketch, 18-20; and religion, 130, 139, 150, 155, 157; and federation and annexation, ch. 6 *passim*, 216, 315, 317; and new imperial relationship, 215, 223, 226-8, 304; and A.N.A., 233, 236; and dock strike, 335-6
Service ministry: formation, 17-18; achievement, 33-40, 42; break-up, 40; annexation and federation movement, ch. 6, 226-8
Service, Robert, 18, 144
Sewerage in Melbourne, 279-81
Sexual *mores*, 167-72
Shakespeare Society, 290
Shaw, W. H., 72
Shearers: conditions, 113-14; Union, 95, 113-15, 121, 334; Chinese, 295
Shepparton, 15, 55, 291, 391
Sherwin, Amy, 283
Shiels, William, 33, 42, 157n., 158, 184n., 307, 318n., 321; on the boom, 259, 269, 270, 285, 328; on Chinese, 300-1; and divorce reform, 305-6
Shipping, 82, 190; *see also* Seamen's Union
Shop Assistants' Union, 106
Shops and Factories Commission, 95, 101-3, 117, 118, 168, 229
Silver mining speculation, 254-5
Simson, Robert, 138
Singleton, Dr John, 92, 149, 154, 163, 167, 174, 328
Sladen, Sir Charles, 38, 219n.
Smeaton, 51
Smith, Bruce, 23-4, 108-10, 116-18
Smith, Calder, 237
Smith, Francis Grey, 66, 251, 259
Smith, Charles, 255n.
Smith, James, 290; cited, 270, 272n., 337-8; attacks Impressionists, 289-90
Smith, Robert Murray, 23, 24, 185, 195-9 *passim*, 203, 204, 208, 223, 334
Smith, Thomas, 165n.
Smith, W. Collard, 39, 42, 103n., 308, 318n., 324; chairman Shops Commission, 100-4
Social Democratic League, 335
Social legislation, 38, 98; *see also* Factory legislation
Socialist League, 335
Society for the Promotion of Morality, 169, 173-4
South Melbourne, 6, 148, 275
Speight, Richard, 34, 81, 115-16, 293; *see also* Railways
Spence, William Guthrie, 97, 107, 120, 123; as secretary A.M.A., 111-12; biog. sketch, 112-13; and A.S.U., 113-15
Spiritualism, 19, 128, 308
Sport, 291-2
'State socialism', 25-6
Stawell, 2, 31, 63-4, 111
Stawell, Sir William, 174, 337
Stead, W. T., 169, 220
Steinfeld, Emanuel, 314, 315, 321

Stephen, G. M., 151
Stephens, James, 100n.
Stewards and Cooks' Union, 95, 116-17
Stewart, J. C., 135
Stewart, Nellie, 290
Stock Exchange of Melbourne, 254, 255, 262, 277
Stock tax, *see* Taxation
Streeton, Arthur, 288-90
Strong, Rev. Dr Charles, 13, 133, 150, 151, 157, 164n., 242, 269; biog. sketch, 134; schism, 134-40; and Australian Church, 140-1; and nationalism, 313
Strong, Professor H. A., 157
Stuart, Sir Alexander, 179-80, 186-8, 195, 196
Stuart, Frank, 71
Sudan expedition, 71, 199-200, 201, 236, 243
Sugar industry, 50, 205
Sugden, Rev. E. H., 143; cited, 89, 153, 156, 272
Sunday Free Discussion Society, 18, 128, 144
Sunday Liberation Society, 157
Sutherland, Alexander, 156, 283
Swallow & Ariell, 70-1, 100, 105, 256
Swallow, Thomas, 50
Swan Hill, 55, 80
Swinburne, George, 74, 253
Syme, David, 18, 37, 41n., 130, 191n., 220; political principles, 26; biog. sketch, 26-7; management of *Age*, 27-9; his power, 29-30; and federation, 316; *see also Age*
Symes, Joseph, 259, 284; described, 145; and secularist movement, 145-7

Table Talk, *see* Brodzky, Maurice
Tailoresses' Union, 95, 101
Talbot, 3
Tariff, *see* Protection
Tariff commission, 25, 35, 75, 192, 221n., 264
Taxation, 35, 327; stock tax, 192, 315-16, 320-6 *passim*
Taylor, G. W., 267, 268
Taylor, Henry, 119
Taylor, Henry d'Esterre, 311
Telegraph, electric, 12, 331
Telephones, 38, 83
Temperance movement, 160-6; in politics, 25, 31, 39, 165-6, 326
Temple, David, 113, 115
Templeton, J. M., 34, 69n.
Templeton, William, 69n.
Terry, W. H., 128
Thomas, Captain A. B., R.N., 203
Thomson, W. K., 293
Thornton, Bishop S., 132, 169
Thurston, Sir John, 208
Timber Yard Employees' Union, 95, 297
Toorak, 50, 249, 252
Topp, A. M., 87
Trade and commerce, 67-9, 247, 255-6; *see also* Commercial classes
Trade unions, 93-123
Trades Hall Council (Melbourne), 22, 40, 92, 93-123 *passim*, 147, 158, 219, 243, 335-6; and politics, 24, 41, 42, 119-21, 122-3, 324; and protection and the *Age*, 30, 120-2, 205, 326-7; formation, 94; expansion, 95-6; and legalization of unions, 97-8; and tailoresses' strike, 101; and Shops Commission, 102-5; and bootmakers' and wharf labourers' strikes, 107-10; and conciliation, 117-19, 334; and anti-Chinese agitation, 296-9; and farmers, 321; *see also* Eight-hours movement
Trades Hall Councils (non-metropolitan), 95, 120, 336
Trade Union Congress, Intercolonial (1884), 96-7, 185
Tramways, 38, 82, 98, 116, 252, 257, 274, 328
Tramways & Omnibus Co., 82, 116
Transport: expansion, 79-82; *see also* Railways, etc.
Trenwith, W. A., 41, 97, 104, 144, 157n., 321, 324; biog. sketch, 107; and boot strike, 106-8; and politics, 120, 123, 324
Trollope, Anthony, 218n., 270; cited, 65, 86
Trustees, Executors & Agency Co., 69n.
Tryon, Rear Admiral Sir George, 203, 208, 213
Tucker, A. L., 20n., 36, 121, 229, 231, 260-1
Tucker, Rev. H. F., 157
Tucker, J. B., 108
Tulloch, Major-General A. B., 230, 330
Turner, George, 231, 324
Turner, Henry Gyles, 19, 23, 33, 66, 77, 90, 130, 132, 157, 164n., 200, 218, 220-1, 230, 278; biog. sketch, 250-1; and banking in the boom, 250-1, 264, 265, 334
Turner (Webster), Martha, 128
Twopeny, R. E. N., 45n., 218n., 230; cited, 22, 30, 45, 66-7, 69, 87-8, 221n., 273, 274, 286, 291

Undenominational Education League, 154
Unemployment, 92-3, 95, 282, 328, 334, 335
Union Bank of Australia, 66-7
Unitarianism, 128, 139, 141, 150

'Vagabond, The' (S. James), 134, 161, 184n.
Vale, John, 162, 164
Vale, R. T., 300, 318n.
Verdon, Sir George, 66, 277, 290
Victoria Permanent Building Society, 162
Victoria Sugar Co., 50
Victorian Academy of Arts, 288

Victorian Alliance for the Suppression of the Liquor Traffic, 161-6, 168
Victorian Artists' Society, 76, 288
Victorian Christian Alliance, 174
Victorian Coal Co., 74
Victorian Farmers' Protection Association, 315, 319-26 *passim*
Victorian Railways Service Employees Mutual Association, 115-16
Victorian Review, 338; cited, 117, 130, 135
Victorian Squatting Co., 247
Victorian Woollen Cloth Manufacturing Co., 75
Vincent, James, 56
Volunteer forces, *see* Defence forces

Wages, 91, 101
Walch, Garnet, 217
Walhalla, 2, 64
Walker, Thomas, 144-5
Walker, W. F., 42, 200, 224, 266, 325
Wallace, D. S., 49, 292
Wallace, J. A., 112
Walters, Rev. George, 141
Wanliss, Newton, 309
Wardell, William, 32, 277
Warracknabeal, 52, 58
Warrnambool, 114, 238n., 320, 331
War scares, 203-4, 331
Water trusts, *see* Irrigation
Watsford, Rev. J., 141-2, 165
Watson, J. B., 64, 249
Way, Professor Samuel, 290
Wedderburn, 52
Weekly Times, 31, 54, 153
Welshpool, 58
Wesleyan church, *see* Methodist churches
Western District, 3, 47, 114, 334
Western District Sheep Farmers' Association, 115
Western Pacific High Commission, 182, 183, 195
Westgarth, William, 223, 275, 286, 337
Wharf Labourers' Union, 95, 99, 108-11, 121, 335
Wheat industry, 51-4, 90, 294, 320
White Cross Union, 170
Williams, Mr Justice Hartley, 130, 132, 229, 301, 309
Williamson, Garner & Musgrove, 290
Wilson, Edward, 30, 223
Wilson, O. E., 233, 308, 309
Wilson, Sir Samuel, 4, 219n., 268, 271
Wimmera, 5, 47, 54, 57, 80, 320
Winchelsea, 113
Windsor, A. L., 27
Winegrowing, 61, 326
Winter, Joseph, 31, 242
Winter, Samuel Vincent, 31, 231
Wisdom, Sir Robert, 211
Withers, W. B., 31
Wodonga, 80, 192
Women: employment, 83-4; franchise, 323
Women's Suffrage Society, 323
Women's Christian Temperance Union, 162, 168, 171
Wood, J. Dennistoun, 223
Woods, John, 41n., 102, 104, 120, 157n., 198, 219, 232n., 266, 318n., 324
Wool manufacturing industry, 75, 326
Woolf, Joseph, 267
Working classes: *see* Artisans; Labourer Larrikins; Trade unions
Workingmen's clubs, 164
Working Men's College, 96, 274
Workingmen's Political Reform Associa tion, 120
'Wowserism', ch. 5 *passim*
Wren, John, 318
Wrixon, Henry, 18, 23, 24, 30, 32n., 33 42, 105, 157n., 222, 266-7, 301, 303, 30
Wyselaskie, J. D., 268

Yarra valley, 61
Yarram, 60
Youl, Dr, 282
Young Men's Christian Association, 157, 174, 249, 292

Zeal, W. A., 323

csn

Mildura
Murray R.
N
MALLEE
Swan Hill
Koondrook
Kerang
Birchip
Boort
Jeparit
Echu
Warracknabeal
Donald
Inglewood
Raywood
St Arnaud
WIMMERA
Horsham
Tarnagulla
Bendigo
Maldon
Maryborough
Castlemaine
Stawell
Talbot
Kyneton
Ararat
Clunes
Smeaton
Wood
Allendale
Daylesford
Creswick
Ballarat
Sunb
Skipton
Bacchus Marsh
Hamilton
Penshurst
Werribee
Caramut
Mortlake
Geelong
Camperdown
Winchelsea
Portland
Koroit
Colac
Cobden
Warrnambool